{ WHAT AMERICA READ }

GORDON HUTNER

What America Read

TASTE, CLASS, AND THE NOVEL,

1920–1960

THE UNIVERSITY OF NORTH CAROLINA PRESS { CHAPEL HILL }

———

THIS BOOK WAS PUBLISHED WITH
THE ASSISTANCE OF THE THORNTON H. BROOKS FUND
OF THE UNIVERSITY OF NORTH CAROLINA PRESS

Designed by Courtney Leigh Baker and set in Whitman,
Serifa, and Bickham Script by Keystone Typesetting, Inc.

Parts of this book have been reprinted in revised form from
the following works: Gordon Hutner, "The 'Good Reader'
and the Bourgeois Critic," *Kenyon Review*, n.s., 20, no. 1
(1998), and "The Meanings of Marjorie Morningstar," in *Key
Texts in American Jewish Culture*, edited by Jack Kugelmass
(New Brunswick, N.J.: Rutgers University Press, 2003).

The paper in this book meets the guidelines for permanence
and durability of the Committee on Production Guidelines
for Book Longevity of the Council on Library Resources.

The University of North Carolina Press has been a
member of the Green Press Initiative since 2003.

Library of Congress Cataloging-in-Publication Data
Hutner, Gordon.
What America read : taste, class, and the novel,
1920–1960 / Gordon Hutner.
p. cm.
Includes bibliographical references and index.
ISBN 978-0-8078-3227-1 (cloth: alk. paper)
1. American fiction—20th century—History and criticism.
2. Realism in literature. 3. Literature and society—United
States—History—20th century. I. Title.
PS379.H86 2009
813'.520912—dc22
2008050469

13 12 11 10 09   5 4 3 2 1

TO *Dale*

———

FOR THE PAST, THE PRESENT,

———

AND THE FUTURE

CONTENTS

ACKNOWLEDGMENTS

I received a great deal of help in writing this book. The first person to thank is Dale Bauer, my most favorite colleague, who read every line on every page in several drafts for more than a decade. Her patience was extraordinary, her instruction luminous, her queries acute and resonant, her corrections insistent and, of course, right. She saved me from a million missteps. No scholar ever had a smarter, more committed interlocutor among his or her colleagues or a nicer one.

Next I have to express my gratitude to the National Endowment for the Humanities, which funded a year-long fellowship so that I could undertake the initial research for the book, a wonderful year when the first inkling of the tale I had to tell came upon me. Another debt I am delighted to acknowledge is to Paul Boyer, the former director of the Wisconsin Institute for Research in the Humanities. Paul generously made available to me a desk, in the basement of the old Observatory where the fellows could enjoy a semester or two of one of the most congenial intellectual atmospheres I have ever had the pleasure to know. We wrote our books in the mornings and afternoons, taking a lunch break when we shared our daily writing interests or decompressed by discussing world affairs. Paul so ably directed us that we took on something of his persona, I think, so whatever in my book is tolerant, poised, and relentlessly inquisitive redounds to Paul's credit. I also thank the Research Board at the University of Illinois for granting funds necessary for the completion of the manuscript.

Of course, many friends and colleagues supported me in my efforts. At the University of Wisconsin, the late Sargent Bush was never bored—or never appeared to be—by my enthusiasm for some long-forgotten article or

recondite book review. Although he did not live to see the book's completion, these pages record his confidence in the project, shrewdness as a
literary critic and historian, and benevolence to a junior colleague. No one
could ever quite match his scholarly meticulousness, but it has been exhilarating to try. At the University of Kentucky, I was blessed with one of the
nation's best cadres of Americanists, including Steve Weisenburger, Dana
Nelson, Virginia Blum, and Andy Doolen. The years of sharing in such a
convivial yet demanding company certainly made an impact on the finished
book. Here in Illinois, I have been fortunate to be among some truly gifted
scholars as well, none the least is Nina Baym, who took many hours out of
her retirement to read and annotate a crucial draft of the manuscript. Our
conversations have inspired me to make the book even better.

Although this study began as a research project and came to life at the
Wisconsin Institute for Research in the Humanities, its vitality developed
through a series of talks at the American Studies Association and the Modern
Language Association, as well as the British Association of American Studies
and the European Association of American Studies. I am very pleased to
thank the several chairs that saw fit to include my panel papers and the
audience members who so vigorously interrogated my arguments. I am also
indebted to hosts who brought me to visit their campuses—Glenn Altschuler
at Cornell, Dan Shiffman at Berry College, David Johnson at Buffalo, Don
Pease at Dartmouth, David Leverenz at Florida, Nancy Bentley at Penn, Jay
Clayton at Vanderbilt, and John Ernest at West Virginia. I am also grateful to
Jack Kugelmass for inviting me to speak at the Key Texts in Jewish American
Culture Colloquium when he was at Arizona State.

It is also a pleasure to recall the warmth with which so many people
responded to my project and how much encouragement they gave along the
way. Larry Buell, Nancy Glazener, Cecelia Tichi, and Trysh Travis were
especially supportive. For a very long time Ross Posnock has been my good
friend, always willing to share his erudition, insight, wit, and concern whenever I asked for it. James L. West answered an urgent query on Fitzgerald,
and Jeff Rubin-Dorsky kindly read an early version of the manuscript and
made many useful annotations.

Among my greatest debts are the ones I owe to the several research
assistants who have helped me at various stages. Foremost is the late Marcia
Reddick, whose resourcefulness and interest in the project helped me to
develop the research techniques that enabled me to define and pursue the

subject. Also at Wisconsin, I must thank David Lacroix, among others. Gena Chattin at Kentucky and Mary Unger and Jason Vredenburg at Illinois were also indispensable. Although I have taught several of the books my study covers, the students in a Cornell American studies seminar on class especially took up the challenge with grace, imagination, and intelligence.

David Lynn at the *Kenyon Review* was wonderful to work with. I thank that journal for permission to republish an early version of the introduction and also thank Rutgers University Press for permission to reprint parts of an essay on Herman Wouk's *Marjorie Morningstar*.

I am very grateful to the three University of North Carolina (UNC) Press readers—Jonathan Arac, Stephen Cox, and Paula Rabinowitz. Their praise thrilled me, and their challenges improved the book immeasurably by making me see my project anew. Sian Hunter is, without a doubt, the most gifted editor I know. Her confidence in this project seemed boundless. I am also grateful to the staff at the UNC Press, especially Paula Wald for her formidable expertise and for her determination to make this manuscript come out right.

Finally, I must thank my wife, Dale Bauer, whose devotion is prodigious. For years, she enabled me to seize countless hours away from my other responsibilities so that I could work a little more on my book, helping me to manage, among other things, a semester's commute to Ithaca, two moves, the birth of our twins, and even a stolen laptop. She even kept our sons, Jake and Dan, from diverting me as easily as I hoped they would and as joyously as they did. All this, even as she continued, without interruption, her own brilliant career. I am the luckiest guy I know.

{ WHAT AMERICA READ }

INTRODUCTION

THE ENVIRONMENT OF FICTION

Why are so few novels remembered while so many thousands are forgotten? Is our literary history incomplete without accounting for these books? These questions, and others like them, have stimulated this study of "better fiction" —novels that were better than formula fiction but not as good as high art. In their time, these novels were within educated readers' reference and memory, but over the years they have passed out of sight. Although these novels frequently won prizes and were often greeted respectfully, even eagerly, in the review columns of important magazines and newspaper supplements, they go unrecollected and unread not because their authors suffered from gender, racial, or political prejudice. On the contrary: because they occupied the very center of the literary landscape, these middle-class realistic novels—and not genre writing like Westerns, romances, or mysteries— constituted the merely ordinary, that is, the fiction against which academic tastemakers later needed to contradistinguish the best. While the unfamiliarity or remoteness of more complex literature or more explicitly ideological fiction frequently necessitates sustained acts of critical preservation so they might be appreciated, the novels I am writing about issue no such challenge. Instead, they comprise the widely read, easily comprehensible fiction that Americans chose for their edification and literary entertainment. These novels mean to please and instruct middle-class America in all its diversity of social marking, economic position, political standing. Strongly pedagogical, these novels often meant to shape public awareness of cultural values as well as individual pursuits, and how they came together.

In presenting this history of modern American realism in its ascendant years, the middle decades of the twentieth century, I am mindful that perhaps no other period of U.S. literary history has been so thoroughly analyzed, in its time or since. Yet this history, although written by so many hands, with so many different missions, has been left significantly incomplete, largely as a result of a critical bias against middle-class readers and their so-called middlebrow taste. Critics and scholars, unlike reviewers, have for a long time understood their job as creating hierarchies of literary achievement, ideologies of taste. Essential as that errand has been, the unfortunate by-product of this zeal to identify a few works by a few writers (who have from time to time been replaced by a few other preferred writers) is the neglect of a vast resource; in turn, that oversight keeps us from fully understanding how cultural values are made, circulated, and recalculated. Taken together, these novels may be said to represent the kind of engaged literary experience that so many readers during the '20s, '30s, '40s, and '50s shared, the quotidian novels that inevitably clued readers to the ways their fellow citizens were thinking, believing, and acting. Arguably, these bourgeois novels were the literary forms of print culture through which Americans were most likely to enter into and perhaps to participate in the public life of the century's middle decades. In a way that I think is underestimated, such books perform the cultural work of helping to shape the public sphere in modern America.[1]

Because there are so many of these books, the first need is to recover them and ascertain their reception. So I will be surveying novels that were scarcely brilliant artistic achievements or dazzling commercial successes, although several of the novels I discuss were both critically recognized and sold by the tens, even hundreds of thousands. Most, however, sold much more moderately; published by large commercial presses—mostly in New York—they were issued in print runs of 1,500, 2,000, or 3,000. They were often good without being great, interesting without being indispensable, accomplished without being profound. Yet why should they disappear when we read so many books from other periods no more fully realized or more vital to our understanding of the nation's literary history and the drama of its cultural production? A great many of the books in my purview fell into disregard, while a few works by a few writers that we do honor—some would say fetishize—might be remembered. The fact is, readers will encounter here a few more or less familiar names, like James Gould Cozzens and John Marquand, but many, I suspect, will be surprised, as I was, to find so many names that they might confess never to have heard before or about whom they have nothing much to say. Of course, these authors were most frequently white and Christian, but some were not, and a small but substantive part of my project has been to find novelists of the middle decades who might be known to a few specialists in race and ethnic literature but who once addressed a wider reading public and whose purchase on that audience's attention has now been obscured. Whatever these novelists' identities, their patron saint was William Dean Howells, not Henry James; Edith Wharton, not Djuna Barnes; Anthony Trollope or John Galsworthy, not Joseph Conrad or James Joyce.

We sometimes see these novels in used bookstores when, looking for something else, we come across titles that give us pause. Some are by authors who may be dimly recalled from scanning shelves, years ago, belonging to an educated relative or family friend who was a member of one of the better book clubs or organizations, like the American Association of University Women. The novels are also the ones that local as well as university libraries routinely try to recycle; literally, they occupy the bargain basement of literary history and can often be had at a dollar a dozen, though once they were estimable enough to be reviewed in prestigious venues.

Although scholars have successfully set about reclaiming authors who have been neglected because of social or race prejudice, these writers are seldom among them. Such projects can do only so much to satisfy the need for reordering and reinterpreting historical contexts, nor is it their ambition to study the mainstream. No less an endeavor of recovery than the *Oxford Companion to Women's Writing in the United States*, whose daunting charge was to create a first-of-its-kind reference book on this voluminous subject, consistently omits middle-class authors, including no fewer than three of the six American women who were Pulitzer Prize novelists of the 1930s. The editors do produce entries on Pearl Buck, Margaret Mitchell, and Marjorie Rawlings, but they miss Margaret Barnes, Caroline Miller, and Josephine Johnson. Such authors are left out because nothing in the ideology of canon revision necessitates extending the categories by which they could *not* be omitted. Barnes, Miller, and Johnson, among dozens of other previously esteemed women authors, are neglected because they appealed primarily to readers of middle-class taste, an identity premise near the bottom of most revisionist agendas, and were unredeemed by great popularity. In contrast to authors like Edna Ferber or Fannie Hurst, who had the saving grace of reaching millions, some of the female novelists whose names surface occasionally in this study—like Ruth Suckow, Helen Hull, Josephine Lawrence, Martha Ostenso, Anne Parrish, Janet Fairbank, and Margaret Halsey—sold well enough and once in awhile even handsomely. They were reviewed widely, praised proportionately, and read loyally. As successful as the *Oxford Companion* is in so many other respects, the recovery of this legion of middle-class women writers, and male authors too, still needs further efforts to resituate them in critical memory.[2]

I stress that these books go missing as a class and as a genre, not as a handful of individual titles whose neglect is worrisome. Since my study does not include the multitude of formula fiction, the books I describe were not always the ones that *everyone* was talking about, but in the world before television, they were a valuable means of circulating not only cultural capital, but also social awareness, if only by providing a few evenings' interesting instruction about the life of the middle class and the state of society. Even to the extent that some of these books were simply holiday or commuter-train reading or weekend or evening-at-home novels, they represent a rudimentary vision of some relative cohesiveness of American life, a shareable set of values and questions about the world in which middle-class Americans live. Rather than get lost in them, readers found themselves through them. These readers were attracted to this literature, I suggest, for its potential, not for escape, but for re-creation—the opportunity for refreshing themselves and their understanding of society, their civic identities as readers. Often, this realist fiction provokes as vigorous an imaginative confrontation with public issues as citizen-readers are likely to find anywhere else in the culture. To this end, such novels are social objects; reading them signified a citizen's interest in the general life going on outside of or shaping the private sphere. Countless copies were given as birthday and Christmas gifts—enjoyable yet serious, though not necessarily weighty tokens of the interest in the world that friends and family inhabit. In such gift giving is coiled a tacit social imperative—read and ye shall understand; taken as a group, these books create a whole storehouse of evidence for determining the history of American middle-class taste and cultural anxieties.

I go so far as to say that their study, from their rise by 1920 and their temporary decline by 1960, discloses a new reserve of modern American fiction: an archive of dozens, perhaps hundreds of titles—books by men and women—that readers might still enjoy as conduits to their history and that scholars might consult in order to perceive ever more acutely the dynamics through which the mainstream secures some values, masks some, disowns still others, how the mainstream assimilates oppositional threats or reimagines its purposes. Rather than make a false claim for these books' privileged place, I wish to recalibrate their interest, especially their contribution to the cultural politics of their era, an interest that was often quite topical and explicit, since they centrally treat issues such as livelihood, intimacy, and marriage as a matter of course, but also history, race, gender, homosexuality, region, religion, law, business, labor, ethnicity, politics, imperialism, mental illness, juvenile delinquency, suburbia, and alcoholism, among dozens of other concerns. These novels' pedagogy was rarely profound, but it was immediate insofar as they were mostly about the challenges that middle-class Americans face—in their time and place or throughout U.S. history.

The neglect of these books' appeal and the misapprehensions about their vitality may also suggest something about the changing role of fiction in twentieth-century American culture, including the gloomy way that academic criticism has inadvertently contributed to the attenuation of the status of literature in the public sphere. Literary scholars will read virtually any other kind of fiction before they read works of middle-class realism. Modernist and New Critical preoccupations favored difficult authors, thus severing college readers from each generation's contemporary fiction on the dubious grounds that they were already equipped to read such presumably unfit or unchallenging works anyway. Even now, in an academic culture reputedly unfettered by modernist precepts about the relation between author and audience or dislocations of time and space or fractured allusions, the teaching of contemporary fiction seldom embraces middle-class experience; indeed, the teaching of contemporary American fiction is still likely to equate the contemporary with the postmodern or experimental writing.

The novels in my purview were readily accessible and were covered by daily newspapers, public opinion magazines, and Sunday supplements. Acknowledged for its artistic expression or cultural wisdom, such writing never needed an expert class of critics to interpret it or scholars to list its seven types of ambiguity. In a basic sense, this fiction never needed academic endorsement to gain its audience, nor did its level of difficulty ever elicit a technical vocabulary to enhance its appreciation—a condition replicated in the way publishers now include book club questions at the back of some contemporary novels. Unlike modernist writing, such fiction meant to be very nearly transparent; its aim was to chronicle and investigate the American culture with which it was contemporary, the world that was simultaneously disappearing and reinventing itself afresh before readers' eyes.

If history is written by the victors, so too is literary history. Throughout this study, I explain how various circumstances influence how this record has been kept and how the books we do remember participate in the literary environment in ways other than rebellion against it. A closer examination of that environment—what critics and reviewers said about books, what other novels were under discussion, what kinds of nonfiction addressed similar ideas—helps to demonstrate how treacherous is the critical ground on which we rest so much confidence and how quickly confounded is our defense of why we remember the books we do.

Although the contingencies of writing literary history have something to do with the reason that these books have been eclipsed over the years, wooden plots or conventional characters are also sometimes to blame. Some books lauded in their time really do not carry well over the generations. My general point, however, is that we really do not know these books as a subgenre well enough to dismiss or ignore them as casually as so many literary historians typically do. And we are often oblivious to them as the result of the antibourgeois prejudice permeating literary academe for decades. That prejudice especially circulated in the twentieth century's middle decades, when the great question for many critics was to determine the revolutionary potential of modern culture, critics who believed it was necessary to choose one radical position or another to save democracy, if democracy could be saved. From such a perspective, mainstream fiction represents the middle-class vision of American life during the years that the middle class came to occupy its central role as cultural arbiter. While several authors embraced radical politics for a time, the dominant social point of view was bourgeois and the political framework usually liberal—in the old, humane sense of the word. With relative degrees of enlightenment, these novelists wrote about all peoples of America—the position of minorities, including homosexuals, as well as the treatment of Native Americans. Scholars of the last twenty years or more often have observed that such groups are sadly underpopulated in so much of U.S. literary history; largely absent in canonical American literature these groups may be, but their presence throughout the broad expanse of twentieth-century realism is readily demonstrated.

Readers may even be startled to learn how much of this fiction is actually *about* the relation between majority and minority cultures.

Several books that I discuss were selections of the Book-of-the-Month Club or the Literary Guild, among other organizations, recognition that once would have probably guaranteed their debased status among critics anxious about the incursions made against elite culture by such institutions. In fact, this fiction is frequently described as "middlebrow," a term of disdain whose use I, in turn, disparage, insofar as the label lazily mystifies class-based values in the name of intellectual distinction. Actually, such "brow"-ism borrows an image that intellectuals in the early twentieth century adopted from anthropologists (who had poached it from nineteenth-century phrenologists and craniologists), who claimed that the height of the brow indicated the potential for civilization. This nomenclature, predictably enough, was also pressed into racist service in debates about immigration and cultural citizenship. Seizing on the resonance, Dwight Macdonald invoked the term for his excoriation of the "midcult"—the world of movies and books and other artistic expressions reinforcing the dull centrism of American democratic thought, typified by Thornton Wilder's *Our Town* and Norman Rockwell's magazine covers. Now, a half century later, with mass culture dominant everywhere, such battles seem like quaint bygones; their reliance on metaphors (not to mention out-of-date ones) seems inadequate to the cultural disputes that have replaced the ones that first yielded the term: the commitment to preserve high culture against the appropriations of the middle has outlasted its urgency. So perhaps we should just give up the word. An ever-diminishing crew of critics ferociously determined to uphold a modernist vision of culture still deprecates the "middlebrow," but by this time, their enemy is really less the midculture's imitations than pop culture's globalizing supremacy.[3]

When I call these novels "middle class," I mean nothing pejorative, certainly none of the modernist disdain for the bourgeoisie. Rather, I use the phrase more for its evocative power than its definitional value. First, I am describing a milieu populated largely by people who make a comfortable enough living that they have the leisure to engage in questions of interiority as well as social appearances. The resolution of their dilemmas will usually be compromises between the conflicting demands of these private and public spheres. Foremost among their private concerns is intimate life, especially courtship and marriage; foremost among their public concerns are the struggles of livelihood, though often they are also witnesses to history or participants in various political and social dramas. The resolution of these conflicts obviously tends to validate the anxieties of the characters' class identifications—who would be surprised? Doesn't any class-identified literature do the same?—though these novels often criticize the most self-satisfied, least generous understandings of the social problems they examine. Typically, the change the novels call for demands a refocusing of attention, not a radical reformation. Their limitation is in the way that these authors imagine circumstances, which tend to be literal-minded, so their realism risks being familiar, even tame. Otherwise, there would be more Dostoyevskies and George Eliots. The efforts of such fiction are not to move the rich or poor into appreciating the worries of the middle class, struggling or otherwise, nor do these novels mean smugly to reinforce the self-consciousness of middle-class life or hold up that life for universal admiration or censure. Instead, these novels situate for readers the social circumstances and psychological and moral ramifications as well as cultural, even political and historical, implications of the way larger public issues make their impact on the private life of the middle class.

When I call these novels or their readers "bourgeois," I do not mean anything derogatory, either. I use the term with respect for its difference but without designating petit or haute, nor as differentiating the urban middle class from its suburban or rural counterpart. I sometimes draw from social historians and theorists in making these designations, since their insights often enliven my reading, but the critical study of the middle class is really a fairly new scholarly enterprise, with just a few books vaulting over the long-term problem of determining the coherence of a class about which it is said some 80 percent of Americans say they belong. Readers who insist on knowing who comprised the middle class or who hope that I will succeed where so many predecessors have failed by defining just what the term "middle class" means will be distressed, but not so much, I trust, that they will miss the chance of learning about this neglected trove of U.S. writing—the fiction written for the American middle class, by the American middle class, about the American middle class.

Instead, I am describing recreational or citizen-readers who as consumers had the means, opportunity, and inclination to keep up with hardback publishing in the '20s, '30s, and '40s, and who continued to support that literature after the paperback revolution in the late '40s and early '50s. Sometimes, the interest in this fiction can be measured in the retail sales of a book, though in general I am less interested in numbers than I am in critical approval to ensure a book's interest. (I might also have used the index of the White House Library, which since 1930 has collected works of nonfiction and fiction that major publishers have considered their best products of the decade, but even that canonization seemed too narrow, though with the White House as the repository, such books obviously enjoy a certain imprimatur of establishing or codifying national consciousness and the nation-state's literary legacy.)

These readers are middle class insofar as they are the implied audience for novels that take their experience as narratable, as stories that can be told, specified, and complicated, with a poised assurance of an expectant audience. Forty years ago, literary critics developed a formal concept of an implied reader; reading dozens and dozens of these novels, and hundreds of reviews and belletristic essays, also led me to appreciate that the general audience to whom so many of these writings were addressed was implicitly middle class, at least to the extent that the characters' problems were the selfsame anxieties of the American middle class. In part, this was a revelation: proletarian literature might be designated by its special class interests; why not these novels? At the same time, understanding that the works were intended for middle-class readers was remarkably commonplace, for, of course, who else had the social investment and leisure interest to consult the realist tradition for its representations of modern life? By invoking "middle class" as an identity more imaginary than a demographically specific entity, I also mean to preserve the looseness of the term, whose very fluidity is essential to my purpose of describing a cultural institution that so fittingly admits of so much contradiction, inconsistency, contingency, appropriative power, assimilative energy, and exclusionary force.

Calling such novels "middlebrow" distracts us from their nuances of class and supports two critical schemas antagonistic to this literature: first, it promotes criticism as an Arnoldian quest for connoisseurship, with dictatorial critics dismissing anything insufficiently highbrow. The unintentional, though by no means unwelcome, result of this hierarchalizing is, then, also to glamorize the lowbrow, as if to challenge decorum by finding in low culture redemptive—that is, pacifying or arousing—properties. The result is that high and low, but not middle, are discussably within a critic's ken.

Second, brow-ism disguises ignorance as superior taste to exempt critics and scholars from reading the stuff, as if to insulate them from the subterfuges of the mediocre and protect them from the danger of mistaking a phony as the real thing. The result is to turn the professional critic and the academic scholar into a "standardized" reader, that 1920s term for conformist ideals, someone who judges by brand names. The irony is that, far from condemning middle-class culture, a good many esteemed academic and nonacademic critics in the middle decades, unlike so many contemporary critics and scholars, actually wrote books that educated readers appreciated: novels, historical narratives, travel accounts, or meditations on the state of American life and letters.

I propose that we come to know this fiction as the twentieth-century continuation of the Howellsian vein of American fiction, a vein that generations of critics have either disparaged (for reasons I will describe) or consciously ignored, since it served neither their highbrow aspirations nor their lowbrow enthusiasms. Traditional scholars may be reluctant to do so now since it violates their good sense: if these books were really so good, they may aver, surely the news would be known by this time. (Dawn Powell's resurrection, led by Gore Vidal, suggests that, for all we know, there might be others, though it is as a chronicler of the New York demimonde, not as a novelist of bad manners in the Ohio of her youth, that formed the basis of her new preferment.) Progressive scholars, on the other hand, often find that redressing the ideological mistakes that result from conservative orthodoxy means that they need to focus their energies on works that never did find the audience they deserve or whose audience was impugned. The fiction I have in mind, however, did have an audience, an appreciative one that just did not have any vested interest in remembering the literary history unfolding before it daily, perhaps because there would have been no reason to suppose that the interests that this literature represented would ever have been endangered. Those books, like the visions of America they represented, endlessly replaced themselves, season after publishing season, thereby giving us a cultural history of the United States in the midst of revising itself. Like the middle class itself, the America that these novels amply witness is not inert but insistently supple, always redefining its boundaries, redesigning its purposes, rearticulating its bewilderments, reaffirming its triumphs, and reenacting its worries.

Sometimes, these books were seen by their reviewers as every bit as compelling as the ones we actually have seized on as the foundation of our twentieth-century literary heritage, like F. Scott Fitzgerald's *The Great Gatsby* (1925). It is also interesting to learn from reading so many reviews just how often critics, by our current estimate, got their job right, how well they recognized, within their inevitable limits, what we now regard as brilliance, even for books we think today they surely would have gotten wrong, like William Faulkner's *The Sound and the Fury* (1929) or Zora Neale Hurston's *Their Eyes Were Watching God* (1937). And when evaluations were split (on Ralph Ellison's *Invisible Man* in 1952, for example), the reasons for that division of opinion could be very telling.

Readers may complain about the amorphousness of "middle-class" writing as a category (though the label is scarcely derided as an inadequate term of derision) and yet, as a Supreme Court judge said of pornography, we know it when we see it. We also generally imagine we know, without the aid of sociologists, economists, political scientists, and cultural theorists (welcome as their efforts are), what makes the middle-class mind what it is and what it is not, though more than a few literary historians might feel apprehensive about readily claiming insight into the policies and procedures of other classes. Should middle-class professors and their mainly middle-class students be surprised to discover that the middle-class mind can translate a thousand inimical attributes into something it can accommodate, can make its vision even more comprehensive; its voice, even more resonant? While some novels merely apologize for a bourgeois point of view, this fiction, as a group, is generally more concerned with examining the kinds of perplexity and threats of discomfiture that the middle class was facing during the forty years in which it extended its cultural domain. Thus, they dramatize any everyday subject in order to criticize, expand, revise, and finally to help reclaim middle-class understanding.

Middle-class writers have been typically described as "minor," which remains a pejorative term among academic critics, though that barb has recently lost some of its sting to the extent that *minority* discourse has been politicized and valorized. Yet *minor* as a literary classification is still a trivializing term: the race and gender implications here are well known. Literary historians also want to ensure that writers are not quieted for having advocated unpopular, even subversive causes, or having voiced the complaints of the oppressed. In academe, the prejudice against the (qualitatively) minor in U.S. literature rose from the fear that virtually the entire national corpus risked being seen, from the British and continental point of view, as minor. Out of such apprehension, only decidedly minor intellects studied minor writers, while major writers appealed, as you would suspect, to major intellects. For many Americanists, defending their field in departments governed by Anglophiles required maximizing the major and minimizing the minor.[4] At the same time, a whole critical apparatus was invented—the New Criticism—to prove the richness, complexity, and coherence of major texts, against the less unambiguous interests and less paradoxical achievements of the minor. New Criticism thus provided a means for sorting out which writers and works were worth studying, a function that helped to cement its postwar prestige. In the last twenty-five years, however, we see that instead of literary expertise, academic criticism is often seen as cultivating its authority through political rather than aesthetic powers of discrimination—at its least exercised, a form of advocacy. Yet criticism, as we now practice it, is supposed to show us how such ideological challenges get formulated and situated. The result is that, in the effort to promote the interests of what used to be thought of as the minor and the marginal, we unwittingly reinforce the major by upholding the power of the canon as a solidifying force. Even though revisionists may see their endeavors as egalitarian and liberatory—to serve the oppressed and to worry the privileged—we risk preserving the very antinomies we distrust: enlisting in the party of the angels, we wind up doing the devil's work.

Although I have undertaken this study in an effort to historicize our twentieth-century literary heritage, the problem facing such revisionism is that we are not sufficiently removed from the era and know it only too well by conventional wisdom. Scholars of earlier centuries have a record, in letters and diaries, of what people read and what they made of their reading. In the twentieth century, despite the changes wrought by the telephone, we also have an extremely full account of readers' interests—in the words of book reviewers. Those accounts of new books seldom achieve the deliberative character of literary criticism or cultural meditation; mostly, they were written by professional readers for amateur ones and were proffered as consumer reports: Will you get your money's worth? Reviews express what educated readers look for by inquiring how closely the novel approaches art, or whether it reads like a sociological tract. Or reviews aim to inform readers whether it will gratify them to know these characters' lives, which is to say whether it is worth their time because it will lead to some sort of sympathetic enhancement or intensification. Reviews communicate to readers the human or affective aspect, though for the most part that turns out to be a middle-class standard of better conduct. At the same time, reviewers mean to instruct their readers as to the public virtue of these books: Will engagement in the plots make readers more modern, more tolerant, more perceptive citizens? So, where appropriate, reviewers also take up a novel's concern with the state of society, or the burden of history, the economic predicament, as well as political consequences.

The novels I study are seldom so finished or rich that their unpacking requires the kind of determined acts of clarification that have been the glory of literary criticism over the last sixty years. Unlike postmodern fiction, they are not so complex that theories of language, time, and space needed to be developed to understand them. Rather, this fiction *wants* to be available: the ironies and ambiguities of the contemporary history these novels play out seem patent, their contradictions readily reconciled. Nor is this history disguised to escape some cultural censor. The books are committed to their realist faith and only infrequently resort to allegory. Of course, there is a fuller, shared life embedded in these texts; that is the point—but there are far too many of them for one person to study at one time. Closely reading eight or nine of them really cannot achieve my purpose of describing the range and scope of what may amount to a new resource in the field, nor will it do simply to create a taxonomy or morphology for them so that others will glean their appeal. The deeper interest of these books, for me, can be developed precisely out of their perceived weakness: how much they are *like* other books—fiction and nonfiction—how explicitly and reliably they register meanings and values abroad in the culture.

Additionally, I hesitate to build my argument on close readings of these novels as works of social consciousness; these books are not so unapproachable that only the minute study of their problematic dynamics of representation will enable their demystification. There are a few novels that represent the range of inquiries I invoke at different junctures, but it is the whole idea of one standing for dozens or a dozen standing for hundreds that has contributed so largely to these books being forgotten. I hope to show that there remains a significant body of literature still to read, a significant body of historical criticism and scholarship still to write. My aim is to describe this repository of a more intricate, enriched understanding of mainstream American life and its formation through the last century, an understanding too important to be left to shibboleths and slogans. Political, social, and cultural historians think nothing of writing a ceaseless procession of tomes about the same era, willing as they are to mine the evidence for fresh insight. Literary historians might do the same. Yet too often, because it is the culture so many academics know best, middle-class life is the one that is studied least.[5] Throughout, I name dozens of novels that I believe Americanists could and should know something about, but perhaps hundreds more can be recovered to create a truer literary historical framework for the era. It is paramount that we glean an understanding of the middle-class annals of American literary history, especially during the era when the American middle class came into prominence as the arbiter of cultural taste and social meaning. So we should exert on these literary works the same scholarly pressure we would apply to the historical artifacts of any other century. Engaging the middle class enables us to see more fully how public consciousness is formed and thus to realize our sense of the state of the nation. Reading this fiction also makes us aware of how precious this resource is, even as it grows increasingly remote.

MODERN AMERICAN FICTION AND THE GOOD READER

In what follows, I introduce readers more fully to my subject by studying an especially vivid moment in the voluminous history of American self-consciousness so that we may observe how the discussion of fiction stages arguments about the sort of persons we are and the kind of public we constitute. This particular hour of critical reflection also allows me to spell out even more explicitly some of the historical issues that set my study in motion. The moment comes near the end of the Great War, when "Civilization in the United States"—the title of the era's most famous compendium of opinion on the subject—was especially open to diagnosis. While the perennial question of America's meaning or promise was then being debated even more contentiously than usual, a polite discussion of the subject was convened during the final summer of the war, when Cambridge University assembled a group of British and U.S. Americanists for its symposium, "The America of Today." Participants included a former secretary of the British embassy in Washington, the U.S. commercial attaché in London, and several academics, most notably George Santayana, but also Yale professor of English, Henry Seidel Canby, whose topic was "Literature in Contemporary America."[6]

Canby would later ascend to the stature of middle-class cultural authority par excellence, one of the most influential arbiters of taste in fiction that mid-twentieth-century literary journalism ever produced and certainly in the years between 1920 and 1937, when his campaign for critics consciously to guide the tastes of citizen-readers was at its most robust. In 1918 he was a forty-year-old professor, the author of a couple of books on the short story and on college culture, who paid his own way to attend the conference. A few years after participating in this symposium and after a stint as the associate editor of the *Yale Review*, he accepted a position as editor of the book review section of the *New York Evening Post*, which led, in 1924, to his assuming the editorship of the newly founded *Saturday Review of Literature*. By 1926, Canby was appointed chairman of the editorial board, as well as guiding intellectual spirit of the Book-of-the-Month Club. From such vantage points, Canby quickly established himself as the citizen-reader's delegated critic, the reader whose "definitions"—what contemporary critics might call "interventions"—could be relied on to summarize a responsive liberality of judgment and insight.

Given the occasion to distinguish the current state of American writing and reading, Canby began his Cambridge address by defining the expectations and achievements of a national literature, like American literature, that does not derive from a nearly homogeneous people: "While our civilization has always been British . . . our blood has always been mixed. . . . We have been like the man in a ready-made suit. The cloth is right, but the cut must be altered before the clothes will fit him." Configuring literary culture as a "ready-made suit" rather than the cloth tailored to fit the particulars of a civilization suggests something fabricated rather than inherited, artificial rather than natural, a literature without an organic relation to the people. It is a powerful image, too, for Canby, who understood his endeavor as helping to produce a better suit—a literary tradition that appealed to middle-class taste, even as he meant to raise it.

According to Canby, the problem facing American literature was that a state of literary "decentralization" prevailed. Although New York was the publishing capital, there was no *literary* capital in America, like Paris or London; writers in Tucson, Minneapolis, or Bangor were "marooned" from others who believed in "the necessity of making not the most easily readable book, but the best." This very lack of center galvanized the "verve of American life," which was not mere pep (that early twentieth-century value for an élan vital) but the result of "new adjustments of race and environment . . . multiplying infinitely all over the United States." Against the monotony of the American cultural style—the same magazines, books, movies, hotels, the same slang and much the same conversation—ran "infinite strainings and divergences," Canby declared. That combination of exigency and difference should prompt American writers to record the "multifarious, confused developments of racial instincts working into a national consciousness," a consciousness that was local before it was social. Seeming to predict the regionalist fervor of the '20s and '30s, Canby wrote that "localization is our difficulty; it is also the only means by which literature can keep touch with life in so huge a congeries as America. If we can escape provincialism and yet remain local, all will be well." American letters will prosper as long as they respect how the specificities of one time and place reverberate throughout America. Then, writing in the United States will open itself to the whole of the republic and its new racial composition.

For Canby, this healthiness spans the four classifications of U.S. literature: aristocratic, democratic, dilettante, and bourgeois. Such traditionally elite writers as Henry James or Edith Wharton comprise the first category, while the second can be associated with Walt Whitman and Edgar Lee Masters as well as the speeches of Abraham Lincoln or Woodrow Wilson. Dilettantism refers to the flood of occasional poetry and fiction from "would-be writers, who in every town and county of the United States are writing, writing, writing what they hope to be literature." Canby jokingly observes that more people seem to be engaged in literary endeavor than in "any single money-making enterprise characteristic of a great industrial nation."

Canby concedes that the fourth category—the nation's "vast bourgeois literature"—is difficult to explain: "It is bourgeois writing that makes visible the rivers and oceans of American writing. . . . One finds magazines (. . . as great a literary force as the book in America) . . . whose entire function is to be admirably bourgeois for their two million odd of readers. And in the more truly literary and 'aristocratic' periodicals, in the books published for the discriminating, the bourgeois creeps in and often is dominant." So pervasive is the middle-class point of view and so complete is its ideological power that bourgeois writing is to be found even where it is not supposed to be. That is so because bourgeois literature confines itself to being true to surface characteristics of life, the world in which so many American citizens believe they are living. Its strength is that, unlike democratic or dilettante categories, it instructs *and* entertains. Its limitation is that it pictures rather than interprets life and risks becoming "standardized," which good literature, Canby stipulates, should never be.

Canby's conviction is that class determines the vitality of American cultural life, whose meanings are sustained by class conventions, signs, anxieties, and taste. Canby seems to be associating himself with Howells's extolling of the pervasive, undemanding prosperity that also risks leavening U.S. culture and rendering it bland and mediocre. Yet he stipulates that a bourgeois literature thrives in America because, unlike in England or France, there are only "gradations" rather than decisive differences among reading publics. In the United States, the bourgeois resonates with qualities not the same as in "static civilizations." Here, all classifications of readers embrace bourgeois writing, resulting in "a literature that is good without being very good, true without being utterly true, clever without being fine." For Canby, this literature performs an essential service in a democratic country, meeting "a necessity for a vast moving upward from generation to generation in the intellectual scale, toward a norm that must be relatively low in order to be attainable." By producing a framework for socialization, this kind of writing helps successive generations to grasp the management of middle-class life and to assimilate its ideals and imagination.

Canby sees the edifying power of the bourgeois spirit as making the aristocratic literary expression more readily available too, even as it helps the best of the democratic tradition to be more fully shared. He postulates that the greatness of our national literature will not come from a coterie's celebration of one genius or another, but from the aggregate middle: "Our expectation" lies in the "slowly mounting level of the vast bourgeois literature that fills not excellently, but certainly not discreditably our books and magazines." He prophesies the coming of "a new era in American literature" once "originality," "energy," and "ability" tackle the "desire of Americans to know themselves." The critic's purpose is not to assail the "flat conventionality of popular writing" but to "crack the smooth and monotonous surface and stir the fire beneath it, until the lava of new and true imaginings can pour through." That middle-class imagination has an even volcanic force once the critic brings it to its eruptive peak.

Thus the critical task lies in gauging accurately this power inhering in the representation of bourgeois America by making it intelligible and giving it voice. This fiction portrays the culture in several moments within the momentum of its unfolding, and it does so by representing middle-class culture in dynamic self-confrontation, that is, in talking to itself. Its upheaval is scarcely revolutionary: Middle-class fiction weighs the current hour against what it knows best, the status quo to which the middle class has been dedicated, and in favor of what it wants most. Only then, Canby declares, will "bourgeois democracy" flourish. As we will see, Canby locates these possibilities in the just appreciation of fiction, like Booth Tarkington's *Alice Adams* (1921), that examines how the middle class balances the shifts modernity brings.

Soon after this address, Canby published *Everyday Americans* (1920), a collection of his writings about American politics, philosophy, religion, literature, and their "consummation," the "Bourgeois American"—the "middle class ideal incarnate," which is "triumphant, or dismal, according to your point of view."[7] In this volume, Canby recurs to the challenge and responsibility of American literature in the postwar world and takes up an issue he had left suspended in his previous assessment: America's "racial problem," by which he does not mean the "Negro Problem" but rather the heterogeneous culture created over the years by the influx of non-British immigrants. Many of the reactionary participants in the controversy over Americanization thought that the new population ratios had kept the United States from becoming "a real nation," since Southern and Eastern European as well as Asian immigration had distanced U.S. culture from its tribal, Anglo-Saxon origins more plainly than ever before. Such differences, Canby observes, have led to radical and positive alterations to our national image, especially the tendency to "think more of character and less of reputation." He is referring here, as he does elsewhere, to some ideal of merit, one that exalts innate talents rather than prevailing typologies, individual achievement over inherited privilege.

Canby's definition of this new literary endeavor not only elevates bourgeois culture at the moment when it is being roundly castigated, but also makes that ascendancy depend on understanding U.S. culture as quintessentially modern, that is, "heterogeneous, brilliant, useful, but disturbing," a prospect that he inevitably associates with the impact of the immigrant population on the host culture, America's British heritage. This New America will need a "mordant, sophisticated, cosmopolitan" literature that is essentially middle class insofar as it is "keenly aware of the need for a more honest and vigorous expression of what America means to-day." Cutting away at the sentimentalities implicit in our idealism, this new writing will attack our "moribund liberalism" and question the "moral standards that have been received as irrevocable because they were American." In this way, Canby demands of modern American literature that it prevail over middle-class consumerism just as it prevailed over the genteel tradition. It should abjure "clever, sentimental writing, which, with sewing-machines, dental pastes, ready-made clothes, and cheap motor-cars, has become one of the standardized products of America." One has to wonder just which authors, in 1918, Canby is enlisting—certainly none of the heroes of the twenties, the expatriates. Perhaps he means Sherwood Anderson or an author like Ernest Poole. Unfortunately, he does not recite their names as part of this peroration, but the other-than-honest, other-than-fresh novelists he means for the new bourgeois authors to overturn are sentimental writers like Zane Grey, Gene Stratton-Porter, or Edith Porter, all of whom had scored successes during the war years.

If Canby's estimate of the potentialities of bourgeois literature is otherwise too generous, here his argument resounds perhaps most recognizably with its time, for it is the middle-class by-product of standardization that is his nemesis, rather than bourgeois taste itself. This modern American literature makes its sensibility felt not by addressing its power of disturbance to please some aristocracy of tastemakers. The new American writing will exert its influence to the extent that it engages and tests the middle class, which for Canby is the means through which cultural instruction is ultimately distributed. That testing comes in the way bourgeois realist novels sometimes oppose the dominant values and prejudices of mainstream culture. Sometimes the result of that confrontation is a fuller understanding of the troubles besetting middle-class culture; sometimes middle-class culture, to its discredit, denies the power of antithesis and takes refuge in its complacency. Throughout the middle decades, as I will show, middle-class fiction pursues these arguments as a central part of the nation's literary culture and as a vital function in formulating and reconfiguring the public sphere.

Canby is not endorsing a middlebrow appropriation of high culture. For him, class tells; and the middle class—the most plentiful, perhaps the most vociferous, certainly the most visible and the most vigorous—tells the most. Its values are the ones that need scrutiny, not from without but from within. It is not enough to accept the given order, like the Puritan tradition and its genteel successors. Rather, an implicit pragmatic faith needs to be summoned: writers of all classifications must sooner or later submit their vision not for middle-class certification, but as part of the bourgeois conversation, a conversation on which the vitality of U.S. culture depends.

Plus, there is no definite divide, Canby notes, in the U.S. reading public, as there is in other countries, where highbrow elitism and lowbrow popularity are also class designated. In the so-called permeable class boundaries of America, the true agent of cultural assimilation might well be a bourgeois sensibility. Canby thus summons a meritocratic ideal of "abilities," one that comprehends the talents of Italians, Greeks, and most especially Jews. That he would single out the contributions of Jews—the group so generally seen as liminal occupants of the nether worlds of rich and poor, Oriental and European, white and colored—as reshaping the American Way, suggests that their difference underscores the cosmopolitanism of the new self-consciousness.[8]

Canby's views, especially concerning the middle class, are by no means the conventional interpretation, either of the contemporaneous state of American society or the richest possibilities of American fiction. In the "battle of the books"—the ongoing culture wars between the conservative New Humanists, like Paul Elmer More and Irving Babbitt, who were troubled by the loss of tradition risked by the new tumult, and the progressive Young Intellectuals, like the early Van Wyck Brooks and his followers, who saw themselves as championing the modern—he aligns himself with neither side. Canby is not especially attuned to the current state of political opinion, for within a few years the Johnson-Reed Act (1924) will turn back immigrant quotas in an effort to restore the primacy of the Northern European–American tradition. Nor were Canby's the views of cultural pluralists like Randolph Bourne or Horace Kallen, who found in the immigrants the possibilities of either a new modern nation or a resuscitation of an American democratic vision. Even though he was by no means committed to a multicultural ideal, his positive sense of the "radical alterations" facing the nation was still diametrically opposed to such influential, reactionary exceptionalists as E. A. Ross or Madison Grant, who argued that immigration was ruining the American social fabric.

At the threshold of the twenties, established literary critics generally did not see the nation's new multicultural aspect as especially salutary. The "point of view in American criticism," according to Stuart P. Sherman (then at his most conservative), was to defend "Puritanism—its deep human passion for perfection"—from antagonists who "are seeking to destroy the one principle which can possibly result in the integration of the national life."[9] Important books of 1918 seemed to stress Sherman's original wisdom, including Pulitzer Prize–winner *The Education of Henry Adams* (though Carl Sandburg's democratic ode to the Midwest, *Cornhuskers*, really was an exception). Willa Cather's *My Antonia*, also of 1918, undermines Canby's argument that the changes immigration introduced could have a tonic effect on the middle class, for in that novel, Americanization ultimately means forsaking ethnic convictions, habits, and charm. The vital power of the immigrant lies not in her capacity to revivify the farm community, but to encourage the American-born narrator's search for freedom, which may be financially rewarding but spiritually debilitating. In fact, U.S. literary scholars of the middle decades typically separated immigrant literature from the New England tradition, the tracing of which remained the most animating tendency in such enterprises as the *Cambridge History of American Literature* (1917–21) or the host of American literature anthologies being prepared for colleges and universities after the war. Few of these encyclopedias found much to say about the cultural diversity of American literature and, in general, were trying to forge a coherent narrative line that made this history comprehensible and patriotic, sometimes nationalistic. Yet, for Canby, the war's liberating result was that the American had become "conscious of his racial heterogeneity. It has turned the X-ray upon his interior processes and revealed a metamorphosis not yet complete."[10] Canby's faith in the middle class to communicate its power of identification across ethnic as well as generational borders certifies this vision of a variegated American cultural landscape. Americanization depends on economic opportunity; instead of the spiritual demands of Puritanism, our modern American culture is truly to be integrated through the shared intensity of a middle-class commitment to prosper and live decently.

Recall that Canby is writing in the years immediately before Sinclair Lewis lambasted the middle class in *Main Street* (1920) and *Babbitt* (1922). The American modernists cast that life as so ferociously smug that combating it became heroic. So powerful has been this view among historians of U.S. literature that it is disconcerting, even now, to observe Canby's devotion to a sensibility he so unabashedly calls "bourgeois." What was the character of this literary and cultural argument? Why has modernism's antibourgeois critique prevailed for so long, especially when one considers just how central a role the middle class ultimately played in promoting modernism? Recent literary scholars have reexamined modernism's power in relation to gender, racial, social, and ideological issues, as well as the philosophical principles underlying its fundamental protest and the formal achievements that this agonism developed.[11] Still to be answered is how centrally the privileging of the modern also codifies a struggle for class preeminence: the battle whereby individuals tried to reascertain their relation to the bourgeoisie, not so much to repudiate it and revile its trivialities, as some surely did, but to escape its stultifications while living in it. (The latter tendency is perhaps why modern critics never forgave Lewis. For all of his corrosive satire, bitter arrogance, outrageous pursuit of bourgeois types to ridicule, he often turned to middle-class consolations.)

That mediating sense of modernist protest also expresses a struggle between the city and the country for cultural prestige, implying a demographic argument over culture, wherein urbanity triumphs over provincialism, as Carl Van Doren so influentially taught. The "revolt from the village" then would also underscore the redefining of class wisdom as well as the reorganizing of class attributes, as they are found from country to city. As much as the allure of modernism was concentrated in a vision of urbanity and a repudiation of the rustic, these opposing principles also screened a perhaps more intense struggle for supremacy, the charm and wisdom of the cosmopolite versus the self-satisfied hypocrisy of the haute bourgeoisie, along with the petit bourgeoisie's small-minded fearfulness. Thus the middle class found itself embroiled in a debate about the distribution of power. That conflict, however, was not the one dramatized so memorably in the 1930s as the tension between capital and labor. Instead, the struggle is a middle-class imbroglio: on the one front, against avant-garde rebellion, and, on the other, against the combined forces of aristocratic and mass culture to authorize status. To win, the middle class followed the lead of the new professional-management class and invested its faith in standards.

The 1920s did not invent the importance of noting standards, but the era gave special resonance to the idea of upholding them.[12] The orthodoxy of citing standards may have begun with the proliferation of IQ testing of the vast number of doughboys in the midst of World War I, though the idea had been circulating for awhile. The metaphor was so ubiquitous that American society was even in danger of seeing itself as bound to a limited set of "standard" choices that Henry Ford's Model T (any color as long as it was black) came to symbolize. And much ink was spilled in deciding whether the middle class had even allowed itself to become too standardized. Standards existed to keep discrimination—for good and for ill—to a minimum, to guarantee quality, to assure the consumer. So it is not altogether surprising that such values would eventually be applied to the discussion of literature. Moreover, the modern aesthetic, with its subversion of decorum, its energy, its primitivism, its tumult would soon elicit the defensive propping that resorting to standards entails.

"Standard" thus emerges as one of the period's keywords insofar as the term resonates with values like the cult of efficiency and with conventional morality locked in dubious battle with the vulgarizing tendencies of modernity, especially its new power to render things evanescent. Standardization comforts the middle-class taste—suspicious of unreceived opinions or any efforts to make anything new, drawn as that taste is to the security of accepted practices, even when it is dazzled by fads and fashions: "To each age its own bogy. To Victorian England the spectre of Philistinism, to our own day the bugbear of standardization." Yet, asks Canby in a *Saturday Review* editorial, "Does the fault lie in standardization or in standards? . . . It is a truism that deviation from the usual is nowhere more frowned upon than in democratic America. Conformity is the price of respectability, and eccentricity is a deadly sin." By virtue of being so "overwhelmingly middle class," this society faces the "great peril" of "having superimposed upon it a set of values emanating from the mediocre rather than the distinguished elements of the community"—values of "material satisfactions and unsubtle aesthetic and intellectual achievement."[13]

Rather than to be feared, scorned, or worried over, this state of affairs presents untold opportunities for the culture industry, including movies, radio, and literature: "What of value may they not standardize!" Libraries and book clubs are means to the "standardization of good taste," for it is not the similarity of taste, but the "similarity of bad taste and bad desire" that puts the republic at risk. Canby concludes, "Standardize reading of the better sort, thinking of the better sort, and automatically you'll destandardize lack of judgment and cheapness of taste." Standardized literature is unhealthy for the nation, but standardized taste can deliver an ideal of good judgment, a new standard of the middle class. However quixotic Canby's vision, he is arguing that regularizing and raising critical taste will ultimately uplift the middle class, at least its tendencies toward "lack of judgment" and "cheapness of taste." It is hard to see whether Canby merely has a misplaced confidence in critics or readers or in his conflicted idea of standards, but his insistence on the possibility puts him squarely in his historical moment.

The question of establishing standards lies at the foundation of the controversies that preoccupied American cultural arbiters and literary observers during the years following World War I. This argument also seems to have laid the groundwork for so many future critical battles—the place of politics; the need first for a New Criticism and, in turn, psychoanalysis and mythology; the embrace of structuralism; postmodernist criticism; the advent of deconstruction, New Historicism, and the culture wars—insofar as the participants imagined the debate between the saviors of culture and the radical agents of destruction or, conversely, between the hidebound conservatives who did not understand how the world was changing and the activist modern intellectuals who did.[14] William Crary Brownell, one of the country's most prestigious New Humanists, sounded a war cry on behalf of the attainments of form in his monograph, *Standards* (1917), which promoted traditional values of criticism amid the new swirl of literary achievements and aspirations.

Among the enemies of the neo-Humanists was Joel Spingarn, a Columbia professor of comparative literature, who actually called for a "new criticism," one that would have the advantage of an "education in esthetic thinking" as well as scholarship—"the discipline of knowledge which will give us at one and the same time a wider international outlook and a deeper national insight." For Spingarn, such a goal could be attained through the training of "taste," which was what American criticism lacked the most, because American life proffered it least of all: "There is a deadness of artistic feeling, which is sometimes replaced or disguised by a fervor of sociological obsession, but this is no substitute for the faculty of imaginative sympathy," which, rather than the appreciation of form, lay "at the heart of all criticism."[15] Canby agreed that the conditions for a "fundamental, creative criticism" were favorable, but there was still much work to do in the "education of the reading American mind." Yet he worried that discipline such as Spingarn sought would not come from academe: "The spade work of criticism is research, investigation into the facts of literature and into its social background. The scholar is sometimes, but not often, a critic. He finds out what happened, and often why it happened. He analyzes. . . . He writes history, but he cannot prophesy, and criticism is prophecy implied or direct.

Few outside the universities realize the magnitude of American research into literature, even into American literature, which has been relatively neglected. A thousand spades have been at work for a generation." Here Canby urges critics to model themselves as good interpreters by writing for "general American readers," even as they must work to train those readers' taste. If intellectuals make the mistake of addressing themselves only to their "coteries" and disdain the "intelligent multitude," they will "never understand them, and so will not comprehend the national literature which it is [the critics'] function to stimulate, interpret, and guide." Thus intellectuals will forsake their standing as prophets, as figures who can rightly assess the present and compellingly envision the future.[16]

Canby's vision of the critic's newly standardized relation to citizen-readers bears an immediate contemporary cultural relevance, for his particular sense of this readership is its "new internationalism." The hybridity of this audience ultimately complicates American literature and criticism and renders them more dynamic. For the "mingling of the peoples" makes the old standards less reliable and necessitates "some general definition of that intellectual emotion we call good reading": How can an Anglo-American tradition that includes Lincoln, Milton, and most of all Franklin be defined for an "intelligent German American" whose tradition is "thoroughly Teutonic?" Canby muses. "How can the son of a Russian Jew . . . who himself has been brought up in clamorous New York, understand Thoreau . . . or Cather, without some defining of the nature of the American environment and the relation between thought and the soil?" Canby's critic equips the reader with a faculty of appreciation, the "intellectual emotion" that recalls Spingarn's view of the "deeper sensibility" empowering a "deeper national insight." The "American critic," by which Canby means "you, O discriminating reader," along with "the professional who puts pen to paper," must stimulate, interpret, and guide the national literature. Canby asks whether, after all, there are "absolute standards" for judging the excellence of literary art. At this "chaotic moment, . . . it is fortunate that the traditionalists have plucked up courage and have been reminding an undiscriminating public that there are standards. But they are safe only when they listen to the criticism of those who study the present as much as the past." "Good criticism," Canby concludes, "must be a collaboration between those who seek the absolute and those aware of the relativity of all human formulas."[17]

This compromise may be too easily described as a middlebrow solution, given its faith in dialogue, productive tension, and an altogether customary respect for mutually defining antinomies. Canby's privileged criterion for appraising a novel's popularity is that it meets some "fixed idea" of a generation, "those wide and slow moving currents of opinion . . . which flow so imperceptibly through the minds of a generation or a whole century that there is little realization of their novelty."[18] "American conceptions of some endurance" are borne along these currents, including such prevailing themes as the belief that "American wives suffer from foreign husbands, that capital is ruthless, that youth is right and age wrong, that energy wins over intellect, that virtue is always rewarded." Or the principle ensuring popularity may be the "value of personality" that has given "short but lofty flights to thousands of native stories." In an essay describing the "cravings" tapped by some novels of the season, such as F. Scott Fitzgerald's very topical *The Beautiful and Damned* and Joseph Hergesheimer's fantasy, *Cytherea*, Canby especially praises Tarkington's *Alice Adams*, which illustrates the triumph when "a popular novelist slurred over the popular elements in order to concentrate upon a study of character."[19] The novel distinguished a lackluster year for fiction, one that witnessed Edith Maude Hull's phenomenal best seller *The Sheik* (published earlier in England) and Dorothy Canfield Fisher's commercial and critical success about the pressures of monogamy, *The Brimming Cup*, along with Dos Passos's war novel, *Three Soldiers*, and Ben Hecht's modern bildungsroman, *Erik Dorn*, along with adventure novels like Zane Grey's *The Mysterious Rider* and Rafael Sabatini's *Scaramouche*.

In singling out the exemplary power of Tarkington, Canby explains that the source of the novelist's popularity is that he replaces a "thinly clad formula" with an artist's "own instinct in the plan." Popularity comes when you "write for the people, and let formula . . . take care of itself." But "writing for the people" is not the same as writing down to the people or trying to manipulate the reader's taste. Even as a writer might try to heighten and refine that taste, it means sharing in a bourgeois power of sympathy. As Canby quotes an anonymous editor on the popularity of such novelists: "They think like the people not for them."

That Tarkington's reputation might need to be resurrected now is a sign of how completely Canby's commonsense view was to be disregarded over the next eighty years. The recipient of two Pulitzers for fiction (*The Magnificent Ambersons*, 1918; *Alice Adams*, 1921), Tarkington had been esteemed as the author of several beloved books, including such celebrated childhood romances as *Penrod* (1914) and *Seventeen* (1916) (whose casual racism now mars their rascally charm—the black boy and the Jewish boy may be playfully insulted but are never excluded from the circle of friends; their integration is required). Not only is he barely remembered for these books, but his more serious efforts to narrate the social history of the Midwest in works like *The Magnificent Ambersons* and *The Midlander* (1923), as well as his vivid social portraits, like *The Plutocrat* (1927) and *The Heritage of Hatcher Ide* (1941), are also forgotten.

Rather than examine the cultural history behind Tarkington's disappearance, among the dozens of novelists who have been forgotten because they made their subject the way Americans live now, we may explore instead why reading this novelist is a civic responsibility and a worthwhile literary experience for Canby. The critic describes *Alice Adams* as a consummate portrait, but that is not the accomplishment most of the novel's admirers cited. According to the stoutly middle-class *Bookman*, the novel is a "great and enduring picture of a slice of American life in the present generation"; "interesting, realistic, and thoroughly American," asserts the *New York Times*. The *Outlook* heralded it as "a closely wrought study of one phase of small-town life" as well as a "clear-cut depiction of American life." Even the progressive *Nation* concurred in evaluating the representativeness of the novel. In comparing Tarkington to the most renowned realists of the day, prominent cultural historian Carl Van Doren comments, a little condescendingly, about the novel's "piercing observation": "Quite possibly Mr. Tarkington has never gone beyond the bourgeois assumptions which his story takes for granted. Well, he has not needed to. Theodore Dreiser would have gone behind them and might have been lost; Edith Wharton might have gone behind them and would have been cruel. Mr. Tarkington sticks to familiar territory and writes with the confident touch of a man who is not confused by speculation." Hypothesizing that if Tarkington's next book improves as *Alice Adams* does over its predecessor, the *Bookman* critic predicts that there will then be "no reason why Mr. Tarkington should not be recorded as the most faithful portrayer of American life as our generation has lived it; for, after all, it has been a generation which has seen life as Mr. Tarkington writes of it. Where others photograph, or penetrate with satirical intent, he sees around." Thus Tarkington's sense of portraiture enables him to explore modern personality in its glimmerings and contingencies, not its stability or integrity.[20]

The magazine and newspaper critics were assured in their assessment of

Tarkington's achievement, leading one to wonder how and why generations of later critics found it utterly negligible. It is impossible to say that Tarkington has been intentionally marginalized, in the way professors use the term to signal the conditions whereby a writer of some aesthetic merit or political viewpoint has been banished from critical memory. Tarkington is largely forgotten because the America he is said to have pictured so faithfully has been so thoroughly obliterated, whereas the America of Fitzgerald and Faulkner is imaginatively preserved. Why is this so? Why does one America remain vivid to a generation of scholars and critics and thus lead them to make pedagogical and historical choices that suppress, intentionally or not, the writers we often speak of as removed—for biased reasons—from the power base of critical consciousness? Why does another picture of American life, one that seemed to a great many readers much more normal at the time, lose its vividness and spirit? Why are the novelists who really did prevail, at least in the minds of the judges of their day, like Booth Tarkington, forgotten along with the America they wrote about?

The American life that *Alice Adams* was supposed to document so perfectly is the tale of one middle-class young woman's negotiation of her family's fortunes, including her shiftless brother's vagaries, the eternal complaining of her mother about the family's diminished social position, and her addled father's uncertain health and ambivalent commitment to business. When Mr. Adams fails in a reckless business gamble, the Adamses are ruined. The scandal is furthered when the brother absconds with money from his employer (and Mr. Adams's competitor), the iron-willed, arbitrarily benevolent Mr. Lamb. This is but half the story, since these are only the circumstances detailing the bourgeois values for doing business in America, which is the socioeconomic framework for Alice's broken romance with Mr. Russell, the most sought-after bachelor in the vicinity. Arthur Russell perceives what the eligible young men in town do not: vivacious, imaginative Alice is the one young woman there worth pursuing. Nevertheless, he backs out of the romance after a disastrous dinner party—a meal even more calamitous than the one in Howells's *Rise of Silas Lapham* (1885)—when the Adams family foibles are revealed all too glaringly, their pretensions left in shambles. The novel closes, however, not with the sentimental contrivance of young Russell putting aside social convention to seize the newly chastened, yet ever-lively Alice, who now sees how her illusions have fomented the very situation she dreaded. Instead, we find her mounting the dreary stairs of a business school, having grasped that she must make her own way: "Well, don't you think," she has asked her father in what amounts to the concluding homily of any realist novel, "since we do have to go on we ought to have learned some sense about how to do it?"[21]

Cloying as some now might find the ending, critics praised it over the "trivial conclusions" Tarkington appended to previous novels. For Canby, the ending is happy but not "illogical." His conviction is that *Alice Adams* succeeds as a character sketch, not as a documentary, insofar as it offers Tarkington the occasion to create a new American icon, the "flapper grown old enough to be skeptical of her illusions," while avoiding the picture of a self-deluded young person seen either in the "poster romance" of "department store writers" or the "sad maturity" rendered by "serious minded" ones. Thus, Canby suggests that this novel is widely read to the extent that it enshrines a new figure in our social life, and in doing so, Tarkington's icon surpasses the conception made available by the breezy sensationalism of mass culture ("department store writers") and the inauthentic philosophizing of "serious minded" elite writers. Canby sees Alice as a "finished characterization in that art of the superficial which this author has made his own and in which he is distinguished."[22]

The novel's appeal for Canby goes beyond the slice of life that other critics have noted. Rather, it invokes one of the two most democratic elements of literary taste—characterization over affective identification, or how a work makes the reader feel. Of all the traditional terms of literary criticism, perhaps the values of characterization are the least examined as well as the ones everyone knows best. Reviews throughout the century exalt the value of character as the sine qua non of a good novel insofar as the quality of characterization is recommended to readers as the means of discovering a figure whose acquaintance they might like to make. Critics may discuss the social construction of gender as well as economic and psychoanalytic formations of personality, but readers—in book clubs or classrooms—invariably want to talk about "character." For the question of a character's interest, it seems, there are no experts in the field. So basic is the conception—from "my favorite character" on—that, except for how a book may make us feel, it virtually seems counterintuitive to talk about almost anything else. "Were people really like that?" "I don't know anyone like that"—these are typical responses that resound with the conviction that books succeed on some basis whereby characters are recognizably like the people we know outside of books, which is to say, to the extent that these characters can be construed to behave, no matter what their time and place, no matter what their social position, as people more or less like us. Professors may writhe under the constraint and may explore a dozen alternative questions—about form, ideology, language, history, about a text's undoing, and broader, perhaps deeper terms for its reception—but much sooner than later, their students will talk most often and most passionately about character. Nor have we, in general, developed a way of treating characterological issues with anything like the skill or nuance with which we have developed taxonomies of genre, plot, or perspective, unless it is to the extent that categories like race, gender, and sexuality have absorbed manifold questions of character, as part of the range of issues they illuminate. If so, it may not be a significant intellectual advancement over E. M. Forster's old distinction between flat characters and round ones—that is, characters who can be described in a single sentence and those who cannot.

Why readers care so much about character is a crucial question, for not only does the discussion of character—those with whom we sympathize and identify and those we do not—keep us locked into a set of identity politics formulated as interpretative issues, but that politics often entails the liberal-democratic ethos of freedom and responsibility, fulfillment and exclusion. Canby's faith in the importance of *Alice Adams* turns on his view that contemporary fiction's office is to register the new figures of American social life to a middle-class audience, from whom they are drawn in the first place. And these characters are presented ultimately to themselves insofar as their presentation is pitched for a middle-class public and its arbiters of taste: "Gradually the familiar figures of the American neighborhood are being caught and figured for us. One day we see them on the door-steps, in elevators, at receptions. The next, we read a book, and there our poor struggling victim of industrial oppression, or giggling flapper, or would-be intellectual is given a name, a story, and a typical individuality. . . . Many writers have had a share in this realization of America, Mr. Tarkington more than most."[23] The critic's job, therefore, is to judge these efforts to constitute this community, even sometimes to police them when those who do not belong invade the vicinity. And whose neighborhood is it? The one in which the "poor struggling victim of industrial oppression," a "giggling flapper," or a "would-be intellectual" are contrasting others—hopeless proletarians, sexually freed and thus trivial women, along with pretentious critics—

antithetical figures that the American middle class uses to constitute itself, in Canby's thumbnail sketch of the enemies of the bourgeois state.

If the modern novelists revolted from middle-class village life, the canonical ones—Ernest Hemingway, F. Scott Fitzgerald, and William Faulkner —took us farther away from the middle class even as they may have transplanted the village. Those writers who attacked the village but who left us in the middle class were the ones we were taught to forget, followed as they were by so many other novelists, each with something to tell us about the generally white, bourgeois, genteel neighborhoods of U.S. fiction. We may no longer see the point in reading about the problems of middle-class persons from another time, but perhaps we should, for as novels like *Alice Adams* show, the key feature of this social topography is the story of the bourgeois consciousness in the midst of adapting and adjusting itself. That self-conception, balancing its "new internationalism" and "native" underpinnings, generates a fiction not of political exclusion or economic deprivation, but of the manners and morals that sustain and fail us, the perplexing world of the middle-class reality, a literary history much richer than many might suppose.

The America these writers brought to the attention of their readers has passed into oblivion and, year by year, has been replaced with another set of surfaces, another source of "confusion," as Jessie Redmon Fauset calls the perplexing changes that the middle class must encounter. Were these novelists good? Yes, but good for what? If that question means do they still instruct us in the practical conduct of our lives, then the answer is not very much. The surfaces of American life have changed too dramatically ever to be represented accurately and richly by an account as old as we will find in the history that follows, though I do point to many books that are replete with current concerns. Does their prose still delight or challenge? Occasionally. These books were written to be read casually, so their prose aimed to be effortless and did not aim to excite in the same ways as do the great novels in the Western tradition. Do writers such as Tarkington speak to our depths— our spiritual needs and fears, dreams and desires? Possibly—yet by showing us how middle-class Americans worry and want, while living amid everyday concerns, they give pleasure and offer guidance perhaps no less wise than scholars find in novels from earlier centuries. Decades hence, few writers of today will be taught in college, but we might project or fantasize that even if they do not illuminate the surfaces of American life eighty years from now, their endeavors to describe some version of our era are worth knowing and important to remember.

REMEMBERING THE PRESENT:
CANON, CLASS, AND CRITICISM

There is no critical conspiracy to keep these books from being read. We simply cannot recall every book that was ever lauded. Perhaps it is just the way of things that many very good books slip through the cracks in the palace of wisdom. Cultural historians and critics should not assign themselves to a special circle of hell and try to recollect *everything*. Americanists have recaptured a great deal of our literary past by refocusing the premises of critical appreciation: we have redressed the New England prejudice, the male, white, and heterosexual prejudices, but we will not—perhaps cannot —give up the antibourgeois prejudice that is often reinforced through a middle-class apprehensiveness about the interest of being middle class.

Consider the critical fortunes of Anzia Yezierska's *Bread Givers* (1925), a novel about a young Jewish woman's achieving identity. By that time, Yezierska had already been celebrated as a Cinderella of the sweatshops who had moved from Hester Street to Hollywood by writing several works of fiction and screenplays. Although she had gained fame for her rendering of the New York ghetto and was even once an answer to a question on the New York State Regents' exam, her star eventually descended. At her death in 1970, Yezierska was just another forgotten writer.

That was the destiny that U.S. literary historians had ordained for her, at least until later in the 1970s when she became one of the first ethnic women writers to be retrieved through the burgeoning spirit of canon reform. Now reprinted and taught as a representative writer in many college and university literature classes (including mine), Yezierska's books quickly became the subject of conference papers, critical essays, and book chapters. A definitive biography appeared; another scholar recounted the tale of the author's love affair with John Dewey. Next to Zora Neale Hurston, no other twentieth-century American woman writer—and certainly no other Jewish American writer—has prospered so much through the new politics of recovery. Yezierska's claim to critical memory will not be so easily lost again, which is as it should be.

Yezierska's most famous novel, *Bread Givers*, appeared in 1925, possibly the annus mirabilis for the novel in modern America, as I will discuss later. The nexus that *Bread Givers* shares with other books of that year includes the anxiety over assimilation, but it might be more tightly focused on the crisis of individualism as well as the complications of gender and its relation to agency. Perhaps most tellingly, this story of a young Jewish woman's coming of age and throwing off patriarchal suffocations forms an ill-fitting triptych with Theodore Dreiser's portrait of Clyde Griffiths in *An American Tragedy* (1925) and Anita Loos's sketch of Lorelei in *Gentlemen Prefer Blondes*— actually a great best seller in 1926—characters who, like Sara Smolinsky, define their self-worth and especially their capacity to love through their material identities in a commodity culture.

As significantly as *Bread Givers* figures in a year that also saw Fitzgerald's *The Great Gatsby*, Willa Cather's *The Professor's House*, Sinclair Lewis's *Arrowsmith* (winner of the Pulitzer Prize), Edith Wharton's *The Mother's Recompense*, and John Dos Passos's *Manhattan Transfer*, the novel was praised not a whit more than another novel of Jewish assimilation in 1925, Elias Tobenkin's *God of Might*. That novel tells the story of an immigrant Jewish man's rise in a small Illinois city, his assimilation, and the ultimate rediscovery of his roots. The struggle of embourgeoisification that occupies the whole of Yezierska's novel, however, is treated with much more dispatch in the tale of Sam Waterman's growth and education. For Tobenkin dramatizes the consequences of making it, not some marvelous fantasy, like Yezierska's, that leaves us at the point of entry. Sara does not wish to tear her new blue serge suit in the ritual act of mourning for her father since it represents her new access to the middle class; Sam Waterman owns the whole emporium. What the novels do share is the staging of the ambivalence that assimilation ineluctably generates, the loss of Jewishness in achieving citizenship. Both characters shed their poverty, and both understand that one cost of their new material well-being is a depleting of spiritual resources, which for Sara Smolinsky is somewhat more welcome than it is for Sam Waterman.

God of Might, like Tobenkin's earlier tale of Americanization, *The House of Conrad* (1918), was roundly praised: in commending its "clear and vigorous English" in addition to its "fine restraint," the *Bookman* pointed out its technical accomplishment and modulation. The *New Republic* so valued the contrast between the dispassionate, direct, and simple exposition of its vision of tragedy that "it might be considered equally valuable as a social document or fiction." Zona Gale, the Midwestern realist, admired it as a "straightforward picture, shorn of adjective, of every quality of ingratiation, packed closely and selectively, communicating no emotion, but adequately producing its clear, cold effect." Writing in the *Saturday Review*, Louis Kronenberger seems most fully to have seized the novel's interest, hailing its elevation of the "persistence of race" over assimilation, intermarriage, and even class.[24]

Elias who? Tobenkin produced five novels between 1916 and 1932 as well as several books of journalism, including one of the first accounts of social conditions in the Soviet Union. You will not find citations about his work in the PMLA, nor is he studied in the new literary histories. Even the encyclopedias of Jewish American writing say little about him, except to note his radical novels, *Witte Arrives* (1916) and *The Road* (1922). Indeed, *God of Might* may well have been the fulfillment of his literary career. His final work, *In the Dark* (1932), went generally unremarked, and the couple of reviews it did garner were content to note its lack of originality.

The reviews of *God of Might* sum up Tobenkin's novel accurately enough, even though he was treated exclusively as a Jewish writer, not an American one. The *Nation* reviewer, J. J. Smertenko, prized the novel's refusal to join in the "shoddy sentimental reactions of those Jews who . . . have contributed popular paeans to the Promised Land." Yezierska herself appreciated his achievement: "With all the passionate sincerity that dominates his work his style is free from adjectives and the overemotionalism of the foreign-born artist"—the very quality that Smertenko, a regular choice among editors for American Jewish titles, found wanting in *Bread Givers*. Having praised *God of Might* in the *Nation* as "ranking with the best Yiddish interpretations of America," he opined in the *Saturday Review* that Yezierska's prose was her undoing, since her skill was too slight to endure the emotional torrents to which her characters are submitted. By contrast, Samson Raphaelson (who wrote perhaps the most famous assimilation narrative, the story from which the first talkie, *The Jazz Singer*, was drawn) preferred Yezierska's book. Although he admired Tobenkin's "air of sanity," "unerring logic," and clear vision of "spiritual unease," he lamented that the author could not appreciate the layers comprising a "fascinating and complex understanding of human nature."[25]

On the basis of their initial reception alone, I cannot find a clear-cut reason to value one above the other, given that the evaluative criteria seem pretty much the same. It may be willfully obtuse to wonder why Yezierska was reclaimed from the deep storage of our critical unconsciousness while Tobenkin seems destined to be discarded. Yes, the time was right for Yezierska, we say, but what does that really mean? That literary and cultural critics make these discriminations according to emerging paradigms? That these norms have lately operated in her favor and that Yezierska has a stronger lobby? Why are contemporary literary historians so content to accept the record made by the very predecessors whose ideological predispositions they mean to contest? I do not say that it is a gross indecency that Tobenkin has been silenced so criminally and ignored so abjectly. His disappearance, if that is the right word for his fate, is really the much more normal, less nefarious dissolving of historical memory, the routine process through which scores of writers talented enough to engage readers in their time pass out of consciousness, pass through the critics' mediation, pass beyond the scholar's ken. Despite our efforts, such cultural amnesia is probably unavoidable and perhaps not entirely unwelcome.

Yet before Yezierska's novel comes to stand too readily for immigrant experience, we might ask what other novels of assimilation were published at about the same time. No one, as far as I know, has yet asked whether *Bread Givers* truly offers a normative and accurate representation of immigrant Jews. Its reflectionist merit is generally accepted at face value, so forceful is the mythology of plucky individualism with which it reverberates. Thomas Ferraro's investigation of the novel's "ethnic passages" suggests that it bears comparison with Mario Puzo's *The Godfather* (1969); on the level of folklore, of course, he is right.[26] Part of *Bread Givers'* appeal—beyond a girl's overcoming her despotic father and passive mother—is that it tells a tale that wanted telling: the struggle to rise out of the tenements into respectability is the fundamental fantasy in Jewish immigrant imagination. This story also enjoys the combined weight of ideological and sentimental approval, at least more so than the tale of a prosperous immigrant's finding his place, although the irony is that both novels close with the discovery of racial consciousness. The readiness to understand Yezierska in this way speaks less to the left side of the hyphen and more to the right. This tendency absorbs the gender parable, even as it enshrines a class-defined story of individualist uplift, in this case, the heroic legend of proletarian exceptionality triumphing over poverty, an American success story that validates both the authenticity of the gifted, determined peasant and the blessings of status. Tobenkin's tale, on the other hand, speaks of the abiding limits of these promises, the disquieting limitation in the relation between identity and class—here, the middle class.

In an inescapable sense, middle-class realism such as Canby describes and *God of Might* represents was meant to be forgotten insofar as the America imagined in this literature was chronically and compulsively re-creating itself. This fiction played a prominent part in defining those changes, at least to the extent that writers took middle-class culture seriously enough to give nuance to its central concerns—of how to live, what to do—yet extending its purview. As much as any other tradition of U.S. writers over the last 125 years, these writers have pertinaciously defined America. In year after year, book after book, the novelists covered in this study create a literary history we forget to our impoverishment, since their fiction reveals the epic story of a nation's self-invention as a modern society through the filter of middle-class experience. In so doing, these novels also instruct readers in their moral duties and civic responsibilities.

{ ONE }

the 1920s

In this chapter, I examine the history of the 1920s as it unfolded rather than the anxious study of its self-consciously modernist literature. I begin with the momentous occasion of William Dean Howells's death to suggest how much the realist tradition survived him. That leads me to survey the middle-class realism that was praised throughout the decade for its efforts to confront modernity. That examination, in turn, helps to reread the critical tenets of the era as well as scholars' sense of important contemporary fiction, an analysis that then takes me into a deeper consideration of the reception of American fiction, with special attention to the year 1925. A review of the plots of this bourgeois literature suggests an emphasis on middle-class culture that the rest of the decade confirms. I further relate that broad view to the larger discussion of bourgeois culture in U.S. fiction. That discussion culminates in a reading of assimilation novels—charting the process whereby foreigners are made into Americans—the meaning of the American dream, and a dire forecast of what is to come. This survey of Americanization novels discloses how truly dedicated is that species of fiction to the middle-class ethos and how deeply involved that ethos was in this salient form of '20s literary expression.

MOURNING HOWELLS

When William Dean Howells died in 1920, his passing symbolized the transition between the end of one era, American Victorianism, and the beginning of another, American modernism. While the moment of his demise coincides with that of the emergence of Sherwood Anderson and Sinclair

Lewis as forerunners to Fitzgerald, Hemingway, and Faulkner, the neatness of this parallel is not as easy as literary historians may have presumed. Howells had already lost sway among the first generation of twentieth-century novelists; even if no writer had yet taken his place as a presiding literary critical intelligence, novelists as widely different from each other as Edith Wharton and Theodore Dreiser had eclipsed his prominence well before the *Age of Innocence* (1920) or *An American Tragedy* (1925). In truth, his doctrines, which once seemed bristling, were now taken as intellectual pieties, compared to, say, the pronouncements of Frank Norris, who had maligned the realism of Henry James and Howells (who had once heralded the younger writer) as the "drama of the broken tea-cup" and the "tragedy of the walk down the lane."[1] In addition, his standing as the nation's literary critic-at-large, humane and even-handed, was also usurped by an intellectual antithesis, journalist H. L. Mencken.

Generations of students have come to know Howells for a remark he made, some forty years before his death, concerning the importance of the American writer's faithfulness to the "more smiling aspects of life," which Howells held to be the "more American." There must always be "sin and suffering and shame" in the United States, he wrote, but these troubles beset individuals, in contrast to the way Tolstoy or Dostoyevsky represented such woe—as the function of an intransigent class structure—in their great trage-dies. Modern readers are likely to know Howells through college syllabus novels like the *Rise of Silas Lapham* (1885) and *A Hazard of New Fortunes* (1890), two different sorts of realism representing his various tendencies. The first follows the moral rise and economic decline of a powerful paint magnate (who scarcely resembles any actual Gilded Age robber baron in his final punctiliousness) by focusing on the development of a central protago-nist; the later novel offers a more general critique of the psychic, social, and political consequences of the transformation of America's natural resources into capital, including urbanization, the plight of labor, the disparities of class, the insufficiency of altruism and inefficiency of collective politics. That novel occupies a broader canvas than *Lapham* and is darker in its implications. Not surprisingly, it was written after Howells had witnessed the Haymarket Riot, which raised his understanding of the systemic basis of evil in America. (In fact, so angered was Howells by the wrongs done to the immigrants accused of anarchist terrorism that he spoke out as forcefully as any public person on their behalf.)

Nevertheless, readers forget that Howells turned more resolutely than any other novelist of his generation to studying the structural composition of many of the *least* smiling aspects of U.S. society in a series of realist novels and satires in the 1890s and 1900s treating such subjects as inherited wealth, race and miscegenation, and evangelical corruption. The misapprehension of Howells as the incarnation of the very genteel tradition he once so aggressively combated masks his identity as the principal architect of U.S. bourgeois realism, fiction written principally to guide middle-class readers through contemporary bewilderments. That is also the literature whose place the modernists had most to derogate and overturn in clearing space for their own agenda.

The reaction to Howells's death, however, reveals that the modernist eclipsing of realism was less an accomplished fact than a critical vision that modernist literary historiographers partially created to promote their own agenda. After he died, Howells was venerated for several accomplishments; none the least, in the words of *Current Opinion*, was he the "great genius of the safe, sane, substantial middle class."[2] His obituaries, along with the reviews of his posthumous novel, *The Vacation of the Kelwyns* (1920), demonstrate that, contrary to conventional wisdom, his standing as an artist and a critic was still significant, not to mention his tense position as the great friend of the late nineteenth century's opposing literary geniuses— "primitive" Mark Twain and "supercivilized" Henry James—whose friendships were routinely invoked amid the appreciations of Howells as the "last of the triumvirate."

One expects hyperbole in obituary notices, but actually these were tempered assessments, as if to acknowledge the gentle example of Howells's style. His critics also modulated their tone. As one observer postulated, Howells's legacy was imperfect. His concentration on the "superficial," his immersion in the tame, shallow world of the middle class, meant that he ultimately did damage to the American novel to the extent that he inaugurated a tradition of reporting—despite his own genius, humor, or artistry. "If his work does not endure," the *Freeman* suggests, it is because "the future will marvel at his having fashioned so much that is lovely out of the unloveliness of the pallid and tepid world that remained, for some reason, the world of his choice." This reaction seems also to predict the ambivalence with which critics read Howells thenceforth: cognizant of his achievement yet impatient with his values and loyalty to the "tepid and pallid" life that middle-class persons presumably lead. His conflicts and dualities never took root the way those of Twain and James did for midcentury critics searching for a premodern legacy for American fiction.[3] On the other hand, his discovery, along with Henry James's, of the life of social intimacy and psychic interiority as the province of middle-class life and the fit subject of critical realism would live on through the twentieth century. If James, who never lost sight of the public world, moved deeper into the inner domain, Howells was determined to make its external, everyday formations the object of his inquiry. It was less the case that he either celebrated or condemned middle-class tribulations and virtues; he did them the honor of taking them seriously as the stuff of serious writing. His most enduring legacy may be how he makes the anxieties of middle-class readers the very subject of his novels, treating that world with a critical edge uncommon for his era, though many readers today do not recognize it as especially sharp. Howells's example discloses how the hoary vision of American fiction as divided into two groups—tender-hearted or tough-skinned, the cult of sensibility or the cult of experience—is really a sort of critical invention, based on perhaps too limited evidence, when the widest comprehension of the twentieth-century realist tradition in America shows that these novels, as I argue throughout, follow neither side of this false binary, but resolutely chart American fiction's supple, capacious middle way.

Surprisingly, Howellsian realism was vivifying even as late as 1920 to the extent that an American fiction that did justice to his vision of a determined if confused middle class was beginning to burgeon. Still, the year was flush with best-selling sentimental, historical, and adventure romances by some of America's best-loved storytellers: Zane Grey, Harold Bell Wright, Joseph C. Lincoln, Irving Bacheller, Eleanor H. Porter, Peter Kyne, and Kathleen Norris all scored big commercial victories. In this respect, 1920 resembled 1919 and 1921 in circumscribing the nation's popular taste, though it was also the year of Lewis's resounding success, *Main Street*, along with the novel that the Pulitzer Prize judges preferred in its place, Wharton's *Age of Innocence*. In addition, 1920 saw critical successes like Zona Gale's story of misbegotten prairie love, *Miss Lulu Bett*, and Floyd Dell's *Moon-Calf*, a tale of a young man from the provinces that led the decade's parade of realist novels espousing the modern temper. Neither Lewis's satire of middle-class mores nor Wharton's of upper-class ones, however, met the challenge evoked in Howells's obituaries of discovering a way of writing fiction that justifies dwelling in middle-class culture amid a world becoming increasingly unlike the past. Perhaps one reason *This Side of Paradise* made its impact that year was that Fitzgerald looked back to the prewar years, not with nostalgia, but as the fearful shape of the uncertain things to come, the new perplexities in how to tell one's delusions from one's desires.

Similarly, Howells's posthumous novel about the 1870s that he finished during the previous decade but had declined to publish also explores the past and its potential for disruption. A reviewer of *The Vacation of the Kelwyns* lauds this story about the troubles that a professor and his family have renting a summer cottage in a Shaker community, citing how the novel discloses its debt to European realism and the representation of the American middle class that Howells tapped through his powers not only to "observe," but also to "chronicle."[4] The words signify. The New Criticism later seized on the former, elevating the power of witness into careful, passionate spectatorship, the Jamesian trapped sentinel, lonely and alienated, raptly watching over and weighing the contact with a changing, sometimes sordid, often brutish social world. The power of chronicling, and exact rendering, was often dismissed, however, as a surface virtue that one may celebrate in Trollope, rather than the more fluid, unfixed narration of Conrad. Ultimately, the critique of chronicling gave way to the derogation of novels as merely reflective—fiction as social documentation for a distinctly ideological purpose, usually progessive.

After Emile Zola, chronicling lost its purchase on creating a reliable record that hinged on the novelist's providing a social epistemology, freighted also with psychological, and even cosmological meaning. Such reports had only a limited use for newly prevailing values for ambiguity, temporal dislocation, and narrative opacity. Instead, the chronicler believes, one may say fetishizes, the phenomenological validity of the extant and the denotative, even deterministic use of material facts. Time and again in reviews of modern American fiction, the impulse to chronicle is disregarded as merely "sociological," in contrast with artistic or literary or imaginative effects. By the 1940s, this tradition even had a name, "problem novels," purportedly illustrating a social ill—alcoholism, juvenile delinquency, sexual repression, mixed marriages, and so forth—that writers were trying at least to publicize and clarify. This impulse was not restricted to polemical works but constituted a narrative commitment to tally that most democratic of subjects—the lives of the middle class. Unlike the naturalists, the Howellsian novelist does not see these problems as predetermined, with the fiction inevitably laying bare the working out of cosmic forces, though on the question of race, Howells himself could be fairly impercipient.[5] Rather, the conviction animating bourgeois realism lies in the belief that a chronicle, giving us the life and times of ordinary citizens, can ultimately help to rehabilitate what is wrong with America.

What were the books of the early '20s that we would not immediately nominate as modernist but might still consider modern realism, books that might have been meant to extend and even to trump Howells but that really follow in the tradition he authorizes? Perhaps nothing could be further in tone from Howells's fiction than the realist satire of *Main Street*, which was, after all, dedicated to Joseph Hergesheimer and James Branch Cabell. Yet in the steady output of novels that captured critical praise and the national attention by surveying the lives of the middle class, Lewis's achievement is supreme. After that controversial success of 1920 came *Babbitt* (1922) and *Arrowsmith* (1925), for which he won even more praise, including the Pulitzer Prize (which he then declined). Lewis followed those triumphs with two critically and commercially successful books: his send-up of hypocritical show-tent clergy, the fiction best seller of its year, *Elmer Gantry* (1927)—which could be compared to Howells's *The Leatherwood God* (1916)—and *Dodsworth* (1929), maybe his most Howellsian book, the story of a retired American businessman's visit to Europe, which rose to second place on the best-selling fiction list. Although the author's reputation later declined steeply—as precipitous a drop as any other American writer may have ever suffered—hard-drinking Red Lewis was the media image of the American novelist in the twenties. Over the years, modern American scholarship has forgotten many of Lewis's books as well as lesser ones by other well-known writers, like Sherwood Anderson's *Poor White* (1920) or Ellen Glasgow's *One Man in His Time* (1922), works even less memorable than those by writers who have entirely dropped out of the canon, such as satirist Harry Leon Wilson, whose *Merton of the Movies* (1922) simultaneously mocked—wonderfully—both the provincial view of Hollywood and Hollywood's dull sense of superiority. Missing too is the modern realist, Ernest Poole, whose novels during the '20s include *Blind* (1920), describing New York tenement life and the Russian Revolution; *Millions* (1922), a family's vigil in anticipation of a large inheritance; *Danger* (1923), the devastation that one neurotic woman wreaks; and *The Avalanche* (1924), where a neurologist (as a precursor of the psychiatrist) struggles with success and materialism.

Other realist novels from the early '20s we might have known more about if the Howellsian legacy had been honored include books about women's new consciousness in the postwar era, such as Alexander Black's *Seventh Angel* (1921), which portrays the New Woman in postwar America, or Mary Briarly's *In His Own Image* (1921), which examines the relations between two working-class and two society women. Other books also devoted to women by better-known writers include Dorothy Canfield Fisher's study of self-determination in marriage, *The Brimming Cup* (1921); Evelyn Scott's tale of a neurotic wife and stepmother, *Narcissus* (1922); and *Adrienne Toner* (1922), the story of an American heiress who imagines that she wants most of all to make others happy, like the English people she lives among, by Anne Douglas Sedgwick, an expatriate whose transatlantic tales were once highly regarded. During these years, Margaret Culkin Banning began her lengthy career as the author of lighter novels about serious subjects, such as *This Marrying* (1920), *The Spellbinders* (1922)—about women entering politics in a Midwestern city—and *Country Club People* (1923).

Were the Howellsian tradition held in higher critical esteem, later students of the novel also might have found out about several novels concerning race relations, like Mary Ovington's powerful study, *Shadow* (1920), or *Nigger* (1922)—Clement Wood's novel about the fates awaiting a former slave and his children—as well as H. A. Shands's highly regarded *Black and White* (1922), concerning the rise of the Ku Klux Klan among tenant farmers in Texas, and Pulitzer Prize–winning novelist T. S. Stribling's first book, a troubling satire about the destiny of a middle-class African American in *Birthright* (1922). Nor were the novels now obliterated from critical consciousness from those years restricted to fiction involving women and blacks. We also have lost an awareness of successful works of mainstream fiction esteemed as significant achievements, books treated in their time in ways indistinguishable from the books we know as major: Owen Johnson, best known as the author of the very popular *Stover at Yale* (1911), whose mature work, *Wasted Generation* (1921), received some celebratory as well as some negative reviews for its critical portrayal of the waste of war, the failure of the social order, and broken love. At the same time, literary historians might have kept sight of critically esteemed books like Mary Maule's story of a disaffected clergyman and his wife, *God's Anointed* (1921); Arthur Train's *His Children's Children* (1923), portraying the breakdown of a family in the generations following the Civil War; *The Able McLaughlins* (1923), Margaret Wilson's Pulitzer Prize–winning novel of nineteenth-century pioneers in Iowa; and popular romancer Kathleen Norris's major critical success, *Certain People of Importance* (1922), about a New England family's westward migration.

OUR TWENTIES

Literary historians now have little way of knowing whether there is a middle-class novel, as a category, worth studying and debating, given the great divide of modern culture that they have inherited and that they have accepted, however tacitly. Throughout the '20s, one can observe efforts that decry modernism and wail over the emergence of a monstrous mass culture at one and the same time. The radical and the sentimental combined to threaten the arbiters of cultural taste to the extent that they both signified an extravagance of expression, offering readers a false choice between two alternatives. The modern versus the sentimental, or popular, signaled counterfeit gods of thought and feeling, of distance and absorption. Modernist threats to bourgeois ideals are patent enough—a literature, as Lionel Trilling once remarked, that bids us to ask questions unmentionable in polite society: Are we happy with our lives, our families, our marriages, our compromises?[6] The case against the sentimental is equally well argued: maneuvered into easy and fixed positions of feeling, readers lose their freedom of thought and responsibility of action. So the argument for studying the popular, as opposed to an avant-garde or its centrist appropriations, turns on the seldom acknowledged yet privileged criterion that the biggest-selling books reveal something truly characteristic about a society—its consuming passions as well as its blind or communal bad faith, especially as that passion is disclosed through sentimental choices and circumstances.

Yet even if we grant that the study of best sellers gives us a clue only about a moment in the culture, and we renounce the impulse to create a typology of best sellers that cuts across the enthusiasms of the day, assigning ourselves instead to the study of these works' means of production and circulation as well as reception, we still would not know why some books are elected to a canon and why other books never get noticed, though they may be devoted to the same subject and, for all any of us know now, are not demonstrably inferior. Missing, I believe, is a sense of the ways literary criticism makes its impact on society, how the talk about books becomes the sound of the culture conversing with itself. The reading public frequently gets excited about novels that cast its concerns into another historical moment or social world, but the pleasures that we find there inevitably depend on their being reflections of contemporary pleasures and worries (as I will later argue about the role of historical fiction in the shaping of literary taste).

What did American fiction look like to the literary critic and general reader of the early '20s? We know something about the landscape of fiction from a range of historical accounts, some of which are by the writers themselves or the critics whose values have been shaped by the ascendancy of one group of writers. Generally trustworthy as they are in representing the important works that prevailing critical taste favors, their dedication to those regnant tastes has resulted in a historical unilateralism. The problem comes not from the historians of the period who were writing immediately in its aftermath, but from later critics and historians who saw so great a need to identify decisive forebears against which to measure new novelists. Especially after World War II, as we shall see, these literary historians did not look to the choices of the '30s, but to the previous postwar era and the novelists to which that volatile time had given rise. Never mind that Hemingway, Fitzgerald, and Faulkner were not the consensus choices of their critics in the '20s. By the late '40s and early '50s, they had attained their imposing prominence, thanks in part to influential collections like Edmund Wilson's of Fitzgerald (1945) and Malcolm Cowley's of Faulkner (1946), not to mention the Nobel Prizes awarded to Faulkner in 1949 and to Hemingway in 1954. Prior to that, at least Hemingway and Faulkner received something like their due.

Although we are so often told that Faulkner was unappreciated and unread by 1945, we might be surprised to learn that he was ranked among readers' ten favorite novelists in the twentieth-anniversary poll of the *Saturday Review of Literature* in 1944 (tied for eighth), while in the same survey, Hemingway—also among the most preferred—alone placed two novels among the readers' favorite ten—*For Whom the Bell Tolls* (number one) and *A Farewell to Arms* (number ten).[7] Already a media darling, Hemingway had committed his powerful myth-making propensities to creating, first, the writer as ultimate competitor (as a deep-sea fisherman, boxer, or big-game hunter), and then, as Papa, the patriarch of literary modernism. Beyond such general approbation and interest was the fascination with these writers, who managed to assert the very personalities, their celebrity, that, according to the New Criticism, artists were in the way of escaping in distancing themselves from their creations. So essays like Mark Schorer's study of Hemingway, "Technique as Discovery" (1950), or anthology choices of Faulkner such as Brooks and Warren made in *Understanding Fiction* (1943), or the valorizing of the unreliable narrator in *The Great Gatsby*, helped to enshrine these figures in the academic assessment of the era as well.

Before 1980 or so, this is the history that so many professors learned when they were in graduate school. This narrative tells us that soon after the Great War, Sherwood Anderson criticized the genteel vision of American rural life with his collection of stories, *Winesburg, Ohio* (1919), followed quickly by Lewis's *Main Street*. Fitzgerald made a splash with *This Side of Paradise* (1920), the novel about golden youth that is said to have initiated the Jazz Age. He sustained his renown with several short stories and then *The Great Gatsby* (1925), which was neither a popular nor a unanimous critical success, but which turned out to be probably the most enduring work of the decade. Lewis scored another hit too, exploding the complacencies of the middle-class businessman in *Babbitt* in 1922. e. e. cummings contributed a war novel, *The Enormous Room* (1922), as had John Dos Passos in *Three Soldiers* (1921), which was followed by Hemingway's stories about postwar malaise, *In Our Time* (1925), and then his monumental *The Sun Also Rises* (1926), which seemed to be the pivotal novel of the decade—the one toward which all others had been heading and the one following which all others had to have in mind. Faulkner's *Soldier's Pay* (1926) and *Sartoris* (1929) were promissory notes for *The Sound and the Fury* (1929) and his '30s masterpieces, while Gertrude Stein was testing the formal properties of language in experimental works like *Geography and Plays* (1922), *The Making of Americans* (1925), and *Composition as Explanation* (1926). Turn-of-the-century novelists Wharton and Dreiser continued to write important books too, but, if they had not lost their audience, they were not winning new readers. There was also a sui generis book by Jean Toomer, *Cane* (1923). In part, this received instruction resulted from the great success of Robert Spiller's *Literary History of the United States* (1948), whose two volumes were republished as a single book in several editions over twenty years, the period when the need to produce American literature professors was likely never greater. No single book is perhaps as responsible for educating a whole generation of Americanists, and the absence—some would say the impossibility—of a suitable successor indicates just how decentered and various the study of American literature(s) has become.[8]

What is missing from this very familiar vision of American literary history? Needless to say, these are more or less the authors that critical partisans of modernism sponsored through the '30s and '40s and especially, as I will describe later, the post–World War II era, and, in the case of Hemingway, Fitzgerald, and Faulkner, turned them into academic industries in the '50s and '60s that rival the output of scholarship devoted to Nathaniel Hawthorne, Herman Melville, Mark Twain, and Henry James. So there is no mention of Booth Tarkington's novels or Willa Cather's *A Lost Lady* or *The Professor's House*, or the Pulitzer Prize she won for a less accomplished book about the war, *One of Ours* (1922). There is no mention of novels by writers who saw themselves as modern and who stood for modern artists but whose works have failed the test of time, like Ben Hecht's *Erik Dorn* (1921) or Floyd Dell's *Moon-Calf* (1920), both once widely admired studies of postwar confusion and alienation, applauded for their sense of sexuality and art as repelling the grossness of provincial middle-class life. Nor is there any mention of Waldo Frank's novels in a similar vein, which appeared throughout the decade. There is no mention either of novels concerning modern women's uncertainties and alienation, like Gertrude Atherton's *Black Oxen* (1923), one of the biggest sellers of its year; nor Edna Ferber's *So Big* (1924), a Pulitzer Prize–winner and best seller too; nor any of Ellen Glasgow's several well-regarded novels. There is no mention of *The Time of Man* (1926) by Elizabeth Madox Roberts, whose string of critically successful novels made her one of the premier writers of the second half of the decade.

Nor is there any inclusion, beyond Toomer's *Cane*, that we would think of as a work of the racial imagination, like W. E. B. Du Bois's *Darkwater* (1920), Walter White's *Fire in the Flint* (1924), or Nella Larsen's novellas (1928, 1929). Indeed, there is not a single mention in Spiller's book of a movement called the Harlem Renaissance. Nor is there any mention of the works of white writers who tried to understand the experience of racial minorities, like Carl Van Vechten's *Nigger Heaven* (1926) and Julia Peterkin's Pulitzer Prize–winning *Scarlet Sister Mary* (1928). Nor of the works of writers who belonged to an ethnic minority, like Yezierska's *Hungry Hearts* (1920) and *Salome of the Tenements* (1923), books considered at least as successful as

Bread Givers. Similarly, writers devoted to the mainstream from within, like Edith Summers Kelley, the author of *Weeds* (1923), are generally forgotten. Even if we were interested solely in studying modern U.S. literary history to learn the new novels most critics of the time thought of as the most important, we would also have to include James Cabell for *Jurgen* (1919), a romance fantasy that authorities censored for its lasciviousness, and Joseph Hergesheimer for *Cytherea* (1922), writers once valued for their skill and their critique of sterility. Their sexual subject matter, which seems no more than naughty to readers of the present day, was held by many to exemplify the new subversive literary spirit. There was no mention either of Thomas Boyd, who enjoyed the highest reputation of all as a war novelist in the 1920s.

CRITICISM IN AMERICA

In forging a canon of '20s writers, the list that Sinclair Lewis furnishes in his 1930 Nobel Prize acceptance speech may give us at least a general understanding of whose careers counted to a writer who the rest of the world deemed the American novelist ablest to stand on an international stage. The authors he names as equally deserving of this honor include Dreiser, Eugene O'Neill, Cabell, Cather, Mencken, Anderson, Upton Sinclair, Hergesheimer, and Hemingway. That list, with some little negotiation (no Wharton?), represented a consensus about the twenties for most of the interbellum period. In firming up such a pantheon of writers, consider two books by Professor Percy Boynton of the University of Chicago, *Some Contemporary Americans* (1924) and *More Contemporary Americans* (1927), where Boynton names the prominent artists of the present moment and makes the case for their importance. He remembers poets—E. A. Robinson, Robert Frost, Edgar Lee Masters, Carl Sandburg, and Amy Lowell (no Ezra Pound, no T. S. Eliot, no Wallace Stevens, no William Carlos Williams)—and dramatists, though none but O'Neill get more than a passing mention, and essayists—the redoubtable Mencken and James Hunecker, who had written vividly about music, along with other works of cultural critique, for the previous quarter century. Novelists elicit the rest of Boynton's attention: the five from the earlier volume include Wharton, Tarkington, Dreiser, Cabell, and Cather; in the second, he adduces three "spokesmen of the moment": Hergesheimer, Anderson, and Lewis. Later, in a textbook, *Literature and American Life*

(1936), Boynton shuffles the lists and nominates the most important writers on "The Contemporary Scene" as Wharton, Anderson, Dreiser, Hergeshei- mer, and Cabell (dropping Tarkington and Cather from the first list and Lewis from the second, even as he adds one or two of his new enthusiasms for the "rediscovery of the frontier"—Ole Rölvaag and Glenway Wescott).

Interestingly, in his 1924 *Encyclopedia Brittanica* article, "Literature in Our Century," Henry Canby nominates the very figures Boynton drops— Lewis, Cather, and Tarkington, along with Zona Gale, as the important writers of the twenties. Later, in *American Estimates* (1929), Canby singles out Cabell and Christopher Morley among contemporary novelists, and, among American novelists since 1914, he suggests that women writers have been extremely successful; Cather and Wharton, he observes, would appear in anyone's top ten list, while Gale, Ferber, Atherton, Anne Douglas Sedg- wick, and Elinor Wylie, the poet-novelist, would also be difficult to exclude. Elsewhere in that collection, he compares Hergesheimer and D. H. Law- rence as typifying the literature of tumult in their respective traditions. A few years later, in *Seven Years' Harvest* (1936), Canby, speaking as editor of the *Saturday Review*, identifies Lewis as the contemporary novelist who has the "gifts of a great social historian" and shares his negative assess- ments of Hemingway and Faulkner, whose *Sanctuary* (1931) was a particular bête noire.[9]

Conventional, even *derrière-garde* as these judgments are, they recur in the critical work that many students of the subject regard as the first full-scale Marxist interpretation of U.S. writing, *The Great Tradition* (1933). There, Granville Hicks also names Wharton, Hergesheimer, Cabell, Cather, Dreiser, Anderson, and Lewis as the '20s novelists whose work counts the most, though he also singles out Elizabeth Roberts and Glenway Wescott. Dos Passos, he says, is the '20s novelist who "has grown steadily during the last decade, and there is no apparent obstacle to his continued growth"— none, that is, but his eventual disaffection, by the end of the '30s, from radical politics. Hicks admires Hemingway's achievements but cannot fore- tell a similarly bright future for him, "with his twin opiates, drink and bull- fighting," or for Faulkner and his "spinning complex melodramas out of his neuroses."[10]

These critics-at-large seem to agree on five or six fiction writers. As the '20s unfold, Tarkington becomes less indispensable, Hergesheimer and Cabell become more essential; Wharton ebbs and returns, Dreiser stays constant, Cather rises. A sample of the many survey course books about American literature reveals what academics thought. In *The New American Literature* (1930), Frederick Pattee, previously the author of the *Feminine Fifties*, a study of nineteenth-century women's writing, notes female writers like Wharton, Atherton, Gale, Cather, and Glasgow, whereas in recognition of Mencken's formidable influence, he gives the critic a whole chapter. For Pattee, the first wave of '20s writers includes "after-the-war-novelists": Hecht, Fitzgerald, and Jim Tully, known for his descriptions of the squalid life of impoverished Irish Americans. Prudently, the professor identifies as someone else's nominations such "undisputed classics" as e. e. cumming's *The Enormous Room*, Elizabeth Roberts's *My Heart and My Flesh* (1927), Wescott's *Goodbye, Wisconsin* (1928), Dos Passos's *Orient Express* (1927)—not *Three Soldiers* or *Manhattan Transfer* (1925), the works now commonly considered the precursors of *U.S.A.*—and, along with some stories by Kenneth Burke, Hemingway's *The Sun Also Rises*. Pattee's book is only given over to the preceding fifty years (it succeeded his *History of American Literature since 1870*, published in 1915), so one would expect it to be more specialized—and it is, meditating on the current vogue of biography, magazine writing, mystery and detective fiction, as well as a consideration of "dime novels." No student of the period should fail to consult it even now.

Russell Blankenship's *American Literature as an Expression of the National Mind* (1931), on the other hand, takes a broader view than Pattee, beginning with a "Background" section that introduces students to the geography and history of the country's several regions as well as providing an overview of America's various races (no mention, however, of Native Americans). Students and professors alike might still learn a good deal about American literature from Blankenship; what other anthologist begins with a detailed consideration of American topography! But Blankenship is not just another nationalist in academic regalia. His section, "The Machine Age," is a responsible account of the '20s, with long discussions of romance and sociology as well as the New Poetry, giving twice as much coverage to "Negro Poetry"— James Weldon Johnson, Claude McKay, Countée Cullen, Langston Hughes— as to T. S. Eliot. In representing the '20s for undergraduates, he iterates Carl Van Doren's thesis concerning the roots of modern American writing in the complex response to the village, with full sections devoted to the defense (newspaperman William Allen White, Booth Tarkington, and Dorothy Canfield Fisher) and to the attack (Lewis and Anderson), while positioning

Cather as "Beyond the Village." For the "new romance," Blankenship singles out Cabell—whose *Jurgen* "seems more clearly than any other novel written in America since *Huckleberry Finn* to bear the promise of relative immortality"—and Hergesheimer, and suggests that Robert Nathan and Donn Byrne will make their presence felt. Both wrote successful books in the '20s and later, though neither, of course, attained the stature that Blankenship predicted.[11]

Ludwig Lewisohn, in his survey book, *Expression in America* (1932), concludes his psychoanalytic investigation of American letters with a section called "Beyond Naturalism," where he studies such modern artists as T. S. Eliot and Eugene O'Neill. The novelists he places in their company, however, are not the modern masters we know, but Cabell, Hergesheimer, and Cather. He predicts that Cather will one day suffer "undue neglect" as a result of the "wild toutings" with which her work is now greeted; this will be a pity, says Lewisohn, because it will mean we risk losing sight of her rare and beautiful talent. Equally prescient about the modern credentials of the other novelists, Lewisohn observes that there is "a sharp and instructive contrast" between the careers of Cabell and Hergesheimer. The former's popularity had resulted from a "silly legal attack" made upon *Jurgen* (1919) for its "salaciousness," charges, says Lewisohn—ever the apostle of sexual freedom—stimulated by "the daydreams of those whose development has been arrested at the threshold of both thought and action." But that popularity is always to be tested by the "rational and virile minds" who find it "almost impossible to read three consecutive pages" of his fantasy romances. Lewisohn contends that Cabell is not really beyond naturalism; he is a "belated romantic" who cannot fashion a novel out of his own time and place: "The fields of earth are on fire under our feet and Cabell offers us the daydreams of a romantic adolescent; there is famine and he goes about hawking expensive and soon cloying sweets." Hergesheimer, on the other hand, has also written of the exotic and distant, but that novelist has sought "to disengage both in the past and in the present the beautiful gesture . . . in which he finds the meaning of life and of the world." For Lewisohn, such historical novels generate "no inner principle of life"; for "an unreligious modern" like Hergesheimer, there is only the "force of human passion" to redeem his work from triviality, and nowhere is that force more vital than in his two "permanent additions to American literature," *Linda Condon* (1919) and *Cytherea* (1922).[12]

Whose word shall we take? How can we explain a literary history so different from the one that has become so normative? What witness to the present might speak authoritatively? It is one thing to suggest that later generations can see more clearly and acutely the dimensions of the present, but of course that is what later generations always say. Obviously, the present always thinks it is the best gauge of the present. The issue is, obviously, whose present, for it cannot be just any member, but the critic young enough not to idolize the past, poised enough to engage the present, and old enough to judge its achievements with a supple, acculturated historical memory—in a word: Edmund Wilson.

Wilson was, for years, the man of letters par excellence in America—critic, fiction writer, historian, cultural arbiter. It is a little sad, though, as a consequence of the changing status of literature in U.S. culture, inevitable, that he has become passé and has so little to say to scholars now, even if so many academics still envy Wilson his claim on the public.[13] Even thirty-five years after his death, twenty-first-century novelists still raise his name as typifying the kind of critic they wish for. It is not so easy now for literary historians to remember Wilson's strong, consistent, and patent appeal. He never had much love for the academy and probably would have disdained, though he could not be surprised by, the turn toward cultural studies, since he himself wrote as much about politics, economics, and popular culture in the United States as he did about literature, perhaps as much as any literary critic ever did, even providing a model for critics of the second half of the twentieth century who resisted the orthodoxy of New Criticism and sought to write about the public issues that reading brought to light.

In *The Shores of Light* (1952), Wilson collected occasional pieces and reviews from the '20s and '30s that he wrote before he settled into his chair as a reviewer for the *New Yorker*. Most were published in the *New Republic*, but he also included articles on '20s writing from his other venues—the *Atlantic Monthly*, *Bookman*, *Dial*, *Nation*, and *Vanity Fair*. These magazines were among the most admired vehicles for shaping literary opinion during the decade, and Wilson's appearance in them helped to solidify his stature, even before he published *Axel's Castle* (1931), his monumental study of modernist writing that traced the development of modernism out of symbolism and naturalism—the first really great book on the new literary aesthetic. That book secured his early renown as the intellectual who could translate the lessons of international modernism, in a way faintly recalling Howells's advocacy of the European realists a half century earlier.

Wilson wasn't interested only in fiction—he wrote about Houdini, burlesque shows, and Greenwich Village—and he often wrote about poets, like Robinson, Stevens, Pound, and Eliot. His several studies of novelists and story writers are not all that surprising: a couple on his college friend Fitzgerald, two reviews of Cather (hated *One of Ours*, liked *A Lost Lady*), Anderson, Ring Lardner, Hemingway, Dos Passos, and Thornton Wilder. Using the reviews to discuss these authors' stature, Wilson also read their fiction primarily to appraise the state of American culture.

The interest of his pieces on Hemingway lies in Wilson's power as a tastemaker. "The Emergence of Ernest Hemingway" recounts how some of Hemingway's writing had come to Wilson's attention and how Wilson's response was brought to the young author's, in turn; it includes Wilson's correspondence with the heretofore unnoticed Hemingway concerning the positive review of the *Three Stories and Ten Poems*, along with *In Our Time*, in the *Dial*, "Mr. Hemingway's Dry-Points." Wilson also collects his end-of-the-decade assessment of the writer, now a celebrity, in "The Sportsman's Tragedy," where he is, typically, at pains to correct other critics' misjudgments. Indeed, other critics are never far from Wilson's mind; he visits with Van Wyck Brooks and Gilbert Seldes (author of the seminal volume on the "vulgar arts" of popular culture studies), as he does time and again with conservatives Irving Babbitt and Paul Elmer More, and with Burton Rascoe, editor of the *Bookman*, among others. Always, Wilson's sense is to praise when possible and, as he puts it, "to clean up" where necessary. His attack on Bernard DeVoto, who had become the editor of the *Saturday Review* in the '30s, was so accurate and acute that Wilson actually anticipated DeVoto's ultimate line several years before DeVoto himself would articulate his provincial assault on '20s expatriate writers.

Wilson can be deadly, as in his assessments of Cabell and Hergesheimer, both of whom represent potential lapses of taste that the sophisticate risks when unguided by Wilson's judgment. His hilarious roundup, "The All-Star Literary Vaudeville," was so naughty that it was first published anonymously, though its authorship was probably an easy guess. There Wilson observes that the American novel, which is supposed to be "our principal glory," is in a bad way and only looks better than English fiction because English novels are at an unusually low ebb. He distrusts Dreiser's preeminence, has no appetite for reading more Lewis once he has been through *Main Street* and *Babbitt*, amusing as they are. Ranked immediately behind these stalwarts are the "provincial fops" Cabell and Hergesheimer, who are cases of a similar kind, since both want very much to be artists: "Except at Cabell's moments of highest imaginative intensity, which are neither very frequent nor very intense, he is likely to be simply insipid," and insofar as Cabell gives the impression of working in a vacuum, "he furnishes a depressing illustration of the decay of the South since the Civil War." To complete the catalog, Cather is a "good craftsman" but "usually rather dull"; Zona Gale is subject to "terrible lapses into feminine melodrama." Among race novels, Toomer's *Cane* is "rather better" than Frank's *Holiday*. (Frank, though talented, is "usually content to invoke an apocalypse.") Dos Passos and Fitzgerald are much more interesting younger writers, certainly more so than the "tawdry" Ben Hecht and the "awfully mild" Van Vechten. Exasperating Sherwood Anderson "could stand to learn something" from Cather and Lewis, though his short stories, along with Hemingway's, Lardner's, and Gertrude Stein's—remote though they may seem from one another—"constitute an impressive group."[14] Wilson's judgments have been so lasting because in some ways he personified taste sophisticated enough to save readers from their bad judgment or blind acceptance of Mencken, who by this time had lost touch with American fiction.

ALL-STAR LITERARY VAUDEVILLE

This excursion into the reception of 1920s fiction indicates that the mainstream were not so happily aware of the achievement of its modernist exemplars as later generations might suppose. In the popular, respected study of the decade's enthusiasms, *Only Yesterday* (1931), Frederick Lewis Allen, the editor of *Harper's*, helps to secure the '20s image when he characterizes the intellectual ferment of these years as "the revolt of the highbrow," a term by which Allen oddly encloses almost anyone who ever had an idea that was critical of or repugnant to middle-class morality. His "highbrow credo" includes a belief in a greater degree of sexual freedom, a defiance of legislative enforcement of propriety, energetic antiprohibitionism, religious skepticism, scorn of the bourgeoisie, a passion for debunking idols, and a fear of mass production and the machine. This sensibility coincides precisely with a vision of the twenties that found great currency during the thirties and that has helped to distort the history of American fiction.

To understand the '20s in ways demanded by the fullness of its literary history, however, means seeing the revolt of highbrows in much more modulated terms than Allen's "informal history" affords. Although the twenties may have roared, they also cleared their throat and often spoke in a well-modulated voice. I am far from suggesting that the decade accepted the preponderant wisdom of bourgeois convention. As V. F. Calverton observes in *The Liberation of American Literature* (1932), the possibilities for liberating American writers came from a rejection of the upper bourgeoisie's vanquishing of the petty bourgeoisie—a victory won even before the '20s began—and a new commitment to the proletariat:

> It will only be generations later . . . that we shall completely realize the full extent to which middle-class rule closed and corrupted the better possibilities of the human mind. . . . Middle-class culture driven to a deception in its economic defense, justifying exploitation as a virtue and competition as a sign of progress, translated the contradiction of its economic life into every form of human endeavor. . . . Nothing was unaffected by this process of intellectual prostitution which it set in motion and was perpetuated by its universities, its privately controlled newspapers and magazines, and its endowed Sunday-schools and churches with lickspittle parsons and priests.[15]

Calverton's complaint seems familiar (and to many unobjectionable) because it has seldom been modified over the last eighty years.

Even if the '20s defined a decade-long battle with middle-class dullness, America was steeped in it. Nowhere does this become more apparent than in its fiction and how it was discussed. One way of seeing this might be to immerse oneself within, not one book or even several books, but the cultural milieu of any given year or two (as scholars have done for 1915 and 1922).[16] While there is something arbitrary about this—a case can probably be made for any year, so why one year and not another?—let's consider a year when American fiction was arguably at its best, 1925, a year when the modern American novel surely might be said to have ascended, with more books by more of the authors we have just seen cited as essential than any other year I can think of: Dreiser, Wharton, Anderson, Dos Passos, Lewis, Cather, Fitzgerald, Glasgow, Hemingway, Ruth Suckow, Van Vechten, Wylie, and Morley. (There was nothing, surprisingly, by the prolific Hergesheimer, except a collection of nonfiction, or Cabell, who published two novels in 1926.) It was also the year of Alain Locke's *The New Negro*, Gertrude Stein's *The Making of Americans*, and William Carlos Williams's *In the American Grain*, along with Yezierska's *Bread Givers*. The novel from that year that ultimately posted the highest sales was Anita Loos's *Gentlemen Prefer Blondes*, though John Erskine's playful historical novel, *The Private Life of Helen of Troy*, also sold astonishingly well. Anne Parrish won the Harper Prize for *The Perennial Bachelor*, a narrative of a man's arrested development and the sisters who support him. Among romances were a Zane Grey (*The Thundering Herd*), a Gene Stratton-Porter (*The Keeper of the Bees*), and a Harold Bell Wright (*A Son of His Father*).

The first notable book appearing in 1925 was the year's Pulitzer Prize winner, Sinclair Lewis's *Arrowsmith*, published in March. Prior to that, the year in fiction seemed unremarkable: playwright Elmer Davis borrowed liberally from *Alice Adams* in his *The Keys of the City*—the first of his two novels that year (which the *New York Times* called a "conventional, rather amusing love story"); in *Runaway*, Floyd Dell tried a story about a woman determined to achieve immortality who befriends a tramp who is also a reporter full of stories. E. Earl Sparling's *Under the Levee*, short stories about the New Orleans demimonde, was marked, said the *Times*, by romance, tragedy, and a "sordid realism." Humorist Irvin Cobb published *Alias Ben Alibi*, about a New York City beat reporter, and historical romancer Rafael Sabatini offered *The Carolinian*, a novel about a husband and wife during the American Revolution, one a loyalist, the other a patriot. Louis Forgione wrote one of the year's several books devoted to ethnic experience in his *Reamer Lou*, the tale of a young Italian man working in the Staten Island shipyards ("Fresh and original and sometimes rather powerful"). In March, the *New Yorker* hailed *Arrowsmith* as a major event, while the *Times* greeted it enthusiastically as following the tradition of *Main Street* and *Babbitt*, noting the character of Leora, Arrowsmith's wife, who was decidedly not a typical angel of domesticity but "gay, wild, fierce and steadfast."[17]

Several noteworthy titles appeared soon after *Arrowsmith*. Dorothy Walworth Carmen, a New England writer, gave a "courageous and truthful" treatment of a minister's moral complexities in *Faith of Our Fathers*; Dawn Powell presented the first of her studies of urban sophisticates, *Whither*, which portrayed a New Woman in New York City; V. R. Emanuel offered *The*

Middle Years, where a suburban nymphomaniac is introduced to a town full of "so many middle-aged Babbitts"; Edward Hungerford's *The Copy Shop* offered another newspaper novel; *Points of Honor* was a collection of stories by Thomas Boyd. Lee Smits's *The Spring Flight* was a highly regarded study of a man's conflict between the moral standards of his faith and his rebellious impulses.[18]

April also saw several memorable books, including *Barren Ground*, Glasgow's story of alienation on the native soil of Virginia ("a contribution of real value to the literary exhibition of American social conditions"), and Fitzgerald's *Great Gatsby* ("a curious book, a mystical, glamorous story of today"). More enthusiastic was the *New York Times* Sunday supplement reviewer about *The Mother's Recompense*—"Mrs. Wharton's best since *House of Mirth*." Actually, several novels devoted to women's experience appeared at about the same time, including Rose Franken's *Pattern*, a psychoanalytic novel that focuses on a woman's fixation on her mother, and Evelyn Scott's *The Golden Door*, which tries to understand a woman's tolerance of a cold, abusive, and adulterous husband. "Old-fashioned" and "sentimental" was popular romancer Faith Baldwin's *Those Difficult Years*, a tale of such typical problems besetting a marriage as in-laws and children. In the fall, Baldwin published a similar book, *Thresholds*, a tale of two sisters and their opposing marriages. Edith Barnard Delano's *The Way of All Earth*, about the heartbreak of keeping up with the Joneses, was considered another "woman's novel" of the season.[19]

For summer reading, several novels concerning modern marriage were reviewed, including Emily Post's foray into fiction, *Parade*, about an impoverished young woman who marries a rich man; her appearance is transformed during her honeymoon, and she becomes captive to this new image of herself. Curiously, two novels about bigamy were reviewed in the same week—one by a woman, in which the perfect man turns out to have a wife and children; the other by a man, who explains how it is possible for a well-meaning man to get himself in such a fix. Adultery was especially worrisome for Thomas Dixon, author of *The Clansman* (1905), who in 1925 offered *The Love Complex*, about a young doctor whose commitment to his work leads him to postpone his marriage to a painter and fabric designer. She eventually falls for another man, in what the *Times* called a "psychological melodrama."[20] There were also several self-consciously modern novels: Herbert Gorman's Joycean *Gold by Gold*; Fulton Ousler's *Sandalwood*, a story of man's struggle against middle-class expectations; critic and cultural journalist

Francis Hackett's effort, *That Nice Young Couple*, about a New Woman who marries on her return from Europe but who eventually has an affair. Cyril Hume's *Cruel Fellowship* is about a young man of reduced circumstances and the social challenges he faces at college. Donald Ogden Stewart's satire, *The Crazy Fool*, tells of a young man's inheriting an insane asylum and his adventures in learning to organize it. Less funny to contemporary taste was the success of Octavus Roy Cohen, who published another of his degrading collections of tales pretending to be comical treatments of African Americans in the South, *Bigger and Blacker*. Obviously, there was a market for such things, since R. Emmet Kennedy's *Black Cameo* had already appeared. A more positive note in the mainstream treatment of blacks was sounded by DuBose Heyward's *Porgy*, which became the basis for George and Ira Gershwin's opera.

Business weighed on the minds of American novelists, including two responses to *Babbitt*: George Hummel's *A Good Man*, which sees business life neither positively nor negatively in its portrayal of a public relations counsel who pursues several interests, including divorce law reform, and Janet Fairbank's *The Smiths*, a novel of the tribulations of a businessman's wife that also aimed to be an epic of Chicago. Later in the summer there came Carl Van Vechten's "cartoon in realism," his "witty, cynical and hard" survey of a group of friends and their activities, including a Wall Street career, *Firecrackers*.[21]

Several novels met the burgeoning interest in regionalism, some treating life in the Midwest, several the South, and a few the Southwest, like Dane Coolidge's *Lorenzo the Magnificent*, which aspires to be a cross-cultural examination of the Mexican takeover of Indian lands. Set more fully in the Anglo perspective is Marshall Hall's Western romance, *Valley of Strife*, and William P. Lawson's *The Fire Woman*, whose hectic plot, about a sect of religious fanatics in Arizona outlawed for their barbarism, the *Times* considered much superior to that of other action novels.

Leading the fall list, the next important novel of 1925, Willa Cather's *The Professor's House*, participates in this enthusiasm for Western American writing, especially in the heroic stature of Tom Outland. The *Times* reviewer was less concerned about this aspect and dwelled instead on the psychological relation between the professor and his favorite student, in what was overall a negative assessment. The following week saw a more positive review of Yezierska's *Bread Givers*, while the next week Sherwood Anderson's *Dark*

Laughter got a mixed notice. More positively reviewed that fall were Louis Bromfield's *Possession*, one of a dozen novels about Midwesterners moving to New York, as well as Nathan Asch's New York novel, *The Office*, a fierce satire of Wall Street; Martha Ostenso's neglected novel of farming in the Northwest, *Wild Geese*, which had won a prize for a manuscript submitted by a first-time author; and Honoré Willsie Morrow's *We Must March*, a romance precursor to A. B. Guthrie's later treatments of the settling of Oregon. Ruth Suckow's *Odyssey of a Nice Girl* and Harry Leon Wilson's *Cousin Jane* were also praised, the former for its portrayal of the limits facing young women, the latter for the painful realism of its approach to female economic dependency.

The *Times* noticed Ernest Hemingway's collection, *In Our Time*—"each story is a sort of extended metaphor"—while John Dos Passos's *Manhattan Transfer* created a much bigger stir: "A powerful and sustained piece of work." Also admired at the end of the season were Christopher Morley's "strange and beautiful" *Thunder on the Left*—a story of twenty-four hours in the lives of adults alternating with scenes from the childhoods they once shared—and Elmer Davis's humorous account of New York City after dark, *Friends of Mr. Sweeney*. The year ended on a stranger note. In December, Dreiser's magisterial *An American Tragedy* was published, along with two novels of seemingly no import. When juxtaposed, however, the three novels suggest a weird, tripartite view of middle-class fiction in the United States. Felix Riesenberg's *P.A.L.* is about a successful inventor who cares only for sales. Believing above all that the public should be sold, he pursues the gullible, until finally one of his products kills someone and he gets bad publicity; the reviewer called it a "mythology" of America. Helen Hull, a popular novelist for years to come, published *The Surry Family*, which relates the life of a farm family, the movement of the children outward, and their lives in the nearby small-town college. Respectively, these two novels write as derisive comedy and as the "accurate limning of the American provincial scene" the very issues that Dreiser attacks—the corrupting power of entrepreneurial capitalism and the falsifications perpetrated in the name of the family and Christian idealism. At the very end of the year, even before the *Times* could take note of it, came the novel that proved to be the year's blockbuster, *Gentlemen Prefer Blondes*.[22]

Over the course of the next eight decades, several of these books have had a turn as the year's greatest work of fiction. Obviously, *Arrowsmith*, but later *An American Tragedy* and *In Our Time*, would also have to be reckoned. When

Dreiser loses favor by the late '40s, *Gatsby* emerges as the crucial book, a judgment perhaps that endures the longest. For some contemporary critics, the most important book might be Wharton's or Cather's or Glasgow's, while for still others Yezierska's. Arguably, the most important work of 1925, for the current generation, might not be a novel at all, but Alain Locke's anthology, *The New Negro*. Yet surely is that collection enriched by reading it in the context of what enlightened white writers were producing. We might say that conferring such a distinction depends on the critic's perspective or ideology, but we also have to see that some books mean a great deal to their time and are remembered for it, while others which may have meant a great deal are not, while a few books, which did not seem to mean as much, are remembered later as having meant or should have meant even more than they did. And, of course, most books meant what they should have meant, then as now.

In examining the year's production of novels in this way, a revisionist historian might point to more memorable, better, or wrongly neglected works. The impulse behind that gesture would again be the connoisseur's superior sense. My point is a little different insofar as I am asking that we recognize that books are championed or not by later generations of critics and readers, and thus are lost to us for no reason except that they did not figure into any reigning ideal of connoisseurship. Yet why should we believe that the books we were taught in school as representing American literary history are the best measure of our cultural heritage, the best lens for our vision of America? Why even now should we turn to *The Professor's House* as a more compelling statement of the United States than, say, Martha Ostenso's *Wild Geese*?

I also mean to point to some unanswerable questions, ones too easily mystified. Our commonsense historical consciousness bids us to recall those works that supposedly spoke for a generation. Or we want to know which books foreshadow greater achievements of the authors we admire, so that even if we do not see *Barren Ground* as itself estimable, it proves important in the development of Glasgow's once quite considerable career. Or we want to know which books, of the many worth remembering for their individual achievement, can claim some combination of topic and style and story and character that leaves us convinced that for a few hours we have been in the presence of art. Or perhaps we want to know which books proved exemplary for other writers.

Generally, readers of a later generation do not find previous popularity a compelling reason to pick up a book, nor does it seem that one year's enthusiasm is another year's grand instruction, so if no one since 1925 has much cared to read and study the deft, lively Harper Prize–winning *Perennial Bachelor*, it does not seem a dire misfortune. But it is lamentable that dozens of such interesting, readable, and valuable novels go missing, a failure of literary historians to do the job of writing the history of the nation's literary production. That history *can* be one of great books—why not?—and it can be one of major authors, or it can be the history of books previously excluded because of prejudices of race, gender, class, ethnicity, and sexuality. Thousands of scholars and critics have devoted their careers to twentieth-century American fiction, yet there ought to be more than the two or three historiographical paradigms to inherit, contest, and refurbish. Of the many literary histories to write, why have we not produced one promoting the full record of our cultural expression, the broad range and thick context of our fiction? Why have literary historians generally understood their mission as endlessly producing interpretations of a few writers and several of their books? That is an important dialogue, but to the extent that it is virtually the only dialogue, it drowns out a multitude of other conversations every bit as important and enriching.

Literary historians want to know which books matter and why. Some academic critics scoff at the imputation of value as something intrinsic and knowable—a counterintuitive classroom gesture that leaves their students stupefied: Why read books from eighty years ago, students query, if the community of literary historians cannot even agree that the ones assigned are the best books, much less the most important books? It satisfies no one outside of English departments—and the reaction is not uniform there either—to say that judgments of taste are no longer the professors' business (though there the disagreement is based less on the need to judge contemporary writing and more on the need to safeguard scholarly investments, usually made twenty, thirty, or fifty years ago); or to say, as well, that value is laden with ideological, potentially suppressive meanings and that the professors' mission is to interrogate or complicate the terms or contingencies on which value is based. As the argument goes, we need to exploit the interest of the external criteria that get tangled up with issues of meaning, questions of significance, and judgments of excellence. In a ballyhooed but limited way, the academic critic's abdication of judgments of excellence in the name of democratic, sometimes radical visions of cultural history turns on a conviction that the idea of cultural authority once undecided or uncertain is now irredeemably bankrupt.

The question might be asked this way: Whose saying some book is good is an opinion worth listening to? A newspaper reviewer's? a magazine critic's? a scholar's? Much of the history of literary criticism in the second half of the twentieth century has been the public's abandonment of the magazine critic and the professors' wresting away what was left of the critic's authority, a power then to be forsaken. Yet the newspaper reviewer, sometimes unaccountably to writers and scholars alike, probably has more say-so over the books that do get attention. Still, was it the newspaper reviewers who made the reputation of, say, Toni Morrison? Who did? Morrison herself? her devoted readers? the prize board members who championed her? the publishers who promoted her? the professors who taught her fiction, the graduate students who featured her in their dissertations, the undergraduates who studied her? book circle participants? Oprah Winfrey and the culture of celebrity in which she flourishes? Is there, following Michel Foucault's "author function," a corollary "critic function" that concatenates the several tests we have for establishing authority?

The impulse behind questions of how literary capital gets circulated is again the expert reader's superior sense of choosing what citizen-readers should remember and of discarding what can safely be forgotten. One may argue that we have needed several hundred books on Faulkner to help us explain to future generations why this author matters so much, that we need so many critical studies to help us discover which ones we truly must have. Yet a few of these books might, without risk to Faulkner's reputation, have been given over to Julia Peterkin or T. S. Stribling, Caroline Gordon, Hamilton Basso, Shelby Foote, or any of the dozens of other Southern writers of the late '20s through the mid-'50s—and there were dozens—whose writings might have benefited from the kind of critical scrutiny afforded to Faulkner. It is one thing—and a good thing—to study, as Lawrence Schwartz did, the enmeshed critical and political processes whereby Faulkner's reputation was constructed after World War II, rescued perhaps from critical underestimation and turned into an industry, but it is another to create so monolithic an ideal that the discussion of other books is stifled.[23]

Why should we believe that the books we were taught in school as representing American literary history are the best lens for our vision of America? They measure our cultural heritage too narrowly. We may neglect a book like Sherwood Anderson's *Dark Laughter* as merely a lesser work of a major writer, now chiefly remembered for one masterfully interwoven collection of sketches as well as for some affecting stories especially useful for teaching students techniques of short fiction, though no less powerful a critic than Mencken hailed *Dark Laughter* as Anderson's best work to date. Yet even this novel has had much more written about it than any of two dozen novels published in 1925 at least as interesting to reviewers and now consigned to oblivion.

In part, writers count for us to the degree that they are the happy beneficiaries of standards of taste, set in place, historically and socially. The admiration for Cabell and Hergesheimer, in the end, could not withstand the new demands that the changes wrought by the Depression and World War II exerted on prevailing criteria of value. Similarly, a beneficiary of these revised standards, like John Steinbeck, could not sustain the revisions of taste in the '50s and '60s, even though his *East of Eden*, a novel that received markedly mixed reviews in 1952, was revived in 2003 as a "classic" by Oprah Winfrey. The logical questions to ask concern when and how the standards that we have for judging the modern American novel were created; how and when the aesthetic judgments favoring modernism assimilate social, economic, and political predispositions such as those distancing the critic from the middle class. Why can so many readers, decades later, agree that Hemingway, not Hergesheimer, speaks to our condition; why Fitzgerald, not Cabell; Wharton, not Elizabeth Roberts—provided that they have read these others? Obviously, some writers never do make it out of their immediate context and are forgotten the next year or the year after. Other writers are fortune's darlings and are remembered for good reasons—and some not-so-good ones, like their alcoholism or their failed marriages, that may have less to do with formal values than we may suppose.[24] But most importantly for this study, why do the books that fall out of favor inevitably treat the middle class, while revenge narratives against the middle class manage to survive? Novels may be popular for all sorts of reasons, but it seems that they cannot be great unless they assail the middle class.

ALL THE FICTION THAT'S FIT TO REVIEW

In surveying the year 1925 in this way, I have relied primarily on the reviews appearing in the *New York Times Book Review*. The *Review* might not have been the most privileged source of the day, in the sense of publishing the most decisive reviews of the most books, and it certainly was not what it has since become, the most authoritative venue for the industry. Its virtue was that it published the largest range of reviews, fiction and nonfiction. In 1925, the paper's Sunday review section did not enjoy its current status as virtually the only place most people, including many of the literati, get their news about books, though the *Times's* efforts to establish itself as the premier newspaper in the United States was already well under way, and its posture of reliable objectivity and unobjectionable taste was already part of its profile. There were dozens of other venues tracking the year's publishing history, and the *Times* might not, at first, seem as reliable a guide as, eighty years later, one would assume, since it certainly chose books to review that favored its cautious politics. It does not describe the year as 1925 might descend to us in the pages of the *Saturday Review* or the *American Mercury* or the *Nation*. At the same time, the *Times* also depended—then as now—on advertising revenue, so the proportion of positive reviews to negatives ones was (and is) extremely high. The voice it was then establishing is precisely why it is still interesting.

Unlike Canby's *Saturday Review*, only a couple of the *Times's* front-page reviews went to fiction (*Arrowsmith* and Lardner's short stories). There were featured reviews of many of the authors one might expect to draw attention, but there was just as much space given to the year's wunderkind, Anne Parrish, among lesser lights. In fact, the weekly roundup reported on mostly now-forgotten books, followed by brief descriptions of seven or eight new books, several of them British. Among the most surprising things for the Americanist of today to discover is the paper's abiding interest in English literature, especially contemporary fiction—Virginia Woolf and Ford Madox Ford to be sure, but also writers whose reputations have not generally survived, like Frank Swinnerton, Rose Macauley, and Margaret Kennedy, standing side by side with Joseph Conrad. In addition, throughout the year some giant—John Donne, James Boswell, Algernon Charles Swinburne, or Thomas Hardy—of English literary history received a reverential homage. Nor did the *Times* content itself with reporting the British scene; its purview also extended to Ladislas Reymont's epic of modern Poland, *The Peasants*, with thoughtful reporting on Marcel Proust and Thomas Mann too. Altogether, the *Times* also mixed coverage of American history and biography with a full range of reviews on international politics, history, and culture.

No other organ had quite the breadth of the *Times*'s weekly supplement, which in 1925 had only recently installed the 32-page format now so familiar —reviews, mixed with an opinion column on topical issues, an omnibus review of interesting articles in the magazines, some publishers' chat, columns of literary queries, and commercial as well as classified ads. For a few years previously, it had been combined with the magazine section and only lately appeared on its own. J. Donald Adams had taken up its editing and brought a new liveliness to the assignments. The weekly supplement had none of Mencken's bite or the *New Yorker*'s insouciance; it avoided the moral earnestness of *Books* or the political partisanship of the *Nation*. Its chief competitor as the weekly arbiter of contemporary fiction was Canby's *Saturday Review*, but that magazine could not take up as many middle-class novels as the *Times*, which performed its job of assessing new books as sensitively as any of its competitors. One must be careful not to claim too much: it was (and is) a newspaper weekly and primarily served as a consumer index of which titles, topics, and authors were up or down. It was urbane about religion but less forgiving of the "new psychology" and modernism. It treated, quite responsively, books about Jewish experience in America and in England (which *is* a little surprising given that the *Times*'s publisher, himself a Jew, was notorious for his self-conscious aloofness—some would say decorously so, others, anxiously so—about covering such concerns). It also reviewed a handful of books by African Americans and was notable among the major venues for reviewing *The New Negro*, though one could not say that it was by any means a beacon in the mainstream discussion of race in the United States, an honor that really should be reserved for the *Dial*.

In the mid-'20s the *Times* commenced its semiannual surveys of fiction, cavalcades that conventionally bemoaned the dullness of the year's production so far even as they also saluted a couple of newcomers and a few favorites. Singled out for praise in the first six months of 1925 were two novels that embody "tendencies of the time," Margaret Kennedy's *Constant Nymph* and William Gerhardie's study of "Europeans cut adrift by the tidal wave of the war," *The Polyglots*. The reviewer also liked novels by English writers such as Rose Macaulay and G. B. Stern. Also recommended were the several books by the American writers one would expect (Lewis, Glasgow, Wharton), along with those whose interest or promise was yet to be generally acknowledged, including the previously cited Floyd Dell and Herbert Gorman, along with Dorothy Walworth Carman, James Boyd (for his histori-

cal novel of the American Revolution, *Drums*), V. R. Emanuel, and an assort-
ment of Indiana novelists (Judge Robert Grant, first-time novelist Lee Smits,
George Shively, and the ever-present Elmer Davis). The standards must have
been pretty high; consider the circumspect estimate of Fitzgerald's "most
skillfully written novel": "'The Great Gatsby' pushes this young novelist
away from youth and toward maturity."[25] In the second roundup, the American novelists to note were, above all, Morley (Anderson and Cather having
produced disappointments), for *Thunder on the Left*, along with Bromfield,
Dos Passos, Helen Hull, Walter Muilenberg (whose treatment of pioneering
the Midwest in *The Prairie* prompted one reviewer to compare it to the work
of Knute Hamsun), Sholem Asch, DuBose Heyward, and John Erskine.

It is one thing to castigate earlier critics for missing the complex appeal of
Barren Ground or *The Mother's Recompense*—which this critic did not—or
The Professor's House, all of which, sooner or later, have scored well, if
unevenly, on the test of time. But *Gatsby*? We cannot say that the novel was
so fully ahead of its time that it could not then be appreciated for the ways it
was later applauded. On the contrary, writing in the *Dial*, the respected
cultural critic Gilbert Seldes prophesies much of *The Great Gatsby*'s later
reputation by remarking that it should be seen as a great leap forward for the
supremely talented author about whom there has always hovered "a grave
question as to what he would do with his gifts." In his latest, Fitzgerald has
"mastered his talents" and "gone soaring in a beautiful flight, leaving behind
him everything dubious and tricky in his earlier work, and leaving even
farther behind all the men of his own generation and most of his elders."
What are the grounds for Seldes's praise? "Scenes of incredible difficulty are
rendered with what seems like effortless precision. . . . The technical virtuosity is extraordinary." Seldes compares the new novel favorably to its
predecessors, admiring its "artistic structure," the novelist's "interesting
temperament," his "abundance of feeling for the characters." The critic then
explains the novel's genealogy, from James via Wharton, and stumbles over
the use of a narrator "who was obviously intended to be much more significant than he is," an intuition that would have seemed a bad joke to those
New Critics who later wrote dozens of journal articles about Nick Carroway's centrality. Seldes also likes the "violent contact" between the novel's
different milieus, though he stops short of fully appreciating Fitzgerald as a
social observer and offers only the by-now-familiar praise: "Fitzgerald has
ceased to content himself with a satiric report on the outside of American

life and has with considerable irony attacked the spirit underneath, and so has begun to report on life in its most general terms." As specific as the report of the Long Island setting may be, it is also "universal." So the critic can conclude that the novel presages a new seriousness and that Fitzgerald can relinquish his identity as the fair-haired boy of the *Saturday Evening Post*—the magazine that paid him so exorbitantly for some unremarkable stories—now that he has "recognized both his capacities and obligations as a novelist."[26]

Seldes gives us a familiar Fitzgerald. That is not surprising inasmuch as the *Dial* was one of the key venues helping to install the critical ideals that have proved so influential. Other critics who should have understood what Fitzgerald was up to were conspicuously less prescient. The *Bookman* considered the novel a "strange combination of satire, burlesque, fantasy, and melodrama," "a satire on present day fame." In a review entitled "Up to the Minute," the critic for the *New York Herald Tribune* thought of *Gatsby* as an advance over the "sociological document" that was *This Side of Paradise*, since the later work is "first and foremost a novel," "almost a perfectly fulfilled intention." However, since the new novel treats the "froth of society," it is at best an "imponderable and fascinating trifle." For this critic, Fitzgerald's "chief weakness" as a novelist was his superficiality, since he did not yet go below the glittering surfaces he reproduced with such virtuosity: "What has never been alive cannot very well go on living; so this is a book of the season only, but so peculiarly of the season, that it is in its small way unique."[27]

In a quirkily positive review in the *Nation*, Carl Van Vechten praises Fitzgerald as a "born story-teller" whose work is "imbued with that rare and beneficent essence we hail as charm"; he singles out the rendering of Gatsby as the "something else" in this novel that skillfully delineates the mundane creatures within the author's imaginative horizon. Van Vechten then pays the author the somewhat backhanded compliment of likening him, despite the "dissimilarity in their choice of material and point of attack," to Booth Tarkington, while pointing out the crucial difference of Fitzgerald's "potential brutality," which bears comparison with Frank Norris. This critic then suggests that really it is Henry James at the core of Fitzgerald's vision, the "theme of a soiled or rather cheap personality transfigured and rendered pathetically appealing through the possession of a passionate idealism." Van Vechten closes by accepting Fitzgerald's own defining talent: "When I read

Absolution in the *American Mercury* I realized that there were many potential qualities inherent in [this author] which hitherto had not been too
apparent. 'The Great Gatsby' confirms this earlier impression. What Mr.
Fitzgerald may do in the future . . . depends to an embarrassing extent on
the nature of his own ambitions." Any embarrassment, however, is Van
Vechten's own abashedness at his having failed to see the completeness of
Fitzgerald's "necessary magic."[28]

In a review obtusely entitled "Scott Fitzgerald Looks into Middle Age,"
Times critic Edwin Clark responds to this magical dimension of the novel,
viewing *Gatsby* first as the work of the "steadiest performer and the most
entertaining" postwar writer and second as a vision expressing "one phase of
the great grotesque spectacle of our American scene." For Clark, the novel's
appeal is generational—the production of a reliable entertainer—and local,
that is, drawing on the new curiosity about the wealthy classes disporting
themselves on Long Island. *Gatsby*'s temper can be found in the "conflict of
spirituality caught fast in the web of our commercial life," a combination of
boisterousness and tragedy that animates the novel with "whimsical magic
and simple pathos that is realized with economy and restraint." All in all, the
"philosopher of the flapper has escaped the mordant but he has turned
grave": "A curious book, a mystical, glamorous story of today. It takes a
deeper cut at life than anything else essayed by Mr. Fitzgerald."[29]

Scribner's seemed intent on anticipating the objections to the novel in
advertising it with a long excerpt from Mencken's review. In a later ad,
Fitzgerald's publisher adduced even stronger acclaim. "Mencken says" was
followed by a corroborating plug from one of the most important of contemporary novelists, "Joseph Hergesheimer says Mencken is right": "It is beautifully written and saturated with a sharp, unforgettable emotion. It gathers
up all his early promise surprisingly soon, and what he subsequently does
must be of great interest and importance." On what basis that these reviews
yield could anyone predict how widely read this novel would be? How much
it would be charged with the responsibility of speaking for modern America
and, in what Van Vechten calls Gatsby's "incredibly cheap and curiously
imitative imagination," the power of illusion at the heart of modernity. At
best, the novel seems to be (1) a fulfillment or justification of Fitzgerald's
early promise; (2) a quintessential tale of the moment and in places a keenly
observed account of the current scene; (3) enlivened by the author's indubi-
table gifts of phrase and maturing sense of form.[30]

One critic astutely suggests that the novel ultimately spans four genres—melodrama, detective story, fantastic satire, Jazz Age extravaganza—and there is a good deal in the academic criticism to confirm this insight. I would also suggest that part of *Gatsby*'s appeal lies not only in the way the narrative orchestrates these several dimensions, but also in the way the novel integrates and, one may say, executes better, some of the novel scenarios then current. In 1925, so many of the books that did excite interest for their modern spirit, like Francis Hackett's *That Nice Young Couple*, Cyril Hume's *Cruel Fellowship*, Donald Douglas's mystical *The Grand Inquisitor*, or Elmer Davis's *Friends of Mr. Sweeney*, focus on the setting that Fitzgerald had made famous, what Van Vechten calls "the aspects and operations of the coeval flapper and cake-eater." The year's fiction was no less filled, as it always is, with novels of broken hearts and disturbed affections, so *Gatsby* exerts this source of appeal too.

At the same time, the novel also makes use of another popular narrative form—the young person from the provinces, like Minnesota, who comes to the great city to find a destiny, such as Larry Barretto's *To Babylon* (about an intelligent Midwesterner who moves to New York, becomes involved with the society crowd and its dinner parties, arrogant families and spoiled children, only to come to certain realizations about his previous aspirations); Louis Bromfield's *Possession* (which traces a young female Ohioan's fortunes in New York); Grove Wilson's *Man of Strife* (in which a Minneapolis newspaperman, despondent over his mother's death and unsatisfied either by his material success or by his marriage, wanders to New York and finds a woman who saves him); and Webb Waldron's *Shanklin* (in which a young man leaves the Midwest on a spiritual quest that takes him around the world, winds up in New York, meets some people with some new political ideas, writes advertising, and searches for an old friend). *Arrowsmith* sort of takes this form too: an idealistic young research physician from the Midwest finds his way to New York, where hypocrisy and corruption test his honest values, and he learns some unsettling things about the modern practice of medicine as well as his own character. (As a story of an imaginative young person in New York City, *Gatsby* also enjoyed some distinguished company in the second half of the '20s, including Wharton's *Hudson River Bracketed*, Claude McKay's *Home to Harlem*, Ludwig Lewisohn's *The Island Within*, and Wallace Thurman's *The Blacker the Berry*.)

The year 1925 had its examples of experiments in narrative point of view to be associated with James or, as one astute reader saw in *Gatsby*, with Conrad, whose *Heart of Darkness* was very much on Fitzgerald's mind when composing the scenario for his own book (a sensitive young man travels to the wilderness, learns of the "horror" to be found there through his meeting of a corrupt older man, a rapacious liar of stupendous proportions, and fears that he has become a liar himself in protecting the older man's memory). Conrad was on a great many readers' and reviewers' minds; his last, unfinished novel had been the feature of the *Saturday Review*'s first table of contents in the previous year, and notes about him and reviews of books about him were everywhere.

What does this constellation of plot summaries and coincidences prove? We might readily concede from our historical vantage point that Fitzgerald's was, after all, the "best" book or most enduring book of the lot, but even then it would not account for the novel's aura, the book that exerted its charm even more forcefully after World War II, in college classrooms of the last fifty years, than it did for its immediate audience—its proportions, wisdom, and style more successfully interpreted than before.

In fact, Fitzgerald's prestige dissipated quickly enough. As his readers know, he was little appreciated in the '30s, but not merely because popular tastes had changed. In a way, he was overly penalized for having been overly lauded. Fitzgerald's great early success initiated a preoccupation among reviewers committed to discovering geniuses, so it was inevitable that critics would desert him in favor of the next new major talent. Fitzgerald's critical invisibility through the '30s is nearly complete, and it is Alfred Kazin who, in 1942, helps to reestablish the stature of *Gatsby*. Two years before, no less a student of modern U.S. fiction than Carl Van Doren, in his *American Novel, 1789–1939*, could praise Fitzgerald's 1925 novel while missing the right appreciative note: "And though he so gave himself to the fashion [for the younger generation that he created] that he passed with it, he wrote *The Great Gatsby* . . . a short realistic novel about a romantic bootlegger that remains one of the brilliant books of a brilliant decade."[31] Indeed, the Fitzgerald who has descended to us—the glamorous, haunted novelist of the Jazz Age—comes primarily through the mediation of Arthur Mizener, whose biography, *The Far Side of Paradise* (1949), restored the gleam to the dazzling celebrity in which Fitzgerald briefly basked. There may be no second acts in America, according to Fitzgerald, but for a few books, like *Gatsby*, there seem to be.

What of the novels that were very much alive, the ones that did create controversy or provoke argument about their worth? It seems as if only Lewis's *Arrowsmith* enjoyed anything like widespread acclaim. Other novels were sometimes paired, as if they were two parts of a puzzle, neither satisfactory in their own right. One such critical juxtaposition was *Manhattan Transfer* and *Thunder on the Left*, which were occasionally reviewed together as offering alternative answers to the difficult question of how to represent our modern era acutely and tastefully. The *New Yorker* yokes them together (along with a play the critic likens to H. G. Wells's *War of the Worlds*), describing Morley's book as the "one likely to please most readers" of the magazine, while stipulating that "you will probably have to read" the Dos Passos novel, since it is "pretty sure to make a lot of noise." *Thunder on the Left*, on the other hand, "embodies a much more intense, and inspired, and searching piece of straight fiction" than readers might expect of Morley, an Algonquin Hotel wag who later created the Baker Street Irregulars for devotees of Sherlock Holmes—whereas *Manhattan Transfer* will provide a "memorable experience," though not necessarily pleasurable, "very much like the real, complete thing" that is life in Manhattan—"a hell of a chaotic futility," "its denizens . . . a scurvy or pitiful lot." Whereas Morley's experiment of alternating chapters concerning adults and the children they once were is "deftly handled," Dos Passos's "Joycean influence is marked, but beneficent." The reviewer never settles his ambivalence: Morley's is the book that will please, but there is a world-weary concession that we also have to read books not merely for pleasure but out of a dimly felt civic duty in the republic of letters—"Dos Passos' Manhattan is not the hypothetical, typical New Yorker reader's"—and that his metropolis is the Manhattan that the magazine's aspirant cosmopolitan readers identify themselves against.[32]

That pairing was made explicitly again in the *Bookman*, that bastion of moderate taste, a review in which the confusions both books register so differently are laid before the reader as possibly the desired effect—"Should a Novel Mean Anything?" In the *Saturday Review*, Canby postulates this similarity of confusing purposes to be the very point to choose, the issue at stake, for the one novel presents modernism as an aesthetic, while the other cultivates the modern as a philosophy. Both novels confront the sense of chaos: one gives us a radical act of representation; the other, a small measure of hope. Canby begins "Thunder in Manhattan" with the conjecture that for later generations of readers, the "most disparate seeming books" of a period, like those by Thackeray and Dickens, reveal more "common characteristics" than contemporaneous reviewers might perceive. So it is, says Canby, of Morley and Dos Passos, two portraitists, two "exponents of what we are in this confused twentieth century."[33]

Dos Passos's world is "multifarious, purposeless, and incoherent." Experience is a "flashing series of movements in which consciousness becomes vivid, so that reality is not in this person or that but in the vividness of their contacts." The "broken narrative of [*Manhattan Transfer*], its shake-up of figures shivering one against the other, its flashes which make no pattern, is tremendously convincing." It seems, after all, that the "city's incoherence is real and man's purposes all illusions." *Thunder on the Left*, however, is committed to making sense of "vagary and confusion": "Morley's week-enders wander in chaotic desires as much as those hard lost souls that flicker through 'Manhattan Transfer,'" but in this novel the individual lashes out against the chaos and "at last he imposes his moral upon the shift of circumstance and bids it take shape and form. . . . What matter if emotions cloud incoherently and there is no pattern into which all of experience fits, these folk have found their own meaning—call it religion if you like."

As complementary as Canby finds these novels, he submits that they ask two decidedly different questions. Dos Passos wants to know "What does life look like in New York?"—that is, a question about representation rather than essence—while Morley's "more fully and more soundly written" book asks a "harder question," "What *is* life?" Dos Passos's Manhattan is a "bad dream where pathetic animals scratch and swallow"; the city's "meaningless entity becomes so real to [the author] that the citizen sinks to a flash and a contact." The Morleyan world is a "waking dream in which the minds of all the characters open to show dark things and light, while chaos just outside our little bit of order is ever pressing in; but it is not a nightmare."

Thus we can see how the terms of the debate over modernity are conceived. Dos Passos's book is to be associated always with "incoherence"— flashes, shivering figures, vividness of contacts—something squalid yet insubstantial, since he does not value the individual's relation to a milieu: "The individual is only a spark from the coil, a point of friction in the whole." But in *Thunder on the Left*, the earnestness of "self-realization" is all: "Life is a mystery, ever threatening, but we are a part of life and may control a tiny share if we will." Here Canby makes clear the terms by which modernity is to be interpreted; the age of satire, he begins by noting, is passed. It is now a question of which portrait will be embraced: nothingness or striving; unpleasantness or "real laughter and beauty and thrill"; "broken pictures, like the sections of a movie film pasted at random" or the "poignancy" of this "loving study of that middle consciousness where thoughts form before they are crystallized by use and wont."

Interestingly, the *Times* did not mean to pair the two novels but coincidentally published reviews of them not only in the same week, but also on the same page. On the strength perhaps of *Three Soldiers*, *Manhattan Transfer* was marked for a feature review, sharing page 5 with Booth Tarkington's latest work of fiction, *Women*, and spilling over to page 10, where "Tragic Trivia of New York" shares space with "Beauty of Style in Christopher Morley's New Novel." What makes this pairing even more intriguing is that the *Times*'s two reviewers seem to anticipate the divergence of opinion Canby exploits as a central question of how we will live with our literature.

The Dos Passos reviewer begins by citing Dos Passos's adherence to Joyce, who is in general a code word for casting "a monkeywrench into the mechanics" of novel writing generally. Instead, the real "meat of this strange book" is the "host of human moths, more or less singed and wilted, who flutter and swarm around the lights of Broadway and Fifth Avenue—tramps, drunkards, wastrels, homo-sexualists, prostitutes. . . . Villagers, waiters, bootleggers, and ruffians." The novel may be a "powerful and sustained piece of work" of "unmade beds, littered dressing tables and dubious bathrooms—of spoiled lives reaching out for mean and momentary alleviations of debauch . . . and grinding, soul-searing poverty. . . . Dos Passos has an exasperated sense of the unpleasant." Of course, the reviewer means that in the most positive light and compares this sensibility to the Brontes'. For the lack of such tempering, "a study that seemed designed to convey the stir and movement of multiple lives too often freezes into a set piece of horror."[34] Perhaps the true term of disapprobation here is not "horror" but "set piece." The *Times* had no need to hide any antimodernism, but an anti-art or anti-intellectual posture was taboo. Invoking the genteel value of discrimination and proportion, the reviewer scolds Dos Passos as an artist who makes bad choices, whose strategies are guaranteed to fail the test of the sensible and balanced.

Morley's reviewer, however, begins by testifying to the care with which the author wrote this "strange and beautiful book," a novel to be commended both for its writing and its philosophy: "Indeed, for sheer beauty and poignancy it ranks with anything published on this side of the Atlantic in the memory of our generation." "Poignancy" again seems to be a primary virtue, a power of feeling based on some mature acceptance, which is to say some representation of the middle-class struggle to accept quotidian life as it is. The reviewer seizes on one such instance to exemplify how *Thunder on the Left* compresses the "riddle of existence" into a child's query at which the author arrives after "probing at the core of life, going through layer after layer of circumstance": "Mother! Tell the truth, it's awfully important, cross your heart and hope to die. Do you have a good time? . . . They won't tell us. They're all liars."[35]

The *Times* reviewer considers this piece of pseudoprofundity—a boy's demand to know whether pleasure and obligation, freedom and responsibility, coexist—clear evidence of the novel's serious effort to come to terms with the challenges of modernity, a seriousness that later in the review he again values for its "poignancy." (If Canby loses control of his vocabulary and sputters "incoherent" at Dos Passos, "poignancy" is the word in season for *Thunder on the Left*.) The critic's admiration for this project is barely to be contained, since it seems to elude trivialization: "'Thunder on the Left' will have a meaning for every sensitive person who has been a child, a mother, a father or a lover. It will not . . . be bid for by the motion-picture producers. Its delicate violins and wistful flutes will not draw the public away from the brass bands that parade our literary Fifth Avenue. But it is important. It should survive." That sense of survival is that which outlasts the mass appeal of transient delights, especially the new, ever-changing cache of novels that movie producers scavenge for plots.

One could also point to the plentiful pseudoprofundity in *Manhattan Transfer* to suggest that it is no likelier than *Thunder on the Left* to flourish, but those who recommended it extolled its modernity. And no reader was more enthusiastic than Sinclair Lewis. Conscious of the hollow encomia passing for critical discussion, Lewis begins his piece in the *Saturday Review* by accepting the burden of assessing what "may veritably be a great book," a "novel of the first importance," one that appeals to both the "idle reader" and the "literary analyst." For Lewis, *Manhattan Transfer* may raise the "vast and blazing dawn": "It *may* be the foundation of a whole new school of novel-writing. Dos Passos *may* be, more than Dreiser, Cather, Hergesheimer, Cabell, or Anderson, the father of humanized and living fiction. And not merely for America but for the world!" *Thunder on the Left* may be embraced for its lesson in how to lead a modern life, but, for Lewis, *Manhattan Transfer* is in the vanguard of a whole method of understanding and writing.[36]

Lewis justifies his zeal by observing that he regards the novel as "more important in every way than anything by Gertrude Stein or Marcel Proust or . . . 'Ulysses.'" Why? Dos Passos has their same capacity for "experimental psychology and style. . . . But the difference is that Dos Passos is *interesting!*" Against the confounded dullness of modernists performing aesthetic experiments for their own sake, Dos Passos imparts a "breathless reality." Elsewhere in the review, Lewis explains that the life Dos Passos renders is a "roaring, thundering, incalculable, obscene, magnificent glory." A novel's "glory," says the author of *Main Street*, *Babbitt*, and *Arrowsmith*, is not to be found in its linguistic or narrative complexities, but in "our American life," which is not a "pallid and improving affair, but the blood and meat of eternal humanity."

For the champions of both Morley and Dos Passos, the survival of their novels depends on rendering a vague yet urgent sense of reality—the bourgeois world where the great secret in a life of responsibility and care, of forsworn or unanswered desires, is whether there is any fun in it. Does the power of pleasure make its way into our life of hypocrisy and deception, or is the highest ideal of our pursuit a struggle to find something like self-acceptance? Or is there really no secret but to attune oneself to the "thousand divinations of beauty without one slobber of arty Beauty-mongering" amid the pervasive degradations of civilization, since the one thing, according to Lewis, that distinguishes Dos Passos is an even Keatsian "passion for beauty and stir of life."

Lewis concedes that many observers will say that this novel enjoys techniques associated with the movies—the sharp cuttings and unblinking camera—but these appraisals miss Dos Passos's intense concern with both the outside and the inside of human beings. What we can observe in the way these two books were read, according to their reviewers, is the way modernist values were going to be admitted into the mainstream. Dos Passos is seen as too sordid and giving too much offense as the mere reporter of our lowest common denominators. Morley, on the other hand, means to elevate us: according to the *Times*, his novel's "stylistic virtues . . . grow out of the fact that there runs through it with almost desperate earnestness a sense of the pain and loveliness that lie at the very heart of life."[37]

The argument is still to be made that Morley and Dos Passos had their partisans, had standing in literary and critical circles; their books were published by important presses like Doubleday and Harper's and were reviewed more prominently than most other novels. Whether the books failed or not, they were unlikely to be ignored, since the whole apparatus for developing literary capital was more or less involved in seeing how deep an impression these books would make on American readers, even to the extent of presenting them as a referendum on modernism in fiction. Forgotten as expressions of an age as these books are now, their authors enjoyed a measure of what contemporary critics call privilege or access—economic or ideological—to the powers of opinion making. Even if one or the other were to be rejected, its argument would at least be heard amid the din of reviewers claiming this book or that the best of the season, the year, or recent memory.

BOURGEOIS AMERICA

The fiction of the second half of the '20s is most notable, not for its classics of American modernism or even the moralism that the Pulitzers glorify, but for the intensity of its efforts to represent a bourgeois America through stories devoted to arbitrating modern troubles. Novel after novel chronicles the pressures facing the New Woman, the challenges of doing business in an immoral age, the trials endured in the suburbs, the frustrations of raising children. Sometimes the obstacles that the characters face are financial, sometimes they are emotional, sometimes their struggles are satirized, sometimes they are rendered as tragic, but always plots of these novels provide marked routes through everyday confusions. According to *Times* critic, John Chamberlain:

> The novelists of America, with some inevitable exceptions, seem to be at their best when dealing with the elemental components of life. Love between the sexes, the fight for livelihood or pleasure or opportunity—it is when they are writing of unsubtle things that Americans . . . are most worth while. . . . Perhaps it is in choice of subject material that the American novelist gains that measure of vitality that seems missing in his English fellow-craftsmen. At any rate, where the English novel often breathes forth an aura of deadness and desiccation, the American product quivers with the quality known as aliveness.[38]

The plots of these novels focused on such "unsubtle things" as how the war has affected relationships or states of mind, how strained the relation between one's livelihood and inner life had become. There were novels about the Western wilderness and novels about Broadway, and one that even brought the two together. Indeed, dozens of novels made a character's successful negotiation of New York City the crux on which an understanding of modernity depended. Of course, the most popular narratives involved intimate lives of characters and how their infatuations, infidelities, divorces, and reconciliations calibrated the meanings of the life going on around them.

These plots guide readers through the entanglements of the psyche when one does not marry for love and, in their competition with romances, instruct readers in the educative, redeeming power of love in a real world, for these novels, like *Alice Adams*, treat love as an essentially modern problem, that is, governed by new uncertainties of being. Fannie Hurst's *Appassionata* (1926) was almost forgiven its turgidity for its modern fable of money in the hands of the new barbarians; her protagonist sees marriage as a domestic trap and takes refuge in her beauty and the stubborn mysticism that is part of her Irish heritage. Consider some other plots circulating in 1926: Wallace Irwin's *Mated* tells the story of a young woman who struggles to renounce the man she loves, since she sees, as he does not, that he is better off without her (Irwin wrote two endings: one aimed at the genteel sensibilities of magazine readers and the "more logical and artistic" one that appears in the book). *The Free Lovers*, by Reginald Wright Kauffman, is the story of a man and woman who go to City Hall during a drunken, passionate escapade and awake to discover that they have a marriage certificate. In Ernest Pascal's *Cynthia Codentry*, a young woman becomes involved with the theater through her father's influence but eventually rejects it in favor of a love affair with a sculptor and decides she cannot be tied down. In a similar vein, Thyra Samter Winslow's *Show Business* tells of an "ugly and unappreciated" Midwestern girl who brings brains and beauty that sophisticated New Yorkers can discern. William C. Bullitt's *It's Not Done* is a novel of ideas satirizing Philadelphia gentility, in the story of an upscale young man whose father demands that he marry someone of their class. He does so, but takes a lover and has sons by both women, which leads to marital and professional complications.[39]

Or consider Bonnie Busch's *Eager Vines*, in which a rich and cultured heroine marries a cruel and selfish Wall Street bigwig, who almost immediately cheats on her. A belated Puritan, she finds divorce out of the question and adopts one child, then four more. When her husband ridicules them, she throws him out and finally changes her stance on the divorce issue. In Larry Barretto's *Walls of Glass*, a Southern woman loses her husband and must make her own way as well as her son's. She has to leave the South, then has trouble getting a job in the North, where she eventually finds help in a neighbor whose own wife is insane. George Shively's *Sabbatical Year* tells the story of a Pennsylvania family whose members' lives have all changed since the war, in which one brother has died. One of the women befriends a pastor, who becomes involved in a scandal with another woman. Mystery writer Hulbert Footner tried his hand at realism in *Antennae*, which describes an urban milieu where one man looks at life disgustedly while another abuses his family and meets with prostitutes. In the end, they both settle down. Frances Newman's *Hard-Boiled Virgin* tells of an ungainly daughter who reads books while her sisters pursue husbands. She struggles with her self-esteem, travels, and becomes a successful author. Margaret Banning's *The Women in the Family* recounts the impact that insanity makes in a family's history by observing how three generations of mental illness play out in the present.

What were the plots of the more memorable or important books of 1926? Ellen Glasgow's *Romantic Comedians* narrates the story of a judge, a widower after thirty-five years of marriage, who considers returning to his previous true love but learns that he dislikes her, then elopes with and is jilted by a fortune-hunting younger woman. The heroine of Willa Cather's *My Mortal Enemy* also elopes, thereby losing a fortune, and then struggles to live within her paltry means, especially once she becomes an invalid locked in a loveless marriage. Dorothy Canfield Fisher's *Her Son's Wife* concerns the challenge to modern domesticity when a mother attempts to control her son's family. Remembered now for its portrayal of white slumming in Harlem, Van Vechten's *Nigger Heaven*, in this context, looks like a conventional story of lovers who face obstacles, discover the truth about their allegiances, and come to an end that depends more on contingencies than the logic of their romance. Finally, the novel that literary history has promoted to the top of the class from this year, Hemingway's *The Sun Also Rises*, tells of an American newspaper writer with a war injury living in Paris who drinks heavily and gets involved in a frustrating romance with a promiscuous aristocrat—a plot that does not seem so radically different from some of these others.

"VERY DEFINITELY AN AGE OF FICTION"

Several articles divining the future of American fiction, especially at the decade's end when taking the literary pulse was in order, declared the modern American novel moribund. For some observers, the dominant sense was that American novels had not sustained the energy of the early '20s, which produced *Main Street, Age of Innocence, Miss Lulu Bett,* and *Moon-Calf.* For others, American fiction was always producing new stars, but the novels that these commentators chose as examples of a new hope for fiction will strike contemporary historians as aberrant, even obscurantist. An early version of this stocktaking appeared in 1927 in the *Bookman.* Editor Charles W. Ferguson wanted to "designate a bevy of novelists" who were distinguishing themselves in the "crowded firmament." His criteria were not merely the commercial and critical success that his "five rising stars in American fiction" had already achieved, both here and in England, but also their combined effect of having "fused new blood" into the contemporary novel, which "a year ago had threatened decadence": From the jeux d'esprit of young intellectuals, critics "have turned to a more serious chronicling of the inner mind. From the unprofitable whanging of Rotarians they have turned to the beam which is in their own eye." Their subjects are more engaging than those of the "naive sophisticates" who supply "accurate photographs of the village mayor and his repressed daughter." For these novelists—Eleanor Carroll Chilton, John Gunther, Ernest Hemingway, Leonard Nason, and Elizabeth Roberts—answer the question, "After unalloyed realism, what?"[40]

The interest of Ferguson's catalog, however, is less its power of prognostication than its sense of what the present moment has to offer a middle-class reader exhausted by the surfeit of critical realism. "Mass production has had its evils," says Ferguson, "yet it has given us a new literary cosmogony," by which the editor means that there are new authors in control of new styles. He distinguishes between women's writing and their concerns for "heads" with men's writing of "tales"—a bad but instructive joke since it identifies the new psychological realism with female experience and the new emphasis on fabulation with men. In the end, his point is to broadcast the news that their combination creates a fresh spirit to relieve the enervation of mid-'20s fiction.

We have to be surprised by Ferguson's assemblage, especially since Hem-

ingway is the only writer generally known to us, while Roberts's claim on
posterity is mostly as a "Kentucky writer." Yet her fiction is as at least
devoted to the historical situation of women as it is to any regional interest,
though it is a common enough gesture of marginalization to assign women's
writing to a lesser genre, as regionalism was understood to be. Still, I am less
interested in disproving Ferguson's wisdom than I am in establishing the
currency of his judgment, the rationales he gives, the achievement he attributes to delineate middle-class taste.

Ferguson's enthusiasm for John Gunther was a minority report. *The Red
Pavilion* (1926), a novel about young Chicago professionals, was denigrated
as a transparent rewriting of Aldous Huxley's *Antic Hay* (1923). Of course,
Gunther never did have a career as a novelist and was much more successful
as a journalist; his accounts of *Inside Europe* (1936) and *Inside U.S.A.* (1947)
were extremely popular cultural guidebooks, and, for generations of high
school students, his *Death Be Not Proud* (1949) was an important lesson in
writing with a voice. Charles Nason's *Chevrons* (1926) was robustly praised
for its portrait of a World War I American recruit, and although Nason wrote
several more works of fiction, he never duplicated this novel's success.
Eleanor Carroll Chilton did produce several estimable novels after *Shadows
Waiting* (1927), though she never recaptured the aura of this first one, which
tells the story of a love affair of a novelist conflicted between the gratifica-
tions of intimacy and the desire for solitude. Although some critics saw
Shadows Waiting as an overwritten and dull "melodrama of the mind," it was
more often praised as a "brilliant and original book," as it was in *Books*; "a
profound, moving, delicately fashioned story, written in exquisite prose,"
declared the *Bookman*; and "simply and solely one of the finest, ablest, most
distinguished and most beautifully written books that America has produced
in a good many years," according to the *New Republic*.[41]

Ferguson's pantheon also includes reputations that have endured, though
here his skewed vision—tilted toward middle-class values—leads us to see
that one source of these writers' appeal is more conventional than we might
at first have supposed. His praise for *The Sun Also Rises* is intriguing. Noting
that "young expatriates who stay drunk most of the time and consequently
say a great many very funny things" comprise the book's cast of characters,
Ferguson observes that the appeal of this book in "dry America" may be that
"we have the pleasure of drunks without having to take them home": "The
novel as a whole affords good weekend diversion." Not only was this classical

work of American modernism understood then as a kind of suburban delight, but also it was recommended as, of all things, appealing to a bourgeois imagination: "It leaves the impression that the author must be a very wild fellow, a gourmand. Yet the fact abides that he is a respectable chap under thirty, with one wife and two children, and anxious to return to the United States of America where prohibition supposedly reigns supreme."

So many sober things have been written about this novel that it is good to be reminded, first of all, that Hemingway still passed Charles Ferguson's respectability test; and, second, that part of Hemingway's original appeal for some readers lay in comic distraction. For that was also the source of the more general admiration elicited by his earlier book of 1926, *Torrents of Spring: A Romantic Novel in Honor of the Passing of a Great Race*, his deliberate satire on the literature of revolt—a "scream," "high-spirited nonsense," "an elaborate and exceedingly witty parody," said various reviewers.[42] *The Sun Also Rises* was by and large a critical success, with readers hailing its "brilliant dialogue," its "casual precision," "some of the finest prose and most restrained prose that this generation has produced": "Written in terse, precise, and aggressively fresh prose, and containing some of the finest dialogue yet written in this country, the story achieves a vividness and a sustained tension that make it unquestionably one of the events of a year rich in interesting books."[43] As a summary statement about modern America, the novel never won the widespread recognition in its own day that its champions claimed for it. Allen Tate, who reviewed both of Hemingway's novels for the *Nation*, preferred *Torrents of Spring* for its "genial satire of the spirituality of roughnecks, the most deftly tempered ribaldry, and the most economically realized humor of disproportion that this reviewer has read in American prose." Tate's praise of *The Sun Also Rises* was stinting: "Hemingway doesn't fill out his characters and let them stand for themselves; he isolates one or two chief traits which reduce them to caricature. His perception of the physical object is direct, and accurate; his vision of character, singularly oblique."[44]

Ferguson, like Tate, misses what so many later critics take for granted but that other reviewers cannot find either: the seriousness and complexity of Hemingway's fiction beyond the level of character study or, as the *Times* reviewer puts it, the "heightened, intimate tangibility" of scene in both his novels and short stories. According to Ferguson, Hemingway, like Gunther, will retain his luster in his season but is destined "to descend periodically and rise again." These authors' brightness "is not so great as that of distant stars, but it appears to be greater, for they are closer to the earth. They will be pointed out by admirers and looked upon quite favorably whenever their time comes to appear."[45]

For Ferguson, Hemingway lacks the wide, organizing brilliance of Elizabeth Roberts, herself a "constellation." The truly discriminating reader is to understand that Hemingway's virtues shine because they are so close to our quotidian life, whereas Roberts's talents, while more remote, are the more impressive. What makes her novel *The Time of Man* (1926) so good—"the strongest novel of this vermilion decade"—is that Roberts so aptly portrays the longings of the American peasantry, in this case Kentucky dirt farmers, in all their self-sufficiency and loneliness. Like many others, Marxist cultural observer V. F. Calverton also admired this novel's unlikely charm: Roberts had "poeticized her material without weakening or diffusing its realism." "A saga of a heroic woman living near the earth," said another. Roberts's subsequent novels were inevitably compared to *The Time of Man*, which remains her most memorable accomplishment.[46]

Ferguson's model of insight and blindness, however, is not merely to be found in the bourgeois mind. Consider Granville Hicks's more politically progressive survey of '20s fiction (whose lame predictions he later mocked). The spectacle Hicks looks out on is not Canby's radiant vista but a "sad business." The decade began hopefully enough with "blissful prophecies" that did not come to pass, so "today we listen patiently to wails of despair and outbursts of denunciation." As Hicks characterizes the common wisdom: "We all know what critics today are saying about the authors who looked so impressive a decade ago. We are told that Cabell is naive, that Lewis is only one short step ahead of George F. Babbitt, that Anderson is diffuse and befuddled, that Dreiser has neither insight nor capacity for clarification, and that Mencken is merely a noisy disseminator of quartertruths and boob-catching platitudes." Still, for Hicks, the critics heralding the twenties are not "altogether asinine," and he calls for a "vigorous analysis" of the authors in question.[47]

He wonders why "the writers of the twenties did not develop, why hatred for shams did not grow into a demand for realities, why a desire to treat the untouched aspects of American life did not become a desire to treat the whole of American life." Perhaps the times lacked a genius, that "popularity was too easily won," that our "national life is as yet too chaotic." Perhaps, also, the flaws were the critics', who "substituted enthusiasm for discrimination." Hicks points to the new critical spirit surpassing Mencken's "cackling hen" school, which was really the last chortling of impressionism. "Today the swing is toward standards"—either those of the traditional humanists in their trumpeting of tradition or those of the younger critics calling for finer methods of discrimination—Clifton Fadiman, Irving Edman, Edmund Wilson, and Yvor Winters, as well as such followers of Van Wyck Brooks as Lewis Mumford, Newton Arvin, and T. K. Whipple. Yet neither sort of criticism can remedy the real trouble with fiction. Contemporary novels are foundering on a new barbarism, by which Hicks means the exaggeration of the middle generation's lack of originality. Against their perilous example, he weighs the fate of those writers who might extend the genre's form and build on the menace posed by Joyce, whose powerful example threatens to "blight their talents." "One watches with interest—but not without perturbation— the careers of Elizabeth Roberts, Glenway Wescott, and Ernest Hemingway." Perturbing Hicks is the anxiety that these newcomers may squander their gifts or have them go unappreciated.

Curiously, the sense that current fiction needs a rehabilitative spirit can be found both in the positive and negative assessments of the U.S. novel at the end of the decade. Many reviewers agreed that '20s writers had arrived at an impasse and could only go so far in imagining a new American modernity. That limit seems to be the novel's imperative to interpret bourgeois lives for a bourgeois audience. Even the bourgeois praise for the era's fantasists—like James Cabell or Elinor Wylie or Eleanor Chilton—is that by the sharpness of their contrast, their imaginations freshen the lives that the middle class lead. Consider, on the other hand, another roster of authors who were making some headway in "aesthetic problems" and who thus stood in happy opposition to the bankruptcy of what this young critic calls the Dreiser school: Clifton Fadiman's roll call in the Nation: Conrad Aiken, Glenway Wescott, and, to some extent, Thornton Wilder. Consider that Fadiman at this point is a (very) young litterateur, not at all the well-known figure he would become; in an important sense, his job is to speak for the young and their apprehension of the art of the novel. For Fadiman, the "whole duty of the young novelist" is dedication to the writer's craft—a tradition associated with Europe— even as young novelists discover in themselves "a reaction away from the democratic sympathies implied in the theme and texture of the work of my elders." Also to be watched, he observes, are Hemingway, Roberts, Nathan

Asch, W. L. River, and Gertrude Diamant ("whose work is for the most part still unpublished"!). The "probably European" resources for young writers— the "nourishing, organic, and exciting literary tradition"—removes from them "the least hint of provincialism." "Rules of their craft" stimulate these artists, not the "stupidity of the mob or the discovery that businessmen get bored with their wives upon reaching the age of thirty-five."[48]

There is little sense that any writers Fadiman singles out continued to develop according to a European model of formal inventiveness, though Roberts published a burst of accomplished novels, whose classic form yielded as impressive a record of critical successes at the outset of a career as any other twentieth-century American novelist, bearing comparison perhaps only with that of Toni Morrison. Conrad Aiken was a Pulitzer Prize–winning poet (1930) for whom writing stream-of-consciousness fiction was a secondary career (he wrote four such novels and one realistic work). Nathan Asch published several novels following *The Office*, including *Love in Chartres* (1927), which was praised for its lyrical use of the interior monologue as a refinement of stream-of-consciousness technique. W. L. River did not have much of a career; the book that earned Fadiman's interest was *Death of a Young Man* (1927), a novel in diary form concerning the thoughts of someone who learns he has but a year to live. Gertrude Diamant, from what I can determine, published *Labyrinth* in 1929, a novel also unflatteringly compared to Huxley's *Antic Hay*, and another novel that got little notice in 1940. In searching for alternatives to the plethora of superficially critical novels, Fadiman uses more widely recognized writers, like Roberts, Hemingway, and Wescott, to promote fiction produced by more dubious, less-heralded choices—Asch, Diamant, and River—whose debt to Europe may have been clearer than Roberts's and no more definite than Wescott's exercises in point of view and Hemingway's stylistic wagers.

In fact, the most popular books of the late 1920s were mystery stories. A slew of classics were published in the years before and directly after the stock market crash, including English writer Agatha Christie's *The Murder of Roger Ackroyd* (1926), two other Poirot novels, and her first Miss Marple. Among Americans' were Dashiell Hammett's *Red Harvest* (1929), Van Dine's *The Bishop Murder Case* (1929), Hammett's *The Maltese Falcon* (1930), Ellery Queen's *The French Powder Mystery* (1930), Leslie Charteris's *Enter the Saint* (1930), and two of Erle Stanley Gardner's in 1933—*The Case of the Velvet Claws* and *The Case of the Lucky Legs*—each of which sold a million copies,

not to mention another Hammett, two other Queens, and two other Gard-
ners, which each sold as many as 1.2 million copies. Why mysteries would
exert such a powerful hold over the American imagination before and after
the Crash invites some likely suppositions, beyond the perennial appeal of
the escape value detective tales hold, about a national hunger to find coherence and the need to find a rational explanation of the woes besetting
American society.[49]

Beyond the promise of mystery novels to purify society, resolve its corruptions, settle its destructive elements, what were the consolations of the
stories that middle-class realists proffered their readers? What do the plots
of American novels look like as a group, say, in the years of our highest
prosperity? Collectively, what is the social imagination of these books and
what do they fantasize about bourgeois America? Again, I am not talking
about the most profitable novels or the most critically revered or even those
that won prizes, though some of these would be included in any catalog of
bourgeois fiction of the time. I refer to the profusion of novels that were
submitted to readers for purchase, the choices the American reading public
were given, even if they were mediated by book clubs or touted by trusted
critics. The interest of these plots, I contend, is the summary of desire that
they create. The plots index a collectively felt sense of challenge to readers'
social aspirations, fears, personal and political virtues. Taken together, they
provide a glimpse into the imaginary life of the republic.

Through the late '20s Americans were offered a variety of realist fiction
that spoke to their fear of marginality and the emptiness at the heart of
modern life. In response, we observe many historical novels whose dominant allure was their explanations of how the past becomes the present, how
our circumstances have been forged for us through the sins of the fathers,
the failures of the sons, the determination of the mothers, and the exertions
of the daughters, or some other permutation. Sometimes, these novels hinge
on reproducing real historical events, like the Salem trials in Esther Forbes's
Mirror for Witches (1928). While the interest of these historical works was
often coiled in the story of generations they told, their general currency
also spoke to an America trying to make sense of its destiny, as in Cather's
novel of the friendship between a French bishop and his vicar, played out
against the backdrop of settling Catholic missions in New Mexico, *Death
Comes for the Archbishop* (1927), as well as Bess Streeter Aldrich's tale of
pioneer women in the Upper Midwest, *Lantern in Her Hand* (1928).

The plots of historical novels are often overlaid with a region's story too, as if to suggest that the development of a locale is central to a family's tale of rise and decline, though the general interest in the history of a region and its mores emerged more fully in the thirties. Some of these novels are about Western wilderness, including the Southwestern desert, though they more often concern the Eastern and Mid-Atlantic states. Along with books about the South and Midwest produced from within their already established traditions, these novels explicitly elaborate more general anxieties of the day. To that end, the many books about race relations in the South and the tension between industry and agriculture in the Midwest, like the haunting grotesquerie of Southern life and the stultifying provincialism of the Midwest, are staples of regionalist mentality.

The same goes for city novels. Throughout the twenties, novels of young people visiting New York, making their way there before finding their way home, are a staple of middle-class interpretations of modernity. Then there are New York novels, like Felix Riesenberg's *East Side, West Side* (1927), a bildungsroman with more in common with novelistic investigations of Chicago and San Francisco than with the startling number of novels about New York City as the premier site of modernity, like Katherine Brush's *Young Man of Manhattan* (1930). Indeed, at least in their belief in the shaping power of environment, such New York City novels may even be more logically associated with tales of the plains of the Dakotas than they are with accounts of Greenwich Village bohemianism.

THE NEW BARBARIANS

In his study of the "assault on democracy" resulting from immigration and the importation of radical ideas to America, Harvard history professor Wilbur Abbott identified the middle class as a critical resource for sustaining any New America. One magazine considered his book, *The New Barbarians* (1925), to be "distinctly a tract on behalf of the middle class," especially since it describes the bourgeoisie so heroically—the "bitterest foe of mere birth and outworn tradition," "the pioneer of movements which destroyed them." Abbott stresses the fluidity of middle-class identity as the source of its strength insofar as the middle class "continually recruited from above and below; and within it are a hundred grades from capitalist to artisan."[50]

Abbott tries to correct the representation of the middle class, especially the ways socialists and communists picture it. First, they mistake capital as the touchstone of the middle class: This self-reliant, capable, energetic, ambitious, and self-respecting class "has something to sell besides its muscles or its birth," the class that has "made us what we are." Second, the middle class carries on the "business of life," not just commerce but social change: it "converted the dream of democracy into a reality," neither obsessed by the past nor dedicated to abolishing it. The bourgeoisie, like the proletarians, "admit the desirability of altering the present system," of mending, not ending, capitalism. Because it believes in amelioration, not revolution, Abbott contends, the middle class offers the best program, since it is "pragmatic," "experimental," "fluid," "evolutionary." It sees society as an organism (not a machine) and accepts no "sacred shibboleth"; it seems "more in accord with human nature and likely to prevail."[51]

This is scarcely the vision of the middle class that the tradition of modern American cultural criticism has authorized. One may turn to Waldo Frank's *The Re-discovery of America* (1929) for a more familiar assessment. There we learn that only over the "grave of Europe" can the "re-discovery of America" take place; only once the world Europe created is dead, as it now seems to be, can a newly vitalizing conception of America take hold. The status of the middle class is central to such a reimagining. For Europe's great foundation in shaping America is exactly the ascendancy of the bourgeoisie, "which dispensed with an inane authority of Spirit, setting its rights squarely on the property which it is possessed." Thus the rulers' authority shifted from divinity to "their real power, wealth, and the middle class, which had the substance of gold without the shadow of spirit moved to unseat them." The American Revolution was the first "great Joust," says Frank, though "everywhere in Europe, Property, uncrowned, battled with Privilege, whose crown grew with the years more flimsy." For Frank, the place of the middle class in the United States was undeniable: "An idea sprung from Europe grew maniacal in America because it was alone."[52] Frank's polemic, like Abbott's apologia, convinced few readers, and both studies earned decidedly mixed reviews. Abbott, a noted professor of European history, was understood to be out of his league as an economist and a sociologist as well as seeming to be a rather overheated spokesman. Frank, on the other hand, was viewed as having written a rich but ill-tempered book—dismissed by some as self-indulgent, muddled, faddish, and superficial while embraced by others as alert and inspiring.

For Calverton, "It would be absurd to think that the literature produced by such a culture could do anything more than reflect its deceptions."[53] The fiction of the second half of the 1920s, for better or worse, tried to do more. The middle-class reading public was always increasing, so it was only to be expected that this audience wanted to learn about itself, gaze at the reflection of its own distortions as it were, by reading novels concerning the problems, obsessions, and rewards of being middle class. That experience was much more various than some monolithic understanding of the middle class might comprehend. For example, Viña Delmar's *Bad Girl*, a vivid tale of how one young working-class woman in New York City struggles to gain respectability, was a best seller of 1928. Novels devoted to middle-class quandaries occasionally sold well and were frequently counted among the critical successes, such as Wharton's *The Children* (1928), which, like several other novels of the day, treated divorce by showing how it affects children. Sinclair Lewis's *Elmer Gantry* (1927) sold mightily and may be the closest thing to a great popular and critical success among the middle-class fantasies I describe.

Actually, such fiction was more readily typified by a very different study of a minister, also from 1927, Reginald Wright Kauffman's *A Man of Little Faith*, which juxtaposes the tribulations of two Protestant clergymen (one an indecisive, unreflective, unfaithful Episcopalian; the other, an intellectual Presbyterian), published just two weeks after Lewis's story of a corrupt evangelical preacher turned corrupt Methodist leader. *Elmer Gantry* was the subject of reviews that alternately admired Lewis's satire or were disgusted by his caricatures, and it was reviewed everywhere as part of the "present preoccupation with ecclesiastical muck-raking." Kauffman's study, in contrast, was generally praised for its "fairness," even if it too steered away from the sentimentality of the previous generation's social gospel novels, in part because Kauffman subordinates the ministers' social experience to their spiritual charge, whereas Lewis sees Gantry's religiosity as a prop for his appetitiveness—his materialist overreaching as much as his sexual adventures. The reception of *A Man of Little Faith* took place mostly in the newspapers, rather than the opinion magazines, so even though Kauffmann was a writer of some standing, the novel did not gain a large national following, quite unlike the interest that *Elmer Gantry* stirred.[54]

Elmer Gantry typifies how these bourgeois fictions sometimes erupt out of extreme cases—conventional class dreams gone awry—but more often they seek to elucidate the everyday drama of ordinary circumstances, in this case injected with a strong dose of licentiousness. Of the great many historical novels, some make the deliberate effort to spirit readers away from modern anxieties like standardization or the ennui that the new technology has wrought. Still, in an age where debates over Americanization were clamorous and where novels about Americanization—like Ole Edvart Rölvaag's *Giants in the Earth* (1927)—could be extremely popular, historical novels cement an abiding picture of American heroism, especially of the Revolutionary War generation, as if to give scale to current middle-class anxieties. At the same time, and perhaps in unconscious response to the burst of immigrant fiction, these historical novels, like regional ones, bring to the fore a heroic spirit in America, one perceived more as the legacy of America's WASP hegemony than as a "re-discovered" America.

The fashion for such books coincides neatly with the vast appetite for biographies of historical figures, especially from the Revolutionary era, including George Washington, Thomas Jefferson, Benjamin Franklin, Ethan Allen, and "Mad Anthony" Wayne (written by Thomas Boyd). Also garnering attention were the collected papers of "Grandmother Brown," whose memories of everyday life spanned the century from 1827 through 1927. There are also political novels, some about politics as a profession, some putative Washington, D.C., exposés. Anomalously, some, like Upton Sinclair's study of the Sacco-Vanzetti case, *Boston* (1928), are about the new radical politics and its ramifications, a subgenre that overlapped at times with the continuing efforts at proletarian fiction.

Reviewers recognized the plots of middle-class fiction and could classify them easily, commenting on the freshness of their variation, for so many narratives responded to celebrated predecessors. For example, Percy Marks's *The Plastic Age* (1924)—itself modeled on Fitzgerald's college novel—stimulated a swarm of imitators, which in turn elicited some novels about professors (who either were adjusting to the new academic circumstances or not), as in Cather's *The Professor's House* (1925), and even a couple about high school. Many middle-class novels centered on the family and observed the problems wrought by dominating mothers; many portrayed the subdued heroics of beleaguered husbands. Novels about men shaking off the effects of a midlife romance or finding freedom in a new affair abounded. Equally numerous were novels about women who leave philandering husbands or who return to the men they left behind when they married for money. The return of lovers from the past, it must be reported, also appears to have been one of the most stressful of American bourgeois fears in the '20s. A striking number of books followed the divergences of two siblings, usually sisters. There were mother-son novels, but perhaps more plentiful were father-daughter fictions—especially tyrannical fathers and imaginative daughters, who, along with sensitive sons of solicitous mothers, had a propensity to grow up to become writers or artists. In fact, this was but one variation of the numerous novels chronicling the education of sculptors, musicians, actors, and playwrights, most of whom had to throw off the narrow-mindedness of their families or the prejudices of small towns.

Sometimes, these stories overlapped with other enduring scenarios, such as the soldier returned from battle, the New Woman seeking emancipation, the young person from the provinces come to the big city. Tales of the provinces themselves, however, can be roughly divided into two groups: the good farm, which has enabled a family to endure for generations; and the bad farm, which for a similar length of time has been the site of corruption, hypocrisy, loveless marriage, sibling rivalry, inheritance arguments, and, most recently, squabbles with immigrants, struggles that occasionally caused a native inhabitant to stay home and transform the bad farm into a good one, even to marry one of the immigrants. In a couple of plots, New Yorkers come to the provinces and have their illusions dispelled by the quality of life found there; in others, the provinces are revealed to be just as filled with duplicity as the city. Sometimes the provinces are also the place of restive laborers in a mill or factory dominating a little city, though many labor novels occur in the metropolis, especially where there are high concentrations of immigrants. The liberal conscience was also a much contested subject in these books, a conflict that sometimes focused on new religious values and cults, social prejudices, or, especially in the South, race relations.

If these plots reveal a middle-class imagination of current circumstances, it should be instructive to consider, beyond the novels we already know or easily have access to, the plots of those books that might have succeeded in the late '20s but did not; or if they did succeed with the public, no record of engagement has descended to us to say why. In the plots from 1927 and 1928 that follow, as I can summarize them, the stories the middle class tells itself of its tensions and aspirations, comic worries and tragic insights, recount an America about to lose its innocence, very much the America studied in the magisterial analysis of middle-class mores and values, *Middletown: A Study in*

American Culture, by Robert and Helen Lynd, which appeared in January 1929. Indeed, the Lynds' chapter titles could serve as the subject guide to any book-length study of the plots in bourgeois fiction: "Getting a Living," "Making a Home," "Training the Young," "Using Leisure," "Engaging in Religious Practices," and "Engaging in Community Activities."

A Georgia-born heroine marries a New Jersey businessman. She meets an old suitor and they both abandon their spouses. The suitor's wife commits suicide; the heroine returns to her husband—a plot the *New York Times* reviewer thought likely to be popular (Elisabeth Cobb Chapman, *Falling Seeds*). A prejudiced and ignorant veteran returns to the United States after difficulties in the army and finds himself an outcast at home until he becomes an official of the Kansas Ku Klux Klan (James Stevens, *Matlock*)—a plot that in salient ways is typical of the war-preparedness fiction that dominates the postwar treatment of World War I. A New York bond salesman quits his job, leaves his fiancée, moves west to the Oklahoma oil fields, then to the Arizona copper mines, where he earns good money and finds true love (Malcolm Ross, *Deep Enough*). The coming-of-age story of a boy in Calumet, Illinois, who reflects on the city's changes as a result of the war, industrialization, and immigration, is played out against the tale of his abortive romance with a Catholic girl (Jacob Wendell Clark, *White Wind*). A feminist writer married to a vain, selfish man still does the cooking, housework, and child rearing, even though she continues to believe a marriage should promote equality (Maude Radford Warren, *Never Give All*). A man in the steel business walks out with other strikers and eventually pursues a literary career in New York (Charles R. Walker, *Bread and Fire*). Four clerks pool their resources and become venture capitalists (George Weston, *The Horseshoe Nails*). Two rich New York families living across the street from each other become entangled in love between two of their children, a lost fortune on Wall Street (and resulting suicide), gambling, a scientific experiment, and love out of wedlock—all recounted on the day of one child's debut (Nathalie Colby, *Black Stream*). A middle-aged married man has a love affair, then makes a reckless business venture, resulting in financial loss, family conflicts, and a lesson to himself, an "admirable" novel with "form, truth, and integrity" (Henry Kitchell Webster, *The Beginners*).[55] A young man studies law at Harvard, works for his father, becomes engaged only to rebel when he discovers he has a child from a previous fling; when the mother rejects the child, he accepts responsibility, only to lose his fiancée (Floyd Dell, *An*

Unmarried Father). A young man, expelled from college, moves to New York City and befriends a man who encourages him to pursue wealth, while another man pulls him to the side of laborers; torn, he finally rejects wealth (Max Eastman, *Venture*). A Jewish family emigrates from Russia, feels a bit superior, and puts too much confidence in Wall Street (Lillian Rogers, *The Royal Cravatts*).

That is not all. An idealistic graduate of Harvard Law School encounters corruption when he enters a lucrative firm and marries a dishonest social climber who seduces his boss to get him a raise (Arthur Train, *Ambition*). A Bowery waitress is discovered by a movie director who brings her to Hollywood. Covering the years 1910–28, Rob Wagner's *Tessie Moves Along* relates a great deal of early movie history as it charts the heroine's path to stardom. A suburban Connecticut family endures the farce of middle-class life, including twisted family relations, unsuitable mates for recalcitrant siblings, and a father's nervous breakdown over finances (Helen Tooker, *The 5:35*). A "poor-white" girl in a Florida village is chastised for being a prostitute and for loving a man supposed to be black; they are routed from town by mob hysteria and move to the Caribbean to live in a hut—"one of the best novels . . . in the present publishing season" (Edwin Granberry, *Strangers and Lovers*). A small-town Midwestern girl goes to an Eastern college and launches a successful academic career (Wanda Franken Neff, *We Sing Diana*). A young man raised only by his mother is forced to visit his father for a summer; although he loathes the prospect, he comes to love his father as well as a young woman he meets (Inez Haynes Irwin, *Gideon*). The protagonist, from a Jewish family that has emigrated from Poland to start a new life, struggles to maintain his cultural identity in modern America and ultimately discovers Zionism (Ludwig Lewisohn, *The Island Within*). A New York family over whom a close-minded great-aunt presides is losing its money, so the children take regular jobs and put their guardian into a nursing home—"the vulgar new triumph over the even more vulgar old" (Larry Barretto, *The Old Enchantment*). In a family of prominent native New Yorkers, the two youngest daughters move out of the old aristocracy and into modern lives on Fifth Avenue (John Wiley, *Queer Street*). A domineering wife and mother clinging to her family's aristocratic past in small-town New England confronts her equally resolute daughter who joins a Greenwich Village theater company (Ann Rice, *Blight*).[56]

Over the years, the typology of this fiction develops, encapsulating not only predecessors but also variations. By 1929, there are still tales of actresses, reporters, and ballerinas, and several concerning the recent crime wave in Chicago, but there is also a significant increase in novels about middle-class marriage. That is not altogether surprising when we remember the extent to which the culture was still digesting the "sex instinct" in Freudian psychology or the hubbub over Margaret Mead's 1928 study, *Coming of Age in Samoa*, which brought adolescent female sexuality to the fore and generated a broad controversy over American mating rituals, especially the cultural threat posed by emancipated, economically independent women. The fantasy of adultery—the great subject of nineteenth-century novels like Hawthorne's *The Scarlet Letter*, Flaubert's *Madame Bovary*, and Tolstoy's *Anna Karenina*—became even more pervasive than it ordinarily might have been. Problems in marriage can be counted on to excite a number of solemn inquiries in any year, but 1929 saw more than its share, including Mary Richmond and Fred S. Hill's legal analysis, *Marriage and the State*—presumably a response to Judge Ben Lindsey's recent polemic in favor of companionate marriage—and works of sociology, like Edward Westermarck's *Marriage*, as well as G. V. Hamilton and Kenneth MacGowan's *What Is Wrong with Marriage?* There were also medical reports, like Dr. Victor Pedersen's *The Man a Woman Marries*, a companion study to his previous popular examination of wives. Bertrand Russell's *Marriage and Morals* was advertised as the most relentlessly "rational" of these inquiries.

These various studies, however, also participated in an ongoing discussion of the place of women. The year 1929 saw the publication of *Sex and Civilization*, a collection of experts documenting the change in attitude about marriage and sexual activity, edited by Calverton and S. D. Schmalhausen. There were also books about women's changing economic position, like Doris Fleischman's *Outline of Careers for Women: A Practical Guide to Achievement*, a collection of forty-three articles by successful women, which followed Mary Raymond Dodge's *Fifty Little Businesses for Women* from the previous year. As if to suggest the clear place of the relation between women and money in fiction, Norah Hoult's short-story anthology, *Poor Women!* narrated the plight of women economically dependent on men. Dorothy Walworth Carman's *Glory and the Parlour* (1929) followed up the success of her earlier satire of suburban conformism and respectability, *Pride of the*

Town (1926), by portraying how one modern woman's choice between career and family reveals both the civil and economic advances made by women in the last half century and the threat of diminishment at every turn.

Such issues always seem to warrant new novels investigating the conditions of the sexes or to retread older answers, especially to marriage and motherhood. Lillian Eichler's *Stillborn*, a tragic if poorly written account, warns against obsessive mother love in treating a woman's right to control the destiny of her child. Myron Brinig's somber *Madonna without Child* describes a forty-year-old spinster's effort to find emotional fulfillment by realizing her maternal instincts in her friendship with a young girl. And the very first novel W. W. Norton and Company published was a "delightfully murderous" satirical attack on a "monster-mother," Lily Bess Campbell's *These Are My Jewels*. Hazel Cole's *Maids Will Be Wives* tells of an intelligent and worldly woman who, coming from a line of family-minded women, chooses a stable domestic life over an adventurous one. After her two children leave home, she experiences a profound loss of purpose, on which the novel closes. This ending raises the question with which so many of these novels are ultimately concerned: "What will modern civilization do with women who are strongly maternal?" Lorna Beers's *A Humble Lear* is a tragic novel of thankless offspring and lonely old age in rural Minnesota, a sort of precursor to Jane Smiley's *A Thousand Acres* (1991). More satirical is Josephine Bentham's *The Outsiders*, about the failed marriage of two entirely incompatible people. Pauline Stiles's *Cloud by Day* examines marriage, with a difference: What happens when a man who is too proud to be supported by his wife loses his livelihood? Nalbro Bartley's *Queen Dick* provides an "able portrait" of a "feminine 'Babbitt'" and her domination of her boring husband, who wakes up to his oppression and leaves her.[57]

Other novels from 1929 about women were not limited to tales of domestic woe. Dawn Powell's *The Bride's House* is a tale of discontent and illicit desire in an Ohio town filled with black sheep and neurotics, "strongly reminiscent of Sherwood Anderson." Helen Grace Carlisle's *See How They Run* portrays the psychological and emotional states of three women from various backgrounds as they pursue their romanticized bohemian life in Greenwich Village. Lola Jean Simpson's *Treadmill* narrates the struggles with uncooperative administrators, officials, and pupils facing an idealistic California high school history teacher. Janet Hoyt's "careful and conscientious" *Wings of Wax* confronts the state of modern education at a large coed university, exposing an administrator's difficulties dealing with the problems of equality between the sexes.[58]

Following the great example of *Babbitt*, novels of 1929 also investigate American businessmen as middle-class subjects. Lewis himself contributed *Dodsworth*, which is as much about the tiresome narcissism of American haute bourgeois women as about the European types the writer satirizes in this tale of a retired businessman's belated recovery from his absorption in commerce and his discovery of self. Jonathan Brooks's *Chains of Lightning*, on the other hand, portrays a millionaire power baron as a sensitive family man who sees his professional misdeeds as just part of his job. Clarence Budington Kelland's *Dynasty* runs truer to type in charting a successful businessman from his beginnings as an assembly-line worker to his conquest of a national corporation fifty years later. Another novel playing more darkly against the story of a worker's rise to power is Thames Williamson's Book-of-the-Month Club selection, *Hunky*, the tale of a Central European immigrant who enjoys his dull routine as a baker's helper until he is replaced by a machine. Also against the type of money romances is a self-consciously alternative vision, like Arthur Train's *Illusion*, which juxtaposes the circus and vaudeville with high-society New York in the story of one man's double life.

The pressure of modern industrial society would also be observed in William Faulkner's *Sartoris*, the story of one old Mississippi family's struggle to survive, which was compared unflatteringly to the many other novels dealing with the decaying South, weakened as the novel was by its "superficial treatment" of major characters and its obscure theme.[59] More highly esteemed was Fiswoode Tarleton's *Bloody Ground*, a series of dialect sketches focusing on a single Southern community. Later in 1929, Faulkner's *The Sound and the Fury* met with several laudatory reviews. Perhaps the Southern novels of that year most thoroughly capturing the critics' imagination, however, were Stark Young's *River House*, which examines the New South through the observation of a father-son conflict, and Thomas Wolfe's more famous *Look Homeward, Angel*.

Stories of race relations as well as tales by white writers about blacks were fairly common in 1929. Ben Wasson's *The Devil Beats His Wife* dramatizes the changing South at the turn of the century by following the conflict between older and younger generations of African Americans. There were also social analyses, like Donald Young's *The American Negro*, a collection of forty essays by blacks and whites on the changes experienced over the last fifteen years;

Howard Odum's *Wings at My Feet: Black Ulysses at the Wars*; and memoirs like Taylor Gordon's record of his rise as a singer, *Born to Be*. Republished in 1929 was Charles Chesnutt's *The Conjure-Woman*, folktales that "deserve the immortality that is Uncle Remus's," as the *New York Times* reviewer reflects.[60]

One of the more successful novels that year was a white author's meditation on race relations, DuBose Heyward's tale of several generations of a genteel, impoverished white family and an upwardly mobile black one that enlists the sympathy of these "quality white folks"—in *Mamba's Daughters*, a Literary Guild selection. As patronizing as we might find Heyward's novel today, it was infinitely more enlightened than Howard Snyder's *Earth-Born*, which the *Times* reviewer saw as a wholly unoriginal collection of the sort of racist stereotypes expected in plantation fiction.

Vera Caspary's *The White Girl*, on the other hand, tells an "exceptionally interesting and thoughtful story" about the life of a mixed-race woman who leaves her parents and passes as white in New York, which, as the reviewer suggests, is a significant subject since there may be twenty thousand people of color in New York who were doing so. Caspary's novel earned nearly as good a review as Nella Larsen's *Passing*, which was seen as "a convincing attempt to portray . . . a vexatious problem" and maybe even a little better than Jessie Redmon Fauset's *Plum Bun*, which is distinguished by having its heroine pass back into the black world. Problems of color are also the core of Wallace Thurman's *The Blacker the Berry*, which observes the tribulations of a light-skinned Negro woman in her hometown, at college, and in Harlem. Claude McKay's *Banjo* might be said to complicate issues of color with issues of class when he pairs an "intellectual Negro" with an easygoing "bum-Negro," an extension that yields "a significance that [the novel] would have lacked if it had been a mere photograph of slum life."[61]

AMERICANIZATION AND THE NOVEL

The spate of books about race relations can also be related to the new interest in novels about the composition of U.S. society. Published in 1929 were several Americanization novels. As we have seen in Yezierska and Tobenkin, the story of creating or achieving an American identity can hinge on a narrative of embourgeoisification, just as the story of the reception of new immigrants turns on the issue of their imagined threat to middle-class order. Drawing from the tradition of bourgeois marriage fiction is Sophie Kerr's *Maeera-Maria*, which treats the question of difference—in race, education, and environment—in the relationship between a mother-in-law of Northern European extraction, whose industrialist son marries a young immigrant Italian woman. An even fuller exploration of the nightmare that difference imports is to be found in Milton Waldman's *The Disinherited*, which describes how a third-generation American Jew is assimilated into a Protestant community as a lawyer and civic leader, only to lose his prestige when a series of curious accidents reveals his heritage. Perhaps the best-known novel of Americanization from 1929, Rölvaag's *Peder Victorious*, dramatizes the steps toward assimilation in its portrayal of the generation succeeding the pioneers of *Giants in the Earth*.

It was a novel about the failure of a Navajo Indian to Americanize and the resistance such efforts meet that appealed to the Pulitzer judges that year: *Laughing Boy* by Oliver La Farge, a young anthropologist and archaeologist, won the prize over *The Sound and the Fury*, Wharton's *Hudson River Bracketed*, *Look Homeward, Angel*, and the much-admired *Farewell to Arms*, which appealed to reviewers as the culmination of Hemingway's efforts and was heralded in giant, full-page ads featuring full-face portraits of the handsome author. Virtually in opposition to the tale of Frederick Henry's separate peace, *Laughing Boy* was hailed for its lyricism, "lucid beauty," and "clear, almost hypnotic style," a "sensitive and important" piece of regional writing.[62]

So resonant was the middle-class story of immigration that throughout the decade American writers of various ethnicities and white Protestant ones found it promising. Middle-class status is usually the ne plus ultra to which the immigrants aspire and against which they define the success of their assimilation. It was not a mere happenstance that William Dean Howells touted Abraham Cahan's *Yekl*, whose tale of two sorts of Americanization (Jake's corruptions and Gitl's triumphs), in gratifying Howells's realist principles more than his democratic yearnings. For all of its ties to the vernacular and regionalist traditions, and for all of its significant tradition of protest, immigrant fiction needs to be understood as the product of the bourgeois imagination: novels of "how I came to be an American" told for middle-class, native-born readers who might learn more about the obstacles in the path to Americanization. The proof of immigrant fiction's middle-class vision lies in the way that it is so often written to assuage anxieties (though sometimes to generate them) about the succession of bloodlines as well as the accession to property. This fiction is concerned centrally, then, to establish or, when told for antipathetic purposes, to challenge the immigrant's rightful stature as an American.

A key moment in a novel from 1923, Yezierska's *Salome of the Tenements*, bears on the relations among immigration, middle-class culture, and democratic ideals. Sonya Vrunsky is a misunderstood tenement girl who wins the heart of the "higher-up" Anglo-Saxon John Manning, an American aristocrat sponsoring a settlement house so that new immigrants may have a place to learn about becoming citizens. For all of the lustful attraction of their otherness, their love is not merely an affair of the senses, but fine feelings too. The novel is given over to Yezierska's conventional dualism of the Jewish female, impoverished yet lush and appetitive, a lover of beauty versus the Protestant male as cold and withdrawn, and so dedicated to family tradition that he is cut off from his personal feelings. *Salome of the Tenements* was actually drawn from two powerful stories, one private, the other public. The latter is the story of Rose Pastor Stokes, a Lower East Side seamstress who married into a well-known New York family, a romance that the newspapers covered obsessively; the private one concerns the love affair the novelist had as an adult student with her teacher, the famous American philosopher, John Dewey.

The characters' personal sources of appeal are freighted with cultural forces: the drive to assimilate and the power to accommodate. The first half of the novel feels like an allegory so driven that it seems to crash through the plot. At a crucial moment, the narrative is occluded when Sonya takes his dictation as John assesses the achievements of the settlement house he has endowed: "We have tried to build a strong foundation for the right kind of womanhood, manhood, and citizenship." The philanthropist continues for a sentence before he gets lost in a "tangle of statistics," unsettled as he is by Sonya's voluptuousness. Undone, John flees the city, but on his return, he is ready to acknowledge the helplessness of his yearning. Following some torrid embraces, the lovers elope.[63]

Unfortunately, we never learn Manning's ideas about how to ensure the right kind of manhood, womanhood, and citizenship, though we can be sure that they are not ones that his marriage to Sonya is likely to confirm. We never learn, according to the weak binary structuring of the novel, what normalizes gender identity or what qualities of citizenship are meant. Nor do we ever learn whether some attributes standardize the relation between the two. The marriage goes so woefully wrong so immediately that Yezierska's vision of the possibilities of Jewish assimilation spelled out in *Salome of the Tenements* challenges the supposedly positive cultural effects of intermarriage. Although critics of immigration decried mixing bloods as mongrelizing Anglo-American stock, other observers saw intermarriage as the most effective way to Americanize. Opponents of assimilation used this biological model to hierarchalize ethnicities. Miscegenation—the term that, in America, usually invokes sexual congress between African and Caucasian Americans—was an equally influential concept in immigration discourse. The "higher-ups," or leisure class, like John Manning's family, could look down on the immigrant masses based on what these guardians of the host culture chose to see as inheritable characteristics rather than confront their racial and class prejudices about who was good enough to become an American and who was not. In this sense of yearning for a time when an equivalency between racial and social identity could be guaranteed and the status quo ensured, arguments focusing on predictable, that is, transmittable, features of race or blood nostalgically favored an antimodern vision of society.

The second half of Yezierska's novel details the mortifications suffered as a result of not knowing the connection between gender and citizenship, or what it means culturally to be a man or a woman in a changing society and what gendered traits of citizenship Manning's settlement means to relay. These anxieties especially apply to the shaping of female cultural identity. After the marriage founders, John withdraws into the steely reserve that presumably stood his Puritan forefathers in good stead. Sonya, however, falls back into her marginalized state before she can begin the arduous process of self-definition, now dis-identifying with cultural ideals of advantageous marriages and easy assimilation and authenticating character through the cultivation of talents and values. Even so, her possibilities are narrow—the sweatshops, service, or marriage. She undertakes to become a clothing designer and, in doing so, helps other immigrant women learn to dress and even to find their civic identities apart from marriage. Her clothes eventually move beyond the Lower East Side and are sold in Fifth Avenue stores, so her imagination of being American comes literally to suit the American women who buy her successful fashions, and thereby teaches them, as Cahan's David Levinsky professed, to signify their identities as American women too. Like the famous Hollywood "moguls," the Jewish producers whose films mediated for Christian America a vision of itself that the producers themselves created out of their yearning to belong, Sonya's dresses make both her and her fancy customers more American.[64]

Yezierska's novel offers a vision of both failed and successful assimilation. The failed one, based on intermarriage, tries to obviate the inheritable class distinctions marking landed American identity and those of immigrant peasants. The successful assimilation involves internalizing the middle-class ethic of hard work and self-cultivation. It still turns on the immigrant's power to adapt, to navigate obstacles. If we now take for granted the meaning of "Americanization" as a general term, it was widely invoked between 1915 and 1924 to describe how the new immigrants were to be molded into cultural as well as legal citizens of the United States. Yet "Americanization" also referred more specifically to a number of formal initiatives that the Department of the Interior had implemented. That socialization meant learning English as well as moral and social discipline, along with knowledge of the political and judicial systems and the conviction that citizens were treated fairly within it. As one French correspondent describes this "curious process": "No strict credo is imposed, and no definite prescriptions have to be accepted. Nor does any discipline have to be taught. It is merely a question of dissolving the original inassimilable qualities of the individual and making him capable of accepting and transmitting the social impulses of the majority and of mingling joyfully with them." This "national and social bond between all the citizens . . . is the most important and efficacious instrument that this great nation possesses . . . for it imposes social peace and moral equilibrium," a means of "pacifying and unifying the nation." While we may see in such accounts how majoritarian culture transacts its ideological authority, the concept of Americanization meant the process of converting immigrants, especially from Southern and Eastern Europe, to the redemptive features of a civil religion, in this case the middle-class vision of individualist fulfillment and familial responsibility.[65]

The voluble discussion of whether and how immigrants could and should be made into citizens clamorously performed the country's effort to define itself during the anxious quarter century, when such debates stirred the United States. An astounding number of books, pamphlets, and articles addressed this great national worry—how well the country was succeeding and how it was failing, the faults of Americans and the foibles of immigrants. For some observers, it was enough to offer immigrants a chance to work at menial labor, while for others it could never suffice merely to exploit their labor and give them a "thin varnish of propaganda." Some saw Americanization more pragmatically as subject to party politics, while others saw the question of trying to assimilate the seemingly inassimilable as risking the vitality of the republic itself. The notorious anti-immigration spokesman Madison Grant subtitles his 1930 anthology (including out-of-context quotations from John Adams, Patrick Henry, Benjamin Franklin, and Alexander Hamilton), *The Alien in Our Midst*, as "Selling Our Birthright for a Mess of Industrial Pottage." His nativist arguments sought to prove, with something like biblical authority, that, like Esau, the nation risked being dispossessed of its cultural legacy if we gratified the needs of our industrial economy for cheap labor. For Grant and his ilk, Americanization and the immigration of some groups were seemingly mutually exclusive, even destructively irreconcilable. As another critic remonstrated, "We didn't bring them here to improve us."[66]

Franklin Lane, President Woodrow Wilson's secretary of the interior, aptly summarized the bewildering blend of sentimental and exploitative motives when he announced that he wanted to "take the foreigner by the hand" and lead him on a guided tour through physical and spiritual America, showing him that America, even at its most impressive, is still "unfinished" and awaits the immigrant's application of labors to make it flower. This curious image posits that the United States is not America until the world's immigrants make their presence felt, that America exists only *in potentia*, awaiting the immigrant to vivify and complete it, that our nation is not the nation we want it to be or expect it to be until the immigrant participates in it. Lane wanted to teach the immigrant that the "march of civilization" demonstrated in the grandeur of America's conquest of the continent is, after all, less the vision of politicians or corporate imperialists than it is the epic of the working man. Immigrants will thus be Americanized when they come to honor their status as laborers, insofar as true Americans prize individual initiative: "We have no philosophy except the philosophy of confidence, of optimism, of faith in the righteousness of the contest we make against nature."[67]

For the honorable secretary, the equation to be drawn is a kind of internalized manifest destiny: immigrants become American to the extent that they identify with the conquest of the continent; they become American to the extent that they see success in the conversion of American resources into wealth, American land into empire, American righteousness into personal salvation. Although Americanization can be achieved through this politicized spiritualization of progress, it is through the offices of the "community council" and school that the immigrant working class can be socialized: "I have asked Congress for an appropriation which will permit us to deliver from bondage . . . millions of children and men and women . . . to liberate them from the blinders of ignorance. . . . We want to interpret America in terms of fair play; in terms of the square deal. We want . . . to interpret America in healthier babies, in boys and girls, and men and women that can read and write . . . in better housing conditions and decent wages. . . . That is Americanization in the concrete—reduced to practical terms."

Let us understand the socioeconomic premises here. These immigrants were largely permitted to enter the United States in order to join a labor force whose living conditions even the secretary of the interior, in 1919, characterized as "bondage," whether it was in the Pennsylvania coal mines, the New York garment industry, the Chicago stockyards, the Western railroads, or factories nationwide. Immigrants, to be Americanized, needed to be given equal opportunities of health, literacy, education, and wages, conditions equal enough to be called "fair play" and a "square deal." Then America would be fulfilling its promises and making its creed concrete, because it would be enabling the immigrant to live out the transformation, the vision we readily call the "American dream," to which I shall turn shortly.

This optimism, however, was also met by dark skepticism, as some analysts, including some immigrants themselves, lamented the difficulties, even the impossibilities, of the task. For example, nativists made much of crime rates among immigrant groups, morals charges, and anything faintly suggesting sexual deviance. Although the Johnson-Reed Act of 1924 was legislated, in part, out of fear that Europe's discontented masses would seek asylum here after World War I, much was made of the immigrants' repatriating to their native countries following the war—either as a proof of their fundamentally mercenary motives or as a reflection of our failed hospitality. It is true that many immigrants always intended to go back; for some, the point was to make money in the United States in order to return to their homelands much better off than they could ever have been had they never left home. Yet it was not at all uncommon either for such immigrants to turn around and pay their families' ways to the United States instead. It is also true, though the point is likely to be obscured by incessant sentimentalizing of the immigrant experience, that some returned home out of frustration and disillusionment; a "pox on Columbus," these immigrants would say when they learned that, instead of with gold, the U.S. streets were paved with stones that immigrants were being paid substandard wages to lay. Of course, most did stay and proved it true, if paradoxical, that beyond what America might make of the immigrants came the more lasting effect of what immigrants made of America.

Native-born Americans often argued that for immigrants to make themselves into good citizens, Americans needed to Americanize immigrants, not by social welfare measures, but through their daily contacts. Instead of holding themselves aloof, Americans should instruct immigrants via the benefit of their own example. Thus, in immigrant narratives, there is usually at least one "old stock" citizen who reaches out to the floundering alien, if only to signify the beneficent possibilities to be discovered in the mainstream. This helpful agent, not surprisingly, is often a teacher, though it can also be a schoolmate, business associate, or lover.

For other observers, immigrants risked becoming Americanized all too easily, insubstantially, and perhaps falsely. According to one critic in the *New Republic*, immigrants "abandon their cultural inheritance with astonishing facility and celerity":

> They acquire almost always in one generation and often sooner the slang, the moral outlook, and the superficial characteristic behavior of the most modern America—the America of movies, headlines and headliners, national fashions and the Hearst newspapers. They are Americanized in the sense that they have yielded to the seductive importunities of popular American occupations, interests, and catchwords, but they are entirely indifferent or actually antagonistic to the most revered household gods of traditional America. They are impatient with its moralism, its affectations, its pretenses, its scruples, its legalism and with the whole of what George Santayana has so aptly described as the genteel tradition.[68]

The criticism here is that immigrants, anxious to blend in, seize on the "seductive," mediated appeals of American glitz and become standardized according to the culture's lowest common denominators. So intense is the desire to assimilate that immigrants mimic, even hysterically, the values they first perceive in America, sign systems that tend to be the most conspicuous, even garish features and facades of the American cultural landscape. In going too fast, they risk going wrong. Even as they adopt the values immediately available to them, immigrants do not grasp some of those cherished ideals that gaudy, trendy America sets itself up to challenge or undo. In this respect, the cultural citizenship of immigrants is always partial, embracing one side of the American dream, such as the vision of rampant individualism, without appreciating the social forces of constraint, in this case, the genteel tradition—the social code of enforced piety that tempers or gives ballast to individualism. The critique, however, is not directed only to the environment of restraint or the artificial life of manufactured freedom. It is also aimed at the cheapness with which immigrants may hold their own traditions, their failure to bring those traditions more meaningfully to bear on the America they inhabit.

Such easy assimilation leaves unfinished the deeper business of Americanization, for the Americans made out of such immigrants, the argument goes, might be too superficial, too inauthentic to count for much as citizens. By internalizing America's worst, they cut themselves off from the deeper wellsprings of American tradition. Another analyst likely spoke for many others in considering the whole controversy over Americanization futile, since the process should be conceived in terms of generations, not years, nor was assimilation anything you could deliberately *do* to people. Katherine Fullerton Gerould observed that Americanization was "either optimism gone mad through ignorance or sheer intellectual dishonesty. Considering the times, it might well be either." For Gerould, the virtue of Americanization would not be proved for a great while—and the sooner the citizenry realized that, the better.[69]

Writers of the era seized on the vicissitudes facing immigrants as the stuff of novels, novels pointed mainly to middle-class readers. For the point of this fiction was not to convince immigrants that successful Americanization could be achieved, but to persuade mainstream Americans that the Americanization of the immigrants was a complex social good. Or not: several of these novels had less to do with "How I became an American" than they did with "What to do with these strangers?" They are now quite obscure, although Peter Kyne, author of *Pride of Palomar* (1921), was, according to one survey, once the fifth most popular author between 1919 and 1926. This work tapped into the reservoir of nativist anxieties by recounting a Californian's efforts to save his ranch from being bought up by the ruthless Japanese. An

Eastern financier holds the mortgage, is eager to make a good deal for himself, and is blind to the peril of selling to the Japanese. Along the way the rancher wins the love, and help, of the financier's daughter who, acting independently, schemes against her father, driven as he is less by democratic faith than by profit. A great best seller, Kyne's novel met with mixed reviews. ("A well-proportioned, vigorous story," said the *Literary Review*; "a remarkable outpouring of sentiment against the Japanese people is the most noteworthy feature," observed the *Times* dryly.)[70]

Other such novels, including Nina Putnam's *Easy* (1924), warning against the dangers of an "unrestricted invasion of small-towns by hordes of foreigners," were less popular as well as less esteemed by critics. "If [these characters] are the representative Americans of the old stock," according to the *Times*, "one cannot feel that their displacement is either surprising or particularly regrettable."[71] *Seed of the Sun* (1921) by Wallace Irwin, on the other hand, was a more widely admired Americanization novel. Here the WASP granddaughter of a town's founding patriarch loses her ranch to an unscrupulous Japanese menace. She is saved from ruin by Leary, a dashing Irishman, whom she at first distrusts, if only because he himself is but one generation removed from being unassimilated. White citizenry thus renegotiates the dream of whiteness, distributing it as a reward for immigrants who identify with mainstream values, serve mainstream socioeconomic purposes, and identify against racially constructed threats to WASP rule. By virtue of his dauntlessness, the Irishman can be transformed into an acceptable member of society if only he will help the Anglo-Protestants keep their land from the scheming, unscrupulous Asian. To the formerly disenfranchised Irish go new acceptance and new standing. Moreover, even if they may no longer have the power they once did, the old stock can be replenished by assimilating the deserving new and thus rearm themselves to do battle another day with their inscrutable, racially differentiated antagonists.

Perhaps the most vigorously waged literary battle of Americanization in the many novels written by European immigrants and their descendants took place in the decade following the Great War. There were stories about more than a half-dozen ethnic groups of the recent arrivals (such as Czech, Hungarian, and Italian novels), as well as novels that looked back to the nineteenth century to chronicle the emergence of others (such as German, Irish, and Norwegian novels). And there were a great many novels about Jews—in New York, of course, but also Philadelphia, South Carolina, Illinois,

California, even in Montana—Jews seemingly everywhere. In covering such a gamut of locations, these books meant, among other things, to edify a curious mainstream public that wanted either to be instructed in the uniqueness of one group or the other—these groups' difference—or to learn about one ethnic group's likeness to the Americans among whom they moved.

Sometimes, as in James Tully's *Shanty Irish* (1928), the autobiographical investigation gives us new respect for the dignity of Irish workers in Ohio, while Louis Forgione's *The River Between* (1928) reminds us of the folkways and heritage of Italian laborers on the New Jersey Palisades. Although the dignity of work is enlisted to redeem the harsh treatments and abuse that immigrants suffer, many of these novels look at love and marriage as the means whereby immigrant or racial traits can be sloughed off, Americanization certified. Sometimes that passage comes through contact with the old stock, sometimes through contact with other immigrants. How interested was America in this story? Consider that Anne Nichols's Broadway smash, *Abie's Irish Rose*, enjoyed a record run of five and a half years (which in an era before *Cats* is remarkable). The play's success was found in the endearing comic lessons it provided for the ways the second generation could overcome the prejudices of first-generation immigrants. Its fame also helped it to crystallize the media image of immigrants in love. Not only did it find a durably hilarious resource in immigrant parents identifying themselves against other immigrants, but casting the immigrant parent as resisting intermarriage also did considerable work. First, that opposition screens nativists' acts of distancing; second, it endorses the native spectator's implied superiority over an immigrant mentality insofar as parental opposition, seen as a humorous source of unfair prejudice, is triumphed over by the believer in the democracy of love. This comic intransigence of the uncomprehending or unsympathetic immigrant parent also suggests how intermarriage among ethnic groups was understood to bring diverse peoples into balance and thus give immigrants a new identity that could be called "American," even if it was not the American identity that nativists held up as an ideal.

Americanization through intermarriage comprises the very drama observed in Ole Rolvaag's second-generation novel, *Peder Victorious* (1929). That novel follows the family fortunes of the heroic Scandinavian pioneers introduced in *Giants in the Earth* (1927), with special emphasis on the development of the youngest son, Peder, whose growth into masculinity is complicated by his special talents at declamation and theatricality, not to mention, in contrast to his brothers, his complete lack of interest in farming. "Peder's Irish Rose," we might call it, because Per and Beret Hansa's gifted son turns his back on evangelical Norwegian Lutheranism, withdrawing from his calling as a minister and discovering happiness in the arms of Susie Doheny. Here the dangers of assimilation are found in his mother's dread of losing her Norwegian hold over her children. In choosing Susie, Peder asserts the freedom from Old World constraints of marrying within the tribe that marks his boldest declaration of independence. The novel's conclusion, in which Beret welcomes her new Irish Catholic daughter-in-law, is meant as a celebration, however qualified, of the New America that such marriages portend.

What was at stake in making novels of Americanization hinge so fully on questions of intermarriage? The reviews frequently observe that as realistic as the muted *Peder Victorious* undoubtedly is, it did not compare favorably to the roaring *Giants in the Earth*, which was an astounding success—forty-four printings in one year—because it is about the second, not the first, generation, whose tribulations are less intense. As the critic in the *Nation* remarked: "Although 'Peder Victorious' is a good book, in fact the best American novel I have seen this winter, it is only a good book; it is not, like its predecessor, a magical, a beguiling, and an enchanting book. . . . We are faced with the fact that the second generation, which built the Western towns, is far less interesting than the first, which drove its rickety covered wagons through the pathless grass of the prairies," an assessment echoed elsewhere: "All the vitality and character that one found so delightful in [*Giants*] are lacking. [Rölvaag] is now concerned with community problems, not with individuals."[72]

The judgment here unself-consciously posits that the first generation's titanic struggle against nature is implicitly more dramatic and more important than the second generation's community building, its Americanization and assimilation. The winters are just as cold, but the challenges are more tepid. Which is to say that there is commodious space in the American cultural landscape for stories of immigrants who vanquish the land and thereby claim their place in society, but less hearty is the welcome for stories about immigrants who merely claim their own natures, and give up their marginality, to enter the American middle class. Consider too that *Giants in the Earth* is praised for its power of mystification ("magical," "enchanting," "beguiling"), while its successor is praised faintly for its concrete, and thus uninspiring realism. Both stories live out Secretary Lane's vision of becoming America by completing America, but we like stories—or our delegated readers, the critics, like stories—about immigrants when they essentially remain immigrants, eternally different, and like them a little less when they not only become citizens but respectable middle-class citizens. In a sense, it is history that diminishes *Peder Victorious*. If the conquest of the wilderness made Americans, as Frederick Turner once argued was the basis for exceptionalism, then we can see that it is Beret, the mother and wife, who is finally subdued, chastened into accepting a world she neither imagined nor chose. Moreover, she resists this fate as long as possible, going so far as (literally) trying to burn down the school where Peder learns his lessons in perfidy. Still, the novel ends with her embracing Peder's choice, since her only alternative is estrangement. In this way the immigrant pioneer is truly overcome; what the wilderness could not do, that is, vanquish the first generation's spirit, the assimilation of the second generation can do merely by repeating marriage vows. Thus, the Americanization first achieved by conquering the wilderness is incomplete and needs this new social discipline. Beret's fate reminds us too of the central role that the mother plays in this fiction, since she is the repository of the Old World values that must be undone or surpassed. In fact, mothers are so often read out of the books—*Salome of the Tenements*, *Shanty Irish*, and *River Between* are true to form—dying early or disappearing, as if Americanization is more easily achieved once a mother's power is curbed, banished, or nullified.

Unlike first-generation narratives (such as *Giants in the Earth*), which establish the complexities of becoming American, the subject of novels like *Peder Victorious* is the "problem of America in the making or America coming of age," says Percy Boynton.[73] Meditating less on Civilization in the United States and more on Middletown, such books do not portray man and woman against cosmic forces or history or the elements. Instead, they place these immigrants amid the humdrum business of merely being American, which is to say in living out the American dream.

By "American dream," I specifically mean the vision of America articulated only two years after *Peder Victorious*, in 1931, by James Truslow Adams in his phenomenally successful *The Epic of America*. This popular history was really popular! It was the eighth best seller among the nonfiction books of 1931 and the number one best seller of nonfiction books in 1932—the single worst year of the Depression. Nor is it hard to guess why this triumphant march through American history would be so well received in troubled times. Its power lies in assuring Americans that they have not been dispossessed of their history, not cut out from the national legacy, that U.S. citizens may yet pursue their dream of freedom and security. Although some say Tocqueville is responsible for the famous phrase and others suggest that it is even older, "American dream" did not come fully into our parlance until Adams devoted his epilogue to spelling out what it was, even feeling the need to italicize the concept as if it had never been formulated before. After listing some of the country's accomplishments, Adams does an about-face. I quote at length partly to show how the historian casts the dream as a middle-class fantasy of individual fulfillment and also to disclose what that vision is ultimately worth as a social ideal:

> It is a difficult dream for the European upper classes to interpret adequately, and too many of us ourselves have grown weary and mistrustful of it. It is not a dream of motor cars and high wages merely, but a dream of a social order in which each man and each woman shall be able to attain to the fullest stature of which they are innately capable, and be recognized by others for what they are, regardless of the fortuitous circumstances of birth or position. . . .
>
> No, the American dream that has lured tens of millions of all nations to our shores in the past century has not been a dream of merely material plenty, though that has doubtless counted heavily. It has been much more than that. It has been a dream of being able to grow to fullest development as man and woman, unhampered by the barriers which had slowly been erected in older civilizations, unrepressed by social orders which had developed for the benefit of classes rather than for the simple human being of any and every class.[74]

Tellingly, Adams immediately recognizes the currency of this "dream of a social order." For the dream's allure for immigrants is that it imagines something beyond the right to pursue material wealth, though of course it argues that as well. The dream fantasizes an individualism that yields a society beyond history, a society where the paralyzing effects of the past can be undone, not merely as an imaginative effect. This vision of classlessness is a middle-class ideal, one that the middle class invents to keep itself viable, for the middle class knows that it only too rarely can enter the upper echelons, just as it knows it must fight fiercely to keep from sliding downward.[75] So Adams describes the American dream as fundamentally a desire for order and justice that is also founded on a middle-class vision of hope and safety, a dream, he continues, that has "evolved from the hearts and burdened souls of many millions, who have come to us from all nations," which is to say central to the immigrant experience.

Adams closes his epilogue, and thus his whole history of America, by quoting *The Promised Land* (1912), the autobiography of Mary Antin, a young Russian-Jewish immigrant. The recently arrived girl describes her assimilation, but not as the salvation one might expect in a book with that title: "And I am the youngest of America's children, and into my hands is given her priceless heritage. . . . Mine is the whole majestic past, and mine is the shining future." Readers may be awed by this optimism, just as they may be taken aback by Adams's faith in Antin's revelation. Antin tells us that she already possesses the America so many of the nativists would deny her, that by virtue of *being* an immigrant, she already holds the "priceless heritage" of America's past and future. For Antin, the dream is only alive to the extent that an immigrant can claim it; past and future can only be made continuous by the present.[76]

WHAT IS HAPPENING TO OUR FICTION?

So asked Robert Herrick, a reputable novelist of some thirty-five years, at the close of 1929. Herrick's query, to the enlightened readers of the *Nation*, articulates the worry and wonder over the state of the novel as it developed through the preceding decade. Although there may have been previous hours in American cultural history when novels elicited as sustained and as apprehensive consideration, the kind of concern to which Herrick's question attested was widespread and general. Throughout the '20s, writers and critics alike were intrigued with the possibilities of the status of fiction in American society. Herrick was neither a brilliant diagnostician nor egregiously wrongheaded; still, his opinions represent a serious effort by a novelist of some standing, in a venue of considerable stature, to give a broad and sober critical account of the future of the modern American novel. A Harvard-educated professor who helped to shape the English department at the University of Chicago, Herrick had been writing critical articles for years, so it was in no way unusual for the *Nation* to turn to him. For Herrick, the decade ended in much the same way as it began, with debates between the need for modernism versus the limits of realism, debates generated in part by the continuing presence of the Howellsian imperative.

This novelist's interrogatory was not like Hawthorne's lament over the popularity of female writers or Melville's complaint about financial worries or James's meditation about the "complex fate" of being American. Here, ostensibly, was not a novelist primarily concerned about claiming a place for his productions or instructing an audience in how to appreciate that work, nor was Herrick lamenting the passing of his historical moment, though of course his deliberations imply all these rationales throughout. Herrick's position was that "our fiction"—"the most fluid form of expression" and "nearer the popular mind than any other"—was at risk because a mounting "amateurishness" had led to the decline of the novel's historic place as a prose epic. The genre that makes our culture communal or integrated was facing several dangers, such as the increasing feminization of literature or the new interiority and an unhealthy interest in psychoanalysis. Yet perhaps the deepest source of Herrick's disquiet was that "authentic craftsmen" (in the tradition of Twain, Howells, James, and George W. Cable) no longer commanded the authority they should have. Now there were too many "free lances" and "casual laborers." More people than ever were reading fiction, meaning both that there were also more feckless writers of fiction than ever before and that so many new readers would not know how to tell the difference.[77]

The new challenges facing fiction writers, and the new rewards for fiction, along with the competition that novels were facing now from film and radio, meant that the prestige novelists should enjoy in contributing to the nation's imaginative life had never appeared more imperiled. Herrick argues that novelists still must strive to create epics in prose and that the novelist's place in society should be nothing less than that of epic poets of earlier civilizations. (Indeed, many novelists of the following decade tried to take up this challenge.) Although Herrick concedes that "what will happen when the present taste for individualistic abandon has run its course is impossible to predict," he still believes that the novel will finally improve its capacity to keep up with the accelerated pace of modernity. Then the novel "will reassume its authority as the interpreter and chronicler of contemporary life," its practitioners proud and "devoted" to their task rather than taking "flyers as in the stock market when the whim or pecuniary exigency moves them," he writes, a mere six weeks after Black Tuesday.

Herrick feels the challenge of the dispossessed. Brought up in the generation that valued the novel as a well-made artifact, he finds himself in a new commodity culture that demands an increasing supply of novels and then values all the wrong kind of things, like the characters' "insides." He does not name the author or give the title, but one of the novels depressing Herrick the most is Ernest Hemingway's *A Farewell to Arms*, which he compares unfavorably to Erich Marie Remarque's *All Quiet on the Western Front*. Both 1929 novels deal with the filth of war, but the American's outsider status guarantees its "amateurish taint." Hemingway's dirt is the squalor of the "boudoir, the brothel, and the bar"—the milieu of the ambulance driver— not the "clean human dirt" of the soldier: "We were amateurs in the great struggle, never rightly understanding what it was all about, often generous and gallant and efficient amateurs, but never quite grown up; so that our literature drawn from that source must have the unsubstantiality and superficiality of the amateur, who does not pay with his blood for his convictions." Herrick's Hemingway personifies this amateurishness (wasted on Herrick is that Hemingway, besides being a dedicated craftsman, really did pay with his blood). If this fiction passes for excellence—an example so disgusting that its author's name must remain unspoken—things have gone very wrong.

This lack of professionalism "pervades our fiction quite generally as in fact it does our national life," says Herrick. Such dilletantism can be found in the voguish treating of appetites so frankly that the only imaginable relation between women and men is the "purely biologic one." The sad result, he argues, is that, for all their sexuality, our novels lack the "deep passions" of "a great literature." A further mark that we, as a people, "rarely take anything with entire seriousness" can be found in our willingness to substitute "chunks of raw experience" for "solid epic form"; even the "brilliant and important books" trading on their literal fidelity to social reality—like Julia Peterkin's works—are classified as "character and background studies" rather than the "noble category of the novel."

So dire is the state of fiction that Herrick can name only a few authors who respect their craft—Wharton, Cather, and Glasgow—or who can approach a "tragic theme" like Upton Sinclair's portrayal of the Sacco-Vanzetti case, *Boston*, or who can, like Sinclair Lewis, deliver "admirably just revelations of average American character," though these writers, he admits, are now the old youth, even as Theodore Dreiser himself, once the Young Turk par excellence, "is fading from the scene" (only four years after *An American Tragedy!*). Where can fiction go to find both the urgency and the substance in chronicling modernity? In what direction can the novel as prose epic move if it is to avert its end as a "lost art"? Herrick finds the answers in the newspaper, as he fancies many others do in this "semiliterate land," where they "get the kind of fictional satisfaction that properly the contemporary novel should give us." In the newspaper, Herrick finds true variety, humor, tragedy, and universality, "so rich in imaginative implications" are the stories that form the "raw material of great novels." Unfortunately, "we have yet no craftsmen sufficiently endowed to fuse, refine, and transform it into enduring art."

Herrick worries that fiction is losing its status, that even the so-called good novels cannot be confused with good literature. Our writers, he fears, are but the expression of our society and our tastes, a milieu more foolish than ever. Herrick's crusty insistence on professionalism actually coincides with the rest of the culture's new emphasis on applied expertise, a culture that, in replacing the gifted amateur Hobey Baker as its sports icon with Red Grange, the cool virtuoso forsaking a college degree for a paycheck, signaled a new expectation for rewarding craftsmanship.

The absence of a prevailing authority appalls Herrick. Neither Sinclair Lewis nor Upton Sinclair, neither Frank Norris nor Theodore Dreiser, can crystallize an orthodoxy amid the "whirlpool" of literary influences and movements. Despite their "professional competence and pride in their art," Wharton, Cather, and Glasgow are no match for the onslaught of aspirants, armed with typewriters, trampling the legacy of the "elder novelists" whose "product had the hallmark of the professional." None command Herrick's idea of general prestige; none define a method or a point of view that inspires emulation and obeisance. In that absence will the woman novelist flourish, and that is a bad thing from Herrick's perspective, because it means the feminization of the American novel.[78] Herrick does not aim to trivialize the accomplishments of artists like Cather, Wharton, or Glasgow; instead, feminization refers to the diminishment of the masculine lineage of novels critical of a culture steeped in corruptions, where the hero must always flee to avoid further degradation (although women can go nowhere). Moreover, these degradations generally result from women pushing their men into the senseless accumulation of social trappings. Bent on success themselves, men must also face such modern perils as women's nerves and hysterical prodding—the situation on which so many of Herrick's own novels hinge. His books never sold well; his writing can be rigid, the plots mechanical, the characters ideological transparencies. Yet more than likely it was the fable that the public rejected: the dilemmas faced by the modern professional man in a culture not nearly as accommodating as the first phase of the Gilded Age. As Kenneth Lynn points out, Herrick suffered from an acute sense of belatedness, but the nostalgia he purveyed was not shared by a readership still fascinated by success.[79]

From Herrick's standpoint, the decade went wrong ten years before, when women's right to vote signaled the chaos overtaking American fiction:

> Quite naturally women are invading the fiction field in ever-increasing numbers, as one of the luxury occupations to which in their need of economic freedom they gravitate, and they are bringing with them their own peculiar interests and emphases. . . . The changes . . . in contemporary fiction . . . bulk large as a whole, above all in the treatment of sexual relations. Instead of less sex or a more spiritualized interpretation . . . there is actually more sex, more biology, and fewer taboos in the modern novel than ever before . . . and a total lack of mystery!

What is wrong with that, we might wonder, except that it panders to the "woman world" where fiction is "mainly consumed"—as opposed to being read and appreciated—a world overseen not only by female writers, but also by their publishers and assistants. This stress on the new sexuality inevitably encourages a fiction freighted with the "new psychology," whose "atrocious jargon" both men and women novelists have "lapped up" in their effort to "ram life in all its variety into the narrow molds of the 'complexes.'" Although the novel, Herrick predicts, will someday absorb whatever it is that psychoanalysis has to offer, its influence so far has been so "disastrous" that writers are well advised to leave it "along with Christian Science to professional practitioners."[80] In Herrick's imagination, the feminization of the novel is worrisome since it harbingers the feminizing of the culture.

Herrick invokes the newspaper as the new source of raw material for the novelist who would create a prose epic. In the paper he finds the evidence of the animating passions of the day, the personalities, the episodes of daily life out of which to shape an American novel worthy of the name. Unfortunately, he did not live to see the whole of Dos Passos's *U.S.A.*, where he may have found a more profound lesson about media representations of reality beyond his own capacity to render it. With such prosaic titles as *The Web of Life* (1900), *The Common Lot* (1904), and, perhaps most telling, *The Real World* (1901), Herrick's own novels were as centrally concerned with the surfaces of American life as he bids American novelists now to make their own. In turning to the newspaper as offering the stuff of the prose epic, Herrick was suggesting, trenchantly, that modern life had become too various and too insubstantial ever again to afford the novelist the straightforward perspective of realism, and that if we want reality, the novelist must seek it in concatenation with the competing stories, of which each tale comprises only a fragment. Nor is it too much to suggest that in Herrick's rustle of the newspaper can be heard the indistinctly expressed anxiety of the novelist who came of age at the end of the nineteenth century that the representation of reality had ultimately failed and that the "real world" he was so sure of documenting had eluded the omniscience of his own realism. His mistrust of women writers concealed for him how decidedly his own aesthetic preoccupations participated in this failure, how realism's categories were less millennial, after all, than Howells ordained. For realism conferred a mixed blessing. On the one hand, it opened subject after subject for representation in the most direct, least affected, more ordinary forms of common expression; on the other, its epistemological limits meant that realism, and its surrogate, regionalism, never could establish the kind of intellectual authority that modernism claimed, one that signaled the authority of revolt. Women writers became, for Herrick, among others, the inverted image of the professional writer's dependency and submission to a new orthodoxy, the limits of their own middle-class imaginations.

As if to register those limits, Herrick's screed could not attend to the testimony concerning the health of U.S. fiction inadvertently issuing from the most celebrated book in the United States in 1929, the most popular novel of the year, a war novel, though not an American one—Erich Marie Remarque's *All Quiet on the Western Front*. Selling millions of copies in several countries, this novel was one of the multitude published about the Great War, but, more than any other, it acquired an international following, perhaps because of its famous, poignant closing image of the delicate freedom of a single bird. That image may summarize how the war's devastating legacy occasions the need to find something to give stability and permanence to the cessation of hostilities. Nowhere more than in the works of the middle-class imagination and the modern realism it sponsored was that need felt so fervently. While we may be tempted to say that *All Quiet* closed the decade with a salutary roundness, crystallizing a final sense of the loss that the war had wrought, it did so in a literary environment that had tried to chronicle how that loss, and its transformations, had been experienced in America and how its urgencies had come to be redefined.

the 1930s

This chapter provides an alternative way of reading the fiction of this decade. I begin by restating the special circumstances under which '30s historiography has been written and then turn to mainstream critical opinion and its sense of the decade's achievements and challenges, pausing to examine the adjudicating of taste that book reviewing played at the time. From that perspective, I turn to the middle-class realism of the era, especially observing several of its principal modes of expression—the woman's novel, the historical novel, the family novel, and the political novel. Along the way, I also study some key episodes in literary history and culture by way of indicating how truly normative this fiction was for American readers.

THE THREATENING THIRTIES

Describing the history of the American taste for fiction in the 1930s requires confronting both the conventional and revisionist beliefs shaping the era's current literary historiography. In this chapter, I build on my reading of the centrality of bourgeois fiction to the 1920s to test the proposition that the literary record of the 1930s has been distorted by critics and historians whose business it was to promulgate a canon. Missing from the account that has descended to us is the middle-class fiction that as a matter of course failed to match canonical premises. It could even be argued that the criteria were fashioned precisely to eliminate these books. As a result, a whole tradition of American novels of the middle class that were bought, read, and discussed throughout the Depression years has been lost. We thus have a history of professional choices rather than of actual reading practices.[1]

The beneficiaries of '30s historiography were once perceived to be the fiction writers valued by the New Critics, sometimes in curious combination with the intellectual circle associated with the *Partisan Review (PR)*—the anticommunist left seeking to fuse radical politics and European modernism. Although the PR's preferences begin with European novelists like Franz Kafka, André Malraux, and Ignazio Silone, not the Southern Agrarian tradition, both groups favored William Faulkner especially. Both camps preferred modernist fiction over the social realism typified by Erskine Caldwell's *Tobacco Road* (1932) or James T. Farrell's *Studs Lonigan* trilogy (1935), which appealed more to the politics than to the aesthetic premises of the PR critics. While most works of social realism would be understood as basically serving the left side of mainstream taste, John Steinbeck's *Grapes of Wrath* (1939) was remarkable insofar as a general audience also embraced it.

The considerable appeal of popular novels, like Pearl Buck's *The Good Earth* (1931) and Hervey Allen's *Anthony Adverse* (1933), whose literary merits were easily maligned, worried guardians of critical taste since the patent success of such books expanded the market for romances or heroic tales of American history, as in the realist historical fiction of Kenneth Roberts and Walter Edmonds, that seemed to distract Americans from their own economic and ideological worries by recalling the nation's past. With the country's imagination engrossed in narratives of how Americans responded to earlier dangers, the literary impact of Depression actualities might be diffused, so it became a matter of conscience for leftist critics to reclaim the socialist and proletarian tradition, first through Walter Rideout's pioneering scholarship.[2] Although novels of labor protest predate the Depression, '30s literature describing the class struggle, industrial strikes, and the lowly state of the American working class may be said to begin with Michael Gold's *Jews without Money* (1930), extending through Grace Lumpkin's *To Make My Bread* (1932), Albert Halper's *Union Square* (1933), Robert Cantwell's *The Land of Plenty* (1934), and, by the end of the decade, Pietro Di Donato's *Christ in Concrete* (1939), which when selected as a Book-of-the-Month Club choice achieved mainstream legitimacy for itself as well as the genre. Among other novels that have descended to later generations as worthy of study were such experimental, even eccentric modernist works as the novels of Nathanael West and Djuna Barnes's *Nightwood* (1936).

Absent from this conventional wisdom is the recognition of the middle-class realism that is essential to understanding the 1930s. These books competed for the readership that literary critics of the day most wished to direct. Yet '30s literary history is so often defined by what these scholars and critics were writing against that the term "the other '30s" has been invoked to distinguish both social realism and classical modernism as the two main veins of fiction in these years, when, in fact, both are minority countermovements to the majoritarian tradition of middle-class realism—especially regionalism, historical fiction, family sagas, and novels of middle-class manners. Without the recovery of this larger range of novels, the continuities of American fiction seem to fade away or fracture. Most readers would not recognize these writers' names, much less be familiar with their works, so even if I listed such different novelists as Josephine Lawrence, John P. Marquand, Michael Foster, Ruth Suckow, George Weller, or Waters E. Turpin, the names might not evoke enough of the variety to suggest the kind of fiction I mean.

Not only does the erasure of these writers misrepresent the actuality, but without a just appraisal of the nature of the bourgeois character of this literary history, our standard version risks losing its revisionist power, since its counterpoint is too cloudy; its corrective power of emphasis is diffused or is misdirected at some notion of the merely popular. Students of the American novel have too little collective understanding of how the works that we now think of as typical were not seen as such in their moment. If Fielding Burke or Tillie Olsen or Tess Slesinger or Tom Kromer, for example, is now given to us as a representative '30s writer, then the contours of that literary history, its preoccupations and omissions, make up a far different chronicle from the one that most '30s readers would have recognized.[3]

Lately, various feminist traditions have recouped the achievements of several women writers, especially Willa Cather, who continued to publish through the thirties, as did Ellen Glasgow and Fannie Hurst. Zora Neale Hurston's is the most famous case of recovery. Especially through the efforts of Robert Hemenway and several black feminist writers and critics in the 1980s, Hurston's work has been fully recuperated, to the point that her once admired but then forgotten novel of 1937, *Their Eyes Were Watching God*, has now attained its rightful place in the canon and become a staple of college literature courses. Lately, too, there has been a vigorous effort to reevaluate some of the better-known modern realist women writers, like Dorothy Canfield Fisher, but, among the middle-class novelists I discuss, too many women writers remain to be rediscovered.[4]

These novels give pleasures other than those of high art or best sellers, now as they did then. Most especially, they create a cultural atmosphere, the place and time in America where choices were made, family issues confronted or buried, relations in the community stirred. They record the daily public drama of the Great Depression played out on private terms and in a minor key. And for the millions of middle-class Americans not living in soul-destroying poverty, life was neither the humiliation of breadlines and soup kitchens nor the degradation of Hoovervilles, though obviously many formerly middle-class citizens were so affected. For the middle-class Americans still buying and reading books, theirs was the more modulated shame of adjustments, compromises, and sacrifices—an embarrassment not of riches but of discomforts, all of which were bound to seem petty in the face of so much greater suffering—then as now. It is not a literature of self-pity or complaint. Neither is it a fiction of hope or desolation, though sometimes its realism falters into an obdurate pathos that seems much like sentimentality, as in Helen Hull's *Hardy Perennial* (1933), the story of a wife who helps her husband through the loss of his business position. Such novels usually did not sell abundantly, though they sold well enough to suggest the existence of an audience more than the equal to that of the fiction that has come to represent the '30s. And the critics took these books seriously too.

The middle-class realism of the 1930s includes the regional writing that saw virtually every square mile of America described in fiction.[5] There were Ohio and Idaho novels, Mississippi and Pennsylvania novels, California, Delaware, and Oklahoma novels, Minnesota and New Mexico novels, novels about the Dakotas and the Carolinas, Colorado and Kansas novels, and more books about Maine (and just about as many about Iowa) than one can imagine. It may have been, as some commentators suggested, that following America's foray into internationalism, regionalism returned after World War I as a neo-nationalist, antimodernist movement seeking easier visions of comprehensibility and history, though not all of these novels can be so described. It may also be, however, that middle-class stories ineluctably find their telling in terms of place and are first of all situated in a here and now, even when that milieu is sometimes located as there and then. In fact, nearly every Pulitzer Prize novel of the thirties was more or less a regional novel, including that favorite of a previous generation's young adults, Marjorie K. Rawlings's *The Yearling* (1938), as well as less memorable ones like T. S. Stribling's examination of corruption in turn-of-the-century Alabama, *The*

Store (1932), Caroline Miller's historical study of backwoods Georgia during the early nineteenth century, *Lamb in His Bosom* (1933), Josephine Johnson's tale of Missouri farm life, *Now in November* (1934), and H. L. Davis's novel of settling the Oregon frontier, *Honey in the Horn* (1935).

These writers, and scores more, were once part of many educated readers' set of contemporaneous references and were never meant to be forgotten. Their books were received as news, especially in the newspaper supplements where they were discussed in detail; a surprising number of these books were reviewed side by side with the period's modernist classics. They were often received on familiar terms: critics suggested how little or how much a new title added to an author's profile, as if to indicate that there was both a general agreement over that stature and a general interest in its development. No historian of the era would feel obliged to catalog these books, nor would a cultural analyst of the day expect the authors to be so thoroughly absent from later chronicles. Throughout the Depression, readers expected fiction to tell the story of how the bourgeoisie live now, and in the hands of writers like Margaret Banning or Josephine Lawrence the troubles of the middle class were dramatized and made culturally meaningful. They wrote about changes in the workplace, support for the aged before Social Security, the social and psychological challenges of living within one's means amid the new realities of the Depression, the economic as well as the social implications of a will's stipulations, a high school reunion, or the trouble in finding good household help, an important subject in a world before labor-saving devices. Their novels were shaped as modern fables, referring domestic problems to a new, bewildering situation, demonstrating strategies of coping with a life that readers recognized and may have felt unprepared to meet. These novels typically disclose the heightened instability of this middle-class world; they recognize the unnerving quality of life and aim to guide readers through the ethical and cultural challenges that the new economic reality occasions. And reviewers respected them for their efforts.

These are not the era's popular melodramas that tried to reassure readers through emotional appeals or the comforts of formula fiction. Nor were they competing with radio soap operas or the movies' screwball comedies as amusements. The popular medium they most resemble is the self-help book so anxiously sought during this period of upheaval: Walter Pitkin's *Life Begins at Forty* (1932), Dorothea Brande's *Wake Up and Live!* (1936), Marjorie Hillis's *Live Alone and Like It* (1936), and a best-selling book of 1938, *The*

Importance of Living, by Lin Yu-Tang, a Chinese observer of modern America who once enjoyed considerable cachet in the United States. All of these advice books were unbendingly middle-class insofar as they promulgated a reliance, perhaps an overreliance, on personal management skills. The conduct manual that outsold them all, Dale Carnegie's *How to Win Friends and Influence People* (1936), transmuted the citizenry's rawest fears into simplistic formulas about reassessing and redeploying those skills as one's human capital.

Yet the fiction that I am describing also needs to be distinguished from the '30s novels that succeeded wildly by appealing to readers yearning for inspiration, for knowledge as assured and assuring "as the earth turns," as one popular romance (which later became a radio serial and then a TV soap opera) was first called. Such readers often turned to stories of modern uncertainties solved by familiar Christian wisdom or vague mysticism, like Lloyd Douglas's *Magnificent Obsession* (1929), whose popularity soared during the early years of the Depression, and *The Green Light* (1935). Sometimes, the novelists most relied on to provide this succor were English: James Hilton, who scored phenomenal successes with *Lost Horizon* (1933), *Goodbye, Mr. Chips* (1934), and *We Are Not Alone* (1937). American practitioners included Rachel Field, whose *Time Out of Mind* (1935) and *All This, and Heaven Too* (1938) were successful examples of the secular writing that one may call middle-class inspirational literature.

Thirties middle-class realism, on the other hand, investigates the practical conduct of this new life. It seldom sees itself as political, though some writers found politics to be a useful setting; it eschews philosophical inquiry and mostly disavows collective response. Its fundamental orientation is that of the bourgeois individual living in history as well as in community, so it also resists the ironic or tragic consciousness preferred by radical and New Critics. To enter into this frame, these novels sometimes begin several generations back, to suggest how the present came into being and thus to see the formation of social, economic, regional, familial, and psychological pressures on the current moment.

One may contend that, in times of such terrible want in America, such aesthetics and politics are just not good enough. So they may deserve to be forgotten. Do these novels bear comparison with Faulkner's *Absalom, Absalom!* or Hurston's *Their Eyes Were Watching God* or Steinbeck's *Grapes of Wrath*? They do—in the limited sense that the more famous ones often treat similar themes and that the plots of such classic novels might resemble middle-class fiction a little more than they first may appear. In another, perhaps much more important sense, the question of their merit is premature, as I have been arguing. A dismissal so cavalier is exactly wrong for the works of the era under discussion, for it was during the 1930s, in the incipient stages of the New Criticism, when the premises of taste, and the means of testing them, were being formulated for the rest of the century. Having neither the political commitment nor the formal attributes that literary critics and historians meant to promote, these novels failed the tests of academic excellence, not because they were bad or foolish, but because the critics who might be seen as shaping literary taste wanted something less middle class than the style and subject in which these books traded and for which they were recognized.

We should read these books to understand better not only our literary, but also our cultural history, since, ultimately, these novels remind us of the intimate relation between public and private spheres, as explored later in the chapter. More often than not, these novels reveal how the typifying modes of the decade overlap, so a novel of middle-class mores often finds expression as a regional work, but it might also appear commingled with modern issues, such as Millen Brand's novel about manic depression, *The Outward Room* (1937), or with the fascination with genealogy, especially turn-of-the-century parents, as in Marquand's *The Late George Apley* (1937).

To explain what these novels are—and to suggest what form their cultural work took and how it was usurped by other discourses—we might recall some of the best-known modes of '30s writing. As we have seen, an ever-growing number of murder mysteries topped the annual best-seller lists. Also popular were works of Americana—historical, social, or biographical memoirs evoking a better time, better leaders, and more comprehensible problems—like James Truslow Adams's *Epic of America* (1931), Carl Carmer's *Stars Fell on Alabama* (1934), Clarence Day's *Life with Father* (1935), or Carl Van Doren's *Benjamin Franklin* (1938). If detective stories fulfilled an appetite for escapist reading, the second seemed to appease a desire for coherence, either folksy or cultural. Less popular Americana were books that also gratified a hunger for truth telling, including such documentary works as Edmund Wilson's *American Jitters* (1932), James Rorty's *Where Life Is Better* (1936), Sherwood Anderson's *Puzzled America* (1935), Erskine Caldwell and Margaret Bourke-White's *You Have Seen Their Faces* (1937), Nathan Asch's

The Road (1937), Ben Appel's *The People Talk* (1940), and James Agee and Walker Evans's *Let Us Now Praise Famous Men* (1941).[6] The frequency with which such poor sellers appeared expresses something of their publishers' willingness to circulate their arguments, perhaps out of a conviction that the times demanded readers' notice of genuine efforts for the country to come to terms with the spectacle of abjection, and even oppression, pervading the U.S. landscape. Lighter reading included warmly welcomed collections of witty opinions, outlandish characters, and remarkable facts, like Victor Heiser's *An American Doctor's Odyssey* (1938), Drew Pearson's *Washington Merry-Go-Round* (1931), and Margaret Halsey's *With Malice toward Some* (1938), along with the surprising best seller of a literary man-about-Manhattan, the *Autobiography of William Lyon Phelps* (1939), and litterateur-radio pundit Alexander Woolcott's incredibly popular *While Rome Burns* (1934)—books the public relished inasmuch as they offered a nostalgic retreat from the present hour or they aspired to make easy sense—easier, say, than the complement of books one might more readily imagine to inventory the Zeitgeist, such as Edward Filene's *Successful Living in the Machine Age* (1932), James Weldon Johnson's *Black Manhattan* (1930), Eleanor Roosevelt's *It's Up to the Women* (1933), the Federal Writers Project's *These Are Our Lives* (1939), and Charles and Mary Beard's *America at Mid-Passage* (1939).

Taken together, these various kinds of writing performed the services of fiction, in an age when fiction—the great middle-class art form—was more of a luxury than it had recently been. They educated readers in moral dilemmas, geopolitical complexities, and social uncertainties. In some prophetic ways, the destruction of the novel so often trumpeted in the '50s—a decline for which '40s wartime journalism is often indicted as misshaping American readers' expectations of fiction—might have been initiated in the '30s, when increasingly fiction lost its cultural charge and capacity to make events novel. Instead, in the years when two or three dollars, the price of a new novel, might be hard to come by, pulp fiction flourished. Indeed, the paperbacking that changed the market for fiction in the 1950s really began in 1939 with the emergence of Pocket Books. While some novels, of course, did well both critically and commercially, including George Santayana's *The Last Puritan* and Thomas Wolfe's *Of Time and the River*, both of 1935, one source of market appeal in '30s middle-class fiction was sheer length; many books extended across 700 pages or more. In part, this was a publishers' reaction to the phenomenal popularity of that 1,000-page extravaganza,

Anthony Adverse. Advertisements, however, suggest that a novel might yield a whole vacation's reading; shared by a family, books could also be a sound leisure value.

NOTHING TO FEAR BUT FEAR ITSELF

In one of his last columns for the *Saturday Review of Literature*, longtime editor Henry Canby makes no mention of Franklin Roosevelt's Inaugural Day injunction, but while meditating, in 1937, on "how books record the dominant emotion of the decade," he names "fear" as the "prevailing time-current," even though the concept does not really get at the range of skepticism, deep pessimism, and alarm with which writers have met the Depression's challenges. Those challenges included the decline of capitalism, the coming of war, the new brutality of daily life, democracy's bankruptcy, the rise of the proletariat, the strong arm of and submission to the state. Treating Oswald Spengler's sense of how works of art manifest the "ruling passion" of a troubled period, Canby also reminds readers of a "more subtle" fear, the "flight from reason to pure emotionalism" and the subsequent exchange of liberties for the joys of powerful eroticism. He elaborates this hypothesis by considering several authors and their styles: Hemingway, whose hard-boiled "books are all books of fear," either of physical danger or spiritual disintegration; Farrell, who seems to fear the "training in toughness" young people receive in a "society careless of civilization"; and John O'Hara, who fears bourgeois vulgarity.[7]

Historical romances, like the decade's "elephantine best-sellers"—*Anthony Adverse* and *Gone with the Wind*—reflect fears at their very core. Hervey Allen's hero, says Canby, "undergoes a spiritual reconstruction symbolic of the need of faith and the willingness for renunciation" characteristic of turbulent periods, while "Miss [Margaret] Mitchell's book . . . responds to the fear in every sensitive heart for the future of another culture also threatened by reconstruction." On the other hand, regionalist works answer the "wide and deep desire to remind us of the good earth from which we sprang," the effects of which on character are more permanent and calculable than the "rootless mechanisms of industrialized urban life." Regionalists speak to the anxiety that the "land is still a home under the sun and rain," even though everything else seems "on the move, speeding toward an uncalculated destination."

Canby passes over "such obvious reflections of malaise" as proletarian novels—"usually the accounts of what a bourgeois intellectual thinks a laborer's mind is like"—as well as the "new crop of exotics" expressing the hope of reaching Nirvana (like James Hilton's popular books), and moves to a category he calls the "syncopaters," writers who react to the era's "growing nervousness" by playing to uncertainty and unrest. The result is a "new speed of sensations" that feels like an "accelerated dance rhythm." To blame are "cheap newspapers," *Time* magazine, a typical Broadway play, the narrative sections of the most successful movies—all designed to "sensationalize," that is, to stimulate and exploit sensations, and thus "to increase the tempo of emotions." Unafraid themselves, agents of this "new speed of sensations" manipulate the public's fear of the new instability, "where no two days are alike and there is no confidence except in the sensations of the moment." As Canby sees it, "When a nation is restless, uneasy, the emotional pressure must be released if there is to be a reaction beyond routine experience. Observe the violent language of European diplomatic language. . . . And thus it is not difficult to relate the jazz intellect of the twenties and thirties to a deep-lying fear of being left behind in the race toward an uncertain future." Though Canby might have named one novelist or another's appropriation of such a style, like Nathanael West, the important point of his examples drawn nearly exclusively from mass culture is that the effects of such syncopation are already widespread. The implications of his assessment will resonate for the next half century of fiction writing.

For Canby, the most "obvious instance," and maybe the most "fortunate," of these fearful expressions is that American historians and biographers now eschew the satiric, disillusioned style that for twenty years was deemed so necessary, primarily because the Depression occasions a realism more sober than ever. Indeed, the "less jittery" historians can model for novelists, dramatists, and poets a new spirit of studying "fearlessly" the "probable results of rapid and inevitable change." For the "fear of change" is "*a ruling passion*" in the thirties, its "worried society unusually afraid that one false step will plunge us into a disaster worse than 1914 or an economic anarchy more devastating than 1929."

Canby concludes that there are "positive signs" of our civilization's attempt to cure itself of the "diseases of undirected progress," efforts that remain largely within the purview of U.S. fiction. Our novels, says Canby, do not go far enough, and "only the loftiest imagination forecasts the lines of the [future's] thinking." Still, the "extraordinary energy" of American fiction, he boasts, more so than the modernism of Thomas Mann or Jules Romains, may serve as a guide to the future of Western civilization. Cautious that this energy might lead down as well as up, Canby commends American literature for being prolific and praises its vigor, variety, and freedom from conventional restraint, however uneven it may be in quality and execution. A "literary psychoanalyst" could see that American literature is conscious of the Western world's general capacity for fear and that it also possesses the power to overcome it.

Has Canby lost his grip? Was American fiction in fact various and vigorous in the late spring of 1937? Not according to the fiction best-seller list representing the period 14 May through 14 June. Number one was the Norwegian novel, *The Wind from the Mountains*, by Trygve Gulbranssen; number two was *Blind Man's Years*, by Warwick Deeping, an extremely popular English writer of the '20s and '30s. Number three was Virginia Woolf's *The Waves*; number four, British formula author E. Phillips Oppenheim's *Ask Miss Mott*; number five, American mystery writer Mignon Eberhart's *The Pattern*. Numbers six and seven were the critically acclaimed *The Outward Room* by Millen Brand and Marian Simms's *Call It Freedom*, a shrewd, unsentimental "light" novel about a divorcée's struggles with loneliness and her sexual feelings ("handled in a forthright, sympathetic, and quite unprudish fashion"). Number eight was Steinbeck's beloved malebonding/workers' tale, *Of Mice and Men*; number nine, *Gone with the Wind*, just down from number one some fifty weeks after publication; and number ten, Jerome Weidman's "scathing portrait of an obnoxious wise guy," *I Can Get It for You Wholesale*.[8]

The month in which Canby is writing lies just prior to the summer titles. In a few weeks, Kenneth Roberts's *Northwest Passage*, the year's biggest fiction best seller, was released. Despite the stranglehold British writing seems to exert on popular tastes, American novels do evince a surprising vigor and variety, including such good novels (from the first half of the year) as Marquand's Pulitzer Prize–winner, *The Late George Apley*; Esther Forbes's Hawthornesque *Paradise*; Daniel Fuchs's *Low Company*, part of his Brooklyn trilogy; Meyer Levin's "landmark in the development of the realistic novel," *The Old Bunch*; Katherine Anne Porter's long story, *Noon Wine*; Stuart Engstrand's *The Invaders*, recounting an Eastern sociologist's visit to the Southwest; Edwin Corle's *People of the Earth*, a "carefully drawn study of a modern Navajo"; Gladys Hasty Carroll's *Neighbor to the Sky*, a "very good though by no means important" Maine novel; Wellington Roe's "intelligent and sound and genuinely moving" saga of the Dust Bowl, *The Tree Falls South*, a precursor to *Grapes of Wrath*; Michael Foster's *American Dream*, a multigenerational narrative of "such generous physiological and psychological comment as to set us dreaming over the long chain of American time"; and William Carlos Williams's *White Mule*, which gave "new texture" and the "world of sound" to the story of an immigrant couple and the "bleak and hostile scene that is America to them."[9]

Later in 1937 two noteworthy novels of social unrest appeared: John McIntyre's labor novel, *Ferment*, "for all men of good will," and Charlie May Simon's "superbly realistic" *The Share-cropper*. In addition, there were several novels on subjects that might surprise readers unfamiliar with the bourgeois tradition, novels praised for their accomplishment and their vision: Lyle Saxon's study of the octoroon class in antebellum New Orleans, *Children of Strangers*; Theodore Strauss's "hair-raising" and "legitimately dramatic" prize-winning novel of lynching, *Night at Hogwallow*; Waters Turpin's novel about the black migration, *These Low Grounds*, and William Brown Meloney's novel of sex and violence, *Rush to the Sun*, which treats desire as "healthy, not sordid." Hemingway published *To Have and Have Not* ("His skill has strengthened, but his stature has shrunk"); and Hurston, *Their Eyes Were Watching God*, of which a reviewer opined, "It is about everyone, or at least everyone who isn't so civilized that he has lost the capacity for glory."[10] American fiction could claim not only the diversity Canby lauds, but also the energetic willingness to meet the several kinds of fears he ascribes to the times. Only an expanded notion of the middle-class cultural production of U.S. fiction, however, will give us this perspective.

AN IMPORTANT, EXCITING, AND DOUR JOB

Struthers Burt, a fiction writer of the middle decades, describes the novelist's challenge as he looked upon the prospects of the 1930s. In asking, "What's left for the novelist?" Burt deliberates over the differences between writing novels in 1931 and five years earlier, when all kinds of plots seemed available to a writer. Now missing, according to Burt, are the conflicts of generations, classes, ideas, religious and other instincts: "The world at present is a very implicit world, marking time and waiting to see what will happen next. Every one knows almost everything there is to be known, and there's not much to get excited about." Such conditions mean the loss of faith in epic types and the "loss of validity of action" in serious fiction, which accounts for "our turning to detective stories when we want action." No longer is it possible to believe in fairy or ghost stories, but "we are still forced to believe, alas, in gunmen and detectives."[11]

In a world that has seen its patterns exposed and virtually all of its traditions and standards challenged, the serious novelist still has the world of the self to explore, the individual in relation to the world, what Burt calls the "man in the taxicab," whose "deepest interest" consists in the decisions he makes. Unlike previous periods of history, Burt argues, decisions can no longer be made on the basis of class or the foundations laid by predecessors. In the last decade, such belief systems have been swept away: "It is almost impossible for us to realize, even those of us who have seen the change, how cataclysmic it has been and how swift; the majority of the world still does not know that the change has occurred. The majority of the world still refers back to the odd, new things it does to patterns that have dissolved." For Burt, this new situation is liberating because it encourages the novelist to check our current follies against our "inherent sanity." No longer need the novel be content to amuse "tired kings or tired businessmen." This freedom to portray the decisions of the man in the taxicab registers the "increasing importance of the serious novelist in the scheme of life and the increasing attention paid to him." The novelist, Burt proclaims, is "one of the leading explorers in this new expedition to find out what man is, and why."

The critical fear at the heart of Burt's argument was rehearsed by many throughout the decade: While novels may be about present urgencies, they should not be propaganda; writers must pursue art, not ideology. The 1930s critic who may have had the heaviest influence on the way we have traditionally understood the decade says something quite similar. In his November 1939 tribute, "A Farewell to the 1930's," Malcolm Cowley wisely if fancifully suggests that novels published after 1932 are ultimately part of Depression literature: "They either revealed its effect on their authors, or studied its causes, or tried to evade it by fleeing to the ends of the earth and the depths of time—only to return with a lesson for tomorrow." He then connects the "literary currents" to three "clusters of events"—the political and social struggles rising out of the crisis; the new position of the United States in world affairs, which resulted from the economic and political problems in Europe; and, finally, the "growth of larger corporations at the expense of smaller ones, the narrowing opportunities for pecuniary success and the changes that followed in middle-class ideals." Literary historians attentive to the first two categories have routinely ignored the third.[12]

Cowley first addresses the proletarian writing born of "hunger and desperation," a literature combining realism with Communist slogans. When the Party dissolved its revolutionary unions and softened its attack on middle-class ideals, leftist writers could produce a more interesting literature, which Dos Passos's *U.S.A.* exemplified at its most ambitious. International events—the Russian Five-Year Plan, the rise of Adolf Hitler, the war in Spain—also helped to direct the novel's "currents" insofar as "people began to feel that this was one of the few countries able to solve its problems by democratic methods." Believing that national security was threatened, some observers concluded that our fate was bound up with Europe's, while others embraced isolationism. Either way, the international situation returned the expatriates who said "long good byes" to Paris, Moscow, and China and "rediscovered" America. In addition, European writers came to the United States, making New York a "capital of world literature." In an early formulation of the idea of a novel's cultural work, Cowley avers that world affairs are "hidden" in some books, "where they deeply affect the intellectual and social background." During this decade too, "Americans have begun to write with their eyes on the world overseas."

Cowley's point that the "closing of the business frontier" in America has supplanted the ethic of "risk and change" with a "small-visioned stability" was a literary topic that "in terms of daily life has still to be explored." The new ideals of the middle class no longer privilege "getting ahead, with hard work and privation willingly endured as the price of ultimate success"; the aim is now security at a lower level—that and making the best of what one has, like Europe before World War I: "There is a growing interest in the amenities of life—in cooking and gardening and decoration, in bridge and croquet, in neighborhood gossip and community affairs. There is a corresponding fear of change, of the private or public misfortunes that might lead to losing one's job." Cowley concedes that the "effects on literature of this process are a little harder to trace" than social struggles and that we are dealing with the middle-class "state of mind," which he also detects in studies about preserving natural resources, like Stuart Chase's *Rich Land, Poor Land* (1936) and Paul Sears's *Deserts on the March* (1935). He also identifies the fundamental middle-classness of best-selling novels like *Anthony Adverse* by suggesting that "a man rising in the world is not concerned with history," since "he is too busy making it." Now, however, "a citizen with a fixed place in the community wants to acquire a glorious past just as he acquires antique furniture. By that past he is reassured of his present importance; in it he finds strength to face the dangers that lie in front of him."

Cowley closes with a summary of '30s writing: "lean years for poetry," "decidedly rich years for autobiography," "lively years for criticism," and "middling rich years for the novel," especially rich in "the hardboiled novel." Perhaps most important of all is Cowley's assessment that the 1930s "will be known as years when the public standing of literature improved, as a result of the greater leisure time for reading." The decade seems to Cowley more interesting than the 1920s and comparable to the era immediately preceding World War I. American literature now lies in the hands of "the number of writers who, by permanent standards, are second-rate, and yet are intelligent and determined to do their best work. Although they will never produce great books, they help to produce them, even lay the groundwork for the appreciation of those books, by creating the necessary background and the nourishing tradition. In such men"—and, he ought to have known, women—Cowley says, "lies the promise of American literature."

PROSPERITY IS JUST AROUND THE CORNER

We take it as a matter of record that the 1920s ended with Black Tuesday. Many observers say that the mood of the country changed so quickly that even the most vigorous act of historical revision could not shake the general conviction that the Crash marked the end of one America and the start of another. Yet the effect of the Crash on middle-class America took shape more slowly; fiction written for the middle class in the early years of the Depression does not confirm the memory that life in the United States had been instantly and irrevocably altered. If anything, American novels in 1930, 1931, and even 1932—severe as those years were—responded little to the new social realities. Nor is this particularly difficult to interpret, for one principal way that the middle class met the Depression was to belittle or ignore its threat. As Robert and Helen Lynd observe in *Middletown in Transition*, "One of the most illuminating aspects of this early period of the depression was the reluctance of Middletown's habits of thought to accept the fact of 'bad times.' This reluctance was related to the tough emotional weighting of the concept of 'the future' in this culture. Then, too, one does not like to admit that the techniques and institutions which one uses with seeming familiarity and nice control are really little-understood things capable of rising up and smiting one."[13]

This general disregard, however, reflects other preoccupations more than it does an insensitivity to the plight of so many less fortunate Americans, though sadly, the middle class sometimes expressed its idealized self-conception of resiliency by insisting on the laziness or spinelessness of those on relief. Despite the appearance of a handful of novels during the first few years of the '30s—fewer than fifteen according to Walter Rideout—concerning the underclass or striking workers, the mainstream of American fiction remained staunchly bourgeois. What is significant in this tendency, according to cultural historian Leo Gurko, "is not so much that America fled from the bitter truth, as that such flight was a logical result not only of our entire historical experience, but of the attitudes established during the period immediately preceding, the period of the 20's."[14]

Thus, the middle-class novel tried to contain the ravages of the Depression through plots enacting the spirit of accommodation or the glory of resilience. The '30s well-known Pulitzer Prize novel, Buck's *The Good Earth*, even made Chinese peasants a model for living with adversity. As if to celebrate the solidity of middle-class culture in the face of its imminent disintegration, Margaret Ayer Barnes's *Years of Grace*, the previous year's winner, honored bourgeois capacities to adjust by dramatizing the life and times of a Chicago wife and mother from her youth in the 1890s to the 1920s. *Years of Grace* was as much a story of the emergence of, and fissures within, the middle class, chronicling as it does the testing of one woman's identity as a wife and mother. It also gave social specificity to the growth of Chicago, then America's second largest city and an important symbol of modernity. Barnes's novel won the Pulitzer Prize over such modernist works as Dos Passos's *42nd Parallel* and Faulkner's *As I Lay Dying* as well as highly regarded novels like Elizabeth Madox Roberts's *The Great Meadow* and Dorothy Canfield Fisher's *The Deepening Stream*, while novels like Michael Gold's *Jews without Money*, Langston Hughes's *Not without Laughter*, and Mary Heaton Vorse's *Strike!* scarcely contended for recognition among the taste-making powers-that-be. One such power, Robert M. Lovett, was probably the critic most responsible for promoting *Years of Grace*. A professor of

English at the University of Chicago, a reviewer of contemporary fiction, and a perennial member of the Pulitzer committee, Lovett touted the novel in the *New Republic* in ways that probably advanced its cause among his fellow committee members: "Mrs. Barnes has written a substantial and satisfying piece of fiction, substantial in the large and immediate sense of life which it conveys, and satisfying in the sureness of its procedure, the rightness of its effect." *Years of Grace* was greeted as "vested in dignity"; its charm reminiscent of the early Wharton. One critic summarized the book's significance: "It is odd . . . that so placid, so unexciting a book should enjoy a wide circulation. Why the success of a story so unadventurous, so lacking in movement? Have we come to a time . . . when the urge toward vicarious experience has worn itself out, when people are turning from the paths of escape—from sentiment, or sophistication, or red-blooded romance—to the reassuring haven of the familiar and average? It will take more than one book to supply the answer, but *Years of Grace* may be sounding the keynote of the more popular fiction of the next decade."[15]

Even though the quiet pleasures this novel so gently excites harbingered a trend in middle-class fiction, the *most* popular novel of 1930, Edna Ferber's *Cimarron*, heroicizing the imposing figures who settled Oklahoma, was about nothing as familiar and average as the tribulations of the Chicago bourgeoisie. Still, it concludes by asserting the inevitable emergence of the middle class to lead the new state into the twentieth century, when the roustabout hero who opens the land is banished from it, while his wife brings her better breeding to the fore and becomes governor! As if to sustain the movement the *Bookman* reviewer descried, several other well-received novels of 1930 did feature milieus similar to Barnes's: Dorothy Carman's *They Thought They Could Buy It*, a tough-minded examination of suburban materialism; Helen G. Carlisle's *Mothers Cry*, about a young widow's struggle to raise four children; Dawn Powell's *Dance Night*, a novel of a young woman's formative experiences in small-town Ohio; and Ruth Suckow's story of Midwestern sisters, *The Kramer Girls*. Each may be said to delve into one dimension or another of *Years of Grace*, though Barnes's novel develops a more broadly historical trajectory than these others.

Barnes's reputation faded, after three more pretty good novels over the next eight years, but her work never captured the imagination of scholars seeking to rectify an author's unjust neglect. She was fairly well admired in her time; all her books were reviewed prominently—mostly favorably—in major venues, and she remained a lecturer of women's clubs for several years after her writing career petered out. At least a dozen others as well respected as Barnes and whose work, over the course of a career, proved consistently interesting to readers—like Anne Parrish, Ruth Suckow, and Josephine Lawrence—have also disappeared with not much less of a trace. These novelists are not to be classed with the era's romancers, like Faith Baldwin, Gladys Carroll, Fannie Hurst, Kathleen Norris, and Mary Rinehart, prolific and quite different writers who generated wide interest and intense loyalty among the thousands of readers who avidly bought (and shared) their books. Some of these popular authors have begun to receive their due, especially Hurst, whose novel, *Imitation of Life* (1933)—and the movies made out if it—has generated a great deal of discussion about the relation between race and class privilege. Indeed, the marks left by Barnes, her sister Janet Ayer Fairbank, Carlisle, Carman, Nancy Hale, Martha Ostenso, Lawrence, Hull, and Parrish are virtually undetectable. Dawn Powell, who could figure in this group, is praised for her novels about New York, not her fiction about young Ohio women shaping their identity.

Occasionally, like Powell, one of these women realists is extracted from the bourgeois tradition because her fiction fits another category, as Jessie Fauset's does with African American literature. Even so, their general eradication reveals the absence of the middle class as an object of inquiry, the limitations with which literary historians have conceived of the era's challenge, as well as a check on the sureness with which Americanists have revised the canon. If these authors are any measure, women's writing during the Depression provides an appropriate lens on the dynamics of revisionism: critical disdain was first directed at the bourgeois ethos, especially as it was found in women's writing; now, it also expresses the historical prejudice against viewing the middle class as a worthy subject. It has been some thirty years since Nina Baym opened up the rich tradition of mid-nineteenth-century American women novelists in *Women's Fiction*; why does so much remain to do for mid-twentieth-century women's writing?

THE PROBLEM OF POPULARITY

We may understand middle-class writers' responses to the Depression when we turn to Sinclair Lewis's first novel after winning the Nobel Prize, *Ann Vickers* (1933). Although the '30s novel for which he is best remembered now is his fable about the coming of fascism to the United States, *It Can't Happen Here*, prior to that his most widely esteemed 1930s novel was *Ann Vickers*, a distended investigation of a New Woman, her loves, and career in prison reform—the fifth leading seller among novels of its publication year. Given his successes in the 1920s, perhaps anything Lewis wrote would sell, but *Ann Vickers* was critically respected in some quarters too. Some reviewers, to be sure, thought that Lewis was losing his once-celebrated satirical skills, and a few questioned his choice of subject as hackneyed or unimportant, though none seem troubled by the misogyny of his characterization of Ann herself. The novel was invariably related to Lewis's oeuvre, but it was also received in the context of the era's reexamining of the relation between the public and private spheres, a context in which so many important novels of 1932 and 1933 participated, including Sherwood Anderson's *Beyond Desire*, Erskine Caldwell's *Tobacco Road*, Ellen Glasgow's *This Sheltered Life*, William Faulkner's *Light in August*, Robert Herrick's *The End of Desire*, Edith Wharton's *The Gods Arrive*, Nathanael West's *Miss Lonelyhearts*, and Anne Parrish's satire, *Loads of Love*. Apparently, by then, the spectacle of the Crash, with business life everywhere in ruins, led novelists to wonder what effects its disillusioning aftermath would have on how Americans conducted intimate life, a concern ultimately dominating middle-class writing for the rest of the decade.

Even Lewis specialists have not had much to say about *Ann Vickers* over the last seventy-five years. At the time, however, male and female reviewers alike lauded the novel for its frank representation of the choices that career women faced. Actually, the novel summarizes a rearguard effort, at the close of the first phase of the Depression, to recall an earlier ideal of female domesticity and to roll back the changes in women's cultural status. In "Heroines Back at the Hearth," critic Louise Maunsell Field describes the dynamic by which "our novelists conspire to remove the modern woman from business life, to which they once helped to introduce her." Lewis takes part in this general attempt to rescind the economic and political liberty that female characters had been granted in the previous twenty years, that is, to have work and personhood count as much as or perhaps even more than marriage as the measure of social worth. For all of Ann Vickers's protests and avowals of passion, says Field, she "never develops beyond the pre-War, pre-suffrage period of her early endeavors, the one to which she definitely belongs."[16]

Field criticizes older authors, like Glasgow and Wharton, as well as such representatives of the "younger generation" as Faulkner, Buck, DuBose Heyward, and Halper for this new, antimodernist twist in female characterization. The reasons for the backlash, she suspects, are twofold. The first, and lesser, one is that the "career woman has ceased to be a novelty" for writers or readers and has achieved her own conventionality, so that younger authors can no longer find enough variety in the type on which to base a novel. And, for a complication of reasons concerning the way culture restrains females, the working woman cannot seem to escape being seen as a type rather than an individual. This is an imaginative failure, one connected to the second explanation, which is much more telling for Field, since it is "closely related to the general divorcement of fiction from present-day reality, a separation," she says, that is "one of the innumerable effects of the depression." Paramount is that the present state of affairs strips business and professional life of its previous glamour, leading novelists to retreat "from the . . . stress typical of our modern life." Despite the increasing number of radical novels, "fiction in general has never had less to do with the realities of its own period than at the present time." Novelists have been returning to the past or choosing "some backwater as yet scarcely troubled by currents from the turbulent present." The nation's fiction, Field worries, like the detective novels read so widely, is by and large an "escape literature," whose pervasiveness proves that "even those of us who have succeeded in keeping our heads above water are yearning to get away from the life and death struggle going on everywhere about us." For Field, fiction needs to do more to establish a truly vital connection with readers: "It may be that the reason why fiction has not held its own during these difficult months as well as have other types of literature lies in this divorcement from reality, whose result has been a general feeling that our novelists seem to have little to show or to say to us which is of value in our present need." Novelists need to face the present, especially the "modern, job-holding or job-hunting woman," whose problems are much more intricate than those of recent fictional heroines.

By asking novelists to take up the Howellsian imperative in the Depression and not to pander to the desire to avoid new challenges, Field abjures social protest literature while she also attacks writers on the right as well as the center for their general failure to address the lives of those who have managed to keep their heads above water—middle-class readers who cannot find themselves in many new novels, certainly not the popular ones, to which they turn for escape. It may be one thing to make a best seller out of Anthony Adverse's adventures in France, New Mexico, and the West Indies, from 1775 to the 1820s, as Hervey Allen did in 1933, but it is another to make heroic or even comprehensible the newly challenging struggle of keeping one's family and property intact. Field's larger point, that the novelists we admire—Wharton and Glasgow on the one hand, Faulkner and Halper on the other—are not meeting this responsibility, is worth preserving. For the general weakness Field finds in both established and highly regarded younger novelists is their reluctance to address middle-class problems, even as in 1933 alone there appeared Hull's aforementioned *Hardy Perennial*, which might seem written with the critic's protests in mind, along with Margaret Banning's *Paths of Love*. Justified as Field's general consternation is in 1933, the decade's middle years witnessed a resurgent middle-class fiction, perhaps as writers absorbed the Depression's recasting of daily life. Modernist literary history asks us to remember 1934 and 1935 for such great or problematic novels as F. Scott Fitzgerald's *Tender Is the Night* and Nathanael West's *A Cool Million*; radical scholars have urged us to remember Jack Conroy's *A World to Win* and Kromer's *Waiting for Nothing*. The years 1933 and 1935 brought forth radical novelist Josephine Herbst's *Pity Is Not Enough* and *The Executioner Waits*, the first two installments in her historical trilogy detailing the breakdown of American middle-class life. But these years also saw such classic yet diverse formulations of the bourgeois spirit and uneasiness as Suckow's *The Folks*, John O'Hara's *Appointment in Samarra*, Glasgow's *Vein of Iron*, and Thornton Wilder's *Heaven's My Destination*.

Vexing Fields is how many novelists have retreated to ever more remote settings and eras, largely to avoid the responsibility of writing about middle-class life today. Surely the success of *Anthony Adverse* demonstrates that this flight impulse can be rewarded. Another side of escape is no less visible in popular female romance, especially in the hands of such writers as Kathleen Norris, Alice Duer Miller, Temple Bailey, Faith Baldwin, and Margaret Widdmer. These sentimental writers are the ones named by Katharine Fullerton Gerould in a *Saturday Review* article of April 1936, "Feminine Fiction," on the appeal that popular women's novelists stimulate at present. A friend and self-appointed rival of Wharton's (and half sister of her former lover, Morton), Gerould had written fiction and thought of herself as both a literary and a cultural critic. Gerould also includes Margaret Banning in this cadre, all of whose members had been publishing for the better part of the preceding fifteen years—a steady output of books, Gerould says, "you cannot imagine any man reading for his own pleasure." In choosing Gerould, the *Saturday Review* was assigning someone well known for her acerbic wit. And she seems to have provided exactly what the magazine wanted. For Gerould, women's romances comprise a vacuous literature, fiction that "states no vital problem for the fastidious mind to solve, that lays on us no duty of moral selection." The pleasures of men's escape literature are the "morality of the fairy tale" and the "logic of the lottery," but feminine fiction adds the "psychology of the window-shopper," glorifying the consumer and giving her the style—clothing, hair color, cuisine, interior decor—that she thinks she desires. "Feminine fiction is less innocent of narcissism. It holds a mirror before the female reader, to see herself in which she needs only a little help from Chanel or Elizabeth Arden or Emily Post."[17]

Such novelists fall short of both realism and romance. Their failure is that "they dare not . . . create a world and abide within its limits, lest they be accused of not knowing something that every up-to-date woman should be aware of." They aspire to sentimentality yet insist that they can also be hardboiled. They must be "admiringly conscious of the simple heart," although "they cannot afford to be ignorant of fashionable perversities." Their realism, on the other hand, seems like an inventory. Because such novels must "permit each woman to see herself in the heroine," their authors are forced to create protagonists who "can be easily copied." Gerould concludes that the sterility of fiction forbidden to be neither realistic nor romantic is only the response of supply to demand: "It is a difficult task that women readers impose on the lady novelist: at once to flatter them and to teach them all the ways of the wicked world." With so tenuous a moral and social charge, it seems foreordained that lady novelists fall back on the "faceless mannequin and the easy symbolism of price tags," producing standardized fiction.

The *Saturday Review* invited Banning to respond. In "The Problem of Popularity," she tries to "controvert" Gerould's failure to differentiate among novelists and to expose her narrowings and oversimplifications, her hopelessness of progress, and her contempt for readers. This last issue especially galls Banning: "Literature will never be at its best in a country which cultivates or even allows a disdain for so large a reading public. It may . . . develop fine writers, precious writers, skilled critics, poets, masters of irony, but it will not develop good, widely-read novelists if the best of its critical tradition holds the popular reading public in contempt."[18]

Banning concentrates on Gerould's knee-jerk failure to distinguish among these writers and their various genres, a mistake resulting in several others. Banning sees telling differences among Gerould's victims, differences she delineates to suggest that her antagonist has not read the very authors she impales: "Mrs. Gerould's lumping of some writers is so careless that it almost proves she had her point made and picked out her illustrations at random. . . . Their common point is their popularity and that . . . is what Mrs. Gerould chiefly disdains. . . . She has no respect for those who write for a large woman's public because she fundamentally scorns such a public. She said so." As Banning explains the weakness of Gerould's position, the bifurcation between popular and "precious" writers closes off a conversation between critics and popular authors, who "would write better than they do" if "this easy scorn were not so common that it creates an unnatural barrier." More important is these novelists' legacy, for they "must be replaced some day, and are the next group to do no better?" According to Banning, "The good novelist seeks and finds a large public, and when his talent is diverted from the mediums which will reach such an audience or when he is taught or encouraged to despise his own readers, he or she is lost. Nor will such a novelist do his best work in a country which separates its readers by sexes."

For a so-called sentimentalist, Banning cogently assesses the consequences of Gerould's thinking. First, Gerould's position reveals the current divisions in literary culture: "We are separating rapidly into two literary camps in this country—those who believe in and cultivate proletarian literature and those who believe in literature which knows no politics and loves fine prose. A few hundred thousand people are included in each group, most of them diligently reading and writing for each other." The problem lies, for Banning, "in between," the rest of the people in the United States "who also can read and do read incessantly." Banning argues that the two warring factions—the proletarians versus the aesthetes—who dominate literary politics and criticism represent neither the literature that most Americans read, nor their critical tastes, since most citizen-readers do not turn to fiction for the ends that either proletarian writing or high style serve. Here Banning also touches on a divided logic troubling the twentieth-century history of American literary criticism. That logic suggests that the critic, like the author, must choose between art and politics. The critic is either a connoisseur of the best literature or an ideologue. The falsity of this choice is patent for Banning, who worries whether the low regard of critics for popular writing will perpetuate itself, in that the novelists will never get better, resulting in the inevitability that the critics will always derogate them. It follows that, however false the division of audiences for fiction, the paradigm of elite connoisseurship versus popular consumption will continue.

For Banning, this is deplorable. She asks why contemporary culture seems unable to produce a Jane Austen or "even" a Louisa May Alcott: "Why don't we penetrate more often the prejudices, the idiosyncrasies, the small contacts, the romantic interludes of ordinary people?" Why, she demands of Gerould, if the "narcissism" of "a great popular audience" (of men and women) does exist, don't writers "give it something to put its teeth into?" And if certain writers have "found the way to approach the minds of these great groups of people," why should they be treated with contempt? She observes that the "literature of escape predominates to a large extent because the literature of reality is not yet great and simple and true enough to capture the imaginations of great numbers of people," something which, says Banning, "could be achieved."

The following week, Henry Canby offered his perspective on the debate he had devised. Though conceding a point to Gerould, the editor favors Banning, "who is a hundred times right in her contention that the snobbish neglect of this popular literature by those whose business it is to direct taste and uphold standards, is culpable." For Canby, the debate resonates with another "curious split," the "chasm" between academic and "unacademic" writing and thinking. ("In criticism few have crossed this gulf, which is why the laborious scholarship of American universities has had so little influence upon our literature.") This division is closely analogous, he says, with a situation familiar to all observers of literary politics—the division between "magazine journalism" and "literary books." Although there is always some passing to and fro between "dominions," they are separate kingdoms, each with its own "familiarities, reputations, and standards of achievement." That we have no Henry Wadsworth Longfellow, James Fenimore Cooper, Edgar Allan Poe, Nathaniel Hawthorne, or Harriet Beecher Stowe results from the "failure of literary opinion to produce the right intellectual climate." The result is a general state of literary ill health: "Our magazine writing today tends to be superficial, artificial, and cheap for pretty much the same reason that our 'serious' literature tends to be esoteric, over-intellectualized, clogged with egoism, muddied with theory, and too often dull." With a public split into highbrow and lowbrow—each despising what the other produces—novelists, "deprived of the stimulus of criticism," are "forbidden to produce real books." The result has been that we esteem literary works for their intrinsic merit—usually understood as a formalist pleasure and thus a sign of their relative unpopularity—or for their availability (often political), a cult of authenticity militating against a modernist cult of profundity and complexity, as if a novel must be one or the other in order to be worthy of study.[19]

BOOKS: THEIR PLACE IN A DEMOCRACY

Popularity was a closely examined question in the thirties for several reasons, not the least of which was the publishing industry's eagerness to identify the properties of best sellers. There were also several sociological surveys of the nation's reading practices, hoping to discover how the habits and choices of American readers might disclose some telling characteristics of the country. In 1930, the year before O. H. Cheyney published his *Economic Survey of the Book Industry, 1930–31*, the results of which were crucial to the reshaping of the publishing business and the concomitant rise of the blockbuster, R. L. Duffus observed that the problem for American readers was not that Americans did not like to read or were indifferent to what the publishers put before them. Instead, the problem was that the publishers did not understand how to compete with movies and radio in distributing books and advertising their interest. Book *publication* might be standardized, Duffus argued in *Books: Their Place in a Democracy* (1930), without endangering book content. "There could be more 'serious' books to choose from than there are now" if publishers learned how to market them. Our own contemporary scholarly concern with book clubs, lending libraries, and reading circles results, in part, from our curiosity in testing Duffus's hypothesis, for such studies of institutions and the means of disseminating cultural capital tell us a great deal about the ways literature circulates, what the citizenry's expectations are, and what institutions developed to excite and then to meet those demands.[20]

Among the best known of these sociological investigations was a survey by Charles Compton, who thought he could distill Americans' reading preferences from his vantage point in the St. Louis, Missouri, library system. Compton's poll, in *Who Reads What?* (1934)—which found that Mark Twain was the U.S. author most Americans liked to read—revealed that taste was not related to age, class, or occupation. Ethnographers of reading who began with a priori views of complexity, class, and audience will surely be disappointed in Compton's findings. For example, William James's *Human Immortality* (1897), he found, was a favorite among a machinist, a cabinetmaker, a lawyer, two physicians, a stenographer, a salesman, a retired farmer, a clerk, and a post office employee.

A much-awaited compilation of research was Douglas Waples's *People and Print* (1938), funded by the "Committee on Studies in Social Aspects of the Depression" (one of thirteen monographs it subsidized). Waples's research spanned several cities, employing more systematic and sophisticated methods of quantifying tastes and social differences than Compton's. From Waples, we learn, in contrast with Compton, a great deal about which authors were popular in what cities—among men and among women, among students, as well as among others in white- and blue-collar occupations—and how new authors fared compared with earlier ones. One can also learn what magazines people bought and where they procured their reading material. In his conclusion, Waples posits that among the changes in the social uses of reading during the Depression was a felt need to "defend class interests," which itself goes through three phases—uncritical, partisan, and highly critical, from which Waples adduces that class-based interest distinguishes readers' tastes.[21]

Such surveys outline the more sociological element of the curiosity about the nation's reading habits, an ongoing conversation whose purposes involve how the circulation of cultural capital through reading is conducted or whether it is incomplete. For literary critics, this conversation reached a high ideological pitch in a series of articles originating in the *Saturday Review* and continuing in the *Nation*. Louis Adamic, author of several books about immigrant and U.S. culture, assessed the interest in proletarian literature among American workers in "What the Proletariat Reads," which appeared immediately before Compton's *Who Reads What?* Adamic learned that workers and labor leaders generally had time to read little besides the daily newspaper, but they did enjoy sensational or special-interest magazines like *True Stories*, *Wild West Tales*, and *Screen Romances*. In fact, Adamic's survey found few laborers even aware of something called "proletarian literature," and their experience of it was mostly negative; they considered it unfaithful to both the spirit and the details of their condition. When, for instance, Adamic queried the women workers in Flint, Michigan, whose story was retold in Catherine Brody's *Nobody Starves: A Novel* (1932), they complained that Brody exaggerated or falsified their circumstances, even making them into bad dressers, a particularly nettling misrepresentation. Responses were as negative or worse in Adamic's other examples.

Adamic's interest in the failure of workers to read the proletarian literature that disaffected young middle-class men and women were writing may well have been to preserve his vision of the United States as the happy site of assimiliationist glory. His overall point is that proletarian literature is really written for the middle class, not the proletarians, and that is not a bad thing if, as Adamic surmises, many middle-class readers are prepared to be radicalized. In addition, fiction about the plight of American workers ought to include descriptions of bosses and management, like Theodore Dreiser's *An American Tragedy* (1925) and Albert Halper's *The Foundry* (1934). Not only are novels written exclusively about one class "puny, unconvincing works," but also this broadening of perspective will gratify the demands of proletarian writing by making the American bourgeoisie unfit for fascism. The present corpus of proletarian fiction is not especially truthful, but proletarian writers should not fear merely telling the "simple, contestable facts about contemporary society," since these are "bad enough." Honest books, Adamic argues, will fill the reader of any class with "shame that we Americans, while having created a marvellous technical machine, have made such a mess of ourselves spiritually and culturally on this continent, which is still offering us the opportunity to build a great civilization."[22]

One author whom Adamic singled out as too narrow in perspective and thus inadvertently dishonest in representing the United States was Robert Cantwell, whose *The Land of Plenty* (1934)—a very good novel, Adamic conceded—missed the opportunity to do even more to convince readers of the workers' right to seize a factory. Cantwell, for his part, thought that Adamic did not know what he was talking about and that there really was a well-informed body of working-class readers. In the *Nation*, several months later, Cantwell contends that Adamic misunderstands proletarian literature if he thinks it is addressed primarily to workers; its aim is to advance the "heritage of human culture." Proletarian fiction is a "cultural product," the value for which is not measured by the size or class affiliation of its immediate audience. For Cantwell, Adamic candidly follows the logic of his beliefs and misapprehensions, but such consistency does not meet the challenge of Adamic's own premises: "Creative literature becomes of such dubious value, its possibilities seem so limited in comparison with the strain and patience it demands, that the inspiration of the individual writer is threatened by his sense of the social meaninglessness of his labor." Instead, Cantwell cites Compton's *Who Reads What?* to suggest that there is within the American proletariat a "growing and groping and eager audience, acquainted with the higher achievement of bourgeois culture. . . . The working class perhaps makes up the majority of serious American readers, even though the majority of the working may not read seriously." So even if Cantwell cannot really dispute Adamic's main charge that the working-class audience for proletarian fiction is limited, he can still uphold the potentially revolutionary point that the workers may yet provide the basis for a highly developed culture.[23] Unanswered is whether these proletarian readers aspire to middle-class status or aim to overturn it.

The general discussion of proletarian fiction, and its audience, as a new phenomenon had begun with reviews here and there, including Granville Hicks's collection of articles in the *New Masses* and an occasional salvo like Michael Gold's attack of Thornton Wilder in the *New Republic* (described in the next section). A month before Adamic's piece, there appeared in the *New Republic* an overview essay by Robert Herrick, who was once again ready to ask what is happening to our fiction. Now at the end of his career, Herrick had just published a utopian fantasy, which might suggest that he was leaving the challenge of realism to a younger generation. For Herrick, there is a real difference between the muck-raking literature ascendant during his own emergence and the new labor fiction, like Lumpkin's *To Make My Bread* and Fielding Burke's *Call Home the Heart* (1932); Conroy's *The Disinherited* (1933); and Cantwell's *The Land of Plenty*, Halper's *The Foundry*, and William Rollins's *The Shadow Before* (1934). He cites George Soule's well-known point that an authentic symptom of a revolutionary age is the appearance of a literature of revolt, "which by spreading conditions and ideas in popular form becomes an active reagent in the change of bourgeois-conditioned minds." Herrick believes that proletarian novels are written by socially conscious individuals "who know the world"—its horror and squalor as well as the physical and spiritual degradations of the masses "who are the helpless, and often sordid, victims of an incoherently motivated society." That pedagogic purpose, however, will only be served to the extent that the "middle as well as the working-class mind is awakened, convinced."[24]

Predating Adamic by a month, Herrick really vacates his argument insofar as the older novelist appreciates that the proletarian writer never intended to address an audience of workers exclusively. Adamic's implied criticism is that there is something false, useless, and ultimately trivial about fiction purporting to be about a milieu whose members themselves find it unengaging or wrongheaded. In this way, Adamic challenges the efficacy and therefore the legitimacy of the cultural work to which this fiction aspires, and he attacks even more fiercely the authority of the sympathetic intellectuals who champion it.

Herrick sees plainly what Adamic has to miss: The literature of social protest is aimed less at finding a solution to the current crisis than at portraying as unforgettably as it can the "economic jungle"—"just how it feels to be jobless or living in terror of losing one's job . . . what the complex of modern machine production means . . . in human terms of the flesh and blood that pays for it." So despite the charges of propaganda with which pundits will criticize proletarian writers for the rest of the decade, it is exactly the relative absence of "rhetorical vehemence" that Herrick admires. Of course, one character or another in any and all of these novels will be called upon to be "more aware than their fellows of the issues," but such intrusions do not detract from the commendable point that these books refuse to proffer a "bright panacea" for the "present turmoil." A key, even "prophetic" point for Herrick is that this fiction immediately replaces the novels so notorious in the '20s—"the neurasthenic school of postwar decadents concerned mainly with sex, gin, and Freud." The new labor writing reveals the "vulgar heaven of the employing class as glimpsed by the mass," the "men in the front office at the push buttons of the industrial system." In addition, this fiction portrays the "final collapse in the eyes of clear-sighted youth" of two venerable superstitions—first, the vaunted superiority of the "American standard of living to any other ever known, which for the vast majority is meaningless"; and second, the constitutional guarantees that the "individual worker may by the exercise of the proper virtues climb the golden ladder of success and enter the ranks of the elect in the inner office."

Herrick names a final American myth that these novels debunk, the "via sacra of Education"—the bourgeois holy tenet that education is the means to upward mobility and redemption. Instead, these novels disclose how "our vast effort to educate has accomplished so little, not even taught the rudiments of a common language, and done nothing discernible to heighten the spiritual tempo of our society." Together, these several forms of exposure create a compelling, if unanticipated brief against the "worthlessness of the social ideals of the successful, of those who by accident or cunning or adaptability . . . have triumphed in the jungle. Their secure haven is not worth the blood and tears it has cost." This argument made on behalf of a generation's overturning the "venerable superstitions" embedded in the ideology of bourgeois individualism signals a triumph of the urgent clarity of youth over the sluggish mystifications of the established order of an "incoherently motivated society." While Herrick reads these novelists through his own ambitions in novels like *The Master of the Inn* (1908), which showed the debilitating effects of the modern city on physical and mental health, he rightly sees the complex positioning of class in these books. The inflections of class on the rhetorical situation of the proletarian novel, according to Herrick, are not like Adamic describes and are so much more specific than Cantwell's "heritage of human culture."

Crucial to Herrick is the experience of these writers who he does not doubt come from the milieu that Adamic says rejects them. These novelists are not giving bourgeois readers a privileged glimpse into the workings of the socioeconomic world that their middle-class status is supposed to protect them from; the writers address the middle class in ways that the middle class wants to reject as wholeheartedly as the proletariat does the representation of the proletariat. Both are inventions, the figures that class imperatives make. The novelists' impulse is pedagogic: These books are meant less to excite revolution and more to instruct readers in class formations, how the middle class is related to the working class and how the working class is separate from the middle—with the author serving as an interpreter who draws the classes into colloquy, albeit a conversation that neither party really wants but one that serves the democratic ideal of disseminating information and raising consciousness—perhaps one that also achieves a modest entertainment value.

In this light, we can upset the critical—and ideological—piety that weighs down and often suffocates the zest that such writers exert. Contrary to the critical fiction that these books were overlooked, most of the novels that Herrick cites as examples received uniformly strong reviews in the mainstream press. The *Times* hailed Lumpkin (*To Make My Bread*) for treating her subject with a "craftsman's and a psychologist's respect"; the *Bookman* said that Burke's *Call Home the Heart* succeeds "in making a great number of contemporary novels seem petty," while the *Christian Science Monitor* described it as standing "full-sized and mature among the many well written but slighter books about mountain folk." The *Saturday Review* called *The Disinherited* one of the season's "outstanding" novels, a book whose "vigor and significance is unusual at any time." The *Times* admired *The Foundry* for its Dickensian "humanity"—its "very great vividness," its "tenderness, vivacity, and punch"; *Christian Century* praised its "fine human sympathy." *The Land of Plenty* was roundly admired for its "extraordinary subtlety and power," a "powerful novel," "subtle and exciting," a work of "deadly devastating accuracy that takes the heart out of you" by "one of the most impressive new talents that has arrived in America in recent years." *The Shadow Before* was lauded with even more uniform enthusiasm: "an important addition to the list of current fiction and another good example of the work our novelists are doing in turning the spotlight on some of the sore spots in our civilization."[25]

Often in these reviews the trope of persuasion is crucial to the critics' sense of the novels' achievement. The main dangers of these novels are that they might be "careless" or indulge in mere reportage or become crudely propagandistic. So it gratifies the critic when they are made exquisite by their subtlety or elegance of phrase and when they resist preaching or go beyond autobiographical experience to disclose "true sympathy." When everyone agrees that a novel is extremely well written, the highest praise is that the book is "powerful" or gives us the "sweep of humanity," or some such phrase that signifies a force outside the self, a strength to be associated with the elements of nature to which the factory that so often appears in these books is habitually compared. As Dos Passos writes of *The Shadow Before*, "This vivid, alive material, so full of sentimental pulsation, is organized almost like a piece of music. The wording appeals continually to the ear, so that your head becomes full of the throb."[26] In effect, the love of the powerful, the compelling force in these books, is the countervailing elaboration of sympathy; it confers on the not-Me all the strength that the Me imagines to inhere in an overwhelming being outside oneself. Not for nothing is "power" also the critical trope reserved for the successful portrayal of African American settings and characters in books by blacks, just as it is also the term of approbation that later stuck to Faulkner. "Power" subsumes artistry, makes difference primitive, makes the other other. It refers as much to the felt strength of authorial feeling as the felt impact of artistic creation. In that way, it reserves for the unvarnished and unlettered the force of what should be true, the legitimation of history, the redemption of beauty. Subject to praise is the authenticity of the experience represented or its putatively transformative effect. For most reviewers, however, the point of sympathy is not the lesson of experience—the dismantling of capitalism for its ravaging of the soul—but the quality of identification, an appeal made to class masquerading as personal. If the rhetoric of bourgeois romance is, as Gerould so archly says, the logic of the shopper's catalog, then the appeal of proletarian fiction is essentially that of the travelog, the report from an exotic milieu among recognizable natives with customs too much like our own for comfort.

THE LITERARY CLASS WAR

If a middle-class history of the novel in the 1930s suggests that the social realism of Depression-era fiction was more various, even richer, than the literature of radical protest taken alone suggests, the history of American literary criticism is another story—putting radical politics in the very forefront. The social urgencies with which critics infused their task gave the discussion of books a new political inflection. Welcoming as this politicizing has been for American literary studies, part of the story of the decline of bourgeois literature in the United States is exactly this loss of critical sponsorship. With so many critics turning leftward and others defending the right, middle-class fiction—its conflicts, ambivalences, ideals—had fewer powerful allies among later literary historians to promulgate its achievement and chronicle its development. Nor did middle-class readers, after the heyday of the *Saturday Review*, have a reliable organ to protect their critical interests. (In fact, by the early '50s the magazine dropped "of Literature" from its title.) The decade's critical consciousness may well have begun with the publication of two essay collections, *Humanism and America*, edited by Norman Foerster, and C. Hartley Grattan's *Critique of Humanism*—a conservative call to an idealized past and a liberal response to this new latitudinarianism—both published in 1930. In the same year, that critical tradition was given an even more reactionary, regionalist dimension in the Agrarians' response to modernity and the changes that Northern industrialism had wrought, *I'll Take My Stand*, by Twelve Southerners. Given the weight it later accumulated as the New Critics' cultural credo, one must struggle to remember that this famous collection excited much less interest at the time than the more broadly focused humanism debate.

That debate centered on the question of who would define standards, the neo-Humanists and their hearkening to classical ideals of art or modern critics and their openness to new forms of expression. That controversy, in large part, supplied the underlying motive for Michael Gold's denunciation of Thornton Wilder as the "prophet of a genteel Christ" in 1930, since that is how the New Masses editor, writing in the New Republic, characterized the well-regarded author of The Cabala (1926), The Bridge of San Luis Rey (1927), and a new book, The Woman of Andros. For Gold, Wilder had emerged as the deputy for the upper-middle-class aspiration to elitism, and Gold's condemnation was vehement enough to set off a flurry of letters so thick that the magazine editors turned to none other than Edmund Wilson, who several months before had published his own balanced review of Wilder's new book, to judge the fairness of Gold's critique. (Wilson's most recent biographer notes that the critic had actually helped Gold publish his article there in the first place.) Wilson tried to be evenhanded, but when he found in Gold's favor, he irritated Wilder's supporters anew, and their letters to the editor resumed. Out of fear that the brouhaha would last forever, the editors turned to Wilson again, eighteen months later, to assess the lessons of the controversy, which he did in the "Literary Class War."[27]

The arguments over The Woman of Andros configured the possibilities of literary criticism to be played out in the decade. Gold meant to provoke: Wilder had begun as a relatively harmless scholastic novelist and playwright but was now seen, a decade before Our Town, as hostile to left-wing hopes of social change. He had created a framework for reintegrating Christian ethics into the bourgeois worldview, and, according to Gold, his novels—about rarefied feelings in exotic places during remote periods—could be viewed as studied, recognizable efforts to make middle-class Americans feel a spiritual kinship with such precious refinement and thus consider themselves morally self-sufficient. Moreover, the phenomenal success of The Bridge of San Luis Rey seemed to exempt his new novels from criticism; Gold worried that the mainstream had apparently found a novelist who could give legitimacy—historical, cultural, and aesthetic—to the ethics of the genteel bourgeoisie. As Gold saw it, the middle class regarded Wilder as a "spiritual teacher" who "wishes to restore . . . through Beauty and Rhetoric the Spirit of Religion in

American Literature," an ideal that sounds more admirable than it actually was, since "religion" here meant the "newly fashionable literary religion" that sees Jesus Christ as the "First British Gentleman." This version of Christianity was "a pastel, pastiche, dilettante religion, without the true neurotic blood and fire, a daydream of homosexual figures in graceful gowns moving archaically among the lilies. It is Anglo-Catholicism, that last refuge of the American literary snob." For Gold, the truly inimical aspect of Wilder's art was that it seemed to be for sissies.

Wilder had to be made to look ridiculous to the intellectuals supervising the choices of a reading public that would be consoled too readily by the novelist's metaphysics. Wilder, Gold asseverates, was nothing more than an apologist whose duty was "to help the parvenu class forget its lowly origins in American industrialism," providing them a "short cut to the aristocratic emotions." The cultural work of Wilder's new book, which would become the third best-selling novel of the year, about love on a distant Greek island thousands of years ago, is to disguise for the bourgeoisie the "barbaric sources of their income, the billions wrung from American workers and foreign peasants and coolies." As a result of treating these readers to a vision of the "human heart when it is nourished by blue blood," Wilder's fiction makes Babbitts everywhere feel "spiritually worthy of that income." Judging in favor of Wilder, however, meant repudiating the possibilities of radical critique, possibilities that seemed reasonable enough to so many Depression-era intellectuals, including those of middle-class origins. Gold's Wilder stood for the blindness of the business leaders of Herbert Hoover's America; his novels, an apparatus of resistance: they gave the bourgeoisie an enhanced sense of their virtues by ratifying their taste in antiques and luxuries. Denying Gold's critique promotes a literature dedicated to exalting bourgeois individualism. How could a critic in good conscience support the muse of the nouveau riche, especially at a time when the "Best People," as Wilson wrote a few months later, do not really know what they are doing and why? Called upon as a referee, Wilson tries to isolate the key issues, taking Gold's argument out of the realm of a simple matter of taste. For Wilson, the critical issues are much more important than the interest of the one book or even Wilder's career. Even though he cannot remember a "disturbance" that has "aroused such an uproar" as Gold's attack, Wilson insists that the "harsh and scurrilous things" Gold says are not the core of the controversy. Gold's view is important because, as one of the few Marxist American critics "of any literary ability," he believes that the "character of literature" is determined by the economic position of the class for whom it is written.[28]

Ultimately, Wilson disputes the rightness of Gold's argument and submits that artists, no less than scientists, can struggle to become independent of the sources of their support, even if they never can detach their minds from the social community—the "organism to which [the artist's] body belongs." He locates Wilder as a kind of publicist for Proust's aesthetic, that is, "the presentable side of impotence, the creeping corruption, the lack of the will to live." Wilder hosts the virus of this "malaise, the frustration, the misery . . . the illnesses of the cultivated people in capitalistic societies," which luxuries and antiquarian pleasures "no more than deaden a little." Wilder prescribes the "pathos and beauty derived from exotic lands of the imagination" as a cure for sick Americans; the "sedative and the demand for it" come from the same source—"a people disposed to idealism but deprived of their original ideals and now making themselves neurotic in the attempt to introduce idealism into the occupations . . . of a precarious economic system the condition for whose success is that they must cut the throats of their neighbors and swindle one another."

This unsigned editorial tried to end the fight, but the tumult continued. The lesson that Wilson drew from this was that the row marked the "eruption of Marxist issues out of literary circles of the radicals into the general field of criticism." The letters seemed to suggest that politics and criticism need clearer boundaries, which led Wilson briefly to suppose that Marxism would change literary criticism. A year and half later, in "The Literary Class War," he reflects that "it became very plain that the economic crisis was to be accompanied by a literary one." The central question for literary intellectuals may no longer be Is It Good? or even Is It Art?, "but what does a revolutionary literature really mean in America? What is bourgeois art?— what is proletarian art? What are the relations between the literature and the art and the dominant social class of a period?"

In formulating his response, Wilson again describes artists' capacity for transcending, if only provisionally, the interests of the dominating class, by likening them again to scientists or engineers. Writers, Wilson explains, are engaged in at least two conversations—one, with each other as a sort of guild, which enables the creation of the art; the other, with the dominating class and its interests, which colors the artist's point of view of his subject as well as his style. These two dialogues correspond to the artist's two worlds, one classless and transnational, existing in the mind's partial apprehension; the other, "the real one of which he is a part." In his effort to discern how partisanship helps us to appreciate art and how it does not, Wilson cites no less an authority than Leon Trotsky on the literature that emerged once "social relations have actually changed." For Wilson, Trotsky empowers a cultivated literary communism that has no wish to do away with the bourgeois art or that sees proletarian art as its antithesis. For Trotsky, "the historic significance and the moral grandeur of the proletarian revolution consist in the fact that it is laying the foundations of a culture which is above classes and which will be the first culture that is truly human."

That "human" quality is also for Wilson the essential one of determining a work's power as art, so he derides the "stupider" Marxists for their failure to grasp the revolutionary power of such instant classics as *Jews without Money* or Edward Dahlberg's *Bottom Dogs*, both of 1930. In addition, dull Marxist journalists who cannot find in Joyce, Freud, or Dostoyevsky and Proust the warrant for their own revolutionary commitment fail to understand how valuable to the future are these modernists' several diagnoses of the sickness of bourgeois society, just as these writers will also have something to teach the proletariat about the "mind of man" in the Marxist state. Wilson's point, following Trotsky, is that the proletariat needs to appropriate the lessons in the breakdown of the bourgeoisie wherever it can; unsurprisingly, some of the profoundest criticism of the bourgeoisie comes from within—as Proust exemplifies so glitteringly for Wilson. Just as Lenin hated capitalism but admired Frederick Taylor's efficiency plans, so must the proletariat "master" artistic techniques as it would mechanical ones and learn from genius whatever its political bent. Why should a writer not be held to the same standards as a chemist or an electrical engineer?

If critics fail to judge the writer as a writer, they are destined merely to gauge literary value on the basis of a work's "literal conformity to a body of fixed moral dogma," which critics, Marxist or Humanist, "elaborate in a void . . . a set of ideal specifications for advancing the end proposed." In this way, academic Marxists are like the very Humanists they despise, except that the Humanist defines that end in the past "where in fact it never existed," while the Marxist projects it in the future, "where it has never existed yet." Still, as dubious as Marxist criticism may be as it is currently practiced, Wilson wants to distinguish it from the "absurdities" with which bourgeois critics have "saddled" it in their effort to discredit it. He proposes that the ferocity of response suggests that in the future arguments about literature will necessarily entail social and political meanings and that the eruption of Marxist argumentation out of the realm of literary intellectuals and onto the pages of the *New Republic* registers a shift in the way that critics talk about literature in this time of crisis.

Apparently Wilson means, in 1932, that the discussion of books can no longer pretend to be apolitical or ahistorical, that the Depression had put radical criticism on an equal footing with any other sort of literary appreciation. By invoking Trotsky's views, Wilson introduces the philosopher not as the maker of doctrine or a propagandist but as a cultivated reader and thinker. The standard move among book critics during the Depression is to worry that a work of radical protest is marred by too much proselytizing. Wilson means to make the conversation between the bourgeois critic and the radical one more productive by abrogating this response. In aligning himself with a Trotskyist vision in the "literary class war," Wilson, who just a few months before had issued an "Appeal to Progressives"—a manifesto intended to wake up *New Republic* readers to the need for a radical overhaul of the liberal agenda—now separates himself from the circle of Marxist literary intellectuals. Wilson's move epitomizes critical argumentation for the rest of the decade—the infighting among various radicals about the object of literary criticism, the formation of an adversary culture of critique, which occasionally would address its mainstream or conservative antagonists but which also grew preoccupied with reviewing its own standards of judgment. Missing, however, from the decade is a critical history that puts radical fiction and radical criticism into the perspective that Wilson glimpsed: a new revolutionary consciousness that was at best part of a general understanding of current events, literary and otherwise.

If, as Gold said, Wilder were ever to deal with any actual America, the effort would reveal his "fundamental silliness and superficiality," as some might have said, five years later, when Wilder—as if in response to his assailant—published *Heaven's My Destination* (1935). Gold may have thought his prophecy came true; even ardent admirers of the book conceded that the vernacular story of the adventures of a reborn traveling religious textbook salesman produced a light, comedic pull, which many saw as a counterweight to the novel's somewhat mystical gravity. For *Commonweal*, the novel was even more significant than the author himself knew: its "verity" of interpretation suggests a "good sardonic etching of this, the most godless of

American ages." While some critics were startled by its difference from the "classic beauty and restraint" of Wilder's previous works, others, including Wilson, believed that *Heaven's My Destination* was his best book.[29]

BUSINESS AS USUAL

In the five years between *The Woman of Andros* and *Heaven's My Destination*, readers of American novels found a great deal to occupy them beyond arguments about the potential for a revolutionary literature. Although the half decade witnessed the rise of proletarian fiction, that phenomenon occupied, even at its highest peak, only a small part of literary discussions. In fact, the "story" of contemporary American fiction that most animated critics and reviewers was the decline of modernist satire and the rise of regionalism, historical fiction, and the family saga, all of which combined, apparently, to replace '20s debunking with a new ideal of earnestness and a new desire for explanation. Regionalism at its most critical certainly permitted some satirical purposes; still, the weight of its achievement might be measured in the solemnity and, to be sure, the sententiousness sometimes invested in its examination of the formative power of place. Similarly, the family chronicle and the historical novel usually did not exploit the ironies possible. It was the age of Thomas Wolfe, not Tom Wolfe. The following sections demonstrate the surprising breadth of that middle-class fiction by revisiting some of its exemplary forms—regionalism, historical fiction, and family sagas—as well as their critical rationales.

The early '30s saw the publication of fiction most commonly associated with the literary values sanctioned by post–World War II academic taste. A few of these books received prestigious support at their appearance: Dos Passos's *42nd Parallel* (1930) and *1919* (1932), Faulkner's *As I Lay Dying* (1930) and *Light in August* (1932), Fitzgerald's *Tender Is the Night*, and West's *A Cool Million* (1934). Henry Roth's *Call It Sleep* (1934) would be recovered in the '50s, but the interest it generated, virtually alone among Jewish immigrant novels, was less the result of its contribution to the growing discussion of Jewish identity than for its Joycean technique, which, of course, was by the 1950s held in especially high regard. Thus the critics endorsing modernism in the academy in the '40s and '50s were not interested so much in recovering forgotten writers but in re-creating the terms of appreciating favorites. As I will explore later, the modern masters of the '20s remained, and it was later up to a new generation of critics to maintain those writers' standing. Yet for all of its brilliant accomplishments, the modernist movement, by the mid-'30s, would have to seem something of a dead letter to readers; indeed, the next masterpiece in the modernist tradition, with the possible exception of Nathanael West's *Day of the Locust* (1939), did not come until 1952, when Ralph Ellison plumbed its aesthetic in *Invisible Man*. Otherwise, modernist fiction no longer inspired the artistic and epistemological upheaval that had once seemed so dangerous, so fruitful and influential, as it had a decade before when *The Sun Also Rises* was published. By 1936, with the appearance of two of the last great works of the tradition—Faulkner's *Absalom, Absalom!* and Dos Passos's *The Big Money*—the modernist tendency of American fiction seemed nearly to have reached a terminus.

What would a history of 1930s American fiction look like if it were not preoccupied with a few modernist achievements? Similarly, how would that history appear were it not concerned with the great popular successes or with the agenda of '30s radicalism? Ignoring such landmarks would falsify modern literary history, but an illuminating account of American culture would thus be found in a detailing of the novels that were read, addressed, and admired by many critics, enjoyed and shared by readers, who often might have considered them to be a source of civic instruction or ethical improvement. Not everyone cared for these books, but they comprised the reading choices that the magazine and newspaper critics considered thought-provoking. These novels were certainly of the moment, "novel" in the sense that they meant to render the new sense of historical, regional, family, class, and psychological circumstances of contemporary consciousness. Since high art was seen in retreat, one of the virtues of "better fiction" was that it was not too good but just good enough—good enough, that is, to be consumed, to serve as intellectual entertainment and a class marker.

Such a history would lack the distorting prejudice that the books defining the Zeitgeist for any generation are those that sold the most copies. Instead, a Zeitgeist might be more fully registered in a citizenry's normative tastes, that is, the combination of books that it sees as important and that later critics see as influential. As Canby meditates in the *Saturday Review of Literature*, the scholar and reader need to consult the "arousable interests of a literary year," for only when books are seen in a dynamic relation to each other and to the life of contemporaneous discourse may they be representative. And for Canby, a year aptly circumscribes those "arousable interests."

He sees these concerns as ideological as well as gendered—since women and men will be stimulated differently—and speculates whether our national taste undergoes the "karma of our utilitarianism," a karma that can be known by seeing books in their dynamic interchange with others of their day. Without understanding these "arousable interests," students may not even know why those books that have earned critical approval or scholarly interest were favored over others, not to mention which others.[30]

Sales figures can tell us much about a book's status as a cultural object (and I often invoke them), but literary historians relinquish a more full contextualized understanding of the range of any year's books when they fix on popularity as the shaping test of the era's preoccupations. Otherwise, sales numbers—which pretend to be a supremely democratic criterion of evaluation—suggest that the calculable distribution of a book also measures the dissemination of its ideas and reveals its importance. Its ideas are thus understood as resonating wherever the book was purchased and for whatever purpose. Sales figures perforce assume receptivity; if a blockbuster did not have some ostensibly fabulous cultural, even totemic value, it would not have sold as much as it did. So, the argument goes, the more people who buy the book, the more readily its significance as a shared mythology might be verified, as if to say that the breadth of a book's purchase is equal to its depth, that its sales are equal to its purchase on the social imagination. It follows that the more people who have bought the book, received it from a book club, or taken it out of the library or discussed it in their reading group, the more its impact can be measured and its significance as a shared fantasy can be certified. In this strictly quantitative measure, however, lies a literary-historical social Darwinism: only the fittest survive. (We remember the books . . . worth remembering!) Yet it also pays to understand the vitality of a kind of book, even if individual titles prove ephemeral.

In this way, sales numbers replace critical argument to winnow out the memorable from the forgettable: Margaret Mitchell's Gone with the Wind, the best seller of 1936 and 1937, becomes a classic of the popular imagination, while Walter D. Edmonds's Drums along the Mohawk, a novel about the troubles facing farmers in upstate New York during the Revolutionary War and the fourth best-selling novel of 1936 and merely the fifth in 1937, is now only mistily recalled, and the Atlantic Prize–winning novel of the year, Winifred Van Etten's I Am the Fox, once second to Mitchell's on the best-seller list, is forgotten. It is not so much that we need to know about other commercial successes, but by privileging the status of the biggest of the best-selling novels, we risk losing sight of many books worthy of interest whose contribution to U.S. literary history we have no way of remembering and whose contribution to the drama of U.S. cultural production might prove informative. Taken together, as Canby urges, these novels create norms for a middle-class consciousness, marking its newest inflections and wrestling with new solutions.

The qualitative argument emphasizes aesthetics, so it excludes most books as not artistically good enough. That is the point of connoisseurship: to weigh according to the privileged premises of taste. That privilege derives from a critically agreed-upon body of knowledge and background, a heritage of sophistication as it were. Part of the appeal of organizations like the Book-of-the-Month "Club" and the Literary "Guild" is that they catered to the wish to join an elite that could make distinctions among many pretenders and award merit to the truly worthy, an aristocracy of good taste that hoped to approximate, even to assume, the expert authority of the "judge" as well as the acumen of the critic. And, of course, the clubs promised to protect the middle-class reader from the embarrassment of making a bad choice—of buying trash one thought was a treasure, though the clubs typically selected books that were neither degraded nor exalted as aesthetic objects.

Whether premises of taste are understood as timeless and transhistorical or seen as responsive to prevailing ideologies and ultimately to fashions, critics interpret, argue, and thus arrive at a semblance of consensus. The result is not only how a book is perceived in its time, but also that later critics remember it as the best example of certain tendencies of the age. No generation can or should be expected to know intimately the ins and outs of such debates, since they record the intensity and gravity of a previous intellectual crisis rather than the one of most concern to the present. Still, the arguments themselves present more than antiquarian interest, because they are part of literary history. It does not gainsay any of the appeal of *Gone with the Wind* to propose that it more accurately discloses mid-thirties taste when it is seen in relation to several contemporaneous works rather than glorified as a one-of-a-kind achievement. This value for reading what also appeared is counterintuitive, for standard literary history has emerged largely as a nineteenth-century narrative, one that instead of nominating and promoting great men, or great authors, as it once did, came to feature estimable works, whose authors have, in turn, to be fetishized, sometimes as great artists but at other times as estimable personalities, including those modern writers we celebrate because their alcoholism, drug addiction, suicide, deviant or merely bohemian social or sexual conduct fulfills a middle-class fantasy of what sort of outlaw a great artist has to be.

Even after the New Criticism, when scholars and literary historians viewed the literary object as a text rather than a work, value-free and objectifiable, this history has become, in one sense, no history at all but a network of intertextual connections. More widely held is the position that this history is the story of dispossession and reclamation—the tale of how some texts, for generally ideological reasons, have been marginalized. One gambit among such historians is to point to the influence that texts had in their time (what could be more convincingly the case than the critical neglect to which Harriet Beecher Stowe's *Uncle Tom's Cabin* had fallen?), or, failing a novel's demonstrable impact, to the popularity it enjoyed. Influence and sales still preserve a value for a text as the historical agent-provocateur. The last quarter century of literary historiography may have successfully dismantled the theoretical underpinnings for the critical premise of a text's autonomy, but to the extent that the object of inquiry is examined for rationales deriving from its influence or currency, its "power" as a repository of ideology, then the history thereby summoned is still the tale of great texts, infinitely sufficient to their purposes.

Beyond sales figures or formal merits or even the passions they stir and the differences they make in individual readers' lives, novels can be appreciated for the force of their cultural responsiveness as well as the clarity and illumination of their surface detail. To that end, their pleasures are not always those that guarantee popular appeal; conversely, the limits to their popularity are not only those that justify the attention of a critical elite. Books signaling the vigor of their encounter with the society that they portray, critic Walter Myers observed, are best aggregated through their concern with the "folksness" typifying the regionalist as well as the proletarian novelists' characterology. These characters do not have "complexity," nor should they be valued solely as typifying locality and class. Along with their "chiefly representative values," says Myers, they index "a wider commonality and an impartial idealism." What cannot be denied the "simple soul" is the democratic potentiality of a "vast" or "epic" pathos, "especially when he is beset with complexities that are beyond him." Seizing on this "folksness" for its ideological currency, historical novels are also less interested in the inner lives of their characters than in the generalizability of the private life and how it forcefully penetrates the public one.[31]

Myers adduces such late '30s treatments of the folk as Elizabeth Roberts's and Marjorie Kinnan Rawlings's as well as John Steinbeck's *Of Mice and Men*, but his larger point is to define a tradition in American fiction, one that we would associate with middle-class aspirations. Both the country and the city provide settings for those folks whose "center of life is the household and family and the labor that maintains them. . . . They fortify themselves by handling familiar objects and by speaking of familiar interests in language usually commonplace and always a bit out of date. They differ, according to times and places . . . but everywhere they are as recognizable as an army with banners." According to Myers, "no more important duty rests upon the American novelist than that of recording folks neither elegiacally nor critically but realistically, without bias but with understanding." These books, like Dorothy Thomas's *Home Place* (1936), do vary in their comforting of "folks hard beset" by the Depression. Conscious as they are of folks' anxieties, these novels aspire to "attain a dynamism beyond the charms of literariness, the glamour of romantic idealization, the vividness of actuality, the intriguements of propaganda, the fervors of prophecy, or even the satisfaction of telling the immediate social truth." These books dramatize the fortunes of the "simple soul," the modern figure cast adrift by modernity: "Then his bewilderment, his inability to know what is destroying him or to express what he suffers can search the depths of pity. . . . His lack of striking personality, his vanishing without any impress on the world, augments the whole effect until it links itself with what we see in the eyes of suffering animals and what we often seem to read in the stars of a possibly dying universe."

For all of their "dynamism," such novels lack philosophical depth. Instead, this fiction is at odds with the values that favor another American realist, not Howells, but Henry James, who codified the values antithetical to those Myers promulgates. In the preface to the *Princess Casamassima*, he stipulates the importance of nuance, bidding the young novelist to be one upon whom nothing was lost; there, he identifies the value of uncertainty and confusion that such subtlety of impression accumulated and against which it was pitted: "If we were never bewildered," James avers, "there would never be a story to tell about us." Bewilderment—and the susceptibility of impression—makes fiction possible, turns the accounting of confusion, not its settling, into an art form.[32]

Contra Myers, James elevates the psychology of slashing out against bewilderment as a modern epistemological heroism and social virtue. And between 1933 and 1943, the critical criteria privileging social and psychological confusion—and the values of profundity that such struggles with bewilderment yielded—were promoted as a basis of American higher critical taste. In this decade, the very years that saw the flourishing of proletarian fiction on the one hand and the historical novel on the other, James was vigorously being reinvented as the major nineteenth-century precursor of American modernism as well as a central figure in the development of modern fiction.[33] To pay homage to this status, the first full-scale appreciation of James was published as an issue of the little magazine *Hound and Horn* (1933). As if to observe the close of a ten-year campaign to install James as the reigning critical spirit of American fiction and thus to complete the dominion of his influence, the *Kenyon Review* marked James's centennial in 1943, amid the first flush of that quarterly's success, by devoting an issue to the range of his career.

HISTORY, FICTION, AND THE DEPRESSION, OR THE WAY WE USED TO LIVE THEN

For an example of Canby's sense of Zeitgeist, consider the "arousable interests" of 1933, one of the worst years of the Depression and a year that neither modernist nor revisionist critics can claim as flourishing. Aside from *Miss Lonelyhearts* and *Ann Vickers*, along with big sellers like Gladys Hasty Carroll's *As the Earth Turns* and Bess Street Aldrich's *Miss Bishop*, proletarian works like *Union Square* or *The Disinherited*, and melodramas like Fannie Hurst's *Imitation of Life*, the novels of 1933 that reviewers considered memorable include books that just might represent prevailing anxieties and wish-dreams at least as well as any others do, books that never make their way into a literary history. The praise reserved for them could be fulsome: James Gould Cozzens's tale of small-town New England, *The Last Adam*, was especially admired; Larry Barretto's "unusually arresting" *Three Roads from Paradise* was "a story of zest, vitality, and richness"; Isabel Paterson's *Never Ask the End*, "a book of delicacy, charm, truth," offered "a complete philosophy for living in these times"; Robert Nathan's *One More Spring*, a Depression fable about New York City homelessness, was "so delightful, original and subtle in its simplicity that adjectives fall short," "a minor miracle"; the "serene mastery of a world passionately possessed" characterized Evelyn Scott's *Eva Gay*; Louis Bromfield's *The Farm* was an "honest . . . deeply felt book and a valuable record" of an Ohio family; and Caroline Miller's historical novel of poverty in the antebellum South, *Lamb in His Bosom*, won the Pulitzer Prize that year, second only to *Anthony Adverse* in hardcover popularity.[34]

Obviously, a list like this could be drawn of books welcomed in their time but disregarded thereafter for any year of the thirties. One way of understanding how memory is activated can be seen through what a populace tries to recollect at the time, as if to say, with psychologists, that there is a consistent line between the way that the past is experienced and the way that the present is lived out. The year 1933 was not a particularly lustrous year for fiction, but it was a fairly strong one for social observation, including history: Mary and Charles Beard published their *Rise of American Civilization*, and the Pulitzer was awarded to Frederick Jackson Turner's *The Significance of Sections in American History*. Popular as American history was, the history of contemporary culture was also widely described, including Gilbert Seldes's *Years of the Locust*, volume 5 of Mark Sullivan's *Our Times*, and most especially Franklin D. Roosevelt's compilation of pre-inaugural speeches, *Looking Forward*, a volume esteemed in the newspapers and opinion magazines for articulating "an unhurried, dispassionate, entirely coherent resume of his political philosophy and of the larger program he hopes to consummate."[35]

Also in 1933, Eleanor Roosevelt exhorted American women to seize the historic challenges before them in *It's Up to the Women*, whose perspective Mary Beard perceived as fundamentally bourgeois. Ignoring Mrs. Roosevelt's privileged background, Beard identified the First Lady's vision of national consolation with the middle-class hope that its values would sustain it during the crisis: "Whereas previous generations could only turn to a Dorothea Dix or a Beatrice Fairfax and a daily paper for sympathetic guidance, this suffering generation may bring its more complex problems to the very center of the nation. Mrs. Roosevelt still sees social arrangements in the bright autumn of bourgeois culture—not in the shadows of a defeated economy or in the confusing glare of insurgency seeking after utopia. Her world of minds and manners is largely bounded by the middle class."[36]

Indeed, the bourgeois self-understanding at the heart of Depression America can be seen in its fixation with books about contract bridge, ostensibly a new way for the middle class to socialize. Ely Culbertson's *Contract Bridge Blue Book of 1933*, number 7 on the year's best-seller list, followed *Culbertson's Summary* and his *Bridge Blue Book*, numbers 5 and 6 in 1931, with the *Summary* rising to number 4 in 1932.[37] It is easy to scorn the middle class for its complacency and historical unawareness—playing cards while one-third of the nation lives in shocking poverty—but bridge may have represented a way of coping with the new life of inconvenience, sacrifice, and constraint with which most of the rest of Americans lived, an ethic of middle-class embarrassment that permeates the historiography of the Depression. On the long shelf of books about these years, there is really precious little written about how the other two-thirds of America lived, a complex silence resulting, in part, from people's self-consciousness, even shame, over their reduced circumstances or their reluctance to see themselves as victims or make much of their discomfiture. That pride, one must concede, could also lead them to express impatience and even contempt for the worse afflicted.[38]

In addition, if the '20s were characterized by intellectual handbooks and narratives like Hendrik Van Loom's *Story of Mankind* (1922), H. G. Wells's *Outline of History* (1925), and Will Durant's *Story of Philosophy* (1926), which endeavored to make history comprehensible through linear narration, '30s history writing tried actively either to concentrate on the shaping power of the past or to escape the current moment. Perhaps the decade's most celebrated example of contemporary history was Frederick Lewis Allen's *Only Yesterday*, which instantly characterized the preceding decade as glorious yet past—and very recently too—as well as to the present. The book's very title marks a division between the '20s, which many readers would still recall vividly, and the '30s, whose present was all too present.

Fleeing history altogether, some books offered guidance through the present turmoil. These ranged from self-help and inspirational works such as Vash Young's *A Fortune to Share* (1931), a businessman's practical advice and pep talk for salesmen, to Dr. Edmund Jacobson's *You Must Relax: A Practical Method for Reducing the Strains of Modern Living* (1934)—still in print in 1978—and Marjorie Hillis's lively guides for single women and those in reduced circumstances, *Live Alone and Like It* (1936) and *Orchids on Your Budget* (1937), as well as Brande's aforementioned polemic against self-pity, *Wake Up and Live!* (1936). Even the nonfiction best seller of 1933—Walter Pitkin's secular inspirational text, *Life Begins at Forty* (1932)—discloses its historicality in catering to the self-definition of a generation that had already witnessed a world war and its aftermath. As Leo Gurko describes its appeal, especially during the first few weeks of the New Deal, "Forty was, of course, the right age, the minimum age . . . for the readers of a book designed to comfort the victims of the crash. Since most people affected by the debacle of October, 1929 were middle-aged, and presumably lacked the psychological resiliency which, by reputation, is a monopoly of youth, messages of hope for the future, assurances that life for them was just beginning, must have seemed like manna from the Almighty."[39]

Throughout the early '30s, the middle class had newly come to see the fragility of its purchase on the so-called American Way of Life. Accordingly, a new, pervasive historical consciousness seems to have enlivened middle-class watchfulness. This is not so surprising, given the anxiety fanned by the incredible success with which Stalin's five-year plans had allegedly galvanized the Soviet economy, at the same time that the United States's was declining. Fiction responded to the claims of history too. *Anthony Adverse*, a historical romance with an overlay of psychoanalytic explanation, might have shown the way for later novelists, and Margaret Mitchell might have created the ne plus ultra, but the sheer enthusiasm for history animating so many plots may never, in America, have been more fully sustained or widely shared. Other eras, like the 1820s or the turn of the twentieth century, had seen a plethora of historical romances, but the 1930s output was acknowledged as unprecedented. Assessing Esther Forbes's *Paradise* in the *North American Review*, Lloyd Morris notes that it does not serve to describe the nation's "increasing preoccupation" with its "insistent" past merely as a "tendency" or "movement," since such labels deaden a "valid, potent form," leading serious writers toward other possibilities, a danger about to beset the historical novel.[40]

According to Morris, "Whenever you set about reconstructing the past, the pressure of the contemporary asserts itself, dictating a selection of elements relevant to the interests and expressive of the aspirations peculiar to your own time." Novels that deal with the past strictly for its own sake may succeed as museum pieces, but by failing to seize on the past as a "useful medium"—as a kind of language—they miss history's ability to "make articulate some elements of a living culture, a heritage of tradition from which we may learn to change the present and shape the future"—an achievement he finds in *The Last Puritan*, *The Late George Apley*, and *Gone with the Wind*. Yet if it is true that the accumulated taste for escape discloses an era's image of what it fears it is not and thus may be said to invert what it is, the need to stage American history in the 1930s reveals that culture's conviction of rupture and discontinuity, a break from the past that historical novels, among other forms of expression, were enlisted to amend or dispel, not to validate.

The episodes to be interpreted within this historical retrospect represent junctures where America might have gone wrong but did not: the English colonial era, including Pocahontas and the Salem witchcraft frenzy; the French and Indian War; the American Revolution (at least a dozen books); Napoleon (a couple of books, including one about his putative descendants in Maryland); Kentucky and Tennessee pioneers, the War of 1812, the Mormon migration, Brook Farm, the Oregon Trail, John Brown, and the Civil War (battles, campaigns, and officers); Iowa, Kansas, and Texas in the postwar era, along with many Reconstruction and carpetbagger novels, such as a study of postwar New Orleans and the octoroon class. Perhaps no Civil War–era subject was more fully explored in the '30s than the assassination of President Abraham Lincoln: works of fiction like *The Man Who Killed Lincoln* (1939), by Philip Van Doren Stern, and Edwin Stanton's incomplete autobiography, *Mr. Secretary* (1940), edited by Ben Ames Williams; a historical analysis of the debacle, *Why Was Lincoln Murdered?* (1937), and Margaret Leech's keenly observed, very popular political study, *Reveille in Washington, 1860–1865* (1941).

If historical novels specify certain moments in the past that, rightly understood, inscribe and celebrate the perception of immediate possibilities, the obvious hypothesis is that, during these hard times American readers developed a special appetite for challenges that elicited their forebears' fortitude, believing that somehow reliving those adversities might spark their hereditary strength now. These historical novels promulgate a generally felt political and social consciousness of U.S. history, in contrast with another '30s effort to write the nation, the Federal Writers' Project (FWP) guide to the states—their cultural attractions, famous and not-so-famous homes, highways, parks, and waterways. Despite the surface-level descriptions, a pronounced historical consciousness invariably made its way into the guidebooks, one not so comforting for the middle class. Robert Cantwell praised this new "portrait" of America as a "fanciful, impulsive, absent-minded, capricious and ingenious" nation with "none of the qualities of the bourgeoisie—the American qualities of thrift, sobriety, calculation and commercial acumen." Rather, the FWP produced "a grand, melancholy, formless, democratic anthology of frustration and idiosyncrasy, a majestic roll call of national failure, a terrible and yet engaging corrective to the success stories that dominate our literature."[41]

If the Writers' Project mapped the forty-eight states culturally as well as topographically and thereby made familiar the rich, contradictory panoply of life in the United States, historical novels aimed to recast and reclaim the consoling American history from which the Depression had alienated the citizenry. In this way, middle-class fiction promotes history—especially the history of traumas recuperated—to keep from seeing the disintegration that the Depression had enacted, the felt separation from history that the middle class was enduring, a new condition of dispossession that the middle class was trying to remedy, in part, through the reading of historical fiction. In another sense, bourgeois fiction exploits the past as a gambit to rehabilitate its vision of the middle class, as well as to express fidelity to a heritage, one that turns as much on class as it does on nation. Instead of transformation, the need that historical fiction may address most sharply is restoration. By turning to a past whose lessons could be enlisted in the present, historical novelists, like the regionalists, contribute a way of making the middle-class cultural consciousness part of the nation's soul, an act of nation making as it were, the circulation of hopes and fears, ideals and anxieties that solidify a society and transform it into a polity, that is, give it the basis for ideological argument or consensus.

In presenting the spectacle of the American past to assuage the middle class of its new worries over its disconnection from the past, historical fiction smoothed over the anxiety of diminishment. Exploiting the past becomes another gambit of the middle class to sustain its vision of itself. Rather than a call to arms in the present, this fiction served to distract, even to make quiescent a populace that partisans of several descriptions were trying to enlist. It promised relief from the sense of dispossession that the Depression caused by giving the middle-class mob the circus of American history to quell its uneasiness. Historical novels like Edmonds's *Drums along the Mohawk* (1936) or Kenneth Roberts's *Northwest Passage* (1937) deployed a power of adhesion derived from their facile resolution of the challenges that history had set. How do they dramatize their acts of nation making? The former portrays the gallant Mohawk Valley yeoman farmers in upstate New

York, who, unaided by a central government, first battled against the British and later against the hostile Iroquois. Can the message be clearer about the plight of the American middle class—to fight both foreign invaders and belligerent natives on American soil? *Northwest Passage*, on the other hand, takes as its interest the explicit connection between the power of representation and the demands of heroism, as much as it connects the story of Robert Rogers, who commanded an American ranger expeditionary force against the Indians in Canada and who later became a governor there, with the tale's narrator, whose ambitions are to follow Rogers and to paint the Indians accurately. Rogers's efforts lead to a court-martial, while the painter's lead him to fulfillment and love. Roberts thus suggests that Rogers compromises his talents by exerting his desires for prestige and power beyond what his considerable talents might merit, while the painter achieves his purpose by striving for realism. Their stories combine to show the resolution of a crisis of national idealism through the hardheaded application of realist principles, yet the novel also predicts the failure to come if the nation, like Rogers, were to mistake mere aggrandizement for the consolations of individualist liberty and responsibility.

Margaret Wallace, one of the *New York Times*'s most reliable fiction reviewers, ponders the political implications of such books in assessing the Revolutionary War novel, *Trumpets of Dawn* (1938), in which Cyril Harris dramatizes the war's effect on everyday people in his story of a young man's departure from his Tory family and his embrace of the cause of liberty. "No equivalent period of time has produced anything like so much critical and intelligent reinterpretation of American history in fiction." For Wallace, this movement toward history represents a shift insofar as novelists were substituting this "new nationalism" for the "experiment in internationalism that has proven so profoundly disappointing."[42]

ATTITUDES TOWARD HISTORY

The War of Independence was the principal site of this reinterpretation, with books about nearly every major personality and famous event. Among the writers turning to the Revolution, Kenneth Roberts had the largest following; his series of interrelated books on the subject punctuated the '30s and early '40s. Even when historians occasionally disputed their accuracy, his lengthy novels remained among the top sellers of their year. Not always sharing the public's enjoyment, critics credited Roberts's extensive learning and his managing of battle scenes, while they chided him for his laughable failure to create believable women, especially as love objects in the rickety marriage plots that propped up such narratives as *Arundel* (1930)—the story of Benedict Arnold's heroic Canadian campaign—and its sequel, *Rabble in Arms* (1933). These two novels were successful enough that Roberts published a book of source material, *March to Quebec* (1938), based on the surviving journals of the veterans of Arnold's company.

Arundel recounts how a young man under General Arnold witnesses firsthand the military genius dauntlessly leading his men on an inspired though costly expedition in bitter winter to confront the British in Canada, a campaign that takes on the epochal scale of Hannibal's crossing the Alps. In the sequel, *Rabble in Arms*, Roberts focuses on the American rebels as combatants motivated more by their marginality to society than political principle. Yet this portrayal of the Patriots as rabble was less an exercise in "folksness" than a reactionary's worry about the claimants of the legacy of democracy. This is not surprising for a novelist who years before he turned to fiction had written a tract against the swarm of new immigrants and the peril in which these newcomers put the country, *Why Europe Leaves Home: A True Account of the Reasons Which Cause Central Europeans to Overrun America* (1922). In both novels, as in his later ones about the French and Indian War and the War of 1812, Roberts aimed to deflate the mythography of the spirit of '76 by scaling down its heroes, especially George Washington, whose generalship disgusted him.

The apex of Roberts's Revolutionary War project was the epic *Oliver Wiswell* (1940), whose 834 pages tell the story of the rebellion from the Tory point of view. The plot focuses on a recent Yale graduate's experience spying for and later fighting alongside the British, with time out in Paris and London, where he counsels a very sensible George III and where he writes the first volume of his history, the Civil War in America, before recrossing the Atlantic to take up arms against the so-called Patriots, all by way of reuniting with Sally Leighton, the rebel girl next door without whose letters he would not have the will to go on.

Wiswell's revolution is a civil war running concurrently with the rebellion and involves three sides, not two: (1) the superior British army led by bumbling generals, who seem, by the imponderable depths of their vanity or the astounding potential of their stupidity or the slyest of political machina- .

tions, intent on losing a war that they have had several opportunities to win handily; (2) the "pock-marked" rebel riffraff who masquerade their malfeasance as a passion for liberty and who see the war as a chance to brutalize their upstanding neighbors and readjust their standard of living—simply the last people on earth whom one would trust to build a new nation; and (3) the quiet, sober, law-abiding Americans who make the colonies work, the industrious, loyal British subjects—merchants, professional men, independent farmers, and honest tradesmen—who do their duty and live decently. Such prudent men would not be inflamed by that mountebank tavern orator and backstairs deal-maker, Samuel Adams, nor were they likely to be swayed by the prestige of a smuggler like John Hancock, who reputedly owed the Crown £100,000. (This founding father, in pledging his sacred fortune, was not kidding.) As a Tory put it in a statement that surely resonated with middle-class readers during the Depression, "We are the conservative people and what has been true of conservative people in all ages and lands is true of us. We dissent from extreme and injudicious measures, from violence. . . . [Loyalist] names are those of the oldest and noblest families whose diligence and abilities founded and built up New England. . . . Their attitude is inspired by conscientious conviction, persisted in in spite of all the outrages that have been done against them, and despite all the outrages they still must suffer."[43]

Through Wiswell's report, readers see the British blunders at Bunker Hill, the narrowness of Washington's escape from New York, and the ragtag retreat of the undisciplined cowards who fought under him. Readers also learn how little the British respected their Tory allies and how they failed to make use of a fighting force that, at the beginning of the revolt, actually represented the majority of the colonists. When Tories were allowed to join the combat, as the Marylanders who routed the rebels on Long Island or the seven hundred North Carolinians who waged the Battle of '96, they performed with the same grit and integrity as they exhibited in building up the land that the rebels were now tearing asunder. Better, at the novel's conclusion, to migrate to Nova Scotia, their new land of liberty, than to remain and have their fortunes seized by the lazy, vicious upstarts who waged war against a legitimate authority. (Mid-Atlantic Tories had already begun the trek to Kentucky.) Though *Wiswell* might have roiled the Daughters of the American Revolution by disclosing the sometimes unseemly patrimony of its members, the novel finally urges readers to see Americans, according to the *New York Times*, as one people descended from both revolutionists and Tories.[44]

Still, Roberts's conservative vision was criticized in magazines as different as the *Nation* and the *New Yorker*, where Clifton Fadiman underlined *Oliver Wiswell*'s immediate message: "Our period is obviously a revolutionary one. The law of action and reaction being what it is, it is only natural that the passion for retaining the *status quo* should be as intense as the passion for remolding the world. . . . Those readers who fear the excesses of democracy or who look with longing upon the relative stability of the pre–second-World-War-period will find a moral lesson in *Oliver Wiswell*."[45] Making a return appearance in this Roberts's novel is none other than Benedict Arnold, who having conspired to deliver West Point to John André, turned to soldiering for the British, as if to prove the stupidity of a Continental Congress that had so myopically failed to give him the charge as Washington's second in command that, in truth, he very likely deserved. In *Oliver Wiswell*, Arnold moves south to Chesapeake to break the rebels' supply lines and to extend the British line of attack. Wiswell can still discern the fearless, accomplished leader whom Washington respected, rather than the vain rogue, always bad with other people's money, who was ultimately to come last in the hearts of his countrymen.

Roberts's Benedict Arnold was the victim of Congress, which had charged him first with illegal plundering and later with abuse of power, promoted lesser generals before him, and refused to give him the command he craved, a fallible man who ought never to have been tempted by the British friends of his Tory wife promising to relieve his financial embarrassments and make him rich. Yet General Arnold already represented an "arousable interest" during the Depression. Early 1930 saw the publication of *Benedict Arnold: The Proud Warrior*, a biography that Henry Steele Commager understood as "clearly the project of an age skeptical of conventional standards of good and evil . . . and sympathetic to a Machiavellian role in the game of war and politics." The author, Charles Sellers, accepted Arnold's explanation that, "ever conscious of my own rectitude," his fear of a French alliance that would undo the colonies led to his perfidy. Two years later, another biography appeared, also pleading for a balanced view, Malcolm Decker's *Benedict Arnold: Son of the Havens*, which attended more to the predictive evidence in his early life of the treason to come. Frank Hough's *Renown* (1938) tried to understand the psychology of Arnold's obsession with glory, a novel that the

Times described as "a moving story, a clear and superbly intelligent piece of writing."[46]

In 1933, Roberts's *Rabble in Arms* completed the story of Arnold's northern campaign by describing the withdrawal of his starving, disease-ridden soldiers to Vermont, his miraculous creation of a fleet to cross Lake Champlain, his abandonment of Fort Ticonderoga, and his stunning success at Saratoga, where he undoubtedly saved the rebellion from a massive British invasion from the north. So persuasive was the vision of Arnold's heroism that critics seldom disputed Roberts's effort to whitewash the traitor by minimizing his bad qualities and by focusing, especially at the close, on his good ones and the debt his country might never have been able to repay. But when the papers of British general Thomas Gage became available, Carl Van Doren demonstrated, in the *Secret History of the American Revolution* (1941), that Arnold had even schemed to get the West Point posting so as to have something truly valuable to betray. By selling the strategic fort, and its 3,000-soldier garrison, for the lavish sum of £10,000 and a good pension too, the high-living general profited more from the war than any other soldier on either side. Previous readers had been ready to charge or excuse Arnold's second wife, but Van Doren explains that Peggy Shippen's role was murkier and Arnold's much clearer than his apologists had cast it.

Conclusively placing Arnold's treachery in the context of other Revolutionary War counterspies, conspirators, and villains, Van Doren's study should have terminated the discussion, but, in 1942, a minor drama, set in heroic couplets, again ascribes Arnold's downfall to his wife's power seeking, as if to testify to the enduring habit of blaming the woman for a man's iniquity. Finally, in 1944, as World War II had progressed and middle-class sympathies changed, Robert Gessner published *Treason*, a novel that places Arnold decisively amid the Tories swarming the colonies, some of whom spoke out against the rebellion and others who disguised their sentiments. The *Herald Tribune* reviewer noted: "By placing Arnold in this milieu of greed, selfishness, luxury and moral flabbiness, Mr. Gessner succeeds in making his final act of treason seem inevitable. . . . It is something of an achievement." Another critic, in the *Saturday Review of Literature*, acutely inferred the novel's subtext as more attuned to the urgencies of World War II than the fading Depression, calling *Treason* "the most cynical novel yet written about the American Revolution," because Gessner "treats frankly the war as primarily a civil conflict with not many more than half the colonists desiring independence, and with the native opponents of self-government more obstructive and insidious than the British themselves." For this reviewer, the author presses too hard the "startling and depressing" parallels between the 1770s and the 1940s: "The property-minded wanted not a better world but a more profitable one. Colonial fascists feared mobocracy and any ·change that would affect business. When the right to exploit and profiteer was challenged, the familiar cry about 'good old American free enterprise' was raised."[47] If *Oliver Wiswell* sought to explain the Revolution from a middle-class Tory point of view, *Treason* saw Arnold's act, in the middle of World War II, as the ultimate gesture of middle-class bad faith.

Why, in the 1930s—in the worst of economic times, with fears of capitalist breakdown and totalitarian possibilities flourishing abroad and at home—would Americans absorb this effort to rehabilitate the reviled Arnold? One might expect a crisis-ridden middle class, apprehensive about its status and its power, to condemn Arnold's selfish amorality and expedient disloyalty. The composite portrait that emerges, however, is of an embattled American who answers George Washington's demand for an "active, spirited officer" but who did not get what he deserved from an unappreciative country and whose lack of self-restraint (the very quality for which Washington is lionized) in his drive to satisfy his taste for wealth leads to his disastrous decision.

This vacillation amid the revived interest in Arnold dramatizes a self-understanding that the middle class had developed and projected elsewhere. Like *Gone with the Wind*, *Oliver Wiswell* finds much of its popularity in championing a lost cause, as Fadiman explains. Roberts's Tories, like Mitchell's slaveholders, enable middle-class Americans to believe, at least for a little while, in an ideology to which they might not otherwise subscribe—the antebellum South, replete with all of its prejudice and privilege; the loyal subjects of the British Crown, with all of the deference to position Americans are supposed to have forsworn. The book that was truly the critical success of 1940, *For Whom the Bell Tolls*, also championed another lost cause, where middle-class Americans might flatteringly compare their struggles to those of the Spanish partisans. (Hemingway's first truly popular book may well have deserved the Pulitzer Prize that year, but the judges spitefully refused, for the first time, to make an award, perhaps because the novel's graphic representation violated genteel taste.) It may be too much to reduce these three novels' commitment to lost causes to one explanation, but, on the surface, both Mitchell's novel and Roberts's are transformed as the plight of the middle class, whereas Hemingway's is demonstrably not, unless the novel's appeal lies in the way it recommends the Spanish partisan cause to the American middle class. Despite the defining ideological differences among the books, middle-class readers may well have identified with their several visions of valiant disenfranchisement, which gave scale and political resonance to their own.[48]

FAMILY, FICTION, AND THE DEPRESSION

The parallels among historical fiction, regionalism, and the family saga are amply evinced in the best-known novel of the 1930s, Margaret Mitchell's *Gone with the Wind* (1936). It is not so much that Scarlett O'Hara's faith—in the soil, a better tomorrow, and her infinite charm—adequately renders the lessons of the Civil War. More to the point, her several faiths bestow a legacy that coincides with the social vision of the soap operas that had grown so popular in the thirties. Mitchell presents the disenfranchised daughter of the plantation class as a prototype for the liberated professional woman of the late '20s and early '30s. In accepting her challenge, readers must commit to several propositions in the present—about the family, materialism, the class predication of desire, even race relations—to say nothing of history— propositions that are sooner or later about middle-class lives.

To suggest how fully *Gone with the Wind* is a thirties novel of middle-class angst amid crushing historical forces, consider that if its title glosses the nostalgia for the lost culture of the antebellum South, its famous ending— "I'll think about it tomorrow. Tomorrow is another day"—points to the sur- vival ethic it issues, though it may smack of sentimental healthy-mindedness. For the years of this novel's ascendancy came precisely when the Depres- sion's ravages had seemed to slacken into a "mood of relaxation." So does Edward Weeks characterize the remission of pressure and worry that helped to establish the novel's claim on the popular imagination. In discerning "What Makes a Book a Best Seller?" Weeks distinguishes this "timeliness" as counting for some 45 percent of a best seller's popularity and submits that the "magnetism" of the story results from reaching us "precisely at the moment when we were ready for it."[49]

Weeks could not know that this novel, stupendous publishing success that it was, would also have the longest shelf life of any '30s novel—and probably always will—the novel that future readers untouched by the Depression respond to most readily of all the books from that decade. Another fictional work of Southern history from 1936—*Absalom, Absalom!*—has no doubt more deeply engaged critics, scholars, and theorists, but no other novel from the 1930s has been read more widely, and read more completely out of its historical context, than *Gone with the Wind*. Obviously, when Weeks wrote, the film, not to mention its hoopla and awards, had not yet transformed the supremely popular book into an indispensable cultural artifact. Yet if we remember that for several weeks during the time Mitchell's novel topped the fictional best sellers, the best-selling work of nonfiction was another publishing sensation, *How to Win Friends and Influence People*, we may be tempted to see both of them more clearly as Depression-era survival manuals, especially to the extent that the nonfiction hit could provide a subtitle for Mitchell's novel. Not only did Dale Carnegie's book offer a regimen of formulas to follow, but it also enshrined a new meaning of success—winning friends and influencing people—that was much more outer-directed than anything an older model, like the monopoly capitalist Andrew Carnegie, would have recognized in his pursuit of wealth and power. In the end, "winning friends and influencing people" enables Scarlett to succeed. Dale Carnegie's rhetoric of diminished expectations teaches readers how to proceed like Scarlett—through ingratiation, impression management, calculated preparation, and seduction.

Gone with the Wind so completely dominated the discussion of fiction in the second half of 1936 that only *Absalom, Absalom!*, *The Big Money*, and James T. Farrell's *A World I Never Made* made an impression throughout the rest of the year. Subject as Margaret Mitchell's novel was to critical condescension for its robust popularity and extravagant plot, it was more generally welcomed as a "part of American folklore"—according to one advertisement. Reviewers might concede that it was by no means a great book, even as they held that it was a better book than highbrow critics allowed. But the novel's combination of history, romance, and family chronicle helped this story of a young woman's negotiation of tough economic circumstances, obstacles of history, and reluctant objects of desire ascend into a new type of cultural narrative. It would be three years until Christopher Morley invented the tough-skinned, soft-hearted working girl in *Kitty Foyle* (1939), but Scarlett O'Hara substantially furthered the idea of the New Woman as beleaguered bourgeois American heroine for Depression readers. As Edward Wagenknecht describes the source of her appeal, "It was exhilarating to watch Scarlett fight and win; even if she did not always employ the most genteel means, at least she did not lie down and die. Futilitarianism and deflation of values had been very smart during the 'twenties, when our economic future seemed secure, but they would not do now."[50] Another critic reminds us that, far from merely approving of methods less than genteel, Mitchell's novel fosters a "vicious individualism," thus glamorizing and romanticizing the same kind of "economic piracy" that Stribling's *The Store*—the Pulitzer Prize winner in 1933—had "sentimentalized and unconvincingly rebuked."[51]

Scarlett O'Hara may well have been the most notorious hard-boiled female protagonist in American fiction, in an era when James Cain, among others, was setting a new tone. Even as Scarlett stood for a traditional American concoction of resilience and resourcefulness poured into the new vessel of middle-class woman, the American man of the old dispensation was enjoying a strange reemergence as well, albeit one tempered through satire or modulated through nostalgia. The professional and kindly man of parts, proud of his family name, generous with his blessings, modest of his accomplishments but determined in his endeavors, enjoyed a resurgence after a few years of nearly total eclipse. Traditional male heroism had been too compromised to model very persuasively; barely a single memorable male realist hero emerges from the decade's first half. There is no central consciousness in Dos Passos's trilogy, except perhaps the all-too-flawed Charley Anderson. There was not much chance that some newly radicalized young person leading a strike was likely to capture the American imagination of individualism. Similarly bloodless are the types Nathanael West creates in *Miss Lonelyhearts*; Fitzgerald moved, in fifteen years, from the ever-engaged Amory Blaine to the more detached Nick Carroway to the listless Dick Diver, whose defeats summarize a culture's deficiencies. From the vigor of Babbitt, who for all his smugness and hypocrisy had exerted a captivating hold on American readers, and Arrowsmith, who for all his mercurial nature and self-deception offered a more compelling alternative to the new corporate American male, and Elmer Gantry, whose venality and self-possession underscored his vitality, Lewis moves to Ann Vickers, who is arguably more assertive than most male protagonists of 1933. Foremost among Faulkner's memorable heroes in the early thirties is the supposed mulatto, Joe Christmas. By the time Hemingway turns to Harry Morgan in *To Have and Have Not* (1937), his '20s masculine ideal seems just about bankrupt.

Recall, for example, the male heroes of Pulitzer Prize–winning novels of the early '30s to see the doldrums into which the white Anglo-Saxon Protestant had fallen. Two heroes, Laughing Boy of Oliver La Farge's novel and Wang Lung of *The Good Earth* are not even "white," though Buck's Chinese peasant farmer could be understood as more Western than Chinese (according to Younghill Kang in the *New Republic*).[52] In Stribling's *The Store*, Miltiades Vaiden combines the worst aspects of Faulkner's Sutpen and Snopes by cheating and then sacrificing his illegitimate black son, who personifies the honest, hard-working man defrauded of his rightful chance to rise.

Obviously, there are vital exceptions: Cozzens's career changed in 1933, when he invented his signature protagonist by focusing on a Yankee doctor in *The Last Adam*, which he followed with a portrait of a liberal minister in *Men and Brethren* (1936) and the range of professional men involved in a murder trial in *The Just and the Unjust* (1942), beau ideals of men whose integrity surpasses their claims to ambition or power. In the second half of the thirties, however, it was much easier to discover a book describing some older American male than a contemporary one as the repository of national virtues, as if to suggest that as the Depression wore on, the recovery of heroic models became increasingly significant. To express the importance of this trend, consider that Canby's final editorial in the *Saturday Review* was devoted to precisely this question, "Heroes for Sale." There, Canby meditates on the failure of American novelists to seek models from the middle-class professions and adduces the success of recent memoirs by doctors. The foremost example of American virility fondly recalled was *Life with Father* (1935), by Clarence Day, an evocation of America in the 1890s, when fathers apparently knew their job and performed it squarely. The humor of this nostalgic memoir proved so popular that Day immediately wrote *Life with Mother*, which also fared well; these were among the top ten nonfiction best sellers from 1935 through 1937. Later, the play drawing on *Life with Father* set a record for consecutive performances on Broadway and inspired several imitators, including the Gilbreths' *Cheaper by the Dozen*.

Part of Day's success can be laid to his father's hardy antimodernism—his impatience with new contraptions, his reluctance to accept the changing, modern order of relations between people. This resistance was near the heart of a Depression era's willful desire to reconstruct the perceived order, certainly the material welfare of the past, the world before the breakup of middle-class stability. In a world as dominated by anxieties over the family's ability to function, that is, to regulate the present and to safeguard the future, Day's image of a father raging against trivial disorders happily contrasted with the nightmare vision Margaret Mitchell offered in the figure of Gerald O'Hara—the once proud individualist now dispossessed, deranged, and, seemingly worst of all, infantilized. (More positively, director of the Works Progress Administration, Orrick Johns would publish a memoir, *Time of Our Lives: The Story of My Father and Myself* [1937], contrasting his life [b. 1887] with his father's [b. 1857] to illustrate the great shift in American cultural life and the renewable possibilities of populism to which each had been heir.) The depth of Americans' desire to reconnect with a simpler, more trustworthy era may also be glimpsed in several books honoring the medical and legal professions, including Victor Heiser's *An American Doctor's Odyssey* (1937), Arthur Hertzler's *The Horse and Buggy Doctor* (1938), and Bellamy Partridge's *Country Lawyer* (1939). In 1938, maybe as a culmination of this pressing retrospect, Carl Van Doren published a Pulitzer Prize–winning biography of the American man of affairs par excellence, Ben Franklin.

In the era when Hollywood brought forward such brash male heroes as Clark Gable and James Cagney, two novels quite memorably registered a different figure of masculine gentility: George Santayana's *The Last Puritan* (1936) and John Marquand's *The Late George Apley* (1937), published less than twelve months apart. The latter may have had the former a little bit in mind, or it might merely have been a publisher's gimmick to invert Santayana's subtitle, *A Memoir in the Form of a Novel*, *A Novel in the Form of a Memoir*, but, as it was reported, the novelists had worked on their books ignorant of each other's project.

Striking as Santayana's success was—who would have supposed that the former Harvard philosophy professor would make such a commercial conquest?—Marquand's book was received even more handsomely. Nor was Marquand, at this point, a likely candidate for the celebrity. Although he had been writing fiction for about fifteen years, up to this time these works had been mainly historical romances along with the popular series of espionage novels detailing the adventures of Mr. Moto. One well-circulated story tells of an agent, accustomed to placing Marquand's magazine fiction without ado, counseling him that his new novel was a humorless fantasy that the author would be wiser to put away and forget.[53] Instead, *The Late George Apley* marked the beginning of the second half of Marquand's career, which lasted through the 1950s—a career so prominent that, twelve years later, in 1949, when he published *Point of No Return*, his picture was featured on the cover of several magazines. Faintly remembered now as a novelist of bygone manners, he was once one of the best known and most appreciated American writers—along with Steinbeck, Hemingway, and Faulkner—in the two decades that followed *The Late George Apley*, and his books may have made the most money of any serious writer.[54]

Marquand's and Santayana's novels were also published in the context of a '30s interest in the heritage of New England. If the country's recent tribulations had caused a searching retrospect in general, New England would have to be a foremost site of reexamination. The enlivening critical rationale for its reassertion as the predominant American subculture comes from its place as the meeting point of two important tendencies of the age—the hunger for historical models and the faith in regionalism. Several historical novels returned American readers to Massachusetts, like Esther Forbes's *Paradise* (1937), and there had already been several best-selling novels sentimentalizing New England life, including *As the Earth Turns* (1933) and Carroll's next book, *Neighbor to the Sky* (1937), as well as Mary Ellen Chase's *Mary Peters* (1934) and Rachel Field's *Time Out of Mind* (1935). As Mencken's influence waned, the time may also have been right to reevaluate the relation between contemporary life and Puritanism. In fact, Perry Miller, the scholar who virtually created American colonial studies, published his first books in the mid-thirties.

Appearing almost immediately between *The Last Puritan* and *The Late George Apley* was a book studying the same culture, a work every bit as successful of its kind—Van Wyck Brooks's *The Flowering of New England*. This highly influential examination of cultural politics and regional landscape was populated by such heroes as Daniel Webster, Nathaniel Hawthorne, and John Quincy Adams. *The Flowering* was not only a critical success—controversially so, since this work of belles lettres was named the Pulitzer Prize for history—but, incredibly, it also ranked as the tenth leading seller among nonfiction books of the year (trailing Hillis's *Orchids on Your Budget*, Noel Coward's memoir *Present Indicative*, and Lancelot Hogben's *Mathematics for the Million*). While some professors disdained *The Flowering*, other scholars and critics embraced it, though, soon after being published in 1941, F. O. Matthiessen's *American Renaissance* supplanted it and became the germinal study of the New England imprimatur of antebellum literature, a book that shaped American literary historiography for a couple of generations. More-over, Brooks's collection defined a great change in this progenitor of the Young Intellectuals, as well as a generational shift. The critic who had once caustically denounced the established cultural arbiters for so poorly "using" the American past had become an unself-conscious nationalist himself, thus marking the ossification of the moving spirit of the cultural critics who had come of age around World War I. Brooks had been a decisive influence on that generation. That *The Flowering* was the kind of apologia those Young Intellectuals once would have disdained suggests that such critics, twenty years on, had lost their adversarial edge and their command of the culture once inflaming their arguments.[55]

Marquand's novel also squanders its rich resource of antagonism. Perhaps the truly remarkable aspect of *The Late George Apley* is that even as it *could* be read as a satire of the conventional man—he who trades the virtue of his convictions for the consolations of caste—it retains enough deference to, even admiration for, the protagonist's lifelong career of saving face. George Apley is presented, through his own words to his son, and his son's to Apley's grandson, as someone who early enough in life cashed in his chances and accepted the protections that high social standing affords. The advice he gives his son and his reflections on the times render Apley without the saving modern grace of ironical self-awareness or wry historical conscious-ness. Apley rails against the Charles River Basin, a Beacon Street esplanade, electric lights, the Great War, and Sacco-Vanzetti; yet even as the spectacle of his self-deceptions may repulse readers, no deeper critique arises. The enshrinement is doubled: Marquand mocks the excesses of fathers but, by relieving his patriarch from confronting his hypocrisy and the sources of his degradation, he preserves Apley's stature. This move insulates the very tem-perament under attack, a failed Oedipal revolt, wanting all the pleasures of desecration and none of the responsibilities. Nor does Marquand, and by extrapolation the reader, ever have to acknowledge his comfort with this half-hearted rebellion.

This ambivalence is very much the form that the reviews of the novel, and its subsequent criticism, take. Reviewers typically concede that the book's formal properties should not work but do; they generally describe Mar-quand's achievement and his failure as deriving from the same source, just as they usually wish to identify Apley as someone who believes in the rights of family over the claims of the individual. The book ends with Apley's death in

1933, having lived long enough to witness, even as he is doomed not to understand, the Depression. Nor did this aristocrat comprehend much of anything throughout the whole unfolding of America's growth since the Civil War, at least in Boston. The reviewers judged the novel as a portrait of a man and a bygone era, and some saw it clearly in the context of Santayana's recent book, that is, an autumnal lament to juxtapose against *The Last Puritan's* satire on the passing of a once vital but now exhausted way of life. Still, they generally considered Marquand's the more complete picture and the more lasting achievement.

The Late George Apley draws closely on the Depression's fascination with the effects of contemporary life on traditional family arrangements. Although part of the novel's appeal lies in its perennial story of Polonius counseling Laertes, its immediate inflection resounds of its participation in a prominent broader cultural discourse of the moment: the discussion of how the changes in social and economic circumstances will affect child rearing, family cohesion, and the transaction of values. Consider the kinds of changes that were then worrying parents. The cumulative effect of articles regularly appearing in magazines and the number of new advice books published near the end of the Depression may lead us to suppose that if life with father or with mother could be evoked for strength, humor, and clarity, life with the children was troubling and confusing. New experts seemed to say that the unscientific ways of the preceding generation no longer applied to modern parents' problems.

Moreover, the Great Depression had created problems that the family itself could not hope to solve. There was a host of magazine articles from the years 1932 through 1937, in a great diversity of venues, whose titles as much as the pieces themselves testify to the nature of these anxieties: "How Much Do We Owe Our Children?" (*Forum*), "Some Recent Changes and Their Effect upon Family Life" (*Home Economics*), "What Kind of World Are Young People Facing?" (*Scribner's*), "Youth in the Depression" (*Survey Graphic*), "Social Change in 1933 and Character Education" (*School and Society*), "Girls on the Road" (*Independent Woman*), "Homeless Girls" (*Ladies Home Journal*), "I Don't Want to Be a Bum: America's 350,000 Boy and Girl Vagabonds" (*Scholastic*), "Half Slave, Half Free: Unemployment, the Depression, and American Young People" (*Harper's*), "Our Muddled Youth" (*American Mercury*), "Plight of American Youth: Study by American Youth Commission" (*School and Society*), "Sons and Daughters of the Depression" (*American Mer-*

cury), "Today's Lost Generation" (*Literary Digest*), "What Next for Youth?" (*Parents*), "Will They Be Better Off?" (*Saturday Evening Post*), "Are Parents Afraid of Their Children?" (*Ladies Home Journal*), "Adaptations of Family Life: Effects of the Depression" (*American Journal of Sociology*). As these titles readily disclose, such articles often express parents' challenges during trying economic times. Yet even as these stories and analyses acknowledge overwhelming circumstances, they generally verge toward a willful optimism.

The Depression contorted the modern American family in ways that may no longer be keenly appreciated, and the fiction of the last few years of the decade vividly records the kinds of family problems that the Depression created, a literature that exhibits the public issues afflicting the private life and family organization. Throughout the late '30s, American novels argue, implicitly and explicitly, that the most telling change the Depression has wrought on manners and mores is to be found in the life of the family. Some of these novels were written by popular women romancers of the day, like Olive Prouty, whose *Lisa Vale* (1938) was seen as an unsuccessful female version of Santayana's and Marquand's Boston novels. (Prouty remains better known for the novel on which is based one of Bette Davis's signature performances, Charlotte Vale, in *Dark Victory* [1939], drawn from a play by George Brewer of the same year.) For others, whose focus was the new grim life of restriction and diminishment, the Depression occasioned tough, anxious appraisals of contemporary domestic circumstances and their ramifications in the public sphere, especially in the fiction of Josephine Lawrence, whose Depression-era books took as their main subject the connection between workplace and home.

How the culture lost sight of Lawrence is difficult to say, since her many novels were regularly, often positively reviewed. Indeed, she was the first writer to have two consecutive books chosen as Book-of-the-Month Club selections: *Years Are So Long* (1934) examines how, in the period before Social Security, elderly people might receive the care and support they needed. *If I Have Four Apples* (1935) was an equally unsentimental portrait of the challenges facing citizens of moderate means during hard times. If the former is "stripped of all sentimentality but full of unspoken compassion," it is also possible that it will "start effective thinking" on what to do about the elderly. The latter is an "entertaining novel" that is also "good clinical reading" about the difficulties of making and sticking to a budget; its implications are immense, since it attacks the ideal of consumerism so crucial to the doctrine of the American Way: "It is a sad commentary on the alertness of the multitudinous watchdogs of the Republic that no finger has been raised to suppress this novel, castigate its author, and discipline the publishers. For it strikes at the very roots of the American Home and Family. It argues that every man should *not* Own His Own Car; that there should *not* be a Car in Every Garage," according to one reviewer. "It is a brave, penetrating, indignant book and it teaches a lesson that only a few Americans don't need to learn."[56]

The public interest of family tension was concentrated in the center of multigenerational novels like Sylvia Chatfield Bates's *The Long Way Home* (1937), Mari Sandoz's *Slogum House* (1937), Rose Wilder Lane's *Free Land* (1938), Agnes Sligh Turnbull's *Remember the End* (1938), as well as several new, up-to-the-minute novels by Margaret Banning, along with Margaret Barnes's continuing dissection of the middle-class home in her treatment of second marriages and suburban life, *Wisdom's Gate* (1938). Held in even higher critical esteem were such novels as Fannie Cook's study of the division between work and motherhood, *The Hill Grows Steeper* (1938), and Anne Parrish's character study of an older woman's realization that her obsessive love for her sons has caused their ruined, futile lives, *Mr. Despondency's Daughter* (1938). Less critical was Hilda Morris's *The Main Stream* (1939), which traces how one family dispersed professionals into the culture.

Male novelists found the condition of domestic circumstances during the Depression equally compelling. Michael Foster's *American Dream* (1937), a multigenerational treatment of the subject, was particularly well received, along with Stuart Engstrand's *The Invaders* (1937), which mediates the story of domestic upheaval through the tale of an Eastern labor organizer's visit to the Southwest; Sidney Meller's *Roots in the Sky* (1938), an account of the relation between spiritual values and family concerns among impoverished Jews in California; and *Bricks without Straw* (1938), Charles Norris's drama of the struggle between the generations, which portrays the process whereby a wayward son becomes an apoplectic parent.

A particularly telling example is Sinclair Lewis's quite forgotten but once heralded book, *The Prodigal Parents* (1938). Though it is commonplace to derogate Lewis's novels of the late '30s and '40s, their very badness curiously indexes the fiction being produced, since Lewis, who once set trends, was always a careful observer of what other novelists were doing and thus teaches us by what he borrowed. Unable to complete the big labor novel he projected, he had found alternative social relevance in a New Woman novel, *Ann Vickers*. The move to *It Can't Happen Here* is ready enough, but he then turns to a middle-aged wish-dream of revenge satirizing the pretensions, smugness, arrogance, and self-deception of the politically minded young, the new generation that is ungrateful for the hard-working honesty, kindly bourgeois virtues to be found in the exemplary Babbitt-father, Frederick Cornplow of *The Prodigal Parents*. As John Chamberlain, who later became a respected conservative observer of American politics but who first won recognition as a literary critic, opines, Lewis's "moral revulsion" has not resulted in a good book; "in his rush to write a tract, Lewis has lost the will to understand the whole inwardness of the situation." Instead of examining the complex relation between family tensions and political reform, Lewis treats the subject with disconcerting levity: "Men can be knaves and still represent the lunatic fringe of a movement whose aspirations toward a decent life are understandable and noble. And middle class Americans can be sober, industrious and kind and still be sadly deficient in brains and political imagination." Honest as Lewis's prodigal parents may be, "it still remains true that Fred Cornplow is dumb about the world of 1938 and hence is undeserving of the adulation which Lewis heaps upon him."[57]

If Lewis's novel was debated only to be dismissed, another family novel of the preceding year, 1937, suffered a revealing lack of critical attention: William Maxwell's *They Came Like Swallows*, an affecting, psychologically deft story of the relations between two young brothers and their beloved mother during the postwar era and the Spanish influenza, as the epidemic was called. Later famous as the editor of the *New Yorker*, a truly powerful figure in the New York literary scene after World War II, Maxwell had written a novel that virtually every critic liked, though no admiring public ever carried the book forward. *They Came Like Swallows* was even selected as a co-nominee for the Book-of-the-Month Club, along with Millen Brand's novel of manic depression, *The Outward Room*, a precursor of William Styron's memoir, *Darkness Visible: A Memoir of Madness* (1990)—a book that sold quite well. So surprised was Bernard DeVoto, the new editor of the *Saturday Review*, that he contrasted critics' lack of interest in championing Maxwell's novel with their support of Virginia Woolf's *The Years* (1937). Woolf's book had earned a broader base of readers, despite its opacities and, for DeVoto, ultimate triviality. In his column "Reviewing the Reviews," De-Voto praised Maxwell's haunting novel for its fineness of touch, its lack of preciosity. Unfortunately, *They Came Like Swallows* landed in an obscurity it did not deserve and would not be reprinted, despite Maxwell's formidable position, for sixty years.

THE AMERICAN WAY

This discourse about the family, like the era's preoccupation with history, corresponds intimately to the vogue of studies appraising the state of American democracy, as if to suggest that the health of the nation and the life of the family are ineluctably tied together, a trope that goes back even to Revolutionary times and the ideology of republican motherhood. In the early years of the Depression, many studies of U.S. democracy diagnosed problems and recommended courses of action. By the end of the decade— after the economy had collapsed again—these studies often found solace in the nation's relative success, the conviction that even if the struggle for economic stability was not yet won, the United States had avoided the worst excesses of those European countries embracing fascism or developing prominent Socialist or Communist parties. Small victory as it was, America celebrated its commitment to facing the sources of economic failure. The country could exult in its vaunted middle-class ideals, if not its actual capacity to meet economic failures or attend to their consequences. A sentimental patriotism underlies this vision of a nation holding onto a dream of individual fulfillment even as it exalts its potential for social cooperation, a national self-image that came to be called the "American Way," a vision some might know primarily through its Hollywood treatment in Frank Capra films, rather than its more nuanced representation in novels.

These studies were legion and included Mauritz Hallgren's *Seeds of Revolt* (1933), a socialist analysis of the failure of the American proletariat to protest its conditions; Rexford Tugwell's *Battle for Democracy* (1935); Ernest Bates's denunciation of the American mania for regulation and repression, *This Land of Liberty* (1930); *American Messiahs* (1935), by an "Unofficial Observer," a study of the country's fascist potential; Alfred Bingham's *Insurgent America* (1935), a voluminous analysis of middle-class life and political possibilities; Lewis Corey's Marxist assessment, *The Decline of American Capitalism* (1934); Thurman Arnold's witty and astute *Folklore of Capitalism* (1937); *Who Owns America?* (1936), edited by Herbert Agar and Allen Tate, a collection of Agrarian essays by many of the contributors to *I'll Take My*

Stand; Alexander Meiklejohn's *What Does America Mean?* (1935); *The End of Democracy* (1937), by decadent architect Ralph Adams Cram; *Forty Years on Main Street* (1937), William Allen White's tour of duty patrolling middle America; Gilbert Seldes's exhortation to the middle class to seize the present hour, *Your Money and Your Life* (1938); and *I Like America* (1938), Marxist critic Granville Hicks's conciliatory overview of mainstream values.

Also addressing the national stakes of the current crisis were Walter Lippmann's *The Good Society* (1937), Max Lerner's *It Is Later Than You Think* (1938), and Western historian Walter Prescott Webb's *Divided We Stand: The Crisis of a Frontierless Democracy* (1938). Among the best known of these books is Harold Stearns's reprise of his earlier compendium on civilization in the United States, *America Now* (1938). John Dewey published *Freedom and Culture* (1939), and Charles Beard, who had coauthored *The American Leviathan: The Republic in the Machine Age* (1930), as if to inaugurate the decade, and who had edited a collection by diverse hands (*A Century of Progress*, 1933) as well as a symposium (*America Faces the Future*, 1932), concluded the '30s by collecting, with Mary Beard, the articles in *America in Midpassage* (1939), a two-volume overview of America since the Wall Street crash. There were a great many others, including many that took up issues of race and gender. Obviously, with such titles, these books intend to perform important work in the project of nation making: they generally announce, for one audience or another, a position that needs reinforcing; if they scarcely succeed in persuading their adversaries, they do not particularly mean to. Their contribution to the culture's sense of itself remains worthy, since they demonstrate just how fully, even in an age of mass media like radio and film, the public sphere is enmeshed in print culture.

Even though most of these books enjoyed modest sales, many were reviewed prominently in the major journals of opinion, arts, and politics, and their handling there—generally by the authors of similar books—seems like something of an event or intellectual occasion, an opportunity to think formally about the country's shaping values. Rarely do these books prove truly influential, though that failure does not seem to have discouraged any pundit from writing one or a publisher from commissioning one. Their combined interest, I suggest, lies in the way they register the variegations of a culture's self-image, the very image that contemporaneous realist fiction at least can be supposed to chronicle and to elucidate. When one of these studies makes an impact, its claim is that it helps us to adjust our understanding of society. Such an alteration turns out to be less practical than rhetorical, since the primary feature of national life that books can change is discourse, though there is always the faith that such a change may affect policy or reshape practice. Aspiring as they do to transform public opinion, they generally fail, or their successes are small. Even as the largest majority of them wind up having no great effect, their contribution is scarcely minor, at least to the extent that they more or less persuasively summarize a country's anxieties, record nuances, and prescribe changes so that, like fiction, they set the boundaries of the country's political imagination. They age quickly, and there is little reason to remember most of them from one year to the next. For all the tenuousness of their path to influence, however, publishers still publish them, perhaps because they bring cachet, but also because the endeavor of constantly revising our interpretation of our society is important, as is its discussion in newspapers and magazines.

We are used to saying, with W. H. Auden, that poetry makes nothing happen, but how much more does most prose do? The dissensus school of American criticism might have said that these studies of U.S. culture are little more than a foreclosing of the possibilities of radical critique, or they fill up the space reserved for honest cultural criticism and keep us from confronting the source of our social and economic deficiencies. (Which, of course, might have been true during the Depression, except that communists themselves joined in the general muting of cultural critique with their often risible efforts to align Marxism with Americanism.) On the other hand, several of these books are nativist, even downright racist, and strive to legitimate a culture's reactionary, antimodernist voices. Rather than a reveille for egalitarian principles, the cumulative effect of such conservative perspectives is to render a vision of America needing no progressive change. Still, the influence of such books as the Agrarians' *Who Owns America?* or Donald Davidson's *American Leviathan*, arguments against centralizing power in the North, or Herbert Agar's *The Pursuit of Happiness*, describing the origins and development of the Democratic Party, three late '30s statements of what has gone wrong with the American dream, is greatly overestimated. A populace that falls under the sway of Father Charles E. Coughlin's speeches or learns the power of collective action from the Silver Shirts really does not seem receptive to the guidance that these serious commentators supply.

Novelists were also broadening their sense of the relation between fiction and contemporary ideology by moving into realms of larger experience than the region, community, family, or the individual. Prominent in this regard were several novels of the late 1930s that dealt with keenly felt political urgencies, the demands on liberalism during the tumultuous times when radical measures seemed more attractive than ever. Whereas U.S. readers are used to fiction ever since Hannah Foster's *The Coquette* (1797) that examines the way public issues exert pressure on the private life, these novels investigate the persons whose individual struggles are subordinate to the guiding forces of history and politics. In this way, they are political without being radical. The tendency of literary historians is too often to imagine politics in a strictly bifurcated way, pitting radical protest against conservative oppression, yet our national politics, as these novels suggest, may be just as accurately portrayed as performing the liberal project of developing compromise, achieving consensus, resisting alienation, and participating meaningfully, a vision perhaps too thoroughly middle class even to be articulated.

Several political novels of the thirties preserved liberalism's appeal even when radical measures seemed to be more necessary than ever. All published by esteemed presses such as Viking or Farrar and Rinehart and issued in runs of several thousands, these novels were often well received and occasionally even feted. The presses allotted a significant budget for their promotion (usually about $5,000), as testimony to their commitment to get the books read. If general interest in any one title was seldom pronounced, a novel might still be picked up by a book club, increasing its circulation as well as stimulating similar novels. Of course, the publishers imagined there was profit in the venture, but their support of such fiction also evinces a willingness to disseminate the arguments about the relation between class and ideology that the novels explore. They include W. L. White's *What People Said* (1938), a view of small-city politics considered artistically deficient but also one that reviewers named as one of the most important books of 1938, and John Hyde Preston's *The Liberals* (1938), which "digs into the foundations of the modern economic structure and exposes much of the rot which undermines it," a sound book, concludes one reviewer, that needed "far more imaginative power." Radical novelist Leane Zugsmith's *The Summer Soldier* (1938) tells the story of several Northern civil rights workers who, like their voting-rights successors twenty-five years later, go South to investigate lynching and learn the complexity of doing good, even as they get their pretenses and hypocrisies beaten out of them. Clyde Brion Davis's

Nebraska Coast (1939) chronicles a young man's rise from farmer to congress-man, and Alice Beal Parsons's *Trial of Helen McLeod* (1938) even features Clarence Darrow as the defense attorney for a society matron charged with sedition as a result of her socialist leanings in the postwar United States. Unduly neglected is Waters E. Turpin's *O Canaan!* (1939), a novel of the black migration northward, whose "social and historical sweep" breaks new ground for the African American novel, according to the *New York Times.* Ideological issues were at the heart of Thomas Dixon's latest, and last, di-atribe against intermarriage, *The Flaming Sword* (1939). His effort to leave an "authoritative record of the conflict of color in America, 1900–1938," ac-cording to *Books,* takes the form of a "vehement melodrama depicting the destruction of American democracy by the red menace," a havoc resulting from the "communistic corruption of the black race": "Whatever you think of the story," the reviewer observes with the Nazi invasion of Poland clearly in mind, "it is not as wildly incredible today as it might have seemed a few short weeks ago."[58]

Critically esteemed yet forgotten from the year that had brought *The Grapes of Wrath,* Dorothy Canfield Fisher's gentle political allegory *Sea-soned Timber* (1939) meditates on the current struggle between democracy and dictatorship, between race hatred and tolerance, in a Vermont village where a financially troubled prep school is offered a great scholarship fund, freighted with anti-Semitic codicils. The headmaster's dilemma is clearly a choice, at this benighted time, between aligning the school and himself with such a hateful beneficiary or with liberal, democratic beliefs, an allegory "of pressing vital significance to every American city and village and main street where the weapons of totalitarianism . . . have made their appearance."[59] On a more explicit level of international politics, Grace Zaring Stone's pseudon-ymous work, *Escape,* was the first best-selling book about Nazis and one of the most popular novels of 1939. (It was rumored to have been written by almost every woman writer but Stone, who had last scored a success in 1930 with *The Bitter Tea of General Yen.*) Frances Parkinson Keyes offered a popu-lar romance, *The Great Tradition,* which follows a German American stu-dent's involvement in the Nazi Party, his rise to prominence, his eventual revulsion and return to the American Way. Even more sensational was Jack Preston's strange *Heil! Hollywood* (1939), warning of a Klan-like rebellion against the power-mad Hollywood autocrats who conduct their business so sadistically. Oscar Schisgall contributed *Swastika* (1939), about a middle-class American family's differing response to the political atmosphere of contemporary Berlin. In *A Half Inch of Candle* (1939), A. Hamilton Gibbs followed the success of earlier work, drawn from World War I, by describing one man's effort in a French parish to seek peace amid the evident mobilization for war.

None of these novels succeeded in the ways we normally measure enduring strength, though a couple did fairly well with critics and those also tended to enjoy good sales. Along these lines, though less explicitly political, was Christopher Morley's *Kitty Foyle* (1939), which was originally titled "Nation Wide," since this story of the "white-collar girl" as the "sharecropper of business" was meant to be seen as "national in scope and significance."[60] Such books were understood as participating to various extents in a new subject that the bourgeois novel was claiming as its own—the public life. In the late '30s, no single work of American political fiction could compete with André Malraux's novel of the Chinese Revolution, *Man's Fate* (1934), in representing crisis. Neither could any of Malraux's subsequent works—not his tribute to anti-Hitlerites, *Days of Wrath* (1935), which was a Book-of-the-Month Club selection, and not *Man's Hope* (1937), his much-praised but ultimately dishonest account of the Spanish Civil War. Before he was ultimately discredited by the left, Malraux had emerged as a new model of the engaged man of letters, the clear-eyed, clear-spoken author who devoted the rigorous objectivity of the archaeologist (as Malraux had first trained to be) to unearthing the keys to moral conduct for the philosophical quandaries that our ongoing political history presents.

It was the general failure of such American novelists, not the bourgeois novelists, to respond fully to the spectacle of a world in crisis that discloses the true blankness of American literary history in the late thirties. That emptiness would become downright embarrassing when Thomas Wolfe published his German travel and political impressions, "I Have a Thing to Tell You"—later part of *You Can't Go Home Again* (1940)—which tried oafishly to put the best face on the Nazis and the German people (avid readers of Wolfe). For better or worse, Faulkner never wrote compellingly when his imagination wandered far from Mississippi; he was never much better than middle-of-the-road in his views concerning race relations. Neither *Pylon* (1935) nor *The Wild Palms* (1939)—often praised then for being his clearest book—did anything to advance the author's reputation as a writer of the public sphere. Hemingway's *To Have and Have Not* (1937) marked a low point in critical esteem, for as much as critics may have admired his usual strengths in dialogue and scene, his vision of disconnection had begun to seem more troubled than troubling.

For Whom the Bell Tolls (1940), however, was a great success—for Hemingway and for American fiction in general, since Hemingway alone of the canonical authors of American modernism had risen to the challenge of imagining the international subject of the American novel. For Whom the Bell Tolls returned to Hemingway a confidence in his grasp of the ethical dilemmas of the times and his ability to represent in Robert Jordan a character whose anxieties responded to a world outside the self. For Whom the Bell Tolls proved invigorating for American fiction because it seemed to uncover new, public resources, just as John Steinbeck in Grapes of Wrath (1939) and Richard Wright in Native Son (1940) had managed to bring social realism to the summit of its achievement. For American fiction, in confronting the grievous work that the Depression forced upon it, had risked provinciality— wasting the great advances by the '20s masters to make it into an international literature. Indeed, a few of the best novels of 1939 were ultimately committed to a regional view of America, including Di Donato's Christ in Concrete, Herbst's Rope of Gold, and, as one may loosely suggest, West's Day of the Locust.

The exigencies of the international Depression and changing political face of Europe helped to encourage a kind of American internationalism. Constricting that imagination is the sentimental nationalism born in the '30s that produced the American Way, a vision we learn from elementary school social studies textbooks, a modernized version of Currier and Ives, a reality that Norman Rockwell paintings evoke at their most simplistic. Under the influence that these national definitions developed, especially through the thirties, we lose sight of the clearly present internationalist impulse that several American novelists found, and that many more have continued to find, animating. Out of the demand to locate national core values, this incipient globalism was, historiographically speaking, squelched, rendered invisible for future generations, yet so many American novelists have written novels about Americans in foreign countries that it would take a full-length study to do justice to this sorely absent subject in American literary studies.

No more powerful focus on core national values might be found in the late 1930s than debates about the American Way. There was even a Harper's

essay competition devoted to the topic, with the four winners assembled as
The American Way (1938).[61] Predicated on a commitment to individualism
supple enough to encompass agrarianism as well as industrialism, the American Way crystallized a vision of the state as a transcendent community of a
mutually constitutive private and public well-being. That fantasy of classlessness makes class the solvent of American difference, aka the American
Dream, as the editors of *Fortune* well knew when they also ran a series of
articles on the subject.

This internationalist vision is observable in the very different careers of
three novelists: Kay Boyle, Julian Green, and Frederic Prokosch. The first
two were holdover expatriates from the '20s who did not return to the
United States until the Nazis made living in France too dangerous. All three
writers were understood by their reviewers to provide a fully cosmopolitan
context to the American novel, and all would eventually be ignored, despite
the many awards and honors they received, precisely because the international cast to their novels enjoyed neither the glitter of Henry James's
beau monde nor the guts of the Abraham Lincoln Brigade. In fact, Green
wrote in French, was understood by French readers to be a French author,
and was elected to the Hall of Immortals. By no stretch can he be considered
in the Howellsian line: his imagination was generally focused on psychological difficulties, the tortured lives of lonely, sensitive people, in such novels as
The Strange River (1932), *The Dreamer* (1934), *Midnight* (1936), and *Then
Shall the Dust Return* (1941). On a more quotidian basis but with her own
energetic experimentalist urge, Boyle examined the complexity of international marriage and love affairs, considering in *Plagued by the Nightingale*
(1931) and *Year before Last* (1932) the tension between the financial rationales and medical dangers of having children. She also published *Gentlemen, I Address You Privately* (1933), about homosexuality; *My Next Bride*
(1934), on American expatriates who must choose between love or money;
and *Death of a Man* (1936), where an American woman renounces her love
for a Nazi doctor, among others. Like Green, Boyle was an accomplished
short story writer too.[62]

Literary historians have wrongly neglected the career of Frederic Pro-
kosch.[63] Winner of the Harper Prize in 1937 and the Harriet Monroe Poetry
Prize in 1941 (he published poetry in the inaugural number of the *Kenyon
Review*), Prokosch wrote several novels devoted to an international stage,

like *The Asiatics* (1935), about an American's travels across Asia; *The Seven Who Fled* (1937), on the struggles of European exiles in Asia; *The Skies of Europe* (1941), concerning Europe on the eve of war; along with a novel, closer to home, on a young hobo's drifting from Wisconsin to Texas, *Night of the Poor* (1939). Later, Prokosch wrote novels about spies in wartime Lisbon, postwar European decadence, the African jungle, and the Indian prince who built the Taj Mahal. Of course, such a career did not fit into the categories of American fiction developed in the '30s and perpetuated in the '50s. Nor could his novels be figured into any of the conventional classifications that American literary historians were developing. As the *Saturday Review of Literature* observes of Prokosch's farewell tour of the Continent, *The Skies of Europe* succeeds in meeting his self-professed greatest desire: to make "an approach to writing which exceeds national limitations, both in its matter and mentality."[64]

The neglect of such writers reminds us that prejudices of class, race, and gender alone do not prop and shape historical evaluation. One constraint apparently enforced on American writers is that the subject matter must be the question of what should concern an American imagination, middle class or otherwise. These novelists' careers ask what represents the scene of an American novel, the answer to which is apparently something set within the national boundaries (and more lately the Caribbean) or written about American nationals. That these novelists are so rarely considered in their time suggests that even before the era of consensus politics, there was a powerful ideology of exclusion at work in the culture. Prokosch and Boyle were read on their own terms in their own day, but literary history has no way of placing them, even now that critics try to envision national literature in a more broadly geopolitical way than their predecessors did. In its commitment to testing the generalizability of its vision by extrapolating the uniqueness of its mapped object, regionalism plays an important part in effecting the vision of homogeneity at the center of this negotiation, since it could be exploited to signify the differences proliferating in the culture, even as the regionalist imagination ultimately revels in the pettiness of those differences. Boyle, Prokosch, and Green, on the other hand, render an American literature not so identifiably American, a literature neither in the United States nor, seemingly, of the United States. Their impulse is antithetical to the regionalist, insofar as they abjure the potential of the American place to shape or frame the real worlds they imagine. Nor are they, in the Jamesian sense, passionate pilgrims who test the efficacy of American values in their conflict with foreign cultures.

Their fiction is American, but not in the sense that it supports any nationalistic or even antinationalistic program—literary or otherwise—of what American writing might be or wishes to become. If Josephine Lawrence gives us a picture of America all too close to home, a domestic world where readers recognize their familiar worlds of discomfort and apprehensiveness, these other writers, often in symbolic allegories, distance themselves from the mainstream of bourgeois American readers by rendering an unrecognizable America, foreign and unknown, one that cannot be appropriated and made our own by an interpretative act of goodwill or a handy new conviction about the way society is put together. Other novelists will find something exotic and unversed on the mainland, a sense of America that can be incorporated with an enhanced, renewed view of the American Way, but these novelists give no such relief or reassurance and wish to go outside our borders to find out about our appetites and concerns. To this extent, they do not typically pretend that they know America from within. Instead, they are consummate outsiders, whose imagination might be false or flawed, as their reviewers attest (since almost all of their books were met with some sort of deep division of opinion), but not inauthentic. The interest that Prokosch and Boyle, and to a limited extent Green, pose for this study can be found in the way they discovered an American sensibility in the world beyond U.S. borders. Indeed, there were other writers of mainstream sensibility doing the same, primarily in the Caribbean, who less successfully developed a point of view American readers would recognize as similar to their own, yet did not derive from the nationalist or exceptionalist mentality permeating so much of the fiction of the era and its underscoring of the American Way.[65] These writers also sought a more fully cosmopolitan perspective.

That cosmopolitanism was not something that we ordinarily associate with '30s writing. On the contrary, when John Steinbeck published *The Grapes of Wrath* at the end of the decade, his novel seemed fittingly to draw almost entirely on several preoccupations of domestic American fiction—labor relations, regionalism, the family, public life, and, perhaps least well understood, the era's crisis of masculinism. So complete is that debt that Steinbeck's novel came to represent the fulfillment of '30s social realism, even as it emerged as a modern classic. In exposing the political and economic frameworks of the misery that migrant workers endured, *Grapes of Wrath* immediately won recognition for its power of sympathy, its urgency. Readers now might be inclined to see that the novel's monumentality rests on commitments more deeply sentimental than ideological, insofar as the novel reads the righting of the workers' abject plight less in the vaguely socialistic vision of union and more as the proper alignments of family feeling and relationship, a vision that also brings *Grapes of Wrath* into an even fuller coinciding with the middle-class fiction of the decade.

the 1940s

I begin this chapter by studying early '40s critical values, first by reading such key cultural texts as Mortimer Adler's *How to Read a Book* and Reinhold Niebuhr's *Faith for Living*, among other important works of the first two years of the decade, to help recuperate the kind of fiction that educated Americans were reading before Pearl Harbor and to trace the continuities in their taste through the war years and after. To that end, I also look at homefront writing, homecoming novels, and the postwar social environment by focusing on the tradition of middle-class realism, a survey that settles on two well-known problem novels of the day, Lillian Smith's *Strange Fruit* and Laura Hobson's *Gentleman's Agreement*. Again, I develop out of these novels the anxious wish to secure middle-class well-being insofar as the fiction serves as conduct manuals for readers who are "learning how to behave," as we also see in several other works of race and female growth and development.

HOW TO UNDERSTAND THE FORTIES

The change in literary history from the Depression through the war years seems obvious: the social realism associated with James T. Farrell and Richard Wright gives way to existential angst and the Cold War. The idea seems to have been that between Richard Wright's *Native Son* (1940) and Ralph Ellison's *Invisible Man* (1952), the only novel that counted was Norman Mailer's *The Naked and the Dead* (1948), as if the era were divided into two monolithic periods—the war and the postwar. Yet the more closely we examine '40s fiction, especially the tradition of middle-class realism, the more interestingly does this decade come into view. We find American novelists challenged by the prospect of war; we also see how in the midst of World War II several versions of realism compete to occupy, some might say to distract, the nation's literary imagination. A fuller understanding of how fiction developed after the war also helps us to see more clearly than we already do how the country responded to the major changes it witnessed in so brief a span, the cultural dynamics displayed in the nation's move from Depression to global power. This shift, in turn, also elucidates many of the shaping interests of '50s fiction.[1]

As the forties begin, the histories tell us, the dominant novelistic virtue is social realism, especially as it presents the case of the dispossessed laborer and the despised minority. For all their monumentality, neither *Native Son* nor *The Grapes of Wrath* was radical enough to escape their fate as Book-of-the-Month Club selections. Yet the emphasis on the realism of the oppressed affords only a limited vision of that twilight period during which the Depression seems to have abated but before America entered the war. To Harry Hansen, whose annual roundup, the "Literary Scene," appeared in *Publisher's Weekly*, 1940 was notable for being normal, lacking "skyrockets, pinwheels and gorgeous bombs."[2] In 1939 and 1940, the giant shadow of Thomas Wolfe figured prominently with the posthumous appearance of *The Web and the Rock* and *You Can't Go Home Again*. According to Hansen, 1940 was also time for a new installment of James T. Farrell's series on Chicago's Irish population—*Father and Son*, which was the second of the Danny O'Neill novels, a better book, reviewers agreed, than any of the *Studs Lonigan* trilogy. (Farrell's 1941 novel, *Ellen Rogers*, also met with acclaim.) Faulkner published *The Hamlet*; *The Last Tycoon* appeared after Fitzgerald's death. Following *Christ in Concrete* in 1939, Ruth McKenney's *Industrial Valley*, and Herbst's *Rope of Gold*, the proletarian movement seemed to have run its course, with the exception of Albert Maltz's *The Underground Stream* (1940).[3]

American middle-class fiction continued to tell its story of victory over the Depression. On the one hand, a satirical critique, like Mari Sandoz's *Capital City*, informed readers that there had been no triumph at all, that American fascism was everywhere on the rise (especially in the Midwest), that anti-Semitism and Negrophobia were rampant, and that the frontier was irretrievably gone, no longer an arena of economic and social redemption. Yet more novels emerged from the Depression with a happier vision of America's social regeneration, novels that, taken together, were leavened with caution—over the war in Europe as well as the economic scene, as we have already seen in Dorothy Canfield Fisher's *Seasoned Timber*. Critics argued, generally, that the day of the topical novel was growing ever shorter. Novelists, they contended, simply could not keep pace with the day-to-day life, for the tempo of life had changed so dramatically that it was impossible to stay ahead of the newspapers—an increasingly familiar complaint. Their anxieties answered not only to the speed of modernity but also to its ephemerality, its heightened susceptibility to change, and its resistance to documentation, in ways that William Dean Howells could not foresee in creating the doctrine of critical realism.

We might dwell over these threshold years because so much is supposed to have changed soon thereafter in the nation's literary life, along with all the changes that came so indubitably with the war. We take for granted, as we should, that the whole cultural history of the country in the twentieth century was irrevocably altered as a result of the upheavals caused by World War II. We can measure the force of these discontinuities—on which so much of contemporary America's cultural identity depends—by comparing the fiction immediately preceding the war with later novels. Those differences may be routinely invoked, but there is little sense of the continuities, at least in literary taste and representation, a sense that helps to explain how much like the fiction of 1940 and 1941 were the novels from the first few years after the war.

The years before the war might be crucial to a fuller understanding of the use and appeal of bourgeois literature because this fiction may represent America in its last unironic moment, that is, the moment before the widespread watching of TV detached us from preceding generations. This cultural watershed also pinpoints a demarcation in the nation's literary history. The novel had warded off the threats that the movies and radio posed during the '20s and '30s, but it could not withstand television nearly as well. By the end of the '50s, we readily postulate, America entered a postliterate age, one of irreversible decline in the general reading tastes, one that transfigured, even eroded, conventional literary values.

America in 1940, however, was still so much a reading culture that it made Mortimer J. Adler's *How to Read a Book* one of the better-selling nonfiction books of the year. Written by a University of Chicago traditionalist, this manual, subtitled "The Art of Getting a Liberal Education," aimed to teach average readers how to read critically—that is, for analysis, interpretation, and significance. Adler's 400-page tract had several purposes but was mainly a brief against contemporary education, especially as it was presided over by the progressive social scientists in the schools of education and, before the heyday of the New Critics, the semanticists of the English departments. Adler also wished to make the case for the kind of liberal education he did admire, the kind that he delivered to his students and that undergraduates were experiencing at the newly founded St. John's College in Annapolis. For Adler, the stakes of the argument were imperative; his last chapter, "Free Minds and Free Men," reminds readers in ways comparable to George Orwell that in an age of such relentless propaganda, the capacity to read analytically and think clearly would ensure that citizens of a democracy were persuaded only by reason, not some baser faculty.

Adler's great concern is teaching average readers to meet the great books —he lists 131 of them—on those books' own terms. He is less interested in the fate of an American university system that he scorned than in fostering adult education, which for Adler might be the last best hope for the resurgence of an educated citizenry—so low was his view of professors and the new academic type, the specialist. In effect, his book goes over the heads of the academic bosses and appeals to educated citizens themselves. For all of Adler's zealous hope for the future of the liberal education—and the discipline of what he saw as "learning from our betters"—he understood quite rightly the middle-class American desire to be educated, an ideal that takes a much more classical shape than the specialists meant to foster. More than sixty-five years later, we no longer imagine that, at a time when we see the proliferation of manuals for "dummies," such a book could sell as successfully as Adler's, though his royalist successor at Chicago, Allan Bloom, addressed a similar state of dissatisfaction in the 1980s to similar effect in his jeremiad, *The Closing of the American Mind.*

While Adler had little to say about specific novels, he understood that fiction was a principal feature of the reading to which the last third of the book, "The Rest of the Reader's Life," is devoted. Novelists comprise only 10 percent of his list of great books, and only Herman Melville and Mark Twain represent U.S. writers, whereas modern novelists are known through James Joyce, Marcel Proust, and Thomas Mann. It seems superfluous even to mention that Adler's greats exclude women and nonwhites (not even Confucius). But enshrined in this roll call of elite culture is a vision of fiction that has proved surprisingly enduring, albeit a canon not quite as unassailable as Adler would like: Henry Fielding and Laurence Sterne, Stendhal, Balzac, and Gustave Flaubert, William Thackeray and Charles Dickens, Dostoyevsky and Tolstoy—in short, the great tradition of British and continental realism.

Adler's "how-to" for reading fiction resembles a program that John Crowe Ransom, whose momentous book, *The New Criticism*, which appeared in 1941, would have approved. Four rules obtain: (1) Don't try to find a "message" in a novel, play, or poem; (2) Don't look for terms, propositions, and arguments in imaginative literature; (3) Don't criticize fiction by the standards of truth and consistency that properly apply to communications of knowledge; and (4) Don't read all imaginative books as if they were the same.[4] In a sense, Adler is instructing general readers of the early '40s in what would eventually become academic dogma in the postwar years. Facilitating that training was a triad of textbooks—*Understanding Poetry* (1938), *Understanding Fiction* (1943), and *Understanding Drama* (1945)—that Cleanth Brooks and Robert Penn Warren, and later Brooks and Robert Heilman, created out of a kindred plan to codify the "intensive reading" that was already being called the "New Criticism." The first edition of *Understanding Fiction* concludes with a peroration that the "underlying significance of all fiction" is found in a writer's "faith" in the significance of experience, "not a mere flux of unrelated items." This tenet valorizes both the cogency of works of artistic complexity and their consistency with a vision of a moral universe: the writer thus has "faith that man is a responsible being, and he tries to validate this faith by the responsible and vital organization of his art."[5] Out of this ethics of formal coherence, Adler too had instructed his readers in how to discover in fiction the illumination they would demand of it throughout their lives.

FAITH FOR LIVING

The desire to wrest this power of illumination from literary works parallels how middle-class citizens also determine meaning in their existence. That spiritual need to find sustenance through interpreting and coming to terms with a threatening modernity marked another crucial book of the year. By 1940, Lewis Mumford was already well ensconced among the premier public intellectuals. Some of his cultural histories and analyses were considered classics, and he could count on a broad audience of thinking people, essentially liberal in their politics and progressive in their attitude toward culture and foreign relations, to engage his arguments. So when J. Donald Adams, editor of the *New York Times Book Review*, panted his approval of *Faith for Living* (1940) in a front-page review, it seemed to augur the enthusiastic admiration that Mumford's previous volume, *The Culture of Cities* (1938), had already secured.

To bolster the spirit of the country by providing an alternative to the alluring despair of a world already embroiled in war, Mumford focused on the positive forces in the United States. Yet *Faith for Living* turned out to be one of Mumford's least memorable books, one that did not achieve an audience among the students of cultural formation who found Mumford such an imposing presence or among the many general readers, then or later. Some readers may have recognized the book, as theologian Reinhold Niebuhr did, as Mumford's effort to revitalize the discussion of liberalism so it could battle the "negative and diabolical religion which is fascism," which many observers saw as the primary threat to the nation's stability. Thus Mumford participated in a series of books on the "destiny of democracy"—as *Books* grouped them together—that meditated on the ways out of the Depression and toward a healthier economy or happier society.[6]

For Mumford, the three principal sites of U.S. decline are the family, the relation between the human spirit and locale, and the cultivation of the individual. Instead of developing these, Americans have allowed a "passive barbarism" or primitivism to overwhelm them in the body politic as well as in their collective soul. That complacency is reflected in novels and the theater, as well as Americans' callousness about violence and morbid interest in the horrible. In general, Mumford warns, the massification of this response deadens the culture's potential; yet as Malcolm Cowley observes in the *New Republic*, "The trouble with [Mumford's] prescription for defending the spirit of democracy is that it means losing the substance of democracy."[7]

Mumford's "faith for living" bears a striking affinity to the lessons of bourgeois novelists at their most discerning. Although realist fiction in 1940 and 1941 did not often explicitly acknowledge the real presence of the fascist threat, many novels examine as the loci of cultural crisis the same three areas Mumford sees as most imperiled. These are among the enduring subjects of middle-class culture—family, the relation to the environment or region, and the development of the self. Beyond the headlines of modernist literary history, novelists were perceived to be trying to fortify middle-class ways of being. T. S. Eliot brought out *The Dry Salvages* and *Burnt Norton* in 1941, but the only novels we would think of from the modernist tradition published in that year were Gertrude Stein's rather inconsequential *Ida* and Fitzgerald's posthumous fragment, *The Last Tycoon*. Guiding modern lights like Theodore Dreiser and John Dos Passos were instead writing mainstream pep talks such as *America Is Worth Saving* and *The Ground We Stand On*. The only true modernist prose classic of the year was not a novel at all but Agee and Evans's *Let Us Now Praise Famous Men*.

On the other hand, in 1941 conservative and progressive critics alike found something deeply resonant in Ellen Glasgow's novel of generational strife, *In This Our Life*, which Cowley, for one, hailed for breaking through its surface optimism to reveal a glimpse of a civilization on the brink of chaos. John Marquand's *H. M. Pulham, Esq.* uses the occasion of a college reunion to deliberate over the meaning of the last quarter century, a meditation on the sojourn of one generation's experience between the Great War and the impending World War II. In Booth Tarkington's *Heritage of Hatcher Ide*, the 42-year-old veteran of American novel writing turns his attention to one of the '30s preoccupying themes and one of his perennial ones—youth versus the older generation in times of economic hardship—out of which he develops a story of how the newly beset privileged class faced their embarrassments and managed their defeats during the Depression.

Among other respected talents who published novels during the first two years of the new decade, several mined the past or the remote to sustain the present. One might cite Louis Bromfield's story of social tension in *Night in Bombay* (1940) or his *Wild Is the River* (1941), a Civil War novel. Willa Cather drew on her memories of an earlier America in *Sapphira and the Slave Girl* (1940), where a daughter works to undo her mother's racism, or two novels of American expansion—Conrad Richter's first installment of his trilogy of the settling Ohio, *The Trees* (1940), and Carl Carmer's *Genesee Fever* (1941)— along with ever-popular Edna Ferber's story of the late nineteenth-century resort, *Saratoga Trunk* (1941). It is true that many of the most esteemed books during these transitional years relayed the Depression's interest in redemptive history, including Caroline Gordon's *Green Centuries* (1941), a tale of the Southern frontier, and Howard Fast's *The Last Frontier* (1941), which chronicled the Cheyenne Indians' trek from Oklahoma to Wyoming, as well as Ben Ames Williams's tale of nineteenth-century Maine, *The*

Strange Woman (1941), and Chard Powers Smith's intriguing study of the gendered distribution of labor at the end of the 1800s in *Ladies Day* (1941).

Beneath the stratum of books by such established novelists ran a vein of fiction much more explicitly engaged with locating a "faith for living" in the present than in scrutinizing the past. These books have passed completely out of our consciousness for no particular reason, except that they do not fit the paradigm of literary history that the world war is supposed to divide. As lively, challenging studies of contemporary mores, such fiction helped to examine America at the present hour—life after the Depression but before Pearl Harbor. The faith such novels sought to confirm would inevitably come to seem outdated, a nostalgic hankering for a moral code that derived from the culture of the Social Gospel. At the same time, these novels about the current state of American flux took up topics like the new hobo life or the drift toward prostitution. One writer that historians of the decade have forgotten, Caroline Slade (surprisingly so, since her husband was president of the Yaddo Corporation, which provided so many fellowships for artists and writers), raised the issue of how women—some on the edge of middle-class life—were turned into sex workers; from book to book, she examined how the temptation takes shape, especially under the aegis of a failing relief system. Especially is this the case in *The Triumph of Willie Pond* (1940), where the heroine turns to the sex trade to support her family.[8]

Similarly, there also appeared several versions of tramp fiction, of which the most famous example is Steinbeck's *Of Mice and Men* (1937), but a form so robust that in 1939 alone there were several variations, including one devoted to wandering girls—Darragh Aldrich's *Girl Going Nowhere*—that tried to give the problem a hopeful twist. At the other end of the spectrum was the comic, hard-bitten tale of three carousing male hoboes in G. S. Perry's *Walls Rise Up*. Also appearing that year was Frederic Prokosch's previously cited *Night of the Poor*, treating a boy's trek from Wisconsin through Texas and the witness he makes of an impoverished, appetitive, murderous America. William Attaway's *Let Me Breathe Thunder*, which was also praised as "poetic," describes the adventures of two young tramps and the Mexican boy they adopt. In 1940, Edwin Corle gives the subject a Southwestern treatment in *Solitaire*.

Perhaps the best way to understand the state of American fiction before America's involvement in World War II is to contemplate the novels reviewed in the weekly supplements of the *New York Herald Tribune* and the *New York Times* on Sunday, 7 December 1941, the day that Franklin Roosevelt said "will live in infamy." Both influential reviews offered retrospectives of the past publishing season. Some novels cited for distinction were works of the regional imagination, like John Selby's "graphic" novel about a Midwestern family's fortune, *Island in the Corn*, or Eloise Liddon's highly praised account of the rise of the Southern slaveholder class, *Some Lose Their Way*, a sort of companion novel to W. J. Cash's *Mind of the South* (1941). Others focused on how society is structured, as might be seen in Hilda Morris's *Landmarks*, about the determining forces underlying the founding of small towns; or Caleb Bruce's novel of a New York suburb as a melting pot, *Knickerbocker Gardens*; or Paul Corey's *County Seat*, the last of his trilogy devoted to an Iowa farming family in the years between 1910 and 1940.

There were a dozen good novels, though by and large not by Americans, about the war in Europe as well as pleasing, escapist stories about exotic places like Peru, the Caribbean, and South Africa. It is surprising to see how little explicit interest U.S. novelists seemed to take in the international crisis, dealing instead in the same three sources of regeneration that Mumford descried—family, the connection between spirit and place, and individual development. Cozzens's story of historical and political tensions experienced by a young American in Europe, *Ask Me Tomorrow* (1940), stands as an important exception. Although Tarkington was closing his career with another well-respected comedy about generational strife, *The Fighting Littles*, and Mary Ellen Chase's new giant best seller about life in coastal Maine, *Windswept*, was considered to be her best regional romance, these years were also notable for new authors like John Faulkner, admired for trying to discover a ground for hope and guidance. His novel about the limits of the Works Progress Administration (WPA), *Men Working*, earned more *uniform* praise by the daily reviewers than his more famous brother's books had recently done. Jerome Ellison's *The Dam* tells of a construction engineer, laid low by the Depression, who turns to the WPA for a chance to restore himself in a novel the *Times* called "huskily sentimental." Thomas Bell's continuing interest in the lives of immigrant Slavs yielded *Out of This Furnace*, while William Attaway's *Blood on the Forge* examined the lives of both white and African American laborers.[9]

In 1941 there were two books to recommend about the oil industry— Edwin Lanham's cautionary tale of striking it rich during the '30s boom,

Thunder in the Earth, and Mary King's portrait of field workers, *Quincie Bolliver*. One white author contributed a much-admired study of African American victimage, inevitably yet felicitously compared to Wright's *Native Son*, Arthur Kuhl's *Royal Road*, which was held to be a more sympathetic book than Elizabeth Wheaton's *Mr. George's Joint*, noteworthy for its authenticity and for "the objectivity of its author" in this portrait of the leisure activities of black workers in Texas. There were also novels about immigrant life, such as Sidney Meller's story of San Francisco, *Home Is Here*, as there were earlier in 1941, in Richard LaPiere's novel of the Chinese in San Francisco, *When the Living Strive*, a sociology professor's experiment with narrative. Popular novelist Kathleen Norris also had a family novel of San Francisco in that year as well. What "faith for living" these novels finally imparted lies in the middle-class wisdom of hard work and democratic opportunity that they promulgated. For such virtues were expected to provide the ballast to a puzzled and shaken nation. The fear that American isolationism would tacitly work to the Nazi advantage, however, was the subject of one of the biggest best sellers of 1941, Douglas Miller's *You Can't Do Business with Hitler*. Later in the year H. R. Knickerbocker's call to arms—*Is Tomorrow Hitler's?*—also warns unmistakably against U.S. "complacency" as "colossal, cosmic, suicidal."[10]

The promise that a faith for living could be discovered in fiction was affirmed, in late 1941 and then again in 1942, by two documents that were once central to the nation's literary conversation but that now need to be retrieved from obscurity. Both critics were held in extremely high regard in ways it now takes a pointed effort to apprehend. Contemporary American literary historians may find it difficult to appreciate Van Wyck Brooks justly, but for the educated reader of the first half of the twentieth century, he was, beyond any professor, among the most admired men of letters in the country. Although Brooks had begun by passionately criticizing the Puritans and the genteel tradition for the materialism they endorsed, he had also by the late '20s turned against the consolations that modernist writers conferred, leading him eventually to align himself with the very forces of conservatism he once battled. By 1941, he was arguing about the deleterious effects of that contemporary American writing in *On Literature Today*, a pamphlet that charged modernists with imbuing the country with a quietism inadequate to the fascist threat, and the monumental *Opinions of Oliver Allston*, a book whose charm has not lasted. The former work is less well remembered and tends to be blurred with Archibald MacLeish's similar claims in *The Irrespon-sibles* (1940), a book that by arguing against the influence of modernist and expatriate writers also helped to polarize the left and the middle on the spectrum of literary politics.

Much better known than the pamphlet was Brooks's *Opinions*. The unify-ing consciousness, "Oliver Allston," is a fictitious man of letters whose ideas are framed by his literary executor, Van Wyck Brooks. Allston, a New En-glander, leaves Brooks to disinter chapbook entries, obiter dicta, and critical views from his literary remains. None of the reviewers much minded the conceit, though few could see the appeal Brooks expected by couching his first-person address in a fictional character. Apparently the frame was sup-posed to imitate an eighteenth-century model of authority, along the lines Henry Adams crafted in his *Education*.

Allston's views on cultural and political affairs, as well as notes on "hu-man nature" and "American traits," make up much of the book, but a good third is devoted to literary history, criticism, and contemporary writing. In fact, the ideas that most struck reviewers were those relating to Allston-Brooks's worry that American writing had grown too concerned with the branches rather than the trunk of the tree of life. This dissociation from the faith for living—indeed, Mumford is singled out, with Robert Frost and Carl Sandburg, for a "courageous confidence in human nature"—has led modern writers into the sneering excesses of a "coterie-literature" in which a truly self-critical sensibility has sagged into formalist snobbery—psychologically diseased and socially harmful. Presided over by the spirits of Chekhov, Joyce, and Proust, along with such native examples as Hemingway and Faulkner, Dos Passos and Farrell, American fiction has lost its grounding—in the family, in the land, in the optimism of the human spirit. Even the greatness of American regionalism suffers from the prevailing hatred of small-town life, which the writers of the thirties so ferociously portrayed.[11]

Allston-Brooks turns to the regional to locate the promise of American literary life, which is not found in the remotest corners of the republic but in the generosity of spirit American writers make of their constraints. Quoting William James on the virtue of residing in America, Allston-Brooks critiques the cosmopolitan notion that only in the European capitals—or in New York—can writers transcend the limits of their backgrounds. The key is to think of region, as one might of one's generation, with a certain detachment, so it might be a resource, not a fetish. If they could do so, our writers might then create a "primary literature," affirming "honor, justice, mercy, love."[12]

Smile or grimace at the evident *derrière-garde* that the *Opinions of Oliver Allston* promotes, readers should not be surprised at how routinely Brooks's argument was seconded. Predictable as it was that the conservative journals endorsed this nativist point of view, we also find that as roughly as his argument is treated by the *Nation* and the *New Republic*, the mainstream press was much kinder to this literary extension of Mumford's vision; Brooks's argument won rousing approval in the *Saturday Review of Literature*, as well as in *Books*. Just as he touted *Faith for Living*, J. Donald Adams gave the first page of the *New York Times Book Review* to Brooks's compendium, since it seemed to the editor that here was "one of the most thoughtful and dynamic books in recent American writing."[13]

As forceful as Allston's impact was on opinion makers, the most influential critic in 1941 was not a promodernist like Philip Rahv or even Edmund Wilson, but the writer who arguably shaped more people's reading taste than anyone else in American history. As the critic who succeeded Henry Seidel Canby as the guiding force of the Book-of-the-Month Club and as the lead book reviewer of the *New Yorker*, Clifton Fadiman passed more judgments on more books in ways that likely had more results than any other figure of the first half of the twentieth century, including his Columbia schoolmate, Lionel Trilling, though the *Oxford Companion to American Literature* does not even record his existence.[14] Moreover, as a radio personality on the much-followed show, *Information Please!*, Fadiman reached an audience that would make today's critics searching for readers beyond academe shudder enviously. Nor did Fadiman betray this office by being fashionable or merely contrary, recondite, or provincial. He tried as best he could to raise the level of American taste without being false to his standards. Inconceivable as it is now, his 1941 anthology, *Reading I've Liked*, ranked seventh in sales among nonfiction books. Seventh!

Reading I've Liked is a 900-page selection of American as well as British and world literature—creative writing, speeches, and journalism—with Fadiman's brief introductions. One can readily see in Fadiman the middlebrow populist of elite culture that Joan Shelley Rubin has studied so intently, but that figure does not cancel out the critic with a surprisingly rich receptivity—someone who, by turns, can appreciate the urbane wit of Ludwig Bemelmans and the profundity of Thomas Mann's meditation on Nazi Germany. While some of the choices, not surprisingly, favor his *New Yorker* associates, his vision of modern American literature is a capacious, democratic one, including Sarah Orne Jewett, Ring Lardner, Hemingway, Steinbeck, Dos Passos, M. F. K. Fisher, Katherine Anne Porter, and Conrad Aiken. For our purposes, the significance of his anthology lies in the vision of American literature it endorses, though part of its interest also has to be the vision of culture it promotes: S. J. Perelman and Bertrand Russell in juxtaposition, or James Thurber and Chief Justice Oliver Wendell Holmes. Perhaps Fadiman, unlike Brooks, reached so many kinds of readers because he valued so many different kinds of writing. That eclecticism also suggests the capaciousness of middle-class taste and the admixture of humor and wisdom it could contain, though his critics might call it simply indiscriminate.

THE WAR AND ALL THAT

Among the younger writers of the early forties, Wallace Stegner stands out as a novelist who explores, in a series of books devoted to the settling, populating, and destroying of the American West, a "faith for living" similar to the middle-class writers of urban and suburban experiences. Stegner, along with DeVoto and Vardis Fisher, conceived of the gorges, mountains, and valleys of the Far West as well as its barren plains, as a fit terrain for examining the complex, even paradoxical moral and social issues played out there. True, Rocky Mountain fiction did not exert a wide, general appeal—maybe not even as much as Southwestern fiction did—but more than one reviewer saw that the new novels devoted to this region warranted further consideration and that the West could really be a literary subject in its own right rather than merely a contrast to the East. Walter Van Tilburg Clark had already won notice in 1940 for the *Ox-Bow Incident*, as an adroitly managed tale of the West that rehearsed the consequences of cattle rustling with the same fineness of perception that might be applied to assigning guilt or innocence in interpreting the onset of the war in Europe—or so its compact allegory of the ethical positions within international relations could be interpreted.

In 1942, Stegner, still in his early thirties, had not yet published a bona fide critical success. His early books—on Iowa, the Western prairie, and young communists—were more or less successful preludes to *The Big Rock Candy Mountain* (1943), the novel that would secure his reputation. As if to prepare readers for the imminent publication of his magnum opus about what a young Westerner makes of the shambles of his family, and what its underlying culture makes of him, Stegner issued a broadside, "Is the Novel Done For?" in *Harper's*, an assessment of the challenges facing American fiction, especially in this time of crisis.[15] Bernard DeVoto was the editor of the magazine, and never was there a stronger proponent of the West as the testing ground of the continental United States's spiritual and ideological empire. Indeed, the novelist's argument met DeVoto's critical needs: in supplying a platform for Stegner, DeVoto was also sustaining a favorite prejudice—the antimodernist diatribe he was about to publish as *The Literary Fallacy*, which followed Brooks and MacLeish in attacking the remoteness of the modern masters—Dos Passos, Hemingway, and Faulkner—and the insensibility of the critics who supported them. Rather forgotten today, DeVoto's little book proved controversial in its moment. With equal vigor Sinclair Lewis, in turn, denounced this notorious attack for its philistinism. DeVoto's argument resonated with MacLeish's nationalistic polemic, criticizing writers who insufficiently propounded democratic, as opposed to radical or alienated, responses to the maelstrom in Europe. MacLeish continued in this vein the next year by issuing the *American Cause*, another meditation on the responsibilities of the artist in a democracy. Unrewarding as later critics and scholars find the DeVoto-MacLeish nationalist arguments against artistic freedom, they give us a clue to what many contemporary students might miss about the '40s, distinguishing the democratic from the reactionary, within the general uncertainties characterizing the debate about the United States joining in the European conflagration.

For Stegner, the literary crisis before the nation had begun several years earlier. That fiction had declined since the Depression seemed a given. There had been a decline in quantity, to be sure—nearly half as many copies of novels (under 15 million) in 1939 were being published than in 1929 (nearly 27 million). Not only did the *Atlantic Monthly* and *Harper's* review fewer books, but they also serialized fewer novels and published fewer short stories. Readers' interest, Stegner says, had turned to journalism, captivated by the new social psychology of the "must-read" books. Such writing applauded facts over truth and thus, especially in wartime, was likely to seem more serious and indispensable, less of a luxury than fiction. During World War II, the sales figures of journalistic accounts of the war, or the events leading up to it, dwarfed the interest in novels. Best-seller lists routinely featured books about battles, diplomacy, and politics, not to mention Ernie Pyle's famous photography collections.

Journalism, Stegner posits, had surpassed fiction in several ways, "coating the pill of information with all the devices of the novel"—beginning with a hook, utilizing dialogue, character, and situation, first-person perspective, all by way of "making plausible implausible facts" instead of what verisimilitude once effected, that is, "making plausible implausible fictions." But the real test for novelists was less the redoubtable advances of journalism than the "domain of the spirit," the "novelist's quarrel with the world." Quoting an anonymous critic who believes that serious writers can no longer escape the sense of doom and victimhood in the influence of Newton, Darwin, Freud, and Marx, Stegner demurs: "If we have lost our consciences, given up our wills to Freud and Marx, transferring the responsibility for our actions to our parents or environment or conditioning, and if our novelists hold up the mirror to show us as we are, we cannot complain . . . if our novelists have cheated us into believing ourselves worse off than we are, then we can complain."

Yet the real problem for novelists, as he saw it, was not complacency or cynicism, but their submission to "effeteness or despair, to be swallowed up by the Zeitgeist, rather than energetically to oppose it." Contemporary novelists "admit too readily that they are prisoners in the world, puppets of economic necessity, bondsmen of psychological necessity, moral waifs, ethical mavericks, religious orphans." Thus, they fail to remember that their greatest challenge as writers is that "America's fate has been always to be compared with perfection." Were they mindful of this, novelists would see that they must abjure the mere ethical "grammar" that the modern philosophers provide, replacing it with "a higher authority," "usage" that is daily life. In short, these writers have betrayed their office: "Aspiring to lead and instruct their society, novelists have been instructing it in a language [of quietude and complacency] it does not understand, and leading it in a direction it does not want to go, and they have done so because they did not understand the language of their own society or accept the direction of its development."

Stegner's article was only one in an ongoing discussion of the responsibilities and prospects of novelists during a time of war. Significantly, it appeared in a venue for the dissemination of middle-class cultural values like *Harper's*, which, along with *Scribner's* and the *Atlantic Monthly*, was the magazine whose articles members of the middle class might be counted on to read and from which they might draw their cultural guidance as middle-class citizens. So it is instructive, though not at all startling, that Stegner's case against American writers would be made there.

More of a jolt was that less than two years later, Diana Trilling, the regular fiction reviewer of the *Nation*, made a similar attack, also in *Harper's*, on the current state of American fiction. Trilling observed that despite the inflationary spiral that came with the war, books had become more affordable, just when, in 1944, paper began to be rationed. The reason that novels, as well as the classics, history, biography, science and technology, and reprints of famous authors, were enjoying this new popularity was a "cultural advance" gaining momentum throughout the interbellum period, mostly the result of the ever-narrowing gap between the privileged and the uncultivated sections of society, the formation of a kind of intellectual no-man's-land, known as the "middlebrow." The emergence of book clubs, lending libraries, and digests (like the *Reader's Digest*) met this ever-increasing demand for certifying the acculturation of consumers that the rise in college-educated Americans, since the '20s, required. Yet even as Trilling approves of this apparent new readiness to live with ideas, she reminds readers that instead of enjoying a "general cultural renaissance" or a "specifically literary one," the country is "in the midst of a period of acute creative poverty," with reviewers answering the call for new fiction to read (and buy) by praising the "next best thing." Rather than await a "truly fine book"—since those are always in such short supply—it is the "keeping abreast of the market that obscures [reviewers'] recollection of what it meant to read Dreiser or Cather."[16]

Trilling was, first of all, an especially expert reviewer, with a talent for exposing fuzzy thinking and bad writing. She did not speak exclusively to the left, but she certainly spoke to its political and social concerns, which were well known to her and with which she had sympathized, briefly, during the early 1930s. Her critical judgments were regularly tendered in a magazine that, by and large, was made up of a minority perspective of the cultural and political arguments of the day, yet her premises would ultimately be the regnant ones. Trilling's remarks will seem familiar, not because they were so readily available at the time, but because the ideas she drew upon, a liberal critique of liberalism, became an everyday critical understanding. For her, the saddest aspect of the recent decline in literary values was that American fiction's deterioration over the past fifteen years had occurred just when the

demand for better taste and learning was growing. American fiction following the first world war—she cites the familiar modern roster—flourished
handsomely but died ignominiously with the advent of the Depression. For
Trilling, the thirties were a wasteland: Marquand, Faulkner, Wolfe, Steinbeck, and Farrell were each flawed (Faulkner was "essentially a virtuoso";
Marquand, a reporter; Wolfe, cursed with a "limited range"; Steinbeck had a
"fatal softness at the bone of his social understanding," while Farrell was
unable "to enlarge upon his own restricted background").

The problem lay in the new relation to the social order, in part brought
about by the war, but more fully by a development of the artist's changing
place in society. The '20s novelist had rebelled, but in the '30s the "progressive and sensitive novelist saw himself as the conscious instrument of social
forces," someone who must "make practical alignments," a difference to be
observed in the contrast between Dreiser's *An American Tragedy* (1925) and
Robert Cantwell's *The Land of Plenty* (1934). When Trilling surveys the current state of that kind of writing, she is moved to wonder whether those who
once made up the "vanguard" were ever "really as promising as we thought
them or whether they simply claimed so much of our hope because they
were so sympathetic to the spirit of the time."

The writers who now are truest to their situation are those who are "as
busy today exhorting to democracy" as they were "exhorting to the class
struggle ten years ago." Inevitably, a "literature of nationalism" has emerged,
rarely as embarrassingly jingoistic as MacKinlay Kantor's *Happy Land* (1943)
or the propagandistic historical novels that exist only to impart a moral for
contemporary society. But, in the end, Trilling is more worried about the
fiction that is unaware of itself as "teaching lessons" in a "national pattern of
thought" to the extent that so much of '40s fiction means nothing less than
saluting the status quo, past and present: "The values of our present-day
novels are the established values. Our fiction would have us love what we
have and hold on to it . . . have us love what we once *had* and recapture it."
Trilling bases her argument about the present "barrenness of scene" by
instead invoking the moral inertia to be found in the theme of "domestic
strength" that animates a giant hit like Betty Smith's *A Tree Grows in Brooklyn* (1943) or a lesser one like Elizabeth Janeway's *The Walsh Girls* (1943),
along with *So Little Time* (1943), Marquand's saga of the middle-aged generation's anticipation of the war. Even Lillian Smith's *Strange Fruit* (1944) is

compromised, able "openly to admit lawless conduct and at the same time condemn it."

Through the representation of "sexual freedom, feminism, insight into economic sources of our social ills," contemporary fiction was "determined to buttress us against the threats implicit in an uncertain political world." Disclosing this subtle, pervasive pattern was the reinvigoration of the new conservatism to which the vogue for religious novels attested. Indeed, throughout the war, several best sellers offered a religious historical theme —notably Lloyd Douglas's *The Robe*, Sholem Asch's *The Apostle*, Franz Werfel's *The Song of Bernadette*—sometimes enjoying high popularity for two years or more. In contrast, just as tellingly, the kunstlerroman failed to generate novels in which artists-in-the-making must contest a concretely particularized, much less fully realized social world or falter into subjectivism.

Like Stegner, Trilling discovers the critical spirit dwelling in nonfiction, not novels. "There is a tempo and change of scene in our current journalism that parallels the movies and in contrast to which our fiction is bound to seem slow and static." Journalism enjoyed the freedom of movement that the war denied novelists and was newly galvanized by reporting worldwide battles, leading Trilling to call journalism the "eyes of modern writing." Moreover, radio coverage demanded a capacity to evoke clear visual images, and the newsreels and photography necessitated reporters who could tell what they saw as honestly as possible. The result was that "our reporters dare to see that they do see; and it is because our novelists do not dare to see or want to that they do not see."

As much as wartime journalism replaced fiction in the national imagination by providing drama as well as supplying the culture with "objects of admiration" and "objects of identification," fiction will not "disappear," since the one sphere journalism seems unable to penetrate—a year before the newsreels of the concentration camps or the reporting of atomic devastation —is the one most central to the novel, the moral imagination. Novelists must reclaim the "free play of critical intelligence" in checking the "confusion of modern life": "If literature is to carry its full share in our future culture, and if fiction is to carry its full share in our literature, the novel will have to meet confusion with art—which, as E. M. Forster has said, is the moral order of the universe."

Citing Forster is felicitous, not because Trilling's husband was soon to publish a monograph on an important modern author whose stature was much higher in the mid-'40s than it is now, but because he evokes the modernist prejudice that fiction has declined, according to Diana Trilling, as a result of history deflecting artists from their modern errand. That mission is not simply to make life hard on the haute bourgeoisie, but to change the ways readers think and the ways they imagine. Literature plays a key role in this upheaval, because literature alone—with the help of the critical cognoscenti—is capable of righting the moral equilibrium, in Forster's sense. It is up to writers to live out an essentially romantic faith in their estrangement from material culture, resistance to social conformity, indignation at economic imbalance. First the Depression, then World War II, made writers "suicidally determined to reform, to comfort, or otherwise to find a place for themselves as anything but artists."

So revolted was Trilling by the novel's descent into the miasma of popular culture that, in considering the implications of journalist John Hersey's *A Bell for Adano* as the Pulitzer Prize–winner for fiction, she proposed that critics might be better repaid by studying popular literature in the form of the detective story or the romantic love story, as actually bringing "us into closer connection with reality than our healthy 'didactic' literature."[17] In pointing to the dangers of didacticism, Trilling recognized the limits of bourgeois fiction as well as any critic, and, rare among modern critics, had actually read enough of it to justify her position. Arguably, the next generation of writers would fail her just as ignobly in their collective inability to render a moral order. Yet contemporaneous writers and critics did not understand themselves to be as timid or as snobbish as Trilling or Stegner characterize them. From at least one point of view, the war had changed the social responsibilities of the novelist, a debate actively conducted in the pages of the *Writer*, a trade magazine that regularly published articles about what writers could do for their country.

A year into the war, Wallace McElroy Kelly speaks to the worry that gave Trilling her animus: writers are growing too conformist. Arguing in "Sincerity and the Novelist" that novelists have been given a new responsibility, one he calls a "patriotic duty," Kelly foretells that "it is for [novelists], as interpreters of the way of life which is being defended, to search that way of life for the ignored significance, the slightest appreciation and affection." "Writers of the American life we cherish" must cast aside "misguided doubts and misdirected cynicisms" and "must come to a newer, firmer faith. And that firm new faith from our deeper self-seeking, should prove to be a very old and warm and solid value which . . . we have too long neglected and the reader has been too long denied."[18]

It does no good to deride Kelly's search for faith as willful unconsciousness and self-blindness, much less a betrayal of the (modernist) dedication to art that makes true literature out of social report. On the contrary, Kelly takes a view antithetical to the modernist aesthetic values Trilling holds up as paramount, for in the deepest sense he is not concerned with art. Nor is he particularly interested in Mammon either. His point is the respectable one that novelists have different challenges at different historical moments, and while some may choose to follow the example of the poet Rilke and say nothing during years of upheaval, Kelly finds that the war "will bring to serious and sincere writers a more positive direction." To be sure, the very concept of the "sincere" was one of the first casualties of World War II, just as the concept of seriousness is one of returning wounded. Even the belief in the prospect of a "positive direction" seems deluded or laughable. What Kelly sees that Trilling does not is a change in the novelist's understanding of the novel's cultural mission, which, for Kelly, is determined to the extent that it serves the reader.

Yet Trilling sees what Kelly and like-minded novelists cannot. To retreat from rebellion is also to renege on the romantic-modernist conception of the artist, Shelley's unacknowledged legislator of the universe as the maker of moral order. Domestic novelist Margaret Banning, again in the *Writer*, answers this general charge about the same time Trilling is making it. For Banning, as a result of the war, not only is the writer's market different but also writers are changed too: "Old or young, male or female, this war makes a writer impatient with any kind of ivory tower." Banning details how writers like Canby and Fadiman, Robert Sherwood, and S. J. Perelman participate in the war effort since "the war takes every talent." For Banning, who wrote books in support of women's contributions to the war effort— *Women for Defense* (1942) and *Letters from England* (1943)—writers who live in time of war find their views changed. "Themes that once appealed to them have been dated or dwarfed by war. They have been proven unreal or trivial." Moreover, readers have grown more sophisticated, though it does not take a great prophet to know that despite demanding an ever-greater realism, they will not want only a literature of disillusion. Instead, based on successful novels with central characters of such "amazing disparity" as *A*

Tree Grows in Brooklyn, Charles Jackson's *The Lost Weekend* (1944), *So Little Time*, and *Strange Fruit*, novelists should be able to deduce that "it appears to be a good time to write truthful stories about anyone who is interesting," which to a culture on the brink of war means something that resonates with their readers' desires to recognize characters whose ways of meeting the life of challenge, upheaval, and change seem like models. If novelists write to that end, they will perform the "sound and useful job" of instructing their readers in the "puzzle of why things are as they are," especially as they appear on the home front.[19]

THE WAR AT HOME

Banning's assurances aside, what did wartime domestic fiction look like and what work did it do? How would we measure the efficacy or power of a national literature in an era of international conflagration where the toll of injury, damage, and death reached unprecedented levels? What becomes of bourgeois fiction? Even Howells, the great architect of the American social novel, lacking what Henry James called the "imagination of disaster," could only take chaos at a glimpse. The Spanish-American War yielded a wonderful story, "Editha," but the Great War left him speechless. What if Howells had not missed the Civil War through his minor diplomatic service in Europe and had been forced, like so many lesser talents, to meet the challenge of modernity at war? What if James himself, who at the end of his career wrote so movingly about World War I's devastation in *Within the Rim* (1918), had been compelled to confront the Holocaust? We remember no great contemporaneous novel of domestic life during the Revolutionary War, the Civil War, or World War I, so perhaps it demands too much of domestic realism that it should endow a literature of enduringly modern sensibility. Not for nothing did Tolstoy's *War and Peace* enjoy a brief renaissance of interest in America at the beginning of World War II. Fadiman even wrote an introduction to a new edition for a culture hungry to learn what it means to be a civilization at war.

The challenge facing writers was a regular subject for debate. Russell Crouse—playwright, Hollywood screenwriter, and president of the American Authors League—maintained that writers were combatants of sorts and exhorted the public to understand that the writers' war effort meant more than publishing new novels to bolster morale; it also encompassed penning thousands of pleas for bonds, as well as promotional articles, scripts, escape literature, and even skits to relieve the boredom of soldiers in the field. Every department of government solicited the Writers' War Board's help. (Well-known journalist and novelist Elmer Davis, ubiquitous in these pages, headed the country's ministry of propaganda, the mammoth Office of War Information.) For Crouse, the time would come after the war for new voices to be heard and old voices to reclaim their audiences: "American writers have won the right to be heard when men sit down to talk about their new world," and he predicts that "they will be heard."[20] Crouse's point was simply that these were not the times to be honing one's craft. Archibald MacLeish, a year after Pearl Harbor, argued that war was very much a writer's battle, but for MacLeish it was a conflict over ideas on which the very future of literature depended. For the poet, the question was whether the "writing of books is good for this time"; the country had lost confidence in the need for books, mostly as a result of the primacy the war effort placed on more streamlined communication—leaflets, newspaper columns, fifteen-minute broadcasts. In refurbishing what had already become a cliché, MacLeish explores the image of words as weapons: "The wars for men's minds . . . are not won with dead shells—with the banalities of unexploding words. . . . They are won by a labor of qualification and definition and illumination which requires for its accomplishment all the machinery of the intellect. And of all the implements which men have devised . . . none is to be compared with the formed and phrased development of concepts to which, for lack of better, we give the name of the book." In the kind of flourish that his detractors saw as posturing, MacLeish calls on writers to help readers discriminate about their democratic faith: facing the "disastrous possibilities of failure" and "inconceivable opportunities of hope," writers must "show us clearly the alternatives with which we are faced and enable us to choose wisely between them, or the war will truly be lost."[21]

The debate over whether the United States should enter the war did excite the nation's appetite for books about the state of our culture, though as late as 1940 not a single "war book" had been a best seller. By 1941, however, four such nonfiction titles succeeded: William Shirer's phenomenally popular account of prewar Germany, *Berlin Diary*; Alice Duer Miller's *The White Cliffs*, a book-length poem in homage to England, which Hitler had begun to bomb in August 1940; Jan Valtin's *Out of the Night*, an account of the Gestapo tactics; and Winston Churchill's selected speeches, *Blood, Sweat and Tears*.

Also circulating was Douglas Miller's forthright plea, *You Can't Do Business with Hitler*. Similarly, onetime agrarian Herbert Agar's *A Time for Greatness* argued that the time for America to join in the war had arrived.

That year middle-class Americans read a curious combination of nostalgia novels and contemporary chronicles from England: A. J. Cronin's *Keys of the Kingdom*, about a Scottish Catholic priest who, after his early years of struggle, goes to China where he serves a long tenure before returning to Scotland to die; that enduring tearjerker was followed by a novel from one of the most beloved writers of the era, the author of *Goodbye, Mr. Chips*, James Hilton, who scored another success with *Random Harvest*, the tale of a well-to-do businessman striving to recover the years his Great War experiences keep him from remembering. Eric Knight, author of the children's classic, *Lassie-Come-Home*, wrote *This Above All*, which ranks as one of the earliest British efforts to come to terms with the war, in this instance through the love affair between a disaffected working-class young man and the rich girl who tries to persuade him that England is worth fighting for. In the previous year, Americans had also bought two other British novels by the tens of thousands—Richard Llewellyn's *How Green Was My Valley* and Jan Struther's giant success, *Mrs. Miniver*, the portrait of a middle-class Englishwoman trying to keep her family together and survive the privations of war with something like ordinary British dignity. (Struther became quite a celebrity in the United States and Canada both for her study of stalwart, reserved English Womanhood and as a lively guest on the popular radio program *Information, Please!*) Both of these English novels were admired, as was novelist Margaret Kennedy's diary of life in England between the fall of Belgium and the height of the Blitz, *Where Stands a Winged Sentry* (1941). Why, however, should American readers divert their attention with English nostalgic fantasies and tales of heroism when they exacted more history and matters of fact from U.S. writers? It may be that the cultural interest English writers summon is always to be found in the charmed vision of another place, like Kismet, at least a place at one remove from the demographic complexities, dashed socioeconomic hopes, and partisan politics besetting the United States. Moreover, Americans' enthusiasm for England suggests how readily they identified with its brave model for resisting Hitler.

As might be expected, books bringing news about the war, especially the documentary literature that culminated in Ernie Pyle's photo-iconography of American soldiers, would remain atop the best-seller lists for the next few years. Even as these books fed the country's appetite for information, they also performed the solemn work of readying Americans to accept the reality of hundreds of thousands of casualties. Most especially was this the case for William L. White's *They Were Expendable* (1942), which in treating the bravery of GIs in the South Pacific, set the tone, certainly the example, for first-person accounts to come. As seriously as Americans read diplomatic memoirs like those of an ambassador to Russia (Joseph Davies's *Mission to Moscow* [1941]), battle reports (*Guadalcanal Diary* [1943], by Richard Tregaskis), or political meditations (Sumner Welles's *Time for Decision* [1944]), readers also turned in droves for the amusement found in *See Here, Private Hargrove* (1942), Marion Hargrove's comic first-person account of making a young American recruit into a GI, or Bob Hope's humorous travelogue of the first of his annual visits to the troops, *I Never Left Home* (1944), the year's best-selling book that helped to transform him from celebrated smart aleck into America's favorite comedian.

In the war's early years, British writers remained popular, in part because American readers found a powerful source of identification with a mother country—nearly 40 percent of Americans still claimed British roots—nor is it surprising that American books sold well in England during these years. Americans eventually moderated their taste for English fiction, turning toward a rejuvenated domestic writing that increasingly faced, as Banning has it, the needs of a domestic reading audience. Rarely realistic enough to suit Diana Trilling's sense of fiction's responsibilities, American novels, beginning in 1942, did try to mediate the challenges that the middle class was experiencing. When novelists tried to write the war at home, they generally failed, and only a handful of notable home-front novels survive, especially *Since You Went Away* (1943) by Margaret Buell Wilder (which was the basis for the three-hanky film of the same name) and *The Time Between* (1942), the story of a ten days' furlough by Gale Wilhelm (now better remembered for her several novels through the '30s and '40s concerning lesbianism). Philip Wylie offered a tale of a group's meditation on death, *Night unto Night* (1944), which followed his controversial, misogynistic study of American values, *Generation of Vipers* (1942), a distasteful collection of essays that is arguably one of the most indispensable works of the war years, having sold so many copies and excited so much comment that it established Wylie, for a few years at least, as one of America's moral arbiters. His critique of "Momism" responded to the cultural puffing of American mothers in order to reconcile them to giving up their sons to battle, an argument that presaged the much broader assault, during the postwar era, on American women who identified themselves centrally as mothers.

Middle-class fiction also extended beyond the historical and regional novels that had been two of the genre's leading forms. While Americans continued to relish a certain exotic escapism in romances by American, British, and Canadian authors, like Marguerite Steen (*The Sun Is My Undoing* [1941]), Daphne DuMaurier (*Hungry Hill* [1943]), A. J. Cronin (*The Green Years* [1944]), and Elizabeth Goudge (*Green Dolphin Street* [1944]), they now also turned for relief from wartime worries to American versions of escape fiction, like Kathleen Winsor's notorious historical bodice-ripper, *Forever Amber* (1944). Some of the most widely read serious romances also had historical and social themes, like Rachel Field's *And Now Tomorrow* (1942), which the *Atlantic Monthly* touted for the Pulitzer; Marcia Davenport's triple-decker generational novel of the Pennsylvania coal country, *Valley of Decision* (1943); and Betty Smith's aforementioned fond, sometimes bittersweet, recollection of an Irish American family and their neighbors at the turn of the century, *A Tree Grows in Brooklyn* (1943).[22]

Beyond the perennial interest in religious novels throughout the century, such works now testified to a growing optimism, or at least the need for a new faith for living, rather than an increased level of piety. Several reviewers called attention to the way world events, as *New York Times Book Review* editor J. Donald Adams put it, had wrought a "revolution in man's inner world." Writing on Independence Day, 1943, Adams sees the wartime enthusiasm for religious fiction as part of a culture's effort to renounce despair: "We are groping, but the groping is definitely in the direction of something to affirm, something in which to believe. The days of negation are as dead as the Lost Generation."[23] We can see in Adams's unconscious condescension the disregard with which such authors as Hemingway, Fitzgerald, and Faulkner were now held by the more conservative side of the literary establishment, which routinely understood them to be corrosively nihilistic, undermining readers' power to believe.

Although the time came when a sizable number of novels were accounting for the war, their commercial success was spotty and their critical success tenuous. Among the best sellers, a few titles were actually about, or tangential to, the war, though none have survived critically intact, including Steinbeck's *The Moon Is Down* (1942); Pearl Buck's study of the invasion of

China, *Dragon Seed* (1942); Hersey's Pulitzer Prize–winning *A Bell for Adano* (1944)—a choice roundly assailed in a year that saw the publication of *Strange Fruit*—and Harry Brown's *A Walk in the Sun* (1944), which many readers regarded as the first really strong U.S. war novel. More consistently popular were larger-than-life historical novels like Louis Bromfield's study of a Nevada matriarch, *Mrs. Parkington* (1943); Hervey Allen's captivity thriller about the French and Indian War, *The Forest and the Fort* (1943); and Irving Stone's story of Jessie Benton Frémont, *Immortal Wife* (1944). After writing a sweeping, contemporary historical novel, *Time of Peace, September 26, 1930 – December 7, 1941* (1942), tracing the movement from the isolationist politics of the '30s to a true appreciation of America's involvement in the war, Ben Ames Williams, an accomplished writer of historical fiction, turned away from both history and politics in *Leave Her to Heaven* (1944), a tale of sisterly intrigue. Also seen through this lens, though for more progressive political purposes, is Howard Fast's faithful account of George Washington, especially his crucial New Jersey campaign, *The Unvanquished*, among the most accomplished novels of 1942 and, later, Fast's novel about the thinking man's patriot, *Citizen Tom Paine* (1943), followed by his ambitious tale of the postbellum South, *Freedom Road* (1944).

How can novelists enter into a cultural conversation as meaningful as the current history being written by journalists? Some, like Steinbeck and Dos Passos, tried by publishing nonfiction like *Bombs Away* (1942) or *State of the Nation* (1944), respectively, or interspersed them with their novels. Dos Passos was one of the few modern masters who actually did try to write seriously about contemporary culture in his *Number One* (1943), which—as Robert Penn Warren specialists know—precedes *All the King's Men* (1946) in imagining a Southern demagogue following the pattern of Huey Long's career.[24]

Mostly the writers we know well kept silent during the war. Faulkner published nothing after *Go Down, Moses* (1942) and Hemingway, nothing (though he participated actively by letting his yacht be used to hunt submarines and serving intermittently as a correspondent in China and later Europe, where he was awarded a Bronze Star for the information he gathered). Only Glenway Wescott actually tried—in a novel about the German occupation of Greece, *Apartment in Athens* (1945)—to imagine how the war affected the interior life. The war years also saw the debuts of writers who would later be understood as minor, and thus unworthy, successors of the previous generation—Carson McCullers, Eudora Welty, Jean Stafford, John Cheever, and Budd Schulberg—though perhaps only Welty (*A Curtain of Green* [1941] and *The Robber Bridegroom* [1942]), Saul Bellow (*Dangling Man* [1944]), and John Cheever (*The Way Some People Live* [1943]) would sustain their initial praise by writing for decades to come. Irwin Shaw published his second book of stories during the war, but the war fiction for which he won so much fame—a collection of stories, *Act of Faith* (1946), and the novel that cemented his reputation, *The Young Lions* (1948)—came later. A host of lesser books from writers as well known as Lewis, Farrell, and Suckow confirms the idea that these years saw so little worthwhile.

Still, during the war, one can point to a dozen books substantive enough to warrant acclaim as rich works of middle-class realism. Jackson's *The Lost Weekend* was received as a powerful, controversial study of alcoholism. When the return of the GIs spawned a plethora of novels about trauma and readjustment, the topic would not seem so unusual, but Jackson's record of one man's descent as a result of his illness was heady stuff in 1944. Later, Jackson turned to other sociopathological "problems"—like the sterility of suburbia and homosexuality—but such books did not uphold his first great claim to success.

The Lost Weekend may well be the best known of a series of books that set up to examine American culture in the raw and the one most likely to be remembered today. Praised just as highly, or even more, were Maritta Wolff's novels, *Whistle Stop* (1941) and *Night Shift* (1942); both succeeded (the former more than the latter) in exciting interest in the lives of working-class Americans, without pursuing the revolutionary agenda of the '30s proletarian writers. Equally lauded was Ira Wolfert's Depression-era novel about the numbers game in Harlem, *Tucker's People* (1943), a forceful attack on monopoly capitalism. Nelson Algren's *Never Come Morning* (1942) was celebrated by critics as diverse as Rahv in the *Partisan Review* and Fadiman in the *New Yorker* for its portrayal of seediness and struggle within Chicago's Polish community.

One of the era's more interesting parables is Frank Fenton's *What Way My Journey Lies* (1946), which made bold to look at the problems of the disabled in a young man who leaves the Midwest for California, where he discovers friendship and fulfillment, but who must be rescued by his brother and brought back home. Such novels were often faulted for their subjectivism, seen as they were in the modernist vein, but in reality they were efforts to make physical and emotional disorders part of the purview of bourgeois fiction. Along these lines, more objectionably, was Alan Seager's unfortunate *Equinox* (1943), which tried to take seriously an incestuous relationship between father and daughter but wound up laying the blame on the daughter— "a mad, bad, and dangerous book," said Diana Trilling, though other critics were much more accepting, even approving, such as *New York Times* reviewer Marjorie Farber: "Exposing the incorrigible moralism of our culture (in its latest disguise) he has seen how we use psychiatric definitions to hide moral judgments."[25]

One development lies in the way that several of these novels were less steeped in the proletarian tradition and more readily located in the Howellsian grain of writers representing social challenges as primarily moral issues. Bourgeois fiction, on the other hand, took immediate shape as the effort to comprehend the cultural stakes of the war, and it was for that, more than anything else, that *Journey in the Dark* was awarded the Pulitzer Prize for 1943, having already received the annual Harper Prize that year as well. Martin Flavin's novel has no audience today, but it was taken then as summarizing national worries and the state of our collective soul. "In Search of America" (review by David T. Bazelon) was the headline at the *New Republic*; "The Rise of Sam Braden" (review by Wallace Stegner), announced the *Saturday Review of Literature*—implying a lineal connection to Howells's own Silas Lapham—and the "Story of an Average American" (review by Horace Reynolds) according to the *New York Times*. *Journey in the Dark* so thoroughly renders the culture of success in the first half of the twentieth century and gives historical background to our society's own formation that this "intelligent and conscientious" novel may be valuable for its sheer obviousness.[26] Flavin tells the tale of Sam Braden, who rises from his impoverished beginnings in Iowa to become, like David Levinsky, a lonely but "successful manufacturer." The difference is that the war stirs the hero out of his life of profit seeking and leads him to a job in a war plant, where he hopes to find meaning in his life.

One historian of the Pulitzer Prize has described *Journey in the Dark* as near the bottom of the list of novels that have won the award.[27] Other readers would contend that the previous year's winner, Upton Sinclair's *Dragon's Teeth*, was the worst, though its defenders could say that its representation of the realities of prewar Nazi Germany performed a mighty public service. Still others might choose the following year's winner, Hersey's *A*

Bell for Adano, as equally deserving this ignominious distinction. It does little good to name the fictions that might have won during the war years, like Smith's *Strange Fruit* (1944), Stegner's *Big Rock Candy Mountain* (1943), Faulkner's *Go Down, Moses* (1942), or Cozzens's highly regarded *The Just and the Unjust* (1942)—a courtroom drama in which the life of a community is put under close social and moral scrutiny and which was perhaps an even better novel than *Guard of Honor*, the Cozzens novel that did win the Pulitzer Prize in 1949. The perception among critics, then as now, was that the Pulitzer committee never chose the best book, but for all the slighted books, several overlooked wartime titles are mostly meaningless today—Conrad Richter's *The Free Man* (1943), Jesse Stuart's *Taps for Private Tussie* (1943), Caroline Gordon's *Women on the Porch* (1944), Feika Feikema's *The Golden Bowl* (1944), or Elizabeth Hardwick's *The Ghostly Lover* (1945).

The novel that most fully achieves the middle-class conception of the home front is John Marquand's *B. F.'s Daughter* (1946). Its predecessor, *Repent in Haste* (1945)—slim by the author's standards—seems less deliberate and less finely observed. In the earlier work, no social world ever really takes shape, without which Marquand's usual interests in the byplay between culture and psychology seem attenuated, in this case the casual bravery and the just-as-casual morality of Marquand's pilot-hero, who returns on a furlough to learn that his marriage is failing. *B. F.'s Daughter*, on the other hand, seeks the socially grounded and perhaps politically nuanced understanding that epitomizes the nation's anxieties and specifies the quality of life for a country at war. Wartime Washington is the locale for a story about the troubled relations between a tycoon's daughter and her husband, an English instructor turned military bureaucrat, one that provides a whole new range of social types, like intellectuals and New Dealers, for Marquand, the "spokesman of the embattled majority" (as Diana Trilling called him), to dissect.[28]

Otherwise, few wartime novels present a richly imagined scene of the home front. Although there were many romances that used the war as their backdrop, one book whose scenario epitomizes the tendency to make sense of the shifting meanings of an America at war, indeed making this subject explicit and direct, is Frances Parkinson Keyes's *Also the Hills* (1943). Keyes enjoyed a reputation for blending the contemporary scene and historical fiction and had a prolific career as what used to be condescendingly called a "woman's writer." In this novel, she turns to the circumstances of the war to give a deep background of a New Hampshire family, the Farmans. The parents are solid farming folk, but in departing from their traditions, their children lead lives summarizing modern American anxieties—the son, a Boston banker who joined the army; the daughter, a WASP beauty who gets entangled, first with a congressman and then with a fascist front organization; another daughter, who, abjuring marriage to the farmer next door, becomes a nurse. At the nadir of the family fortunes, the son's widow—a Creole beauty—comes to the farm to have the Farmans' grandchild. Not only is she a gracious spirit of redemption, but the money she brings also allows the Farmans to modernize and save the family homestead. "Loads of women will love it," observed reviewer Mabel Ulrich.[29]

Although *Also the Hills* turns on the presence of the Creole to restore the divisions in a white family, the home-front novel that might most effectively appeal to the contemporary taste is not about the World War II home front at all, but the world of the segregated South immediately following World War I. As much as any other book of the wartime era, Lillian Smith's *Strange Fruit* excited readers and critics alike. Banned in Boston (for obscenity), the book's treatment of miscegenation and murder—at the safe remove of two decades—made the country examine its taste for fiction, a taste that this Southern liberal writer understood was shaped by one's experience of race in the United States. The book shredded the nation's fabrication of unity, its fiction of working together for a common goal, and made readers see, under the aspect of one conventional if privileged white man's doomed passion for the light-skinned African American beauty who adores him, the cultural impasse that the United States would face again and again in the postwar era, one that came to be known as the "American Dilemma."

RACE AND THE IDEOLOGY OF TASTE

That Smith's novel exerted the appeal it did in the middle of a war seems unlikely, yet a careful look at the environment of fiction in the first half of the forties suggests that Americans were more conscious of race, and of the need to improve race relations, than might immediately be supposed. Literary historians' sense of race and the '40s always begins, as it needs to do, with Richard Wright, just as the collective sense of the civil rights era effectively begins with the return of black GIs, who were now determined to pursue the rights at home that they had fought to uphold in Europe and the

Pacific. All that is true enough, but such realities cannot account for the strange interest the country took in *Strange Fruit*.

Smith's novel and the study of race relations that Gunnar Myrdal undertook in *American Dilemma* (1944) were published just a few months apart. Both books were saluted for the light they cast on the "Negro problem," which may be defined as the white person's sense of how America could practice democracy without disturbing its systemic racist practices, especially segregation. In 1944, even the mildest arguments for integration met with a great deal of resistance. The conventional liberal position on segregation was ameliorative: out of fear of civil disorder, whites were reluctant to break up segregationist excesses. Instead, the liberal hope was that if accommodations had to be separate, they should also be, as nearly as possible, equal.

Or so the case was made in the *Atlantic Monthly* that year by David Cohn, a Mississippi journalist known for his liberal perspective. Cohn observed that whites and blacks who contemplated breaking down the wall of segregation by federal fiat needed to be cautious, not headstrong: "I have no doubt that in such an event every Southern white man would spring to arms and the country would be swept by civil war." Cohn concluded that as hopelessly permanent as segregation was, race relations could still be improved once blacks and whites agreed that the problem was, after all, "incapable of a solution."[30] If such thinking typifies one side of the presiding wisdom, more enlightened ideals were articulated in the *American Scholar*. In 1944, Otelia Cromwell, who had compiled a schoolbook of African American literature and who later wrote a biography of Lucretia Mott, published "Democracy and the Negro," in which she takes issue with exactly this sort of liberal "warning." Now it reads like a prologue to the civil rights movement: Cromwell reminds her Phi Beta Kappa readership that Southern segregation cannot exist without the compliance of other sections of the country and that a nation where the newspapers seem to foster race prejudice is "playing with dynamite." She recounts stories of the color bar closing in the Washington bureaucracy even in time of national emergency, tales so demeaning that she italicizes her exhortation that "*thoughtful Americans ought to acknowledge the mockery in what passes for democracy in their own country.*" She urges blacks to persist and reminds them to draw strength from the example of women's struggle for justice: "Acts of repression may increase in number, but neither violence nor sugar plums can muzzle the power of thought—thought that will keep acute the Negro's awareness of the rights that should be his."[31]

Cromwell's essay provoked no controversy at all in the *Scholar's* pages. Instead, the debate there was focused on American reading practices. The magazine had recently published "Why 100,000,000 Americans Read the Comics," an essay to which Cleanth Brooks and Robert Heilman replied in detail. Their position piece then gave literary academic Darrel Abel the chance to criticize these "intellectual critics"—in much the same way that a later generation of academics attacked "theory"—for its calculating formalism. Brooks responded with "The New Criticism: A Brief for the Defense," offering his once-famous reading of "Tears, Idle Tears."

This triangulated argument among America's comic book readers, the academic critics who meant to raise the country's appreciation for form, and the professors who feared that formalism was sucking the breath out of literary studies, was further mediated through an essay by Dorothy Canfield Fisher in the same issue as Cromwell's deliberations on democracy and African Americans. Out of her seventeen years' experience as a Book-of-the-Month Club (BOMC) judge, Fisher reflects on the "changing tastes of American readers," a phrase she puts in quotation marks as if to stress her remove from such a hackneyed topic, since neither she nor anyone else, she concedes, really knows. As Fisher recalls wondering during the exciting days when she first joined the BOMC Editorial Board, "Who was I to tell any fellow Americans what to buy?" The piece surveys the unlikely successes of several club choices, even as she cogitates on the uncertainty of predicting club favorites to observe: "What readers seem to like to find in a book is the feeling of contact with living, vital personalities. The traditional classification by subject matter—biography, travel books, humor, fiction, and so on—is quite irrelevant, since apparently what people enjoy in a book is meeting a fellow man that interests them."[32]

Fisher's perspective is important, especially given the editorial decisions she made and the influence she exerted over Richard Wright's *Black Boy* as well as for the familiar middle-class criterion of critical engagement she invokes, the capacity of a book to present a "fellow man." Out of deference to her record in supporting Wright's previous novel and her eminence, Fisher was asked to prepare an introduction for the autobiography, which she recalled she felt "very much honored to do." In fact, it was Fisher who not only reviewed Wright's new book for the BOMC, but also, in the spring of 1944, determined to sever the narrative at the point of young Richard's move to Chicago, thereby in a stroke dividing the book in two, which she, and ultimately Wright himself, imagined to have the effect of making it more acceptable to the club's predominantly white, middle-class clientele. Fisher guessed that these readers would delight in meeting the "living, vital personality" of young Wright, the rogue-naïf, rather than the urbanite flirting with communism. Nor does she suggest that Wright, who had already begun to think that the Southern years had their own unity, minded her judgment.[33]

Native Son and Black Boy were the two books by which African American experience was best known during these years, and so it would remain until Ralph Ellison's Invisible Man appeared in 1952. Beyond the fiction of Ann Petry and Chester Himes, however, at least two other books might have competed for preeminence, but neither the Negro Caravan (1941), edited by Sterling Brown, Arthur Davis, and Ulysses Lee, nor New World A-Coming: Inside Black America (1943) by Roi Ottley, could claim the imaginative resonance of Wright's works. Negro Caravan is a famous anthology welcomed in its time as "stirringly written," "entertaining and impressive," and, condescendingly, a "great book by a great people."[34]

Actually, New World A-Coming, a newspaperman's inquiries, bears comment as one of the few books written by an African American published by a major commercial press (Houghton Mifflin) for wide circulation. The book sold well and earned good reviews: "Eloquent and fearless," said the New York Herald Tribune, which gave it a full-front and three-fifths-of-the-second-page treatment in its weekly supplement. If some complained about journalese, other readers praised Ottley's miraculously suspending his anger to show the reality of black urban experience and the need for change. So important was it, raved the New York Times, that New World A-Coming should be on the desk of every "editor, preacher, politician, leader . . . everybody."[35]

The "Negro problem" for American literature that emerges, however, is not that African American culture is too negligible or that its literary production is too inconsequential. Rather, it is close to invisible. Sadly, most novels by African Americans at the time were almost never published by the major houses, which might have improved the books' chances of getting reviewed. Failing that support, it is no wonder that this literary heritage no longer seems even to exist. From what I can gather, there were not a great many novels in circulation, and the few there were have been consigned to oblivion. Contemporary literary historians know about Attaway's *Blood on the Forge* (1941), a story of three brothers who leave their Kentucky farm to work in the Pennsylvania steel mills, but perhaps too little about George Washington Lee's *Beale Street Sundown* (1942), his follow-up to a BOMC selection of several years before, *River George* (1937); Carl Ruthven Offord's *The White Face* (1943), a novel about two Georgia sharecroppers who move to Harlem for a better life, only to fall into the hands of pro-Nazi agents; W. Adolphe Roberts's New Orleans novel, *The Royal Street* (1944); and *The Case of Mrs. Wingate* (1944) by filmmaker Oscar Micheaux. Nor do we know about the interests or merits of such books as Katheryn Campbell Graham's *Under the Cottonwood* (1941), Deadrick Franklin Jenkins's *It Was Not My World* (1942), Annie Green Nelson's *After the Storm* (1942) and *The Dawn Appears* (1944)—two of her four novels—Adam Clayton Powell Sr.'s *Picketing Hell* (1942), a spiritual autobiography told in fiction, Edward Gholson's *From Jericho to Jerusalem* (1943), Curtis Lucas's *Flour Is Dusty* (1943), Thomas Roach's *Victor* (1943), Ruth Thompson's *What's Wrong with Lottery?* (1943), Chancellor Williams's *The Raven* (1943), Wade Gray's *Her Latest Performance* (1944), Lewis A. H. Caldwell's *The Policy King* (1945), and Odella Phelps Woods's *High Ground* (1945). I can find no record that any were reviewed in a mainstream venue.

Strange Fruit, on the other hand, was reviewed everywhere. Published by Reynal and Hitchcock, it first appeared in February 1944; by May, it had established itself as number 1 on the *New York Times* best-seller list, where it stayed for several months until ultimately surpassed by an even greater succès de scandale, Winsor's *Forever Amber*. In 1945, Smith's novel was taken to Broadway for an undistinguished run and then soon passed from the scene. This explicit story of love and race made Lillian Smith an estimable figure, though previously she had enjoyed regional notoriety as the founding editor of the liberal magazine, *South Today*, which had grown over the years to a circulation of about ten thousand at its peak. She published one other novel later in her career, also about Southern small-town immorality, *One Hour* (1959), but the manuscripts for the five that preceded *Strange Fruit* were destroyed when some local boys set her house afire, presumably enraged by her being a lesbian. A determined integrationist, Smith died in 1966 after another two decades of strenuously advocating African American civil rights.

It is no exaggeration to say that for much of the last sixty years, this once notorious book had been forgotten by American literary historians, despite the recognition it enjoyed among Southern cultural historians; indeed, a historian rather than a literary scholar wrote the only biography we have of Smith.[36] Now the novel has been made available in paperback editions and, in the last fifteen years, has generated its own scholarship. Yet were it not for its association with Billie Holiday's mournful song, and the novel's interest in interracial love and lynching, Smith's book might not have made much of a dent on the present. Despite Smith's own experiments with point of view, the literary critical establishment discovered its favorite Southern novelist in Faulkner, whose critical reputation was—in a matter of months—to be sparked anew by Malcolm Cowley's famous Viking introduction. (Cowley reviewed *Strange Fruit*—positively—though he thought it lacked Faulkner's power.) Lillian Smith was not just any Southern liberal but, by several accounts, the most forceful liberal of the pre–civil rights era. That she was also a vigorous anticommunist would not have endeared her to the left; she was just as severely anti-Agrarian, so she would have found no critical succor in that quarter either. In the *Sewanee Review*, a young New Critic, Robert W. Daniel, predicted accurately enough that in twenty years no one would remember *Strange Fruit* (comparing Smith's treatment of blacks unfavorably to Forster's representation of Indians in *Passage to India*), while invoking the example of Harriet Beecher Stowe's *Uncle Tom's Cabin* as a predecessor of polemical novels that time forgets. Moreover, *Strange Fruit*'s popularity was inevitably colored by its sensationalism, leading some critics to dismiss Smith as a serious artist, certainly not as much of an artist as she wished to see herself. That sensationalism—sex, murder, homosexuality, and lynching—was underscored by the use of "fuck"; its being banned in Boston boosted sales nationwide but did little for the book's critical reputation. Controversy ensued when, despite threats, DeVoto, who had held that the strength of Smith's novel was its willingness to address social concerns, orchestrated a purchase that led to obscenity charges being drawn. The tumult did not subside until First Lady Eleanor Roosevelt quietly intervened, and the criminal complaint was dropped.

Many reviewers agreed that *Strange Fruit* should be praised for its down-to-earth realities and its stirring tale. The critic for the *Virginia Quarterly Review* summarized the responses, first distinguishing the "New York" review in which the writer's "critical consciousness is equipped with a slot marked 'south' into which 'Strange Fruit' fits neatly as a nickel in a subway turnstile. . . . 'Tender' . . . daring . . . he writes, '. . . pity . . . terror . . . man's inhumanity to man.' But this, after all, is not criticism; it is merely conditioned reflex."[37] The second category of review addresses the novel's commercial success, which would be unfair to the novelist, "for her aim is not cheap and her manner is not shoddy." Finally, there is the review that treats the book as a "serious work of art." Although such a critic begins with praise, "the collapse is inevitable because Miss Smith's purpose is not to present a tragic effect of racial prejudice on individual lives, but to shock the people of the United States into action that will benefit the Negro. The propagandist who turns to fiction always narrows and solidifies the flow of experience until it loses human shape and becomes a sword to strike with." A year later, in the *Saturday Review*, when Smith answered her critics, she struck each of these themes. Her motives for writing *had* been impugned as commercial or political. No one, not even the reviewers who praised it as a social tract, took seriously enough the story about the tragic waste of humanity that she intended.[38] By Christmas, the novel was named in several annual top ten lists.

Other important novels of 1944 include Jean Stafford's *Boston Adventure*, Jackson's *The Lost Weekend*, and Joseph Pennell's *History of Rome Hanks and Kindred Matters*, a novel sometimes cited as a neglected masterpiece. Upton Sinclair scored a hit with *Presidential Agent*, which by this time had positioned Lanny Budd, his Zelig-like witness to the century, as a secret agent in prewar Nazi Germany; Saul Bellow made his debut with *Dangling Man*, his dramatic meditation of a young man about to enter the army. Somerset Maugham's *The Razor's Edge* was the best-known novel in English of the year. In such a milieu, the success of *Strange Fruit* seems all the more anomalous. As the reviewer in the *Virginia Quarterly* attests, *Strange Fruit* seems to have been appreciated as a regional novel, since it was readily apprehended as Southern and thus was part of that vital '30s trend. Despite the appearance of two Montana novels in 1944, however, regionalism was declining as the war progressed; nor was Smith's novel strictly an effort to give the South an unsentimental rewriting of *Gone with the Wind*, which Smith had reviewed favorably in her own magazine.

So why did a novel about sexual relations between a promising young black woman and a directionless young white man of the comfortable classes—a story about the rural South of twenty years before—engage so many readers during the critical period of the months leading up to the

D-Day invasion, when America's triumph was by no means secure? The key to *Strange Fruit's* interest may well lie in its subordinating questions of race and sex to questions of class, especially middle-class solidity. Nonnie Anderson comes from respectable blacks—she was a college student—while Tracy Deen is from an established white family. Their love affair threatens Tracy's parents' sense of social order; he seems unwilling to desist with Nonnie and, worse, to let go of the girl from his own circumstances, at least until he finds religion. The trouble really begins when Tracy then feels obliged to provide a husband for Nonnie, who is carrying his baby. (Can we really suppose that a white man would imagine that to be his responsibility to a black woman, since the most liberal reaction for a young man of Tracy's class would have been to give a pregnant black woman money?) He finds that spouse in Henry, his primitive former servant and childhood playmate—a consideration Nonnie finds unendurable. Tracy's love blinds him to his class duty, which then sets off the turbulent events to follow, including his own murder. In these respects, the shocking aspect of *Strange Fruit* is the heavy risk to class stability with which the plot is freighted.

Rather than an aberration, Smith's novel was a book of its day inasmuch as it was one of several that year conjoining race and region. I have already mentioned another best seller, Fast's reconstruction novel *Freedom Road*, which met with mixed critical success. Also appearing in 1944 were Frances Gaither's *The Red Cock Crows*, a historical novel about a slave revolt, and Lonnie Coleman's *Escape the Thunder*, an "all-Negro novel" by a white author that was neither "innocent of lynchings" nor "a quaint story of lovable darkies." A committed student of the South, Hodding Carter published *Winds of Fear*, a well-regarded novel connecting racism and fascism and fixing blame on the disparity of power. Also receiving positive reviews was Edith Pope's *Colcorton*, a miscegenation tale of the granddaughter of a slave trader and the fate of her ancestral home.[39]

As much as 1944 witnessed the continuation of some dominant trends of '30s fiction, it was also one of the most productive years for pondering race relations. Since the summer of 1943 had seen riots in Detroit, Harlem, and Beaumont, Texas, there was a pronounced need to discuss—some might say contain—racial injustice. Several relevant books and pamphlets were hurried into print, such as Howard W. Odum's *Race and Rumors of Race*, Rayford Logan's *What the Negro Wants*, Edwin Embree's *American Negroes: A Handbook*, Earl Brown and George Leighton's *The Negro and the War*, *Meet the Negro* by Karl E. Downs, and *Color: Unfinished Business of Democracy* (a special issue of *Survey Graphic*, the pop sociology magazine whose special issue, twenty years before, on the Harlem Renaissance became Alain Locke's *The New Negro*). Such occasional works took their place in the ever-growing library of books issued throughout the war years devoted to race in America, an output that included *12 Million Black Voices*, which Wright compiled, and *Black Metropolis*, a sociological study of Chicago, for which he wrote an introduction. In addition, dozens of books in the middle and late '40s rehearsed the lessons in hypocrisy learned by African American soldiers, especially those who were forced to return to segregation, both in various Southern training camps and in most of the battle units in which they served. To that same end, humorist Margaret Halsey described her experiences as a United Service Organizations (USO) hostess witnessing racism in *Some of My Best Friends Are Soldiers* (1944), a work of light fiction, and *Color Blind* (1946), her more serious take on the same subject, which the *Christian Century* called "certainly the most readable book ever written about the 'color problem.'"[40]

The weightiest contribution to the race writing of this moment was not occasioned by the riots or even the war but had actually been initiated several years before when the Carnegie Commission invited Swedish economist Gunnar Myrdal to survey the status of African Americans. His 1,400-page tome, *American Dilemma*, was completed at the end of 1942 and was more than a year in production. Touted as the next in a series of distinguished reports from perceptive foreign visitors, like Tocqueville or Lord Bryce, it left a decisive impression. Although leftist critics held that *American Dilemma* isolated race from the larger question of labor and capital, and some older black conservative critics believed that the study discovered what they had presented years ago, most readers agreed with W. E. B. Du Bois in finding the report "overwhelming."

In the mainstream press, the book was a great success and was reviewed by some of the leading students of race relations. For J. Saunders Redding, in the *New Republic*, Myrdal's conviction that the "American dilemma" of how to treat blacks turned on the disparity between American creed and deed revealed that the "Negro problem" is not regional but lies "in the heart of the American." Influential sociologist Robert S. Lynd, writing in the *Saturday Review*, echoes this point while praising Myrdal for his comprehensive survey of the "vast and ugly reality of our greatest failure." Lynd seconds Myrdal's indictment of the Northerner for thinking that African Americans should enjoy their rights as citizens as long as they did so somewhere else, approving Myrdal's conclusion that, in America, there was no "somewhere else." Moreover, Lynd upholds Myrdal's view that, lacking any general moral will to reform, the American citizenry looked to such comforting vagueness of "education" and "leadership" to counter its "mere passivity" in solving the country's profoundest ills.[41]

The whole array of African American periodicals also scrutinized *American Dilemma*. *Phylon*, a journal of opinion and affairs, offered a double review —one by Du Bois, the other by E. A. Reuter. An eminent sociologist, Reuter faulted the study not so much for its technique but for its lost opportunity, seeing Myrdal's report as a "competent performance" rather than the "superior" presentation that the situation warranted. Du Bois immediately understood that instead of a defeat for the social sciences, the book should be seen as underscoring the *failure* of that mode of inquiry as the latest discipline— following theology, "natural science," biology, and psychology—to be enlisted in the epistemological struggle to meet the challenge of race in the United States. According to Du Bois, what makes *American Dilemma* so "monumental and unrivalled" is that Myrdal insists that the "Negro problem" needs to be seen as a moral issue, not principally as a sociological one.[42]

American Dilemma's influence, especially on educators, social scientists, teachers, and all manner of other professionals, including, presumably, Supreme Court justices, was incalculable. Myrdal's investigation sustained what the riots fomented, an activist impatience to get on with the job of integration. Profound as this impact was, however, it was part of a concatenation of publishing events, not the least of which was Lillian Smith's novel; her example heartened Southern liberals most of all, for at last someone—a woman from one of the oldest families in Georgia—was finally speaking out in ways that others would hear. Americans listened to that voice in large part because it addressed them, through the vital personalities of the kind Dorothy Canfield Fisher believed American readers wanted to meet, in the class terms they could appreciate.

LEARNING HOW TO BEHAVE

As prominent a political and economic question as race poses in the American forties, it also raises another sort of anxiety, about conduct, for middle-class Americans. As we will see, worries about how the performance of middle-class well-being might be ascertained, exerted, and confirmed permeate the fiction of the postwar era. To an important extent, even minor works like Margaret Halsey's previously cited *Color Blind* and *Some of My Best Friends Are Soldiers*, which recount how prejudice violates middle-class standards of taste, underscore this crucial lesson. Such concerns about how the middle class should treat minorities emerge as an even more apparent cultural instruction in a few years, when novelists turn to the general question of anti-Semitism. But it is important to realize that, for the middle class, the postwar era is awash with uncertainties about how to act in both the private and public spheres. As if to answer this general interest, late in 1946 prominent historian Arthur Schlesinger Sr. published a modest account of etiquette books in America, tracing their evolution and preoccupations. Only seventy-one pages in text, the book would scarcely serve as a prelude to Schlesinger's forthcoming monumental study of recent U.S. history, *Paths to the Present* (1949). Still, unpretentious as it was, *Learning How to Behave* resounds faithfully with the concerns of the postwar world and the fiction that addressed them.

For Schlesinger, a historical analysis of conduct manuals should ring with a true triumphalism, to the extent that they tell the story of how good manners vanquished American crudity. Schlesinger calls this evolution the "leveling-up process of democracy," which, mirthful moments aside, reveals nothing less than the "common man's struggle to achieve a larger degree of human dignity and self-respect."[43] Eighteen months after the end of World War II, this famous scholar's little study makes an ideological point as contemporaneous as his magisterial study of the historical ascent of democracy. America's rise as a world power can readily be understood as a victory of this spirit—of knowing how to present yourself, how to negotiate troubles and bewilderments, how to tally your worthiness in a time of uncertainty, unstable values, and vaguely limned relations. And this sense of American society would come to prevail over the postwar era even as a prelude to the conformist years to follow.

In fact, the years after the war witnessed a surge in etiquette books, as well as personal and social management manuals. (As it also did after World War I: recall that Emily Post's monumental guide, the most famous of these, was first published in 1922.) It is easy to see how a society as self-conscious as America in the years following the Allies' victory, the nation to which so many other countries now looked upon as a model, developed an ever-broader taste for books about itself than before. Indeed, this period also marks the rise of American studies internationally, the curriculum for which the U.S. Information Agency publicized by way of disseminating American nationalist and exceptionalist values.

Yet this self-consciousness was not some simple boosterism, for one of the great concerns clouding America in 1945 and after was how to win the peace—domestically as well as internationally—before the Cold War set in. How would Americans manage themselves, their unprecedented opportunities and social challenges? After they had won the war to preserve the American Way of Life, what would be the character of that life, cultural critics wanted to know, and what were its difficulties? That critical spirit was soon to be squashed by anticommunist jingoism, but the record of the '40s reveals that, after World War II, American writers immediately moved to answer such questions, and their success in doing so was typically seen as the response to a mandate. Or so the new social fiction was explained and evaluated by the reviewers, who often saw their task as judging how well the novelists discharged these duties. Novelists implicitly pursued Schlesinger's sense of American upward mobility as "Learning How to Behave"; right conduct was something that a country, like its citizens, could learn to perform. Among the first citizens whose experiences mattered most were the returning GIs, as they maneuvered through the great changes in the workplace and in their communities that had occurred in their absence. Often these soldiers returned from the war damaged by their tours of duty— anxiously suffering from the memory of brutality they either observed or in which they had participated and for which little in their prewar lives could have ever prepared them—though certainly many were improved by their transformation from boy next door to savior of democracy. Before taking up those novels, however, I turn to a kind of novel meant to help citizens to learn how to behave amid new social fluidities, confusions, and realignments. These books are now largely forgotten, but their lessons in class protocols function also as a primer in nation making, whose instructions often parallel the dramatic intensity of returning veteran novels.

With this in mind, we might recall one of the most critically successful American novels of the second half of 1945, and a fairly popular seller too, Josephine Pinckney's *Three O'Clock Dinner*. This story dramatizes an argument that Lionel Trilling would spell out two years later, when he codified the primacy of realism for the history of fiction in "Manners, Morals, and the

Novel." For Pinckney, the battle for civilization—Schlesinger's sense of the "struggle to achieve a larger degree of human dignity and self-respect"—culminates in a formal dinner party in Charleston. While Pinckney (whose South Carolina roots went back to the illustrious cousins who signed the Constitution) held that Charleston was the incidental ground for this modern tale of love and class, most reviewers responded warmly to the rich social texture afforded by "this complete tour of Charleston and beautifully planned tour de force as well." Here the skirmish is between two families, the arriviste Hessenwinkles and the aristocratic Redcliffs. At the party announcing the marriage of a Redcliff heir to a lusty Hessenwinkle daughter—who clearly does not know how to behave—the spectacle of her vulgarity shocks his family and leads to a breakup and the revelation of an interracial baby. Through their newly awakened power of love, and their superior manners, the Redcliffs work through this debacle, teaching readers how to act in a society in flux.[44]

Throughout the latter '40s, American realists turned doggedly to the very novelty of contemporary life for their subject. What was new in America, after sixteen years of international depression and conflagration, was a darker, more tenuous sense of an American dream, even as that dream would soon be mass produced, advertised, and consumed on an unprecedented level. The spectacle of American materialism occupying the collective mythology of the 1950s, however, is not yet solidified. Rather than the systematic healthy-mindedness we associate with the Eisenhower years, there is a lingering awareness of the destruction, even doom, that had so recently been a part of so many Americans' experience. If Americans were eager for a change, they were also mindful of distress. The middle-class literary strategy was to examine the precariousness of the dream; more than one critic complained that this tendency signaled a laziness of the novelists' critical faculty, since books all too often became test cases about the moral underpinnings of the age. Reviewers were impressed by this seriousness of purpose, but some were also dismayed at the typicality of the proceedings and the lack of imagination in an author's moral position—whether or not it was critical of the status quo.

Not surprisingly, war novels and back-from-the-war novels dominated the fiction of the second half of the decade and seemingly every American soldier who could write was ready to try his hand at a novel. We remember the famous ones like Norman Mailer's *The Naked and the Dead* (1948) and

Irwin Shaw's *The Young Lions* (1948), but literally hundreds of them were published during the several years following the war. While Mailer's and Shaw's were best sellers, novels about the war—a type followed fairly closely in the reviews—rarely achieved great popularity, though a few, like John Horne Burns's *The Gallery* (1947) and Alfred Hayes's *The Girl on the Via Flaminia* (1949), were substantial critical successes. *The Gallery*, about the encounters between American GIs and Italian civilians in Naples during the occupation of 1944, made *A Bell for Adano* seem like the sentimental tripe some earlier readers had suspected. Burns's photographic realism gives postwar readers a glimpse into the life of VD hospitals and homosexual meeting places, as well as into the amusement promenade of the title—details that were seldom included in letters from the front. Before Mailer's novel wrested the mantle away, *The Gallery* was usually conceded to be the best of these books.

Like *The Gallery*, *The Girl on the Via Flaminia* is a "brutal yet compassionate" treatment of the U.S. occupation of Italy; it focuses on the relationship between a lonely American GI and an honorable, though demoralized Italian woman. Hayes's style was obviously in Hemingway's debt, and his novel was inevitably compared to *A Farewell to Arms*. Not so strangely, as the postwar years unfolded, American writers moved away from the scene of battle and toward the psychology of survivorship. Wright Morris's *The Man Who Was There* (1945) developed the conceit of examining the lives of one dead GI's survivors; Ben Field, in *The Last Freshet* (1948), relates the story of a logger who supports the widows of the two sons he lost in the war and ends by marrying one of them. Elizabeth Janeway's *The Question of Gregory* (1949) traces the effects of a son's death on his parents, who are further unsettled when they learn a few days later of Franklin D. Roosevelt's death—the father becomes a wanderer; the mother returns to her wealthy family.

Novelists struggled to make fiction out of a war that had transmuted the reality of everyday life so completely that it seemed unmoored. Van van Praag records the fear and tension of a day in combat that unhinges his protagonist in *Day without End* (1949). Paul Gallico describes the meanings and effects of a wartime romance in *The Lonely* (1949). That same year, Kay Boyle, who had already written three war novels, offers in *His Human Majesty* the story of a ski troop training in the Rockies, made up of representatives of Nazi victims —Jews, Norwegians, Dutch, Poles, French, English, and Americans—who are preparing an assault on Europe. Implausible as the plot sounds (and it was based on a real operation), the reviewers were a little dismayed that Boyle does not bring off a "miracle": "One always expects the impossible of Kay Boyle—and almost always gets it. For she has an . . . unmatched . . . faculty for capturing the well-nigh inexpressible and impaling it upon her sharp, incandescent prose," observes the *Herald Tribune*.[45]

While the public only occasionally made popular successes of these novels about the war, they had a fairly strong interest in nonfiction books about battle and military policy, books that generally outsold the scores of war novels in the years immediately following the war and that frequently landed on the best-seller lists, like George C. Marshall's *General Marshall's Report* (1945), which was the last installment of the chief of staff's record of the war effort. Among nonfiction best sellers in 1946 alone, there appeared two biographies of Roosevelt, a White House memoir, two war books, and an "anatomy of peace" during the same year that the inspirational *Peace of Mind* scored a great success with its vision of the relation between Judaeo-Christian ethics and psychoanalysis, a book that sold even more copies the next year.[46] Maybe because there were so many of them, these novels managed to treat virtually every theater, and situation, of the war, sometimes very frankly; their commercial appeal was oddly limited, however. Readers seldom favored these books, as if to suggest that the country wanted to have the story told (or thought it did) but then did not want particularly to listen. Still, we would watch: many of these books were written in cooperation with a publisher and reprint house for remuneration that Hollywood widely advertised. Payments were one thousand dollars for a five-page outline; once accepted by all parties, the sum would be paid out to an author over ten weeks during which the ex-GI would produce a thirty-page synopsis and twenty thousand words of manuscript. If accepted, the author would receive an additional thousand dollars, then royalties and a movie option.

Movie industry interest, and the taut suspense of a journalistic account, led authors to focus on an exciting incident, like William Wister Haines's *Command Decision* (1947) concerning the destruction of Hitler's jet factories, though such novels could not provide the scope that Mailer or Shaw did. Some novels, such as Stefan Heym's *The Crusaders* (1948), aspired to a large-scale rendition but by substituting a logic of accumulated detail or types, failed on the level of character or psychology. Or works of fiction sought breadth at the expense of a sustained narrative line, like James Michener's *Tales of the South Pacific*—awarded the Pulitzer Prize in 1948—in its portrayal of the lives of combatants, nurses, and Seabees. (As a musical, Michener's story would be explicitly deployed to encourage a society more tolerant of racial others, though this note does not enter into the reviews of his book.) War novels could also involve isolated, out-of-the headlines experiences of the war, like Gore Vidal's *Williwaw* (1946), his first book, about passengers on a freighter in a storm at sea. Vance Bourjaily's *The End of My Life* (1947), on American ambulance drivers with the British armies in Syria and Italy, was an especially bitter tale of a war whose every locale seems to have had at least one novel written about it.

There was also an intense effort to bring the war home and thus to reveal the clash in attitudes and experiences that would foretell what the returning GIS would soon know. Hiram Haydn's *Manhattan Furlough* (1945) encapsulates many features of the genre in an early version, when his army sergeant–hero feels obliged to visit the parents of a man he had trained. Nearly losing his sanity, he is brought back by an understanding friend and a loving young woman. In *The Journey Home* (1945), Zelda Popkin essays a broader social canvas. Here, a lieutenant returning with battle fatigue finds himself on a train from Miami to New York and encounters an isolationist senator, his lascivious daughter, a grateful war widow, and several other modern American types, like the young female magazine designer who turns out to be the girl of his dreams.

James Gould Cozzens's *Guard of Honor*, the 1949 Pulitzer winner, may have been the most successful. In a novel that is less about the war than the effects of the war on contemporary life, including the moral laxity that war's constant senses of contingency and expediency have promoted, Cozzens minutely scrutinizes three days of corruption, cover-up, and ethical watchfulness at a Florida military base, where racial prejudice has come to a head. Similarly but in a more displaced way, issues of moral responsibility were reassessed in the little spate of novels by authors of substantial reputation on the *maquisards*, the French patriots who, after the war, zealously continued to pursue collaborationists. Boyle, in *A Frenchman Must Die* (1946), Prokosch, in *Age of Thunder* (1945), and Albert Guerard (later a literary scholar and critic), in *Maquisard: A Christmas Tale* (1945) all turn to this subject to refine questions of guilt—doubts and charges that rarely arise in mainland novels about the United States.

Sometimes, issues of morality could only be retrieved through allegorical renderings of the war as the means of achieving freedom and peace, most notably James R. Ullman's tale of mountain climbing in the Swiss Alps, *The White Tower* (1945). In the several books about the occupation of Germany, novelists confronted ethical nuances: first in *The Liberators* (1946) by Wesley Towner, but more notably, in David Davidson's widely admired, *The Steeper Cliff* (1947), which describes an American officer, ashamed that he sat out the war, grappling with the heroic example of an anti-Nazi Bavarian. William Gardner Smith's *Last of the Conquerors* (1948), the story of a young German woman's love for an American black soldier stationed in Mannheim, examines the moral arguments against the hypocrisy of a segregated army. By 1949, representing postwar Germany had reached a new sophistication in John Hawkes's surrealist fiction, *The Cannibal*.

Questions of lost innocence, however, were more generally pronounced in novels about the veterans' return, where GIS might find the occasion either to test new convictions or confront the paltry values of their old homes. Set against the famous image of a serviceman kissing a swooning nurse in Times Square on V-J Day—an image at once romantic and domestic, at once marking the end of the war and the beginning of the peace—as an authorizing story of a soldier's return, is the much more everyday tale of the process whereby American veterans were bidden to rechannel all that they had learned about the depreciation of the self so necessary for military discipline, if they wished to prosper by the ethic of individual responsibility that awaited them at home. Further set against the unthinking delight and relief of this kiss was the national uncertainty over how ex-GIS could forget how to live by orders and to learn all over again the challenge of self-direction. Dozens of articles, pamphlets, and books—*Parents' Magazine* even featured a "Do's and Don'ts"—explained how and why "readjustment" would be difficult. It has been something of a national illusion that, because the war was so relentlessly mythologized as the "good war," American soldiers were quick to forswear the cloud of disaster and death they carried with them. Historical markers like the fiftieth anniversary of D-Day or veterans' aggrieved reaction to *Saving Private Ryan* (1998) reveal that many GIS had not put the past behind them at all but had still to remember, repeat, and work through their traumas.

By far the most telling way of registering the sense of change was in the veterans' relations with wives and girlfriends. The felicity that so many anticipated turned out to be vaporous. One may wish that the Times Square kiss betokened future relations between the sexes—its nostalgic combination of assertiveness and absorption might be at the root of its general appeal—but the reality was that women were frequently beaten, brutalized, raped, and killed by poorly readjusted veterans. So many marriages failed that the nation's divorce rate doubled what it was in 1939. More than half a million marriages failed in 1945 and 1946; for ten months in Oklahoma City and Dallas, divorces even outpaced weddings. Beyond the war's having rendered some ex-GIS unfit for intimacy, many marriages obviously had been made in haste and probably would never have succeeded under ordinary circumstances. In addition, the war had occasioned so much adultery, at home and overseas, that ex-soldiers and wives were both counseled not to confess or to feel guilty about infidelities that resulted from loneliness, frustration, and bewilderment. Another explanation for the high divorce rate was that the war led many servicemen as well as women in the workplace to a new purchase on life, and a primary way of exercising that sense was to renounce stifling marriages made in youthful ignorance and impatience.[47]

With demobilization, a slew of novels about the experience of coming home—as one of the very first was called—appeared; dozens followed in the next decade, including some of the era's most famous books: *The Man with the Golden Arm* (1949), Nelson Algren's hard-boiled tale of an ex-GI who returns to his sordid corner of Chicago a morphine addict, and Sloan Wilson's *The Man in the Gray Flannel Suit* (1955), which used the idea of readjustment to test the materialism of the new conformity. The central subject of these books was to be found in the close scrutiny of the veteran's new life, the tradition of middle-class fiction to which ex-GI novels generally belong. These novels have less to do with battle fatigue (as post-traumatic stress syndrome was called) or bad cases of nerves (as neurotic disorders were known) than with the dynamic between the ex-GIS' burdens of war and the social scene that greeted their return. A few novels, to be sure, studied the psychologically wounded, but even these usually represented mental disorder for the edification of the middle class. Such tales might even be presented as parables, like *The Perfect Round* (1945), Henry Robinson's fantasy of a man obsessed with repairing a merry-go-round.

Coming-home novels focused on the problematic process of reconciliation with a society changed during the ex-soldier's absence. American novelists seemed captivated by *this* story. Not only did the actual combatants try their hand at writing these novels, but so did established novelists whose careers had otherwise flourished—for example, John Marquand's tale of middle-class New England WASPs in *Point of No Return* (1949) or Ann Petry's *Country Place* (1947), both of which take this skeletal plot and develop other interests. In his second novel, *In a Yellow Wood* (1947), Gore Vidal also gave the form a try, a story of a day and a night of a New York socialite having to make choices, including the allure of homosexuality, before returning to a job at a brokerage firm.

Sometimes resolution came through political action, as in Lester Cohen's *Coming Home* (1945), where an ex-soldier battles against city corruption; sometimes, through humanitarian feelings, as in Robert Lowery's esteemed *Find Me in the Fire* (1948), or, perhaps most often, through the love of a good woman. Summarizing many of the subject's possibilities was *That Winter* (1948), by Merle Miller, a highly praised story of how three ex-GIs sharing an apartment in Manhattan reach very different ends: a wealthy young man commits suicide when he cannot cope with having been severely wounded, a self-hating Jew accepts his identity and returns to the family business in California, and the narrator, a poor Midwestern kid, comes to terms with his grief and guilt once he visits the understanding widow of a buddy whose death he had blamed on himself.

Most of the novels, however, had little to say about the psychological effects of war, even when they did refer to "battle fatigue" or "nerves," though there were several important exceptions, like Carl Jonas's *Beachhead on the Wind* (1945), which tells of the disorientations that military life has caused for seven sailors. Peter Packer's *Inward Voyage* (1948) chronicles a son's ordeal of readjustment, his hopes of marriage, and his despair over his father's Parkinson's disease. Betsey Barton's *The Long Walk* (1948) was one of the few novels that looked at the problems of the permanently wounded. Gertrude Mallette's *Once Is Forever* (1946) takes up that subject through the lens of the women who love them.

As one might expect, a great many infidelities and divorces activate these plots, as if to document how the process of reharmonizing with the world will be more vexed than simply reclaiming the loving woman left behind. Alice Parsons's *I Know What I'd Do* (1946) tells of the fissures that the wartime atmosphere of pervasive adultery leaves on a community. Here, a veteran whose wife has been rumored to have been unfaithful, a circumstance he would choose to ignore, is led to murder when the Ku Klux Klan (operating in his upstate New York village) interferes. A doctor saves the day, and, indeed, throughout these books various professionals (including several well-meaning psychiatrists) surface briefly, if only to explain, with sometimes painful glibness, the resistance to the adaptation that the ex-soldiers have to make.

These novels frequently made ex-GIS' encounters with the home front the palimpsest through which to interpret the range of postwar social complexities. Consider one of the first such fictions, *Sons of the Morning* (1945) by Otto Schrag, who had fled Germany and had previously written a novel on the Kansas locust plague. *Sons of the Morning* presents the story of two vets—one with his French fiancée—who return to their New England village only to find themselves objects of suspicion and ill-will, the source of which is murky to them. Ultimately, a wholesome American girl straightens out the confusion. Although several critics did not forgive the sentimental comity so important to this émigré writer, one well-known reviewer praised the book for being a "post-war" novel: "This is . . . a story not of a brave new world of triumphant democracy and scientific achievement, but of plain people—those who went and those who stayed—struggling to recover from a shock that had upset familiar ways, thrown habits and emotions into new alignments."[48]

Like *Sons of the Morning*, the overwhelming majority of these books are long forgotten. Why they have ceased to matter seems to me a normal circumstance of literary history: they were written to be replaced—perhaps by the spate of juvenile delinquent, sensitive youth, and suburbia novels of the early '50s—in the way that middle-class realism always recreates itself via the next version of America needing analysis. Consider the premises and plots of several books appreciatively reviewed in their day: Charles Dwoskin's *Shadow over the Land* (1946) attacks a fascist front organization playing on the confusions of an ex-GI and a bereaved young woman; Leslie Waller's *Show Me the Way* (1947) describes one vet's conversion to a vision of individual responsibility when he witnesses anti-Semitism and racial prejudice. In Grace Breckling's *Dream without End* (1950), a well-to-do family confronts a changing America in the persons of a son, who gives up his engagement to join the one-world movement, and a sister, who leaves for Alaska with a mill worker. Jeanne Wylie's *Face to Face* (1952) tells of two foster brothers who return to their Midwestern college town to run the local newspaper and who daily meet new challenges, such as black segregation and campus subversives. Charles Gorham's crude and violent *The Future*

Mr. Dolan (1948) looks forward to the delinquent hero in his portrait of a nineteen-year-old veteran who returns to the Irish slums of New York an amoral killer.

Nor were these stories limited to the challenges men faced. Maritta Wolff's *About Lyddy Thomas* (1947) explores how one young woman's experiences as a factory worker during the war quicken her resolve to divorce her shiftless, alcoholic abusive husband on his return. A startlingly vivid psychological portrait, Wolff's novel describes Lyddy Thomas's harrowing effort to live independently, even as it gives a series of social sketches of several other women's experiences in surviving the war. The power of *About Lyddy Thomas* comes from Wolff's detailing Lyddy's psychological state and the close study of contemporary mores that make her resolve at once so difficult and so crucial to uphold, for whatever else has happened to her husband, the war has changed her, enabling her to resist the subjugation he would visit upon her.

Ultimately, the largest majority of these books tranquilize for the middle class the trauma from which so many returning soldiers suffered, and through their representations of adjustment, disclose a process that either makes the line of demarcation clear and treatable, as some critics urged, or checks the seamlessness of character—individual and cultural—despite the disruptions of war. Most of all, these books regularly show an America urgent to believe in a coherent, comprehensible society, where ex-GIs and their loved ones alike can learn again how to conduct themselves.

THE BEST YEARS OF OUR LIVES: RACE AND THE MIDDLE-CLASS NOVEL

Among the most surprising features of the postwar literary landscape is the number of novels that focus on the veterans' experience with African Americans, homosexuals, Jews, and assorted criminals, really a catalog of the dispossessed. Having gained a much more complex understanding of the world, veterans could now be seen as enlisting in a war for the American Way of Life at home, too, by defending beleaguered minorities. David Alman's *World Full of Strangers* (1949), in which an ex-GI returns home to serve as a New York City social worker, challenged that norm. Increasingly alienated from a city made up of so many immigrant slum dwellers, the vet succumbs to bribery, becoming ever more ruthless as a result of his corruption.

Yet with the victory over Germany and Japan, the pluralist spirit flourished anew, a spirit that had been galvanized earlier in the decade by *Common Ground*, a magazine dedicated to the philosophy of its editor, Louis Adamic, who popularized a vision of ethnic inclusiveness. Even though the magazine itself had a precarious existence, George and Helen Papashivly's *Anything Can Happen*, a compilation of their reports from the magazine, recounting incidents of the good fortune that awaited recent immigrants like themselves, was one of the biggest best sellers of 1945. This sense of "social unity"—the name of the "Committee" that sponsored the magazine for its eleven-year run (from 1940 to 1951)—led *Common Ground* to combat the forces of prejudice as well as any superficial rhetoric of Americans brought together, in the melting pot again, for a shared goal.[49] The articles concentrated on a vision of America as unreservedly one of e pluribus unum. Immediately following the victory in Europe, Adamic published *A Nation of Nations*, his vision of an amalgamated America, a travelogue in which he locates stories of hundreds of citizens whose background is other than Anglo-Saxon and who have risen to places of local prestige. In October 1945, Wallace Stegner, in conjunction with the editors of the photo-magazine *Look*, published another such panorama of American difference, *One Nation*, also to contest the prejudice festering in the body social, despite the easy wartime rhetoric of unity.

Dozens of novels in the late '40s hate intolerance, racial segregation, and anti-Semitism especially, an era that saw another important coming-home novel, Hobson's *Gentleman's Agreement* (1947), to which I will soon turn. As the '40s closed, right up until Ellison's *Invisible Man* (1952) and James Baldwin's *Go Tell It on the Mountain* (1953), there was a series of novels about the relations between whites and blacks, including an all-but-forgotten tradition of whites writing about blacks in the hope of inspiring racial tolerance among whites. In fact, in the second half of 1945, scarcely a year after Myrdal's *American Dilemma* and but a few months after Richard Wright's *Black Boy*, two major efforts to explain the races to each other were published—the landmark sociological study of Chicago, *Black Metropolis*, and the now forgotten but once esteemed *A Primer for White Folks* by white Northerner, Bucklin Moon, a novelist and social observer who spent his career trying to understand the problems of race, especially in the American South. No less a student of racial dynamics than Ralph Ellison called the *Primer* "a vivid statement of the strengths and weaknesses of the new mood born in the hearts of Americans during the war." For Ellison, Moon's book is notable because it reveals something "practically missing from American writing since *Huckleberry Finn*"—"a search for images of white and black fraternity."[50] Moon later published a novel, *Without Magnolias* (1949), which aspired to give the much sentimentalized South the truly honest scrutiny that had eluded previous authors.

Without Magnolias, winner of the annual George Washington Carver Prize for the best book by or about African Americans, gives novel form to the double consciousness that Du Bois so famously describes in *The Souls of the Black Folk* (1903). The narrative divides according to color lines, as we observe blacks and whites in all the variety of their complications and conflicts, just as Moon also shifts attention to the self-made world of African Americans. One consistent source of praise for Moon was that he avoided the "invective and exacerbation" that so often characterized the "increasing pile of novels about negro life in America."[51] But most of these books were by white—not black—writers, and, in the postwar years, were quite self-consciously part of a new challenge. While these novels aimed to particularize the complex world of race relations, sixty years later they can sometimes seem a little too conventional to matter much. Nevertheless, for the literary historian, their absence in the discussion of race in U.S. literary history is an injustice that ought to be corrected. For these books testify to mainstream efforts to imagine the brotherhood of which Ellison wrote and the American-African presence that Toni Morrison stipulates as crucial to any right conception of U.S. cultural identity. Yet, apparently, the only white writer whose imagination of race mattered to later chroniclers of the era is Faulkner, whose *Intruder in the Dust* (1948) actually seems less searching and more ordinary when placed in this historical context.

White novelists also tried occasionally to imagine the inner lives of black folk. Edwin Peeples's *Swing Low* (1945), for example, tells of one farm couple's benighted move to the city, where they meet prejudice and injustice and are forced to return to the country. Like Peeples, Alice Nisbet's *Send Me an Angel* (1946), a story of a woman's love for her "imbecile" son and the no-good husband who returns to cause his death, met with decidedly mixed reviews. Both were praised by white reviewers for their "great tenderness" in portraying individual black characters, even as they can be "unintentionally patronizing" in treating the race as a "mass," according to Bucklin Moon.[52]

Just as split was the view of those writers who concentrated on the reality of race relations. Among the most critically acclaimed of these novels is Fannie Cook's *Mrs. Palmer's Honey* (1946), the first winner of the George Washington Carver Prize, about the transformation of a domestic servant into a labor leader. Otherwise, few were marked critical successes. Helped by its status as a BOMC choice, *Kingsblood Royal* (1947) scored an unlikely hit in Sinclair Lewis's tale of a man who thought he was white; when he discovers his black identity, he resolves to live out his racial fate, not in the repressive South but in a North that cannot conceal its hypocrisy and racial bias. Many reviews used the novel to assess Lewis's achievement at the end of his career, applauding his successful tract but lamenting the bankruptcy of his imagination, as his foray into race consciousness appears conventional. Isador Young's novel of a young black woman of the Brooklyn slums, *Jadie Greenway* (1947), did have a popular audience and was well regarded, even if we no longer remember it. The novel, according to one reviewer, was told with "painful realism . . . and the vernacular . . . makes for difficult and distressing reading," though the same critic touted it, in the condescending but once acceptable way, as "a modest but effective *Tree Grows in Brooklyn* for the colored people."[53]

In part as a legacy of *Strange Fruit*, several novels tried to portray interracial sexual relations too, but these often failed, like two books by David Alman, *Hourglass* (1947), which observes the consequences of the rape of a young black woman by three white men, and *The Well of Compassion* (1948), which is the story of a white woman who marries a black artist, not for love or even for forbidden allure, but because she thinks it will enhance her art. He, in turn, marries her out of a desire to escape the black world. Of course, neither gets what they wish for, and their divorce is inevitable. More successful were first-time authors Mark Harris, writing a kunstlerroman that includes an interracial marriage, *Trumpet to the World* (1946), and Irwin Stark, whose *The Invisible Island* (1948)—a precursor to Evan Hunter's *The Blackboard Jungle* (1954)—tells of a teacher who goes to Harlem to alleviate his guilt at having been classified 4-F, thus paying tribute to his best friend who died overseas. Somewhat more original, and seemingly drawn from autobiographical materials, was Worth Tuttle Hedden's *The Other Room* (1947), about a conservative young Southern woman who learns on her arrival that the out-of-state teaching job she has accepted is at an all-black college. She stays on—to learn both the basics of racial equality and the power of interracial love. A few reviewers valued the book's right-mindedness, but others wished that it had been more skillfully told. Some novelists, of course, eschewed craft altogether and hoped to exploit the new attention to race, such as John Henry Hewlett, whose *Harlem Story* (1948) relates the love affair of two African Americans who, unbeknownst to each other, are both trying to pass as white.

Better intentioned but also unsuccessful was Clifton Cuthbert's novel of Harlem jazz life, *The Robbed Heart* (1945), which features an interracial romance between a white musician and a middle-class African American woman. A much stronger urban tale of race is *Duke* (1949), by Hal Ellson, a white social worker, whose novels over the next decade or so describe the life he observed of teenage gangs. Throughout the late '40s, African American authors sought alternately to portray the demands of the black community as well as the problems of living in a white-dominated society. Besides Willard Motley, whose hard-boiled, though racially uninflected tale of the Chicago streets, *Knock on Any Door* (1947), has been a curiosity to literary historians, Chester Himes and Ann Petry are the novelists who published a couple of books each during the interim and who most readily come to mind as the African American novelists in the hiatus between *Black Boy* and *Invisible Man*.[54]

Petry had grown up in Old Saybrook, Connecticut, and moved to New York where she worked as a journalist, an experience that helped her further to understand issues facing black Americans. She took up some of those concerns in *The Street* (1946), which began her literary career. Himes wrote *If He Hollers Let Him Go* (1945), a home-front novel about a factory worker's struggle with racial and class prejudice. "An honest, bitter, but not very original book," opined the *New Yorker* reviewer, encapsulating all three of the responses that other reviewers were likely to emphasize. Two years later, Himes wrote another labor novel, *Lonely Crusade*, which Arna Bontemps called "provocative," maintaining that Himes's talent was readily apparent, though other reviewers complained of the novel's length, the author's bile, and the story's melodrama. Taken together, the two books give nuance to Himes's early efforts in reshaping the subject matter of black life in terms of class struggle in a world where color counts for everything.[55]

Besides William Gardner Smith, who would publish two more books twenty years later, two other African American novelists emerged in this era only to disappear. Both made the relation between color and class the focus of their books; both won praise everywhere the books were read, and both, as far as I can determine, never published again. Alden Bland, in *Behold a Cry* (1947), dramatizes the racial and economic problems facing the African American migrants to Chicago after World War I. Willard Savoy, in *Alien Land* (1949), describes a middle-class father's resistance to the seductions of passing for white and his rupture, and ultimate reconciliation, with his lighter-complexioned son, who is resolved to live as a white. An "exciting, as well as frightening journey," observed the reviewer in the *San Francisco Chronicle*. Most white reviewers agreed, even if some praised while others lamented the novel's explicit concern for social justice over art. In the *Saturday Review of Literature*, Petry also held that the novel suffers from too much speech-giving, but when Savoy resumes the narrative, "the book is wonderfully alive, moving at a headlong pace." Bontemps, writing in the *Herald Tribune*, welcomed the "newest Negro novelist" and praised *Alien Land*'s "conviction" and "rugged" style.[56]

ANTI-SEMITISM AND THE FORTIES

Southern culture, race, crime, violence, guilt, and the socioeconomic foundations of its explanations are only the most immediate reference points in describing how the middle class imagined otherness in postwar America. Nearly as powerful a stimulus to the question of the place of minorities in U.S. culture was the understanding of American Jews' presence in a nation that emerged so victorious from the war. To that end, at least one important book organized the feelings of many citizens on the subject. Moreover, there was an increasing appetite for hard-hitting tell-all fiction, novels undertaking to unveil the corruption of American institutions and customs. *Gentleman's Agreement* (1947) is by far the best known of these, but the tendency it represents is also observable in a Canadian novel, Gwethalyn Graham's *Earth and High Heaven* (1944), which treats anti-Semitism in Montreal during World War II, a work that won huge audiences and was translated into ten languages.

Novels opposing anti-Semitism were already an identifiable index to American social anxieties. Especially in the late '40s, with the newsreel images of Hitler's death camps fresh in citizens' memories, American fiction made the exposure of Jew-hating a cause célèbre, one that glorified the nation's spiritual health. Besides Bellow's *The Victim* (1947), appearing around the same time as Hobson's novel, there were books like Arthur

Miller's early novel, *Focus* (1945), a story of a Gentile who, by donning glasses, is mistaken for a Jew and encounters prejudice (finally made into a movie fifty-five years later). Abraham Bernstein's description of job discrimination, *Home Is the Hunted* (1947), was also a returning vet novel and something of a failure on both counts. *Whisper My Name* (1949), by Burke Davis, tries to show race hatred's deleterious effects on a Jew who finally learns that the community in which he has been passing for years has always known the truth. Esteemed novelists like Josephine Lawrence in *Let Us Consider One Another* (1945) and Mary Jane Ward in *The Professor's Umbrella* (1948) also took up the issue as it appeared in a mixed marriage or in college politics. Norman Katkov gave an interesting twist to the subject by exploring a Jewish family's opposition to a mixed marriage and by exposing the seldom-acknowledged reality of Jewish contempt for Christians in *Eagle at My Eyes* (1948). The most lauded of these novels—it won the Harper Prize in 1946—was by Jo Sinclair (Ruth Seid); her *Wasteland* presents a character study of Jake Braunovitz, who takes the name "John Brown" in order to succeed in business. His self-hatred ultimately leads him to a psychiatrist's office, and the novel gives itself over to demonstrating the efficacy of the psychoanalytic method, while picturing Braunovitz's family and his efforts to achieve a stable identity. Although critics debated Sinclair's command of the stream-of-consciousness technique, one interesting review placed her novel in another context: "It is a fascinating, detailed account, faithful in its delineation of a situation common to America, repeated in every industrial city and town, duplicated in every tenement. For it is not primarily a Jewish story. . . . It is an American story, the story of a predominantly Anglo-Saxon culture and the differences it presents to people reared in peasant societies of Slavic or Latin countries."[57]

Stories about American Jews in the years following World War II were generally about a member of the middle class being hated, as opposed to Jewish American novels of the '30s, which were more often about being poor or illiterate. These books mark a transition between the proletarian novels and the embourgeoisification narratives, like Herman Wouk's *Marjorie Morningstar* in the '50s. The reviewer, Thomas Sugrue, accurately enough designates the import of this context for Sinclair's book, yet there were dozens more novels about Jews than about other groups. Not to the extent of African Americans, Jews emerged as the social minority, not the class contrast, by which to measure the purity of American democracy. Previously,

J. H. Wallis, a popular romancer, wrote *The Niece of Abraham Pein* (1943), a mystery tale in which a Jew is persecuted by his anti-Semitic neighbors, who prosecute him for the murder of his missing daughter, as seen through the eyes of a fair-minded attorney enlisted to protect the integrity of the judicial system, a Gentile's view of how anti-Semitism endangers the Gentile world. Later, Harry Sylvester's *Moon Gaffney* (1947) revealed anti-Jewish prejudice, among other racial hatreds, in Brooklyn's middle-class Irish neighborhoods.

Laura Z. Hobson's *Gentleman's Agreement* (1947) is the novel that most clearly has special resonance for the years following the end of World War II, but before the time when Americans were happy and unself-conscious again. What was America interpreting itself to be in the early postwar years and how did anti-Semitism signify? The United States needed to understand itself as not Europe—that is, not the place where devastation and destruction would be visited on a civilian population, where rubble replaced statuary as the iconographic display of civilization. Now that its heart was no longer young and gay, America interpreted itself as the place where its innocence—its sense of its rightness—could be squared with its mightiness, and its responsibility, as a world power. Yet even to the willfully innocent American mind, that was not easy to do. It required settling some moral accounts at home. In order to *be* America—to itself and the rest of the world—the United States had to answer questions, especially how it would treat its minorities. It had to wrestle, as we have seen, with the "Negro Problem," what Myrdal redefined as the gap between American creed and American deed. For the key to the way the United States could live up to its image was to confront how it expected African Americans to fight and die for freedoms abroad that they could not share in at home.

The United States had also to redress its guilt in incarcerating Japanese Americans, which it began doing in Morton Grodiuz's powerful book *America Betrayed* (1949). The nation had to struggle as well with the second-class status it conferred on its mestizo and Chicano peoples, for that would disclose the way America was truly part of the Americas, not Europe. As always, it would have to face the grimmest truths, as it had tried in the past to do, of how it persecuted its indigenous peoples. Yet in the way that America could be reinvented as America and prove to itself that it was not Europe, it had to confront the country's affinity for the great European prejudice: it had to examine its own pervasive anti-Semitic customs and accept its Jews as part of the body social and the body politic. Not a syllable by any foreign observer suggests the urgency of this concern; yet, in 1947 and 1948, the issues of what it meant to be a Jew in America and what it meant to discriminate against Jews would be very nearly as pressing a cultural anxiety as racism against blacks. So compelling was the consciousness of the Nazis' effort to exterminate European Jewry that it may have seemed that only with the resolution of this issue could the United States truly begin the international business of being America.

To this end, the country was deeply divided, as it had been throughout the decade. As early as 1940 *Life* magazine ran a three-part series on anti-Semitism in America, while litterateur Maurice Samuel addressed this socially tolerated prejudice in a meditation, *The Great Hatred*. In the 1920s, the fear of Jewish immigration had been one of the driving anxieties behind congressionally mandated cutbacks, and throughout the '30s quota systems prevailed at American colleges and universities; into the 1940s, professions were closed to Jews, and housing covenants existed openly—discrimination that would continue for years. Jews were seen as controlling the movies— actually they did not, as the Protestant-owned New York banks owned the studios—or were scorned as capitalist fagins, on the one hand, and perpetrators of international Marxist/Zionist conspiracies, on the other. Among the most popular radio shows of the '30s was that of Father Charles Edward Coughlin, the Detroit priest whose anti-Semitism got bolder as his following grew. Even marginal "salesmen of hate," like Gerald L. K. Smith and Gerald Winrod, prospered, editing their spurious newsletters and directing fascist organizations like the America First Party or Action America, among other like-minded reactionary coalitions.

Even during World War II, hatred for Jews in the United States seemed little to abate. Polls suggested that Jewish Americans were perceived to shirk their duty and to find ways out of the service, a sad falsehood given the fact that Jewish men died in the war according to their percentage of the population; Jewish soldiers even won medals for heroism at a rate a few percentage points higher than the national proportion would have demanded. In the late '40s, America would have to admit what it did not want to know in the early '40s—that the Jews turned away before the war perished in the Nazi death camps. Throughout the '30s as well as throughout the war, Hitler's treatment of the Jews was recounted by reliable sources in the Protestant press, the magazines and newspapers to which churchmen and -women subscribed. Yet during that time, stories of mass murder and countless acts of inhumanity were discounted as propaganda, atrocity tales, or unverified accounts, though reports from previously trustworthy correspondents, from the mid-thirties on, kept being filed. "So it was true!" said one editorialist for a Protestant church publication, the *Sign of the Times*, in a May 1945 reflection on a visit to a Nazi death camp.[58] It was not simply that readers of the respectable church press, in ignoring these accounts, contributed to an atmosphere in which anti-Semitism was permitted to thrive. More subtly, this willful disbelief meant that anti-Semitism was understood not as something to be ashamed of or denied but tolerated.

If soldiers came back from Europe with the news that prejudice *is* terrible, it was news to many of their waiting families. So rife was anti-Semitism in the years right after the war that several publications typified the urgency of the liberal conscience, stirred by newsreels of the death camps, to raise the question forcefully. Articles appeared in many of the opinion magazines, especially Norman Cousins's reports in the *Saturday Review of Literature*, about a beating at the University of Iowa during the summer of 1947 and Bruce Bliven's eight-part series in the *Nation* describing the agents, rationales, victims, and dynamics of anti-Semitism. European intellectuals also tried to come to grips: Max Horkheimer and Theodor Adorno had already addressed the cultural and psychological formation of anti-Semitism in the as-yet untranslated *Dialectics of Enlightenment* (1944), and Jean-Paul Sartre, now enjoying his period of greatest favor in the United States, published an English translation of *Anti-Semite and Jew* (1948).

No one more thoroughly personified the institutionalized ethic of hatred at home than Mississippi congressman John E. Rankin, who, from his seat in the U.S. House of Representatives, called Walter Winchell, the famous publicist and radio personality, a "little kike." Not a single member of Congress rose to denounce Rankin. Laura Hobson was appalled and saw in this episode the approach to the "coming home" novel on which she was working. She immediately understood that Congress's indulgence meant complicity, that the silence of Rankin's colleagues revealed how vulgar anti-Semitism and genteel anti-Semitism complemented and sustained each other. With this in mind, she reconstructed her novel-in-progress about the America to which the GIs return so that it would expose how anti-Semitism flourished here. Her book's mission became nothing less than the education of a public unwilling to see its involvement in the very sin Rankin's remark ramified.

Gentleman's Agreement was one of the most controversial and successful novels of 1947. First excerpted, near the end of 1946, in *Cosmopolitan* magazine, the novel was immediately destined for Hollywood. While none of the so-called Jewish moguls, who typically disparaged the commercial viability of subjects having to do with Jews, would touch the film rights, Darryl Zanuck, producer of *The Jazz Singer*, *Little Caesar*, and *The Sound of Music*, gambled on its market and cultural appeal. He was right: the movie, starring Gregory Peck (who had already begun the string of roles that would make him the icon of WASP moral authority), was the Academy Award–winning Best Picture for 1948.

In Hobson's novel, Philip Green is a well-regarded investigative journalist who passes as a Jew for two months or so, in response to his new editor's demand that he do something really big and fresh on the question of American anti-Semitism—one "hell of a stiff assignment," they agree.[59] As it happens, the idea for this magazine series is first suggested by the editor's recently divorced niece, Kathy Lacey, the New Woman who finds herself drawn to the equally susceptible widower. They fall in love, but their ultimate union is threatened when she thinks that he takes too seriously the crowding a lifetime of felt prejudice into eight weeks of posing as a Jew. Then she fears that Phil Green thinks she subscribes to the very prejudices she has helped him to uncover, but, worse, she also thinks she might as well. Whether they can resolve their difficulties is left unanswered, though on the last page they seem ready to try.

Excluded from the Book-of-the-Month Club, which had already chosen *Kingsblood Royal* (1947) as its latest socially conscious new work of fiction, Hobson's novel immediately gained a wide following, the result of being distributed by the less prestigious but more popular Dollar Book Club. *Gentleman's Agreement* would certainly have reached a broader audience than the other important novel of 1947 concerning anti-Semitism, Bellow's *The Victim*. Positive as some responses were, Hobson's novel mostly garnered respectful assessments—"readable and effective," said the *Christian Science Monitor*; sometimes begrudgingly, "special pleading," observed *Catholic World*. Readers would respond favorably, or so the *Survey Graphic*, the popular sociology magazine, predicted: "The book's enormous value is in the very way it cheerfully falls in with the style and manner of 'women's fiction.' Wearing this seemingly innocuous guise, it manages to describe anti-Semitism with a thoroughness that a professor of sociology might envy. . . . There will be those who will object to this book because it is tastelessly written. They will be overlooking one of its greatest assets." The reviewer, James Reid Parker, goes on to observe: "Women who wouldn't touch *The Nation* or *The New Republic* [or the *Survey Graphic*] with a ten-foot pole are going to read 'Gentleman's Agreement' as they sit under the dryer."[60]

For this reviewer, opinions gleaned at the hairdresser's are obviously not those that one encounters in magazines of politics and letters and must be inferior to them. Thus, Hobson is perceived as translating a story of cultural reconciliation into the story of love gone awry, to the extent that the bourgeois marriage plot, conventional as we may find it, is fundamental to this latest romance of the republic. Will Phil Green's sympathetic identification with Jews and his determination to lay bare American anti-Semitism keep him from marrying Kathy Lacey, or will they each find in their complex feelings about Jews the opportunity, in the postwar era, to realign their torn and confused lives? Beyond this, as semitough-guy author of *What Makes Sammy Run?* (1941) and *The Harder They Fall* (1947), Budd Schulberg asserts in the *New Republic* that such sources of appeal "don't blunt the sharp, hard point of this welcome, timely, able tract." For Schulberg, "Mrs. Hobson deserves whatever prizes a push-me-pull-you democracy can bestow on one of its more responsible citizens. . . . Mrs. Hobson's novel is a Stop-Look-Listen-and Do-Something warning for every American."[61]

Like abolitionists writing about the ills of slavery for a Northern white audience, Hobson takes the decisive step of rendering anti-Semitism's impact on Gentiles, male and female, for the novel is almost entirely unconcerned with the inner lives of Jews. We see only a few—Phil's secretary, a deracinated self-hating passer; his boyhood pal, Dave, a war hero who finds himself unable to accept a good job in New York because he faces discrimination in his search for appropriate housing for his family; and a scientist-philosopher who dispenses sage advice. We are meant to observe the effects of hating Jews on Christians, whether they are Phil's social-climbing sister, Kathy's snobby sister, or Phil's son, who becomes the victim of anti-Semitic abuse when neighborhood kids give him a rough time once they suppose that the family is Jewish. ("Now you know it all," says Dave, "There's the place they really get at you—your kids. Now you even know about that. You can quit being Jewish tomorrow. There's nothing else.") The effect of the boy's traumatic moment on Kathy is to assure him of his privilege, that he, like she, should be "glad" that he is a Christian and that "it would be awful" to be otherwise: "It's just a fact, like being glad you were good-looking instead of ugly, or comfortably fixed instead of poor, healthy instead of crippled, young instead of old." Thus Hobson stages the various rationalizations that enable anti-Semitism to flourish: "It was purely a practical recognition," for Kathy, "not a judgment of superior status." For Phil, "the biggest thing about the whole business" is that such realistic understandings are precisely the problem: "It's just that I've come to see that lots of nice people who aren't [anti-Semitic] *are* [anti-Semites'] unknowing helpers and connivers. People who'd never beat up a Jew or yell kike at a child. They think antisemitism is something way off there, in a dark crackpot place with low-class morons."[62] As the novel shows, such citizens will still patronize restricted hotels, still enjoy the favor of being Christian in America.

Writing in *Commentary*, Diana Trilling derogates the novel for its complete susceptibilty to the "sterility of our fashionable liberal ideal": "Were such values Mrs. Hobson's alone, they would not be worth noting. But these identical touchstones of moral and psychological health appear in novel after novel of the liberal persuasion. Surely no totalitarian ideal has ever projected a more complete regimentation of the psychic life of a nation than our present-day liberal ideal. Does the liberal society that Mrs. Hobson envisages allow no distinction between Jew and Gentile? For that matter, it allows no distinctions between human beings." For Trilling, the danger of *Gentleman's Agreement* is that it monistically sets aside, in the name of tolerance, the cultural pluralism that "complicates our notion of both society and the individual, and makes a place for saving human differences which can often be even political salvation."[63]

Obviously, Trilling's aim is to resist the encroachments of liberal culture, which she identifies as the deliberate work of bourgeois fiction, but so thoroughly under way is this new hegemony in America that her efforts seem futile. The following year, Carey McWilliams, the author of the influential study of race relations *Brothers under the Skin* (1942), published the second part of that investigation, *A Mask for Privilege: Anti-Semitism in America* (1948). As if to bear out Hobson's argument, that book describes how anti-Jewish discrimination was given its impetus, during the early years of the Gilded Age, by the top ranks of society from whom anti-Semitism still drew its strength. McWilliams's study was immediately recognized as "penetrating and cool-headed," "a brilliant and comprehensive analysis . . . of this grave threat to American democracy and security." Some reviewers saw the book as "absorbing, uncompromisingly honest and almost frightening," but even those who objected to its "superficiality" and "dogmatic attitude" conceded that this analysis was "useful in pointing out the dangerous spread of anti-semitism in America," praising McWilliams for "urging efforts at a cure."[64]

Anti-Semitism would become more explicitly the nation's business in the debate to adjust the laws concerning the admission of displaced persons from Europe. The machinations of several congressmen in resisting President Harry S. Truman's call for immediate succor for Jewish refugees seem like something out of the anti-immigration arguments of the '20s. Not only were quotas on refugees placed at 1920 levels, but also the same need to check the threat of subversive politics (by checking the threat to the gene pool) was again invoked. One Wisconsin representative called for refugees with "good blood": "We don't want rats; we've got enough of them already." So when Congress, following Truman, called for the admission of 200,000 Displaced Persons (DPS), to be registered by 21 April 1947, the Senate subcommittee cut the number in half, while confining eligibility to those DPS who had been in the Nazi camps by 22 December 1945, thus restricting the potential number of Jewish refugees, since many concentration camp survivors had not by then been designated as displaced. Moreover, the Senate subcommittee on immigration also stipulated that 50 percent of the visas be reserved for agricultural workers and 50 percent of the total be admitted from Baltic states annexed by Russia after the war, moves seen as transparently discriminatory, since Jews not already in the cities had gravitated there after the war; Jews in the Baltic states had already been slaughtered.[65]

This bill was worked into a compromise with a congressional one that, after all the wrangling, kept its anti-Semitic character intact. Reluctantly, Truman signed into law this new "gentleman's agreement" called the Displaced Persons Act of 1948. While several members of Congress condemned the legislation, it was not until the next session that the most glaring evidence of its deliberately exclusionary character—the 22 December 1945 cutoff date—could be undone. By that time, many Jewish refugees had made their way to Israel, which had declared its nationhood in May 1948. At precisely the moment when America could have opened its doors, it shut them, just as it had a decade before when it closed its borders to thousands of European Jewish refugees. For all of the novel's powerful influence, it demands too much of *Gentleman's Agreement* to effect so dramatic a change.

BETWEEN TWO WARS

The historical self-consciousness of the era directly following World War II might be measured in the sheer number of novels that were devoted to examining the recent past and, often, its shaping of the present. In a form carried over from the 1930s, many novels were committed to cultivating a plot of land and a family's fortunes as historical exempla of character- as well as nation-building. Subjects were as diversified as Elizabeth Howard's *Before the Sun Goes Down* (1946), a tale of two families in Gilded Age small-town Pennsylvania, and Sholem Asch's *East River* (1948), a story of the New York Jewish immigrants. In *Our Own Kind* (1946), Edward McSorley inscribed the history of an Irish family in turn-of-the-century Providence, Rhode Island, while Gerald Brace gives the genealogy of another New England family in *The Garretson Chronicles* (1947). Paul Wellman's *Walls of Jericho* (1947), a tale of feuding Kansas families, may have been the most successful novel in his very long career as an entertaining storyteller. *The Quarry* (1947), a historical novel by Mildred Walker, returned to racial themes, this time in the enduring friendship between a woebegone Vermont villager and the escaped slave he befriends. The year 1948 saw the most accomplished of the genre, *Raintree County*, Ross Lockridge's tempestuous epic of lust and the abiding memory of the Civil War in Indiana, also a best seller. That same year brought out another Kansas novel, Joseph Pennell's *The History of Nora Beckham*, which followed his critical success, *The History of Rome Hanks* (1944). Another noted sequel was Betty Smith's move from the turn-of-the-century Irish neighborhood of *A Tree Grows in Brooklyn* to the 1920s in *Tomorrow Will Be Better*, the fifth best-selling novel of the year.

The tumult of the preceding three decades was so ripe a subject that the interbellum years were mined time and again in the brief period before the Cold War. One of the most commercially successful novels of the year was *Dinner at Antoine's* (1948), Frances Parkinson Keyes's rendition of political, financial, and social circumstances of the Louisiana bayou from the end of World War I through World War II. And one of the most critically successful was Edmund Wilson's *Memoirs of Hecate County* (1946), which treated the milieu of the cultivated rich during the years before and after the Depression. By 1948, the form, having fully moved from romance to realism, pursued a conviction of doom, especially to be seen in Martin Dibner's tale of four sad young men of the Class of 1933 during the years of the Depression and then the war, *Bachelor Seals*. A European novel about the lead-up to the previous war, Robert Briffault's *Europa: The Days of Ignorance* (1935) made a deep impact on U.S. writers, including May Sarton, who wrote of Belgians, not Americans, during the interbellum period, in *Bridge of Years* (1946); Richard Plant transferred the story to Frankfurt before the burning of the Reichstag in *Dragon in the Forest* (1948). In another American adaptation, Hiram Haydn's group portrait of six young people in the late 1920s, *Time Is Noon* (1948), promised to be "among the most widely discussed recent novels," if only because "in our present moment of crisis," "few readers are likely to escape the sense of being personally involved by it."[66]

Kenneth Davis's *Years of the Pilgrimage* (1948), still another Kansas novel of misspent passions, was set in the present but was told in flashbacks. Neil S. Boardman's *The Long Home* (1948) shifts the scene to Minnesota, where the illegitimate son of a conventional family joins the labor movement in the '30s but loses his faith in the party and then loses his girlfriend. Dorothy West brings the story to Boston and the doings of a young African American woman, Cleo Judson, "a chronicle," says Arna Bontemps, "of twisted lives" in *The Living Is Easy* (1948).[67] David Lord's *Joey* (1949) marries the interbellum novel with the family novel, mixed with the second-generation immigration story, by tracing the history of the American-born son of a Jewish family in Los Angeles.

If the recent past, as ever, was seen as a rich field for fiction's investigation of the secret of current realities, the present was a cultural and political spectacle that required continual unmasking. In 1946, the tell-all was Frederic Wakeman's exposé of the radio advertising business, *The Hucksters* (later made into a film with Clark Gable). While Hobson's Philip Green wants to "blow the lid off" anti-Semitism, Schulberg is doing the same for boxing in *The Harder They Fall* (1947). Also in the spirit of an inside look was a book by Harold Robbins, who began his career with a serious novel about moviemakers' greed and corruption in *The Dream Merchants* (1949), a subject treated farcically in Ludwig Bemelmans's *Dirty Eddie* (1947). There Bemelmans—now chiefly remembered as the children's book author-illustrator who created the enduring favorite, Madeline, but who for years enjoyed a reputation as a cosmopolitan wag and travel writer—satirized Hollywood moviemaking by making a pig the star.

Other professions were also skewered, none more thoroughly than journalism, including *New York Times* book reviewer William Du Bois's *Island in*

the *Square* (1947), a retrospective account of a '20s New York newspaperman; Jerome Weidman's *The Price Is Right* (1949), a story of cut-throat
competition for a top job in the New York news syndicate; and John Brooks's
The Big Wheel (1949), which was perhaps the most successful at extrapolating moral issues out of the inside stuff of editorial offices. Occasionally, these
novels could be satiric, such as Charles Harrison's send-up of poll taking,
which by this time had become a national sport, *Nobody's Fool* (1948), a
theme recurring in Shepherd Mead's satire on opinion surveys and the
discovery of the perfect index in one small-town fellow, *The Magnificent
MacInnes* (1949).

Lionel Trilling's *Middle of the Journey* (1947) is now the best known and
most estimable of these works examining the ethical stakes of the relation
between power and ideas, but it should also be recalled as helping to create a
context for novels about politics and contemporary history. Samuel Hopkins
Adams's *Plunder* (1948), a novel about the attempt of some corrupt Washington officials to fix the Army-Navy game, seemed to surpass itself as an
inside look and to venture social commentary on the kind of scapegrace
profiteers drawn to national politics. Another novel along these lines was
Merle Miller's *The Sure Thing* (1949), an account of a young State Department official who is subjected to an unjust investigation. The reviewers
generally held Miller's character in low regard, but no less an observer than
John Kenneth Galbraith, writing in the *New York Times*, demurred: "Mr.
Miller has made the thirty-six hours of FBI interrogations, press exposes,
political denunciations, empty regrets, frightened condolences, welching
friends, fear and loneliness as real as the smell of burning flesh."[68]

Although the Cold War had not yet got its name, we already start finding
novels about the perceived confrontation to come between world powers.
These novels make an explicit effort to confront the changes in American
political culture and to write about them in ways that middle-class readers
would especially find engaging. A year before George Orwell's *1984*, Gerald
Heard brought out *Doppelgangers: An Episode of the 4th, the Psychological,
Revolution* (1947), "a fantastic tale of the future in which two opposing
dictatorships fight for supremacy": "a thoroughly exciting and stimulating
book, combining a horror story, a political and philosophical treatise, a study
of modern revolutions, with other elements, that made Aldous Huxley's
Brave New World a gruesome satire on what man's life might be like if a
police dictatorship were ever run by cold-blooded scientists."[69] Novels about

nuclear destruction had also begun to appear: Pat Frank's satire, *Mr. Adam* (1946), tells of the struggle to perpetuate the human race in the story of the only male, a geologist, to survive an explosion of the great nuclear fission plants and who did not lose his potency. (Frank followed *Mr. Adam* with another satiric novel, *An Affair of State* [1948]—about State Department bureaucracy and the young official who discovers a plot to overthrow Stalin but whose friendship with a Russian officer makes him untrustworthy.) Previously, Otto Schrag offered a more somber parable in *Bedrock* (1948), the story of a surgeon's alienation from a world hovering on mass destruction who finds fulfillment, ironically enough, in the desert. The point is less to extol these writers than to remember the interest of what they did write, novels that complicate the history of American fiction in the postwar era as complacent or unresponsive to the shift in social codes and ideological values, a tradition that we will see continued throughout the 1950s.

GIVE US OUR DREAM

As much as any other novel, *Give Us Our Dream* (1947), by Arthémise Goertz, aptly summarizes the postwar hopes and apprehensions of middle-class Americans who lived through World War II. Written on Long Island about the inhabitants of an apartment house there by a Southern woman recuperating from the ordeal of confinement and disease in wartime Japan, this example of light fiction moves through a series of episodes reminding us of Mr. Bennett's wisdom in *Pride and Prejudice* that "we live to make sport for our neighbors and to laugh at them in our turn." Here we follow Mrs. Marsan, who, binoculars in hand, studies her neighbors and tries to help them sort their way through the human comedy. Consider how the *Saturday Review* recommended the novel's attractions to readers: "The grand coffee-party with Adrian's arty talk, Mrs. Marsan's malapropisms, and Jessamine's mad, irrelevant comments; the innocently wicked scene in which Mrs. Marsan informs the preacher concerning real Christianity: the hilarious reading aloud of 'Tess of the D'Urbervilles' with the sound literary criticism of the cleaning lady who is listening."[70]

As much as the novel trades on middle-class superficiality, it stimulates readers to ask, What is the dream that Americans wanted their culture to "give" them? The story of those hopes is perennially the business of middle-class novels, insofar as they narrate national fantasies, desires that popular culture instills but that can never be fulfilled, even as they also chronicle the combined material and social aspirations of citizens—the dream of solvency, independence, and betterment. This vision of a beneficent America lies at the heart of postwar images of the national dream, the desire America is imagined as gratifying. Surely this is the understanding that animates such popular fictions as *Mr. Blandings Builds His Dream House* (1946) and Edward Streeter's *Father of the Bride* (1949), two postwar novels satirizing the new American consumerism that were also made into beloved films. On the other hand, several novels exploited the world of work to characterize the vitality of American social and economic aspiration. For example, Josiah Greene, an army sergeant at the time he won the Macmillan Prize for the best manuscript by a member of the armed forces, made an Eastern dairy the center of *Not in Our Stars* (1945) in a story of the interwoven lives of workers and managers, a novel praised roundly for its "biting veracity"; Orville Prescott, writing in the *Yale Review*, called it one of the year's notable books—"vital, intense, dramatic, and mature."[71] If at its worst, the novel seems dull and overly detailed, it still means to argue the limits of defining the pursuit of happiness when workers have insufficient responsibility and too little participation in the business decisions that affect their lives. Along similar lines, Thomas Bell further pursued this apprehension of a worker's alienation in *There Comes a Time* (1946), whose protagonist is no longer one of this writer's beleaguered proletarians but a middle-aged bank teller who overcomes paralyzing uncertainty by joining a union and involving himself concretely in the world outside his desires. Alternatively, in *Shadow of Heaven* (1947), Alfred Hayes describes a world-weary labor organizer who has lost faith in the cause.

In the years following World War II, contemporary novels devoted to the complicated relation between family and work sought a form that went beyond the multigenerational saga. Books dramatizing the tension between wanting love and wanting prestige, wanting money and wanting peace, tried to do so in the relative short compass of one generation, like Dan Wickenden's 1945 tale of a failed patriarch, *The Wayfarers*—"a skillful, soft-spoken novel about a middle-class family in a Middle Western town." According to the *Times*, "in a quiet way [it is] as true and intelligent a new novel as you are likely to encounter at the present moment." Wickenden describes a widowed father's coming to terms with the children he neglected during a decade-long bereavement. (*Commonweal* especially liked *The Wayfarers'* sense of proportion: "In writing about the America of those years [imme-diately before the war] it is difficult to leave out the approaching storm from overseas; it is to Mr. Wickenden's credit that he does not overstress, as most of his contemporaries do, the after-the-fact political predictions in which his characters occasionally indulge." Less felicitously, Allan Seager's *The Inheri-tance* (1948) moved from intimations of incest in his preceding novel (*Equi-nox* [1943]) to the dark tale of a Michigan bank president's son who finds his father's cache of pornography after his parents die in a car accident. He also learns of his father's unsavory business practices and discovers how small his financial inheritance really is. Yet so committed has he been to respecting the elder generation that he can only express the revulsion of his "inheri-tance" in a series of mediated acts of irresponsibility rather than outright repudiation—a drunken brawl, the public display of a prostitute—until he is committed for insanity. An "honest, effective, brilliantly written novel," intones the *Times*. In a novel like poet Howard Nemerov's *The Melodrama-tists* (1949), the family is seen as seeking separate ways of escaping reality, turning to religion and psychiatry, promiscuity, and even the Royal Canadian Mounted Police.[72]

If such books witness the distortions of hope and ambition, and ra-tionalized failures, Albert Maltz's *Journey of Simon McKeever* (1949) reminds readers of the restorative power of desire and the redemptions of merely trying. Here an elderly man searches for the fountain of youth in the form of a quest to cure his arthritis. But along the way, he discovers a sense of himself as his own agent, not the victim of forces of good and evil, but someone of courage and responsibility who is determined to write a book that will make his story known to others and thus to realize his dream of surviving. Praised as something even finer than a "tender little book," it was viewed as a repository of hope: "In this tightly plotted short novel, Mr. Maltz achieves an effect all too rare in current fiction—an affirmation of faith in man's courage, in man's will to put things right in a badly off-center world." Other reviewers appreciated the interest but were less enthused about the achievement: "Albert Maltz has once again attempted to fuse a fine talent for storytelling with an urgent sense of our social problems. It is an attempt illuminated from time to time by vivid characterization and by the author's faith in the underlying kindness of the average man, but as a story it strains credibility and as a message is forced."[73]

The power of dreams as a cultural referent appears throughout the half decade and helps to determine the range and character of American self-consciousness. To that end, novels of artists, writers, and intellectuals usefully criticized how a culture understood its dreams. Mary McCarthy and Wallace Stegner offered novels where the life of dreams collides with the life of ideas and the pretensions of those trying to live it. McCarthy's utopia of such desires, *The Oasis* (1949), mocks American intellectuals who repair to a magic mountain only to learn that they cannot really escape the banalities of everyday life. In *Second Growth* (1947), the scene of conflicting demands on life made by year-round villagers and the professors and writers who share a New Hampshire community during the summer marks, for Stegner, the difference that not only results in class tension, but also represents the vitalizing of a culture's shared center.

Two novels of 1947 interrogate our national fantasies in ways more attuned to a later multicultural moment, and both were important commercial successes. Both aimed to fix the character of the nation's dream life, one through a grimly realistic survey of the American "green world," the other through the romance of New York City, the capital of American desire at a particularly exciting moment: Marcia Davenport's *East Side, West Side* and John Steinbeck's *The Wayward Bus*, a more ambitious novel than the smaller one from that year—*The Pearl*—that later won favor with high school English teachers through the '60s and beyond. Though lacking the sales support of book club status, Davenport's novel was one of the year's great successes at the bookstores, while *The Wayward Bus* had trade as well as book club and armed services sales of more than half a million copies, sales that placed it just behind ever-popular Frank Yerby's *The Vixens* at sixth in the year's top ten. Part of the charm of these books came from their effort to define the postwar age even allegorically. Davenport's sense of American possibilities is recounted through the career of a woman—the daughter of a Jewish actress and an Irish contractor—who gives up her life as a famous philanthropist's spouse when she meets a returning war hero, also the son of an interfaith marriage. By contrast, Steinbeck creates a "medieval palimpsest" of characters (including Juan Chicoy of Irish Mexican heritage) caught amid their journey at a roadside gas station that becomes a sort of "Grand Hotel" and the locale for the revelation of their dashed hopes in order to impart a vision of the diversity of American dreams.[74]

Despite these authors' attempts to comprehend a broad scope of class and ethnicity in their descriptions of American aspirations, both efforts generally failed to impress critics, well received among readers as they may have been. According to the *New Yorker*, Davenport's "picture of the greedy, reckless life [in Manhattan] in the first days of peace is admirably done," a setting that allows the author to demonstrate how subordinate are the lives of the well-to-do to the working and middle classes in this "travelogue-cum-etiquette" book. Steinbeck, for his part, examines the new sense of American heterogeneity, especially in its various forms of sexual feelings and practices, to be found in the mixture of Americans arbitrarily recorded on a bus manifest, a catalog of desire whose scope surpasses *Tortilla Flat* (1935) or *Cannery Row* (1945). Critics, however, routinely dismissed *The Wayward Bus* as a disappointing effort by an excellent writer: "Very natural and funny, and at times very candid, is the talk. . . . But for all [the] animal magnetism and photographic reality, one ends by wondering if American life is actually so empty, so devoid of meaning, so lonely."[75]

INVISIBLE WOMEN

The life of desire in postwar novels, of course, finds its primary expression in the narratives of intimate relations, novels frequently dedicated to staging the reinvention of American women after the war. The most forceful impetus for this transformation can be traced to the wartime experience of many American women. Many of those women who had entered the workforce and created lives without men now underwent a dramatic shift in their attitudes toward courtship, romance, marriage, and child rearing as a result of their newly grasped freedom. The fiction of the second half of the 1940s amply testifies to this explanation, usually in case studies of American New Women. Some novels read like psychological treatises, whereas others only superficially describe a fissure in the history of American gender roles: sometimes the argument is encased in a historical novel and occasionally in an antisentimental romance. Yet the dominant form remains the novel of bourgeois experience and manners.

Perhaps the best remembered of these was a predecessor tale, one not written by a woman and not even much recollected as a novel, but more so as a Hollywood film, James Cain's *Mildred Pierce* (1941). That movie is often discussed in feminist film criticism, largely because of the fantasy it perpetuates of male visions of New Womanhood, but also because of the embattled relationship between mother and daughter, issues clearly present in Cain's novel too. By the end of the war, however, enough women had experienced enough of a changed social reality that the fiction might be expected to tell a different story. In the late fall of 1945, Elizabeth Janeway published *Daisy Kenyon*, which most reviewers agreed was an unworthy successor to her critically successful first novel, *The Walsh Girls* (1943), a tale of the two very different daughters of a pompous minister. In the new book, Janeway offers a sort of historical novel of the years 1940–42, a slick story of adultery on the home front. Critics scorned Janeway's failure either to satirize or to condemn the illicit lovers, especially since the novel ultimately favors marriage over mere liaison. In its false sympathy, says Diana Trilling, *Daisy Kenyon* was an especially revealing instance of the new American moral earnestness— the culture's easy readiness to condemn the true hollowness of the book.

Josephine Johnson's *Wildwood* (1946) returned her to critical favor as she moved away from the social realism of her previous effort, *Jordanstown* (1937), and back to the psychological realism of her Pulitzer Prize–winning novel, *Now in November* (1934). The new novel explores the loneliness of Edith Pierre, an introspective girl adopted by elderly cousins, as she grows into maturity. So cloistered is she that their death leaves her friendless and lost. Indeed, the novel recounts the process whereby women are led to withdraw from the world and end enslaved to their surroundings, infantilized and doomed. Later in 1946, Elinor Rice published *Mirror, Mirror*, which seems to be a polar opposite in that its heroine represents a New Woman who is fiercely determined to succeed as a fashion designer but who discovers the misery of dominating a marriage. Rice's novel was praised for its "honesty"; indeed, Diana Trilling describes Mona Biro as a "narcissist" who is also the "very prototype of the modern career woman." Trilling reviewed it in relation to Marquand's *B. F.'s Daughter*, which, we have seen, was the critics' consensus choice as the nation's home-front novel. In that book, to the extent that it shares in the typology of women's fiction, Polly Fulton learns the hard way about the consequences of her restless desire for fulfillment beyond domesticity. "There is no question," says Trilling, "but that the twin virtue to traditional domesticity is political conservatism."[76]

Women writers contest this vision throughout the rest of the decade in novels that specify efforts to contest gender inequality, especially, as we saw in Marita Wolff's *About Lyddy Thomas*, as a result of the war and its legacy. How those experiences helped to shape the quest for female subjectivity becomes apparent in Nancy Ross's *The Left Hand Is the Dreamer* (1947), a novel praised everywhere for its beautiful prose and its "lyric study of a woman, awakening to integrity." For some reviewers, however, the ideas were underdone, despite the author's aspiration of writing "a brief for the relevance of love in an age seemingly dedicated to destruction," as the *New York Times* reviewer summarized it. The generally liberal perspective of these case studies coincides with the structural critique that feminism was to wage in the '60s and '70s. Nor is it too much to hazard that these books helped to create the intellectual and cultural milieu out of which, twenty years later, Betty Friedan's *The Feminine Mystique* was fermented.[77]

One may contrast Ross's exemplary story of a woman's coming into self-possession with a cautionary tale, Martin Yoseloff's *The Girl in the Spike-heeled Shoes* (1949). If Ross suggests that a woman can find wholeness through the choice of her own lover, without social interference, Yoseloff tries to discipline his young woman. This "Magdalene of the juke joints" has been saved from a life of delinquency by marriage to a middle-class guy but now risks returning to her working-class origins when her GI husband goes AWOL to live with another woman. Luckily, she listens to the good advice of a priest. Not only is Maybelle then redeemed by bourgeois ideals of intimacy, but also she is further sustained by the church's wise counsel. Apparently, from this point of view, you cannot be a good woman without some help. Despite a satisfactory review here and there, and several acknowledgments of its verisimilitude, the novel never won much of an audience.[78]

Nor did Yoseloff, but consider the works of writers whose reputations have survived, to one extent or another. Conrad Richter departed from his historical trilogy of Ohio to write a story of fidelity by imagining in *Always Young and Fair* (1947) the case of a young woman who, after losing a fiancé in the Spanish-American War, tries to keep alive his memory by refusing an ardent suitor. Later, afraid of aging, she relents and marries the man though he no longer loves her. A male reviewer in the *New York Times* praises Richter's "graceful lucidity"; a female reviewer in the *Herald Tribune* asks for a "deeper probing of the human heart and mind." As a kind of countervision of the perils of renunciation, the great succès de scandale of the late '40s was John O'Hara's steamy and, for many, repulsive 600-page tale of a shallow, wealthy woman's history of sexual adventurism. Scorned by reviewers—liberal and conservative—*A Rage to Live* (1949), predictably, was among the best-selling novels of the postwar years.[79]

Some of the most successful novels about New Women were actually about old women, or women of a previous generation, who might still provide models of a kind of success. Some were books about the ferocious determination of women of times gone by, like Natalie Anderson Scott's *The Husband* (1949), a historical novel about a wholesome woman and her abusive husband in eighteenth-century Massachusetts, and Mabel Seeley's *Woman of Property* (1947), a punishing account of a turn-of-the-century small-town Midwestern woman, brutalized by her father, who scrambles for money, makes four marriages along the way, but loses the man she really loves. Seeley's novel was surprisingly well reviewed, since critics routinely conceded how hackneyed was the plot of this first serious literary effort by a fairly successful mystery writer. Victoria Lincoln's *Celia Amberley* (1949), a psychological portrait of an adolescent girl in the years immediately following World War I, was by no means the startling popular success that *February Hill* had been in 1934, but it was considered to be a "distinguished piece of fiction," especially for its treatment of the emotional pressures on a young woman by the "utter inadequacies of this environment," that is, the privileged world of the newly rich and Radcliffe College of the mid-1920s.[80]

Sometimes these novels were given over to depictions of women who set terrible but instructive examples. One such book was Peggy Munsterberg's *The Last Leaf* (1947), a "wise and objective and fair" account of a middle-aged spinster's effort to free herself from the past and live in the present. It tells of the "timeless problem of the overdominated, frustrated and genteel spirit unable to cope with the realities of the world": "a first novel of no small merit and distinction," observed the critics. Similarly, Mary Ellen Chase's short novel *Plum Tree* (1949) epitomizes the general conversation that so many of these novels, taken together, illustrate: a nurse who presides over a women's old-age home and aspires to be the symbol of grace in her charges' lives is challenged severely by three eccentric pensioners. The *Saturday Review* praised the novel as "[a] capsule of compassion made memorable by Miss Chase's almost unbearable awareness of the human heart."[81]

The New Woman novel was inextricably connected to the Sensitive Young Woman novel, too. Eleanor Estes's *Echoing Green* (1947) traces the development of one young woman into her twenties. After her father drinks himself to death, the family's struggles increase, until finally, on her mother's death, she moves to New York to begin a new life—"a warm, well-realized characterization," says the *New York Times*. We have already seen the contours of

Josephine Lawrence's career as an author who writes about women's private issues in response to more public circumstances—housing, aging, financial insecurities, intermarriage. In 1948, she contributed to this ongoing discussion of the stature of the American New Woman in *The Pleasant Morning Light*, a chronicle of three marriages that cousins feel pressured to make after the war, a story largely about generational tension. In 1949, Lawrence published *My Heart Shall Not Fear*, a story of three generations surrounding a dying young mother. Not as successful, according to one of her reviewers, as the best of her previous work, the novel "gives a clear and sympathetic picture of many dilemmas that confront young people and their families in A.D. 1949."[82] One such New Woman novel became famous because it represents the battle that a young woman claiming her identity has to wage, Mary Jane Ward's *The Snake Pit* (1946); the heroine is committed to an insane asylum to combat the manic depression that accompanies her new marriage. Ward's book rose to the tenth best-selling novel of the year.

There are so many more of these novels. Why are their authors virtually invisible? In part, American women writers would be slighted in the years that followed for not being veterans of the recent war. Thus their contributions were typically considered less important than those of the male writers who were themselves under critical indictment for not having written novels worthy of Fitzgerald, Hemingway, and Faulkner. The residual effect of these women writers' invisibility was a diminution of the value of domestic fiction, on the one hand, but, on the other, a consistent level of misprizing the achievements of women writers in the decades to come. So much of the historiography of the postwar era is a narrative of omission and neglect, beginning in the late '40s, when the search for a way of interpreting the relative weakness of the literary scene led critics to lose sight of the centrality of women writers and turn their attention to males. For it was then that the inordinate critical demands on American fiction also began to interpret the middle-class novel as too trivial to warrant serious attention. The result was the loss of a crucial mission for the novel to serve.

the 1950s

This last chapter observes the waning of the middle-class novel in the twentieth century before its revival in the 1980s. I begin by assessing the cultural opinion of the early fifties, first by looking at the kind of documents, like the famous colloquium, "Our Country and Our Culture," that usually mark this discussion, along with less heralded but no less revealing essays and lectures that, along with the changes in awarding various prizes, vividly disclose the place of American realism. Although I describe some effects of the paperback revolution and point to the impact films and TV were having on American taste, I focus on the fiction that critical historiography rendered invisible, particularly John Aldridge's influential study, *After the Lost Generation* (1951). That interest in the middle class also helps me to reread the literary history of the Cold War as a (middle-) class struggle. Maligned as domestic fiction is, I also show how it tried to sustain its relevance in such novels of social difference as Herman Wouk's *Marjorie Morningstar* (1955) or in fiction devoted to the national crisis of ethics, such as Frederick Buechner's *The Return of Ansel Gibbs* (1958). I end with a closer reading of civil rights fiction and the '50s problematic vision of the future.

AMERICAN FICTION AND AMERICAN VALUES

The literary historiography of the 1950s is so entrenched that there does not seem to be another way of understanding the decade.[1] Briefly put, following the war, American readers waited vainly for a new generation of novelists to spell out contemporary cultural terms. In the face of that failure to establish a newly lost generation came an array of middlebrow novels ultimately too paltry to create a literary tradition that could stand up either to a comparison with the generation that came of age after the first world war or to the onslaughts that popular culture was making on national taste, especially through television and the movies. Thus, for critics, the effect of overcompensating for their predecessors' undervaluing the literature of the post–World War I writers was, in turn, undervaluing the literature that was now being produced.

In this sterile state, the story goes, the middlebrow emerges an evermore urgent critical target insofar as it threatens the vitality and integrity of true artistic accomplishment. Leading intellectuals were often enmeshed in intramural debates about their place in a society where progressive politics had lost its following and where the "eggheads" had been soundly defeated, not once but twice in Adlai Stevenson's failed presidential campaigns of 1952 and 1956. Consensus visions of the culture, like Louis Hartz's *Liberal Tradition in America* (1955), a study of political history since the American Revolution, had the effect of prodding intellectuals to assail the midcult more ferociously than ever since the middlebrow had become the symbol—and engine—of the resistance that had balked the elite from providing its tonic of art and ideas to a "mass" society seemingly more obdurately lowbrow than ever.

To some degree, fiction accorded with this view. The plethora of war novels was followed increasingly by sensational novels, usually having to do with intimate life but sometimes contemporary politics too, while regionalism and family chronicles seemed to have ebbed away, as if to express the culture's turn away from tradition and toward a more atomized individualism. A softened naturalism moved out of the city and approached the suburbs, though there remained a hard-core determinist interest in juvenile delinquents and inner-city social ills (frequently told from a sociological viewpoint). Social problem novels increasingly hinged on the merely intimate, so that a starkly autobiographical fiction resulted, with writers reporting less and less on the public sphere. In part, it seemed that as the war writers searched for the subject of their next books, they were invariably drawn to the next phase of their existence as the grounds of fictive experience—the personal life, with a new candor concerning sex.

Novels also grew increasingly psychological, not in the modern sense of committing narrative to replicating the workings of the mind but in the journalistic style of allegorizing a conventional understanding of Freudian premises. Historical fiction also lost the realistic edge with which its practitioners over the preceding twenty years had sought to complement the always popular romance style. Much of this decline in literary values was attributed to Hollywood's allure for authors who had been upended by the shrinking market for fiction and the resulting cutbacks among publishers of hardcover fiction, as a consequence of the explosion of the paperback industry. Moreover, technical innovations like Cinemascope and the increasingly normative use of color photography and spectacle—plus the industry's power of hype—gave movies a much bigger share of the entertainment dollar than ever and created a product against which middle-class fiction could only compete by becoming more sensational and vulgar itself. Thus, presumably, critical realism, with its ever-diminishing audience, abdicated its proper subject—the way the middle class lives now—and settled into a moral and aesthetic morass. It became platitudinous to speak of the end of the novel or the death of literature, by which was largely meant the demise of the Howellsian novel as entertaining its reader by a sharp focus on contemporary life.

Literary values received passing infusions of life from maverick fiction, like the Beat Generation's, or in the antirealism of the early postmodernists, like John Barth. This often experimental writing turns out to be the fiction that has generally represented the 1950s in college courses and in the decade's scholarly afterlife. But overall, the novel as an art form was often seen as decaying. Some pious novels and a few scandalous ones appeared in the second half of the decade, but no new Hemingway or Faulkner surfaced; in fact, not even the real Hemingway or Faulkner could serve as a luminous example for the next generation of novelists. By the late '50s, both were exhausted, and by the early '60s, both were dead. Steinbeck's limits had become too unmistakable. Marquand's powers as a social observer diminished even as the world of manners on which he focused had fallen into eclipse. Cozzens scored his biggest hit, *By Love Possessed* (1957), not by adhering to the values that had made his reputation but by adapting his practices to the new demand for sensationalism. John O'Hara remained successful, as did Edwin O'Connor. Several rising novelists of the '40s continued to write—like Cheever, Welty, Mary McCarthy, Bellow, Elizabeth Spencer, Wright Morris, and Mailer—and several new ones developed—like James Baldwin, John Updike, Bernard Malamud, Flannery O'Connor, Herbert Gold, J. F. Powers, Jessamyn West, Shirley Ann Grau, and Philip Roth—

but no new vision of the middle-class novel ever fully took shape. The challenges and excitements of the preceding thirty years seem, in this casual history, to dissipate, until we are left with a literature so moribund in the '60s and '70s (what Barth himself called a "literature of exhaustion" and what Warner Berthoff would also call a "literature without qualities") that the new realism of the '80s and '90s seems unimaginable.[2]

The search for a rich middle-class realism was more sorely tested in the 1950s than at any other time since World War I. Year by year, fewer works of bourgeois realism were being published and reviewed in the major venues. The critical debates about the death of the novel, or the loss of faith in mimesis in the face of the New Novel in France, translate into questions about the capacity of Howellsian realism to give depth, texture, and meaning to everyday life. Obviously, there are always successes, but the failure goes deeper; even for supporters, the realist novel frequently seemed to be in its death throes, its aesthetics doomed and its political inertia and cultural exhaustion too profound to accommodate the changes within the culture. Throughout the '50s, magazines of all descriptions ran columns and symposia to discuss this extinguishing of the "bright book of life," as Alfred Kazin, following D. H. Lawrence, would later describe the novel.[3]

What were the tastes for fiction at the start of the decade? Little seems to distinguish 1950 from the years immediately prior. In 1950, the most popular novel was ostensibly Roman Catholic, but it was also well suited for a nation soon to experience great economic prosperity: Henry Morton Robinson's *The Cardinal* traces the ascendant career of an American priest from the beginning of the first world war through the beginning of the second. While critics differed over the novel's success—some saw the characters as pasteboards; others praised the book as a "performance of remarkable virtuosity" —its motive, as one reviewer said, was to attack "complacent materialism" and thus to interpret contemporary American life as a spiritual struggle in an unaccommodating world.[4] By contrast, Frances Parkinson Keyes's *Joy Street* (the number two best seller) examined the newly diverse ethnic and racial society by showing one aristocratic Boston family opening its home to all kinds of Americans.

Two distinct critical failures but great commercial successes might also be described as concerned about the public meanings of private travails: neither Daphne du Maurier's study of the wastrel children of a theatrical couple, *The Parasites* (number six), nor Kathleen Winsor's *Star Money* (number five), about the sexual misadventures of a successful novelist awaiting the return of her husband from the war, lived up to the possibilities of their interest in exploring the emptiness or tawdriness of the current moment. More successful in that regard was a cautionary tale of a writer's pursuing Mammon rather than art, Budd Schulberg's *The Disenchanted*, which follows the sad, if familiar story, obviously drawn from F. Scott Fitzgerald's life, of a modern writer's degradation in Hollywood, of how true artistic genius is mistreated in the American dream's own factory town and how crass materialism trumps art every time. Other popular novels looked to history for a precursor of the current loss of faith, as did Mika Waltari's sixteenth-century picaresque tale, *The Adventurer* (number nine)—a sequel to the chart-topping novel of the previous year, *The Egyptian*. Frank Yerby's costume drama, *Floodtide* (number seven), looks to the American past in the tale of a bound-to-rise young man who yearns to enter high society in 1850s Natchez, Mississippi. Just as romantically and portentously, Gwen Bristow's sentimental romance of women's socialization in early California, *Jubilee Trail* (number eight), tells of the happy joining together of a respectable widow and a showgirl along the trade route between Sante Fe and Los Angeles, perhaps an early lesson, drawn from the war years, about the solidarity of women amid the aggressions of a male culture.

Dreary as some of these popular books might have been, perhaps the grimmest performance among the year's most commercially successful novels was Hemingway's feeble effort to apply his aesthetic to the recent war, *Across the River and into the Trees* (number three), which several critics considered to be a self-parody. Reviewed everywhere and respected almost nowhere, it sold extremely well. Not only did the novel disappoint critics and reviewers looking for something like *For Whom the Bells Tolls* (1940), but even Hemingway's strong supporters conceded its badness. The World War II novel from 1950 that critics did acclaim was something Hemingway could never have even imagined, John Hersey's memorable chronicle of the Warsaw Ghetto, *The Wall* (number four), which, alone among the best sellers, was virtually an unqualified critical success. Hersey's success may have even limited the popular attention that some critics also believed Ned Calmer's *The Strange Land* deserved, a work of fiction told from twelve perspectives, perhaps the best World War II novel that no one has ever heard of.[5]

But if this summary of the year's most widely purchased and best-known books suggests an overwhelming meagerness, the literary history is really much fuller. The forgotten novels that critics did care about were often books with a great deal to tell readers about the decade's social and spiritual situations: *Stranger and Alone*, by J. Saunders Redding, explores the life of a black student at college and his feelings of treachery as a young African American who "by collaborating with the despoilers of the south do insidious damage to us all," as Ralph Ellison put it. Ellison considered the novel "sociologically important," even if he did not think much of the quality of the account, though Ann Petry considered the novel "first-rate" and moving.[6] Robert Wilder, author of several novels about Southern corruption, published *Wait for Tomorrow*, the story of an ex-king's scheme, with the aid of a Texas oilman, to enter the United States, and the New York journalist who ultimately restores his moral self amid their duplicities. Veteran novelists like Samuel Hopkins Adams in *Sunrise to Sunset* and Ben Ames Williams in *Owen Glen* scored solid successes with historical fictions. One of the best debut novels of 1950 was *Homeward Borne*, by Ruth Chatterton (who already had had a career as an actress), the tale of a young New England wife of a Southern aristocrat who adopts a Polish-Jewish refugee boy and divorces her unsympathetic husband. The year also saw the first novel of Frederick Buechner, who would be hailed throughout the decade for psychologically layered, sometimes mannered and allusive fiction like *A Long Day's Dying*, a school novel exploring the intricacy of mother-son relations and the shaping of homosexual identity. Nancy Wilson Ross, author of several novels devoted to the practice of psychology in everyday life, pursues father-son relations in *I, My Ancestor*, which enjoyed uniformly strong reviews.

Among novels receiving the very best notices was another debut, Brendan Gill's *The Trouble of One House*. Known better now as a journalist and humorist, Gill offered a serious character study of a dying woman who elicited both love and hatred from all who knew her. Critics admired the "chaste, austere, and disciplined" prose and the finely controlled ironies (according to the *New Yorker*, which was not above raving about one of its own). Robert Penn Warren's *World Enough and Time*—concerning an infamous 1820s murder, a duel between a lawyer and a politician over an adultery known as the "Kentucky Tragedy"—was celebrated for its wisdom and profundity, even if a few critics thought it overlong at 512 pages. Conceding that Warren was really trying to write four novels in one, Malcolm Cowley still called the book Warren's richest work of fiction, while novelist Elizabeth Janeway observed that the book demonstrates how Warren was clearly still stretching the extent of his talents, which was "good news for American literature."[7]

As complex as the process of prize giving and prestige conferring is, it proved daunting to select a Pulitzer Prize winner from this group; in fact, the judges chose Conrad Richter's *The Town*, the last of his trilogy, which he began a decade earlier with *The Trees* (1940) and sustained with *The Fields* (1946), about the settling of the Ohio frontier. Observing the fortunes of one family, now settled, after their trek from Pennsylvania and their early struggles, *The Town* plays out as a drama of ideas between a son of the new generation and his pioneer-stock mother. Like *Peder Victorious*, Richter's novel about the founding of a city does full justice to the idea of a middle-class fiction "based upon the lives of ordinary people . . . as your neighbors or mine in any ordinary American community," according to Louis Bromfield, a theme echoed throughout the reviews.[8] *The Town* also comes in the long line of Pulitzer winners praising rural American women, who express a vision of individual fulfillment through hard work. To this purpose, the protagonist, Sayward Wheeler, means to dispel her son's illusions about Robert Owen's collectivism, which, she opines, only exacerbates individual dissatisfaction, instead of "making your young ones work off their own troubles."[9] Her rebuke, however, is less a response to the Cold War than a defense of the older generation's belief in individualism of redoubtable effort rather than therapeutic fulfillment.

So unsatisfying had the Pulitzer become for ascertaining the achievements in fiction that a new organization had emerged in 1949 to present the National Book Award (NBA). Never having truly garnered the broad enthusiasm of the literary community, the Pulitzer, as we have seen, often opted for mediocrity in the name of merely (pretty) good taste. Recall that it was founded on the principle of honoring the fiction depicting the "wholeness" of American life, not the excellence of artistic achievement, and in many ways the prizewinners remained true to Pulitzer's originating conception. That was the source of its troubles for the literary community. After World War II, publishers especially came to resist the hegemony that the Pulitzer had claimed, and three groups—the American Book Publishers Council, the American Booksellers Association, and the Book Manufacturers Institute—banded together to sponsor this new award. These publishers meant to invigorate mainstream art by supporting its most challenging exemplars, rather than rewarding what the Pulitzer did. This new prize would be reserved for books "worthy of a distinguished role in our general intellectual and cultural life."[10] (The commercial origins of the NBA eventually showed through, and during the mid-'70s it too became associated too closely with the interests of the publishing industry, and a new prize for artistic accomplishment, the Pen/Faulkner Award, was invented.) Through the '50s and into the '60s, however, with its open deliberations—in contrast with the Pulitzer Prize, which had been reluctant even to disclose its jurors' names— the NBA evoked a more assured understanding of a year's best in American fiction. Boldly had it made this point by first honoring Nelson Algren's *The Man with the Golden Arm* over the Pulitzer choice, A. B. Guthrie's rousing yarn of American expansionism and Conestoga wagons, *The Way West*.

The NBA would go on to make consistently livelier and, many might say, more honest choices about a year's best novel. Consider that in 1953 it selected *Invisible Man* over *The Old Man and the Sea*, as the Pulitzer did not. It chose Bellow's *Adventures of Augie March* in 1954, when the Pulitzer declined even to give a prize, and in 1959, the NBA went for *The Magic Barrel*, by Bernard Malamud, over Robert Lewis Peters's *The Travels of Jaimie McPheeters*. In only one year, 1955, did the prizes overlap, for the very questionable choice of Faulkner's *A Fable*—over Harriette Arnow's *The Dollmaker*, Hamilton Basso's *The View from Pompey's Head*, Randall Jarrell's *Pictures from an Institution*, and Wright Morris's *The Huge Season*—though with Malcolm Cowley, one of Faulkner's greatest supporters and a critic who had written one of *A Fable*'s very few adulatory reviews, on the board of judges, it would be hard to imagine any other outcome. Ironically enough, the NBA closed the decade by giving the prize for 1960 to none other than Conrad Richter for his much more experimental study of experiencing the past, *The Waters of Chronos*, which the judges selected over a work very much in the Pulitzer's tradition of social piety, Harper Lee's *To Kill a Mockingbird*. In 1951, the NBA winner was not a novel at all but Faulkner's *Collected Stories*, a choice that may have been an effort to compensate for the Pulitzer's history of slighting the novelist's masterpieces—LaFarge's *Laughing Boy* over *The Sound and the Fury* (1929); T. S. Stribling's *The Store* over *Light in August* (1932); and Margaret Mitchell's *Gone with the Wind* over *Absalom, Absalom!* (1936).

These years witness more fully than the publication of Cowley's famous introduction to the Viking *Portable Faulkner* the moment when the novelist's stature became ordained and his effect on the academic prejudice against the middle-class novel much more patent. One reviewer noted that the book would "certainly strengthen the case of those critics who have steadily maintained that Faulkner is the greatest living American writer." Irascible Norman Podhoretz, on the other hand, claimed that *A Fable* was very likely Faulkner's worst novel, though it would mean rereading *Pylon* (1935) to be certain, an "ordeal" he avowed he could not face.[11] The enshrinement of Faulkner, along with Fitzgerald and Hemingway, as a sultan of American literary modernism often sounds the note of rectifying past wrongs and conferring on these writers the aura seemingly denied to them twenty-five years before. The implication is, generally, that these novelists were denied access to the larger audience that they deserved, either because critics had not yet learned to appreciate them or because general readers could not see their true value, neither of which was all that true. Sometimes the praise for these writers is tinged with compensatory guilt, as if contemporary critics were determined not to replicate a previous generation of critics' blindness. Then the case for these writers' defense was waged with a hostile eye on the past, as if to say that the current generation of critics was by and large more trustworthy than their predecessors, who had failed to protect these national treasures. Inasmuch as these three writers were also among the first twentieth-century American authors to be read around the world, their critical safekeeping became more than a domestic chore assigned to daily reviewers but an international responsibility requiring true critical discrimination. Especially was this true for Faulkner, who, unlike Hemingway and the deceased Fitzgerald, actually continued to produce, though by no means at the level of his previous masterpieces. It was, after all, in 1950 that Faulkner was awarded the Nobel Prize for literature; even if that recognition seemed belated, it also seemed more fully merited than the awards given to other Americans like Sinclair Lewis (1930) and Pearl Buck (1938).

Yet now that there was presumably a ready, astute, and larger audience for his work, and critics who could interpret the work, Faulkner could barely produce enough that would justify his recognition. In fact, the *Collected Stories* comes right after *Intruder in the Dust* (1948) and *Knight's Gambit* (1949), a year before *Requiem for a Nun* (1951) and then, after a brief hiatus, *A Fable* (1954) and, the next year, a collection of hunting stories, *Big Woods* (1955). Two better-known novels, *The Town* (1957) and *The Mansion* (1959), complete the decade's production, which is at least as hectic a pace as the one Faulkner followed between 1929 and 1937. But the new works did not earn the esteem that the earlier books had. The sobriquet of "greatest living American writer" might have even seemed something of a dull joke to Faulkner, since the new works were so inferior to the ones he had produced fifteen and twenty years prior, when such a title might have more meaningfully conveyed broad acknowledgment and deep appreciation. Emerging in these years as America's presiding novelist, the twentieth-century author about whom more has been written than any other figure, comparable only to Henry James as the distant second to Shakespeare, Faulkner thus became the site for critics and scholars to discover an originating myth of American modernism that appealed to those in the center of the political spectrum as well as to liberals and conservatives, too.

Leaving aside the question of any author's need to be acclaimed, what was in it for critics in the early '50s to assert Faulkner's predominance so righteously? For one thing, perhaps there is a sort of competition among critics for the honor of being most discerning among a writer's champions. Second, the critic can be seen as performing a kind of national service—of initiating the populace in the status of its literary resources—a function that fits nicely with the era's cultural sentimentalism. Sometimes, of course, that service degenerates into boosterism, but it frequently brokers a vision of America assumed to be in season, allowing the "greatest living novelist" label to be used as an endorsement of a given view of the state of culture (witness Bellow for the New York intellectuals).[12] Several critics have already read Faulkner and his critics alike for the purpose of analyzing the limitations of past liberalism.[13] Faulkner's public statements on race and the need for African Americans not to agitate, for example, are now embarrassing, but, in the early '50s, they may have seemed to make good liberal sense, not too radical but surely enlightened and, for some, generous (except for his vow to shoot protesting blacks rather than white Mississippians if he had to choose).

One of the critic's crucial jobs, historically, is to uncover the context for a text's political meanings. Yet critics no less than novelists operate within their historical limits, even though critics, like novelists, often see themselves as enjoying a wider or deeper perspective than other observers. That does not mean that authors do not have much to say about the politics or social conditions under which they work or that critics do not have much to reveal about how those political and social meanings surface in the shaping of literary meanings and values, but it does suggest that those determinations will be more contingent than critics' puncturing of others' assessments. Within the reading of "greatness" for public consumption, critics protect themselves from their time-bound judgments to avoid the occupational hazard of merely being wrong, which also might mean their vision of the culture is askew. So Faulkner's example for critics working within the era's consensus politics was almost overwhelming; the problem came about when that consensus was dismantled. Then one could still admire Faulkner's achievement but no longer had to accept his shaky grasp of history and his Dixiecrat point of view.

If Hemingway looms as the nation's media vision of a novelist of broad experience, Faulkner becomes the country's image of the writer as artist, just as Marquand stands as a postwar icon of a writer as social observer. In serving his country this way, Faulkner—far more than Hemingway, who achieved fame as a tenacious craftsman as well as a sportsman—is distinguished as a thinking novelist, whose hard-drinking signifies his pain, even his vulnerability (unlike Sinclair Lewis, whose drinking signified the tough edge of his nonconformity). In Faulkner's pain is found the writer's romanticized ability to see into the spiritual and social circumstances of American modernity and to divine the truth from which we trust him not to shirk.

Thus, Faulkner's status as the "greatest living American writer" is different from that of others who have enjoyed the appellation, like Howells or Tarkington. Faulkner is understood as a truth-teller, bearing a message too profound for the common run of realist writers to seize. Toni Morrison, by contrast, as our contemporary "greatest living writer," is seen as telling us heart-truths—a gendered and racialized part of her appeal, whereas Philip Roth, as our "greatest living writer," makes us confront the dark truths about our psyches and the republic, while John Updike, as our "greatest living writer," gives us the truth of the lyrical apprehension of our lives. Alternatively, Don DeLillo or Thomas Pynchon may also be our "greatest living novelist" because of the chaos or paranoia they perceive and their sympathy with postmodern entropy. Through his alcoholism, his reputation for incomprehensible prose, his willingness to rummage through the past as well as through the recesses of the self, Faulkner becomes the figure of the U.S. writer as conscious mind, the secretary of the American inner state. Surely his Nobel Prize speech, which is remembered way beyond proportion to its vision, amply testifies to this exaltation. His praise of stoical acceptance in the face of the threat of nuclear annihilation, among the forces that so

potently threaten to obliterate mankind, much less unseat American identity, is supposed to be courageous and dignified, though it too readily accepts
the status quo rather than seek any deeper structural revolution of spirit or
vision. Indeed, in the name of embracing mankind's perdurability, it accepts
the very powers threatening humanity. Like another antiromantic Romantic
philosopher, Margaret Fuller, he "accepts the universe." For readers and
critics cowed by the reigning forces of destruction and willing to controvert
their quietism into a virtue and call themselves principled—now with the
rhetoric of Faulkner at their bidding—the vision of Lear-like endurance
seems cheaply bought.

Faulkner himself did little to cater to the stature he was awarded as a sort
of cultural sage or seer, though two other '50s publishing ventures, *Faulkner
at Nagano* (1956) and *Faulkner at the University* (1959), and later, after his
death, *Faulkner at West Point* (1964), suggest his cooperation—and certainly
his publishers' desire—to circulate the ideas of this active mind, whose
pronouncements on writing especially become noteworthy to the extent
that they are Faulknerian. This ventilation was inevitable since, by 1950, the
tendency to propose representative cultural terms was peaking. As part of
the national self-consciousness of the midcentury, many critics and pundits
opined on the state of American society, history, and letters, partly to define
the nation's course—past, present, and future—and partly in response to the
threats to democracy first descried by the anticommunist left and then, even
more urgently and distortedly, by McCarthyism. It was, to be sure, an era
of historical test cases, with seemingly every development weighted for
its representative or predictive value as an expression of the "American
state of mind."

THE AMERICAN STATE OF MIND

Addressing an audience of graduating seniors at Pomona College in the
spring of 1950, poet Archibald MacLeish spoke of the guiding sense of
purpose that citizens could recite to define their country and their culture.
That American sense of direction, he observed, needed fresh articulation
now that McCarthyism had transformed traditional American courage and
character into new, overheated apprehensiveness: "How could *we* fall from
ourselves so far? And into such morbid and unmanly fears? Into such spite-

ful hatreds? Such hysterical suspicion of each other and ourselves? . . . Such ignorant forgetfulness of the great meaning of our past?"[14]

MacLeish's admonitions were not the paranoid fantasies of the cultural nationalist who, a decade before, had worried about the role of "irresponsible" modernist writers in weakening American resistance to various forms of totalitarian regimes. Now he is concerned with the wasting effect on language that writers might deploy in the name of giving American ideals a life. For MacLeish, as for so many others, that viability was to be understood in terms of the possibilities for individual as opposed to collective well-being. The greatest risk of McCarthyism lies in the way it debilitates individual freedom of thought, the "live and passionate belief in man," without which "democracy is a rhetorical formula which will collapse whenever fear assaults it: which any demagogue can undermine." Citizens especially need to be armed with knowledge of the nation's purpose, of ensuring, through its colleges and universities, a polis activated by a "belief in the absolute value of freedom and independence of the individual mind."

Such watchfulness over this freedom of mind as well as consciousness of the nation's sense of mission especially attracted intellectuals. A revealing occasion for this scrutiny came near the close of 1951, when William Barrett declared that for all of its busy industry, "literary production in America" had declined so disastrously that realization of this failure "must be a very painful and embarrassing situation to all Americans whose patriotism is not a self-deception."[15] Barrett rejected the usual explanations for recent American fiction's failure to achieve international distinction, dismissing those that pointed to the weak position of the writer in American society, the culture's relative newness, or its lack of tradition, as well as the morass of mass culture. Barrett looks for a "deeper cause": "American life in our own time tends away from the emotional and organic depths out of which the greatest literature has sprung." The problem is the "facile liberalism" that makes the contemporary novel false to life: "What matters in the end, both for values and to art, is the depth of life as a felt thing: and it is this, and not some intellectual explanation, that is lost whenever we say that the meaning of life has been lost. And if our young writers now experience the life around them as meaningless, it is this meaning they have lost."

Elsewhere Barrett describes how, "in American fiction, the values seem to become uncertain when they are to be held consciously; and therefore the educated middle classes appear as the social stratum where nihilism has made its chief inroads." The nihilistic middle class? Barrett contends that there the conflict between traditional norms and America's roots as a radical break from tradition reaches an impasse. The current situation, he argues, can be differentiated from the one that challenged Russian writers in the nineteenth century: "We can hardly expect a Tolstoy or Dostoyevsky in America when the deepest experience of these writers is not an organic and recognized part of American life: our extrovert civilization has developed other means of adjusting to life without their spiritual struggles. We have the crack-up and the breakdown, neurosis and maladjustment, but we do not have the tragic sense of life." So the "American sense of life," if it even survives, may develop into something quite different from what we know. Barrett castigates much of contemporary fiction as imitative, that is, a "kind of make-believe of serious literature," and points to a recent Pulitzer winner —Cozzens's *Guard of Honor* (1949)—as an example insofar as it "lacks depth, its characters are the kind of decent and struggling Americans whose perplexities about life [in this case concerning duty, racial prejudice, and ethics] are only practical problems to be solved, while the ultimate or primitive things, never articulated and faced, are hardly more than faint shadows in the background."[16]

The particular occasion for Barrett's assessment was the publication of a book that once had a strong influence on the way we understand postwar literature, though it has been awhile since scholars of the field felt obliged to cite it: John Aldridge's *After the Lost Generation*, already mentioned in another context. The work became famous for its expostulation of contemporary fiction's limitations as a general failure to live up to the examples of Hemingway, Fitzgerald, and Dos Passos. (The narrative complexities of Faulkner might have been too daunting for Aldridge.) Searching for a new tradition in the novelists who came of age after World War II, Aldridge found writers like Norman Mailer, John Horne Burns, Alfred Hayes, Merle Miller, and Vance Bourjaily to be inadequate when compared to their predecessors. Never mind that Dos Passos, after his turn from the left, had been disowned for years; that Hemingway did not enjoy a true commercial success until 1940, more than a decade after his status as a postwar writer was cemented; or that Fitzgerald, after years of neglect, was just beginning to be rehabilitated.

Aldridge's analysis purported to explain the conundrum that, even though so many writers participated in World War II, so few works of literary merit have resulted. Where were the geniuses? Aldridge constructs an antinomy between the '20s avant-garde and late '40s and early '50s mainstream novelists. Contemporary writers, he contended, either elaborated their style or faltered into journalism or hollowly asserted the need for belief, a devaluation of contemporary writing waged at the time it could perhaps least afford it. In the immediate postwar years, the middle-class novel, like *The Hucksters* (1946) and *Gentleman's Agreement* (1947), had shown possibilities of making itself into a substantial vehicle for public debates about the state of the culture, but its critical denigration in the early '50s, on the grounds that it was not equal to the fiction that addressed the contingencies of the postwar world of 1920s America, discouraged the discussion over its vitality. *After the Lost Generation* did not do this dubious work alone, nor was it universally admired (it received a very bad notice in the *New York Times*), but its argument had remarkable circulation, as if it were propagating a myth that reviewers of contemporary fiction were especially eager to believe in. And professors of American literature, too.

Moreover, Aldridge defined contemporary writers by their want of a generation: "Lacking the focus of negation and loss, a new world to discover, and a single perspective for protest, the new writers are deprived as well of group solidarity. They form no distinct generation in the old sense; they champion no cause; they share no common aim; they are impelled by no awareness of a common artistic mission. It is the sum of their rejections that even though they have never known the values that were lost to them thirty years ago, they cannot make a new or substitute value of their art."[17] Implicit here is the expectation that every generation can adhere to the standard of the putative coherence of the American modernists, which, as we have already seen, their critics never would have pinpointed thirty years before, even if those critics sometimes noted kinships, proclaimed schools, traced influences. Lacking in Aldridge is any real effort to analyze what constitutes a generation beyond the synchronicity of birthdates and experiences, so that one wonders what, if any, generation might have actually claimed the status he affords the modernists.

Finding "less relevant" those writers that others might see as crucial and thus enabling him to keep silent or distort their contributions to and qualifications of this norm, Aldridge calls the roll of the postwar generation of such ex-GIs as Vance Bourjaily, Norman Mailer, Merle Miller, John Horne Burns, Irwin Shaw, and Gore Vidal, as opposed to James Baldwin, Paul Bowles,

Frederick Buechner, Truman Capote, and Wright Morris. No Richard Wright or Saul Bellow (already the author of the *Dangling Man* and *The Victim*), no Chester Himes or William Gardner Smith, not to mention Eudora Welty, Jean Stafford, Mary McCarthy, Flannery O'Connor, Ann Petry, Shirley Jackson, or Carson McCullers, extend or complicate Aldridge's all too limited sense of generation.

Although many critics similarly concluded that the novel in the United States had declined in both status and achievement, the actual debate about its vitality followed various directions and advanced different worries. Some critics viewed the new fiction as dull, its social vision as formulaic. Others worried about the incursion of the vast new paperback industry into literary production and the danger of writing for a mass culture. Some critics despaired over the diminution of traditional possibilities of American heroism, especially as that was seen through the lens of public ethics, not to mention the incipient stages of the breakdown in the power and status of males in terms of the "organization man," as well as the stirring of the women's movement. Others saw the challenges of U.S. fiction coming from the new conformism, the '50s version of '20s standardization, especially evident in the new suburban landscape. Some worried about a political scene dominated by suspicion and a ruthless disregard of democratic principles, while others found hope—and others despair—in novelists' new interest in drug addicts, homosexuals, African Americans, Jews, juvenile delinquents, or their combination.

Arguments focused on such questions as how to measure literary greatness, the loss of a novel-reading public, the rise of television, the new paperback industry, the residual wartime preference for nonfiction, and the failure of U.S. novelists to dramatize meaningfully, or even give a name to, the new American society. Whatever the immediate concern of the critics, postwar American novelists were faulted for not carrying the burden that their predecessors were presumed to have shouldered in the '20s. Indeed, the fiction of the early '50s, as it is read today, consists largely of the lingering modernism of Ellison's *Invisible Man* or Bellow's *Seize the Day*. Some authors survive as interesting voices from one movement or another, like Shirley Jackson, James Baldwin, Jack Kerouac, Norman Mailer, or J. D. Salinger. A handful of others have been recuperated for their social or political interest, like John Okada (*No-No Boy*), though they may have made no general impression in their moment; a few others have been remembered for an extremely popular book, like Grace Metalious's *Peyton Place* or Sloan Wilson's *Man in the Gray Flannel Suit* and *A Summer Place*. In general, contemporary scholars of American culture have accepted the judgment of '50s critics like Bernard DeVoto, who derogated the way '50s novelists tried to come to terms with the postwar era, including the atomic age and anticommunism. In doing so, they perpetuate, unwittingly, the critical scorn for their efforts to register and confront the way we lived then—the situation of women, relations between the races, rebellious youth, and the crisis of ethics pervading public life.[18] Half a century later, if we find it hard to recall just how and when American fiction lost its general hold on the people it was written to entertain and instruct, it may be because we have enshrined that same disdain. In part, that residual disregard comes from the way the '50s have been treated in the literary histories. Instead of seeking to provide the full history of fiction in the decade, academic critics tended to celebrate the early postmodernist works of Barth or the aesthetic challenges in, say, Vladimir Nabokov's extraordinary *Lolita* (1955), finding in nonmimetic forms the hope of rediscovering the ferment of the '20s.

During the '50s, as we shall see, the novel could still vigorously negotiate modernity for the middle class, though ultimately that mediation was becoming less pervasive, even if occasionally it could still arouse intense interest. What we can observe through the decade's unfolding is how the realistic artifact meant to edify citizen-readers becomes a consumer item positioned to compete with TV and Hollywood. For one crucial difference between the middle-class novel and those of earlier decades comes in the smaller niche middle-class fiction occupies. This change partly results from genre crossing, in that pulps and romances more actively venture into the middle-class territory of the novel, so the novel competes not only with mystery and detective fiction, as in years past, but also with spy thrillers and sensational works on a seemingly unprecedented scale. As the years play out, the novel seems to matter less as a coherence-making agent in American cultural life in helping to shape the consciousness of the public sphere than, say, Rachel Carson's *Silent Spring* (1963). While there are many exceptions, the novel increasingly lives out the logic of its packaging over the preceding thirty years and becomes merely another consumable differentiated for a season; in this way, its packaging weighs heavily as part of its cultural worth. This transformation of the novel's status cannot be blamed solely on the publishers who were developing the blockbuster sensibility or on the Hollywood producers whose options on books changed the novel's capital. Nor can guilt be assigned merely to those writers who retreated from their errand of making the novel matter. The question that remains is how the bourgeois novel continued, despite its decline, to animate the ideas shaping postwar American consciousness.

WHY READ DULL NOVELS?

If 1950 was less than a fertile year for American fiction, it also suggested how little things were about to change, except perhaps to get worse. In a year-end roundup of 1951 for *Publisher's Weekly*, well-known reviewer Joseph H. Jackson, in "Fiction Is Neither What It Was Nor What It Might Be," meditated on the worsening prospect for "indifferently good" American novels; he speculated that the novel in the United States was "relatively weak," while nonfiction was "fairly strong." Jackson rehearses the "root causes": an anxious political and social age that seems incapable of sparking works of genius, writers' growing difficulty in earning a living, the proliferation of other media competing for readers' diminishing attention, and the pervasive influence of book clubs, a problem held by some to be so deleterious that there were even government proceedings to determine whether book clubs were, after all, legal.[19]

Jackson gives a fairly normative description of the year's best: best sellers included James Jones's epic, *From Here to Eternity*, which won the NBA, though its sales were surpassed by another war novel, Herman Wouk's Pulitzer Prize–winning *The Caine Mutiny*. Also commercially successful were such good books as Marquand's portrait of a general in the postwar peace, *Melville Goodwin, USA*. Critically as well as commercially successful novels that also undertook deeper probings of the mind included Solomon Asch's religious novel, *Moses*, and J. D. Salinger's "immensely sensitive" *The Catcher in the Rye*. While there were other popular hits, including new works by such veteran best-selling romancers as Frank Yerby and Frances Parkinson Keyes, the novelists that American readers had traditionally looked to as the country's standard-bearers—Lewis, Bromfield, Faulkner, Dos Passos, O'Hara, William Saroyan, or, more recently, Mailer, Shaw, even Capote—all handed in books of uneven achievement. Jackson does not explain this phenomenon, except to observe that at least two such novelists produced works of "high quality": Shirley Jackson's *Hangsaman*, a psychological study of a sensitive young woman and her domineering father, and Jessamyn West's *The Witch Diggers*, a Midwestern farm novel that discovers an American gothic sensibility ultimately the equal of another book, *Lie Down in Darkness*, a story of Southern degeneration by a new novelist, William Styron.

Also worthy of Jackson's mention is Alice Tisdale Hobart's *The Serpent-Wreathed Staff*, a study of the medical profession and the often-trumped desire to do good, which critics believed it behooved doctors to read; Wright Morris's *Man and Boy*, a "poisonous," "slashing," "murderous" satire of a self-satisfied woman; Virginia Sorenson's *The Proper Gods*, a tale of postwar adjustment and the making of a Mexican American; and Hilde Abel's *The Guests of Summer*, about a young woman's "deeply moving" yet "disciplined" coming-of-age at an Adirondack summer hotel, not unlike Allegra Goodman's *Kaaterskill Falls* (1999). Jackson does not mention other books that were well thought of: James Agee's *The Morning Watch*, a schoolboy tale of "tension, loneliness and longing," or Robert Bowen's well-reviewed story of an American prisoner of war in the Philippines, *The Weight of the Cross*, which was so good it overshadowed another accomplished novel about race in the wartime Philippines, Benjamin Appel's *Fortress in the Rice*.[20] Also cited were Shelby Foote's begrudgingly admired *Love in a Dry Season*, a tale of moral deterioration in the South; Herbert Gold's *Birth of a Hero*, a stream-of-conscious portrayal of a middle-class, middle-aged man learning the deepest proportions of ordinary life, which began Gold's illustrious career; Caroline Gordon's satire of intellectuals in Tennessee, *The Strange Children*; McCullers's collection of short fiction, *The Ballad of the Sad Café*; and Edwin O'Connor's satire of a pompous radio commentator (like Walter Winchell), *The Oracle*, a portrait of how public exposure reveals the worst tendencies of the shallower celebrities that the mass media help to create.

The overall picture of the early '50s that these novels help to depict is a more nuanced, less simplified world, with values more open to debate, than we typically recall. Taken together, they might tell us that the general air of uneasy conformity and suspicion permeates the enforced fiction of well-being. Perhaps our culture has no use for these novels because the country renounces its use: in 1952, the need to think of the United States enjoying an uncomplicated prosperity led intellectuals not to confront the complexities of American society but to assess the distinctions among the social classes, reveling in the brute honesty of the folk culture of the masses while despising the forces of mediocrity in bourgeois culture and engaging in such sideshows as the measuring of brows.[21]

In 1952, *Harper's* editor Bernard DeVoto registered the complaint against middle-class fiction when he asked, "Why Read Dull Novels?"—an opinion piece in which the well-known gadfly addressed U.S. fiction's decline in quality after World War II. DeVoto decried the proliferation of bad "good books," not merely trashy or popular books but novels he disparaged for their kinship to the "how-to" books then flooding the market: "How to live under the threat of the atom bomb, how to raise money to pay three sets of alimony, how to get along with your children, how to use the waste space behind the furnace, how to make an outboard motor out of old roller skates," books that would sell better if their "clumsy and meretricious veneer of fiction . . . is scraped off."[22] In a similar vein, Arthur Mizener had written about "What Makes Great Books Great?" just a couple of weeks before in the *Times Book Review*, arguing that "abiding moral insight," not "implications for today," distinguishes a novelist like Faulkner from those who merely exploit the current interest in race relations or who only "encourage people to enjoy the insidious pleasures of righteousness unearned by understanding."[23] Greatness was less about timeliness than timelessness. To understand why two noted critics would adjudicate these questions, it helps to recall that, by contrast, the early '50s also saw the rise of the nonbook—titles that sold stupendously but were really about very little. Although such books had been popping up now and then on best-seller lists, it was only since 1949 that they truly multiplied: 1951 saw such best sellers as *Betty Crocker's Picture Cook Book* (number one); *The Baby* (number two), a collection of humorous candid photographs; *Look Younger, Live Longer* (number three), which sold even better in health food stores than it did in bookstores; *How I Raised Myself from Failure to Success in Selling* (number four); and *Your Dream Home* (number seven), along with a book drawn from Walt Kelly's quasi-political cartoon strip, *Pogo*.

Such novels as DeVoto belittles draw their appeal from the various how-to books helping readers in the '20s to figure out the new "plastic age"; in the '30s, they guided the middle class through the Depression; and in the 40s, they tried to interpret the country's several social challenges and sources of disillusionment. By the '50s, these bad good books—like Wilson's *The Man in the Gray Flannel Suit* and Allen Drury's *Advise and Consent*—tried to meet such cultural demands as explaining conformity, the power of suburban malaise, and the tortuous ways of government corruption; their success ultimately diminished, DeVoto explains, partly because so many novelists trivialized human experience by passing off the "bitterness, gloom, pessimism, cynicism, and ethical anarchy of current fiction" as a tragic sense of life: "Who says my experience is tawdry and my pain and happiness without meaning? That little twirp?—the hell with him," DeVoto huffed.[24]

For DeVoto, these novels' explicit social purpose is exactly what's wrong with them. That purpose is overdetermined. Replete with insufficiently nuanced characters, uninspired plots, and thinly imagined social scenes, these novels are too simple to engage society in the ways in which their authors so obviously hoped and out of which their publishers—perhaps waiting for another *Uncle Tom's Cabin*—so crazily expected to reap a profit. DeVoto says, "The worst novels . . . try to deal justly and honestly with the substance of experience but fail because they are tawdrily imagined and wretchedly written."

Consider DeVoto's arguments in light of the great cultural preoccupation with the atomic bomb and the fiction that it motivated. Although much has been written about the effect of the Cold War on the development of American criticism, novels actually written about the atom bomb, or anticommunism for that matter, among other hot-button issues of the early '50s, seldom come to scholarly attention.[25] Denounced in the contemporary criticism of the Cold War's rhetoric of consensus is the prevailing liberal humanism that supposedly restrained a progressive or radical agenda. The result has been a tremulous historical awareness of the range of cultural expression in an era we think we know well, so close is it to our own. That history generally understands '50s fiction to be so much a failure that it is best studied in its avant-garde movements. In part, the academic championing of '50s postmodernism is an Oedipal victory: the older generation's embrace of Hemingway, Faulkner, and Fitzgerald over "better fiction" left room for the trouncing of modernist masters by postmodernists, but no room for reengaging the middle-class writers whom both modernists and their successors meant to overturn. Thus the period's own stylizing of the great has meant that fewer and fewer novels have entered into our scholarly consciousness. Instead, the social fiction of the '50s continued to take up the cultural anxieties of the time. If we want to know why we should read these so-called dull novels, it is perhaps because their dullness is a misnomer. They are dull because they are not something else, something that suits a different critical agenda. In the 1950s, this fiction was said to decline because it could not do what another generation's did, as virtually no other generation of English-speaking novelists, except perhaps the British Victorian writers, had done— invent the domestic literature of its time as a world literature. Arguably, '50s writers were presented with the more modest but nonetheless vital opportunity to write the social history of their time. There may not be the master-works that other decades might claim, but the generality of accomplishment might be wider and higher than historians have heretofore assessed.

An initial way of framing these novels' range of accomplishment can be gleaned from antinuclear fiction. In 1950, just a few months after the Soviet Union exploded its first nuclear bomb, science fiction writer Judith Merril turned her hand to realism, *Shadow on the Hearth*, which may have been the first book to portray nuclear war with the recognizable face of a domestic drama. Already several A-bomb novels had been published, and these mostly fantasized about the political circumstances under which nuclear war was possible or they sought to conjure an accommodating vision of destruction. Rather than a propagandistic work that could be pressed into the service of anticommunists, Merril's novel makes a space for another kind of discussion —women's struggle during the fallout. The title tells a great deal, as the plot observes the several crises that a Westchester housewife and mother faces after a foreign enemy drops the big one on Manhattan, where her husband works. Mrs. Mitchell must conquer such difficulties as losing her electricity, stopping a gas leak, dealing with a hysterical neighbor, combating marauders, fending off the sexual overtures of a self-important Civil Defense marshal, harboring a nuclear protester, and treating her little girl's radiation poisoning. Only when the enemy surrenders can Mrs. Mitchell, on the last page, greet her husband who, despite suffering shock, manages to find his way home.

While *Shadow on the Hearth* portrays nuclear war as a domestic threat, the book's more powerful achievement is to be found in the dramatic immediacy it gives to the class-consciousness of the pervasive conversation regarding survival, even as Merril animates its gendered terms. To see the novel's part in this discussion, consider the articles published in the various magazines of the day and how they meant to portray and allay atomic bomb worries: "A-Bomb Won't Do What You Think" (*Collier's*), "How You Can Survive an A-Bomb Blast" (*Saturday Evening Post*), "If the A-Bomb Burst" (*Popular Mechanics*), "Train Hundreds on How to Handle A-Bomb" (*Science Digest*). The principal lesson of Merril's novel is that although its security and comfort may be lost, the middle-class family is up to the challenge of nuclear confla-gration. Middle-class tenacity and resourcefulness—the virtues that brought the bourgeoisie its stability—ensure the family's survival. It may be a silly wish-dream, but, naively or not, *Shadow on the Hearth* speaks to a certain level of resolve.

None of the other books about the A-bomb have enjoyed much of a revival, and there is no particular reason, beyond its rendering of a middle-class woman's fantasy, that this book should be remembered. Merril's claim to critical attention was reserved solely for her science fiction, and despite novelist-reviewer August Derleth's praise for her skill, the novel's style would not pass muster with DeVoto, nor would it win acclaim for its politics. The *Times* dismissed it, exaggerating that the heroine's "few days' ordeal . . . seems more like a somewhat uncomfortable picnic than a manifestation of tragedy," but the *Saturday Review*, still the bulwark of bourgeois liberalism, applauded Merril's achievement in telling this "awesome and frightening story" from the point of view of a suburban housewife. For this reviewer, the moral that runs through the story is almost too obvious. "Men and women can go through the worst disasters if they are not conquered by fear or doubt but go bravely about their allotted tasks. A united family is the solid base on which civilization rests."[26]

No less gendered and no less an exercise in middle-class survival con-sciousness was a novel, five years later, from a writer we might have more cause to remember, especially because his war novel a few years earlier had been highly esteemed. Vance Bourjaily wrote several novels over four de-cades, enjoying special favor among fellow artists in the '60s and '70s. His second book, *The Hound of Earth* (1955), turns on the alienating guilt of a young scientist who realizes how his work on the Manhattan Project has been used. He immediately walks away from both his job and his family and keeps walking for seven years. The novel begins as we catch up with the disaffected Al Pennington working in the stockroom of a San Francisco department store during the Christmas season. It is one thing to turn your back on the American government's war machine, but to renounce the consolation of bourgeois family life entails grim consequences.

This novel met with decidedly mixed reviews. Some disparaged the "in-souciance" of treating "a decent man in a sorely distempered society," though others considered the novel "possessed of the sort of whimsical despair that the situation demands." One critic found in it "an affirmation . . . solidly in the humanist tradition," while Herbert Gold, writing in the *Nation*, held that the book "endures past a first reading as an effective drama about how difficult it is to be both responsible and an individual in contemporary America."[27] That variety partly reflects the divided opinion of the novel's emphasis on middle-class survival: as one may phrase it, Is the novel's reducing of the question of nuclear survival to such a level, and the attendant trivializing it risks, adequate to its investigation of its interest in responsibility and individual fate?

One principal difference between these survivor novels is their interest in sex—barely present and hushed in *Shadow on the Hearth*, visible and talkative in *The Hound of Earth*. Domestic as Merril's vision is, Bourjaily treats readers to a compendium of '50s heteronormative sexual worries: lesbian rape, telephone booth masturbation, even a child-molesting Santa Claus. Yet such conduct is not portrayed as aberrant, but as part of everyday life in the postwar society from which Al cannot absent himself even when he tries. For at least one critic, this element of sexual anxiety makes the novel lose its force as a meditation on the consequences of the bomb: "Hiroshima . . . seems to have little direct connection with the[se] sexually tormented, uselessly confused characters."[28] From Merril, we learn that even in the face of a nuclear disaster, your neighbor may still feel a little randy; in Bourjaily, we learn that in a world under a mushroom cloud, neurosis and perversion will touch everyday sexual relations.

That outlaw element, however, may even come to define the question of nonconformity that underlies the novel's greatest purport. Two years later, Lewis Dabney, describing in the *Nation* how fiction's loss of "public relevance has come with the loss of its intellectual and critical dimensions," mounts the case for novels that confront "the moral and political problems posed by the age of conformity." Citing *The Hound of Earth* and *Invisible Man* as *the* two contemporary novels that can suggest a "new school of articulate dissenting fiction," Dabney praises their moral engagement, even as he concedes that they both sacrifice the personal to the public and thus "proceed from the central weakness that they do not fully explore their subject, the problem of how to live with integrity in contemporary American society." As influential as Ellison's novel became, Bourjaily's book inspired no new school. Instead, *The Hound of Earth* represents a middle-class fantasy of dispossession that the specter of nuclear annihilation signifies, turning the

A-bomb into a screen for narrating and detailing the social, sexual, psychological, and cultural worries of the American middle class—and in that regard Bourjaily's novel also typifies a national literature we have lost.[29]

THE AGE OF CONFORMITY

Lost in the misvaluing of middle-class fiction is the omnipresent work of designating the place of middle-class culture in relation to the well-being of American intellectual life. Early in the 1950s, the *Partisan Review* (PR) took up this crucial subject when it published a three-part symposium that has become a watershed moment in the history of '50s intellectual life in the United States, a document to which many observers have turned. "Our Country and Our Culture" poses questions about the intellectuals' responsibilities and the qualifications they would attach to any affirmation of American life. The editors mainly wanted to know if intellectuals had become too cozy with material well-being and now were venturing too close to the political center. Had the recent prosperity, PR wondered, encouraged American cultural analysts to suspend their vigilant scrutiny of capitalist suppression, or had these intellectuals—some of them children of immigrants—finally rediscovered America, finding themselves newly at home with American social ways and rationales?

So the editors asked about thirty prominent writers and thinkers to contemplate the issue. The responses come from an array of the era's notable cultural thinkers, including Newton Arvin, Norman Mailer, Reinhold Niebuhr, David Riesman, Lionel Trilling, Louise Bogan (the only female), Sidney Hook, and C. Wright Mills, along with a dozen other usual suspects. Often, the respondents try to evade the question of the new spirit of affirmation, making fine distinctions about the critical endeavor while insisting on the consistency between their own pre- and postwar politics, as if to suggest that they had never had any communist-inspired ideas. Some intellectuals had come to terms with their role over the preceding fifteen years. As Arthur Schlesinger Jr. observes, "Next to Hitler, even Babbitt began to look good."[30] Delmore Schwartz, on the other hand, is less forgiving:

> The intellectual will to conformism is formulated in terms of the startling discovery that the middle class is not entirely depraved, that liberalism does not provide an answer to all social questions, and that a state

of perpetual revolution in literature and art is neither an end in itself nor the chief purpose of literature or revolution. Who, apart from the intellectuals who make these extraordinary revelations, is helped, comforted and illuminated? During a period of economic prosperity, the middle class has no more need of intellectuals to defend it than the editors of the *Saturday Review* need James Joyce as a novelist, Pablo Picasso as an illustrator, and T. S. Eliot as an editor.[31]

In such distinguished company, one of the most thoughtful responses was Louis Kronenberger's. A poet, playwright, drama critic, and cultural observer who lived out an eighteenth-century ideal of urbanity and wit, Kronenberger is not a figure from that era who has endured, nor was he ever particularly influential. Yet he responded to the PR's questions with at least as much verve and insight as any of the best-known contributors by stating that the problem is neither eager conformity with American material beneficence nor silent, willing capitulation to mass culture, since these targets are too easy: "If American intellectuals are to be of any use, they must . . . associate themselves with American life." Kronenberger's intellectual, like the vigorous Renaissance man, must identify privilege with participation, not elitism and withdrawal. The intellectual does so, not for "matey or pseudo-democratic reasons" but because "a lack of highbrow concern leaves mass culture not just more arid, but infinitely more aggressive":

> The trouble isn't just intellectual snobbery or a worry over backing the wrong horse: it springs also out of an intense current fear of the trivial, of the minor, so that no one asks how good something is on its own terms, or whether it has distinction, but only how central or integral or symptomatic it is, and whether it has importance. This highbrow attitude strikes me at times as born of the most flagrantly middle-brow impulse: it worships "major" art exactly as America generally worships size. And the point is not just how pretentious this may be, but also how ill-considered: surely any sound cultural tradition must be kept alive and in good order by its minor art. . . . [Works of minor art] are the constants of any creditable culture; and they guarantee not only a certain amount of good art, but also a certain number of people who can appreciate it.[32]

For Kronenberger, the highbrow disparaging of modest artistic accomplishment is every bit as smarmy and small-minded and middlebrow as the middlebrow's insecurity or smug complacency about its own power of cultural arbitration. In describing the fear that the guardians of elite culture have for the "minor," which they mistake for the trivial, Kronenberger points to a key element of '50s intellectual life, one that has affected the circulation of aesthetic and social values and the health of the arts ever since. The highbrow disdain for the middlebrow's appropriation of elite culture, especially those achievements and sensibilities that most forcefully appealed to middlebrow readers, meant that mass culture—the basely popular and overly commercial—was left free to be as "aggressive" as it could be. Without a viable middle-class culture, held accountable by critics such as emerged in the '20s and '30s—like Henry Seidel Canby, Dorothy Canfield Fisher, and later Clifton Fadiman—not only was highbrow art not strengthened but also its remoteness increased, while the influence of popular culture, at its most vapid and brainless, proliferated. Kronenberger would prefer that intellectuals know the minor achievements under their purview—which to my mind includes the mainstream works of middle-class realism forgotten as a result of their middle-class appeal. Not only does the appreciation of the minor make the appreciation of the major more honest, but it also means that intellectuals must stay in touch with the breadth of the culture over which they must keep watch. Intellectuals need to abjure their connection to that culture as embracing the august or sheerly popular and include as well the richness of expression and thought that minor works voice or exemplify.

CONFORMITY AND THE MIDDLE CLASS

As we have seen, "middlebrow" comes out of Van Wyck Brooks's effort to establish a middle ground of culture wherein intellectuals could make themselves useful not only as thinkers but also for the practices they instructed a community to establish. The effort failed as an approach to culture, even if the so-called middle way ultimately emerged, first in the late '30s and then in the middle and late '40s, again as the key to American politics. Avoiding extremes and taking the best of opposing principles, middlebrow intellectuals wanted to do for the culture what consensus intellectuals, like Arthur Schlesinger Jr., were understood to do for American politics. Unfortunately, American cultural dynamics did not align themselves so neatly. Middle-class culture—for all of its lapses of intellect, will, and tragic imagi-

nation—bridged the distance between mass culture and high art; its contribution was that it buttressed them both and thus both kept alive their
connection and kept real their distance. Sometimes those failures led to
diminishments and trivializations, but often middlebrow-ism could lead to
the preserving of significant cultural achievements.

Grace Metalious's short, unhappy career instances a telling version of this
dynamic. *Peyton Place* could be considered on any list of key texts from the
decade not only for its great commercial success, but also for its curious role
in shaping a mid-'50s feminist view. What made the book so scandalous in
1956 is not likely even to register today—sex across class lines. This was
nothing new for French fiction, to be sure, but to an American audience
beset with anxieties about fitting in, where the middle class can use sex to
solidify its position and sometimes to ameliorate its status, while the upper
class means to police and even to turn back any effort by the lower classes to
use sex to transform social standing, the novel was certainly controversial.

Beyond the panting descriptions of sexual acts, the underlying scandal of
the book resided in violating conformist imperatives, or as the *New Yorker*
critic put it, in the "uniform paleness of [the novel's] characters and . . .
dullness of the homes, genteel or sordid, in which they spend their humorless, ungenerous lives."[33] Throughout the fifties, writers and critics struggled
with the perception that American life had grown hopelessly conformist and
that the very vehicle for the criticism of this point—the bourgeois novel—
exemplified the result of this seemingly new ethos in American social life.
The self-consciousness of this conformism may be too momentous to allow
us to see that American society has always been materialistic. So many
influential books and magazine articles address the anxiety over the country's conformist turn that the critique of conformity was, paradoxically,
inescapable. In the film that gave the '50s critique of conformity so much of
its currency, *Rebel without a Cause* (based on a short story of little standing),
the point is less that its protagonist's rebellion is essentially purposeless:
there are no great wrongs or crushing inequalities to rectify. Beyond the
angst of adjusting to a new high school, his revulsion at the barrenness of the
new suburbs, and the hypocrisy of his parents, the hero lacks a motivating
idea amid the embarrassment of material comforts and his disquieting sense
that intimate life does not minister to the sense of scale one experiences at
the Palomar Observatory.[34]

One can certainly admire this film's direction, the actors' luminous performances, and its memorable dialogue yet still see that the alienation it enshrines, a vision that has become even emblematic, tells us little about the potential for repudiating '50s conformity. More to the point, its popularity may even suggest how double-voiced the decade was. At the very moment that the '50s are supposed to reveal their potential for aggressive nonconformity and the tragedy of isolation, it falters into a bourgeois melodrama about the enduring value of intimate life. Similarly, the movie's analog among novels—a book that could have been titled "A Rebel without That Much of a Cause," Wilson's *Man in the Gray Flannel Suit* (1955)—mutes its capacity for rebellious instruction by returning its rebel, Tom Rath, a public relations man helping his boss kick off a national campaign for mental health, to the well-being of suburban fulfillment. The novel closes as the happy couple goes on a shopping trip as they prepare for a getaway. What begins as an exemplary tale of how a veteran integrates his memories of World War II and the consequences of his efforts to cope with its uncertainty and horror turns out to be an optimistic vision of how the American middle class, once it brings to light its capacity for entropy, can still prosper. Financially as well as morally: not only are Tom and his wife set to make a bundle from converting his family estate into subdivisions, but his felicity comes and is ultimately blessed by the local magistrate, Judge Bernstein, who sees all and whose smile of approbation is reserved for the book's closing image.

The debilitating power of conformity, however, was exposed and assailed in books from the first half of the decade whose impact on U.S. social life has been quite estimable: *White Collar* (subtitled the *American Middle Classes,* 1951), *The Lonely Crowd* (1950), and *The Organization Man* (1956). Each posed a critique of social well-being; each took the American middle class to task for its all-encompassing embrace of the very stimuli and rewards that guaranteed the middle class its anxious feelings of inconclusive striving. While each discovered its own province in describing the deleterious consequences for the nation's spirit that conformity wields, each understood how anxious conformity gives a name to deeper structural failures of a democratic America, especially consumer capitalism. Several commentators have understood the implications for cultural production that these famous nostrums outlined, but Lionel Trilling, early on, discerned the implications of David Riesman's *Lonely Crowd* for modern American fiction. Lamenting that novelists ought to envy sociologists for taking up the province of manners and morals that writers ceded, the kind of cultural epistemology for which

Sinclair Lewis had been praised in the '20s, Trilling explains that Riesman's inquiries rival Stendhal's *The Red and the Black* in representing for a society how its gifted individuals, its "inner-directed" free agents as opposed to "other-directed" performers, pursue fulfillment. Trilling is surprised that his Columbia students do not share Julien Sorel's romantic ambitions but see themselves instead as "organization men," thus confirming for the critic that Riesman has something important to teach American writers as well as the public at large. In a review of Riesman's *Individualism Reconsidered* (1954), two years later, Trilling wants to know why "no American novel of recent years has been able to give me the sense of the actuality of our society that I get from Mr. Riesman's book, nor has any novel been able to suggest . . . the excitement of contemplating our life in culture as an opportunity and a danger."[35]

The answer for Trilling is that American novelists are increasingly insensitive to the material world and decreasingly curious about the social. For Trilling, the charges of malfeasance can be seen in the intellectual attributes that lead to the kinds of questions Riesman poses and that novelists, with the exception of John O'Hara, do not:

> What actually is going on in our family life? in our modes of consumption? in our factories? in our board-rooms? in our schools? on the cinema screen? in the theater? in the courts? in the judge's chambers? in the political caucus and in the political caucuses not only of our majority parties but of marginal groups? And who but Mr. Riesman would give serious attention to the cultural implications of the social, ethnic, and intellectual characteristics of the editorial boards of student law reviews? Or consider at length the development of American football as the reflection of our social conditions and expression of our social ideals? Or examine American Zionism objectively as a manifestation of elements of specifically American feeling?[36]

These are questions a society needs to examine, the ones that the novelist wrongly forsakes or neglects in searching for some more rarefied sense of mission or, obversely, in settling on some simplistic sense of intimate life. According to Trilling, we ought to remember that the roots of this novelistic tradition are not American but European, crucially Balzac, as he had spelled out in the late '40s essay, "Manners, Morals, and the Novel." By "manners," Trilling does not mean the rich, formal codes of expression and gestures associated with the Old World, or with the wealthy or old-fashioned, but the "culture's hum and buzz of implication," which is the way social life is conducted, the manifest if sometimes evanescent series of gestures and inflections through which people communicate with each other and perform their purposes. And for Trilling, this kind of social expression takes place in the here and now, a material world whose features are crucial.

Later readers may empathize with Trilling's frustrations. As we have seen, the NBA and Pulitzer Prize for 1954 went to *A Fable*, which by no stretch of the imagination qualifies as a kind of sociology, maybe the only Faulkner novel that has actually receded in importance since its publication. (One may observe that at last Faulkner had written his war novel; the trouble is that this allegory of the Passion Week was about World War I, not World War II.) Nor would the other nominees for the NBA that year meet Trilling's requirements, including Milton Lott's *The Last Hunt*, a tale of buffalo hunting in the 1870s and Frederick (Feikema) Manfred's *Lord Grizzly*, which recovered mountain legends from the 1820s. Still, there was Arnow's memorable study of the working poor of the urban north, *The Dollmaker*, and Basso's examination of the comfortable classes of the Old and New South, *The View from Pompey's Head*; Wright Morris's finest novel to date, *The Huge Season*, the study of a middle-aged man's reflections on his youth in the 1920s; and Frank Rooney's *The Courts of Memory*, a family chronicle that reviewers compared to the work of John Marquand. (The next year Marquand himself would write much the kind of novel Trilling asked for, *Sincerely, Willis Wayde*, which portrays the ascent of a businessman.) As cogent as Trilling's brief for a commitment to fiction's material documentation of class and social condition was, it could not persuade critics determined to promote even the most overwrought works of a modernist master out of a nostalgia for an earlier era.

THE SECOND SEX AND THE NOVEL

Trilling was basically right to lament that the novel of social inquiry—the novel that teaches the middle class about professions and changing social and economic conditions—was in retreat. As bleakly as he saw the absence of the social novel in America, its disappearance yielded an accompanying turn toward the novel of sensibility, except that sensibility had shifted toward sexuality and farther away from feeling. In part, this happens as a result of the advent of therapeutic culture and the belief that individual experience will provide the only sources of redemption and fulfillment. The turn toward sexuality is also fiction's way of staying ahead of movies, which were subject to the industry's notorious code. The advancing preoccupation with sexuality also resulted from middle-class fiction's competition with the flourishing pulp novel trade during these years, the upshot of a coarsening of American culture—itself a partial outcome of the wartime experience of so many American men, who apparently returned home with a whole new way of cursing.[37] Whatever the origins, the turn from social experience to sexual life becomes obvious, with more and more novels taking liberties of representation that neither Howells nor James would have thought possible in their complaints about the strictures on telling America the truth about the social life of the passions.

With the exception of the Kinsey reports on men (1948) and women (1953), arguably no book did as much to make sex central to the culture's consciousness as the publication of Simone de Beauvoir's *The Second Sex* in an English translation (1953), for it conferred international intellectual glamour on what had been a fairly vocal domestic discourse. Beauvoir's book expanded the discussion of women's place in the New America, even though her remarks about American women were few and, according to many readers, uninformed. Part literary history, part philosophy, part anthropology, part sociology, *The Second Sex* was greeted with spirited reviews; many praised its scope, learning, and zeal—even those such as the one in the *Scientific American* that faulted its method as well as its logic.

The controversy that Beauvoir's book generated was part of a larger cultural discussion of the role of women in contemporary society. Indeed, nonfiction books about women's "destiny" abounded in the first half of the '50s—including such well-known volumes as the Kinsey *Sexual Behavior in the Human Female* (1953) and Ashley Montagu's *Natural Superiority of Women* (1953)—titles focused on general concerns, such as collections like the proceedings of a Cooper Union symposium edited by J. E. Fairchild, *Women, Society, and Sex* (1952), along with Elizabeth Bragdon's *Women Today: Their Conflicts, Their Frustrations and Their Fulfillments* (1953). These books aimed to negotiate the great change America's women had experienced in the preceding decade, the shift from the workplace back to the home that the returning veterans and the new prosperity demanded. Some books aimed to cement in place ideals of bourgeois fulfillment, while others tried to claim space for alternative visions, especially for women's economic potential, like Beth Bailey McLean's *Young Women in Business* (1953) or M. W. Zapoleon's *A College Girl Looks Ahead to Her Career Opportunities* (1957), not to mention (on the other side of the spectrum) Agnes Nestor's memoir, *Woman's Labor Leader* (1954), which recounts her career as an organizer of the Women's Trade Union League.

Others pointedly addressed the new consciousness that recent changes had wrought: Sidonie Gruenberg's *The Many Lives of Modern Woman* (1952) —which the *Nation* described as the "most logical analysis yet available of the development of the American woman's life pattern"—along with *The Challenge of Being a Woman* (1955) by Helen Sherman and self-help books like *How to Be a Happy Woman* (1952) by Ardis Whitman. Many books also treated women's role models, like notable female figures in American history, such as Margaret Whitton's *These Were the Women* (1954), or like the makers of the feminist tradition, *The Revolt of American Women* (1952) by Oliver Jensen or *Bold Women* (1953) by Helen Woodward Beal. There were also several books devoted to the heroism of ordinary women, as in Elizabeth Logan Davis's *Mothers of America* (1954)—about the influence of a Christian home on famous Americans—or, alternatively, James Horan's *Desperate Women* (1952)— accounts of famous American spies and outlaws.[38]

Whatever their orientation, these books often gave a glimpse of the vision that Betty Friedan so memorably described a decade later. And if they generally exerted little effect on material conditions for women, the *Second Sex* and the data in *Sexual Behavior in the Human Female* were furiously debated at the time. The Kinsey *Report* followed the spectacular impact of its predecessor volume on American men, while the *Second Sex* was poised to win general interest: Beauvoir had become a public figure in France, partly as a result of the cultural and psychic nerve that her book had touched and partly as an effect of her national visibility as the companion of the philosopher who had given the postwar era a vocabulary for discussing postwar alienation. Jean-Paul Sartre's *existentialism* became a buzz word for contemporary anxieties over freedom, and he emerged as the media image of disaffected intellectualism. This postwar philosophical guide to misconduct emerged as the perfect European import; its message would threaten Americans most deeply and the dismissal or intellectual vanquishing of which would mean the most glorious victory of all—the restoration of American freedom as an abiding principle, as if McCarthyism, along with the new social conformism of the middle-class suburbs, had not cast it into such serious doubt. Beauvoir's book fell neatly into place in these discussions, since reviewers made the fate of American womanhood, especially its middle-class idealization, the focus of the French philosopher's threat.

Among the most significant novels in the decade's arguments over women's place is one that unwittingly exhibits a compelling model of the "second sex." A half century after *Marjorie Morningstar* was published in 1955, it must mystify contemporary scholars of U.S. culture, including American Jewish studies, that it was considered an important cultural event. Having emerged after the war along with so many other veteran-authors, Herman Wouk followed his first books—about the radio business and a Manhattan coming-of-age tale—with a novel that truly captured the American reading public's imagination, the Pulitzer Prize–winning study of guilt and moral authority in wartime, a conflict between military command and citizen-sailors, *The Caine Mutiny* (1951). That novel proved so engaging that it later became a successful stage play and a memorable film, which is the form in which we are now most likely to remember it. At the height of its popularity, Wouk's book sold better than any other twentieth-century novel except *Gone with the Wind*.

Readers and critics wondered what Wouk's new novel would be like. Had he developed into a serious artist, or was he destined to remain a writer for the slicks? When *Marjorie Morningstar* appeared in the first week of September—the traditional time for publishers to begin promoting their fall schedule—it was reviewed prominently in the weekly supplements, sometimes assigned the very first page. But the novel earned decidedly mixed responses. Some reviewers praised the book overmuch, while others despised it; a few saw it in the "great tradition" of Victorian fiction, while others found it proof positive that Wouk was ultimately nothing more than a middlebrow moralist.

As a literary work, *Marjorie Morningstar* has not endured. Indeed, the novel has stimulated only a handful of journal articles and some passing references in histories of Jewish American writing or brief notes in cultural analyses of Jewish American women or film—most luminously by Joyce Antler and Stephen Whitfield, not to mention Barbara Ehrenreich, whose interest in the novel is limited to its portrayal of emasculation.[39] Wouk's book is rightfully subjected to the critique that, whatever its ostensible intentions, it catalogs misogynistic and anti-Semitic typologies, combined notably in the "Shirley" figure: the '30s material girl who mothered the Jewish American princess of the postwar era—soon to be memorialized by Philip Roth in *Goodbye, Columbus* (1959).

While *Marjorie Morningstar*'s popularity resulted in large part from its book club affiliations—a Book-of-the-Month Club selection and a *Reader's Digest* condensed version—significantly, it was also the novel that the most people paid retail to read. Those customers were not merely Jewish club women who thought they might recognize themselves in the Morningstar story. Why would a book about the search for identity undertaken by a bourgeois Jewish maiden become *the* best-selling novel of 1955? The truly fascinating aspect of *Marjorie Morningstar*, I suggest, is that it *was* a crossover book, very likely the first novel about American Jews that American Gentiles read avidly. The reviews demonstrate why Jewish intellectuals hated the book. Why shouldn't they, since it was ultimately an attack against them and a counterassault on their attack on the bourgeois reading public? Why, however, did Christian America find the book spellbinding? As Leslie Fiedler put the conundrum, "What is truly strange is not that Marjorie should seem representative to the bourgeois Jewish community, but that she should also strike the American community at large as a satisfactory image."[40] The answer, he thought, was that the Jewish suburban housewife emerged as a "proper symbol of interfaith 'tolerance'" in the same year that Will Herberg published his classic sociology of American religion, *Protestant-Catholic-Jew*, which advanced the parity among religions as expressions of the American Way of Life.[41] In a year when Edward Steichen's *Family of Man*—and its celebration of the vision of unity in diversity—was the number two nonfiction best seller, Fiedler, however well known for his sometimes outlandish judgments, explains how Marjorie Morgenstern solves the problem of American difference. Wouk's novel won its audience less as a work of the American Jewish imagination than as a female's coming-of-age story. Its reputation has faltered less because its intervention in American Jewish cultural politics is now irrelevant, than because, as a female bildungsroman, it is even clunkier now than it was five decades ago.

Remember that in 1955 Jewish American fiction had scarcely been invented. In fact, Jewish American writing is not even a category in the first edition of that canon-shaping volume, *Literary History of the United States* (1948). There, Abraham Cahan's 1917 novel, *The Rise of David Levinsky*, is cited as an example of Yiddish literature, when, in fact, the book was written in English, having been drawn from a series of magazine articles. Saul Bellow's career had already begun to flourish with the success of the *Adventures of Augie March* (1953), though he had not yet published *Seize the Day* (1956) and was almost a decade away from *Herzog* (1964). Bernard Malamud had not yet published *The Assistant* (1957)—his first novel exclusively devoted to the Jewish American experience—while Philip Roth was just beginning to write his early short stories. In 1955, there is scarcely enough of a critical mass to warrant a category. That is not to say that there wasn't a great deal of Jewish American writing, only that it had not yet distinguished itself from the middle-class traditions of family fiction, the '30s proletarian tradition or the liberal tradition of '40s social fiction, or the capacious confines of immigrant fiction, of which Jews were certainly the largest ethnic group reporting. Widely read as it was, *Gentleman's Agreement* is primarily about a Gentile's experience of anti-Semitism rather than Jewish American social life. Similarly, there were books by Jews and about controversial Jewish characters, but the resulting tumult was reserved mainly for Jewish readers. Exceptions, like Budd Schulberg's *What Makes Sammy Run?* (1941) or Jerome Weidman's *I Can Get It for You Wholesale* (1937), were portraits of unlikable social types whose purport Jewish readers could debate as being good for their people or not. The culture at large scarcely registered these earlier books' power to define a whole ethnic group, much less American society as a whole.

What occasions the popularity of this story of a young Jewish woman's education at the end of the Depression? Marjorie Morgenstern means to become an actress, debates a long time whether to have an affair, and ultimately chooses the kind of man her mother would have picked for her when she becomes Mrs. Milton Schwartz of Westchester County, New York. The critical consensus has been that the novel celebrates the collapsing of Jewish identity within the American bourgeoisie; its primary appeal is its case for middle-class ideals of conformity disguised in its updated brief on behalf of female purity. Other fiction best sellers in 1955 included that other monumental book about conformity and the suburbs, *The Man in the Gray Flannel Suit*; one of the great critical successes of that year was also a novel that peeled away the compromises and humiliations that go into making the successful conformist, John O'Hara's *Ten North Frederick*. (Two phenomenally popular novels of the same year actually celebrated nonconformity by substituting its residual power of correction into something amusing—

naughtily, in the case of Patrick Dennis's *Auntie Mame*, and slyly subversive, in Mac Hyman's *No Time for Sergeants*, which as a stage play gave Andy Griffith his comic persona, the bumpkin whose inability to comprehend the ways of military and social authority renders that authority foolish.) Although the rejection of social orthodoxy would arguably be contained in another best-selling novel of that year, Françoise Sagan's sensational tale of an adolescent girl's complex feelings about her father's remarrying, *Bonjour Tristesse*, the nonfiction best sellers frantically addressed the anxious maintenance of basic values, including two books from Christian tradition: Norman Vincent Peale's vision of achieving success through Jesus Christ, *The Power of Positive Thinking*, and Billy Graham's *The Secret of Happiness*.

The year 1955 witnessed other novels by writers who were either admired at the time or would later be prized more highly than Wouk: Nabokov's *Lolita*, Mary McCarthy's *A Charmed Life*, and Robert Penn Warren's *Band of Angels*. Yet *Time* made Wouk its cover story (on 5 September), lauded his observant practice of Judaism, and praised *Marjorie Morningstar* as sustaining a conservative revolt against the modernist fiction of the last thirty years—especially its "skeptical criticism, sexual emancipation, social protest, and psychoanalytic sermonizing"—by lavishly enshrining bourgeois consolations, thus eliciting the particular scorn of modernist intellectuals.[42]

Marjorie Morningstar certainly militates against the independent life and derides the freethinking of Greenwich Village so urgently that it seems incredible that Marjorie could be waylaid from her upper-middle-class destiny for very long at all. If the book warns the bourgeoisie against any inattention to preserving its gains, the argument need not be compelling, since the vision of nonconformity is so tendentious.[43] That point is dramatized explicitly in a passage to which almost every commentator on the novel refers—Noel Airman's "Dear Marjorie" letter. There, the posturing bohemian (né Saul Ehrmann) argues that it is actually Marjorie who has led *him* astray, seducing him with visions of writing a Broadway success, making him unfaithful to his true nonconformist self. Of course, the fundamental weakness of his attack lies in his refusal to take any responsibility for his decisions.

The responses to *Marjorie Morningstar* disclose the sources of its claim on the American imagination in the '50s insofar as these reviews dramatize ongoing debates concerning the spiritual as well as social condition of American Jews, although, taken together, they also help to reveal the novel's cultural agenda. In the *New York Times*, Maxwell Geismar conceded that the novel was "very good reading indeed" but that the "values of true culture," like the "impulses of real life," are "remote from its polished orbit." Not surprisingly for Geismar, a longtime student of political fiction, Wouk's interest in Marjorie's career is how it situates the "problem of revolt and authority," which in this novel, he says, is "settled by a final bow to . . . the proprieties of social class." The *New York Herald Tribune*'s critic, on the other hand, saw *Marjorie Morningstar* as bearing comparison to the Victorian authors Wouk admired, describing it as "a modern Jewish *Vanity Fair* . . . spacious, abundantly peopled, shrewd, observant, humane." For the *Herald Tribune*, the novel's grand achievement is its characterization, not of Marjorie, but of an "American family."[44] The book begins as a work of Jewish American imagination and ends as a national fantasy of domestic strength.

Implicit in these reviews are the conflicts with which many other critics also grappled. What does it mean to call a book a Jewish *Vanity Fair* and then describe it as a portrait of an American family? Such thinking might participate in the warm accommodationism, lively assimiliationism, and happy prosperity that led so many social observers and rabbis to worry over the "Changing Status of American Jewry."[45] By 1955, the movement of a large number of second-generation Jews out of the cities into the suburbs had led cultural analysts to question the effects of the migration on American Jewish identity, a demographic corollary to the story of embourgeoisification. What does it mean to see the novel as resolving modernist issues of "revolt and authority" by submitting them to bourgeois proprieties? Is Marjorie's career important because she chooses Mamaroneck over Montmartre? Was it ever in doubt? Sooner or later seemingly every critic recurs to what it means for Wouk alternately to reward and punish Marjorie by packing her off to the suburbs, the wife of a lawyer and the mother of four children.

Critics on the left were both gratified and horrified by this resolution, gratified that their suspicions were right—this is what happens if you listen to your mother—and horrified that the mother's vision could be taken seriously, a fear that Norman Podhoretz most notably articulated in his eloquent review, "The Jew as Bourgeois." Podhoretz found the novel's argument troubling because it signaled to him how little demand a generation had made of its youth, how hysterically it tried to become—in one of the keywords of the decade—"mature," which led to an unnaturally abbreviated period of revolt and a craven desire to find authority in conventional bourgeois order. (Fifteen years later, Podhoretz acidly criticized the next younger generation for its disrespectful, even contemptuous refusal of bourgeois maturity!) For Podhoretz, the problem could be found in pandering to the taste of readers who had even less purchase on their sense of having a biography than Marjorie herself.[46]

Mainstream critics, however, found Marjorie's destiny anything but discouraging, even if they had qualms about the literary quality of the novel. Several reviewers were dismayed by its length—more than five hundred pages—a book that despite being "rich in minor treasures and to be respected for the scope and seriousness of its intention" said *Commonweal*, "promises more than it delivers." At the same time such reviewers admired the general level of "sustained virtuosity and calm, unjudging insight of the misguided, frequently vain, people who inhabit this fortunately small world," according to the *Christian Science Monitor*.[47] *Marjorie Morningstar* was generally fortunate in its reviewers too, not that it received many puffs, but even the attacks were often incisive. Many of those adversarial critics enjoyed abiding respect, like Isaac Rosenfeld, Meyer Levin, and Ludwig Lewisohn. In England, curiously, *Marjorie Morningstar* gained a more uniformly positive reaction. Although the *Times Literary Supplement* murmured about the length, the *Spectator* hailed it as "damned nearly the Great American Novel," "essential reading for anyone interested in transatlantic writing." The "breadth and depth of . . . vision" is "remarkable"; "the sheer professional achievement of the thing is exhilarating"; "at his best [Wouk] emerges . . . as one of the most important writers now working in America."[48] So much for the English gift of understatement.

For American critics, the "breadth and depth" of vision were precisely at issue, and the defense did not go well. In the *Partisan Review*, "For God and the Suburbs," Isaac Rosenfeld wages a predictable assault. First, the book makes too much of Marjorie's long vigil over her virginity. "Somehow all of this is supposed to show that psychoanalysis is nonsense and intellectuals are bums, and that the accumulated folk wisdom of the Bronx and Central Park West is superior to sex, bohemianism, the new pediatrics, and the eating of crustaceans and pork." For Rosenfeld, the novel is quintessential middlebrow entertainment, "made not only to withstand but to thrive on disparagement." The sense here is not simply that the middlebrow is impervious to criticism. Wouk, says Rosenfeld, is "faking," sociologically, whereby he lays down his position on Jews in American society without having anything truly to say. Wouk's study of Jewish social and family life, according to Rosenfeld, boils down to accepting the proposition that Mom is always right. Even as Wouk exposes Mrs. Morgenstern to ridicule, he winds up siding with her, as if to say that the solution for Jewish life in America is to head out to the suburbs but be sure to bring along the tallith and tefillin.[49] Wouk's approval of Marjorie's mother participates in the deep ambivalence over motherhood pervading the middle and late '50s: while father may know best, mother must be persuaded to embrace motherhood as a profession, however inferior, in order to validate the superiority of spouses and children. Abnegation becomes impossible to distinguish from aspiration.

Redeeming Marjorie from her failed efforts of self-invention, however, is her identification with the Jewish war dead. Seeing her kinship with the victims of the Holocaust, in Wouk's scheme of things, gives her a scale she can never achieve through any paltry dream of theatrical glory, a love affair, or matronly status. Moreover, Wouk is, ideologically, just as phony, argues Rosenfeld: in an effort to make respectability respectable, the novelist skewers anything resembling intellectual engagement; for this novelist, all intellectuals are pseudo-intellectuals. The seducer who Marjorie ruins in turn, Noel Airman—his very name signifying the lightness of his character and his lack of substance—is destroyed because his pursuit of the pleasure principle has rendered his love for Marjorie crippling. Wouk's argument challenges bohemians as having insufficiently distanced themselves from their middle-class roots and asks whether, after the requisite measure of theatrical gesturing, they have not fully eradicated the would-be burgher within. The Nation sounded similar notes: "Celebrating the virtues of triumphant mediocrity, [Wouk] applauds the well-upholstered life, the basic values of home, family, religion. The intellectual is the villain . . . doomed to spiritual sterility." One should expect that some reviewers, fiercely protecting intellectual life from middlebrow smothering, would respond in these ways, but the animus against antimodernism also finds a special target: "Only when Marjorie realizes the error of her ways and turns to sanctified breeding, does she achieve contentment. And contentment—as mother, wife, and ladies' auxiliary member—is the most basic of all Wouk's 'basic' values."[50]

One rudimentary move of the reviewers, in their taking up Wouk's assailing of subversive values, was actually to look past the titular heroine to the novel's insulting treatment of modern articles of intellectual faith and then to the upper-middle-class life for which Marjorie seems so terribly destined. Nor did one need to be Jewish to disparage her. Writing in the liberal Christian magazine *Commonweal*, R. T. Horchler sees Marjorie as the central source of the novel's weakness: "She is tiresomely imperceptive and a painfully slow learner. At the novel's end she has muddled through to a happy establishment . . . but all of her decisions have been made by instinct and accident, and she knows very little more about the world than she did when she was seventeen."[51]

Marjorie is not really supposed to stand as a vivid and vivifying young woman of substantive conviction; nor is she meant to compete with another recent representative of young Jewish women's life-affirming powers. Published also in 1955 was Albert Hackett's *Diary of Anne Frank*—the stage adaptation of her diary—a text, it has been argued, that assimilates the Nazi victim by turning a "young girl" into a heroine of studied universalism. At least one critic, Nora Magid, a regular reviewer for the opinion magazines of the day and eventually the literary editor of the *Reporter*, did assert that the weakness of Wouk's book was neither its conflation of Jews with the bourgeoisie nor its brief for the stability of middle-class virtue over the chaos of modernist thought. Instead, for Magid, writing in the *New Republic*, the book's danger and vast emptiness were to be found in the novelist's failure to imagine Marjorie Morgenstern as a woman. Magid turns Wouk's sense that young Marjorie was "very bored with the problems of being a girl" into the author's "problem" in "never having been one," in that "he cannot tell a girl's story from a girl's point of view." Even though she praises the novel's "vivid and enormously complex" environment, Magid alone seizes on the basis of an insufficiently imagined central character around whom all else revolves to derogate the novel's aspirations, seeing it as "a soap opera with psychological and sociological props."[52]

The reasons that this banal love story achieved the status it did are not to be found alone in its Jewish context or even its middle-class meanings. If it were, other novels the year before or after might have succeeded a little better than they did. Consider the fate of Eliot Wagner's *Grand Concourse* (1954), the tale of an impoverished Bronx Jewish family, whose anchor, Julie, the daughter, secretly yearns for escape and love. So true to the Jewish family experience is it that the *New York Herald Tribune* reviewer praises its social vision and reservoir of emotion: "Anybody who wants to know what the Bronx is like will find it in this deeply felt book." While the *Times* demurred over *Grand Concourse*'s aesthetic accomplishment, it recommended this "study in frustration" and the author's "remarkable gift for describing the backgrounds against which his people move."[53] Six months before *Marjorie Morningstar* appeared, Ann Birstein's *The Troublemaker* (1955), a story about the second-generation daughters of a middle-class Jewish family, met with polite reviews. (It followed her debut novel *Star of Glass* [1950], which portrayed a young Jewish woman of the times to more mixed reviews.) Most found her characterizations engaging but wished Birstein had put them toward a broader, less timid purpose. Leonard Bishop's *Days of My Love* (1953) tells of a second-generation daughter who wants to be an artist; despite the "disorder" of its "tumult," according to the *Times*, its "achievement is considerable."[54] Nor did other Jewish novels bearing comparison to Wouk's fare well. Michael Blankfort's *The Strong Hand* (1956), the benighted love story of an Orthodox rabbi and a war widow, was commended as instructive by reviewers, including one who found it "strangely evocative": "Above all it presents an accurate interpretation of the ethical meaning of Judaism far removed from the soap opera and kosher food treatment that Herman Wouk accorded it in 'Marjorie Morningstar.'"[55]

During these years, serious or middlebrow novels about the careers of young middle-class women did not exactly flourish, though Rona Barrett would write an extremely popular treatment, *The Best of Everything* (1957). Romances were plentiful, novels about marriage—and adultery—abounded, but mainstream novels that meditated over the shaping of a woman's identity were less prominent. In retrospect, *Marjorie Morningstar*'s appeal was less its representation of Jewish American culture than as a book about placating the national anxiety over women in modern culture—for whom a theatrical young Jewish woman might seem an apt model not only of religious and social tolerance, but also an implicit, if inverted, demand for gender tolerance too. The novel's force, then, is less to be understood as a middlebrow rationalization of "basic" values or even as a portrayal of a middle-class American family, though obviously it also fulfills those purposes. *Marjorie Morningstar*'s claim to national attention centered on the part it played in *limiting* the possibilities of fulfillment for American women, for whom Jewish American women—mobile and college-educated as so many were—might figure either as a stereotype or as a historical model, or both. Wouk's dubious achievement—the sad source of his book's appeal—was not only to help to persuade a generation of "Shirleys" that they made the right choice, but also, by trivializing Marjorie's career, to convince them that, finally, they had no choice, a lesson that makes all the more lamentable that so many women testified to sharing in Marjorie Morgenstern's experience.

Shameful as *Marjorie Morningstar* is, the guilt is not entirely Wouk's. The book could not be read as the debilitating vision it is because for so many years the Jewish American literary establishment was so thoroughly a male preserve, one that regarded the "World of Our Mothers" merely as an afterthought to the "World of Our Fathers." The irate reviewers' conjecture that Wouk is validating Mrs. Morgenstern as the moral center of the novel asserts a Jewish version of the anti-Momism permeating midcentury U.S. culture. In the name of class warfare—that is, the struggle to dismantle middle-class orthodoxy under the auspices of modernist cosmopolitanism—the reviewers of *Marjorie Morningstar*, one may say, join in a communal act of condemning the mother by silencing the daughter. What makes the daughter worthy of their violent repudiation is that she is, after all, merely a middle-class young woman, damned if she aspires to self-invention, denounced if she lives out her so-called destiny as a lawyer's wife in suburbia, precisely at the time that the middle class was fleeing the city. Thus, the reviews of the book recapitulate and perpetuate national anxieties about modernity and women's mobility, along with conventional Jewish cultural and gender politics. Marjorie's humbling is a foregone conclusion; its meanings are portentous.

FICTION AND ETHICS

The receding of the Howellsian tradition can be quantified in the number of books reviewed and the shrinking number of venues for their discussion, a phenomenon that generally does not show up until the 1960s but that is already under way. The *New York Times Book Review* and the *New Yorker* continued to broker books, but the *Herald Tribune*, the *Times*'s erstwhile competitor, would soon cease publishing. The *Saturday Review* operated through the '60s, but, with each passing year, it lost more of its purchase on the shaping of American cultural life. Having already dropped "Literature" from its title, it would ultimately abandon its commitment to fiction as well. No major publication interested in assessing the achievement of new fiction is born until the *New York Review of Books* comes into being as a result of the newspaper strike of 1964 (though eventually it too would informally drop "Books" from its title).

As if these factors were not enough, reviewing also suffered in prestige when critics despised and mocked the ambitions and experience of a large portion of the book-buying public—the middle class—and scholars, as a group, turned away from the interest of middle-class social experience in fiction and settled their attention on formal achievements. To top it off, the avant-garde was understood to be taking its cues from French writers whose "new novel" proved too unrewardingly difficult for many readers. Stripped of conventional plot and character, content to glory in Barthelmesque triviality or Barthian self-referentiality, American postmodern fiction would develop its own audience by the 1960s, but it seldom captured the imagination of the larger book-buying public.

All of this sounds like a recipe for disaster, with books being published that never found an audience. That decline, nearly imperceptible from year to year, became quite apparent through the '60s, but the lament that the novel was dead or in decline was already audible in the '50s. On the one hand, the phrase meant that the aesthetic assumptions of the nineteenth-century novel had expired, that the first half of the twentieth century had transcended its lessons, and now the art form had exhausted its possibilities. *Novel* means something new and, by this time, no experiment seemed left to freshen the genre, no new wager for the artist to make and still be writing a novel; its whole repository of possible technical innovations, empty. Even though that was what scholars might have understood, it is less sure that critics meant the same thing. For them, the novel was in decline or dead not only because of these artistic issues but also because its history had somehow completed itself. Its practitioners could never overtake Joyce, and in America, new writers could not, obviously, compete with the generation that ascended after World War I. Compared to Hemingway, Fitzgerald, Dos Passos, and Faulkner, the newer writers had less artistic capacity and cultural warrant in making U.S. literature an international one. The novel had turned so deeply inward that the result for many observers was a literature transitory and fungible, without any vivid understanding of the way Americans lived at that time.

For most readers, however, the death of the novel meant its passing as a vehicle of social instruction. For them, the novel became defunct when it relinquished or forfeited its Arnoldian charge of criticizing life, of trying to make sense of its sources of turmoil and their contours. Less and less did American writers make bold to face this challenge—of using fiction to point the moral way. In part, one may argue that the new hip sensibility disregarded such a square tendency to find in fiction an implied manual of what to do and how to live, but it would be a mistake to view the reading public to be under such sway, despite the enormous popularity of, say, *On the Road* (1957). Jack Kerouac's appeal was not just to the dropout, who might find something consoling and familiar in the alienation driving Sal Paradise, but to the middle class. Such readers knew him as a kindred spirit, at least in his living out the fantasy of reckless driving through the dark fields of the republic, open to adventure and, of course, freedom, a bourgeois escape fantasy that John Updike evokes in having Rabbit Angstrom drive off at the close of his 1960 novel, *Rabbit, Run*. The audience for such fiction may not have been strait-laced suburbanites, but those middle-class readers who may otherwise have been entertained by the music of Tom Lehrer or the political humor of Mort Sahl. To suggest the relevance of Sal Paradise and Dean Moriarty's manic flight as a middle-class cultural fantasy, consider that in just a few years a TV show, *Route 66*, capitalized on the myth, turning Sal and Dean into clean-cut kids in a Corvette. Whatever its permutation, the appeal of *On the Road* remains an essentially ethical one of disclosing a hedonism whose appeal could accurately be gauged by a middle class unhappy and frustrated by its abiding bargain with deferred gratification.

Yet the desire to create a "living novel" manifested itself with writers' interest in portraying stories of public values. Among the several concerns of middle-class novels of the late '50s is one that has received too little attention: the question of ethics. Partly shaping this issue was a political scandal that resulted when Sherman Adams, an assistant to President Dwight D. Eisenhower, resigned—under pressure from fellow Republicans during a midterm election year—after having sworn under oath to a congressional committee that he had not advanced the cause of industrialist Bernard Goldfine, who, it was later revealed, had given Adams gifts. Although Americans witnessed greater corruption in office before and since, what was startling about the Adams affair was not only that an embarrassed Ike had called Adams a man of integrity, but also that such shoddiness did not comport with the image of Protestant establishment respectability on which Adams had traded. It seemed to send shock waves through a populace that had already witnessed the Army-McCarthy hearings and would soon suffer further disillusionment through the unseemliness of another American aristocrat, the corrupt prince of high culture and quiz show competitor, Charles

Van Doren. In a sense, the Adams affair may have been an early episode in the decline of the WASP that was to play out over the next twenty years.[56]

The Adams episode once had the power to specify a whole cultural sense of turpitude and moral failure. Even as it did so, it also helped to temper a spate of American writing whose main purport was to expose the ethical instabilities in contemporary political culture. Critically speaking, the novel might have been dead or dying, but these novels offered some of the remaining vital signs of the tradition of middle-class realism. For their strength invariably might be found in the way they validated the middle-class order of things in American social life.

Best known of these works must be Allen Drury's *Advise and Consent* (1959), an operations manual about the rigors of a Senate confirmation hearing, which won the Pulitzer Prize though it has no standing now. Also recalled from this milieu was Gore Vidal's drama about the machinations in nominating a presidential candidate, *The Best Man* (1960). As much as these are middle-class entertainments, with their inside look at practical politics, the novel most fully emphasizing a middle-class imaginary might be Frederick Buechner's *The Return of Ansel Gibbs* (1958). Buechner, a novelist as well as a minister, wrote some psychological novels during his career and, once he was ordained, moved more and more into religiosity, so much so that by the 1970s, religion dominated his fiction completely. Still, in his first phase, he focused on the challenges of living in a secular society.

The Return of Ansel Gibbs is an exception in Buechner's oeuvre, at least to the extent that it is probably his most straightforwardly reportorial plot. The novel concerns the nomination of a liberal man of political affairs to a cabinet post, a figure who had been instrumental in the Capitol during the war but who has since retired. That appointment is an anathema to a McCarthyesque senator, Edward Farwell, who despises Gibbs's acculturated bearing and his intellectual understanding of culture and politics. In an ill-fated decision, Gibbs agrees to meet his antagonist on television, a confrontation moderated by Robin Tripp, who is not only well known for his talent at luring guests into embarrassing disclosures and compromising displays, but who also happens to be the son of a business associate whose moral lapses, years ago, Gibbs could not overlook and who ended as a suicide. And—here is the unlikely part—young Tripp is also the fiancé of Gibbs's daughter, Anne. On air, Gibbs reveals himself as truly detached, and despite his being, in the liberal watchword of 1952 and 1956, the "best we

have" (as supporters of Adlai Stevenson described the presidential nomi-
nee), he gets the worse of the exchange. Under Tripp's skillful manipulation,
Gibbs is no match for the bloodless, media-savvy demagoguery of his oppo-
nent, a humiliation that, in turn, leads his daughter to break off her engagement, since she is bright enough to blame her fiancé for Gibbs's debacle.
Ultimately Gibbs recovers himself, through the aid of a minister (very much
like Reinhold Niebuhr) attending to the impoverished people of East Harlem, who had once been Gibbs's philosophy teacher at Harvard. At the close,
he decides to go to Washington to have the president withdraw his nomination, but changes his mind yet again when circumstances lead him to sympathy for Tripp, who finally wins Anne back. Gibbs realizes that, rather than
being a heartless bureaucrat, he really can feel for people, and thus is worthy
of serving America.

The interest of the plot is that it makes political dynamics a vehicle for
bourgeois fulfillment. Buechner is especially good on exposing how the new
mass medium of TV creates false heroes and unwitting victims through its
own particular rules of engagement. Yet Buechner knows little about the
way politics work; his figure of a man of affairs as a man of scruples owes
more to a religious imagination than experience. Even Arthur Winner, the
lawyer-hero of the previous year's succès de scandale, *By Love Possessed*,
performs more convincingly as a man of affairs—in this case, a lawyer—
distracted by ethical qualms. In *The Return of Ansel Gibbs*, the marriage plot
seems like a sop; Tripp's suppressed hatred for Gibbs at having fired his
father so many years before never fully persuades us of the young man's
conscious or unconscious revenge motive, as if Buechner were incapable of
having the son decide to ruin Gibbs's life just for the fun of it, so intoxicating
is the power of TV and the egotism of the men who master the medium.

Buechner's moral vision, however, comes not only on the heels of Sherman Adams's disgrace, but as part of the public worry over the character
of American political leaders of whom Adams is only one example, an
unwitting victim of the general skepticism that resulted from the fall of
Joseph McCarthy, not to mention the residual scandal—and the tale of
homosexual favoritism—over the part that his aide Roy Cohn played in the
Army-McCarthy hearings. Consider the tenor of dozens of magazine articles
of the middle and late '50s. Not only is the Adams case covered in several
articles appearing in *Time*, *US News*, and *Newsweek*, but also it is the subject
of feature articles in *Commonweal*, *Christian Century*, *Businessweek*, *National*

Business, the *New York Times Magazine*, *Life*, the *Saturday Evening Post* ("Why Must Republicans Always Clobber One Another?"), and *Look* ("Must There Always Be a Mess in Washington?"), even as it provides the moment that John F. Kennedy used to define himself against in his well-received book, *Profiles in Courage* (1956), about the brave integrity of politicians past, and in an article on the "Education of an American Politician." The year 1957 also witnessed articles on political ethics that included "Morals for Gentlemen" and "Private Interests of Public Servants" (*New Republic*) as well as "Political and Personal Morality" (*Saturday Review*), among many others.

Public concern about ethics in political life resonates with larger anxieties about national fortitude and readiness to withstand Cold War threats, especially after Sputnik indicated the Soviets' technical superiority. That fortitude was also attacked from within by John Kenneth Galbraith in his controversial treatise, *The Affluent Society* (1958), which diagnosed the ills of superfluous production and advertisement. Moreover, gnawing at the center of American dreams of well-being during the era is the unmistakable, unsettling realization that racial divisions had gone too far for too long and that the country was at a critical juncture, whether it was the Montgomery, Alabama, bus boycott of 1956 or the federalizing of the National Guard in Little Rock, Arkansas, in 1957. The perception of an undivided America, the vision of an uncomplicated common prosperity, seemed destined to crack.

CIVIC LESSONS

Fiction writers during the civil rights era responded to segregation, both in the North and the South, especially in the period between the Eisenhower and Kennedy administrations. The principal novel concerning race relations, written by a white American of the time, was *To Kill a Mockingbird*, published in October 1960. The book has had an amazing shelf life— advanced by a Hollywood movie, along with its required status in high schools throughout the United States, and in countless local theater productions. Yet how the critical response helps to illuminate cultural values for integration is less well understood. What we will see is that Harper Lee's novel converses with the literary critical debates as well as political and social discourses of the moment, including the election year of 1960.

How it does so requires a larger understanding of how deeply middle-class culture has shaped the reception of modern American fiction. Two novels by white Americans, published no less than three months after Lee's, were devoted to the crisis of integration in the North. These books focused on blockbusting, the unscrupulous realtors' practice of integrating Northern suburban neighborhoods first by obscuring the identities of black purchasers and then by stimulating panic selling through a variety of unsavory scare tactics. *Peaceable Lane* (by Keith Wheeler) and *First Family* (by Christopher Davis) were positively received, and both were seen as making important contributions (on the pro side) to the discussion of integration. The simultaneity of publication suggests something about how American writers confronted segregation and suggests how some white writers really were enmeshed in representing racial issues.

Lee's novel is remembered largely because of the civics lesson it imparts, especially for a literary establishment altogether eager to see racial injustice as a regional rather than a national problem and altogether eager to demonize the South, where segregation seemed de jure as opposed to the North where it seemed de facto. Wheeler's and Davis's novels, however, teach that segregation is just as much the province of the Northern suburban middle class as it is the gentry's and rednecks' of the unreconstructed South (as if the middle class played no part there). Such overdetermined cultural memory eclipses historical realities and disguises the extent to which class biases distort how cultural historians and critical observers understand such challenges.

Both *Peaceable Lane* and *First Family* constellate a range of American middle-class anxieties, particularly about the suburbs, mining that world for its fictional resources, most especially the participation in civil rights writing. The suburbs are susceptible of such critical discussion.[57] Suburbia has generally been judged by what it is not—neither urban nor rural—signifying as it does that infinite American nowhere—the land no one else wanted or that could no longer be made to pay. Even the names are virtually the same, a world without identity, without depth, and virtually without history, a world, as one may say, that seems like a precursor of the virtual communities of the Internet. Yet the easy derogation of suburbia seems wrong, even desperate, especially when we consider just how fully suburban culture, values, and aspirations shape American politics and social life. It was one thing to deride the suburbs in the postwar era, when a housing shortage first aroused the need for commuter villages like Levittown, resulting in poorly made "little boxes." It was one thing to disdain the suburbs as the spiritual wasteland that kids, hankering for authenticity, found there in the '60s, even as their parents may have discovered them to be a "split-level trap"—the name of a psychological study of the effects of living in suburban New Jersey.[58] It is even one thing to despise the suburbs for their relentless spawning of shopping plazas and strip malls—the soulless residuum of what America's social life once was.

The suburbs, however, can claim to be the preeminent U.S. culture, the normative American social environment. When we talk about them now, we can speak with the same confidence in their power and range of cultural definition as the nineteenth century felt about agricultural life, with the same conviction that the first half of the twentieth century had of the city's vibrancy and resource, as locales of political and social meaning: suburbanites now elect our president, generate mainstream policies, absorb and assimilate their antagonists. They are the territory ahead that replaces the boulevard of broken dreams, the world elsewhere now enveloped by the city's outer ring. The suburban novel through the '50s and '60s did not truly displace the regional novel of the '30s, but it did aim, as did the normative fiction of the '30s and '40s, to interpret American modernity by making place into the setting of shifts in ethical standards as well as the grounds of social change. In this regard, the suburbs are every bit as important as the wilderness was to James Fenimore Cooper, the sea to Herman Melville, the middle border to Hamlin Garland, the country of the pointed firs to Jewett, the prairie to Cather, or la frontera to Sandra Cisneros; every bit as important as the city was to James T. Farrell, Wright, or Bellow. And it may be that, in trying to make this new locale into an object of cultural inquiry, these suburban novels ultimately proved to be the precursors of the critical realism that has reasserted itself in the last twenty years of the twentieth century and into the twenty-first, now that the suburbs too have accumulated more of a complex history, more political valence, more social diversity.

While the suburbs might not have found their Tolstoy or Dostoyevsky in the 1950s, most literary historians point to The Man in the Gray Flannel Suit as the paradigmatic example of the genre in the '50s, largely because it corroborated so well the anxieties codified in William Whyte's influential Organization Man. Although it would ultimately be surpassed by Richard Yates's Revolutionary Road (1961), Wilson's book was the best-known novel of its day to examine how the suburbs could be imagined as the place where the domestic side of alienated man's quandaries gets worked out. Like Organiza-

tion Man, it looks closely at the dislocated emotional lives of commuters and thus also operates as a study of American masculinity. By analyzing what happens to husbands and fathers as they negotiate the 5:16 P.M. to Westport, Connecticut, *The Man in the Gray Flannel Suit* is given over to the concept of commuting between worlds rather than a fully committed portrayal of what gets worked out behind the picture window. Indeed, the story of the deleterious effects of such fissures on women contributed largely to *The Feminine Mystique*, which is, after all, partly a product of an outraged suburban imagination. One may even suppose that fundamental flaws in relations between women and men might be naturalized or obscured in the city or the country, but made unavoidable in suburbia. Be that as it may, middle-class novels through the second half of the '50s anxiously tried to interpret the changes in American social organization: some addressed politics, some psychology, but their investigations proceeded out of the conviction that American society was witnessing a substantial change, that suburbanization meant, in the immediate sense of things, new scenes and subjects for realist fiction. In the larger sense, suburbanization meant a redistribution of cultural capital to be found in the new nexus between country and city and thus signified a crucial historical, and geographical, shift.

Several novels constellate these changes, most of them published in the second half of the '50s and the early '60s. Although these works invoked various visions of tragedy and humor, the claim that the suburbs most exerted on the level of national fantasy was as a place of rampant adultery (especially between neighbors), where children discover sex early and where teens engage in it promiscuously. *The Devil in Bucks County* (1959), by Edmund Schiddel, for example, describes the life of the Barksdales—Bill, a successful, hard-working TV producer; his wife Lillian, who finds comfort in the arms of the deliveryman of the local bakery; and Laurie, the teenage daughter infuriated by her mother's immorality—which the *New York Times* praised for its surprising power of compassion. In *Copper Beech* (1960), by Ariadne Thompson, a haughty suburban man discovers that his wife has been shot dead by her Lawrentian lover, the local tree pruner, a novel generally regarded as trite, though the *Times* saw its redemption: "Shrunken from poetry and philosophy to a suburban female, practical point of view, the story has an oddly distressing reality. . . . The very limitations of the characters add poignance to their sense of loneliness, and to the author's pleas for love within the possible." A novel like Irving Wallace's *Chapman*

Report (1960), which takes the view of a sexologist's survey, still lives a little in the cultural memory because of its once infamous, low-minded interest in extramarital affairs; a more sensitive book of the preceding year, Marjorie Lee's *Lion House*, has been forgotten, though it was read in its time as "a subtle and frightening novel," a story of wife swapping that eventuates in a lesbian relationship.[59]

Perhaps these books are forgotten for the good reason that the America they documented has reshaped itself as compulsively as the suburban developments they depict; the lines and shadows that need so much nuance in one decade pass out of memory by the next. Beyond these novels' efforts to chronicle the new dream life of Americans, they move vigorously into the public sphere and draw on another vein of midcentury fiction: the social problem novel. Ultimately, the troubles that beset the suburbs are as much about difference, especially race and class, as they are about gender, since the suburbs would impose a Jeffersonian scheme of order. They reflect the perennial distrust of the cities in the shaping of the American community, and, historically, over the chaos of postwar America, a chaos so fervently felt that it generated the militant conformity we are now likely to associate with the "nifty fifties." So craven was the desire for order, so desperate the fear of the other, that the suburbs—developed in so many ways out of the "white flight" stripping cities of their middle class—exemplify the vision of white, middle-class utopia, the lawns neatly cut and meticulously tended to approximate the very measure of rural, at least antiurban, nostalgia.

Wheeler's *Peaceable Lane* tells the story of what happens when a successful African American graphic artist buys a house in a segregated New York suburb. A variety of social types populate this suburban street, and their reactions to discovering that their new neighbors are black helped readers of the day to determine their own moral positions. Most of the whites respond badly, though some are moderate by inclination or are forced into tolerance by their reluctance to sell their home for less than market value. Sometimes, the reactions can bring a split between spouses who see the matter quite differently. Some reactions are inevitably made out to be subject positions: embourgeoisified American Jews act one way; less assimilated Jewish refugees from Nazi Germany, another. The novel's protagonist, Matt Jones, is an ad man, originally from Wyoming, who discovers that his black business associate, a man he thinks of as a friend, is about to buy the house next door. At first, Jones sides with his white neighbors and engineers a plan to purchase the property through a consortium, but the chicanery feels all wrong, especially after a visit to his friend's tastefully decorated Harlem apartment. The real villain in the piece is neither the white liberal nor the arrogant black artist, Winters, a cosmopolite who turns into a suburbanite only to save his son from the mean streets and not because there is a touch of Babbitry to him, a man who adamantly refuses a submissive place among whites. Nor is the primary antagonist the most virulent neighborhood racist or the outraged patrician torn between his pride and worldliness. The villain is not even some greedy real estate agent trying to make a fast buck.

Despicable as many of the whites are, the object of hatred that Wheeler constructs is a black realtor who lives to blockbust, to break up neighborhoods by stampeding anxious whites into panic selling. He says that he is motivated by feelings for his people, but in Wheeler's scheme of things, the most animating feeling he has is a deeply ingrained hatred of whites. He is certainly not a race man, enjoying no connection to one of the national organizations, like the NAACP. Wheeler's realtor cares nothing for the feelings of the one black man who prefers to live among whites than among blacks; he cares nothing for the vision of bourgeois individuality that the novel inscribes. From the polish of his demeanor to his slick business maneuverings, to his whispering telephone campaign, to his strong-arm associates, his villainy succeeds because he hates so implacably.

Peaceable Lane ends with peace restored after Winters dies in an auto accident, the result of his much remarked-upon high-spirited driving, a peace that results from his neighbors' acceptance of their situation. The novel's reviews were surprisingly good: the major newspapers admired it, as did opinion magazines like the *Atlantic Monthly* and the *New Yorker*, as an "effective, in fact, rather terrifying" vision of "something that might happen in a town one knows and of situations it would take courage and integrity to face." But the *Saturday Review* critic may have gotten it right when he criticized the novel as a "fast-moving, heavily plotted social fable whose characters are shiny market-researched products right off the assembly line of the cliché factory. . . . There is a lesson here in this that deserves better realization."[60]

Christopher Davis's *First Family* was published in early January 1961, during the interregnum between Dwight Eisenhower and John F. Kennedy. The novel charts the consequences, especially for young people, when an African American family moves into a comfortable white section of a Midwestern city. Readers are supposed to be engaged by the fragile psychology of Scotty—young, gifted, and black. That emphasis is meant to depoliticize the story by focusing it on the inner lives of the characters, though of course we are completely uninterested in these lives but for the occasion of integration their collision yields. Again, readers are given lessons in the art of blockbusting; again, we observe how spouses react to the situation; and, again, the white characters model a range of moral choices—from haughty contempt, to vulgar rudeness, to liberal inadequacy. Again, violence at the close brings peace to the neighborhood.

The novel's reviewers were almost uniformly ambivalent about the book, in equal measure. Some called it shrill and dreary; others chide its vision of "Negro super-people." The *Times* reviewer complained that this "well-padded integration vehicle" sacrificed artistry, while the *Herald Tribune* applauded *First Family* as "daring and controversial." *Time* compared it favorably to *Peaceable Lane*, while the *Saturday Review* held that the novel was less the "powerful tract" than Wheeler's book was, though certainly it was more a work of literary art.[61]

The interest of these books would be negligible but for two reasons. The first is their grasp of race relations in the late '50s and the way they take up a subject very much in the air within a few years of the *Brown v. Board of Education* case and of the integration of Little Rock, Arkansas, schools. The question of integration in the North was more or less focused on issues of real estate, rather than segregation laws, as in the South. In the North, African Americans faced redlined districts and racial steering; in the South, the police dogs of Bull Connor, public safety commissioner of Birmingham, Alabama. While many ex-urbanites did not think of themselves as racist in moving from the city in pursuit of their own home and not out of fear of the city's growing racial divide, the social reality, as the builder of Levittown knew, was that owning a home meant the need to control its market value, which, for many places like Levittown, devolved into the position that neighborhoods must be kept white.

This new America sought mainly to be a white America, with working-class blacks living in segregated communities nearby and the black bourgeoisie someone else's problem. How critical this issue was can be seen in the 1960 presidential election, when John F. Kennedy complained of the Republican administration's failure to support a law, unanimously endorsed by the Civil Rights Commission, banning discrimination in federally assisted housing. In fact, Kennedy's campaign was helped to victory through the support of 70 percent of the African American vote, though it took him two years to throw the weight of executive action behind efforts to challenge residential segregation with, as he called it, but a "stroke of the presidential pen." A few years later, the effect of this legislation would be felt, tumultuously, in places like Forest Hills, New York, where white enclaves would be undone and housing made available to all.[62]

The novel that has emerged from the fall publishing season of 1960 as the book to remember introduced many, many readers to the way fiction could give moral clarity to the sullied life of social experience, especially race relations. *To Kill a Mockingbird* is the white liberal novel par excellence, demonstrating how a sensitive young person learns about a complex world, where injustice and prejudice seem prescribed, and who comes to a larger understanding of the urgent challenge to be tolerant. As distinguished as its service has been in the battle for civil rights, the novel was not an immediate critical success. It sold well, both as a Literary Guild selection and through word of mouth, yet critics did not take it all that seriously. Sometimes it was praised as a "most persuasive plea for racial justice" and for its characterization of Atticus Finch, a vivid portrait of a Southern white liberal, but just as often it was seen as an incomplete achievement, "delightfully deceptive" to be sure, but inadequately bringing together two dominant themes of contemporary Southern fiction: "the recollection of childhood among village eccentrics and the spirit-corroding shame of the civilized white Southerner in the treatment of the Negro."[63]

Nothing in the reviews indicates that the book was going to be long cherished, though the *New York Times* reviewer presciently suggested that it would make a good movie; none of the reviewers were particularly illustrious or the reviews especially luminous. Most praise was reserved for it being a successful first novel, a ponderous irony given that it would be Lee's only one. If one or two reviews commended its timeliness, no reviewer foresaw what a contribution it would make to whites' participation in the civil rights movement. It was generally seen to be among the better efforts of a kind of fiction we have completely forgotten about today: the novels by white liberals about unjust racial politics, largely in the South. Actually, several novels appeared during these years that recommend themselves to our attention and were part of the intellectual and literary milieu reviewers so comfortably cited in responding to Harper Lee. Thomas Sterling's *Strangers and*

Afraid (1952) is told through the twin narratives of a black convict who escapes from the South and a well-known white activist for social change. Esteemed novelist Herbert Gold's *Prospect before Us* (1954) relates the consequences when a well-intentioned white businessman goes along with the African American who, trying to put teeth into an antidiscrimination ordinance, asks for a room in the man's hotel. Grace Breckling's *Walk in Beauty* (1955) dramatizes a story from the 1920s at a woman's college in the North, where two half sisters from the South cause a tragedy when it is revealed that the older one is part black. Douglas Kiker (whom some remember as a TV news reporter) wrote *The Southerners* (1957), about a navy man who returns to the South to find himself in the middle of the first school desegregation case there. L. H. Rogers's *Birthright*, also of 1957, chronicles the experiences of a schoolteacher and her defiant stand against segregation as well.

Lee Bergman's *None So Blind* (1957) is the tale of another schoolteacher whose conscience forces him to testify against the same racist his lawyer-father is defending against a heinous charge of race prejudice, in something of a precursor to Lee's famous novel. Francis Gwaltney's *Numbers of Our Days*, inspired perhaps by the recent unrest caused by the Little Rock school desegregation; Ruth Chatterton's story of desegregation, *Southern Wild*; Elizabeth de Vegh's "distinguished and beautiful novel" (about the intersection of the separate lives of blacks and whites in New Jersey), *Knot of Roots*;[64] Brainard Cheney's *This Is Adam*, a historical novel about greed and the relations between the races at the turn of the century; W. L. Coleman's study of miscegenation, *Southern Lady*; and Robert Molloy's anatomy of a Southern murder, *Afternoon in March*, were all respected books from 1958 variously devoted to the cause of desegregation, interracial relations, and civil rights. In 1959, several more were published, including *The Intruder*, Charles Beaumont's novel of Ku Klux Klan resistance to integration; playwright Garson Kanin's highly praised historical jazz novel, *Blow Up a Storm*; another Molloy novel, *Reunion*; C. B. Jones's desegregation novel, *The White Band*, also about a racist citizens' council; and Harvard freshman Philip Stone's callow novel of Southern politics, *No Place To Run*. The year 1960 also saw Rachel Maddux's memoir, in the form of a novel, of her friendship with an African American family in the segregated South, *Abel's Daughter*, and 1961 offered another half-dozen titles.

Beyond enumerating all these is the obvious, though often forgotten, point that white writers often did write about blacks, and while most of the reviews of these novels were fixed on the question of whether they recorded memorable characters or provided insights unavailable from the growing list of nonfiction books, several novels did manage to win some recognition for the cultural errand they performed. True enough, some pandered to stereotypes of Southern racists, and several of the blacks that the novelists portrayed faintly resemble Uncle Tom himself, yet there is still enough variety and complexity in the range of these books to warrant their rereading. Like the books on political ethics in the last few years of the decade, the antisegregation novels of the era close the '50s struggle to maintain mainstream fiction as a source of social critique, one that remains crucial to any true literary history of the period.

NOVEL WRITING FOR THE SIXTIES

The turn from the public sphere that we have observed as an increasing tendency characterizing the 1950s was vitiated by the concomitant embrace of autobiographical fiction marking the era. So warned William E. Barrett in an article in the trade journal, *The Writer* (July 1960).[65] Not to be confused with the longtime coeditor of the *Partisan Review*, this William Barrett had published several novels, perhaps the best known of which was *Lilies of the Field* (1962). Seldom regarded as a subtle thinker—his plots usually turn on crises of faith in engaging settings, skillfully told with narrative drive—Barrett describes the challenges facing the aspiring novelist and finds that the worst obstacle to good writing is the predilection for the personal found in so many new novels, a tendency novices ought to avoid: "The autobiographical novel represents the path of least resistance, the simplest way to write, demanding little experience of the author, only a rudimentary knowledge of drama, and little skill. It is not immediately apparent to the young writer that the autobiographical formula is a creative dead-end street which will take him into a writing career, but with a fatal limitation blocking his progress and development." For Barrett, the current era was the first to acclaim autobiographical fiction as a standard to be imitated, and he sees World War II as the dividing line in the history of the critical taste for fiction since so many postwar novels turn on personal experience. Moreover, "the post-war student . . . was encouraged to write autobiographically. . . . He did not learn that the true creative artist looks outward rather than inward for his material, that he seeks an understanding of other lives and draws upon his own emotional experience only for the purpose of reaching that understanding."[66]

Perhaps the worst effect of the primacy of the autobiographical in fiction was that the reliance on the personal report lent itself to a denial about the possibility of meaning, that is, "since the authors lacked the power of interpretation, they denied that human experience has meaning," an untenable position for the true realist.[67] Barrett's solution seems somewhat limited: young writers should turn to writing biographies, since then the novice would learn, with the life of an interesting person spread before him, how to select important details, which would impart a "sense of meaning" that helps the author to develop incidents. Thus "he will reach outside of himself to discover other people about whom to write and in the structure of biography, he will find the secret of the novel." Otherwise, Barrett worries, novelists of the '60s, like so many of the '50s, will be washed out with the tide of history.

As at the beginning of every decade, critics are often asked to judge the current state of the novel or make predictions about the fiction that the next ten years will bring. Along such lines, the editor of the Saturday Review, Norman Cousins asks, "What's Wrong with the American Novel?" Nothing but that it is "full of people not worth knowing"—rather a sad commentary when juxtaposed against Barrett's complaint about the autobiographical impulse. Cousins continues: "The surprising thing is to find how adroit and readable these novels can be without ever bringing a human creature to life."[68] So even as these novelists are drawing too incessantly on their own lives, unknowing of the way true interest evolves in a person's history, their characterizations can seem meager and dull.

By the end of the year, however, it is possible to see '60s production in a more favorable light. If the first books are supposed to be the most autobiographical of all, there are several to go along with To Kill a Mockingbird that are worth remembering: John Knowles's schoolboy classic, A Separate Peace; James Leo Herlihy's story of a disintegrated family resisting the easy bourgeois pieties of repair, All Fall Down; Peter Beagles's graveyard fable about the likeness of the living and nonliving, A Fine and Private Place; and Philip McFarland's A House Full of Women, which recounts a harrowing time in a boy's life where everything that seems possible to go wrong does, a novel, the reviewers agree, that avoids melodrama but that fails to achieve tragedy. Seymour Epstein's scenes from a young marriage breaking apart,

Pillar of Salt, was also much esteemed, as was Barbara Probst Solomon's debut novel, the history of a romance across ethnic and class lines, *The Beat of Life*.

Beyond first novels, there appeared several novels by relatively new practitioners that seemed great developments in their careers or, as in the case of William Styron's *Set This House on Fire*, may have needed to be derogated to compensate for the easy approbation awarded to its predecessor, *Lie Down in Darkness*. On the positive side of the ledger were John Updike's *Rabbit, Run*, marking substantial growth over *Poorhouse Fair*; Flannery O'Connor's *The Violent Bear It Away*; and new books by less youthful writers like Wright Morris, whose *Ceremony in Lone Tree* seemed at least as good as anything he had yet written and probably better, and Herbert Gold, a key figure of the era who has never seemed to get his due and whose *Therefore Be Bold* was generally considered a little marvel of capturing adolescent love. No less autobiographical, Vance Bourjaily's *Confessions of a Spent Youth* might have been a case in point for Barrett, since critics disagreed on how successfully the novelist had worked through the material of his sexual pursuits against the backdrop of the war years.

The year 1960 also saw several accomplished novels that had little to do with autobiography: Harvey Swados's *False Coin*, which examines the corruptions and hypocrisies that power brings to an artist, even as it also reveals virtues, and Elizabeth Spencer's *The Light in the Piazza*, a novella nearly universally admired for its psychological tension and power. Also much praised was Gerald Brace's *Winter Solstice*, a portrait of middle-class New England life—its disappointments and muted rewards. *On a Lonesome Porch* was Ovid Williams Pierce's novel of Reconstruction, where two women enjoy a friendship on a North Carolina hillside, a situation vaguely similar to Charles Frazier's *Cold Mountain* (1997). Another Southern novel, *Walk Egypt*, Vinnie Williams's study of a young woman's discovery of religion in the north Georgia hills, bore a comparison to Elizabeth Roberts's Kentucky fiction. Guy Owen also explores the relation between the South and religious fanaticism, but includes the complications of race and violence in *Season of Fear*. Less historical was William Hoffman's timely, well-wrought study of race and contemporary Southern mores, *A Place for My Head*.

Among the other admired novels of the year, John Hersey's satiric fable about American education, *The Child Buyer*, was much discussed during the autumn. Unlike anything he had written previously, the book might be compared to works like Jonathan Swift's "A Modest Proposal" or, in the American tradition, Mark Twain's *Mysterious Stranger* as an indictment of existing institutions and government interference through the veil of satire. Critics were surprised to find that James Purdy's *The Nephew* succeeded so well, since his earlier productions had seemed too mystifying. They also lauded Paul Horgan's historical novel of the Southwest and the Apache wars, *A Distant Trumpet*, while Jacquin Sanders pursued his own genre, the historical comedy, in a novel about the Puritans' "deflowering of New England," *Look to Your Geese*. Novels of contemporary history include Jo Sinclair's chronicle about an elderly Hungarian woman, a refugee from the 1956 revolution, *Anna Teller*, and Julius Horowitz's esteemed study of urban poverty, *The Inhabitants*, a book perhaps as prescient and as moving as Michael Harrington's *The Other America* (1962). Also garnering accolades was Mildred Walker's *Body of a Young Man*.

And of course there were others.

One lesson to remember as we close the decade that many considered the end of the ascendancy of middle-class realism is that, despite the sense that the vitality of this novel form was steadily dwindling, a remarkable number of valuable novels that most literary historians have never heard of were still published and commended. Readers continue to enjoy them or be disturbed by them, to have their sense of social reality inflected by them. If they have entered the dustbin of literary history, it is only because historians themselves have no use for them, not because they have no use-value, for we may not yet have asked of them the questions through which these novels' several kinds of appeal might be made known and remembered.

CONCLUSION

For some readers, the history of the American novel will always be one of its formal changes—from Cooper, through Hawthorne and Melville, to James and onward through Hemingway and Faulkner, on through the early post-modernists, culminating in Pynchon or DeLillo or Morrison. At various points, for these readers, lesser lights will have something to add. The pleasures of reading American novels this way are patent, but the enthusiasm for studying the novel's formal changes—up to and out of realism—does not admit of the kind of pleasure that middle-class fiction affords, the complex appeal, not of form, but of modern social history. Perhaps readers who so choose should be left alone with these linguistic artifacts, many of which are so fully realized that they will stand, deservedly, for a very long time in the annals of fiction. Other readers care less for form and want to read American novels in terms of their potential for change—and these readers will examine fiction for its power to imagine a world beyond the one in which the middle class resides and maybe presides. The struggle of the comfortable classes to remain comfortable, despite the ruptures and vagaries of history, admits of little heroism to such readers, though, as I hope to have shown, that struggle in its fullest proportions seems even epic, insofar as it commands the perspective of America envisioning what the country has become.

My study of middle-class fiction, in part, has asked that scholars and readers turn to novels they may never have heard about in order to gain a clearer understanding of the unfolding shape of American literary and cultural history. Readers need not give up their preference for Hurston or Hemingway, but they might seek a richer understanding of the historical and social milieu in which these writers wrote, a context that is significantly distorted if the centrifugal powers of middle-class conditions of production, circulation, and reception are not acknowledged or understood. Once readers do that, they will see that middle-class fiction accommodates a whole range of novels, at least as much as any other category can define. Middle-class novels, I have tried to show, help us to organize ways of seeing the variegations and patterns of American cultural history; their nearly total absence from scholarly discussion expresses nothing less than their suppressed centrality to the nation's literary heritage.

What should we do with this knowledge? Students need not go about reading these books closely, validating some for further study and eliminating others, in order to establish a countercanon. My point is not to engineer some shift in the object of academic inquiry—away from the traditional works of modernist or postmodernist formal invention and toward realist convention, or away from proletarian or multicultural writing and toward the bourgeoisie. Instead, my hope is that these books will emerge in all their complementarity and supplementarity, wherein lies what may be their full power of distinction and contradistinction. Studying middle-class fiction should help us to see more clearly the accomplishments of the novelists we do cherish, though it will be gratifying if other scholars find in the many titles I have named works that they can use for the production of deeper cultural knowledge and historical awareness. These books, I have argued throughout, are part of our literary environment and cultural milieu; a history that ignores their place is partial and necessarily distorted. In that sense, it is bad history and needs to be corrected.

But how would a new history take shape? I would discourage a student from writing a dissertation, for example, on three or four of these writers, or seven or eight, for several reasons: primarily, these individual writers are not important *because* they have been forgotten; they are important because they have been forgotten as a *group*, one that wrote not just for an implied class of readers, but the general audience for serious fiction. Yet the books that they have left behind need not be relegated so peremptorily as they have been. Instead, I see everything to be gained from bringing these works to bear on some analysis of a single text by any preferred writer, so that these forgotten novels may qualify and contextualize better-known works. For instance, I have suggested at various places that novels of immigration remain popular through much of the period of this study, so that scholars of

American literary ethnicity simply cannot afford to limit their awareness of the history of their subject to a handful of novels. If future scholars of modern American writing are persuaded that Faulkner is also interesting for the light T. S. Stribling or Hamilton Basso throws, all the better for Faulkner. If we are interested in the relation between the Caribbean islands and North America, it would be a shame to lose sight of the several dozen novels valuable American writers have devoted to the subject, just as it would be lamentable to lose sight of the American writing staged throughout the world, especially as we move toward a critical value for globalization. Or we might read American novelists who have written, sometimes with more heat than light, but often with light, about the American Southwest. Some popular romancers were imperial apologists, but bourgeois realists by and large were not, though it is instructive to see how they missed what present-day critics might wish that they had seized about a part of the United States that more famous novelists have ignored or treated sketchily. I have already mentioned, in the 1950s, the surprising range of white writing about race, and while it is traceable throughout the forty years of my survey, white writers also tried—sometimes out of false consciousness, sometimes out of liberal sympathies (however problematic)—to make sense of a more diverse country than our current revisionism can appreciate. Finally, reading middle-class fiction takes seriously the incontrovertible place women writers have occupied in this century. Throughout this book I have been concerned to cite them and their achievements, just as I have been glad to note the contributions of so many women reviewers and critics, long forgotten but once much recognized and respected.

Such attention would alleviate our ignorance of the more compendious library of American literature than the one in which we currently conduct our research. Once upon a critical time, it was imperative to argue how a writer was unlike his or her peers. To that end, the connections between writers might have to be minimized or erased so that the author's true originality, true modernity, could receive its due. Such a vision fit nicely with reigning preoccupations of the text's uniqueness. Even though that sort of genius-mongering has passed into critical eclipse, we still preserve a notion of an author whose authority derives from some measure of specialness— whether it is political affiliation, racial or ethnic identity, gender or sexuality, though, as a matter of course, those have inspired a complex understanding of how language works to define the subtleties of this special character. What I have tried to do here is to suggest how a collective sense of authorship—this time of the middle class—presents another kind of fiction for which we might still develop an even more engaged rhetoric than the vision of cultural work I have evoked throughout.

I would argue that essays and books on well-known writers should also attend to how much they had in common with the work of their compeers, sometimes their friends, their colleagues, and even their rivals. Very likely, we will still prefer our long-standing favorites or the new enthusiasms that replace them, but we would also know more fluently than we do the figures with whom better-studied writers competed or the literary milieu of which these writers were conscious and against whom they identified. Were we to do so, we might know more about, say, American attitudes toward prostitution or the Philippines than we know only from critiques of one or two very pointed texts. Surely we would know more about race relations or the dynamics among minority cultures and between those cultures and the mainstream as well. We would also know more about disability novels. We would know more about historical values in America as well as scientific ones. We would know more about regions, more about geography. We would know more about everything, rather than settle for the bracing, often brilliant critiques to which the great American novelists have treated us. We would understand more about the possibilities of a national culture. We may still want to criticize that culture, but we would know more about why we understand America as we do.

Why won't we read these books? I am as aware as anyone that a stroll through the fiction section of any college or university library is bound to reveal dozens, even hundreds of titles that register absolutely nothing for even an extremely well-trained specialist. So much fiction has been written in America over the last hundred years that it seems Sisyphean to want to account for it; even the most dedicated scholar of contemporary fiction, say the fiction of the last fifteen or twenty years, cannot keep pace with a year's production. At the same time, it is no empty appeal to identity politics to say that preserving this record and knowing it much more intimately is a job that falls to those readers and students who identify modern American literature as their area of expertise. In this sense, I have meant to hold us to account by asking whether we are well read if we know so little of the very literature out of which our scholarly favorites have emerged, since I cannot make the point strongly enough that these are the novels the canon has been defined against, the literature of the not great, but of the pretty good.

Because these are not great works, we may have a difficult time offering them to undergraduates, who can often readily see their limits as works of art compared to other novels that they are required to read. From my experience, the students' discussion is usually the livelier for that recognition; without the aura of great literature or important writing to inhibit their talk, the students are quicker to debate the novels' interest, the portrayal of lives they see as familiar enough and remote enough to be eminently worthy of comment. I am not suggesting that we teach *Man in the Gray Flannel Suit* instead of *Invisible Man*, but their juxtaposition might be especially productive: surely it would cast a stronger light on the Invisible Man's experience of alienation, given the "invisible" black characters in Wilson's novel. Unfortunately, only a few titles are even in paperback, though it might not cost too much to reprint them, since many have not had their copyright renewed. Someone determined to teach one of these books could certainly do so now via desktop publishing, so even if reprint houses and university presses could not be persuaded to bring them forward, teachers could still make them available to students very affordably. Because some of the more familiar novels have multiple listings as used books over the Internet, students can also find their own inexpensive hardback copies, if they choose.

Middle-class fiction is precisely the kind of writing that figured in debates about the death of literature, especially the exhaustion of the novel as an art form and as a cultural vehicle. The question, however, was less about the illegibility of modern art and more about the paucity of realist masterpieces. The idea was that now that writers had fully experimented with concepts such as plot and character, demystifying them and exposing their essential artifice, realism would not be able to generate any new purchase on the demand to represent the life of social experience, experience that had become too fluid to be readily comprehended in the phenomenological validity of the here and now. Yet the predictions heard throughout the fifties and sixties about the end of the novel have not really come true, though some may wish to argue that the fiction of the sixties and seventies made, on the whole, a sorry lot of evidence for the defense. Works of promise and achievement there always were, but the perception that the realist novel had lost sway seems undeniable. Why this should be has less to do with the fiction actually being written than the culture's changing needs. One may wish to blame the realistic novel's seeming decline on the emergence of made-for-TV movies (in a world before cable TV) or Hollywood in general, or such new aesthetic interests as those developed by Eastern European as well as Central and South American fiction writers, but it seems to me more reasonable to say that despite the appearance of several valuable realist works, the twenty-year span between 1960 and 1980, like the one opening the century, is really an era waiting for a redefinition of realism, in that these decades are testing new realist incarnations while nervously holding on to existing ones. Only with the emergence of magical realism and minimalism at the end of the '70s and the concomitant reaction of neorealism can we see a renewed purchase on the middle-class novel.

At the beginning of this study, I expressed the hope that its lessons were also applicable to the study of the novels of the last twenty-five years. I mean that, first of all, we might widen our canon of the contemporary writers to include those for whom the bourgeois experience is crucial to their vision. It is surprising to me that, however consensual the choices of the most important writers of the last twenty-five years, they are rather seldom taught as contemporary fiction, which often is content to describe contemporary writing for its interest in formalist innovation or multiculturalism, which, to my mind, is like reading any historical period for one theme—productive, illuminating, but scarcely representative of an era's accomplishments or characteristic concerns. The official version of contemporary fiction, as the academy describes it, is a very incomplete context for understanding the presence of middle-class lives, when, in fact, middle-class lives constitute so much of the emotional drama of contemporary fiction.

A look at the fiction of 2006 will suggest how vital the tradition still is. The novels recommended for the National Book Award (NBA) included Ken Kalfus's *A Disorder Peculiar to the Country*, a study of a marriage breaking up in the aftermath of 9/11; and Dana Spiotta's *Eat the Document*, the tale of '70s fugitive radicals who come to terms with their crime decades later. Even Jess Walter's satiric parable of terrorism, *The Zero*, resonates within the rubric. Among the *New York Times Book Review*'s "notable" novels are titles by Updike (*The Terrorist*) and Roth (*Everyman*) that also reveal such continuities, just as there are works by past masters like Richard Ford (*The Lay of the Land*) and Anne Tyler (*Digging to America*). Allegra Goodman offered *Intuition*, about cancer research and its consequences, while another established writer, Alice McDermott, published the most fully domestic novel of the year, *After This*. Younger novelists kept the form alive in such works as Nell Freudenberger's *The Dissident*, which portrays the effects—comic and serious—of a visiting Chinese performance artist and a wealthy Beverly Hills dysfunctional family, and Heidi Julavits's *The Uses of Enchantment*, which connects the complications of a mother-daughter relationship with larger questions of memory, fantasy, mental health, and history. In an even more ambitious way, Richard Powers's *The Echo Maker*—the winner of the NBA for fiction and a Pulitzer Prize finalist—configures similar issues put to the broader concerns of identity, neuroscience, and ecology.

Over the last thirty years or so, some of the most important contemporary writers have been quite critical of the concerns of middle-class realism, like Russell Banks, whose *Continental Drift* (1985) does the middle class the honor of taking its vision seriously enough to dissect its wounds from a hemispheric, even cosmological perspective. Or a novel like Anne Tyler's *Amateur Marriage* (2004), whose sympathetic if relentless critique of middle-class marriage ends up damning the second half of the American Century. Similarly, we might read Jane Smiley, Jane Hamilton, Richard Russo, and dozens of other writers for whom the middle-class experience is the central reality they can imagine. Consider, for example, the completion of Updike's *Rabbit* trilogy—before he decided to write the story as a tetralogy. *Rabbit, Run* signals not the beginning of a new aesthetic but the culmination of an older one, whereas *Rabbit Is Rich* (1981) harbingers the intense investigation of the interior life under the aspect of the social realism that would mark so much of the following twenty years of American fiction, an era bisected, if you will, by *Rabbit at Rest* (1990), which is closer in achievement to its predecessor than *Rabbit Is Rich* was to *Rabbit Redux* (1971), the weakest *Rabbit* book, most critics agree, since its realist representation of middle-class life gives way to its fascination with the novel's antibourgeois skepticism. That uneasiness is expressed in the novel's last line when Rabbit, temporarily at rest, lies with his estranged wife in a local motel room, wondering whether this wan facsimile of middle-class virtue suffices: "OK?" Rabbit asks. Is this attenuated version of domestic stability enough to meet the social and political challenges the novel has voiced? As a novel marking the two realisms Updike undertakes, the lyric documentary style of the first and the more closely observed social analysis of the third (and fourth) installments, *Rabbit Redux* fails out of the insubstantiality of its social vision and the commensurate thinness of the changes Harry Angstrom purportedly undergoes.

I do not mean to make too much of the grid that Updike's tetralogy inadvertently creates. The more important point is that by the '80s, perhaps out of a reaction to the failed aesthetic gambles of the '60s and '70s, novelists again turned to a deeper, less broad but more intense realism to accommodate a cultural vision increasingly mediated and dispersed. There are so many books to discuss that literary historians, including those who would address a more general audience than a scholarly one, need to take up the challenge of studying them, of using their skills as readers and teachers to help the literature of our time count more. Otherwise, that literature may also be lost before we know it.

POSTSCRIPT

In writing a book devoted to the middle-class realism of mid-twentieth-century American fiction, three concerns of method and scope persisted. Since I was describing a subject of previously unregistered proportions, I first had to determine what kind of literary history I was writing: my research entailed a host of social, cultural, often political, sometimes material, as well as aesthetic ways of assessing the contours of this fiction, so rather than a thematic study, I needed to construct a format capacious enough to incorporate the array of interests that these novels aroused. And, second, since I was addressing the absence of a historiographical interest in this literature, my study would also have to be about critical values as well as their shaping. Perhaps most vexing of all, I had to consult the needs of potential students of the subject, whom I considered to be readers who care about American fiction and who may know its critical history well but who would also like to learn more about it. That audience included scholars and students as well as other readers who might want a deeper background.

To write a literary history that met these difficulties and that comprehended its salient questions, I developed multiple strands of inquiry to be followed throughout and that were often interwoven. These included, first, a history of the novels that generally appealed to what I saw as recreational readers (readers who understood these novels as the opportunity to re-create themselves), readers who were also what I call citizen-readers, that is, readers for whom these novels offered opportunities of civic engagement: educated, mainly middle-class readers who embraced the realist literature that critics identified as "better" than formula fiction. So I was freed from writing only about popular books and came to see that classifying books as either popular or elite was a way of *not* treating the vast store of American novels that were neither works of genius nor best sellers. The readers of these novels may or may not have been interested in popular literature, but pursuing the popular was not necessarily the defining aspect of their appetite for fiction. Mostly, these readers were looking, as the reviewers understood, for something edifying as well as entertaining, and they turned—not to genre fiction that mythologized the conquering of evil or the purging of social ills through the allegory of an astute detective or the integrity of a cowboy loner—but to realism for guidance on how to think about modern life. At the same time, these readers proved less interested in masterpieces, including those we now associate with the modernist movement, than they were in what might be described as a consistently high level of modest achievement, and for that they turned to magazine critics and newspaper reviewers for their cue about what was worth reading and why. I found, amid yearly roundups in places like the *New York Times Sunday Book Review*, an unending supply of well-regarded titles I had never heard of. I was then led to encounter hundreds of books—reading a season's overviews of new novels and features on authors, predictions of the most promising of the new novelists, roundups of books already considered wrongly forgotten. Sometimes I would happen upon reviews of books because they were placed next to one I was searching for, or perhaps another book was included in an omnibus review of the one I was tracking down. The *Book Review Digest* was absolutely indispensable—it saved me time, but, more important, it sparked a myriad of new inquiries. All in all, I read about two hundred novels by nearly as many authors.

Ultimately, I discerned an archive coming before my eyes. So little had been written about this plethora of novels that, in order to develop a way of talking about them, I had next—my second line of inquiry—to turn to those reviews, the dailies as well as those in the opinion magazines, journals, belles lettres quarterlies, and newspaper supplements, to help me appreciate the range of the corpus as well as the reputation of the novels. It was intriguing to learn that reviewers hailed some of these novels with astounding encomiums: "the greatest novel of its time," "the best American book since *Huckleberry Finn*," "the novel by which the decade would be remembered," "the best book of the year." And I found that despite my suspicion of the reviewers' exuberance and exaggeration, the books were often pretty good. Although I sometimes would find a critical article or two about a writer once well known but now only familiar to a lone researcher, the field, measured against the wealth of commentary on Hemingway, Faulkner, and Fitzgerald—or Wright, Hurston and Bellow, or even Dos Passos, Wolfe, and Steinbeck—seemed virtually blank. Eventually I did find critical books, surveys of one decade or another, or long-out-of-date thematic studies that gave appreciative nuance to a handful of the novels, but I also kept finding more novels by authors I was never asked to know about in graduate school, writers whose unfamiliar names sent me scurrying to long-out-of-print reference books. The more of these novels I read, the more I chided my ignorance, the less I thought I knew about the history of the twentieth-century U.S. novel that I had been studying for some thirty years.

These reviews were often at odds, not just in the sense that books sometimes met with mixed reviews, but also in how they reflected ongoing cultural arguments. Magazine reviews especially revealed that more was at stake in the evaluation of books than the maintaining of consumer confidence in which the daily newspapers were often invested. At stake was the way contemporary fiction could be understood as participating in a larger discourse—especially the role of the middle class as the arbiter of social value, a conversation among critics that was deeply concerned with the health of the culture. That discovery led to my third strand, the contemporaneous discussion of the character of current fiction and its relevance for the polis. Those debates were found, as they still are to some extent, in the journals of arts and ideas, as well as in the magazines of a political tendency and those that saw themselves primarily interested in mediating the cultural interests of their middle-class readers. Here I discovered the critiques by those readers generally unaffiliated with academe, the kind of men and women of letters of whom Edmund Wilson is still the best known. Not all of them were truly intellectuals: some were tastemakers, like Henry Seidel Canby, while others were litterateurs, people who made their living by their pen, voiced opinions—on a variety of subjects (literary and otherwise)—and even wrote novels themselves. Of these, a second roll call emerged: critics who were reliably incisive and whose judgments still seem resonant, including a number of forgotten women, critics like Mary Colum or Louise Field or Margaret Marshall, among others.

These critical discussions turned on general concerns about the culture, so that chronic arguments about "what's happening to our fiction?" coincided with "what is to be done?" articles that the largely middle-class readers of the novels also found in their periodical reading. Often the novels themselves were on momentous themes, topics under more or less daily scrutiny, such as race relations. Occasionally, novels led the discussion in the way that *The Jungle* (1906) changed government regulation of the meatpacking industry; few novels could really be quite so decisive, but that is not to say that their general status was degraded or trivial. Several helped to generate a new social understanding, like Laura Z. Hobson's *Gentleman's Agreement* (1947). Thus, the fourth strand of my study was to follow how these novels, as a group, resonated with key nonfiction works of their era. For that, I became less interested in generating a reading of an exemplary text than in demonstrating the way a spate of novels variously specify or signify on a discussion of a social issue in which they take part. To that end, my research necessitated connecting the literary and cultural issues to such defining issues as the health of the middle class, the possibilities of youth, the burden of history, the status and well-being of the family, prejudice, returning war veterans, and nuclear war, among many others.

Out of these several threads a story emerged about the contribution of the middle-class novel and its place in the shaping of public consciousness, the part that the literary works play in helping to make the nation—an issue normally considered in studies of nineteenth-century American literature yet seemingly less pressing in twentieth-century studies, where scholars often rely on received historical opinion and even personal memory. Yet whenever I would describe my project, I frequently faced the question of what aesthetic value these novels have—a suspicion that feminists and African Americanists had continually to encounter twenty years ago—as if to say that, lacking any ideological interest as a result of their middle-class identification, the only redeeming quality would have to be formal composition, a residual interest in aesthetic achievements that, for scholarly purposes, had otherwise fallen into disuse. Or my academic interlocutors would ask what makes these books worth reading, at a time when so many hands are engaged in recovering works forgotten or marginalized because of their politics or because of the race, gender, sexuality, or ethnicity of their authors. What was the urgency—or need—of recovering (of all things) the literary taste of the middle class?

There seems to me no good reason to abjure reading these books simply because no one has heretofore read them as formulating a tradition. For example, many scholars interested in the work of recovery will be startled to learn, as I was, how deeply concerned these novels are in issues of American-ization, for which most of the authors showed an abidingly liberal and sometimes boldly egalitarian commitment. Indeed, there is scarcely a social problem that students of marginalized American fiction research that is not sympathetically addressed or given immediacy in the broad range of middle-class fiction. Not only will such scholars enhance the specificity of their understanding of the mainstream, but they will also see how broadly and agitatedly the mainstream flowed. Moreover, professors and students will find that there is often a correspondence, even a predictive quality, between the social concerns of middle-class fiction throughout the century and in our own time, since middle-class values tend to remain constant even if their antagonists undergo confusing new permutations. Teachers may readily ful-fill their desire to choose representative works in making up a syllabus of them, though most will only want an occasional title to complement canoni-cal works and can easily use these books to enact debates about value, about class identification, or a host of other classroom exercises. Nor do I suggest anywhere that these novels should substitute for the fiction of proletarian protest, though in their treatment of middle-class life, they ought to extend the questions we raise in teaching literature's class attributes.

In order to organize such a wide range of materials, I made two choices. The first was to write a history rather than a critical monograph that might have highlighted eight or ten exemplary writers. Such a monograph was tantalizingly beyond me because, in being merely representative, it would disable my telling what I thought of as the whole story of this fiction and its place in the nation's literary and cultural history. Nor did I entertain any great desire to canonize these works by insisting on one and not another; on the contrary, my desire was to prompt interest in the whole range of these books, so readers can recover part of the wealth of our national literature, and scholars of many persuasions can find new titles to incorporate into their research. I also realized that the form of analysis in which I had been trained—close reading and interpretation—would not serve me especially well, since what was the point of reading in detail novels that I knew so few people had also read or, I worried, would read? (I cannot tell you the number of times I took out a novel from a university library only to learn that the book had no bar code and not been checked out in thirty, fifty, or seventy years.) Thus I had to surrender as the object of literary inquiry a knotty text needing a consummately trained interpreter to unravel its matrix of critical, historical, and cognate issues and public discourse through which a novel's meanings are associated. I learned to study instead the combination of reviews a book received or the shadings of the arguments among critics. But I did read closely the makeup of a best-seller list or the roll of prizewinners and competing nominees. As a result, my book also aims, in part, to recount American literary history from the perspective of its unfolding by observing how several books devoted to a kindred topic or the thematic contours of a year's array of fiction—and the welter of responses—locate significant historical changes.

In each decade, I take up particular books when their study is especially instructive for an era's concerns, and these are generally novels that met with both critical and commercial success. Without the constricting organizational logic of a series of paradigmatic readings, however, I can trace the development of a tradition by following variations and innovations played out over the forty-year period that observed the flourishing of American culture in the mid-twentieth century, especially the rise of the middle class. That commitment led me to see how subordinate to this history are the ones with which students are more familiar: the emergence of U.S. modernist fiction as part of an international literature and its ultimate decline—which has been our conventional way of reading these decades—or the radical novels that were once shunted aside as a result of this preoccupation. Many feminist novels were pointedly overlooked, to be sure, but more women writers, I learned, have been ignored because their vision was bourgeois. To that purpose, I examine the domestic literary scene and its arguments about taste, the mainstream tradition of the critical realism that William Dean Howells initiated.

My project has been to examine the books to which middle-class readers turned in order to gain counsel or succor and to comprehend those concerns through the lens of the middle class's voluminous reading—fiction, nonfiction, essays, history, and more. Others have turned to the varieties of formula writing as well as radio, TV, and film, or other forms of broadly cultural expression, but no one, as far as I know, has concentrated on the ethos of middle-class fiction over these four decades. Because the films especially are often better known (and frequently often drawn from the fiction I read), it sometimes seems reasonable to expect that I will engage in a study of Hollywood's treatment of this fiction, but that is not the story I have to relate. Throughout, I mean to show that the features and themes of this fiction evince and corroborate these novels' class interests. For the most part, the plots revolve around a crisis or two inspired by modern circumstances for which the characters' upbringing has left them largely unprepared, so the characters' true essence will win out, even in a newly diminished state. The novels mostly believe in progress, not in its most expansive prospect but as a quiet faith. Sometimes their social values are actively progressive—and once in awhile a writer moves in and out of partisan identification—but generally the vision is liberal, in the old sense of being tolerant, decent, generous, and humane. The novels try to eschew sentimental conclusions, although those efforts will not always succeed for today's readers, who are sometimes apt to mistake the characters' realistic resolve for brimmingly romantic or sentimental optimism.

The novels' sense of crisis may address the "way we live now," just as they may also express the trials of the recent past. These challenges posing consequences for contemporaneous readers to inherit may have been convulsed during the previous generation, or they may have happened long ago and thus comprise the very foundation of modern life, but their forebears' clarifying example needs to be recalled to guide the middle class through its current confusions. In fact, the narrative logic of a great many novels is that of the genealogy: we watch how the achievements or corruptions of an earlier generation are perpetuated or complicated by its successors, only to be lived out and settled by the following one. "What happens next?" as Thomas Mann begins his chronicle of the fortunes of the German bourgeoisie, *Buddenbrooks* (1901), the informing question of realist fiction and the animating one for the middle class. Is our security stable? Will the children do their part to ensure the success of future generations, or will they prove degenerate? Is there coherence to the life we have made, or is it simply a parade of anxieties to be negotiated?

Many novels strive to be up-to-the-minute bulletins from the front, the trench warfare of how the middle class is supposed to sustain its self-image and well-being amid new sources of turmoil. In this respect, many works of middle-class realism emerge as "problem" novels—especially flourishing in the '40s—books devoted to exposing a newly comprehended social ill (racism, mental illness, alcoholism, etc.), often with the intent of exposing some new threat for a middle-class public curious to learn more about it, or presumably curious enough that publishers would print novels devoted to the subject. Committed as these novels are to scrutinizing manners and morals, they also make much of the puzzlements of courtship and marriage, just as they do the turbulence of growth and education. For the middle class, however, these issues do not need to be solved conventionally; instead, the charge of these writers seems very often to be to expand the convention—of love, sexuality, and gender identity—in order to accommodate new challenges and thus to assimilate their threat, which may be what the middle class does best and why it is often so mistrusted. Because the novels explore and extend the confines of middle-class sensibility, it is not surprising that so many of their protagonists are in business, but that does not mean that crises are necessarily to be decided in favor of capital over labor. What we find in this fiction is that the self-conception of the middle class is decidedly more various than its critics might have it, the chance of discovering oneself to be an exception more patent, which of course some critics would see as part of the snare of middle-class sensibility.

In focusing on this mainstream literary experience, I have also tried to expand the revisionist imperative set forth by feminist, radical, African American, Chicano/a, Asian American, and Native American literary historians. Indeed, my study has been made possible by their efforts to shake loose the enshrined understanding of how American writing has been made coherent and assessed. In a small way—greatly to be acknowledged but only mildly to be insisted on—my book joins their program, as I am also writing against an elite understanding of the achievement of fiction in the United States, an overly rarefied understanding rife with a prejudice one might call "antibourgeois." As trivial as that sounds to some, its omnipresence and vitality continues, wrongly, to stultify and muddle the appreciation of U.S. fiction. Rather than urge a return to the great works or to curb the emergence of previously marginal literatures, I write to magnify the ways readers can study the history of the U.S. novel and the cultural dynamics of its production.

Committed as my study is to the mainstream culture, its motivating impulse does not lie in the movement called "whiteness studies," although that is a nexus of my concerns. Whiteness studies takes as its mission the need to understand Caucasian culture as a legitimate topic of critical inquiry. It does not do so in some reactionary way, such as trumpeting the superiority of Northern European American experience in the name of elevating whites to a privileged status in the culture, but by investigating the folkways and social practices of the dominant culture, so its peculiarities,

instabilities, and disruptions are not forgotten as readily as a majority community might wish, which is its relevance for my undertaking. So I also
endeavor to keep in view the limits of the American middle-class point of
view, not from the perspective of those who have assailed it anyway but
within its own terms, that is, when a novel's moral imagination, and, by
extension, the middle-class view of itself, is fissured or mired in bad faith.
This demand is especially challenging in confronting issues of race and the
social acceptance of otherness. Even though the writers I cover are predominantly white and Christian, their race fictions are much more diverse than I
believe has been understood. Indeed, the middle class itself offers a mixed
record on thinking about race. Some prevailing racist attributes, I am sorry
to say, marked how white writers portrayed the experience of ethnic and
racial minorities. Yet it is also true, much more so than is remembered, that
some white middle-class representations of racial and ethnic otherness are
respectful, well meaning, and even wonderfully democratic, perhaps more
impressive in this regard than the record of canonical writers. In making a
case for the cultural contribution of a middle-class sensibility, I have also
been mindful of other limits, which are at least as many as the foibles of the
elite or of the poor. The shortcomings of bourgeois points of view are legion,
and in searching for the happier, more productive elements of the middle-
class imagination, I have tried not merely to champion them. For my main
purpose has been to demonstrate the need to study these books more fully.
Interested readers can find in them a resource, while students of the subject
can learn much by historicizing their vision and expression.

NOTES

INTRODUCTION

1 See Tompkins, *Sensational Designs*. This study is surely one of the key analyses of the last twenty-five years, and its influence has been decisive insofar as so many Americanists have followed its basic wisdom of testing how novels register, codify, and negotiate cultural meanings and values, what Tompkins calls "cultural work." Other books key to my study are Janice Radway's *A Feeling for Books*, which takes up some similar subjects but which develops a very different value for reading, one closer to absorption rather than re-creation or civic activity. I have also learned from Joan Rubin's *The Making of Middlebrow Culture*, which to my mind misses the class interests of her subject. I am grateful for David Minter's *A Cultural History of the American Novel*, which in a sense provided an outline of what I then no longer needed to do in my study. Much later did I find Rita Barnard's useful, evocative essay, "Modern American Fiction," and, even later, Peter Stonely and Cindy Weinstein's *A Concise Companion to American Fiction*.

2 Along with the *Oxford Companion to Women's Writing in the United States*, I have benefited from several important recovery efforts that have been concluded during the course of writing this book, especially Deborah Lindsay Williams's *Not in Sisterhood* and, more recently, Jamie Harker's *America the Middlebrow*, which relates modern American women writers to their nineteenth-century counterparts instead of the Howellsian tradition in which, I argue, they participate.

3 On the historical question of reading, there were a plethora of periodical articles on the changing importance and function of reading in the era following World War I, some of which related the changes to the rise of college-educated readers. See, e.g., Maurice, "A New Golden Age in American Reading," and Dana, "Changes in Reading." My discussion of middle-class culture is indebted to Pierre Bourdieu's works of social analysis, esp. *Distinction: A Social Critique of the Judgement of Taste*, esp. 292–94, and *The Field of Cultural Production*, esp. 161–75, though I have tried to be mindful that few analogies to the twentieth-century shaping of the American mid-

dle class strictly apply. Rather than attempt here to answer the predictable, though perhaps impossible, question of what exactly do we mean when we say "middle class," I want to challenge the idea that the literature it produces is negligible by definition, even if its governing sensibility scarcely needs—some would say does not deserve—the nurturance that the academy affords. The antibourgeois prejudice was reinforced by the succession of methodologies and critical ideologies shaping American literary history, first, through the mastery of New Critical tenets, later through deconstruction, then through the new pluralism, and now through transnationalist vision. Actually, the lessons learned from gender and race revisionists have frequently guided me through this reconsideration of class-based values of reading. My book thus owes a substantial debt particularly to Nina Baym's *Woman's Fiction*.

4   See esp. Vanderbilt, *American Literature and the Academy*, and Shumway, *Creating American Civilization*.

5   Several recent books have made middle-class culture their object of inquiry, especially Sherry Ortner's work in social anthropology, *New Jersey Dreaming*. Also see Moskowitz, *Standard of Living*, and Bledstein and Johnston, *The Middling Sort*.

6   Canby, "Literature in Contemporary America."

7   Canby, "The Bourgeois American," *Everyday Americans*, 175–83, esp. 165.

8   Ibid. Canby continues that the key factor in these changes was the "rise to intellectual influence and cultural and social power of aliens . . . most of all Jews—[who], unlike the earlier immigrant, do not cherish as their chief wish the desire to become in every sense American." The arrival of such groups has resulted in a "new America"—"heterogeneous, brilliant, useful, but disturbing"—that has "made us sensible of . . . the new alignments inevitable for the future." American critics must count on the "cosmopolitans of brains and ability among us" and not bend to nativist clamor, as Canby describes the challenges to self-consciousness that the changing demography poses for national literature.

9   Sherman, *The Genius of America*, 226.

10   Canby, *Education by Violence*, 84–85.

11   Studies in the relation between the middle class and modernism include Catherine Turner's *Marketing Modernism*.

12   On the question of standardizing American culture, the literature is voluminous. See N. Roosevelt, "America's Cultural Deserts Begin to Blossom," 2, 17. Also see Duncan Aikman, "Not Quite Standardized Yet." Also responding to the complaint that standardization has rendered U.S. culture as arid is H. K. Norton, "An Age of Alarums."

13   Canby, "Standardization," 12 February 1927. Also see two other Canby editorials on standards, 6 October 1928 and 18 October 1930.

14   Several studies cover this 1920s version of the "culture wars"; among the best remains Ruland's *Rediscovery of American Literature*.

15   J. E. Spingarn, "The New Criticism," 304–5.

16   Canby, *Definitions*, 294–95.

17   Ibid., 296–97.

18   Ibid., 68.

19   Ibid., 69–70.

20   *Bookman*, 21 July 1921, 449; *New York Times Book Review*, 22 May 1921, 22; *Outlook*, 24 August 1921, 658; *Nation*, 3 August 1921, 125.

21   Tarkington, *Alice Adams*, 430.

22   Canby, "Twenty-Two," *Literary Review*, 21 May 1921, 3.

23   Ibid.

24   On *God of Might*, see Paterson, "A Shelf of Recent Books"; D. B. Woolsey, *New Republic*, 20 May 1925, 348; Zona Gale, *International Book Review*, 25 May 1925, 375; and Kronenberger, "A Racial Problem."

25   On *God of Might*, see J. J. Smertenko, "The Assimilated Jew," *Nation*, 29 July 1925, 146, and *Saturday Review of Literature*, 10 October 1925, 192; Yezierska and Raphaelson, *New York Herald Tribune*, 25 October 1925, 20.

26   Ferraro, *Ethnic Passages*, 53–86. Also see Ammons, *Conflicting Stories*, 67–68.

CHAPTER ONE

1   Norris, *Responsibilities of the Novelist*: see "A Plea for Romantic Fiction," 213–20, esp. 215, and "An American School of Fiction?," 193–200.

2   "Safe and Sane Genius of William Dean Howells."

3   "Mr. Howells' World," *Freeman*, 26 May 1920, 248. Cf. L. Trilling's assessment in his study of Howells, "The Roots of Modern Taste."

4   "Mr. Howells' World"; E. F. E., "Living Voice of Mr. Howells."

5   Although several essays in the last few years have confronted Howells's treatment of race—especially his novella, *An Imperative Duty*—none surpass Kenneth Warren's treatment in *Black and White Strangers*. Also see Jarrett, "Entirely *Black* Verse from Him Would Succeed."

6   L. Trilling, "On the Teaching of Modern Literature," esp. 7–8.

7   See "*SRL* Poll on Novels and Novelists."

8   For an excellent historical explanation of the shaping of this important book, consult Kermit Vanderbilt, *American Literature and the Academy*. For a more critical assessment of the historical relation between the study of American literature and the university curriculum, see David Shumway, *Creating American Civilization*.

9   Canby, *Seven Years' Harvest*. On Lewis, see esp. 133–39; on Faulkner, see 79.

10   Hicks, "The Twenties in American Literature."

11   Blankenship, *American Literature*, 692.

12   Lewisohn, *Expression in America*, 533–34.

13   See "State of American Writing, 1999."

14   E. Wilson, "All-Star Literary Vaudeville," *Shores of Light*, 229–36, esp. 230–35. The article first appeared anonymously in 1926.

15   Calverton, *Liberation of American Literature*, 476.

16   Consider, e.g., North, *Reading 1922*, and Manganaro, *Culture, 1922 and After*.

17 On *Keys of the City*, see "In Indiana"; on *Under the Levee*, see *New York Times Book Review*, 19 April 1925, 15; on *Reamer Lou*, see "A Laborer's Life"; on *Arrowsmith*, see Morgan, "Lewis Assails Our Medicine Men."

18 On *Faith of Our Fathers*, see "In a First Novel the Worldly Affairs of the Clergy"; on *The Middle Years*, see "American Marriage."

19 On *Barren Ground*, see Brock, "Southern Romance Is Dead"; on *The Great Gatsby*, see Edwin Clark, "Scott Fitzgerald Looks into Middle Age"; on *The Mother's Recompense*, see Hutchison, "Mrs. Wharton Brings 'The House of Mirth' Up to Date"; on *Those Difficult Years*, see "This Perfect World"; on *The Way of All Earth*, see "Redemption by Work."

20 Reviews of the two bigamist novels appeared in the *New York Times Book Review* on 5 July 1925, 13. Their titles are *Married Men*, by Jane Burr, about an actress who discovers that her perfect man has a wife and children, and John Chichester's *The Bigamist*, about a lawyer who marries first for position and then for the love he left behind. On *The Love Complex*, see "Mr. Dixon's Thriller."

21 On *Firecrackers*, see "New York of 1924."

22 On *In Our Time*, see "Preludes to a Mood"; on *Manhattan Transfer*, see Stuart, "John Dos Passos Notes the Tragic Trivia"; on *Thunder on the Left*, see "Beauty of Style in Christopher Morley's New Novel"; on *P.A.L.*, see "Get-Rich-Quick"; on *The Surry Family*, see "Commonplace Folk."

23 See L. Schwartz, *Creating Faulkner's Reputation*.

24 For an excellent account of reclaiming one gifted writer from obscurity, see Cox, *The Woman and the Dynamo*.

25 "Fifty Books of Fiction."

26 Seldes, "Spring Flight."

27 Paterson, "Up to the Minute."

28 Van Vechten, "Fitzgerald on the March."

29 E. Clark, "Scott Fitzgerald Looks into Middle Age."

30 Scribner's advertisement, *New York Times Book Review*, 7 June 1925, 22; Van Vechten, "Fitzgerald on the March."

31 C. Van Doren, *American Novel*, 327.

32 *New Yorker*, 28 November 1925, 18.

33 *Bookman*, March 1926; Canby, "Thunder in Manhattan."

34 Stuart, "John Dos Passos Notes the Tragic Trivia."

35 Ibid.

36 S. Lewis, "Manhattan at Last!"

37 Stuart, "John Dos Passos Notes the Tragic Trivia."

38 Chamberlain, "Six Months in the Field of Fiction," 2.

39 On *Show Business*, see "A Small-Town Girl," *New York Times Book Review*, 14 March 1926, 6.

40 Ferguson, "Five Rising Stars."

41 On *Shadows Waiting*, see Parsons, "Another Way of Hacking at Wine Chests"; "The Editor Recommends"; and R. L., *New Republic*, 13 April 1927, 231.

42 On *Torrents of Spring*, see "Mr. Hemingway Writes Some High-Spirited Nonsense."

43 On *The Sun Also Rises*, see C. B. Chase, *Saturday Review of Literature*, 11 December 1926, 420.

44 On *The Sun Also Rises*, see Tate, "Spirituality of Roughnecks" and "Hard-Boiled."

45 For *The Sun Also Rises*, see "Marital Tragedy," *New York Times Book Review*, 31 October 1926; Ferguson, "Five Rising Stars."

46 Ferguson, "Five Rising Stars"; Calverton, *Survey*, 1 November 1926, 160.

47 Hicks, "The Twenties in American Literature."

48 Fadiman, "Whole Duty."

49 See Cawelti's classic formulation of the cultural appeal of detective fiction, *Adventure, Mystery, and Romance*.

50 Abbott, *The New Barbarians*, 35. On *The New Barbarians*, also see *Independent*, 21 March 1925, 331.

51 Abbott, *The New Barbarians*, 91.

52 Frank, *Re-discovery of America*, 60–61.

53 Calverton, *Liberation of American Literature*, 477.

54 Kauffman's novel was not as widely reviewed as *Elmer Gantry* but received positive assessments. The *New York Times*, "Protestant Clergymen," praised its "good deal of verisimilitude"; it was not "sensational, nor is it startling, except possibly to those who willfully blind their eyes," but it also was grouped together with Lewis's novel as "ecclesiastical muck-raking," according to the *Saturday Review of Literature*, April 1927, 767.

55 See " 'The Beginners' and Other Recent Works."

56 On *Strangers and Lovers*, see John Carter, "Mr. Granberry's Fine Novel"; on *The Old Enchantment*, see "Vulgarity Triumphs."

57 On *These Are My Jewels*, see "Murderous Satire"; on *Maids Will Be Wives*, see "The Maternal Woman"; on *Queen Dick*, see "A Selfish Woman."

58 On *The Bride's House*, see "Macabre Intensity," *New York Times Book Review*, 12 May 1929, 7; on *See How They Run*, see "Three Blind Mice."

59 On *Sartoris*, see "A Southern Family," *New York Times Book Review*, 3 March 1929, 8.

60 On *The Conjure-Woman*, see "Negro Folktales."

61 See " 'The White Girl' and Other Recent Works." On *Passing*, see "Beyond the Color Line," *New York Times Book Review*, 28 April 1929, 14; on *Banjo*, see " 'Banjo' and Other Recent Works of Fiction."

62 On *Laughing Boy*, see Wallace, "A Romance of the Navajo Country."

63 Yezierska, *Salome of the Tenements*, 87.

64 See Gabler, *Empire of Their Own*.

65 Fay, "Protestant America," 1194.

66 Gerould, "Comedy of Americanization," 82.

67 Lane, "How to Make Americans."

68 "The Rise of the 'New' American."

69 Gerould, "Comedy of Americanization," 82.

70 "The Pride of Palomar," *Literary Review*, and *New York Times Book Review*. For

evidence of Kyne's popularity, see *Publishers' Weekly*, 12 March 1927, 1045–53. Kyne ranks right between romancers A. S. M. Hutchinson and Harold Bell Wright. *The Pride of Palomar* is rated twenty-second, one notch above *Babbitt*.

71 On *Easy*, see "The Invading Horde," *New York Times Book Review*, 16 March 1924, 14.

72 On *Peder Victorious*, see Parsons, "Prairie and Fjord."

73 Boynton, *Rediscovery of the Frontier*, 134–39.

74 J. T. Adams, *Epic of America*, esp. 404–12.

75 Cf. Barbara Ehrenreich's study of middle-class angst, *Fear of Falling*.

76 J. T. Adams, *Epic of America*, esp. 416–17 (quotation, 417).

77 Herrick, "What Is Happening to Our Fiction?"

78 See Hergesheimer, "The Feminine Nuisance in American Literature." Cf. F. N. Hart, "The Feminine Nuisance Replies."

79 Lynn, *Dream of Success*.

80 Herrick, "What Is Happening to Our Fiction?" Herrick's anxiety about psychoanalysis seems like standard antimodern stuff too, insofar as literary criticism in the United States has never been all that enamored with talk of compulsions and complexes. A couple of books were published in the '20s and early '30s, then virtually nothing until Frederick Crews's landmark study of Hawthorne in 1966.

CHAPTER TWO

1 I do not mean to gainsay the many excellent studies of the '30s that scholars have produced, and they are legion. I am only arguing that the paradigms under which they have been written come from the false dichotomy of pitting modernist classics against proletarian writing, a bifurcation in turn legitimated by the claim that neither is popular, like romances and formula fiction. This kind of thinking has led historians to imagine that these are the era's only kinds of fiction writing. A notable exception to this is the work of feminist scholars trying to reclaim "middlebrow" writers, including Fannie Hurst, Pearl S. Buck, and Dorothy Canfield Fisher. I contend that these writers are more comprehensible as a group when seen under the aegis of class. One such study, relating these women writers to the nineteenth-century sentimental tradition that Jane Tompkins addresses in her reading of Stowe, is Jamie Harker's *America the Middlebrow*, which features readings of Canfield Fisher, Buck, and Josephine Herbst.

2 Supplementing Walter Rideout's well-regarded pioneering study, *Radical Novel in the United States*, is Alan Wald's two-volume history, *Exiles from a Future Time* (2002) and *Trinity of Passion* (2007). Two richly provocative revisionist studies of '30s radicalism are Irr's *The Suburb of Dissent* (1998) and Szalay's *New Deal Modernism* (2000).

3 Daniel Aaron's *Writers on the Left* (1965) and James Gilbert's *Writers and Partisans* (1968) helped to cement the history of proletarian protest as the privileged history of '30s writing.

4 See Constance Coiner's luminous study, *Better Red* (1998), and Paula Rabinowitz's *Labor and Desire* (1991).

5 See Richard Brodhead's *Cultures of Letters* (1993). Brodhead is primarily concerned with the earlier tradition of regionalism, but he also describes the active impulse in the '20s and '30s. Also see Thomas Lutz, *Cosmopolitan Vistas* (2004). A very helpful study is Robert L. Dorman's *Revolt of the Provinces* (1993). The bibliography of '30s commentary on regionalism is immense, but one representative forum of the discussion appeared as "Regionalism: Pro and Con," by Joseph E. Baker, an English professor at the University of Iowa, and Paul R. Beath, who was a delegate from Nebraska to the Democratic National Convention that year, in *Saturday Review of Literature*, 28 November 1936.

6 Of the many books to consult on this subject, the definitive study remains William Stott's *Documentary Expression and Thirties America* (1973).

7 Canby, "Significant Reading of a Literary Year." Also see Canby, "The Threatening Thirties," 3–4, 14.

8 "The Best-Selling Books," *New York Times Book Review*, 4 July 1937, 64.

9 On *The Old Bunch*, see Strauss, "A Novel of Youth in Chicago"; on *People of the Earth*, see Eda Lou Walton, "A Modern Navajo"; on *Neighbor to the Sky*, see Walton, "A Return to the Soil of Maine"; on *The Tree Falls South*, see Marsh, "When the Good Earth Blows Away"; on *American Dream*, see Young, "A Wide-Sweeping Novel on American Generations"; on *White Mule*, see Kazin, "'White Mule' and Other Recent Works."

10 On *Ferment*, see Marsh, "Mr. McIntyre's Novel"; on *Night at Hogwallow*, see Van Gelder, "Lynch Mob"; on *Rush to the Sun*, see "A First Novel That Has Power"; on *To Have and Have Not*, see J. Donald Adams, "Ernest Hemingway's First Novel in Eight Years"; and on *Their Eyes Were Watching God*, see Tompkins, "In the Florida Glades."

11 Burt, "What's Left for the Novelist?"

12 Cowley, "A Farewell to the 1930's."

13 Lynd and Lynd, *Middletown in Transition*, 15.

14 Gurko, *Angry Decade*, 36.

15 G. Holt, "Fledgling Fiction."

16 Field, "Heroines Back at the Hearth."

17 Gerould, "Feminine Fiction," 3–4, 15.

18 Banning, "The Problem of Popularity," 3–4, 16–17.

19 Canby, "The Ethics of Popularity."

20 R. L. Duffus, *Books*, xi. Recent years have seen an explosion of interest in seventeenth-, eighteenth-, and nineteenth-century reading habits in America. After landmarks like Carl Kaestle's study (Kaestle et al., *Literacy in the United States*, 1991) and Janice Radway's work on the Book-of-the-Month Club (*A Feeling for Books*, 1997), more remains to do in twentieth-century studies. Although some of that will be repaired when the History of the Book project publishes its later volumes, retarding the development of modern studies of the book trade again is the antibourgeois

prejudice that is less likely to affect earlier centuries, the scholarship of which recognizes that middle-class reading is a primary site of inquiry.

21 Waples, *People and Print*. Also see Waples, "Do People Read What They Like?"

22 Adamic, "What the Proletariat Reads." Although working in an earlier time frame, Eric Schocket offers the concept of the "class transvestite" to describe those middle-class authors who mime working-class traits and expression in order to authenticate their touristic studies of the lower. See Schocket, "Middle-Class Melancholy and Proletarian Pain," *Vanishing Moments*, 105–42, esp. 118–24.

23 Cantwell, "What the Working Class Reads."

24 Herrick, "Writers in the Jungle."

25 On *To Make My Bread*, see "A Novel of the Southern Mills"; on *Call Home the Heart*, see Archer Winsten, *Bookman*, June 1932, 319, and "A Heart Divided"; on *The Disinherited*, see C. Simpson, "A Powerful Novel of Social Revolt"; on *The Foundry*, see Kronenberger, "Albert Halper's Vivid New Novel," and *Christian Century*, 19 September 1934, 1178. On *The Land of Plenty*, see H. Gregory, "The World within a Factory"; *Boston Evening Transcript*, 29 May 1934, 3; Kronenberger, "Portrait of a Factory"; and Strauss, "Robert Cantwell's Novel and Other Recent Works." On *The Shadow Before*, see *New York Evening Post*, 17 March 1934, 11.

26 Dos Passos, "The Business of a Novelist."

27 Dabney, *Edmund Wilson*, 152. Also see M. Gold, "Wilder: Prophet of the Genteel Christ."

28 E. Wilson, "Literary Class War."

29 M. Gold, "Wilder: Prophet of the Genteel Christ"; Shuster, "George Brush"; E. Wilson, "Mr. Wilder in the Middle West."

30 Canby, "Emotion and History." At various points in my argument, I follow Canby's model of describing a year's production of novelistic interests, but, obviously, one year can be an arbitrary bracketing too. So I sometimes include information when the publishing interests of two or three years are germane. In that way, I hope to preserve Canby's more serious point that a deeper insight into a novel's currency comes from expanding the moment of popularity beyond one publishing season and examining a novel's affinities with other recently published, roughly synchronous works.

31 Myers, "The Novel and the Past."

32 James, *Art of the Novel*, 63.

33 For a wise, incisive explanation of the history of James criticism, see Posnock, *Trial of Curiosity*, esp. chap. 3, " 'On a Certain Blindness': Henry James and the Politics of Cultural Response," 54–79.

34 Cozzens's *The Last Adam*, generally considered his best novel up to that time, and most of his successive books, were leading up to the ones that made him most famous, the Pulitzer Prize–winning *Guard of Honor* (1948) and *By Love Possessed* (1957). See Chamberlain, "Small-Time Life in Connecticut," *New York Times Book Review*, 27 August 1933, 7. On *Roads from Paradise*, see Lisle Bell, *Books*, 8 January 1933, 6; Barretto actually had a long and respected career. On *Never Ask the End*, see

Ellen Glasgow, *Books*, 8 January 1933, 3. See Paterson, *Books*, 5 February 1933, 5. The anonymous reviewer in the *Nation* (1 February 1933, 127–28) also suggests that Paterson "provides a complete philosophy for living in these times." On *One More Spring*, see Chamberlain, ("Gentile Satire in 'One More Spring'"): "Some day Americans will wake up to the fact that they have a writer worth cherishing in Mr. Nathan." On *Eva Gay*, see Lovett, "Diagram of Pain." On *The Farm*, see J. Donald Adams, "Mr. Bromfield's Family Chronicle."

35 Houghton, "What President Roosevelt Hopes to Achieve."

36 Mary Beard, *Books*, 15 November 1933, 7.

37 I follow the statistics from *Publishers' Weekly*, which Alice Hackett compiled in *70 Years of Bestsellers, 1895–1965*, 147–48.

38 See Watkins, *The Hungry Years*, 104–5.

39 Gurko, *Angry Decade*, 84–85.

40 L. Morris, "More Historical Novels."

41 Cantwell, "America and the Writers' Project."

42 Wallace, "A Fine Novel of Revolution."

43 K. Roberts, *Oliver Wiswell*, 258.

44 See Duffus, "Kenneth Roberts' New Novel."

45 Fadiman, "A Little Theorizing."

46 Commager, "The 'Traitor'"; Sellers, *Proud Warrior*. Also see Gaither, "Intrepid Traitor"; Cordell, "American 'Loyalists'"; Salomon, "Tory Through and Through"; Soskin, *Books*, 3 May 1939, 6.

47 Rice, Rev. of *Treason*; R. A. Cordell, *Saturday Review of Literature*, 20 May 1944, 28.

48 See Fadiman, "A Little Theorizing."

49 Weeks, "What Makes a Book a Best Seller?"

50 Wagenknecht, *Cavalcade of the American Novel*, 425.

51 Here, as elsewhere, I have relied on W. J. Stuckey's informative 1966 study, *The Pulitzer Prize Novels*, 108.

52 Kang, "China Is Different."

53 See Birmingham, *The Late John Marquand*, 85.

54 Ibid., 224.

55 For an account of Brooks's "reentrenchment," see Nelson, *Van Wyck Brooks*, esp. part 3, 199–263.

56 On *Years Are So Long*, see *Saturday Review of Literature*, 7 July 1934, 793; on *If I Have Four Apples*, see Bénet, "Instalment Living."

57 Chamberlain, "Literature," in *America Now*, esp. 42–43.

58 On *The Liberals*, see Feld, "'The Liberals' and Other Recent Works"; on *O Canaan!*, see Marsh, "People of a Great Migration"; on *The Flaming Sword*, see *Books*, 17 September 1939, 12.

59 On *Seasoned Timber*, see Soskin, "When World Problems Invade Vermont." Similar commendations were also issued by Hicks, "The Swastika in Vermont," and Marquand, "Freedom of the Mind." The *New York Times* (Field, "Dorothy Canfield's New Novel") also praised it as summarizing "clearly and well many of the doubts

and differences of this most doubtful and very difficult time." Even the conservative *Yale Review* (Ralph Thompson, "Outstanding Novels") found much to praise, comparing it as "no less militant" than Sinclair Lewis's *It Can't Happen Here*. For a broader view of the novel in Canfield Fisher's career, see Erhardt, *Writers of Conviction*, 88–91.

60 See Hartung, "Stone Walls Do Not," and R. Thompson, "Outstanding Novels."

61 See Corbin, "Four Views of the American Way of Life"; Childs, "Roads to the Future"; and R. M. B., "American Leeway."

62 Boyle scholarship has been more active in the last few years, including the publication of her lost novella, *Process*, edited and introduced by Sandra Spanier. Also see Austenfeld, *American Women Writers and the Nazis*.

63 A recent appreciation of Prokosch appeared in the *New York Review of Books*, 6 January 2005.

64 Loveman, "The Clearing House," 16 August 1941.

65 For a study of the relation between border writing, the Caribbean, and middle-class realism, see Hutner, "In the Middle: Fiction, Borders, and Class."

CHAPTER THREE

1 The best survey of 1940s fiction remains Chester E. Eisinger's indispensable *Fiction of the Forties*. More recently, see Tony Hilfer, *American Fiction since 1940*.

2 Hansen, "Literary Scene in 1940."

3 Hicks, "The Shape of Postwar Literature."

4 See Adler, *How to Read a Book*, esp. 373–89.

5 Brooks and Warren, *Understanding Fiction*, 600.

6 Niebuhr, "Challenge for Liberals."

7 Cowley, "Shipwreck."

8 For a broader context, see Halford E. Luccock's long-forgotten *American Mirror* (1941), including chap. 5, "The Impact of the Depression," esp. 122–23.

9 On *The Dam*, see Marsh, "WPA Workers."

10 On *Mr. George's Joint*, see Brickell, "A Fresh Talent from the South"; on *Is Tomorrow Hitler's?*, see Kittredge, "Eloquent Warning."

11 V. W. Brooks, *Opinions of Oliver Allston*, 201.

12 See "Nationalism and Regionalism" in ibid., 256–72, esp. 259.

13 J. Donald Adams, "Life and Literature in America."

14 The broad outlines of Fadiman's career are to be found in Rubin's *Making of Middlebrow Culture*, 320–27.

15 Stegner, "Is the Novel Done For?"

16 D. Trilling, "What Has Happened to Our Novels?"

17 D. Trilling, *Reviewing the Forties*, 133. Trilling made a more crucial impact on the discussion of contemporary fiction in her time than is commonly understood. Her relative lack of standing reminds us of a dozen female magazine and newspaper critics and reviewers who have suffered an even worse fate, insofar as they were not

married to an illustrious man of letters like Lionel Trilling. Diana Trilling's case is doubly unfortunate, insofar as she has often been seen as a mere appendage. Although she secured her appointment as a reviewer for the *Nation* at her husband's suggestion, it was her brio and conviction that won her reviews the prestige they enjoyed. Self-assertive as she was, Trilling was also, at times, the object of misogynistic sneers (sometimes by her husband's associates). Two predecessors of mine in appreciating her contributions are James Seaton's "Making Double Judgments: The Criticism of Diana Trilling," in his *Cultural Conservatism, Political Liberalism*, and Lewis Simpson's "A Poetic of Cultural Politics," in his *Imagining Our Time*, esp. 134–37.

18 Kelly, "Sincerity and the Novelist."

19 Banning, "In Print and in War."

20 Crouse, "Writers and the War."

21 MacLeish, "Books in This World at War."

22 See Michael Szalay's New Deal reading of Betty Smith's novel in his *New Deal Modernism*, 184–94.

23 J. Donald Adams, "Speaking of Books."

24 See Keith Perry's useful study, *The Kingfish in Fiction: Huey P. Long and the Modern American Novel.*

25 D. Trilling, "Fiction in Review," 18 September 1943; Farber, "Freudian Nightmare."

26 Clifton P. Fadiman, *New Yorker*, 23 October 1943, 84.

27 Stuckey, *The Pulitzer Prize Novels*, 129–32.

28 D. Trilling, "Fiction in Review," 23 September 1946.

29 On *Also the Hills*, see Ulrich, "The Conn. Family."

30 Cf. Anonymous, "I Changed My Name"; Cohn, "I've Kept Mine."

31 Cromwell, "Democracy and the Negro."

32 Fisher, "American Readers and Books," 191.

33 For a study of Fisher's influence on Wright and the history of her editorial intervention, see Karem, *Romance of Authenticity*, 77–84.

34 On *Negro Caravan*, see Meachem, "Negro Writers Speak for Themselves," and Kreymborg, "March of a Noble Race."

35 On *New World A-Coming*, see Feld, "World of the American Negro Today," and R. Holt, "Tenth of a Nation."

36 See Loveland, *Lillian Smith*; also see Sosna, *In Search of the Silent South*. The newest criticism on *Strange Fruit* has tended to emphasize the issues of interracial sex and lesbianism.

37 D. S. Norton, "Past and Present," 474. The hypocrisy resonated in the halls of Congress, where Senator Bilbo and Congressman John E. Rankin, both of Mississippi, used their offices in time of war to warn the nation against miscegenation and to filibuster against poll tax reform, as well as to plead for clearing homeless blacks from Washington, D.C., alleys and to urge their deportation!

38 Ibid.; L. Smith, "Personal History of 'Strange Fruit.'"

39 On *Escape the Thunder*, see N. B. Baker, "Release." While Smith herself disliked

Colcorton, averring that Pope was "not intellectually and socially prepared" to undertake her theme, despite her "talent for fiction" (*New Republic*, 26 June 1944, 853), that was something of a minority report, for *Colcorton* received excellent reviews in the *New Yorker*, *New York Times Book Review*, and *Yale Review*, among others.

40 On *Color Blind*, see *Christian Century*, 9 October 1946, 1215.

41 Redding, "The Negro: America's Dilemma"; Lynd, "Prison for American Genius."

42 Reuter, "The American Dilemma," and William Du Bois, "The American Dilemma," *Phylon* 5 (1944): 114–24.

43 Schlesinger Sr., *Learning How to Behave*.

44 On *Three O'Clock Dinner*, see William Du Bois, "Pluff Mud, Oleanders and Drains," *New York Times Book Review*, 23 September 1945, 5.

45 See *New York Times Book Review*, 10 April 1949, 5.

46 See Heinze, "*Peace of Mind.*"

47 There are various first-person accounts of a soldier's "assimilation" and its problems, including Lang's intense "A Reporter at Large: Everyone Walks Too Slow," and E. L. Jones's "The Soldier Returns." Also see Nisbet's "The Coming Problem of Assimilation," and Daly's "Peace: It's a Problem!" Of the many books devoted to the subject, Baruch and Travis's *You're Out of the Service Now: The Veteran's Guide to Civilian Life* is a particularly vivid account. Among the multitudinous magazine articles about the various facets of postwar servicemen's experience, also see Berrigan's comparison of the new itinerant class with the '30s hoboes in "New Men Travel the Old Roads."

48 Mary Ross, *Weekly Book Review*, 18 November 1945.

49 In *The Cultural Front* (447–49), Michael Denning claims that the Committee on Social Unity was a Popular Front organization.

50 Ralph Ellison, *New Republic*, 22 October 1945, 535.

51 Ralph Ellison, *New Yorker*, 9 April 1949, 120. Also see Ann Petry's review ("No Mobs, No Fiery Crosses") for her praise of the novel's realism: "It is an extraordinarily successful book, for the seamy side of race relations comes through as a powerful undercurrent, revealed largely through conversations in bars and barber shops, at parties."

52 On both novels, see B. Moon, "Deep South." Also on *Send Me an Angel*, the *New York Times Book Review* (Parke, "Cabin in the Cotton") praises its "power of truthfulness" and "drama of unadornment," while Coleman Rosenberger in the *New York Herald Weekly Book Review* worries that the "quiet precision of the writing" manages to support a plot far more melodramatic than the brief novel can sustain.

53 On *Jadie Greenway*, see Bullock, "Across the Bridge."

54 See Butcher, "Our Raceless Writers," for a contemporaneous consideration of African American novelists' treatment of whites, which includes positive assessments of Petry's *Country Place*, a critical view of Dorothy West's *The Living Is Easy*, and a negative judgment of Will Thomas's *God Is for White Folks*.

55 On *If He Hollers Let Him Go*, see *New Yorker*, 3 November 1945, 102; on *Lonely Crusade*, see Bontemps, *New York Herald Weekly Book Review*, 7 September 1947, 8.

56 On *Alien Land*, see *San Francisco Chronicle*, 8 May 1949, 21, and Bontemps, "A 'White Negro' 'Passes.'"

57 On *Wasteland*, see Thomas Sugrue, *Weekly Book Review*, 17 February 1946, 3.

58 W. R. Ross, *So It Was True!*, 233–34.

59 Hobson, *Gentleman's Agreement*, 12. For a fuller consideration of the novel, see Hutner, "Our Hearts Were Young and Gay." Hobson's book has elicited little criticism in the last sixty years, though the movie has come in for its share of discussion. The film *Crossfire* is generally understood as Hollywood's first major effort to treat anti-Semitism, but, interestingly, that movie replaces homophobia with anti-Semitism—in some ways, a more palatable form of social deviancy—in the novel *The Brick Foxhole* (1945) by Richard Brooks. Indeed, *Crossfire* is less about anti-Semitism than postwar malaise. As Joseph Samuels (played by dapper Sam Levene) tells an obstreperous soldier (Robert Ryan) at a bar, "Now we start looking at each other again. We don't know what we're supposed to do; we don't know what's supposed to happen. We're used to fighting, but we just don't know what to fight. You can feel the tension in the air. A whole lot of fight and hate doesn't know where to go. A guy like you maybe starts hating himself. Maybe one of these days we'll all sort of shift gears. Maybe we'll all start liking each other again." The soldier kills him. See Weber, *Haunted in the New World*, 99.

60 On *Gentleman's Agreement*, see H. S. Hayward, *Christian Science Monitor*, 21 March 1947, 12; *Catholic World* (June 1947), 285; James Reid Parker, *Survey Graphic* (May 1947), 312.

61 Schulberg, "Kid-Glove Cruelty."

62 Hobson, *Gentleman's Agreement*, 200, 192.

63 D. Trilling, "Americans without Distinction," 292.

64 On *A Mask for Privilege*, see *New Yorker*, 20 March 1948, 110; James G. MacDonald, "Hidden Motives"; R. H. M., *Christian Science Monitor*, 30 March 1948, 12.

65 Dinnerstein, "The Tide Ebbs."

66 On *Time Is Noon*, see "Swift-Paced, Dramatic, Thoughtful Story."

67 On *The Living Is Easy*, see Bontemps, "In Boston."

68 On *The Sure Thing*, see Galbraith, "Hunt for a Heretic."

69 On *Dopplegangers*, see Harrison Smith, "Fighting Man or Stuffed Goose."

70 On *Give Us Our Dream*, see Cordell, "Lilt on Long Island."

71 On *Not in Our Stars*, see Andrea Parke, *New York Times Book Review*, 16 September 1943, 6, and Prescott, "Outstanding Novels," 1946.

72 On *The Wayfarers*, see Flagg, "The Private Life of a Widower," and *Commonweal*, 13 July 1945, 315; on *The Inheritance*, see Van Gelder, "Neuroses in Athens, Michigan."

73 On *The Journey of Simon McKeever*, see William Du Bois, "Tales of a 'Spunky Septuagenarian,'" and Rugoff, "Pilgrim—and a Message." Albert Maltz had a creditable career as a novelist and screenwriter (including *This Gun for Hire*, *Naked City*,

and an Academy Award–winning short film on race relations, *The House I Live In*). Maltz had been indicted for contempt of Congress in 1947 for refusing to name names to the House Committee on Un-American Activities, an inquiry that came as a result of his partisan standing during the '30s, when he wrote several proletarian plays and a mammoth novel, *The Underground Stream* (1940). Maltz also wrote a war novel, *The Cross and the Arrow* (1944), and a collection of essays, *The Citizen Writer* (1950). For a fuller appreciation of his career, see Salzman, *Albert Maltz*.

74 On *The Wayward Bus*, see Chris Baker, "Mr. Steinbeck's Cross-Section."

75 On *East Side, West Side*, see *New Yorker*, 25 October 1947, 133; on *The Wayward Bus*, see Edward Weeks, *Atlantic Monthly*, November 1947, 179.

76 On *Mirror, Mirror*, see D. Trilling, "Fiction in Review," 1946.

77 On *The Left Hand Is the Dreamer*, see McGrory, "Fine Novel of a Woman's Choice."

78 On *The Girl in the Spike-heeled Shoes*, see esp. Jack Conroy, *Chicago Sun*, 16 October 1949, 13.

79 On *Always Young and Fair*, see Sullivan, "Silver Threads among the Gold," and Rose Feld, *New York Herald Weekly Book Review*, 30 May 1947, 10.

80 On *Celia Amberley*, see *Christian Science Monitor*, 18 October 1949, 14.

81 On *The Last Leaf*, see Richards, "Martha's Puritan Bondage"; on *Plum Tree*, see Catharine Mereddith Brown, *Saturday Review of Literature*, 17 December 1949, 26.

82 On *Echoing Green*, see De Grace, "Jemmie's Progress"; on *My Heart Shall Not Fear*, see M. Ross, "A Warm Human Appeal."

CHAPTER FOUR

1 For an argument associated with my own, see Morris Dickstein, *Leopards in the Temple: The Transformation of American Fiction, 1945–1970*. Dickstein views the arrival of "outsiders" as a key source of American fiction's development, though I will show that this element of estrangement is more central to the bourgeois tradition than Dickstein's argument allows.

2 See Barth, "Literature of Exhaustion," and Berthoff, *A Literature without Qualities*. For a contemporaneous version of these arguments, consider J. Brooks, "Some Notes on Writing One Kind of Novel."

3 See Kazin, *Bright Book of Life*. For examples of the many symposia, see Hicks, "The Living Novel," as well as special issues of the *American Scholar*—e.g., "What's Wrong with the American Novel?" 24, no. 4 (Autumn 1955): 464–503, whose participants included Ralph Ellison, Jean Stafford, and William Styron, among others. Less focused on fiction is the previous year's "The Future of Books in America" 23, no. 2 (Spring 1954): 197–215.

4 On *The Cardinal*, see "The Universal Church," *Atlantic Monthly*, May 1950, 82, and *San Francisco Chronicle*, 9 April 1950, 15.

5 For reviews of *The Strange Land*, see H. F. West, "War's Smell and Taste," and J. H. Thompson, "Ten Soldiers in Never-Never Land." For a list of best sellers, see Alice Hackett, *70 Years of Best Sellers, 1895–1965*, 184.

6 On *Stranger and Alone*, see R. Ellison, "Collaborator with His Own Enemy," and Petry, "Race Betrayal."

7 On *The Trouble of One House*, see *New Yorker*, 21 October 1950, 132; on *World Enough and Time*, see Janeway, "Man in Conflict." Other critics praised the realist-historical novel of the Plymouth landing, Ernest Gebler's *The Plymouth Adventure*, or Jesse Stuart's latest local color rendering of Kentucky hill people, *Hie to the Hunters*.

8 On *The Town*, see Bromfield, "Another Volume."

9 Richter, *The Town*, 311.

10 Trimmer, *The N.B.A. for Fiction*, xi, n. 21.

11 Podhoretz, "Faulkner in the Fifties," *Doings and Undoings*, 13.

12 See *Atlantic Monthly*, October 1950, 90.

13 Cf. studies of Faulkner by Schwartz (*Creating Faulkner's Reputation*) and Sundquist (*Faulkner*).

14 MacLeish, "American State of Mind."

15 Barrett, "American Fiction and American Values."

16 Barrett, "The Literature of Nihilism."

17 Aldridge, *After the Lost Generation*, 243. Cf. John Hazlett, *My Generation*. Also see Soto, *The Modernist Nation*, esp. 17–56.

18 Very influential in this respect is Ihab Hassan's crucial study, *Radical Innocence*.

19 Jackson, "Fiction Is Neither What It Was Nor What It Might Be."

20 On *The Morning Watch*, see *New Yorker*, 7 April 1951, 118.

21 For an especially rich understanding of brow-ism, one that seldom is remarked on by literary scholars, see Daniel Belgard's acute reading in *The Culture of Spontaneity*, 233–44.

22 DeVoto, "The Easy Chair: Why Read Dull Novels?"

23 Mizener, "What Makes Great Books Great?"

24 DeVoto, "The Easy Chair: Why Read Dull Novels?"

25 The happy exception is Canaday's *The Nuclear Muse*. Also see Winkler, *Life under a Cloud*.

26 On *Shadow on the Hearth*, see Cournos, "No Hiroshima," and Harrison Smith, "Atom-Bombing Here." Also see *Chicago Sunday Tribune*, 2 July 1950, 3.

27 On *The Hound of Earth*, see Charles J. Rolo, *Atlantic Monthly*, April 1955, 81, and Herbert Gold, "Fugitive from a Chain Reaction."

28 McMahon, "One Man's Revolt."

29 Dabney, "The American Novel in the Age of Conformity." For further background, see Howe, "This Age of Conformity." Also see Chase, "Neo-Conservatism and American Literature."

30 Schlesinger Jr., "Our Country and Our Culture."

31 Schwartz, "Our Country and Our Culture."

32 Kronenberger, "Our Country and Our Culture."

33 On *Peyton Place*, see *New Yorker*, 20 October 1956, 197.

34 See Medovoi, *Rebels*, esp. 182–86.

35 L. Trilling, "Two Notes on David Riesman," *A Gathering of Fugitives*, 92.

36 Ibid., 95.

37 Fussell, *Wartime*.

38 On *The Many Lives of Modern Woman*, see Keene, "The Modern Marriage."

39 See Ehrenreich, *The Hearts of Men*, 27–28. Also see Antler, *The Journey Home*, 235–36, 266; Prell, "Cinderellas Who (Almost) Never Become Princesses"; and Antler, *You Never Call, You Never Write!*, 108–9, 115.

40 Fiedler, "The Breakthrough."

41 See Bush and Moore, "Will Herberg's *Protestant-Catholic-Jew*."

42 On *Marjorie Morningstar*, see "Wouk Mutiny."

43 See Long, *American Dream and the Popular Novel*, 90.

44 On *Marjorie Morningstar*, see Geismar, "Roots and the Flowering Tree," 1, and Bullock, "Herman Wouk Spins a Tale."

45 See Teller, "Changing Status of American Jewry." Also see Smertenko, "The Emerging Hyphen"; Gersh, "The New Suburbanites of the 50's"; and A. I. Gordon, *Jews in Suburbia*.

46 See Podhoretz, "The Jew as Bourgeois." Also see Fitch, "The Bourgeois and the Bohemian."

47 On *Marjorie Morningstar*, see Horchler, "Life and the Dream," and E. W. Foell, *Christian Science Monitor*, 1 September 1955, 7.

48 Metcalf, "New Novels."

49 I. Rosenfeld, "For God and the Suburbs."

50 Ibid.; "Wouk in the Pulpit," *Nation*, 22 October 1955, 347.

51 Horchler, "Life and the Dream."

52 Magid, "The Girl Who Went Back Home."

53 On *Grand Concourse*, see *New York Herald Weekly Book Review*, 14 November 1954, 15, and Don M. Mankiewicz, "Doomed in Advance," *New York Times Book Review*, 12 December 1954, 27.

54 On *Days of My Love*, see Gilbert Millstein, "Life of a Salesman," *New York Times Book Review*, 8 March 1953, 26.

55 On *The Strong Hand*, see *San Francisco Chronicle*, 4 March 1956, 22.

56 Cf. Schrag, *Decline of the WASP*.

57 See Irr, *Suburb of Dissent*; Jurca, *White Diaspora*; and Hoberek, *Twilight of the Middle Class*. For all of these studies' useful intervention, they tend to concentrate on the familiar works of their respective eras. Jurca is especially incisive in her chapter on *The Man in the Gray Flannel Suit*.

58 See Gordon, Gordon, and Gunther, *Split-Level Trap*.

59 On *Copper Beech*, see Otis K. Burger, "The Endless War between the Sexes," *New York Times Book Review*, 8 May 1960, 27; on *The Chapman Report*, see Daniel Talbot, "In a Swamp of Erotica," *New York Times Book Review*, 29 May 1960, 18; on *The Lion House*, see Caroline Tunstall, "In the Cages of Exurbia," *New York Herald Tribune Weekly Book Review*, 11 October 1959, 7.

60 On *Peaceable Lane*, see Weeks, "The Negro as Our Neighbor"; *New Yorker*, 24 December 1960, 61; Cooney, "Real Estate: Restricted."

61 On *First Family*, see Kelly, "Racial Clash in Courtland Park"; Feld, "Subtly Moving Novel"; *New York Herald Tribune Lively Arts*, 5 February 1961, 37; "Haunted Castle"; and Cooney, "Real Estate: Restricted."

62 On race and the suburbs, see Polenberg, "The Suburban Nation," *One Nation Divisible*, 151–63. Further reading includes Masotti, *Suburbia in Transition*; Keating, *Suburban Racial Dilemma*; and Haar, *Suburbs under Siege*.

63 On *To Kill a Mockingbird*, see LeMay, "Children Play."

64 On *Knot of Roots*, see M. Ross, "Two Worlds Meet." This novel also received laudatory reviews in the *Booklist*, the *Manchester Guardian*, and the *Times* of London, but somehow the *New York Times* missed it.

65 Also see "Fiction in Decline," *Library Journal*, 1 June 1960, 2128; Hicks, "As Fiction Faces the Sixties" and "The Case for Fiction in 1960"; and H. Gold, "Fiction of the Sixties."

66 W. E. Barrett, "Novel Writing for the Sixties."

67 Ibid., 7.

68 Cousins, "What's Wrong with the American Novel?"

BIBLIOGRAPHY

BOOKS

Aaron, Daniel. *Writers on the Left*. 1965. New York: Oxford University Press, 1977.

Aaron, Daniel, and Robert Bendiner, eds. *The Strenuous Decade: A Social and Intellectual Record of the 1930s*. Garden City, N.Y.: Anchor, 1970.

Abbott, Wilbur. *The New Barbarians*. Boston: Little, Brown, 1925.

Adamic, Louis. *My America, 1928–1938*. 1938. New York: Da Capo Press, 1976.

Adams, James Truslow. *The Epic of America*. Boston: Little, Brown, 1931.

Adams, Michael C. C. *The Best War Ever: America and World War II*. Ed. Stanley I. Kutler. The American Moment. Baltimore: Johns Hopkins University Press, 1994.

Adler, Mortimer J. *How to Read a Book: The Art of Getting a Liberal Education*. New York: Simon and Schuster, 1940.

Agar, Herbert, and Allen Tate, eds. *Who Owns America? A New Declaration of Independence*. Boston: Houghton Mifflin, 1936. See esp. "Literature as Symptom," by Robert Penn Warren (264–79).

Aldridge, John W. *After the Lost Generation: A Critical Study of the Writers of Two Wars*. 1951. Freeport, N.Y.: Books for Libraries Press, 1971.

———. *In Search of Heresy: American Literature in an Age of Conformity*. New York: McGraw-Hill, 1956.

Alexander, Charles C. *Nationalism in American Thought, 1930–1945*. Ed. David D. Van Tassel. Rand McNally Series on the History of American Thought and Culture. Chicago: Rand McNally, 1969.

Allen, Frederick Lewis. *The Big Change: America Transforms Itself, 1900–1950*. 1952. New York: Harper and Row, 1988.

———. *Since Yesterday: The 1930s in America, September 3, 1929–September 3, 1939*. New York: Harper and Row, 1972 (reissued 1986).

American Writers' Congress. *The Writer in a Changing World*. Ed. Henry Hart. New York: Equinox Cooperative Press, 1937.

Ammons, Elizabeth. *Conflicting Stories: American Women Writers at the Turn into the Twentieth Century*. New York: Oxford University Press, 1991.

Antler, Joyce. *The Journey Home: Jewish Women and the American Century*. New York: Free Press, 1997.

———. *You Never Call, You Never Write! A History of the Jewish Mother*. New York: Oxford University Press, 2007.

Austenfeld, Thomas Carl. *American Women Writers and the Nazis: Ethics and Politics in Boyle, Porter, Stafford, and Hellman*. Charlottesville: University Press of Virginia, 2001.

Austin, Mary. *Beyond Borders: The Selected Essays of Mary Austin*. Ed. and intro. Reuben J. Ellis. Carbondale: Southern Illinois University Press, 1996.

Baltzell, E. Digby. *The Protestant Establishment Revisited*. New Brunswick, N.J.: Transaction Press, 1991.

Baritz, Loren. *The Good Life: The Meaning of Success for the American Middle Class*. New York: Knopf, 1989.

Baruch, Dorothy W., and Lee Edward Travis. *You're Out of the Service Now: The Veteran's Guide to Civilian Life*. New York: D. Appleton-Century, 1946.

Baughman, James L. *The Republic of Mass Culture: Journalism, Filmmaking, and Broadcasting in America since 1941*. Ed. Stanley I. Kutler. The American Moment. 2nd ed. Baltimore: Johns Hopkins University Press, 1997.

Baxandall, Rosalyn, and Elizabeth Ewen. *Picture Windows: How the Suburbs Happened*. New York: Basic Books, 2000.

Baym, Nina. *Woman's Fiction: A Guide to Novels by and about Women in America, 1820– 1870*. Ithaca, N.Y.: Cornell University Press, 1978.

Beach, Joseph Warren. *American Fiction 1920–1940*. 1941. New York: Macmillan, 1960. See esp. "Lay of the Land" (3–21) and "John P. Marquand: The Moonlight of Culture" (253–70).

———. *The Outlook for American Prose*. Chicago: University of Chicago Press, 1926.

Beard, Charles A., and Mary R. *America in Midpassage*. Vol. 2. New York: Macmillan, 1939.

Beard, Mary R., ed. *America through Women's Eyes*. New York: Macmillan, 1933.

Belgrad, Daniel. *The Culture of Spontaneity: Improvisation and the Arts in Postwar America*. Chicago: University of Chicago Press, 1998.

Bell, Millicent. *Marquand: An American Life*. Boston: Little, Brown, 1979.

Bendiner, Robert. *Just around the Corner: A Highly Selective History of the Thirties*. New York: Harper and Row, 1967.

Benét, Stephen Vincent, Erika Mann, McGeorge Bundy, William L. White, Garrett Underhill, and Walter Millis. *Zero Hour: A Summons to the Free*. New York: Farrar and Rinehart, 1940.

Berthoff, Warner. *A Literature without Qualities: The Decline of American Writing since 1945*. Berkeley: University of California Press, 1979.

Biel, Steven. *Independent Intellectuals in the United States, 1910–1945*. Ed. James

Kirby Martin. American Social Experience Series. New York: New York University Press, 1992.

Bird, Caroline. *The Invisible Scar*. New York: David McKay, 1966.

Birmingham, Stephen. *The Late John Marquand: A Biography*. Philadelphia: Lippincott, 1972.

Blackwell, Louise, and Frances Clay. *Lillian Smith*. New York: Twayne, 1971.

Blankenship, Russell. *American Literature as an Expression of the National Mind*. New York: Henry Holt, 1931.

Bledstein, Burton J., and Robert D. Johnston, eds. *The Middling Sort: Explorations in the History of the American Middle Class*. New York: Routledge, 2001.

Blum, John Morton. *V Was for Victory: Politics and American Culture during World War II*. New York: Harcourt, Brace, 1976.

Bolte, Charles G. *The New Veteran*. New York: Reynal and Hitchcock, 1945.

Botshon, Lisa, and Meredith Goldsmith, eds. *Middlebrow Moderns: Popular American Women Writers of the 1920s*. Boston: Northeastern University Press, 2003.

Bourdieu, Pierre. *Distinction: A Social Critique of the Judgement of Taste*. Trans. Richard Nice. Cambridge: Harvard University Press, 1984.

———. *The Field of Cultural Production: Essays on Art and Literature*. Ed. and intro. Randal Johnson. New York: Columbia University Press, 1993.

Bowman, James Cloyd, ed. *Contemporary American Criticism*. New York: Henry Holt, 1926.

Boyd, Ernest A. *Portraits: Real and Imaginary*. New York: George H. Doran Co., 1924.

Boyle, Kay. *Process: A Novel*. Ed. and intro. Sandra Spanier. Urbana: University of Illinois Press, 2001.

Boynton, Percy H. *America in Contemporary Fiction*. Chicago: University of Chicago Press, 1940.

———. *Literature and American Life: For Students of American Literature*. Boston: Ginn, 1936.

———. *More Contemporary Americans*. Chicago: University of Chicago Press, 1927.

———. *The Rediscovery of the Frontier*. Chicago: University of Chicago Press, 1931.

———. *Some Contemporary Americans*. Chicago: University of Chicago Press, 1924.

Bradbury, Malcolm. *The Modern American Novel*. Ed. Alan Ryan et al. OPUS series. Oxford: Oxford University Press, 1983.

Brier, Peter. *Howard Mumford Jones and the Dynamics of Liberal Humanism*. Columbia: University of Missouri Press, 1994.

Brodhead, Richard H. *Cultures of Letters: Scenes of Reading and Writing in Nineteenth-Century America*. Chicago: University of Chicago Press, 1993.

Brogan, Denis W. *The Era of Franklin D. Roosevelt: A Chronicle of the New Deal and Global War*. New Haven: Yale University Press, 1950.

Brooks, Cleanth, and Robert Penn Warren. *Understanding Fiction*. New York: F. S. Crofts, 1943.

Brooks, John. *The Great Leap: The Past Twenty-Five Years in America*. New York: Harper and Row, 1966.

——. *Showing Off in America: From Conspicuous Consumption to Parody Display*. Boston: Little, Brown, 1981.

Brooks, Van Wyck. *America's Coming-of-Age*. 1915. New York: Viking, 1930.

——. *On Literature Today*. New York: E. P. Dutton, 1941.

——. *Opinions of Oliver Allston*. New York: E. P. Dutton, 1941.

Brown, Earl, and George R. Leighton. *The Negro and the War*. New York: AMS Press, 1942.

Brown, Francis J., and Joseph Slabey Roucek, eds. *One America: The History, Contributions, and Present Problems of Our Racial and National Minorities*. 1945. Rev. ed. New York: Prentice Hall, 1946.

Brown, Ina Corinne. *Race Relations in a Democracy*. New York: Harper and Brothers, 1949.

Bryer, Jackson. *Fifteen Modern American Authors: A Survey of Research and Criticism*. Durham: Duke University Press, 1969.

Burlingame, Roger. *Of Making Many Books: A Hundred Years of Reading, Writing, and Publishing*. 1946. University Park: Pennsylvania State University Press, 1996.

Burnett, Whit, and Hallie Southgate Burnett. *Story: The Fiction of the Forties*. New York: E. P. Dutton, 1941.

Burnham, James, ed. *What Europe Thinks of America*. New York: John Day, 1953.

Burt, Struthers. *Escape From America*. New York: Scribner's, 1936.

Cahan, Abraham. *The Rise of David Levinsky*. 1918. New York: Harper, 1964.

Calverton, V. F. *The Liberation of American Literature*. New York: Scribner's, 1932.

——. *Sex Expression in Literature*. New York: Boni and Liveright, 1926.

Canaday, John. *The Nuclear Muse: Literature, Physics, and the First Atomic Bombs*. Madison: University of Wisconsin Press, 2000.

Canby, Henry Seidel. *American Estimates*. New York: Harcourt, Brace, 1929.

——. *American Memoir*. Boston: Houghton Mifflin, 1947.

——. *Definitions: Essays in Contemporary Criticism*. 2nd ser. New York: Harcourt, Brace, 1924.

——. *Education by Violence: Essays on the War and the Future*. New York: Macmillan, 1919.

——. *Everyday Americans*. New York: Century, 1920.

——. *Seven Years' Harvest: Notes on Contemporary Literature*. New York: Farrar and Rinehart, 1936.

Canby, Henry Seidel, Amy Loveman, William Rose Benét, Christopher Morley, and May Lamberton Becker. *Designed for Reading: An Anthology Drawn from* The Saturday Review of Literature, *1924–1934*. New York: Macmillan, 1934.

Cargill, Oscar. *Intellectual America: Ideas on the March*. 1941. New York: Macmillan, 1948.

Carnegie, Dale. *How to Win Friends and Influence People*. New York: Simon and Schuster, 1936.

Casdorph, Paul D. *Let the Good Times Roll: Life at Home in America during World War II*. New York: Paragon House, 1989.

Castronovo, David. *Beyond the Gray Flannel Suit: Books from the 1950s That Made American Culture*. New York: Continuum, 2004.

Cawelti, John. *Adventure, Mystery, and Romance: Formula Stories as Art and Popular Culture*. Chicago: University of Chicago Press, 1976.

Charvat, William. *The Origins of American Critical Thought, 1810–1835*. 1936. New York: Russell and Russell, 1968.

Cleaton, Irene, and Allen Cleaton. *Books and Battles: American Literature, 1920–1930*. Boston: Houghton Mifflin, 1937.

Cohn, David L. *Love in America: An Informal Study of Manners and Morals in American Marriage*. New York: Simon and Schuster, 1943.

Coiner, Constance. *Better Red: The Writing and Resistance of Tillie Olsen and Meridel Le Sueur*. Champaign: University of Illinois Press, 1998.

Cooke, Alistair. *America Observed: From the 1940s to the 1980s*. Comp. Ronald A. Wells. New York: Knopf, 1988.

Cooney, Terry A. *Balancing Acts: American Thought and Culture in the 1930s*. Ed. Lewis Perry. Twayne's American Thought and Culture Series. New York: Twayne, 1995.

Cowley, Malcolm, ed. *After the Genteel Tradition: American Writers since 1910*. 1937. New York: Norton, 1964.

———. *Exile's Return: A Literary Odyssey of the 1920s*. 1934. New York: Viking, 1956.

———. *The Literary Situation*. 1947. New York: Viking, 1954.

———. *Think Back on Us . . . : A Contemporary Chronicle of the 1930's by Malcolm Cowley*. Ed. Henry Dan Piper. Carbondale: Southern Illinois University Press, 1967.

Cox, Stephen. *The Woman and the Dynamo: Isabel Paterson and the Idea of America*. New Brunswick, N.J.: Transaction Press, 2004.

Crane, Milton, ed. *The Roosevelt Era*. New York: Boni and Gaer, 1947.

"Creative Art in Fiction." *Outlook*, 24 August 1921, 658.

Crowley, John W. *The Dean of American Letters: The Late Career of William Dean Howells*. Amherst: University of Massachusetts Press, 1999.

Currell, Susan. *The March of Spare Time: The Problem and Promise of Leisure in the Great Depression*. Philadelphia: University of Pennsylvania Press, 2005.

Dabney, Lewis. *Edmund Wilson: A Life in Literature*. New York: Farrar, Straus, and Giroux, 2005.

Davidson, Donald. *The Attack on Leviathan: Regionalism and Nationalism in the United States*. 1938. Gloucester: Peter Smith, 1962.

Degler, Carl N. *Out of Our Past: The Forces That Shaped Modern America*. 1959. Rev. ed. New York: Harper and Row, 1970.

De Mille, George E. *Literary Criticism in America: A Preliminary Survey*. 1931. New York: Russell and Russell, 1967.

Denning, Michael. *The Cultural Front: The Laboring of American Culture in the Twentieth Century*. New York: Verso, 1996.

DeVoto, Bernard. *The Literary Fallacy*. Boston: Little, Brown, 1944.

———. *The World of Fiction*. Boston: Houghton Mifflin, 1950. See esp. "Alice's Adventures in Utopia" (47–68).

Dickstein, Morris. *Leopards in the Temple: The Transformation of American Fiction, 1945–1970.* Cambridge: Harvard University Press, 2002.

Diggins, John Patrick. *The Proud Decades: America in War and in Peace, 1941–1960.* New York: Norton, 1989.

Doren, Carl Van. *The American Novel, 1789–1939.* 1940. New York: Macmillan, 1946.

Dorman, Robert L. *Revolt of the Provinces: The Regionalist Movement in America, 1920–1945.* Chapel Hill: University of North Carolina Press, 1993.

Drake, St. Clair, and Horace R. Cayton. *Black Metropolis: A Study of Negro Life in a Northern City.* Intro. Richard Wright. New York: Harcourt, Brace, 1945.

Drake, William A., ed. *American Criticism, 1926.* New York: Harcourt, Brace, 1926.

Drew, Elizabeth A. *The Modern Novel: Some Aspects of Contemporary Fiction.* New York: Harcourt, Brace, 1926. See esp. "Sex Simplexes and Complexes" (53–73) and "The American Scene" (135–52).

Duany, Andres, Elizabeth Plater-Zyberk, and Jeff Speck. *Suburban Nation: The Rise of Sprawl and the Decline of the American Dream.* New York: North Point Press, 2000.

Duffus, R. L. *Books: Their Place in Democracy.* Boston: Houghton Mifflin, 1930.

———. *Democracy Enters College: A Study of the Rise and Decline of the Academic Lockstep.* New York: Scribner's, 1936.

Eastman, Max. *The Literary Mind: Its Place in an Age of Science.* New York: Scribner's, 1935.

Edwards, Brian. *Literature and National Cultures.* Geelong, Victoria: Deakin University, 1988.

Ehrenreich, Barbara. *Fear of Falling: The Inner Life of the Middle Class.* New York: Pantheon, 1989.

———. *The Hearts of Men: American Dreams and the Flight from Commitment.* Garden City: Anchor Press/Doubleday, 1983.

Eisinger, Chester E. *Fiction of the Forties.* Chicago: University of Chicago Press, 1963.

Elias, Robert H. *"Entangling Alliances with None": An Essay on the Individual in the American Twenties.* New York: Norton, 1973.

Embree, Edwin R. *American Negroes: A Handbook.* New York: John Day, 1942.

England, Robert. *Twenty Million World War Veterans.* London: Oxford University Press, 1950.

Erhardt, Julia. *Writers of Conviction: The Personal Politics of Zona Gale, Dorothy Canfield Fisher, Rose Wilder Lane, and Josephine Herbst.* Columbia: University of Missouri Press, 2004.

Exman, Eugene. *The House of Harper: One Hundred and Fifty Years of Publishing.* New York: Harper and Row, 1967.

Fadiman, Clifton P. *Any Number Can Play.* Cleveland: World Publishing, 1957.

Fairchild, Henry Pratt. *Race and Nationality as Factors in American Life.* New York: Ronald Press, 1947.

Farrar, John. *The Literary Spotlight.* New York: George H. Doran, 1924. See esp. "Joseph Hergesheimer" (287–94).

Ferraro, Thomas. *Ethnic Passages: Literary Immigrants in Twentieth-Century America.* Chicago: University of Chicago Press, 1993.

Fiedler, Leslie A. *An End to Innocence: Essays on Culture and Politics.* 1948. Boston: Beacon Press, 1955.

Francis, Elizabeth. *The Secret Treachery of Words: Feminism and Modernism in America.* Minneapolis: University of Minnesota Press, 2002.

Frank, Waldo. *The Re-discovery of America: An Introduction to a Philosophy of American Life.* New York: Scribner's, 1929.

Franklin, Jay. *1940.* New York: Viking, 1940.

French, Warren. *The Social Novel at the End of an Era.* Preface by Harry T. Moore. Carbondale: Southern Illinois University Press, 1966.

Friedan, Betty. *The Feminine Mystique.* New York: Dell, 1963.

Fussell, Paul. *Class: A Guide through the American Status System.* Illustrated by Martin de Avillez. New York: Touchstone, 1983.

———. *Wartime: Understanding and Behavior in the Second World War.* New York: Oxford University Press, 1989.

Gabler, Neal. *An Empire of Their Own: How the Jews Invented Hollywood.* New York: Crown, 1988.

Gans, Herbert J. *Popular Culture and High Culture: An Analysis and Evaluation of Taste.* New York: Basic Books, 1974.

Gebler, Ernest. *The Plymouth Adventure: A Chronicle Novel of the Voyage of the Mayflower.* Garden City, N.Y.: Doubleday, 1950.

Geismar, Maxwell. *American Moderns: From Rebellion to Conformity.* New York: Hill and Wang, 1958.

Gerould, Katharine Fullerton. *Modes and Morals.* New York: Scribner's, 1920.

———. *Ringside Seats.* New York: Dodd, Mead, 1937.

Gilbert, James B. *Writers and Partisans: A History of Literary Radicalism in America.* New York: Wiley, 1968.

Glazener, Nancy. *Reading for Realism: The History of a U.S. Literary Institution, 1850–1910.* Durham: Duke University Press, 1997.

Glicksberg, Charles I. *American Literary Criticism, 1900–1950.* New York: Hendricks House, 1952.

Goldsmith, Arnold L. *American Literary Criticism, 1905–1965.* Vol. 3. Boston: Twayne, 1979.

Gordon, Albert I. *Jews in Suburbia.* Boston: Beacon Hill, 1959.

Gordon, Richard E., Katherine K. Gordon, and Max Gunther. *The Split-Level Trap.* New York: B. Geis Associates, 1961.

Gorman, Paul R. *Left Intellectuals and Popular Culture in Twentieth-Century America.* Chapel Hill: University of North Carolina Press, 1996.

Goulden, Joseph C. *The Best Years: 1945–1950.* New York: Atheneum, 1976.

Graebner, William. *The Age of Doubt: American Thought and Culture in the 1940s.* Boston: Twayne, 1991.

Grattan, C. Hartley, ed. *The Critique of Humanism: A Symposium*. New York: Brewer and Warren, 1930. See esp. "Drift and Mastery in Our Novelists," by John Chamberlain (257–80).

Greene, Suzanne Ellery. *Books for Pleasure: Popular Fiction, 1914–1945*. Bowling Green, Ky.: Bowling Green University Popular Press, 1974.

Gregory, Ross. *America, 1941: A Nation at the Crossroads*. New York: Free Press, 1989.

Gross, John J. *John P. Marquand*. New York: Twayne, 1963.

Gurko, Leo. *The Angry Decade*. New York: Dodd, Mead, 1947. See esp. "Last Echoes of America First" (260–83).

Haar, Charles M. *Suburbs under Siege: Race, Space, and Audacious Judges*. Princeton: Princeton University Press, 1996.

Hackett, Alice Payne. *70 Years of Bestsellers, 1895–1965*. New York: R. R. Bowker, 1967.

Hackett, Francis, ed. *On American Books*. New York: B. W. Huebsch, 1920. See esp. "The Literary Capital of the United States," by H. L. Mencken (31–38), and "The Recent American Novel," by Francis Hackett (52–59).

Haines, Helen E. *What's in a Novel*. New York: Columbia University Press, 1942. See esp. "The World We Live In" (83–103) and "History in Fiction" (105–32).

Halberstam, David. *The Fifties*. New York: Villard, 1993.

Haldeman-Julius, Emanuel. *The Big American Parade*. Boston: Stratford, 1929.

Halsey, Margaret. *The Folks at Home*. New York: Simon and Schuster, 1952.

——. *With Malice toward Some*. New York: Simon and Schuster, 1938.

Hamburger, Philip. *J. P. Marquand, Esquire: A Portrait in the Form of a Novel*. Boston: Houghton Mifflin, 1952.

Handlin, Oscar. *Race and Nationality in American Life*. Boston: Little, Brown, 1957.

Harker, Jamie. *America the Middlebrow*. Amherst: University of Massachusetts Press, 2007.

Hart, Henry, ed. *The Writer in a Changing World*. New York: Equinox Cooperative Press, 1937.

Hart, James. *The Popular Book: A History of America's Literary Taste*. New York: Oxford University Press, 1950.

Hassan, Ihab. *Radical Innocence: Studies in the Contemporary American Novel*. 1961. New York: Harper and Row, 1966.

Hatcher, Harlan. *Creating the Modern American Novel*. New York: Farrar and Rinehart, 1935.

Hazlett, John Downtown. *My Generation: Collective Autobiography and Identity Politics*. Ed. William L. Andrews. Wisconsin Studies in American Autobiography. Madison: University of Wisconsin Press, 1998.

Hegeman, Susan. *Patterns for America: Modernism and the Concept of Culture*. Princeton: Princeton University Press, 1999.

Hicks, Granville. *The Great Tradition: An Interpretation of American Literature since the Civil War*. 1933. New York: Biblo and Tannen, 1967.

——. *I Like America*. New York: Modern Age Books, 1938.

——. *The Living Novel: A Symposium*. New York: Macmillan, 1957.

Hicks, Granville, Michael Gold, Isidor Schneider, Joseph North, Paul Peters, and Alan
  Calmer, eds. *Proletarian Literature in the United States: An Anthology*. Critical intro.
  Joseph Freeman. New York: International Publishers, 1935.

Hilfer, Tony [Anthony Channell]. *American Fiction since 1940*. New York: Longman, 1992.

———. *The Revolt from the Village, 1915–1930*. Chapel Hill: University of North Carolina
  Press, 1969.

Hoberek, Andrew. *The Twilight of the Middle Class: Post–World War II American Fiction
  and White-Collar Work*. Princeton: Princeton University Press, 2005.

Hobson, Laura Z. *Gentleman's Agreement*. New York: Simon and Schuster, 1947.

Hoehling, A. A. *Home Front, U.S.A.* New York: Thomas Y. Crowell, 1966.

Hoffman, Frederick J. *The Modern Novel in America*. 1951. Chicago: Gateway, 1956.

Horowitz, Daniel. *The Anxieties of Affluence: Critiques of American Consumer Culture,
  1939–1979*. Amherst: University of Massachusetts Press, 2004.

Hughes, Carl Milton. *The Negro Novelist: A Discussion of the Writings of American Negro
  Novelists, 1940–1950*. New intro. Arthur Ashe. New York: Carol Publishing Group,
  1990.

Hull, Helen R., and Michael Drury, eds. *Writer's Roundtable*. New York: Harper, 1959.

Humble, Nicola. *The Feminine Middlebrow Novel, 1920s to 1950s: Class, Domesticity, and
  Bohemianism*. Oxford: Oxford University Press, 2001.

Irr, Caren. *The Suburb of Dissent: Cultural Politics in the United States and Canada during
  the 1930s*. Durham: Duke University Press, 1998.

James, Henry. *Art of the Novel*. New York: Scribner's, 1934.

Jarrett, Gene Andrew. *Deans and Truants: Race and Realism in African American
  Literature*. Philadelphia: University of Pennsylvania Press, 2007.

Joad, C. E. M. *The Babbit Warren*. New York: Harper and Brothers, 1927.

Johnson, Charles S., and Associates. *To Stem This Tide: A Survey of Racial Tension Areas in
  the United States*. Boston: Pilgrim, 1943.

Jones, Howard Mumford. *The Theory of American Literature*. 1948. Reissued with a New
  Concluding Chapter and Revised Bibliography. Ithaca, N.Y.: Cornell University Press,
  1966.

Jumonville, Neil. *Critical Crossings: The New York Intellectuals in Postwar America*.
  Berkeley: University of California Press, 1991.

Jurca, Catherine. *White Diaspora: The Suburb and the Twentieth-Century American Novel*.
  Princeton: Princeton University Press, 2001.

Kaestle, Carl F., Helen Damon-More, Lawrence C. Stedman, Katherine Tinsley, and
  William Vance Trollinger Jr. *Literacy in the United States: Readers and Readings since
  1880*. New Haven: Yale University Press, 1991.

Kammen, Michael. *American Culture, American Tastes: Social Change and the 20th
  Century*. New York: Knopf, 1999.

Karem, Jeffrey. *The Romance of Authenticity: The Cultural Politics of Regional and Ethnic
  Literatures*. Charlottesville: University Press of Virginia, 2004.

Kazin, Alfred. *The Bright Book of Life: American Novelists and Storytellers from Hemingway
  to Mailer*. Boston: Little, Brown, 1973.

——. *On Native Grounds: An Interpretation of Modern American Prose Literature*. New York: Reynal and Hitchcock, 1942.

Keating, W. Dennis. *The Suburban Racial Dilemma: Housing and Neighborhoods*. Philadelphia: Temple University Press, 1994.

Kennedy, David M. *Freedom from Fear: The American People in Depression and War, 1929–1945*. New York: Oxford University Press, 1999.

Kohn, Hans. *Readings in American Nationalism*. New York: Van Nostrand Reinhold, 1970.

Kryder, Daniel. *Divided Arsenal: Race and the American State during World War II*. Cambridge: Cambridge University Press, 2000.

Kunitz, Stanley, ed. *Authors Today and Yesterday*. New York: H. W. Wilson, 1933.

Kunitz, Stanley, and Howard Haycraft, eds. *Twentieth-Century Authors: A Biographical Dictionary of Modern Literature*. New York: H. W. Wilson, 1942.

Kunitz, Stanley, and Vineta Colby, eds. *Twentieth-Century Authors, First Supplement: A Biographical Dictionary of Modern Literature*. New York: H. W. Wilson, 1955.

Lawrence, Margaret. *The School of Femininity: A Book for and about Women as They Are Interpreted through Feminine Writers of Yesterday and Today*. New York: Frederick A. Stokes, 1936.

Lawson, R. Alan. *The Failure of Independent Liberalism, 1930–1941*. New York: Putnam, 1971.

Lee, Alfred McClung, and Norman Daymond Humphrey. *Race Riot*. New York: Dryden Press, 1943.

Levenson, Leah, and Jerry Natterstad. *Granville Hicks: The Intellectual in Mass Society*. Eds. Susan Porter Benson, Stephen Brier, and Roy Rosenzweig. Critical Perspectives on the Past. Philadelphia: Temple University Press, 1993.

Levine, Lawrence W. *The Unpredictable Past: Explorations in American Cultural History*. New York: Oxford University Press, 1993. See esp. "American Culture and the Great Depression" (206–30).

Lewisohn, Ludwig. *Expression in America*. New York: Harper and Brothers, 1932.

Lingeman, Richard R. *Don't You Know There's a War On? The American Home Front, 1941–1945*. New York: Putnam, 1970.

Literary Prizes and Their Winners. New York: R. R. Bowker, 1946.

Logan, Rayford W., ed. *What the Negro Wants*. Chapel Hill: University of North Carolina Press, 1944.

Logan, Spencer. *A Negro's Faith in America*. New York: Macmillan, 1946.

Loggins, Vernon. *I Hear America: Literature in the United States since 1900*. New York: Thomas Y. Crowell, 1937.

Long, Elizabeth. *American Dream and the Popular Novel*. Boston: Routledge, 1985.

Loveland, Anne. *Lillian Smith: A Southerner Confronting the South*. Baton Rouge: Louisiana State University Press, 1986.

Lovett, Robert Morss. *Edith Wharton*. New York: Robert McBride and Co., 1925.

Lowenthal, Leo. *Literature, Popular Culture, and Society*. Palo Alto: Pacific Books, 1961.

Luccock, Halford E. *American Mirror: Social, Ethical, and Religious Aspects of American Literature, 1930–1940*. New York: Macmillan, 1941.

Lukacs, John. *A New Republic: A History of the United States in the Twentieth Century*. New Haven: Yale University Press, 2004. Rpt. of *Outgrowing Democracy*. 1984.

Lutz, Thomas. *Cosmopolitan Vistas: American Regionalism and Literary Value*. Ithaca, N.Y.: Cornell University Press, 2004.

Lynd, Robert S., and Helen Merrell Lynd. *Middletown in Transition: A Study in Cultural Conflicts*. New York: Harcourt, Brace, 1937.

Lynn, Kenneth. *The Dream of Success: A Study of the Modern American Imagination*. Boston: Little, Brown, 1955.

Macy, John, ed. *American Writers on American Literature*. 1931. New York: Tudor, 1934. See esp. "Negro Literature," by Walter White (442–51), and "Contemporary Fiction," by Llewellyn Jones (487–502).

Manganaro, Marc. *Culture, 1922 and After: Conversations in Anthropology and Literary Study*. Princeton: Princeton University Press, 2002.

Maritain, Jacques. *Reflections on America*. New York: Scribner's, 1958.

Masotti, Louis H., comp. *Suburbia in Transition*. Ed. and intro. Masotti and Jeffrey K. Hadden. New York: Franklin Watts, 1974.

Matthiessen, F. O. *From the Heart of Europe*. New York: Oxford University Press, 1948.

Maurois, André. *From My Journal*. Trans. Joan Charles. New York: Harper and Brothers, 1948.

McCole, C. John. *Lucifer at Large*. 1937. Essay Index Reprint Series. Freeport, N.Y.: Books for Libraries, 1968.

McElvaine, Robert S., ed. *Down and Out in the Great Depression: Letters from the "Forgotten Man."* Chapel Hill: University of North Carolina Press, 1983.

———. *The Great Depression: America, 1929–1941*. New York: Times Books, 1984.

McWilliams, Carey. *Brothers under the Skin*. 1942. Rev. ed. Boston: Little, Brown, 1964.

———. *The New Regionalism in American Literature*. Ed. Glen Hughes. University of Washington Chapbooks (No. 46). Seattle: University of Washington Book Store, 1930.

Medovoi, Leerom. *Rebels: Youth and the Cold War Origins of Identity*. Ed. Donald E. Pease. New Americanists. Durham: Duke University Press, 2005.

Michaud, Régis. *The American Novel To-Day: A Social and Psychological Study*. Boston: Little, Brown, 1928.

Michaels, Walter Benn. *Our America: Nativism, Modernism, and Pluralism*. Durham: Duke University Press, 1995.

Millgate, Michael. *American Social Fiction: James to Cozzens*. 1964. New York: Barnes and Noble, 1967.

Minter, David. *A Cultural History of the American Novel: Henry James to William Faulkner*. Cambridge: Cambridge University Press, 1994.

Morris, Lloyd. *Postscript to Yesterday, America: The Last Fifty Years*. New York: Random House, 1947.

Moskowitz, Marina. *Standard of Living: The Measure of the Middle Class in Modern America*. Baltimore: Johns Hopkins University Press, 2004.

Moton, Robert Russa. *What the Negro Thinks*. Garden City: Doubleday, Doran, 1929.

Munson, Gorham. *The Awakening Twenties: A Memoir-History of a Literary Period.* Baton Rouge: Louisiana State University Press, 1985.

Myrdal, Gunnar, with the assistance of Richard Sterner and Arnold Rose. *An American Dilemma: The Negro Problem and Modern Democracy.* 1944. Twentieth Anniversary Edition. New York: Harper and Row, 1962.

Nash, Roderick. *The Nervous Generation: American Thought, 1917–1930.* Chicago: Rand McNally, 1970.

Nelson, Raymond. *Van Wyck Brooks: A Writer's Life.* New York: E. P. Dutton, 1981.

Norris, Frank. *The Responsibilities of the Novelist and Other Literary Essays.* New York: Doubleday, Page, 1903.

North, Michael. *Reading 1922: A Return to the Scene of the Modern.* New York: Oxford University Press, 1999.

Nye, Russel. *The Unembarrassed Muse: The Popular Arts in America.* New York: Dial, 1970.

Oliver, J. Eric. *Democracy in Suburbia.* Princeton: Princeton University Press, 2001.

O'Neill, William L. *A Democracy at War: America's Fight at Home and Abroad in World War II.* Cambridge: Harvard University Press, 1993.

Oppenheim, James. *American Types: A Preface to Analytic Psychology.* New York: Knopf, 1931.

Ortner, Sherry. *New Jersey Dreaming: Capital, Culture, and the Class of 1958.* Durham: Duke University Press, 2003.

Ottley, Roi. *"New World A-Coming": Inside Black America.* Boston: Houghton Mifflin, 1943.

Oxford Companion to Women's Writing in the United States. Ed. Cathy N. Davidson and Linda Wagner-Martin. New York: Oxford University Press, 1995.

Page, Kirby, ed. *Recent Gains in American Civilization.* New York: Harcourt, Brace, 1928. See esp. "American Literature Moves On," by Mary Austin (183–203), and "A Critique of American Civilization," by John Dewey (253–275).

Pattee, Fred Lewis. *The New American Literature, 1890–1930.* New York: Century, 1930.

Patterson, James T. *Grand Expectations: The United States, 1945–1974.* Ed. C. Vann Woodward. Oxford History of the United States. New York: Oxford University Press, 1996.

Pells, Richard H. *The Liberal Mind in a Conservative Age: American Intellectuals in the 1940s and 1950s.* New York: Harper and Row, 1985.

——. *Radical Visions and American Dreams: Culture and Social Thought in the Depression Years.* 1973. Urbana: University of Illinois Press, 1998.

Perry, Keith. *The Kingfish in Fiction: Huey P. Long and the Modern American Novel.* Baton Rouge: Louisiana State University Press, 2004.

Perry, Ralph Barton. *Characteristically American: Five Lectures Delivered on the William W. Cook Foundation at the University of Michigan, November–December 1948.* New York: Knopf, 1949.

Peterson, Theodore. *Magazines in the Twentieth Century.* 1956. Urbana: University of Illinois Press, 1958.

Phillips, Cabell. *The New York Times Chronicle of American Life: From the Crash to the Blitz, 1929–1939*. New York: Macmillan, 1969.

Podhoretz, Norman. *Doings and Undoings: The Fifties and After in American Writing*. New York: Noonday Press, 1964.

Polenberg, Richard. *One Nation Divisible: Class, Race, and Ethnicity in the United States since 1938*. New York: Viking, 1980.

Posnock, Ross. *Trial of Curiosity: Henry James, William James, and the Challenge of Modernity*. New York: Oxford University Press, 1991.

Quinn, Arthur Hobson. *American Fiction: An Historical and Critical Survey*. 1936. Students' Edition. New York: Appleton-Century-Crofts, 1964.

Rabinowitz, Paula. *Labor and Desire: Women's Revolutionary Fiction in Depression America*. Chapel Hill: University of North Carolina Press, 1991.

Radway, Janice A. *A Feeling for Books: The Book-of-the-Month Club, Literary Taste, and Middle-Class Desire*. Chapel Hill: University of North Carolina Press, 1997.

Rapson, Richard L., ed. and intro. *The Cult of Youth in Middle-Class America*. Lexington, Mass.: D. C. Heath, 1971.

Rideout, Walter B. *The Radical Novel in the United States, 1900–1954: Some Interrelations of Literature and Society*. Cambridge: Harvard University Press, 1956.

Riesman, David, Nathan Glazer, and Reuel Denney. *The Lonely Crowd: A Study of the Changing American Character*. 1950. Abridged by the authors. Garden City, N.Y.: Doubleday, 1953.

Roberts, Cecil. *And So to America*. Garden City, N.Y.: Doubleday, 1947.

Roberts, Kenneth. *Oliver Wiswell*. New York: Doubleday, Doran, 1940.

Robertson, James Oliver. *American Myth, American Reality*. New York: Hill and Wang, 1980.

Rose, Arnold, and Caroline Rose. *America Divided: Minority Group Relations in the United States*. New York: Knopf, 1948.

Rosenberg, Bernard, and David Manning White, eds. *Mass Culture: The Popular Arts in America*. Glencoe, Ill.: Free Press, 1957. See esp. "Is There a Best Seller Formula?," by Frank Luther Mott (113–18); "Who Reads What Books and Why?," by Bernard Berelson (119–25); "The Book Business in America," by Alan Dutscher (126–40); "The Problem of the Paper-Backs," by Cecil Hemley (141–46); "Majority and Minority Americans: An Analysis of Magazine Fiction," by Bernard Berelson and Patricia J. Salter (235–56); and "The Middle against Both Ends," by Leslie A. Fielder (537–47).

Ross, Andrew. *No Respect: Intellectuals and Popular Culture*. New York: Routledge, 1989.

Ross, Ishbel. *Taste in America: An Illustrated History of the Evolution of Architecture, Furnishings, Fashions, and Customs of the American People*. New York: Crowell, 1967.

Ross, W. Robert. *So It Was True! The American Protestant Press and the Nazi Persecution of the Jews*. Minneapolis: University of Minnesota Press, 1980.

Rubin, Joan Shelley. *The Making of Middlebrow Culture*. Chapel Hill: University of North Carolina Press, 1992.

Ruland, Richard. *The Rediscovery of American Literature: Premises of Critical Taste, 1900–1940*. Cambridge: Harvard University Press, 1967.

Salzman, Jack. *Albert Maltz*. Twayne's U.S. Authors Series (No. 311). Boston: Twayne, 1978.

——, ed. *The Survival Years: A Collection of American Writings of the 1940's*. New York: Pegasus, 1969. See esp. "The Irresponsibles: A Declaration," by Archibald MacLeish (173–84); "Primary Literature and Coterie-Literature," by Van Wyck Brooks (185–203); and "Kulturbolschevismus Is Here," by Dwight MacDonald (204–12).

Satterfield, Jay. *The World's Best Books: Taste, Culture, and the Modern Library*. Ed. Roger Chartier et al. Studies in Print Culture and the History of the Book. Amherst: University of Massachusetts Press, 2002.

Schaub, Thomas Hill. *American Fiction in the Cold War*. Ed. Paul S. Boyer. History of American Thought and Culture. Madison: University of Wisconsin Press, 1991.

Schermerhorn, R. A. *These Our People: Minorities in American Culture*. Ed. Howard Becker. Heath's Social Relations Series. Boston: D. C. Heath, 1949.

Schlesinger, Arthur M., Sr. *Learning How to Behave: A Historical Study of American Etiquette Books*. New York: Macmillan, 1947.

Schocket, Eric. *Vanishing Moments: Class and American Literature*. Ann Arbor: University of Michigan Press, 2006.

Schrag, Peter. *The Decline of the Wasp*. New York: Simon and Schuster, 1971.

Schrieke, B. *Alien Americans: A Study of Race Relations*. New York: Viking, 1936.

Schwartz, Larry. *Creating Faulkner's Reputation: The Politics of Modern Literary Criticism*. Knoxville: University of Tennessee Press, 1988.

Seaton, James. *Cultural Conservatism, Political Liberalism: From Criticism to Cultural Studies*. Ann Arbor: University of Michigan Press, 1996.

Seguin, Robert. *Around Quitting Time: Work and Middle-Class Fantasy in American Fiction*. Ed. Donald E. Pease. New Americanists. Durham: Duke University Press, 2001.

Seldes, Gilbert. *The Great Audience*. New York: Viking, 1951.

Sellers, Charles Coleman. *Benedict Arnold: The Proud Warrior*. New York: Minton Balch and Co., 1930.

Severo, Richard, and Lewis Milford. *The Wages of War: When America's Soldiers Came Home—From Valley Forge to Vietnam*. New York: Simon and Schuster, 1989.

Shannon, Christopher. *Conspicuous Criticism: Tradition, the Individual, and Culture in American Social Thought, from Veblen to Mills*. Ed. Thomas Bender. New Studies in American Intellectual and Cultural History. Baltimore: Johns Hopkins University Press, 1996.

Sherman, Stuart P. *Americans*. New York: Scribner's, 1924. See esp. "Mr. Mencken, the Jeune Fille, and the New Spirit in Letters" (1–12).

——. *The Emotional Discovery of America and Other Essays*. New York: Farrar and Rinehart, 1932. See esp. "Speaking to Successful Executives and Business Men Only on the Literary Profession" (115–31).

——. *The Genius of America: Studies in Behalf of the Younger Generation*. New York: Scribner's, 1924. See esp. "The Superior Class" (127–43).

Shumway, David. *Creating American Civilization: A Genealogy of American Literature as an Academic Discipline*. Minneapolis: University of Minnesota Press, 1994.

Simpson, Lewis P. *Imagining Our Time: Recollections and Reflections on American Writing.* Baton Rouge: Louisiana State University Press, 2007.

Sklar, Robert, ed., intro., and notes. *The Plastic Age, 1917–1930.* New York: G. Braziller, 1970.

Smith, Bernard. *Forces in American Criticism: A Study in the History of American Literary Thought.* New York: Harcourt, Brace, 1939.

Sosna, Morton. *In Search of the Silent South: Southern Liberals and the Race Issue.* New York: Columbia University Press, 1977.

Soto, Michael. *The Modernist Nation: Generation, Renaissance, and Twentieth-Century American Literature.* Tuscaloosa: University of Alabama Press, 2004.

Spingarn, Joel Elias. *Creative Criticism and Other Essays.* 1917. New, enlarged ed. Port Washington, N.Y.: Kennikat Press, 1964.

Stearns, Harold, ed. *America Now: An Inquiry into the Civilization of the United States.* New York: Scribner's, 1938. See esp. "Literature," by John Chamberlain (36–47).

Stevens, George, and Stanley Unwin. *Best-Sellers: Are They Born or Made? ("Lincoln's Doctor's Dog").* London: George Allen and Unwin, 1939.

Stonely, Peter, and Cindy Weinstein. *A Concise Companion to American Fiction, 1900–1950.* Oxford: Blackwell, 2007.

Stott, William. *Documentary Expression and Thirties America.* New York: Oxford University Press, 1973.

Strasser, Susan. *Satisfaction Guaranteed: The Making of the American Mass Market.* New York: Pantheon, 1989.

Strunsky, Simeon. *The Living Tradition: Change and America.* New York: Doubleday, Doran, 1939.

Stuart, Jesse. *Hie to the Hunters.* New York: Whittlesey House, 1950.

Stuckey, William J. *The Pulitzer Prize Novels: A Critical Backward Look.* Norman: University of Oklahoma Press, 1966.

Sumner, Gregory D. *Dwight Macdonald and the Politics Circle: The Challenge of Cosmopolitan Democracy.* Ithaca, N.Y.: Cornell University Press, 1996.

Sundquist, Eric J. *Faulkner: The House Divided.* Baltimore: Johns Hopkins University Press, 1983.

Susman, Warren I., ed., intro., notes. *Culture and Commitment: 1929–1945.* New York: George Braziller, 1973.

——. *Culture as History: The Transformation of American Society in the Twentieth Century.* New York: Pantheon Books, 1984.

Szalay, Michael. *New Deal Modernism: American Literature and the Invention of the Welfare State.* Ed. Stanley Fish and Fredrick Jameson. Post-Contemporary Interventions. Durham: Duke University Press, 2000.

Tarkington, Booth. *Alice Adams.* Garden City, N.Y.: Doubleday, Page, 1921.

Taylor, Lloyd C., Jr. *Margaret Ayer Barnes.* New York: Twayne, 1974.

Tebbel, John. *The American Magazine: A Compact History.* New York: Hawthorn Books, 1969.

——. *Between Covers: The Rise and Transformation of Book Publishing in America*. New York: Oxford University Press, 1987.

——. *A History of Book Publishing in the United States*. Vol. 3: *The Golden Age between Two Wars, 1920–1940*. New York: R. R. Bowker, 1978.

——. *A History of Book Publishing in the United States*. Vol. 4: *The Great Change, 1940–1980*. New York: R. R. Bowker, 1981.

Thompson, Graham. *The Business of America: The Cultural Production of a Post-War Nation*. London: Pluto Press, 2004.

Thorp, Willard. *American Writing in the Twentieth Century*. Cambridge: Harvard University Press, 1960. See esp. "Caste and Class in the Novel, 1920–1950" (110–42).

Tompkins, Jane P. *Sensational Designs: The Cultural Work of American Fiction*. New York: Oxford University Press, 1985.

Trilling, Diana. *Reviewing the Forties*. New York: Harcourt Brace Jovanovich, 1978.

Trilling, Lionel. *A Gathering of Fugitives*. Boston: Beacon Press, 1956.

——. *Speaking of Literature and Society*. Ed. Diana Trilling. The Works of Lionel Trilling Series. New York: Harcourt Brace Jovanovich, 1980.

Trimmer, Joseph. *The N.B.A. for Fiction: An Index of the First 25 Years*. Boston: Hall, 1978.

Turner, Catherine. *Marketing Modernism between the Two World Wars*. Amherst: University of Massachusetts Press, 2003.

Twelve American Novelists. *The Novel of Tomorrow and the Scope of Fiction*. Indianapolis: Bobbs-Merrill, 1922.

Twelve Southerners. *I'll Take My Stand: The South and the Agrarian Tradition*. 1929. New York: Peter Smith, 1951.

Tyler, Parker. *The Hollywood Hallucination*. 1944. New York: Creative Age Press, 1970.

Vanderbilt, Kermit. *American Literature and the Academy: Roots, Growth, and Maturity of a Profession*. Philadelphia: University of Pennsylvania Press, 1986.

Van Doren, Carl. *The American Novel, 1789–1939*. 1921. Rev. and enlarged ed. New York: Macmillan, 1940.

——. *Three Worlds*. New York: Harper and Brothers, 1936.

Van Doren, Mark. *The Private Reader: Selected Articles and Reviews*. 1942. New York: Kraus Reprint, 1968.

Van Gelder, Robert. *Writers and Writing*. New York: Scribner's, 1946.

Wagenknecht, Edward. *Cavalcade of the American Novel from the Birth of the Nation to the Middle of the Twentieth Century*. New York: Henry Holt, 1952; New York: Holt, Rinehart and Winston, 1967.

Wald, Alan M. *Exiles from a Future Time: The Forging of the Mid-Twentieth-Century Literary Left*. Chapel Hill: University of North Carolina Press, 2002.

——. *Trinity of Passion: The Literary Left and the Antifascist Crusade*. Chapel Hill: University of North Carolina Press, 2007.

Waldmeir, Joseph J. *American Novels of the Second World War*. Paris: Mouton, 1969.

Wallach, Mark I., and Jon Bracker. *Christopher Morley*. Boston: Twayne, 1976.

Waples, Douglas. *People and Print: Social Aspects of Reading in the Depression*. Chicago: University of Chicago Press, 1938.

Warfel, Harry R. *American Novelists of Today*. New York: American Book Co., 1951.

Warren, Kenneth. *Black and White Strangers: Race and American Literary Realism*. Chicago: University of Chicago Press, 1993.

Watkins, T. H. *The Hungry Years: A Narrative History of the Great Depression in America*. New York: Henry Holt, 1999.

Watson, Goodwin, ed. *Civilian Morale*. New York: Reynal and Hitchcock, 1942.

Watts, Emily Stipes. *The Businessman in American Literature*. Athens: University of Georgia Press, 1982.

Weber, Donald. *Haunted in the New World: Jewish American Culture from Cahan to the Goldbergs*. Bloomington: Indiana University Press, 2005.

Wecter, Dixon, F. O. Matthiessen, Detlev W. Bronk, Brand Blanshard, and George F. Thomas. *Changing Patterns in American Civilization*. Preface by Robert E. Spiller. Philadelphia: University of Pennsylvania Press, 1949.

Whitfield, Stephen J. *The Culture of the Cold War*. Baltimore: Johns Hopkins University Press, 1991.

Wilcox, Leonard. *V. F. Calverton: Radical in the American Grain*. Ed. Susan Porter Benson, Stephen Brier, and Roy Rosenzweig. Critical Perspectives on the Past. Philadelphia: Temple University Press, 1992.

Willenz, June A. *Women Veterans: America's Forgotten Heroines*. New York: Continuum, 1983.

Williams, Deborah Lindsay. *Not in Sisterhood: Edith Wharton, Willa Cather, Zona Gale, and the Politics of Female Authorship*. New York: Palgrave, 2001.

Wilson, Edmund. *The American Jitters: A Year of the Slump*. 1932. Essay Index Reprint Series. Freeport, N.Y.: Books for Libraries Press, 1968.

——. *The Shores of Light: A Literary Chronicle of the Twenties and Thirties*. New York: Farrar, Straus and Young, 1952.

Wilson, Robert N. *The Writer as Social Seer*. Chapel Hill: University of North Carolina Press, 1979.

Winkler, Allan M. *Life under a Cloud: American Anxiety about the Atom*. 1993. Urbana: University of Illinois Press, 1999.

Wood, James Playsted. *Magazines in the United States*. 1949. 2nd ed. New York: Ronald Press, 1956.

Wylie, Philip. *Generation of Vipers*. New York: Farrar and Rinehart, 1942.

Yezierska, Anzia. *Salome of the Tenements*. New York: Boni and Liveright, 1923.

ARTICLES

Abbott, Lawrence F. "The Middlebrows." *Outlook*, 2 November 1927, 281+.

Abramson, Ben. "The Influence of Books." *Saturday Review of Literature*, 24 July 1937, 13.

Acklom, Moreby. "People Don't Know They Want Books." *Bookman*, October 1919, 135–37.

Adamic, Louis. "What the Proletariat Reads." *Saturday Review of Literature*, 1 December 1934, 321–22.

Adams, Frank S. "Rationing Cuts Down Greatest Book Sales in History." *New York Times Book Review*, 8 August 1943, 4, 18.

Adams, J. Donald. "Mr. Bromfield's Family Chronicle." *New York Times Book Review*, 20 August 1933, 6.

———. "Speaking of Books." *New York Times Book Review*, 4 July 1943, 2.

———. "Speaking of Books." *New York Times Book Review*, 7 September 1947, 2.

Aiken, Conrad. "American Writers Come of Age." *Atlantic Monthly*, April 1942, 476–81.

Aikman, Duncan. "Not Quite Standardized Yet." *Harper's*, September 1928, 507–15.

Albrecht, W. P. "War and Fraternity: A Study of Some Recent American War Novels." *New Mexico Quarterly* 21 (Winter 1951): 461–74.

Alden, Robert. "Written for the Reader Who's Running for the 7:02." *New York Times Book Review*, 17 January 1960, 6.

Aldridge, John W. "The New Generation of Writers: With Some Reflections on the Older Ones." *Harper's*, November 1947, 423–32.

Allen, Frederick Lewis. "Best-Sellers: 1900–1935." *Saturday Review of Literature*, 7 December 1935, 3–4, 20, 24, 26.

Allen, Hervey. "History and the Novel." *Atlantic Monthly*, February 1944, 119–21.

"America's Literary Stars." *Literary Digest*, 22 July 1922, 28–29, 44–50.

"America's So-Called Literature." *Living Age*, March 1930, 62–63.

"The American Spirit in Fiction." *Common Ground* 3, no. 2 (Winter 1943): 118–19.

Amis, Kingsley. "The Delights of Literary Lecturing." Special Issue, *Harper's*, October 1959, 181–82.

Anonymous. "I Changed My Name." *Atlantic Monthly*, February 1946, 72.

Appel, Benjamin. "Mr. Average America and Books." *Publishers' Weekly*, 29 June 1940, 2400–2401.

———. "The Paperback Revolution." *Saturday Review*, 28 November 1953, 13–14, 45–48.

"Are People Starving in America?" *Literary Digest*, 2 April 1932, 12.

Arnold, Aerol. "The Social Novel as a Best Seller." *University of Kansas City Review* 8 (October 1941): 59–64.

Arvin, Newton. "Fiction Mirrors America." *Current History* (September 1935): 610–16.

Asheim, Lester. "Book Business Looks at Itself." *Saturday Review of Literature*, 2 June 1951, 18–19, 27–28.

Asheim, Lester, Knox Burger, Harold Guinzburg, John Hersey, Walter Pitkin Jr., and Irita Van Doren. "The Future of Books in America." Transcript of discussion held at the home of Irita Van Doren on 14 January 1954. *American Scholar* 23 (1954): 197–215.

Atherton, Gertrude. "Is There a Moral Decline?" *Forum* 65 (March 1921): 312–15.

———. "Why Is American Literature Bourgeois?" *North American Review* 178 (May 1904): 771–81.

Auchincloss, Louis. "Marquand and O'Hara: The Novel of Manners." *Nation*, 19 November 1960, 383–88.

Austin, Mary. "Folk Literature." *Saturday Review of Literature*, 11 August 1928, 1–3.

——. "Regionalism in American Fiction." *English Journal* 21 (February 1932): 97–107.

"Author Meets Businessman." *Fortune*, December 1952, 111, 226.

Bacon, Josephine D. "Is American Literature Bourgeois?" *North American Review* 179 (July 1904): 105–17.

Bagger, Eugene S. "Intellectual America." *Atlantic Monthly*, February 1921, 200–205.

Bailey, Sydney D. "How I Left the Middle Class." *Christian Century*, 25 November 1959, 1375.

Baker, Joseph E. "Four Arguments for Regionalism." *Saturday Review of Literature*, 28 November 1936, 3–4, 14.

Ballowe, James. "Marquand and Santayana: Apley and Alden." *Markham Review*, February 1971, 92–94.

Banning, Margaret Culkin. "Changing Moral Standards in Fiction." *Saturday Review of Literature*, 1 July 1939, 3–4, 14.

——. "In Print and in War." *Writer*, July 1944, 195–97.

——. "Nobody Reads in Hammocks." *Saturday Review of Literature*, 30 July 1938, 11–12.

——. "The Problem of Popularity." *Saturday Review of Literature*, 2 May 1936, 3–4, 16–17.

——. "Who Escapes?" *Saturday Review of Literature*, 17 July 1937, 3–4, 14–15.

Barrett, William. "American Fiction and American Values." *Partisan Review* 8, no. 6 (November–December 1951): 681–90.

——. "Novel Writing for the Sixties." *Writer*, July 1960, 5–8.

——. "We're On the Road: A Critic Discovers America and Sees the Forces That Shape Its Literature." *New York Times Book Review*, 10 May 1959, 1, 30–31.

Barth, John. "The Literature of Exhaustion." *Atlantic Monthly*, August 1967, 29–34.

Barzun, Jacques. "America's Passion for Culture." *Harper's*, March 1954, 40–47.

Bass, Altha Leah. "The Social Consciousness of William Dean Howells." *New Republic*, 13 April 1921, 192–94.

Beach, Joseph. "Eight Novelists between Wars." *Saturday Review of Literature*, 29 March 1941, 3–4, 17–19.

Beath, Paul Robert. "Four Fallacies of Regionalism." *Saturday Review of Literature*, 28 November 1936, 3–4, 14, 16.

Belgion, Montgomery. "Another Man's Poison." *Saturday Review of Literature*, 29 January 1927, 541–42.

Benedict, Stewart H. "The Pattern of Determinism in J. P. Marquand's Novels." *Ball State Teachers College Forum* 2, no. 2 (Winter 1961–62): 60–64.

Benjamin, Curtis G. "How Bad in the Big Book Business." *Saturday Review*, 9 October 1954, 11, 32.

Benjamin, Robert Spiers. "Out of Thin Air." *Publishers' Weekly*, 12 July 1941, 88–91.

Bennett, Jesse Lee. "What We Read and Why We Read It." *Bookman*, October 1925, 119–26.

Berelson, Bernard. "Who Reads What and Why?" *Saturday Review of Literature*, 12 May 1951, 7–8, 30–31.

Berrigan, Darrell. "New Men Travel the Old Roads." *New Republic*, 26 May 1947, 13–15.

Bessie, Simon Michael. "American Writing Today: A Publisher's Viewpoint." *Virginia Quarterly Review* 34, no. 1 (Winter 1958): 1–17.

Björkman, Edwin. "An Open Letter to President Wilson on Behalf of American Literature." *Century Magazine*, April 1914, 887–89.

"Black Boy." *Ebony* 1 (November 1945): 26–27.

Blackiston, Elliott. "Writing in Time of War." *Writer*, February 1942, 50–51.

Bliven, Bruce. "The Cold Pogrom." *New Republic*, 15 December 1947, 22–24.

——. "For 'Nordics' Only." *New Republic*, 8 December 1947, 18–21.

——. "Myths about the Jews." *New Republic*, 24 November 1947, 21–24.

——. "Prejudice Is Curable." *New Republic*, 29 December 1947, 22–25.

——. "The Revolution of the Joneses." *New York Times*, 9 October 1960, 28, 120–21.

——. "Salesmen of Hate." *New Republic*, 17 November 1947, 20–23.

——. "U.S. Anti-Semitism Today." *New Republic*, 3 November 1947, 16–19.

——. "What *Is* Anti-Semitism?" *New Republic*, 22 December 1947, 16–18.

Blythe, Samuel G. "A Clear Call to the Center." *Saturday Evening Post*, 6 January 1934, 8–9, 67, 70.

Bodenheim, Maxwell. "Criticism in America." *Saturday Review of Literature*, 6 June 1925, 801–2.

Bolwell, Robert Whitney. "Concerning the Study of Nationalism in American Literature." *American Literature* 10 (January 1939): 406–16.

Bontemps, Arna. "Famous WPA Authors." *Negro Digest*, June 1950, 43–46.

——. "The Two Harlems." *American Scholar* 14 (1945): 167–73.

"Book Boom for Negro Authors: Once-Hungry Writers Finally Hit Pay Dirt in Publishing House." *Ebony* 1 (November 1945): 24–25.

Boorstin, Daniel J. "The Place of Thought in American Life." *American Scholar* 25, no. 2 (Spring 1956): 137–50.

Booth, Bradford A. "The Novel Has Attained Its Full Dignity." *Library Journal*, 15 February 1950, 239–42.

Botkin, B. A. "Regionalism: Cult or Culture?" *English Journal* 25 (March 1936): 181–85.

Bourjaily, Vance. "The Lost Art of Writing for Television." Special Issue, *Harper's*, October 1959, 151–57.

Bowen, Elizabeth. "A Matter of Inspiration." *Saturday Review of Literature*, 13 October 1951, 27–28.

Boyd, Ernest A. "American Literature or Colonial?" *Freeman*, 17 March 1920, 13–15.

——. "Charting the Sea of Fiction." *New York Times Book Review*, 22 June 1924, 1, 25.

Boyd, James. "The Elusive American and the Ex-European." *Scribner's*, July 1922, 26–28.

Boynton, H. W. "Some American Novels of Quality." *Bookman*, May 1918, 340–47.

Brandon, Alfred N. "What Are Adults Reading?" *Library Journal*, 1 February 1956, 336–41.

Breit, Harvey. "J. P. Marquand." *The Writer Observed* (New York: World, 1956), 47–51.

——. "The Literary Market Place Today." *New York Times Book Review*, 18 May 1947, 1, 37.

Brickell, Herschel. "A Fresh Talent from the South." *New York Times Book Review*, 26 October 1941, 5.

——. "The Literary Landscape." *North American Review* 235 (April 1933): 376–84.

——. "The Present State of Fiction." *Virginia Quarterly Review* 25 (January 1949): 92–98.

Bromfield, Louis. "'I Know What I Like.'" *New York Times Book Review*, 5 July 1925, 2, 26.

Brooks, Cleanth. "Literature and the Professors: I. Literary History vs. Criticism." *Kenyon Review* 2 (1940): 403–12.

——. "The New Criticism: A Brief for the Defense." *American Scholar* 13 (Spring 1944): 285–95.

Brooks, Van Wyck. "Fashions in Defeatism." *Saturday Review of Literature*, 22 March 1941, 3–4, 14.

Brown, E. K. "The National Idea in American Criticism." *Dalhousie Review*, July 1934, 133–47.

Brown, Herbert R. "The Great American Novel." *American Literature* 7 (1935–36): 1–14.

Brown, John Mason, and Maxwell Geismar. "John P. Marquand." *Saturday Review*, 13 August 1960, 14–15, 39.

Brown, Sterling A. "Negro Character as Seen by White Authors." *Journal of Negro Education*, April 1933, 179–203.

Brustein, Robert. "Why American Plays Are Not Literature." Special Issue, *Harper's*, October 1959, 167–72.

Bunker, John. "Nationality and the Case of American Literature." *Sewanee Review* 27 (January 1919): 82–91.

Burgum, Edwin Berry. "Our Writers are Winning Victories Too." *College English* 6, no. 4 (January 1945): 185–93.

Burke, Kenneth. "A Decade of American Fiction." *Bookman*, August 1929, 561–67.

——. "Symbolic War." *Southern Review* 2 (1936): 134–47.

Burman, Ben Lucien. "Wanted: New Gods." *Saturday Review of Literature*, 28 December 1946, 7–8, 29.

Burt, Struthers. "What's Left for the Novelist?" *North American Review* 232 (August 1931): 118–25.

Bush, Douglas. "American Writers Come Back from the Wars." *New Republic*, 30 October 1950, 21–24.

——. "Making Culture Hum." *Bookman*, August 1929, 591–95.

——. "Scholars, Critics, and Readers." *Virginia Quarterly Review* 22 (April 1950): 242–50.

Butcher, Philip. "In Print . . . Our Raceless Writers." *Opportunity*, July–September 1948, 113–15.

Calcott, Emily. "The New Look in American Books." *Wilson Library Bulletin* 25, no. 2 (October 1950): 153–57.

Calverton, V. F. "The Bankruptcy of Southern Culture." *Scribner's*, May 1936, 294–98.

——. "The Challenge of the New American Literature." *Current History* (August 1930): 882–88.

——. "The Negro and American Culture." *Saturday Review of Literature*, 21 September 1940, 3–4, 17–18.

——. "Proletarianitis." *Saturday Review of Literature*, 9 January 1937, 3–4, 14–15.

Cameron, Anne. "The Double Gold Rush: The Transition from Stakes to Scripts." *Saturday Review of Literature*, 30 October 1943, 10–11.

Campbell, Walter S. "Re-Tooling for the War Market." *Writer*, August 1943, 231–33.

Canby, Henry Seidel. "Alas, the Poor 'Twenties!" *Saturday Review of Literature*, 10 May 1930, 1021, 1025.

———. "Americans Own America." *Saturday Review of Literature*, 7 September 1935, 8.

———. "Emotion and History." *Saturday Review of Literature*, 18 September 1936, 8.

———. "The Farm and the Novel." *Saturday Review of Literature*, 27 July 1929, 1, 4.

———. Introduction. Special Issue, *Saturday Review of Literature*, 5 August 1944, 11–13.

———. "The New Humanists." *Saturday Review of Literature*, 22 February 1930, 749–51.

———. "Post Mortem." *Saturday Review of Literature*, 14 June 1930, 1121–23.

———. "The School of Cruelty." *Saturday Review of Literature*, 21 March 1931, 673–74.

———. "The Threatening Thirties." *Saturday Review of Literature*, 22 May 1937, 3–4, 14.

———. "Thunder in Manhattan." *Saturday Review of Literature*, 16 January 1926, 489, 495.

Canby, Henry Seidel, Christopher Morley, and William Allen White. "Books of the Fall." *Saturday Review of Literature*, 10 October 1936, 16, 26, 28.

Cantwell, Robert. "America and the Writers' Project." *New Republic*, 26 April 1939, 323–25.

———. "What the Working Class Reads." *New Republic*, 17 July 1935, 274–76.

Carter, Michael. "Book-of-Month Author Talks for AFRO: Richard Wright Believes Fear, Not Sex, Governs Race Relations." *Afro-American*, 13 January 1945, 1, 19.

Cason, Clarence E. "On Henry W. Grady: Some Marginal Notes." *Sewanee Review* 39 (October–December 1931): 466–71.

Castle, Marian. "The Decline of Nice People." *Bookman*, November 1931, 317–19.

Cerf, Bennett A. "Books That Shook the World." *Saturday Evening Post*, 3 April 1943, 19, 84–86.

Chamberlain, John. "The Negro as Writer." *Bookman*, February 1930, 603–11.

———. "Six Months in the Field of Fiction." *New York Times Book Review*, 24 June 1928, 2, 26.

———. "Six Months of Glittering Diversity in the Field of Fiction." *New York Times Book Review*, 4 December 1927, 3, 22.

———. "Small-Time Life in Connecticut." *New York Times Book Review*, 8 January 1933, 7.

Chase, Richard. "Is There a Middle Way in Culture? Clifton Fadiman and the Middlebrow." *Commentary*, July 1955, 57–63.

———. "Neo-Conservatism and American Literature: Traditional Impulse and Radical Idea." *Commentary*, March 1957, 254–61.

Childs, Marquis W. "Roads to the Future." *Saturday Review of Literature*, 28 May 1938, 10–11.

Clapp, Verner W. "Why Do People Read?" *Library Journal*, 1 June 1951, 917–19, 935.

Clark, Edwin. "Six Months in the Field of Fiction." *New York Times Book Review*, 26 June 1927, 5, 18.

Clark, Harry Hayden. "Nationalism in American Literature." *University of Toronto Quarterly* 2 (July 1933): 492–519.

———. "Suggestions concerning a History of American Literature." *American Literature* 12 (November 1940): 288–96.

Cohen, Elliot E. "Letter to the Movie-Makers: The Film Drama as a Social Force." *Commentary*, August 1947, 110–18.

———. "Mr. Zanuck's 'Gentleman's Agreement': Reflections on Hollywood's Second Film about Anti-Semitism." *Commentary*, January 1948, 51–56.

Cohn, David L. "I've Kept Mine." *Atlantic Monthly*, April 1946, 42.

Colum, Mary M. "Life and Literature: Fiction and Fact." *Forum* 97 (January 1937): 33–38.

———. "Self-Critical America." *Scribner's*, February 1930, 197–206.

Commager, Henry Steele. "The 'Traitor.'" *Books*, 9 March 1930.

Compton, Charles H. "The Librarian and the Novelist." *South Atlantic Quarterly* 26 (October 1927): 392–403.

"Constructive Class Consciousness." *New Republic*, 9 November 1927, 300–302.

Coolidge, Calvin. "My Principles of Citizenship." *Forum* 63 (January 1920): 30–38.

Cooney, Thomas E. "Good News on Paperbacks." *Saturday Review*, 11 June 1955, 20, 36–37.

———. "Three Books on Modern American Society." *Saturday Review*, 26 January 1957, 12–13.

Corbin, John. "The Forgotten Folk." *North American Review* 211 (September 1920): 308–18.

———. "Four Views of the American Way of Life." *New York Times Book Review*, 22 May 1938, 2.

Cordell, Richard. "American 'Loyalists.'" *Saturday Review of Literature*, 20 May 1938, 5.

Corey, Lewis. "The Crisis of the Middle Class: I. The Middle Class under Capitalism." *Nation*, 14 August 1935, 176–78.

———. "The Crisis of the Middle Class: II. The Middle Class under Fascism." *Nation*, 21 August 1935, 207–10.

———. "The Crisis of the Middle Class: III. The Middle Class under Socialism." *Nation*, 28 August 1935, 238–41.

Cory, Herbert Ellsworth. "The Critics of Criticism." *Dial*, 16 November 1914, 371–74.

Cousins, Norman. "Bystanders Are Not Innocent." *Saturday Review of Literature*, 2 August 1947, 7–9.

———. "What's Wrong with the American Novel?" *Saturday Review*, 1 October 1960, 26.

Cowley, Malcolm. "American Literature in Wartime." *New Republic*, 6 December 1943, 800–803.

———. "A Farewell to the 1930's." *New Republic*, 8 November 1939, 42–44.

———. "Haven't You Read These Novels?" *New Republic*, 30 March 1953, 26–30.

———. "The War against Writers." *New Republic*, 8 May 1944, 631–32.

Cram, Ralph Adams. "The Forgotten Class." *American Review* 7 (April–October 1936): 32–46.

"Creative Art in Fiction." *Outlook*, 24 August 1921, 658.

Cromwell, Otelia. "Democracy and the Negro." *American Scholar* 13, no. 2 (Spring 1944): 149–61.

Crouse, Russell. "Writers and the War." *Writer*, September 1944, 267–68.

Crowell, Chester T. "Back to Bread and Circuses." *Outlook and Independent* 150 (1928): 1233–34.

"Culling the Sweet and Bitter Fruits of Six Months' Fiction." *New York Times Book Review*, 5 December 1926, 5, 34, 38.

Curtis, Alberta. "Radio and Reading: Do Broadcasts Compete with Books?" *Saturday Review of Literature*, 8 June 1940, 11–13.

Curtiss, Philip. "Lost: The Gentle Reader." *Atlantic Monthly*, June 1934, 673–80.

Dabney, Lewis. "The American Novel in the Age of Conformity." *Nation*, 23 February 1957, 167–69.

Daiches, David. "Britons Find It Jolly Good Reading." *New York Times Book Review*, 5 September 1954, 1, 14.

——. "The Scope of Sociological Criticism." *Epoch* 3, no. 2 (Summer 1950): 57–64.

Daly, Maureen. "Peace: It's a Problem!" *Ladies' Home Journal*, May 1947, 207–12, 288–93.

Dana, John Cotton. "Changes in Reading." *North American Review* 216 (December 1922): 823–32.

Dane, Clemence. "American Fairy-Tale." *North American Review* 242 (Autumn 1936): 143–52.

Dangerfield, George. "English Ebb, American Flow." *Saturday Review of Literature*, 3 April 1937, 3–4, 26, 28.

Davenport, Walter. "Race Riots Coming." *Collier's*, 18 September 1943, 11, 79–84.

Davidson, Carter. "The Immigrant Strain in Contemporary American Literature." *English Journal* 25, no. 10 (December 1935): 862–68.

Davidson, Donald. "The 43 Best Southern Novels for Readers and Collectors." *Publishers' Weekly*, 27 April 1935, 1675–76.

——. "Regionalism and Nationalism in American Literature." *American Review*, April 1935, 48–61.

Davis, Anne Pence. "A Novelist Competes with the Headlines." *Writer*, July 1942, 195–99.

Davis, Robert Gorham. "The Continuing American Ideal: How Plural Is Our Culture?" *Commentary*, May 1958, 369–78.

——. "Creative Writing in Wartime: On the Significance of the Fiction We Salvage from the Chaos of War." *New York Times Book Review*, 24 June 1945, 1, 16, 18.

"Decline in Reading." *America*, 4 June 1955, 259.

"The Decline of Good Manners." *Literary Digest*, 16 January 1932, 22.

Dempsey, David. "The Revolution in Books." *Atlantic Monthly*, January 1953, 75–77.

Derleth, August. "America in Today's Fiction." *Publishers' Weekly*, 3 May 1941, 1820–25.

DeVoto, Bernard. "American Novels: 1939." *Atlantic Monthly*, January 1940, 66–74.

——. "The Easy Chair: The Sixty-Cent Royalty." *Harper's*, January 1952, 41–44.

——. "The Easy Chair: Why Read Dull Novels?" *Harper's*, February 1952, 65–69.

——. "Fiction and the Everlasting If: Notes on the Contemporary Historical Novel." *Harper's*, June–November 1938, 42–49.

——. "Fiction Fights the Civil War." *Saturday Review of Literature*, 18 December 1937, 3–4, 15–16.

——. "The Pulitzer Prize Winners." *Saturday Review of Literature*, 8 May 1937, 3–4.

——. "Snow White and the Seven Dreads." *Harper's*, November 1938, 669–72.

——. "They Turned Their Backs on America: Writers of the Twenties Missed the Real Meaning of the Time." *Saturday Review of Literature*, 8 April 1944, 5–8.

——. "The Threshold of Fiction." *Harper's*, December 1939–May 1940, 221–24.

Dupree, Gordon, Ronald Mansbridge, and J. R. Cominsky. "The Battle for the Book." *Saturday Review*, 2 June 1956, 5–7, 33–34. See esp. "Can Johnny's Parents Read?," by Dupree (5–7, 34), and "Books Are Hard Work," by Mansbridge (7–8, 33–34).

Edmonds, Walter D. "A Novelist Takes Stock." *Atlantic Monthly*, July 1943, 73–77.

"Effect of Television on Reading Is Estimated in Recent Surveys." *Publishers' Weekly*, 21 April 1951, 1707–9.

Ellis, Robert. "Why One Novelist Won't Write about Negroes." *Negro Digest*, April 1949, 65–67.

Erskine, John. "American Business in the American Novel." *Bookman*, July 1931, 449–57.

——. "Present Tendencies in American Literature." *New York Times Book Review*, 23 December 1923, 3.

——. "William Dean Howells." *Bookman*, June 1920, 385–89.

[A European]. "Intellectual America." *Atlantic Monthly*, February 1920, 188–99.

Fadiman, Clifton P. "The American Novel of the Truce." *Saturday Review of Literature*, 5 August 1944, 19–21.

——. "The Best People's Best Novelist." *Nation*, 15 February 1933, 175–77.

——. "The Decline of Attention." *Saturday Review of Literature*, 6 August 1949, 20–24.

——. "Immigrants among the Novels." *Bookman*, January 1929, 588–90.

——. "A Little Theorizing," *New Yorker*, 23 November 1940, 75–77.

——. "The Whole Duty of the Young Novelist." *Nation*, 18 April 1928, 445–47.

Farber, Marjorie. "Freudian Nightmare." *New York Times Book Review*, 22 August 1943, 5.

Farnham, Marynia F. "The Pen and the Distaff." *Saturday Review of Literature*, 22 February 1947, 7–8, 29–30.

Farrar, John. "The American Tradition." *Bookman*, February 1924, 609–14.

——. "The Condition of American Writing." *English Journal* 38, no. 8 (October 1949): 421–28.

Farrell, James T. "The Decline of the Serious Writer." *Antioch Review* 17 (Summer 1957): 147–60.

——. "The End of a Literary Decade." *American Mercury*, December 1939, 408–14.

——. "The Frightened Philistines." *New Republic*, 4 December 1944, 764–69.

——. "The Language of Hollywood." *Saturday Review of Literature*, 5 August 1944, 29–32.

——. "The Last Writers' Congress: An Interim Report on Its Results." *Saturday Review of Literature*, 5 June 1937, 10, 14.

Faulkner, William. "On Privacy, the American Dream: What Happened to It." *Harper's*, July 1955, 33–38.

Fay, Bernard. "Protestant America." *Living Age*, July 1928, 1193–1201.

"Feature Editors Discuss 'Book Page Situation' at Annual Convention." *Publishers' Weekly*, 9 December 1950, 2421–23.

Fenton, Charles A. "The Writers Who Came Out of the War." *Saturday Review*, 3 August 1957, 5–7, 24.

Ferguson, Charles W. "Five Rising Stars in American Fiction." *Bookman*, May 1927, 251–57.

———. "Give the Public What It Wants." *Publishers' Weekly*, 2 January 1937, 32–33.

———. "Who Reads Religious Books?" *Saturday Review of Literature*, 10 July 1937, 3–4, 14–15.

Ferguson, Milton J. "Days of '39." *Library Journal*, July 1939, 529–30.

"Fiction for Today." *Common Ground* 4, no. 4 (Summer 1944): 109–10.

"Fiction Reading Decreases." *Publishers' Weekly*, 5 January 1935, 53.

Fiedler, Leslie. "The Breakthrough: The American Jewish Novelist and the Fictional Image of the Jew." *Midstream* (Winter 1958): 15–35, esp. 30.

Field, Louise Maunsell. "American Novelists vs. the Nation." *North American Review* 235 (June 1933): 552–60.

———. "Heroines Back at the Hearth." *North American Review* 236 (August 1933): 176–83.

———. "What's Wrong with the Men?" *North American Review* 231 (March 1931): 234–40.

———. "What's Wrong with the Women?" *North American Review* 232 (September 1931): 274–80.

"Fifty Books of Fiction of the Past Six Months." *New York Times Book Review*, 28 June 1925, 3, 22.

Firkins, O. W. "Undepicted America." *Yale Review* 20 (September 1930): 140–50.

Fisher, Dorothy Canfield. "American Readers and Books." *American Scholar* 13, no. 2 (Spring 1944): 179–91.

Fitch, Robert E. "The Bourgeois and the Bohemian." *Antioch Review* 16 (Summer 1956): 131–45.

Foerster, Norman. "American Literature." *Saturday Review of Literature*, 3 April 1926, 677–79.

Follett, Wilson. "Down the Sooty Fiction Chimney." *New York Times Book Review*, 24 June 1923, 1, 24, 27.

———. "Literature and Bad Nerves." *Harper's*, June–November 1921, 107–16.

Ford, Nick Aaron. "Battle of the Books: A Critical Survey of Significant Books by and about Negroes Published in 1960." *Phylon* 22, no. 2 (June 1961): 119–34.

"Four Dollars' Worth of Books per Year per Capita." *Publishers' Weekly*, 2 December 1950, 2352.

Frank, Waldo. "In Defense of Our Vulgarity." *New Republic*, 3 February 1926, 298.

———. "Our Folk: The Re-Discovery of America: XVI." *New Republic*, 18 July 1928, 219–22.

Fuess, Claude M. "Can Writers Be Too Objective?" *Saturday Review*, 22 March 1952, 11–12, 37.

Gaines, Francis P. "The Racial Bar Sinister in American Romance." *South Atlantic Quarterly* 25 (October 1926): 396–402.

Gale, Zona. "Period Realism." *Yale Review* 42 (August 1933): 111–24.

Gallup, George. "The Favorite Books of Americans." *New York Times Book Review*, 15 January 1939, 2, 16.

Gardiner, Harold C. "The Future of American Reading." *America*, 30 January 1954, 447–48.

Garis, Roy L., and V. F. Calverton. "Are Aliens Lowering American Standards?" *Current History* 24 (August 1926): 666–77.

Geismar, Maxwell. "Decline of the Classic Moderns." *Nation*, 7 May 1955, 402–3.

George, W. L. "This Generation of Literary Paragons." *New York Times Book Review*, 16 March 1924, 2.

"George Washington Carver Award Given to Bucklin Moon." *Publishers' Weekly*, 5 February 1949, 819.

Gerould, Katharine Fullerton. "The Comedy of Americanization." *Saturday Evening Post*, 29 October 1921, 21, 82.

———. "Feminine Fiction." *Saturday Review of Literature*, 11 April 1936, 3–4, 15.

———. "This Hard-Boiled Era." *Harper's*, February 1929, 265–74.

Gersh, Harry. "The New Suburbanites of the 50's." *Commentary*, March 1954, 209–21.

Gibson, Richard. "A No to Nothing." *Hudson Review* 13 (Spring 1951): 252–55.

Gitler, Robert L. "The Printed Word Will Stay." *Library Journal*, 1 March 1951, 376–79.

Glasgow, Ellen. "Heroes and Monsters." *Saturday Review of Literature*, 4 May 1935, 3–4.

Glick, Nathan. "Marquand's Vanishing American Aristocracy: Good Manners and the Good Life." *Commentary*, May 1950, 435–44.

Glicksberg, Charles I. "Farewell to a Decade." *Twentieth Century* 149 (January 1951): 61–68.

Gold, Herbert. "Fiction of the Fifties." *Hudson Review* 12 (Summer 1959): 192–201.

———. "Fiction of the Sixties." *Atlantic Monthly*, September 1960, 53–57.

———. "The New Upper-Middle Soap Opera (A Tribute to Herman Wouk, Sloan Wilson, Cameron Hawley, and Makers of Fine Face-Cream Everywhere)." *Hudson Review* 9 (Winter 1956–57): 585–91.

———. "The Writer as Nag." *Nation*, 18 January 1958, 54–56.

Goodman, J. A., and Albert Rice. "Big Books: The Story of Best Sellers." *Saturday Evening Post*, 17 November 1934, 31–34, 94–97.

Goodrich, Marc. "Along the Appian Way to Main Street." *New York Times Book Review*, 31 May 1925, 2.

Goodwin, George, Jr. "The Last Hurrahs: George Apley and Frank Skeffington." *Massachusetts Review* 1 (Spring 1960): 461–71.

Gordon, Milton M. "*Kitty Foyle* and the Concept of Class as Culture." *American Journal of Sociology* 53 (November 1947): 210–17.

Grattan, C. Hartley. "The Trouble with Books Today." *Harper's*, November 1951, 31–36.

———. "Upton Sinclair on Current Literature: A Summary of a Conversation with C. Hartley Grattan." *Bookman*, April 1932, 61–64.

"The Great American Novel." *Bookman*, March 1927, 3–4.

Green, Alan. "Tradewinds." *Saturday Review*, 6 August 1955, 4–5.

Greenhill, Robert. "This Best of All Possible Literary Worlds." *New York Times Book Review*, 22 April 1923, 2.

Gregory, Horace, Muriel Rukeyser, Marshall Schacht, and Granville Hicks. "'Good News' in American Literature: A Symposium." *New Masses*, 12 October 1937, 17–19.

Guilfoil, Kelsey. "Josephine Lawrence: *The Voice of the People*." *English Journal* 38, no. 7 (September 1949): 365–70.

Hackett, Alice Payne. "New Novelists of 1945." *Saturday Review of Literature*, 16 February 1946, 8–10.

Hackett, Francis. "The Critic and the Criticized." *New Republic*, 17 September 1919, 198–99.

———. "New Novelists of 1944." *Saturday Review of Literature*, 17 February 1945, 12–14, 41.

———. "New Novelists of 1946." *Saturday Review of Literature*, 15 February 1947, 11–13.

———. "Pardon Me!" *New Republic*, 24 March 1937, 207–8.

———. "Stuffed Shirts and Red Shirts." *Saturday Review of Literature*, 4 April 1936, 3–4, 25.

Haines, Helen E. "Books and Book-making in the United States." *Library Journal*, 1 September 1922, 699–704.

Halprin, Lee S. "American Liberalism, Literature, and World War II." *Minnesota Review* 3 (Winter 1963): 179–91.

Halsey, Van R. "Fiction and the Businessman: Society through All Its Literature." *American Quarterly* 11 (Fall 1959): 391–402.

Hansen, Harry. "American Literary Output in 1942." *Publishers' Weekly*, 16 January 1943, 236–37.

———. "The First Reader." *Publishers' Weekly*, 18 January 1936, 199–201.

———. "The Literary Editor Looks at 1944." *Publishers' Weekly*, 20 January 1945, 216–18.

———. "Literary Scene in 1940." *Publishers' Weekly*, 18 January 1941, 216–18.

———. "1943 from the Literary Desk." *Publishers' Weekly*, 22 January 1944, 284–86.

Hardwick, Elizabeth. "The Decline of Book Reviewing." Special Issue, *Harper's*, October 1959, 139–43.

Hart, Frances Noyes. "The Feminine Nuisance Replies." *Bookman*, September 1921, 31–34.

Hart, Irving Harlow. "The Most Popular Authors of Fiction in the Post-War Period, 1919–1926." *Publishers' Weekly*, 12 March 1927, 1045–53.

Hartung, P. T. "Stone Walls Do Not." *Commonweal*, 17 March 1939, 854.

"Has America a Literary Dictatorship?" *Bookman*, April 1927, 191–99.

Hatch, Robert L. "Movies: Gentleman's Agreement." *New Republic*, 17 November 1947, 38.

"The Haunted Castle." *Time*, 10 February 1961, 80.

Hayes, H. Gordon. "The Narrowing Gulf between Rich and Poor." *Harper's*, July 1947, 57–60.

Hazard, Eloise Perry. "First Novelists of 1947." *Saturday Review of Literature*, 14 February 1948, 8–11.

Hazlitt, Henry. "Who Reads the Classics Now?" *Nation*, 16 April 1930, 449–51.

Heiskell, Andrew. "Have the Newer Media Made Reading Obsolete?" *Library Journal*, 1 October 1950, 1577–81.

Hergesheimer, Joseph. "The Feminine Nuisance in American Literature." *Yale Review*
10, no. 4 (July 1921): 716–25.

Herrick, Robert. "The Background of the American Novel." *Yale Review* 3, no. 2 (January
1914): 213–33.

——. "What Is Happening to Our Fiction?" *Nation*, 4 December 1929, 673–75.

——. "Writers in the Jungle." *New Republic*, 17 October 1934, 259–61.

Herzberg, Max J. "1946: Year of Doubt." *English Journal* 36, no. 3 (March 1947): 109–15.

Hicks, Granville. "American Fiction since the War." *English Journal* 37, no. 6 (June 1948):
271–77.

——. "As Fiction Faces the Sixties." *Saturday Review*, 2 January 1960, 14.

——. "The Case for Fiction in 1960." *Saturday Review*, 31 December 1960, 9.

——. "The Highbrow and the Midcult." *Saturday Review*, 13 August 1960, 16.

——. "Marquand of Newburyport." *Harper's*, April 1950, 101–8.

——. "Our Novelists' Shifting Reputations." *English Journal* 40, no. 1 (January 1951): 1–7.

——. "The Shape of Postwar Literature." *College English* 5, no. 8 (May 1944): 407–12.

——. "The Twenties in American Literature." *Nation*, 12 February 1930, 183–85.

Hill, Helen. "A Local Habitation." *Sewanee Review* 39 (October–December 1931): 460–65.

"Historicals, Film Books, Anthologies among Paper-Cover High Spots." *Publishers'
Weekly*, 31 May 1952, 2202–5.

Hobson, Laura Z. "Trade Winds." *Saturday Review*, 12 September 1953, 6, 8.

Hoggart, Richard. "A Matter of Rhetoric? American Writers and British Readers."
Nation, 27 April 1957, 361–64.

Holt, Guy. "Fledgling Fiction." *Bookman*, September 1930, xvi–xviii.

Horchler, R. T. "Life and the Dream." *Commonweal*, 4 November 1955, 123.

"How the American Middle Class Lives." *Scribner's*, December 1929, 694–99.

"How 'Best Sellers' Are Made." *Literary Digest*, 9 January 1926, 66–67.

"How the Critics Sell Books: An Interview with Isabel Paterson Who Conducts 'Turns
With a Book Worm' for the *Herald Tribune*." *Publishers' Weekly*, 3 December 1932,
2103.

Howe, Irving. "Mass Society and Post-Modern Fiction." *Partisan Review* 26 (Summer
1959): 420–36.

——. "This Age of Conformity: Notes on an Endless Theme; or, A Catalogue of
Complaints." *Partisan Review* 21, no. 1 (January–February 1954): 7–33.

Howells, W. D. "Professor Barrett Wendell's Notions of American Literature." *North
American Review* 172 (January 1901): 623–40.

Hutner, Gordon. "In the Middle: Fiction, Borders, and Class." *CR: The New Centennial
Review* 2, no. 1 (Fall 2001): 89–108.

"Increase in Number of $3.50 Novels Brings Up Average Price of Fiction." *Publishers'
Weekly*, 9 September 1950, 1033–34.

Jack, Homer A. "Lillian Smith of Clayton, Georgia." *Christian Century*, 2 October 1957,
1166–68.

Jack, Peter Monro. "The James Branch Cabell Period." *New Republic*, 13 January 1937,
323–26.

Jackson, Joseph Henry. "Fiction Is Neither What It Was Nor What It Might Be." *Publishers' Weekly*, 19 January 1952, 198–204.

Jacobson, Dan. "Why Read Novels?" *Nation*, 14 November 1959, 343–45.

Janeway, Elizabeth. "Fiction's Place in a World Awry." *New York Times Book Review*, 13 August 1961, 1, 24.

Jenkins, Herbert F. "The Nation's Appetite for Fiction." *Publishers' Weekly*, 24 September 1921, 973–75.

Johnson, Burges. "The Alleged Depravity of Popular Taste." *Harper's*, January 1921, 209–15.

Johnson, Gerald W. "American Writing, American Life: A Critic Maintains That Our Novels Misrepresent Us to the Outside World." *New York Times Book Review*, 1 May 1949, 1, 17–18.

Johnson, James Weldon. "Race Prejudice and the Negro Artist." *Harper's*, June–November 1928, 769–76.

Johnson, James William. "The Adolescent Hero: A Trend in Modern Fiction." *Twentieth Century Literature* 5, no. 1 (April 1959): 3–11.

Johnson, Lavinia Lowery. "Publication of Negro Literature Has a Bright Outlook." *Library Journal*, 1 February 1948, 182–84.

Johnston, Eric. "Movies: End of an Era?" *Fortune*, April 1949, 98–102, 135–50.

Jones, Edgar L. "The Soldier Returns." *Atlantic Monthly*, January 1944, 42–46.

Jones, Howard Mumford. "The Limits of Contemporary Criticism." *Saturday Review of Literature*, 6 September 1941, 3–4, 17.

Jones, John Paul. "Middle-Class Misery." *Survey*, April–December 1932, 402–4.

Josephson, Matthew. "Chicago: A Modernistic Portrait." *Outlook and Independent*, 30 January 1929, 165+.

———. "Leane Zugsmith: The Social Novel of the Thirties." *Southern Review* 11 (1975): 530–52.

———. "The Younger Generation: Its Young Novelists." *Virginia Quarterly Review* 9 (April 1933): 243–61.

Kandel, I. L. "The New Illiteracy." *School and Society* 25 (November 1950): 348.

Kazin, Alfred. "The Alone Generation: A Comment on the Fiction of the 'Fifties." Special Issue, *Harper's*, October 1959, 127–31.

Kelley, Florence Finch. "What America Means to Mr. Meiklejohn." *New York Times Book Review*, 5 January 1936, 3, 17.

Kellogg, Vernon. "Race and Americanization." *Yale Review* 29 (July 1921): 729–40.

Kellor, Frances A. "What Is Americanization?" *Yale Review* 27 (January 1919): 282–99.

Kelly, Wallace McElroy. "Sincerity and the Novelist." *Writer*, December 1942, 359–61.

Knopf, Alfred A. "Book Publishing: The Changes I've Seen." *Atlantic Monthly*, December 1957, 155–60.

Komroff, Manuel. "Russian Manners for American Novels." *New York Times Book Review*, 23 March 1924, 2.

Kronenberger, Louis. "Are Reviewers Too Polite?" *Saturday Review of Literature*, 16 April 1938, 13–14.

———. "Our Country and Our Culture." *Partisan Review* 19 (July–August 1952): 439–45.

———. "A Time to Speak Words of Praise." *New York Times Book Review*, 12 July 1953, 1.

Kunitz, Stanley. "American Poetry's Silver Age." Special Issue, *Harper's*, October 1959, 173–79.

La Farge, Oliver. "Alien Races in Fiction." *North American Review* 244 (Autumn 1937): 202–5.

Lamont, Thomas W. "What a Capitalist Reads: One Man's Literary Meat: Part 1." *Saturday Review of Literature*, 4 December 1943, 12–15.

———. "What a Capitalist Reads: One Man's Literary Meat: Part II." *Saturday Review of Literature*, 11 December 1943, 7–10.

Lane, Franklin K. "How to Make Americans: Take the Foreigner by the Hand—Show Him the Spirit of the Nation." *Forum* 61 (April 1919): 399–406.

Lang, Daniel. "A Reporter at Large: Everyone Walks Too Slow." *New Yorker*, 23 October 1943, 44–47.

Law, Robert Adger. "Mrs. Peterkin's Negroes." *Southwest Review* 14, no. 4 (July 1929): 455–61.

Leisy, Ernest E. "American Literature in Colleges and Universities." *School and Society* 6 (March 1926): 307–9.

Lerner, Max. "Capitalism as Magic." *Nation*, 8 January 1938, 46–47.

"Letter to a Young Man about to Enter Publishing." Special Issue, *Harper's*, October 1959, 184–90.

Lewisohn, Ludwig. "The Crisis of the Novel." *Yale Review* 22 (May 1933): 533–44.

———. "The New Literature in America." *Nation*, 23 March 1921, 429.

Lindeman, Eduard C. "The Common Man as Reader." *Saturday Review*, 9 May 1953, 11–12, 46–47.

Littell, Robert. "The Great American Novel." *New Republic*, 15 July 1925, 211.

Loveman, Amy. "The Clearing House." *Saturday Review of Literature*, 3 October 1936, 18.

———. "The Clearing House." *Saturday Review of Literature*, 17 October 1936, 19–20.

———. "The Clearing House." *Saturday Review of Literature*, 16 August 1941, 7.

———. "The Plight of the Novelist." *Saturday Review*, 12 December 1953, 28.

Lovett, Robert Morss, H. L. Mencken, J. Middleton Murry, Morris R. Cohen, Dickinson S. Miller, Clive Bell, and Francis Hackett. "The Function of Criticism." *New Republic* [Literary Supplement], 26 October 1921, 247–65. See esp. "Criticism Past and Present," by Lovett (247–49), "The Motive of the Critic," by Mencken (249–51), and "The Critic as Witness," by Hackett (261–65).

"Low Readership Level in U.S. Shown by Gallup Poll." *Publishers' Weekly*, 11 February 1950, 893.

Lunt, Storer B. "The Heritage of the Printed Word." *Saturday Review of Literature*, 18 August 1951, 2.

Macauley, Robie. "Fiction of the Forties." *Western Review* 16, no. 1 (Autumn 1951): 59–69.

MacDonald, James G. "Hidden Motives of the Anti-Semitic Myth." *New York Herald Weekly Book Review*, 21 March 1948, 1.

MacDonald, William. "The Decline and Fall of Liberty in the United States." *New York Times Book Review*, 31 August 1930, 2.

MacLeish, Archibald. "American State of Mind." *American Scholar* (Autumn 1950): 398–408, esp. 407–8.

———. "Books in This World at War: Their Part in the Task ahead of Us Is of the Greatest Importance." *New York Times Book Review*, 6 December 1942, 1.

———. "On the Teaching of Writing." Special Issue, *Harper's*, October 1959, 158–61.

Macleod, Norman. "Notes on Regionalism." *Sewanee Review* 39 (October–December 1931): 456–59.

"Making Americans Out of Immigrants." *Outlook*, 30 June 1920, 419.

Marcus, Steven. "The Novel Again." *Partisan Review* 29 (Spring 1962): 171–95.

Marquand, John P. "Apley, Wickford Point, and Pulham: My Early Struggles." *Atlantic Monthly*, September 1956, 71–76.

Marshall, Margaret, and Mary McCarthy. "Our Critics, Right or Wrong." *Nation*, 23 October 1935, 468–69, 472.

———. "Our Critics, Right or Wrong, Part 2, 'The Anti-Intellectuals.'" *Nation*, 6 November 1935, 542–44.

———. "Our Critics, Right or Wrong, Part 3." *Nation*, 20 November 1935, 595–96, 598.

———. "Our Critics, Right or Wrong, Part 4, 'The Proletarians.'" *Nation*, 4 December 1935, 653–55.

———. "Our Critics, Right or Wrong, Part 5, 'Literary Salesmen.'" *Nation*, 18 December 1935, 717–19.

Martin, Edward S. "W. D. Howells." *Harper's*, July 1920, 265–66.

Maurice, Arthur B. "A New Golden Age in American Reading." *World's Work*, March 1920, 488–507.

McCarthy, Mary. "The Revolt of the American Authors." *Listener*, 26 November 1953, 901–2.

McDowell, Tremaine. "Regionalism in American Literature." *Minnesota History* 20, no. 2 (June 1939): 105–18.

McWilliams, Carey. "Localism in American Criticism: A Century and a Half of Controversy." *Southwest Review* 19 (July 1934): 410–28.

———. "The Zoot-Suit Riots." *New Republic*, 21 June 1943, 818–20.

Melcher, Frederic G. "Book Prices Much Below the Cost of Living Figures." *Publishers' Weekly*, 2 December 1950, 2352.

———. "Our Heritage in Books Is in Need of Re-Emphasis." *Publishers' Weekly*, 24 March 1951, 1418.

Mencken, H. L. "The National Literature." *Yale Review* 28 (July 1920): 804–17.

Menninger, Karl A., Philip Wylie, Ashley Montagu, Phyllis McGinley, Margaret Mead, and Olive R. Goldman. "A SR Panel Takes Aim at the Second Sex." *Saturday Review*, 21 February 1953, 26–31, 41.

Merz, Charles. "Behind the Blocs: A New Explanation of Our Growing Sectionalism." *Harper's*, June–November 1925, 76–81.

Metcalf, John. "New Novels." *Spectator*, 7 October 1955, 470–71.

Miller, Merle. "The Book Club Controversy." *Harper's*, June 1948, 518–24.

——. "The Book Clubs." *Harper's*, May 1948, 433–40.

Miller, Nellie B. "Is America Ill? A Literary Diagnosis and Dosage." *Independent*, 5 June 1926, 661–63.

Miller, Perry. "Europe's Faith in American Fiction." *Atlantic Monthly*, December 1951, 52–56.

Millett, Fred B. "American Literature (1940–5)." *English Journal* 36 (Spring 1947): 170–77.

"Millions of Critics." *Newsweek*, 2 January 1950, 54–55.

Mizener, Arthur. "The Novel of Manners in America." *Kenyon Review* 12, no. 1 (Winter 1950): 1–19.

——. "What Makes Great Books Great?" *New York Times Book Review*, 9 March 1952, 1.

Moon, Bucklin. "Is the Boom in Race Novels Over?" *Negro Digest*, March 1950, 73–77.

More, Paul Elmer. "The Modern Current in American Literature." *Forum* 79 (January 1928): 127–36.

Morgan, Henry Stuart. "Lewis Assails Our Medicine Men." *New York Times Book Review*, 8 March 1925, 1.

Morris, Lloyd. "Skimming the Cream from Six Months' Fiction." *New York Times Book Review*, 6 December 1925, 2.

Morris, Wright. "Death of the Reader." *Nation*, 13 January 1964, 53–54.

"Mr. Faulkner Exhausts the Future." *Nation*, 26 October 1957, 274–75.

Muirhead, James F. "Must American Literature Defy Its Traditions?" *Independent and the Weekly Review*, 18 March 1922, 269–70.

Muller, Edwin. "Radio v. Reading." *New Republic*, 19 February 1940, 236–38.

Muller, Herbert J. "Literary Criticism: Cudgel or Scales?" *American Scholar* 8 (July 1939): 285–94.

Mumford, Lewis. "American Condescension and European Superiority." *Scribner's*, May 1930, 518–27.

——. "Reflections on Chicago." *New Republic*, 27 February 1929, 44–45.

——. "What Has 1932 Done for Literature?" *Atlantic Monthly*, December 1932, 761–67.

Munson, Gorham B. "The Embattled Humanists: Introducing a New Character into the Current Drama of Ideas." *Bookman*, December 1928, 404–10.

——. "Stocktaking at Thirty-three." *Saturday Review of Literature*, 24 August 1929, 69–70.

Murphy, John J. "Elizabeth Madox Roberts and the Civilizing Consciousness." *Register of the Kentucky Historical Society* 64, no. 1 (January 1966): 110–20.

Myers, Walter L. "The Novel and the Past." *Virginia Quarterly Review* 14 (Autumn 1938): 567–78.

Nathan, Paul S. "Books into Films." *Publishers' Weekly*, 17 July 1948, 216.

——. "Books into Films." *Publishers' Weekly*, 16 October 1948, 1764.

——. "Books into Films." *Publishers' Weekly*, 3 May 1952, 1867.

"The New Middle Class." *Literary Digest*, 2 June 1923, 102.

[A New York Publisher-Bookseller]. "Fewer and Better Books." *Atlantic Monthly*, January 1925, 56–64.

Nichols, F. B. "Middle Western Growing Pains." *North American Review* 240 (June 1933): 546–51.

Nisbet, Robert A. "The Coming Problem of Assimilation." *American Journal of Sociology* 50, no. 4 (January 1945): 261–70.

Nock, Albert Jay. "The Return of the Patriots." *Virginia Quarterly Review* 8 (August 1932): 161–74.

Norton, Dan S. "Past and Present." *Virginia Quarterly Review* 20 (Summer 1944): 474–80.

Norton, Henry Kittredge. "An Age of Alarums." *Century*, 30 April 1930, 192–202.

——. "I'd Rather Be Standardized." *Review of Reviews*, July 1930, 78–80.

Oppenheimer, Franz M. "Lament for Unbought Grace: The Novels of John P. Marquand." *Antioch Review* 18 (March 1958): 41–61.

"Original Paperback Publishing Grows: Its Merits and Effects Are Debated." *Publishers' Weekly*, 3 May 1952, 1831–33.

"Our Literature and Ourselves." *Nation*, 28 October 1925, 481.

Overstreet, H. A. "Books Make the Times." *Saturday Review of Literature*, 6 August 1949, 82–83, 88.

Paterson, Isabel. "A Shelf of Recent Books." *Bookman*, May 1925, 347.

Pattee, Fred Lewis. "American Literature in the College Curriculum." *Educational Review* 16 (May 1924): 266–72.

"Peeved Look at Publishing." *Time*, 16 December 1957, 98.

Pell, Herbert C. "A Contented Bourgeois." *North American Review* 245 (1938): 340–49.

Perry, William. "What Do You Read, My Lord?" *American Scholar* 6, no. 3 (Summer 1937): 271–81.

Pfaff, William. "The Naked, the Dead and the Novels." *Commonweal*, 7 September 1951, 529–30.

Pick, Robert. "A Refugee Looks at Anti-Semitism Here: The Difference between European and American Patterns." *Commentary*, September 1948, 207–13.

Podhoretz, Norman. "The Jew as Bourgeois." *Commentary*, February 1956, 186–88.

"Portrait of Mr. Nobody." *Business Week*, 6 October 1951, 102–4.

Prescott, Orville. "Books or Bullets." *Publishers' Weekly*, 30 January 1943, 512–14.

——. "A Handful of Rising Stars." *New York Times Book Review*, 21 March 1943, 13.

——. "Outstanding Novels." *Yale Review* 35 (December 1946): 382.

——. "Outstanding Novels." *Yale Review* 37, no. 3 (March 1948): 573–76.

Pringle, Henry F. "Literature at the Crossroads: An Inquiry into the Buying of Books." *Outlook*, 7 March 1928, 380–81.

——. "Middle-Class Squeeze." *Nation's Business*, November 1951, 42–43, 60–61.

Pritchett, V. S. "The Vanished Luxury of a Private Art." *New Republic*, 30 October 1950, 18–21.

Quinn, Arthur Hobson. "The Art of William Dean Howells." *Century Magazine*, September 1920, 675–81.

Rabinowitz, Nancy S., and Peter J. Rabinowitz. "Legends of Toothpaste and Love: Margaret Ayer Barnes and the Poetics of Stupidity." *Paperson Language and Literature* 78 (1982): 132–50.

Rahv, Philip. "Fiction and the Criticism of Fiction." *Kenyon Review* 18 (Spring 1956): 276–99.

———. "Self-Definition in American Literature: Experience and Fulfillment." *Commentary*, December 1957, 530–37.

———. "The Slump in American Writing." *American Mercury*, February 1940, 185–91.

———. "Twilight of the Thirties." *Partisan Review* 6, no. 4 (Summer 1939): 3–15.

Ransom, John Crowe. "The South Is a Bulwark." *Scribner's*, May 1936, 299–303.

Rascoe, Burton. "Neglected Books." *American Mercury*, August 1940, 495–98.

———. "The Tough-Muscle Boys of Literature." *American Mercury*, November 1940, 369–74.

"Rates Us Low as Book Readers." *Science Digest*, October 1958, 24.

Raushenbush, Winifred. "How to Prevent Race Riots." *American Mercury*, September 1943, 302–9.

Redding, J. Saunders. "American Negro Literature." *American Scholar*, Spring 1949, 137–48.

Ribalow, Harold U. "From *Hungry Hearts* to *Marjorie Morningstar*: The Progress of an American Minority Told in Fiction." *Saturday Review*, 14 September 1957, 46–48.

———. "Jewish Life in the American Novel." *American Mercury*, July 1950, 109–17.

"The Rise of the 'New' American." *New Republic*, 10 May 1922, 301–2.

R. M. B. "American Leeway." *Christian Science Monitor*, 14 May 1938.

Roberts, Kenneth. "The Memories of John P. Marquand: Marsh Mud, Harvard Sawdust, and Stuffed Shirts." *Saturday Review*, 15 September 1956, 14–15.

Roberts, S. C. "British Publishing after Two Wars." *Saturday Review of Literature*, 13 October 1951, 28–29, 51.

Rogers, W. G. "The 1949 Literary Output Was Not Memorable, Not Negligible." *Publishers' Weekly*, 21 January 1950, 222–24.

Rolo, Charles J. "1950: A Literary Roundup." *Publishers' Weekly*, 20 January 1951, 216–20.

Roosevelt, Nicholas. "America's Cultural Deserts Begin to Blossom: Our Depressing Standardization Viewed in the Light of What Has Gone Before." *New York Times Book Review*, 19 July 1925, 2, 17.

Rosenfeld, Paul. "The Authors and Politics." *Scribner's*, May 1933, 318–20.

Rovit, Earl H. "The Regions versus the Nation: Critical Battle of the Thirties." *Mississippi Quarterly* 13 (Spring 1960): 90–98.

Russell, Charles Edward. "Take Them or Leave Them: Standardization of Hats and Houses and Minds." *Century Magazine*, June 1926, 168–77.

"The Safe and Sane Genius of William Dean Howells." *Current Opinion*, July 1920, 93–96.

Salomon, Louis B. "Tory Through and Through." *Nation*, 23 November 1940, 509.

Sancton, Thomas. "The Race Riots." *New Republic*, 5 July 1943, 9–13.

Schlesinger, Arthur, Jr. "Our Country and Our Culture." *Partisan Review* 19 (September–October 1952): 590–93.

———. "Our New-Found Leisure Won't Bore Us If Some of It Is Employed in Reading." *Saturday Evening Post*, 18 April 1959, 10.

Schulberg, Budd. "The Writer and Hollywood." Special Issue, *Harper's*, October 1959, 133–37.

Schuyler, George S. "What's Wrong with Negro Authors." *Negro Digest*, May 1950, 3–7.

Schwartz, Delmore. "Our Country and Our Culture." *Partisan Review* 19 (September–October 1952): 593–97.

Seaver, Edwin. "The Age of the Jackpot." *Saturday Review of Literature*, 15 February 1947, 9–10.

Seldes, Gilbert. "Spring Flight." *Dial*, August 1925, 162–64.

Seligman, Daniel. "The 'Business Novel' Fad." *Fortune*, August 1959, 104–5, 178–79.

———. "The New Masses." *Fortune*, May 1959, 106–11, 257–58.

Sheerin, John B. "Shall We Conform or Think?" *Catholic World*, July 1956, 241–45.

Sherman, Caroline B. "Farm Life Fiction." *South Atlantic Quarterly* 27 (July 1928): 310–24.

———. "Farm Life Fiction Reaches Maturity." *Sewanee Review* 39 (October–December 1931): 472–83.

Sherman, Stuart P. "American Style." *Bookman*, November 1922, 257–64.

———. "For the Higher Study of American Literature." *Yale Review* 31 (April 1923): 469–75.

———. "The National Genius." *Atlantic Monthly*, January 1921, 1–11.

———. "The Point of View in American Criticism." *Atlantic Monthly*, November 1922, 620–31.

Siegfried, Andre. "Social Changes in America." *Atlantic Monthly*, November 1933, 546–48.

Simpson, Lewis P. "Introduction: Recovering Elizabeth Madox Roberts." *Southern Review* 20, no. 4 (October 1984): 749–51.

———. "The Sexuality of History." *Southern Review* 20, no. 4 (October 1984): 785–802.

"Situation of American Writing, 1999." *American Literary History* 11, no. 2 (1999): 215–353.

"Six Undistinguished Months in the Contemporary Novel." *New York Times Book Review*, 21 December 1924, 5, 23.

Slichter, Sumner H. "The Growth of Moderation." *Atlantic Monthly*, October 1956, 61–64.

Smertenko, John J. "The Emerging Hyphen." *Harper's*, August 1951, 63–71.

Smith, Harrison. "Ten New Talents." *Saturday Review of Literature*, 17 February 1951, 7+.

———. "Thirteen Adventurers: A Study of a Year of First Novelists, 1947." *Saturday Review of Literature*, 14 February 1948, 6–8, 30–31.

Smith, Henry. "On Living in America." *Southwest Review* 16 (October 1930): 22–31.

Smith, Howard. "The American Businessman in the American Novel." *Southern Economic Journal* 25, no. 3 (January 1959): 265–302.

Smith, Lillian. "Personal History of 'Strange Fruit': A Statement of Purposes and Intentions." *Saturday Review of Literature*, 17 February 1945, 9–10.

Smith, Rebecca W. "The Southwest in Fiction." *Saturday Review of Literature*, 16 May 1942, 12–13, 37.

Snow, C. P. "Which Side of the Atlantic?" *Harper's*, October 1959, 163–66.

Spiller, Robert E. "What Became of the Literary Radicals?" *New Republic*, 18 November 1946, 664–66.

Spingarn, Arthur B. "Books by Negro Authors in 1940." *Crisis*, March 1941, 76–77.

——. "Books by Negro Authors in 1941." *Crisis*, April 1942, 114–15.

——. "Books by Negro Authors in 1942." *Crisis*, February 1943, 45–46.

——. "Books by Negro Authors in 1943." *Crisis*, February 1944, 49–50.

——. "Books by Negro Authors in 1944." *Crisis*, February 1945, 49–50.

"*SRL* Poll on Novels and Novelists." *Saturday Review of Literature*, 5 August 1944, 61.

Stearns, Harold. "America and the Young Intellectuals." *Bookman*, March 1921, 42–48.

Stedmond, J. M. "The Business Executive in Fiction." *Dalhousie Review* 42 (Spring 1962): 18–27.

Stegner, Wallace. "The Anxious Generation." *College English* 10, no. 4 (January 1949): 183–88.

——. "Fiction: A Lens on Life." *Saturday Review of Literature*, 22 April 1950, 9–10, 32–34.

——. "Is the Novel Done For?" *Harper's*, December 1942, 76–83.

Stern, Philip Van Doren. "Books and Best-Sellers." *Virginia Quarterly Review* 18, no. 1 (Winter 1942): 45–55.

Stout, Rex. "Books and the Tiger: Rex Stout Discusses Some of the Beliefs That Are Weapons for War against the Axis." *New York Times Book Review*, 21 March 1943, 11.

Strauss, Harold. "The Illiterate American Writer." *Saturday Review*, 17 May 1952, 8–9, 39.

Strunsky, Simeon. "About Books, More or Less: The American Idiom." *New York Times Book Review*, 26 April 1925, 4.

——. "About Books, More or Less: Barbarians and Decadents." *New York Times Book Review*, 1 March 1925, 4.

——. "About Books, More or Less: Chromosomes and Hyphens." *New York Times Book Review*, 22 March 1925, 4.

——. "About Books, More or Less: The Closed Door." *New York Times Book Review*, 21 February 1926, 4.

——. "The Rediscovery of Jones." *Atlantic Monthly*, July 1931, 1–8.

Stuart, Henry Longan. "Fifty 'Outstanding Novels' of the Last Six Months." *New York Times Book Review*, 27 June 1926, 3, 24–25.

Swados, Harvey. "Paper Books: What Do They Promise?" *Nation*, 11 August 1951, 114–15.

——. "Paper Books: What Do They Promise? [part II]." *Nation*, 18 August 1951, 134–35.

Tarkington, Booth. "Rotarian and Sophisticate." *World's Work*, January 1929, 42–44, 146.

Tate, Allen. "Spirituality of Roughnecks." *Nation*, 28 July 1926, 89.

Teachout, Terry. "Justice to John P. Marquand." *Commentary*, October 1987, 54–58.

"Television Will Bring Many Changes in Home Life." *Science Digest*, April 1945, 27.

Teller, Judd L. "The Changing Status of American Jewry." *Midstream: A Quarterly Jewish Review* (Summer 1957): 5–14.

Thompson, Charles Willis. "The Books That Never Die: But Where, Oh, Where, Are the Best Sellers of Yesteryear?" *New York Times Book Review*, 26 July 1925, 2, 17.

Thompson, Ralph. "Outstanding Novels." *Yale Review* (Summer 1939): viii.

Thorp, Margaret. "The Motion Picture and the Novel." *American Quarterly* 3 (Fall 1951): 195–203.

Towne, Alfred. "Homosexuality in American Culture: The New Taste in Literature." *American Mercury*, August 1951, 3–9.

Townsend, R. D. "The Book Table: A Test of Taste." *Outlook*, 14 December 1921, 617–18.

Tracy, Henry C. "The Bookshelf." *Common Ground* 1, no. 4 (Summer 1941): 129–34.

———. "The Bookshelf." *Common Ground* 4, no. 3 (Spring 1944): 107–12. See esp. "Toward the American Creed" (107–9) and "The American Scene" (109–11).

———. "The Bookshelf." *Common Ground* 6, no. 4 (Summer 1946): 106–12. See esp. "Answered in Fiction" (109–10) and "White Man's Burden" (110–12).

Trilling, Diana. "Fiction in Review." *Nation*, 18 September 1943, 330–31.

———. "Fiction in Review." *Nation*, 23 November 1946, 589–90.

———. "Fiction in Review." *Nation*, 21 February 1948, 218–19.

———. "What Has Happened to Our Novels?" *Harper's*, May 1944, 529–36.

Trilling, Lionel. "Is Literature Possible?" *Nation*, 15 October 1930, 405–6.

Tyree, Wade. "Time's Own River: The Three Major Novels of Elizabeth Madox Roberts." *Michigan Quarterly Review* 16 (Winter 1977): 33–46.

Umland, Rudolph. "On Editing WPA Guide Books." *Prairie Schooner*, 1939, 160–69.

[An Unassimilated Foreigner]. "The Failure of the Melting-Pot." *Nation*, 24 January 1920, 100–102.

Utley, Clifton M. "How Illiterate Can Television Make Us?" *Commonweal*, 19 November 1948, 137–39.

Uzzell, Thomas H. "Mob Reading: Romantic Ingredients of the Super Best Seller." *Saturday Review of Literature*, 20 November 1937, 3–4, 16, 18.

Van Doren, Carl. "American Realism." *New Republic*, 21 March 1923, 107–9.

———. "*The Nation* and the American Novel." *Nation*, 10 February 1940, 212–14.

———. "Toward a New Canon." *Nation*, 13 April 1932, 429–30.

Van Zile, Edward S. "Our Barnyard School of Fiction." *New York Times Book Review*, 4 May 1924, 2.

Viereck, Peter. "Babbitt Junior: The New Philistinism." *Georgia Review* 5 (Summer 1951): 150–56.

Wagenknecht, Edward. "Novelists on the Threshold." *Virginia Quarterly Review* 19 (October 1943): 628–32.

Walcutt, Charles Child. "The Regional Novel and Its Future." *Arizona Quarterly* 1 (Summer 1945): 17–27.

Walker, C. Lester. "Big Boom in Good Books." *Saturday Review*, 8 February 1958, 16, 38.

Wallace, Margaret. "Young Women Novelists Steal the Headlines." *Independent Woman* 31 (April 1952): 107–8.

Walters, Raymond, Jr. "Intellectuals in Gray Flannel Suits." *Saturday Review*, 14 September 1957, 28.

Waples, Douglas. "Do People Read What They Like?" *Publishers' Weekly*, 5 September 1931, 930–33.

"War Books Are Leading the Best Seller List." *Publishers' Weekly*, 12 July 1941, 85–86.

"The War Is a Best Seller." *New Republic*, 11 May 1942, 621.

Weeks, Edward. "What Makes a Book a Best Seller?" *New York Times Book Review*, 20 December 1936, 2, 15.

Weltner, George. "A 'Liberal Gentile' Looks at Himself." *Commentary*, July 1948, 35–39.

West, Geoffrey. "Joseph Hergesheimer." *Virginia Quarterly Review* 8 (January 1932): 95–108.

West, Ray B., Jr. "Four Rocky Mountain Novels." *Rocky Mountain Review* 10 (Autumn 1945): 21–28.

"What Books Are Wanted? Dr. Albert Guerard, Author and Critic, Pronounces Literary Theories to Booksellers in California." *Publishers' Weekly*, 21 June 1930, 3004.

"What Do Readers Read?" *Publishers' Weekly*, 26 May 1934, 1924–25.

"What Is Literary Authority?" *Nation*, 18 March 1925, 282.

"What *SRL* Reviewers Are Giving at Christmas." *Saturday Review of Literature*, 5 December 1942, 14–15.

Whipple, T. K. "Literature in the Doldrums." *New Republic*, 21 April 1937, 311–14.

White, William Allen. "The Challenge to Democracy: It Is a Glib Shibboleth." *Vital Speeches of the Day* 4, no. 16 (1 June 1938): 494–96.

———. "The Challenge to the Middle Class." *Atlantic Monthly*, August 1937, 196–201.

"Who Are the 'Classic Authors' of Today?" *Literary Digest*, 15 March 1924, 46–50, 54.

"Who Reads What?" *Publishers' Weekly*, 9 January 1937, 120.

"Why the Middle Classes Do Not Count." *Literary Digest*, 7 May 1921, 16.

"Why Reading Is Essential in a Democratic Society." *Publishers' Weekly*, 9 February 1952, 807.

"William Dean Howells." *Nation*, 22 May 1920, 673.

Williams, Stanley T. "Who Reads an American Book?" *Virginia Quarterly Review* 28, no. 4 (October 1952): 518–31.

Wilson, Angus. "The Revolution in British Reading." *American Mercury*, December 1951, 47–54.

Wilson, Edmund. "The Best People." *Scribner's*, March 1932, 153–57.

———. "The Economic Interpretation of Wilder." *New Republic*, 26 November 1930, 31–32.

———. "Literary Politics." *New Republic*, 1 February 1928, 289–90.

Wittke, Carl. "Melting-Pot Literature." *College English* 7 (January 1946): 189–97.

Wolf, Irwin D. "Is Prestige an Adequate Substitute for Profit?" *Publishers' Weekly*, 2 June 1951, 2294–99.

Wolfe, Bernard. "Angry at What?" *Nation*, 1 November 1958, 316–22.

Woolf, Virginia. "American Fiction." *Saturday Review of Literature*, 1 August 1925, 1–3.

"The Wouk Mutiny." *Time*, 5 September 1955, 48–49.

Wylie, Philip. "Memorandum on Anti-Semitism." *American Mercury*, January 1945, 66–72.

Yerby, Frank. "How and Why I Write the Costume Novel." Special Issue, *Harper's*, October 1959, 145–50.

CHAPTERS AND ESSAYS

Aaron, Daniel. "The Hyphenate Writer and American Letters." 1964. In *American Notes: Selected Essays*, 69–83. Boston: Northeastern University Press, 1994.

Aldridge, John W. "The Search for Values." 1951. In *The American Novel since World War*

II, ed. and intro. Marcus Klein, 39–57. Greenwich, Conn.: Fawcett Publications, 1969.

——. "The War Writers Ten Years Later." In *Contemporary American Novelists*, ed. Harry T. Moore, 32–40. Carbondale: Southern Illinois University Press, 1964.

Babbitt, Irving. "The Critic and American Life." 1928. In *American Literary Criticism: 1900–1950*, ed. Charles I. Glicksberg, 288–306. New York: Hendricks House, Inc., 1951.

Barnard, Rita. "Modern American Fiction." In *The Cambridge Companion to American Modernism*, ed. Walter Kalaidjian, 39–67. Cambridge: Cambridge University Press, 2005.

Barnes, Margaret Ayer. "The Period Novel." In *What Is a Book? Thoughts about Writing*, ed. Dale Warren, 213–19. Boston: Houghton Mifflin, 1935.

Benedict, Stewart H. "The Business Novel." In *Papers of the Michigan Academy of Science, Arts, and Letters*, 447–53. Ann Arbor: Michigan University Press, 1960.

Boyd, Ernest A. "Ku Klux Kriticism." In *Criticism in America: Its Function and Status*, ed. Irving Babbitt et al., 309–20. New York: Haskell House, 1969. Originally published in *Nation*, 20 June 1923.

Brodhead, Richard H. "Regionalism and the Upper Class." In *Rethinking Class: Literary Studies and Social Formations*, ed. Wai Chee Dimock and Michael T. Gilmore, 150–74. Social Foundations of Aesthetic Forms series, ed. Jonathan Arac. New York: Columbia University Press, 1994.

Brogan, Denis W. "On Reading American Fiction." 1940. In *American Themes*, 117–29. New York: Harper and Brothers, 1948.

Brooks, John. "Some Notes on Writing One Kind of Novel." In *The Living Novel: A Symposium*, ed. Granville Hicks, 39–57. New York: Macmillan, 1957.

Bush, Andrew, and Deborah Dash Moore. "Will Herberg's *Protestant-Catholic-Jew*: A Critique." In *Key Texts in American Jewish Culture*, ed. Jack Kugelmass, 258–74. New Brunswick, N.J.: Rutgers University Press, 2003.

Calverton, V. F. "Social Forces in American Literature." In *Behold America!*, ed. Samuel D. Schmalhausen, 673–703. New York: Farrar and Rinehart, 1931.

——. "Sociological Criticism of Literature." 1925. In *American Literary Criticism: 1900–1950*, ed. Charles I. Glicksberg, 226–43. New York: Hendricks House, Inc., 1951.

Canby, Henry Seidel. "Literature in Contemporary America." In *The America of Today: Being Lectures Delivered at the Local Lectures Summer Meeting of the University of Cambridge, 1918*, ed. Gaillard Lapsley, 199–212. Cambridge: Cambridge University Press, 1919.

Chamberlain, John. "Literature." In *America Now: An Inquiry into the Civilization of the United States*, ed. Harold Stearns, 36–47. New York: Scribner's, 1938.

Clark, Clifford E., Jr. "Ranch-House Suburbia: Ideals and Realities." In *Recasting America: Culture and Politics in the Age of Cold War*, ed. Lary May, 171–91. Chicago: University of Chicago Press, 1989.

Dinnerstein, Leonard. "The Tide Ebbs." In *Antisemitism in America*, 150–55. New York: Oxford University Press, 1994.

Farrell, James T. "The Categories of 'Bourgeois' and 'Proletarian.'" 1936. In *American Literary Criticism: 1900–1950*, ed. Charles I. Glicksberg, 427–38. New York: Hendricks House, Inc., 1951.

——. "The End of a Literary Decade." In *Literature at the Barricades: The American Writer in the 1930s*, ed. Ralph F. Bogardus and Fred Hobson, 204–10. University, Ala.: University of Alabama Press, 1982.

Fiedler, Leslie. "Negro and Jew: Encounter in America." In *The Collected Essays of Leslie Fiedler*, vol. 1, 451–70. New York: Stein and Day Publishers, 1971.

——. "William Faulkner, Highbrows' Lowbrow." In *The Collected Essays of Leslie Fiedler*, vol. 1, 331–38. New York: Stein and Day Publishers, 1971.

French, Warren. "Fiction: A Handful of Survivors." In *The Forties: Fiction, Poetry, Drama*, ed. Warren French, 7–32. Deland, Fla.: Everett/Edwards, 1969.

——. "General Introduction: Remembering the Forties." In *The Forties: Fiction, Poetry, Drama*, ed. Warren French, 1–4. Deland, Fla.: Everett/Edwards, 1969.

Gannett, Lewis. "Books." In *While You Were Gone: A Report on Wartime Life in the United States*, ed. Jack Goodman, 447–64. New York: Da Capo Press, 1974.

Gold, Herbert. "Fiction of the Fifties." In *Recent American Fiction: Some Critical Views*, ed. Joseph J. Waldmeir, 36–44. Boston: Houghton Mifflin, 1963.

Gold, Michael. "Wilder: Prophet of the Genteel Christ." In *Literature and Liberalism: An Anthology of Sixty Years of* The New Republic, ed. Edward Zwick, 190–94. Washington, D.C.: New Republic Book Co., 1976. Originally published in *New Republic*, 22 October 1930.

Heinze, Andrew. "*Peace of Mind*: Judaism and the Therapeutic Polemics of Postwar America." In *Key Texts in American Jewish Culture*, ed. Jack Kugelmass, 225–43. New Brunswick, N.J.: Rutgers University Press, 2003.

Hicks, Granville. "Writers in the Thirties." In *As We Saw the Thirties: Essays on Social and Political Movements of a Decade*, ed. Rita James Simon, 78–101. Urbana: University of Illinois Press, 1967.

Hutner, Gordon. "Our Hearts Were Young and Gay." In *American and European National Identities: Faces in the Mirror*, ed. Stephen Fender, 143–57. European Papers in American History (No. 4). Keele, Staffordshire, England: Keele University Press, 1996.

Jarrett, Gene. "Entirely *Black* Verse from Him Would Succeed." In *Deans and Truants: Race and Realism in African American Literature*, 29–51. Philadelphia: University of Pennsylvania Press, 2007.

Jehlen, Myra. "The Novel and the Middle Class in America." In *Ideology and Classic American Literature*, ed. Sacvan Bercovitch and Myra Jehlen, 125–44. Cambridge: Cambridge University Press, 1986.

Kazin, Alfred. "John P. Marquand and the American Failure." 1958. In *Contemporaries*, 122–30. Boston: Little, Brown, 1962.

Macdonald, Dwight. "By Cozzens Possessed." January 1958. In *Against the American Grain*, 187–212. New York: Random House, 1962.

MacLeish, Archibald. "The Irresponsibles." 1940. In *A Time to Speak: The Selected Prose of Archibald MacLeish*, 103–21. Houghton Mifflin, 1941.

Prell, Riv-Ellen. "Cinderellas Who (Almost) Never Become Princesses: Subversive Representations of Jewish Women in Postwar Popular Novels." In *Talking Back: Images of Jewish Women in American Popular Culture*, ed. Joyce Antler, 127–38, 268–70. Hanover, N.H.: University Press of New England, 1998.

Roth, Philip. "Writing American Fiction." 1961. In *The American Novel since World War II*, ed. and intro. Marcus Klein, 142–58. Greenwich, Conn.: Fawcett, 1969.

Rubin, Louis D., Jr. "Trouble on the Land: Southern Literature and the Great Depression." In *Literature and the Barricades: The American Writer in the 1930s*, ed. Ralph F. Bogardus and Fred Hobson, 96–113. University, Ala.: University of Alabama Press, 1982.

Shapiro, Edward. "Will Herberg's *Protestant-Catholic-Jew*: A Critique." In *Key Texts in American Jewish Culture*, ed. Jack Kugelmass, 258–74. New Brunswick, N.J.: Rutgers University Press, 2003.

Tipple, John. "Prologue: The Businessman and the Politician." In *Crisis of the American Dream: A History of American Social Thought, 1920–1940*, 18–34. New York: Pegasus, 1968.

Trilling, Lionel. "The Roots of Modern Taste." In *The Opposing Self: Nine Essays in Criticism*, 67–91. New York: Viking, 1955.

———. "On the Teaching of Modern Literature." In *Beyond Culture: Essays on Literature and Learning*, 3–27. New York: Viking, 1968.

Wald, Alan. "Revolutionary Intellectuals: *Partisan Review* in the 1930s." In *Literature at the Barricades: The American Writer in the 1930s*, ed. Ralph F. Bogardus and and Fred Hobson, 187–203. University, Ala.: University of Alabama Press, 1982.

Warren, Robert Penn. "Literature as a Symptom." In *Who Owns America? A New Declaration of Independence*, ed. Herbert Agar and Allen Tate, 264–79. Boston: Houghton Mifflin, 1936.

Wilson, Edmund. "The Literary Class War." In *Literature and Liberalism: An Anthology of Sixty Years of The New Republic*, ed. Edward Zwick, 194–201. Washington, D.C.: New Republic Book Co., 1976. Originally published in *New Republic*, 4 May 1932.

REVIEWS

Adams, J. Donald. "Ernest Hemingway's First Novel in Eight Years." Rev. of *To Have and Have Not*, by Ernest Hemingway. *New York Times Book Review*, 17 October 1937, 2.

———. "Life and Literature in America: Van Wyck Brooks Sets Down Some Important Convictions about Them." Rev. of *Opinions of Oliver Allston*, by Van Wyck Brooks. *New York Times Book Review*, 14 December 1941, 1.

———. "The New Novel by Hemingway: 'For Whom the Bell Tolls' Is the Best Book He Has Written." Rev. of *For Whom the Bell Tolls*, by Ernest Hemingway. *New York Times Book Review*, 20 October 1940, 93.

———. "The Regeneration of America: Lewis Mumford's Call for a New Faith in Living." Rev. of *Faith for Living*, by Lewis Mumford. *New York Times Book Review*, 8 September 1940, 1, 29.

"A First Novel That Has Power." Rev. of *Rush to the Sun*, by William Brown Meloney. *New York Times Book Review*, 29 August 1937, 6.

Algren, Nelson. "Between Two Races." Rev. of *Alien Land*, by Willard Savoy. *Chicago Sun-Times*, 20 April 1949, 56.

"American Marriage." Rev. of *The Middle Years*, by V. R. Emanuel. *New York Times Book Review*, 22 March 1925, 8.

Amidon, Beulah. Rev. of *Without Magnolias*, by Bucklin Moon. *Survey*, September 1949, 495–96.

Arvin, Robert Hawkins. Rev. of *Find Me in Fire*, by Robert Lowry. *Commonweal*, 10 September 1948, 528–29.

Baker, Chris. "Mr. Steinbeck's Cross-Section." Rev. of *The Wayward Bus*, by John Steinbeck. *New York Times Book Review*, 16 February 1947, 1.

Baker, Joseph E. "Regionalism in the Middle West." Rev. of *The Folks*, by Ruth Suckow. *American Review* 4, no. 5 (March 1935): 603–14.

Baker, Nina Brown. "Release." Rev. of *Escape the Thunder*, by Lonnie Coleman. *New York Times Book Review*, 13 August 1944, 7.

" 'Banjo' and Other Recent Works of Fiction." Rev. of *Banjo*, by Claude McKay. *New York Times Book Review*, 12 May 1929, 5.

Barrett, William. "The Literature of Nihilism." Rev. of *After the Lost Generation*, by John W. Aldridge. *Saturday Review of Literature*, 9 June 1951, 13.

Barzun, Jacques. "Read, Do Not Run." Rev. of *How to Read a Book*, by Mortimer J. Adler. *Saturday Review of Literature*, 9 March 1940, 6–7.

Bazelon, David T. "In Search of America." Rev. of *The Big Rock Candy Mountain*, by Wallace Stegner, and *Journey in the Dark*, by Martin Flavin. *New Republic*, 8 September 1943, 659–60.

Beach, Joseph. "The Decade of the Doomed." Rev. of *Some of Us: An Essay in Epitaphs*, by James Branch Cabell. *Nation*, 3 December 1930, 622.

———. "The Marquand World: An Acerb Comment on Our Fumbling between Wars." Rev. of *So Little Time*, by John P. Marquand. *New York Times Book Review*, 22 August 1943, 1, 25.

"Beauty of Style in Christopher Morley's New Novel." Rev. of *Thunder on the Left*, by Christopher Morley. *New York Times Book Review*, 29 November 1925, 10.

" 'The Beginners' and Other Recent Works of Fiction." Rev. of *The Beginners*, by Henry Kitchell Webster. *New York Times Book Review*, 16 October 1927, 8.

Bell, Lisle. Rev. of *City of Angels*, by Rupert Hughes. *New York Herald Tribune Books*, 16 March 1941, 11.

Bénet, William Rose. "Instalment Living." Rev. of *If I Have Four Apples*, by Josephine Lawrence. *Saturday Review of Literature*, 4 January 1936, 5.

Berle, A. A., Jr. "Lewis Corey Examines American Capitalism." Rev. of *The Decline of American Capitalism*, by Lewis Corey. *Nation*, 12 September 1934, 305.

Bontemps, Arna. "In Boston." Rev. of *The Living Is Easy*, by Dorothy West. *New York Herald Weekly Book Review*, 13 June 1948, 3.

——. "A 'White Negro' 'Passes.'" Rev. of *Alien Land*, by Willard Savoy. *New York Herald Tribune Weekly Book Review*, 17 April 1949, 6.

Bourne, Randolph. "Clipped Wings." Rev. of *The House of Conrad*, by Elias Tobenkin. *Dial*, 11 April 1918, 358–59.

Boyd, Ernest A. "Readers and Writers." Rev. of *Melting-Pot Mistake*, by Henry P. Fairchild. *Independent*, 13 February 1926, 192.

Breit, Harvey. "W P and A." Rev. of *Men Working*, by John Faulkner. *New Republic*, 11 August 1941, 196.

"Brilliance on Darkness." Rev. of *How to Read a Book*, by Mortimer J. Adler. *Time*, 18 March 1940, 94–96.

Brock, H. I. "Southern Romance Is Dead." Rev. of *Barren Ground*, by Ellen Glasgow. *New York Times Book Review*, 12 April 1925, 2.

Bromfield, Louis. "Another Volume in Mr. Richter's Fine Frontier Saga." Rev. of *The Town*, by Conrad Richter. *New York Herald Tribune*, 23 April 1950, 5.

Bullock, Florence Haxton. "Across the Bridge." Rev. of *Jadie Greenway*, by I. S. Young. *New York Herald Tribune Weekly Book Review*, 5 October 1947, 5.

——. "Career of a Complete Escapist." Rev. of *No Stone Unturned*, by Josephine Lawrence. *New York Herald Tribune Books*, 5 January 1941, 3.

——. "Herman Wouk Spins a Tale in the Great Tradition." Rev. of *Marjorie Morningstar*, by Herman Wouk. *New York Herald Weekly Book Review*, 4 September 1955, 1.

Burke, Arthur E. "Aframerican Cross Section." Rev. of *Without Magnolias*, by Bucklin Moon. *Crisis*, June 1949, 187.

Burt, Struthers. "The Poison in Our Body Politic." Rev. of *Gentleman's Agreement*, by Laura Z. Hobson. *Saturday Review of Literature*, 1 March 1947, 14.

Canby, Henry Seidel. "Kentucke." Rev. of *The Great Meadow*, by Elizabeth Madox Roberts. *Saturday Review of Literature*, 15 March 1930, 821.

——. "New England Renaissance." Rev. of *The Flowering of New England*, by Van Wyck Brooks. *Saturday Review of Literature*, 22 August 1936, 3–4, 15.

——. "Twenty-Two." Rev. of *Alice Adams*, by Booth Tarkington. *Literary Review*, 21 May 1921, 3.

Carter, John. "Dreiser Reduced Literature to Its Own Level." Rev. of *Theodore Dreiser*, by Burton Rascoe. *New York Times Book Review*, 9 August 1925, 5.

——. "Jewish America in a Problem Novel." Rev. of *God of Might*, by Elias Tobenkin. *New York Times Book Review*, 22 February 1925, 5, 28.

——. "Mr. Granberry's Fine Novel of 'Poor-White' Life in Florida." Rev. of *Strangers and Lovers*, by Edwin Granberry. *New York Times Book Review*, 19 February 1928, 11.

C. C. Rev. of *Satan's Sergeants*, by Josephine Herbst. *Saturday Review of Literature*, 21 June 1941, 19.

Chamberlain, John. "Books of the Times." Rev. of *The Decline of American Capitalism*, by Lewis Corey. *New York Times Book Review*, 12 September 1934, 21.

——. "Gentle Satire on 'One More Spring.'" Rev. of *One More Spring*, by Robert Nathan. *New York Times Book Review*, 5 February 1933, 7.

——. "The New Middle Class." Rev. of *Insurgent America*, by Alfred M. Bingham, and

The Crisis of the Middle Class, by Lewis Corey. *Saturday Review of Literature*, 28 December 1935, 6–7.

——. "The Promised Land." Rev. of *The Great Meadow*, by Elizabeth Madox Roberts. *New Republic*, 2 April 1930, 197–98.

——. "Van Wyck Brooks' Revenge on His Critics." Rev. of *Opinions of Oliver Allston*, by Van Wyck Brooks. *New York Herald Tribune Books*, 23 November 1941, 5.

Clark, Edwin. "Scott Fitzgerald Looks into Middle Age." Rev. of *The Great Gatsby*, by F. Scott Fitzgerald. *New York Times Book Review*, 19 April 1925, 9.

Clinton-Baddeley, V. C. "Fiction." Rev. of *The Dove Found No Rest*, by Dennis Gray Stoll, *Journey in the Dark*, by Martin Flavin, and *Bitten by the Tarantula*, by J. Maclaren-Ross. *Spectator*, 1 February 1946, 124–25.

Colum, Mary M. "The Double Men of Criticism." Rev. of *A Time to Speak*, by Archibald MacLeish. *American Mercury*, 8 June 1941, 762–68.

Commager, Henry. "For Fifty Years a Literary Dynamo." Rev. of *Howells: His Life and World*, by Van Wyck Brooks. *New York Times Book Review*, 11 October 1959, 1, 16.

"Commonplace Folk." Rev. of *The Surry Family*, by Felix Riesenberg. *New York Times Book Review*, 27 December 1925, 16.

Conroy, Jack. "Negroes in the South." Rev. of *Without Magnolias*, by Bucklin Moon. *Chicago Sun-Times*, 13 April 1949, 51.

Cooney, Thomas E. "Real Estate: Restricted." Rev. of *Peaceable Lane*, by Keith Wheeler. *Saturday Review*, 22 April 1961, 25.

Cooper, Frederick Taber. "The Soul of America." Rev. of *The House of Conrad*, by Elias Tobenkin. *Publishers' Weekly*, 16 February 1918, 536–37.

Cordell, Richard A. "Lilt on Long Island." Rev. of *Give Us Our Dream*, by Arthemise Goertz. *Saturday Review of Literature*, 28 June 1947, 30.

Cournos, John. "No Hiroshima." Rev. of *Shadow on the Hearth*, by Judith Merrill. *New York Times Book Review*, 18 June 1950, 12.

Cowley, Malcolm. "A Faith for Writing." Rev. of *The Writer in America*, by Van Wyck Brooks. *New Republic*, 9 March 1953, 19–20.

——. "Mr. Brooks Dissenting." Rev. of *Opinions of Oliver Allston*, by Van Wyck Brooks. *New Republic*, 24 November 1941, 705–6.

——. "Mr. Brooks Dissenting: II." Rev. of *Opinions of Oliver Allston*, by Van Wyck Brooks. *New Republic*, 1 December 1941, 738–39.

——. "Shipwreck." *New Republic*, 9 September 1940, 357-58.

Creekmore, Hubert. Rev. of *Reflections in a Golden Eye*, by Carson McCullers, and *Satan's Sergeants*, by Josephine Herbst. *Accent* 2 (1941): 61–62.

Creighton, Alan. Rev. of *Coming Home*, by Lester Cohen. *Canadian Forum* 25 (August 1945): 120.

Daiches, David. "Writers' Shop Talk." Rev. of *The Living Novel*, ed. Granville Hicks. *Saturday Review*, 16 November 1957, 19–20.

"Decayed Gentility." Rev. of *The Sound and the Fury*, by William Faulkner. *New York Times Book Review*, 10 November 1929, 28.

De Grace, Therese. "Jemmie's Progress." Rev. of *Echoing Green*, by Eleanor Estes. *New York Times Book Review*, 30 November 1947, 22.

De Kay, Drake. "The Color Line." Rev. of *Blood on the Forge*, by William Attaway. *New York Times Book Review*, 24 August 1941, 18, 20.

DeVoto, Bernard. "The Brahmin Way of Life." Rev. of *The Late George Apley*, by John P. Marquand. *Saturday Review of Literature*, 2 January 1937, 5.

———. "John Dos Passos: Anatomist of Our Time." Rev. of *The Big Money*, by John Dos Passos. *Saturday Review of Literature*, 8 August 1936, 3–4, 12–13.

———. "Roberts' Rangers." Rev. of *Northwest Passage*, by Kenneth Roberts. *Saturday Review of Literature*, 3 July 1937, 5.

Dos Passos, John. "The Business of a Novelist." Rev. of *The Shadow Before*, by William Rollins Jr. *New Republic*, 4 April 1934, 220.

Doughty, Howard. "Writers Turn from Defeat to Affirmation." Rev. of *Writers in Crisis: The American Novel between Two Wars*, by Maxwell Geismar. *New York Herald Tribune Weekly Book Review*, 28 June 1942, 3.

Du Bois, William. "Tales of a 'Spunky Septuagenarian.' " Rev. of *The Journey of Simon McKeever*, by Albert Maltz. *New York Times Book Review*, 8 May 1949, 5.

Duffus, R. L. "Kenneth Roberts' New Novel." Rev. of *Oliver Wiswell*, by Kenneth Roberts. *New York Times Book Review*, 24 November 1940, 1.

Eastman, Max. "Whitman, Brooks, Groucho Marx." Rev. of *American Giant: Walt Whitman and His Times*, by Frances Winwar, *Opinions of Oliver Allston*, by Van Wyck Brooks, and *Many Happy Returns: An Unofficial Guide to Your Income Tax Problems*, by Groucho Marx. *American Mercury*, March 1942, 366–71.

"The Editor Recommends." *Bookman*, 27 April 1927, 213.

Edman, Irwin. "Discovery of America by Its Own Writers: In Alfred Kazin a Major Critic Roams from Howells to Steinbeck." Rev. of *On Native Grounds*, by Alfred Kazin. *New York Herald Tribune Books*, 1 November 1942, 1–2.

E. F. E. "The Living Voice of Mr. Howells." Rev. of *The Vacation of the Kelwyns: An Idyl of the Middle Eighteen-Seventies*, by William Dean Howells. *Boston Evening Transcript*, 29 September 1920, 4.

Eimerl, Sarel. "The Critics and Cozzens." Rev. of *Love Possessed*, by James Gould Cozzens. *New Republic*, 16 September 1957, 17.

Ellison, Ralph. "Collaborator with His Own Enemy." Rev. of *Stranger and Alone*, by J. Saunders Redding. *New York Times Book Review*, 19 February 1950, 4.

"Elusive Possessions." Rev. of *The Heritage of Hatcher Ide*, by Booth Tarkington. *Times Literary Supplement*, 23 August 1941, 405.

Eshleman, Lloyd. "Fiction." Rev. of *Satan's Sergeants*, by Josephine Herbst. *Commonweal*, 6 June 1941, 162–63.

Fadiman, Clifton P. Rev. of *Journey in the Dark*, by Martin Flavin. *New Yorker*, 23 October 1943, 78.

Fearing, Kenneth. Rev. of *Coming Home*, by Lester Cohen. *New York Times Book Review*, 13 May 1945, 11.

Feld, Rose. " 'The Liberals' and Other Recent Works of Fiction." Rev. of *The Liberals*, by John Hyde Preston. *New York Times Book Review*, 21 August 1938, 6.

———. "Negro from Nazareth." Rev. of *Royal Road*, by Arthur Kuhl. *New York Times Book Review*, 19 October 1941, 6.

———. Rev. of *I Know What I'd Do*, by Alice Beal Parsons. *New York Herald Tribune Weekly Book Review*, 5 May 1946, 10.

———. Rev. of *Men Working*, by John Faulkner. *New York Herald Tribune Books*, 10 August 1941, 6.

———. Rev. of *Satan's Sergeants*, by Josephine Herbst. *New York Herald Tribune Books*, 4 May 1941, 8.

———. "Subtly Moving Novel of Racial Conflict." Rev. of *First Family*, by Christopher Davis. *New York Herald Tribune Lively Arts*, 5 February 1961, 37.

———. "The World of the American Negro Today: The Gospel of 'Golden Slippers' Is Dead; He Asks Equal Rights." Rev. of *New World A-Coming*, by Roi Ottley. *New York Herald Tribune Weekly Book Review*, 15 August 1943, 1–2.

Ferguson, Otis. "The Incredible City." Rev. of *What Makes Sammy Run?*, by Budd Schulberg, and *City of Angels*, by Rupert Hughes. *New Republic*, 31 March 1941, 442–43.

Field, Louise Maunsell. "American Youth and the Depression." Rev. of *The Heritage of Hatcher Ide*, by Booth Tarkington. *New York Times Book Review*, 23 February 1941, 6.

———. "Dorothy Canfield's New Novel." Rev. of *Seasoned Timber*, by Dorothy Canfield. *New York Times Book Review*, 5 March 1939, 6.

Flagg, Nancy. "The Private Life of a Widower." Rev. of *The Wayfarers*, by Dan Wickenden. *New York Times Book Review*, 8 July 1945, 6

Flint, F. Cudworth. "A Cycle of New England." Rev. of *The Flowering of New England*, by Van Wyck Brooks. *Virginia Quarterly Review* 13, no. 1 (Winter 1937): 122–26.

Foerster, Norman. Rev. of *Opinions of Oliver Allston*, by Van Wyck Brooks. *American Literature* 14 (March 1942): 95–97.

Frank, Grace. "Crisis in Pawlet, N.Y." Rev. of *I Know What I'd Do*, by Alice Beal Parsons. *Saturday Review of Literature*, 27 April 1946, 45.

Frazier, E. Franklin. "Race: An American Dream." Rev. of *An American Dilemma: The Negro Problem and Modern Democracy*, by Gunnar Myrdal. *Crisis*, April 1944, 105–6, 124.

Gaither, Frances. "Democracy—the Negro's Hope." Rev. of *An American Dilemma: The Negro Problem and Modern Democracy*, by Gunnar Myrdal, with the assistance of Richard Sterner and Arnold Rose. *New York Times Book Review*, 2 April 1944, 7.

———. "Intrepid Traitor." *New York Times Book Review*, 13 March 1944, 5, 15.

Galbraith, J. K. "Hunt for a Heretic." Rev. of *The Sure Thing*, by Merle Miller. *New York Times Book Review*, 21 August 1949, 8.

Geismar, Maxwell. "The Roots and the Flowering Tree." Rev. of *Marjorie Morningstar*, by Herman Wouk. *New York Times Book Review*, 4 September 1955, 1.

———. "Sad Young Men of World War II." Rev. of *That Winter*, by Merle Miller. *Saturday Review of Literature*, 24 January 1948, 15.

"Get-Rich-Quick." Rev. of *P.A.L.*, by Felix Riesenberg. *New York Times Book Review*, 20 December 1925, 24.

Godfrey, Clare. Rev. of *Royal Road*, by Arthur Kuhl. *New York Herald Tribune Books*, 16 November 1941, 14.

Gold, Herbert. "Fugitive from a Chain Reaction." Rev. of *The Hound of Earth*, by Vance Bourjaily. *Nation*, 23 July 1955, 79.

Gold, William Jay. "Of Mississippi Folk." Rev. of *Men Working*, by John Faulkner. *Saturday Review of Literature*, 9 August 1941, 7.

Gorman, Herbert S. "Cabell as One of the Great American Romancers." Rev. of *James Branch Cabell*, by Carl Van Doren. *New York Times Book Review*, 29 March 1925, 11.

Gregory, Horace. "The World within a Factory." Rev. of *The Land of Plenty*, by Robert Cantwell. *Books*, 29 April 1934, 6,

Grieser, Norman. Rev. of *That Winter*, by Merle Miller. *New Republic*, 16 February 1948, 29–29.

Griffiths, Joan. "A Limited Device." Rev. of *Gentleman's Agreement*, by Laura Z. Hobson. *Nation*, 3 May 1947, 521.

Hackett, Francis. "Literary Critics." Rev. of *The World of Washington Irving*, by Van Wyck Brooks, *American Renaissance*, by F. O. Matthiessen, *The Literary Fallacy*, by Bernard DeVoto, *Puritanism and Democracy*, by Ralph Barton Perry, and *The Intent of the Critic*, by John Crowe Ransom. *American Mercury*, March 1945, 367–74.

Hampson, John. Rev. of *Spenlove in Arcady*, by William McFee, *No Stone Unturned*, by Josephine Lawrence, and *Owen Glendower*, by John Cowper Powys. *Spectator*, 27 March 1941, 312.

Hansen, Harry. " 'Unfinished Business of Democracy.' " Rev. of *An American Dilemma: The Negro Problem and Modern Democracy*, by Gunnar Myrdal, with the assistance of Richard Sterner and Arnold Rose. *Survey Graphic* 33 (1944): 183–84.

Hardwick, Elizabeth. "Much Outcry; Little Outcome." Rev. of *That Winter*, by Merle Miller, and *Other Voices, Other Rooms*, by Truman Capote. *Partisan Review* 25, no. 3 (March 1948): 374–77.

Hauser, Marianne. Rev. of *The Dam*, by Jerome Ellison. *New York Herald Tribune Books*, 27 April 1941, 10.

Hayes, Dorsha. "No Longer the Forgotten Men." Rev. of *The Dam*, by Jerome Ellison. *Saturday Review of Literature*, 3 May 1941, 11.

Hays, Arthur Garfield. "Primer for the Race of the Living." Rev. of *New World A-Coming*, by Roi Ottley. *Saturday Review of Literature*, 18 September 1943, 16.

Hayward, Henry S. "Combating Racial Intolerance." Rev. of *Gentleman's Agreement*, by Laura Z. Hobson. *Christian Science Monitor*, 21 March 1947, 18.

Hazlitt, Henry. "Walter Lippmann's Prescription for the Good Society." Rev. of *The Good Society*, by Walter Lippmann. *New York Times Book Review*, 26 September 1937, 3, 30.

"A Heart Divided." Rev. of *Call Home the Heart*, by Fielding Burke. *Christian Science Monitor*, 12 March 1932, 5.

Hicks, Granville. "The Swastika in Vermont." Rev. of *Seasoned Timber*, by Dorothy Canfield. *New Republic*, 12 April 1939, 284.

Holsaert, Eunice S. "Sally's Dilemma." Rev. of *I Know What I'd Do*, by Alice Beal Parsons. *New York Times Book Review*, 12 May 1946, 14.

Holt, Rackham. "A Tenth of a Nation." Rev. of *New World A-Coming*, by Roi Ottley. *New York Times Book Review*, 15 August 1943, 3.

Houghton, W. M. "What President Roosevelt Hopes to Achieve." Rev. of *Looking Forward*, by Franklin Delano Roosevelt. *Books*, 19 March 1933, 1.

Hutchison, Percy A. "Love and War in the Pages of Mr. Hemingway." Rev. of *A Farewell to Arms*, by Ernest Hemingway. *New York Times Book Review*, 29 September 1929, 5.

——. "Mr. Marquand's Novel of the Boston Brahmin Tradition." Rev. of *The Late George Apley*, by John P. Marquand. *New York Times Book Review*, 3 January 1937, 3.

——. "Mrs. Wharton Brings 'The House of Mirth' Up to Date." Rev. of *The Mother's Recompense*, by Edith Wharton. *New York Times Book Review*, 26 April 1925, 7.

"In a First Novel the Worldly Affairs of the Clergy." Rev. of *Faith of Our Fathers*, by Dorothy Walworth Carman. *New York Times Book Review*, 15 March 1925, 8.

"In Indiana." Rev. of *Keys of the City*, by Elmer Davis. *New York Times Book Review*, 22 February 1925, 8.

Janeway, Elizabeth. "Man in Conflict, Mind in Torment." Rev. of *World Enough and Time*, by Robert Penn Warren. *New York Times Book Review*, 25 June 1950, 1.

J. D. A. "Miss Roberts's Kentucky Saga." Rev. of *The Great Meadow*, by Elizabeth Madox Roberts. *New York Times Book Review*, 2 March 1930, 1.

Johnson, Gerald W. "An American Dilemma." Rev. of *The Negro Problem and Modern Democracy*, by Gunnar Myrdal, with the assistance of Richard Sterner and Arnold Rose. *New York Herald Tribune Weekly Book Review*, 13 August 1944, 2.

Jones, Howard Mumford. "Life in the Dustbowl." Rev. of *The Tree Falls South*, by Wellington Roe. *Saturday Review of Literature*, 22 May 1937, 12.

——. "Opinions of Van Wyck Brooks." Rev. of *Opinions of Oliver Allston*, by Van Wyck Brooks. *Saturday Review of Literature*, 15 November 1941, 5, 20.

——. "What Is Literary History?" Rev. of *A History of American Letters*, by Walter Fuller Taylor, *Literature and American Life*, by Percy H. Boynton, and *The Puritan Pronaos: Studies in the Intellectual Life of New England in the Sixteenth Century*, by Samuel Eliot Morison. *Saturday Review of Literature*, 8 August 1936, 10.

Kang, Younghill. "China Is Different." Rev. of *The Good Earth*, by Pearl S. Buck, and *The Tragedy of Ah Qui and Other Modern Chinese Stories*, trans. Kyn Yr Yu and E. H. F. Mills. *New Republic*, 1 July 1931, 185.

Kazin, Alfred. " 'White Mule' and Other Recent Works of Fiction." Rev. of *White Mule*, by William Carlos Williams. *New York Times Book Review*, 20 June 1937, 7.

Keene, Frances. "The Modern Marriage." Rev. of *The Many Lives of Modern Woman*, by Sidonie M. Gruenberg. *Nation*, 11 October 1952, 335.

Kelly, Janes. "Racial Clash in Courtland Park." Rev. of *First Family*, by Christopher Davis. *New York Times Book Review*, 5 February 1961, 41.

Kittredge, Eleanor. "An Eloquent Warning to Us That the Hour Grows Late." Rev. of *Is Tomorrow Hitler's?*, by H. R. Knickerbocker. *New York Times Book Review*, 14 December 1941, 9.

Klaw, Barbara. Rev. of *Coming Home*, by Lester Cohen. *New York Herald Tribune Weekly Book Review*, 13 May 1945, 6.

Kreymborg, Alfred. "March of a Noble Race." Rev. of *The Negro Caravan*, ed. Sterling A.
Brown, Arthur P. Davis, and Ulysses Lee. *New York Times Book Review*, 21 February
1942, 13.

Kronenberger, Louis. "Albert Halper's Vivid New Novel." Rev. of *The Foundry*, by Albert
Halper. *New York Times Book Review*, 9 September 1934, 6.

———. "Portrait of a Factory." Rev. of *The Land of Plenty*, by Robert Cantwell. *Nation*,
13 June 1934, 679.

———. "A Racial Problem." Rev. of *God of Might*, by Elias Tobenkin. *Saturday Review of
Literature*, 4 April 1925, 643.

Krutch, Joseph Wood. "An Invitation to Minerva." Rev. of *Opinions of Oliver Allston*, by
Van Wyck Brooks. *Nation*, 13 December 1941, 615–16.

———. "The Peasants." Rev. of *The Time of Man*, by Elizabeth Madox Roberts. *Saturday
Review of Literature*, 28 August 1926, 69.

"A Laborer's Life." Rev. of *Reamer Lou*, by Louis Forgione. *New York Times Book Review*,
1 March 1925, 14.

Laidler, Harry W. "A Communist Examines Capitalism." Rev. of *The Decline of American
Capitalism*, by Lewis Corey. *Survey Graphic* 24 (January 1935): 41.

Lardner, John. "The Mislaid Generation." Rev. of *That Winter*, by Merle Miller. *New
Yorker*, 24 January 1948, 78–80.

Lazarus, H. P. "In Solitary." Rev. of *Satan's Sergeants*, by Josephine Herbst. *Nation*,
31 May 1941, 646.

LeMay, Hardy. "Children Play; Adults Betray." Rev. of *To Kill a Mockingbird*, by Harper
Lee. *New York Herald Weekly Book Review*, 10 July 1960, 5.

Lerner, Max. "Lippmann Agonistes." Rev. of *The Good Society*, by Walter Lippmann.
Nation, 27 November 1937, 589–90.

Lewis, Sinclair. "Manhattan at Last!" Rev. of *Manhattan Transfer*, by John Dos Passos.
Saturday Review of Literature, 5 December 1925, 361.

Locke, Alain. Rev. of *What the Negro Wants*, by Rayford W. Logan. *Survey Mid-Monthly* 81
(March 1945): 95.

Lovett, Robert Morss. "Chicago." Rev. of *Chicago: The History of Its Reputation*, by Henry
Justin Smith and Lloyd Lewis. *New Republic*, 4 September 1929, 76–77.

———. "Diagram of Pain." Rev. of *Eva Gay*, by Evelyn Scott. *New Republic*, 17 May 1933,
24–25.

———. Rev. of *Years of Grace*, by Margaret Ayer Barnes. *New Republic*, 23 July 1930, 298.

Lynd, Robert S. "Prison for American Genius: 'The Vast and Ugly Reality of Our
Greatest Failure.'" Rev. of *An American Dilemma: The Negro Problem and Modern
Democracy*, by Gunnar Myrdal, with the assistance of Richard Sterner and Arnold
Rose. *Saturday Review of Literature*, 22 April 1944, 5–7.

MacBride, James. "Reconversion Blues." Rev. of *That Winter*, by Merle Miller. *New York
Times Book Review*, 25 January 1948, 5.

MacDonald, William. "A Jeremiad over the State of American Capitalism." Rev. of *The
Decline of American Capitalism*, by Lewis Corey. *New York Times Book Review*,
9 September 1934, 5, 20.

Magid, Nora. "The Girl Who Went Back Home." Rev. of *Marjorie Morningstar*, by Herman Wouk. *New Republic*, 5 September 1955, 20.

Malcolm, Donald. "Drugstore Culture." Rev. of *Mass Culture*, ed. Bernard Rosenberg and David Manning. *New Republic*, 29 July 1957, 16–17.

Marquand, John P. "Freedom of the Mind." Rev. of *Seasoned Timber*, by Dorothy Canfield. *New York Times Book Review*, 4 March 1939, 5.

———. "Tarkington and Social Significance." Rev. of *The Heritage of Hatcher Ide*, by Booth Tarkington. *Saturday Review of Literature*, 1 March 1941, 7.

Marsh, Fred T. "Of Men and Work." Rev. of *Men Working*, by John Faulkner. *New York Times Book Review*, 10 August 1941, 6–7.

———. "Mr. McIntyre's Novel." Rev. of *Ferment*, by John Thomas McIntyre. *New York Times Book Review*, 11 July 1937, 4.

———. "People of a Great Migration: A Novel of Negroes Who Went from South to North." Rev. of *O Canaan!*, by Waters E. Turpin. *New York Times Book Review*, 16 July 1939, 4.

———. "When the Good Earth Blows Away." Rev. of *The Tree Falls South*, by Wellington Roe. *New York Times Book Review*, 23 May 1937, 7.

———. "WPA Workers." Rev. of *The Dam*, by Jerome Ellison. *New York Times Book Review*, 4 May 1941, 7, 23.

Match, Richard. "Six Stalled Marriages." Rev. of *About Lyddy Thomas*, by Maritta Wolf. *New York Herald Tribune Weekly Book Review*, 23 November 1947, 16.

"The Maternal Woman." Rev. of *Maids Will Be Wives*, by Hazel Cole. *New York Times Book Review*, 19 May 1929, 8.

Matthiessen, F. O. " 'The Great Tradition': A Counter-Statement." Rev. of *The Great Tradition*, by Granville Hicks. *New England Quarterly* 7 (June 1934): 223–34.

Maynard, Theodore. Rev. of *Opinions of Oliver Allston*, by Van Wyck Brooks. *Thought* 17 (1942): 136–38.

McFee, William. Rev. of *The Perennial Bachelor*, by Anna Parrish. 1925. *Current Reviews*, ed. L. W. Smith, 228–32. New York: Henry Holt, 1926.

McGrory, Mary. "A Fine Novel of a Woman's Choice between Two Worlds." Rev. of *The Left Hand Is the Dreamer*, by Nancy Wilson Ross. *New York Times Book Review*, 16 February 1947, 3.

McLaughlin, Michael J. Rev. of *What the Negro Wants*, ed. Rayford W. Logan. *Catholic World*, April 1945, 89–90.

McMahon, Joseph H. "One Man's Revolt." Review of *The Hound of Earth*, by Vance Bourjaily. *Commonweal*, 18 March 1955, 639.

Meacham, William Shands. "The Negro's Future in America." Rev. of *What the Negro Wants*, ed. Rayford W. Logan. *New York Times Book Review*, 5 November 1944, 28.

———. "Negro Writers Speak for Themselves." Rev. of *The Negro Caravan*, ed. Sterling A. Brown, Arthur P. Davis, and Ulysses Lee. *New York Times Book Review*, 29 March 1942, 3.

Miller, Perry. "A Friendly Restoration of William Dean Howells." Rev. of *Howells: His Life and World*, by Van Wyck Brooks. *New York Herald Tribune Weekly Book Review*, 11 October 1959, 1.

Monaghan, John. Rev. of *The Opinions of Oliver Allston*, by Van Wyck Brooks. *Commonweal*, 9 January 1942, 300.

Moon, Bucklin. "Deep South." Rev. of *Swing Low*, by Edwin A. Peeples. *New Republic*, 7 May 1945, 649.

Moon, Henry Lee. "Hectic Harlem." Rev. of *New World A-Coming*, by Roi Ottley. *New Republic*, 6 September 1943, 342.

Morey, C. R. "Critical Reading and a Troubled World." Rev. of *How to Read a Book*, by Mortimer J. Adler. *Commonweal*, 7 June 1940, 149–51.

Morris, Lloyd. "More Historical Novels." Rev. of *Paradise*, by Esther Forbes. *North American Review* 243, no. 2 (Summer 1937): 395–400.

——. "A Swift-Paced, Dramatic, Thoughtful Story." Rev. of *Time Is Noon*, by Hiram Collins Hadyn. *New York Herald Weekly Book Review*, 28 March 1948, 3.

"Mr. Bromfield's Family Chronicle." Rev. of *The Farm*, by Louis Bromfield. *New York Times Book Review*, 20 August 1933, 6.

"Mr. Dixon's Thriller and Other New Summer Novels." Rev. of *The Love Complex*, by Thomas Dixon. *New York Times Book Review*, 5 July 1925, 12.

"Mr. Hemingway Writes Some High-Spirited Nonsense." Rev. of *Torrents of Spring*, by Ernest Hemingway. *New York Times Book Review*, 13 June 1926, 24.

"Murderous Satire." Rev. of *These Are My Jewels*, by L. B. Campbell. *New York Times Book Review*, 17 February 1929, 6.

Murdock, Kenneth B. "Flesh and Blood Puritans." Rev. of *Paradise*, by Esther Forbes. *Saturday Review of Literature*, 27 February 1937, 6–7.

"Negro Folktales." Rev. of the *The Conjure-Woman*, by Charles W. Chestnutt. *New York Times Book Review*, 3 March 1929, 9.

N. E. M. Rev. of *Journey in the Dark*, by Martin Flavin. *Catholic World*, January 1944, 410–11.

"New York, New York!" Rev. of *That Winter*, by Merle Miller. *Atlantic Monthly*, March 1948, 107.

"New York of 1924 in a New Van Vechten Novel." Rev. of *Firecrackers*, by Carl Van Vechten. *New York Times Book Review*, 9 August 1925, 6.

Nicholson, Marjorie Hope. "Reading and Education." Rev. of *How to Read a Book: The Art of Getting a Liberal Education*, by Mortimer Adler. *Yale Review* 30 (Autumn 1940): 184–88.

Niebuhr, Reinhold. "Challenge for Liberals." Rev. of *Faith for Living*, by Lewis Mumford. *Nation*, 14 September 1940, 221.

"A Novel of the Southern Mills." Rev. of *To Make My Bread*, by Grace Lumpkin. *New York Times Book Review*, 25 September 1932, 7.

Overstreet, H. A. "On the American Agenda." Rev. of *What the Negro Wants*, ed. Rayford W. Logan. *Saturday Review of Literature*, 4 November 1944, 15.

Parke, Andrea. "A Cabin in the Cotton." Rev. of *Send Me an Angel*, by Alice Nisbet. *New York Times Book Review*, 8 December 1946, 10.

Parsons, Alice Beal. "Another Way of Hacking at Wine Chests." Rev. of *Shadows Waiting*, by Eleanor Chilton. *Books*, 20 February 1927, 7.

——. "Prairie and Fjord." Rev. of *Peder Victorious*, by O. E. Rolvaag. Trans. Nora A. Solum and Rolvaag. *Nation*, 13 March 1929, 317–18.

Paterson, Isabel. "Up to the Minute." Rev. of *The Great Gatsby*, by F. Scott Fitzgerald. *New York Herald Tribune*, 19 April 1925, 6.

Petry, Ann. "No Mobs, No Fiery Crosses." Rev. of *Without Magnolias*, by Bucklin Moon. *New York Herald Tribune Weekly Book Review*, 10 April 1949, 4.

——. "Race Betrayal." Rev. of *Stranger and Alone*, by J. Saunders Redding. *Saturday Review of Literature*, 25 February 1950, 18.

Poore, Charles. "Books of the Times." Rev. of *Gentleman's Agreement*, by Laura Z. Hobson. *New York Times Book Review*, 27 February 1947, 19.

"Preludes to a Mood." Rev. of *In Our Time*, by Ernest Hemingway. *New York Times Book Review*, 18 October 1925, 8.

"The Pride of Palomar." Review of *The Pride of Palomar*, by Peter B. Kyne. *New York Times Book Review*, 2 October 1921, 12, and *Literary Review*, 22 October 1921, 107.

"Protestant Clergymen." Rev. of *A Man of Little Faith*, by Reginald Wright Kauffman. *New York Times Book Review*, 27 March 1927, 14.

Ransom, John Crowe. "Sociology and the Black Belt." Rev. of *Shadow of the Plantation*, by Charles S. Johnson. *American Review* 4, no. 2 (December 1934): 147–54.

Redding, J. Saunders. "The Negro: America's Dilemma." Rev. of *An American Dilemma: The Negro Problem and Modern Democracy*, by Gunnar Myrdal, with the assistance of Richard Sterner and Arnold Rose. *New Republic*, 20 March 1944, 384–86.

"Redemption by Work." Rev. of *The Way of All Earth*, by Edith Barnard Delano. *New York Times Book Review*, 24 May 1925, 9.

Reuter, E. B. Rev. of *What the Negro Wants*, ed. Rayford W. Logan. *American Journal of Sociology* 50 (January 1945): 317–18.

Rev. of *About Lyddy Thomas*, by Maritta Wolff. *New Yorker*, 15 November 1947, 136.

Rev. of *An American Dilemma*, by Gunnar Myrdal. *Catholic World*, 1944, 181–82.

Rev. of *The Dam*, by Earl Jerome Ellison. *Booklist*, 1 June 1941, 464.

Rev. of *Gentleman's Agreement*, by Laura Z. Hobson. *Catholic World*, June 1947, 285–86.

Rev. of *Journey in the Dark*, by Martin Flavin. *Commonweal*, 12 November 1943, 100.

Rev. of *Men Working*, by John Faulkner. *Booklist*, 1 October 1941, 35.

Rev. of *Men Working*, by John Faulkner. *Christian Century*, 13 August 1941, 1007.

Rev. of *Men Working*, by John Faulkner. *Time*, 11 August 1941, 68–71.

Rev. of *Royal Road*, by Arthur Kuhl. *Catholic World*, January 1942, 507.

Rev. of *Royal Road*, by Arthur Kuhl. *Christian Century*, 15 October 1941, 1276.

"Reviewing Reviews: *Northwest Passage* by Kenneth Roberts." *Saturday Review of Literature*, 14 August 1937, 16.

"Reviewing Reviews." *Saturday Review of Literature*, 16 January 1937, 19–20.

"Reviewing Reviews." *Saturday Review of Literature*, 19 June 1937, 21–22.

"Reviewing Reviews: William Maxwell's 'They Came Like Swallows.'" *Saturday Review of Literature*, 17 July 1937, 20.

Reynolds, Horace. "The Story of an Average American." Rev. of *Journey in the Dark*, by Martin Flavin. *New York Times Book Review*, 24 October 1943, 4.

Rice, Jennings. Rev. of *Treason*, by Robert Gessner. *New York Herald Tribune Weekly Book Review*, 12 March 1944, 6.

Richards, Anne. "Martha's Puritan Bondage." Rev. of *The Last Leaf*, by Peggy Munsterberg. *New York Times Book Review*, 16 March 1947, 16.

Robins, J. D. "A Great Migration." Rev. of *The Great Meadow*, by Elizabeth Madox Roberts. *Canadian Forum* 10 (1930): 296.

Rosenberger, Coleman. "Southern Negroes in Chicago." Rev. of *Behold a Cry*, by Alden Bland. *New York Herald Tribune Weekly Book Review*, 9 March 1949, 7.

Rosenfeld, Isaac. "For God and the Suburbs." Rev. of *Marjorie Morningstar*, by Herman Wouk. *Partisan Review* (Fall 1955): 565–69.

Ross, Alan. "War's Aftermath." Rev. of *That Winter*, by Merle Miller, and *The Sky Is Red*, by Giuseppe Berto. *Times Literary Supplement*, 9 October 1948, 565.

Ross, Mary. "Out of a Black Past." Rev. of *East By Day*, by Blair Niles. *New York Herald Tribune Books*, 19 January 1941, 2.

——. Rev. of *The Heritage of Hatcher Ide*, by Booth Tarkington. *New York Herald Tribune Books*, 23 February 1941, 8, 10.

——. "Two Worlds Meet, Quietly and Happily." Rev. of *Knot of Roots*, by Elizabeth Baynes De Vegh. *New York Herald Weekly Book Review*, 25 January 1959, 5.

——. "A Warm Human Appeal." Rev. of *My Heart Shall Not Fear*, by Josephine Lawrence. *New York Herald Weekly Book Review*, 17 April 1949, 10.

Ross, Virgilia Peterson. "The Chronicle of a Family." Rev. of *Years of Grace*, by Margaret Ayer Barnes. *New York Herald Tribune Books*, 29 June 1930, 3.

Rothman, Nathan L. "Angel of Doom and Babes in the Woods." Rev. of *Find Me in Fire*, by Robery Lowry, and *The Last Profession*, by Jacques Laurent. *Saturday Review of Literature*, 7 August 1948, 18.

Rugoff, Milton. "The Magic of William Faulkner." Rev. of *Go Down, Moses*, by William Faulkner. *New York Herald Tribune Books*, 17 May 1942, 2.

——. "Pilgrim—and a Message." Rev. of *The Journey of Simon McKeever*, by Albert Maltz. *New York Herald Tribune Weekly Book Review*, 15 May 1949, 8.

——. Rev. of *Blood on the Forge*, by William Attaway. *New York Herald Tribune Books*, 24 August 1941, 8.

——. Rev. of *That Winter*, by Merle Miller. *New York Herald Tribune Weekly Book Review*, 25 January 1948, 6.

Sadler, Coral. "Racial Blueprint." Rev. of *What the Negro Wants*, ed. Rayford W. Logan. *Crisis*, December 1944, 395, 398.

Schlesinger, Arthur, Jr. "Portrait of America, Warts and All." Rev. of *As Others See Us: The United States through Foreign Eyes*, ed. Franz M. Joseph. *New York Times Book Review*, 20 December 1959, 1, 14.

Schulberg, Budd. "Kid-Glove Cruelty." Rev. of *Gentleman's Agreement*, by Laura Z. Hobson. *New Republic*, 17 March 1947, 36.

"A Selfish Woman." Rev. of *Queen Dick*, by Nalbro Bartley. *New York Times Book Review*, 21 April 1929, 17.

Seligman, Ben. "The Briefcase Man." Rev. of *White Collar*, by C. Wright Mills. *New Republic*, 17 July 1951, 20.

Shannon, J. B. Rev. of *What the Negro Wants*, ed. Rayford W. Logan. *American Political Science Review* 39 (February 1945): 197–98.

Sherman, Beatrice. "Home Front Romance." Rev. of *Also the Hills*, by Frances Parkinson Keyes. *New York Times Book Review*, 28 November 1943, 6, 24.

Shuster, George. "George Brush." Rev. of *Heaven's My Destination*, by Thornton Wilder. *Commonweal*, 22 March 1935, 604–5.

Simpson, Clinton. "A Powerful Novel of Social Revolt." Rev. of *The Disinherited*, by Jack Conroy. *Saturday Review of Literature*, 2 December 1933, 305.

Slade, Caroline. "Unofficial Truth." Rev. of *Men Working*, by John Faulkner. *Survey Mid-Monthly* 77 (November 1941): 340.

Smith, Bradford. "Personal Upheaval." Rev. of *About Lyddy Thomas*, by Maritta Wolf. *Saturday Review of Literature*, 29 November 1947, 17–18.

Smith, Harrison. "Atom-Bombing Here." Rev. of *Shadow on the Hearth*, by Judith Merril. *Saturday Review of Literature*, 2 July 1950, 3.

——. "Fighting Man or Stuffed Goose." Rev. of *Doppelgangers*, by Gerald Heard. *Saturday Review of Literature*, 15 March 1947, 14.

Smyth, Frances. "Malty Russell." Rev. of *No Stone Unturned*, by Josephine Lawrence. *Saturday Review of Literature*, 8 February 1941, 20.

Soskin, William. "When World Problems Invade Vermont." Rev. of *Seasoned Timber*, by Dorothy Canfield Fisher. *Books*, 5 March 1939, 5.

——. *Books*, 3 May 1939, 6.

Spingarn, Joel Elias. "The New Criticism." In *Criticism in America: Its Function and Status*, by Irving Babbitt et al., 9–45, 1924. New York: Haskell House, 1969.

Stearn, Bernhard J. Rev. of *What the Negro Wants*, ed. Rayford W. Logan. *Political Science Quarterly* 60 (June 1945): 306–7.

Stegner, Wallace. "The Rise of Sam Braden." Rev. of *Journey in the Dark*, by Martin Flavin. *Saturday Review of Literature*, 13 November 1943, 7.

Stong, Phil. "Coal Gestapo in Pennsylvania." Rev. of *Coming Home*, by Lester Cohen. *Saturday Review of Literature*, 2 June 1945, 22.

Stout, Rex. "A Jew for Two Months—What He Learned." Rev. of *Gentleman's Agreement*, by Laura Z. Hobson. *New York Herald Tribune Weekly Book Review*, 9 March 1947, 5.

Strachey, Richard. "Mainly American." Rev. of *Mario and the Magician*, by Thomas Mann, *Exit*, by H. B. Wright, *Ol' Man Adam an' His Chillun*, by Roark Bradford, *Black Soil*, by Josephine Donovan, *Years of Grace*, by Margaret Ayer Barnes, and *The Forty-second Parallel*, by John Dos Passos. *Nation and Athenæum*, 1 November 1930, 169–70.

Strauss, Harold. "A Novel of Youth in Chicago." Rev. of *The Old Bunch*, by Meyer Levin. *New York Times Book Review*, 28 March 1937, 6.

——. "Robert Cantwell's Novel and Other Recent Works of Fiction." Rev. of *The Land of Plenty*, by Robert Cantwell. *New York Times Book Review*, 29 April 1934, 7.

Stuart, Henry Longan. "Family Decadence and Tragedy the Theme of Prize Novel." Rev.

of *The Perennial Bachelor*, by Anne Parrish. *New York Times Book Review*, 6 September 1925, 9.

——. "John Dos Passos Notes the Tragic Trivia of New York." Rev. of *Manhattan Transfer*, by John Dos Passos. *New York Times Book Review*, 29 November 1925, 5–10.

Sugrue, Thomas. "A Post-War Novel—Strictly Down-to-Earth." Rev. of *About Lyddy Thomas*, by Maritta Wolf. *New York Times Book Review*, 10 November 1947, 22.

Sullivan, Richard. "Silver Threads among the Gold." Rev. of *Always Young and Fair*, by Conrad Richter. *New York Times Book Review*, 30 March 1947, 4.

Sylvester, Harry. Rev. of *Men Working*, by John Faulkner. *Commonweal*, 29 August 1941, 451–52.

Tate, Allen. "Hard-Boiled." Rev. of *The Sun Also Rises*, by Ernest Hemingway. *Nation*, 15 December 1926, 642–43.

Taylor, Graham. "This Is Chicago!" Rev. of *Chicago: The History of Its Reputation*, by Lloyd Lewis and Henry Justin Smith. *Survey*, 1 November 1929, 160–61.

T. D. J. "Negroes, but Not Men." Rev. of *Without Magnolias*, by Bucklin Moon. *Phylon* 10, no. 3 (3rd Quarter 1949): 275–76.

Terry, C. V. "Impasse." Rev. of *Alien Land*, by Willard Savoy. *New York Times Book Review*, 3 April 1949, 20.

"This Perfect World." Rev. of *Those Difficult Years*, by Faith Baldwin. *New York Times Book Review*, 10 May 1925, 9.

Thompson, John H. "Ten Soldiers in Never-Never Land." Rev. of *The Strange Land*, by Ned Calmer. *Chicago Sunday Tribune Books*, 19 February 1950, 3.

Thompson, Lovell. "Eden in Easy Payments." Rev. of Sears Roebuck Catalogue: Spring and Summer 1937. *Saturday Review of Literature*, 3 April 1937, 15–16.

"Three Blind Mice." Rev. of *See How They Run*, by Helen Grace Carlisle. *New York Times Book Review*, 30 June 1929, 4.

Tompkins, Lucy. "In the Florida Glades." Rev. of *Their Eyes Were Watching God*, by Zora Neale Hurston. *New York Times Book Review*, 26 September 1937, 29.

Trilling, Diana. "Americans without Distinction." Rev. of *Gentleman's Agreement*, by Laura Z. Hobson. *Commentary*, March 1947, 290–92.

Trilling, Lionel. "Four Decades of American Prose." Rev. of *On Native Grounds*, by Alfred Kazin. *Nation*, 7 September 1942, 483–84.

——. "Some Are Gentle, Some Are Not." Rev. of *The Troubled Air*, by Irwin Shaw. *Saturday Review of Literature*, 9 June 1951, 8–9.

"Turbulent Folkways of the Ghetto in a New Novel." Rev. of *Bread Givers*, by Anzia Yezierska. *New York Times Book Review*, 13 September 1925, 8.

Ulrich, Mabel S. "The Conn. Family." Rev. of *Also the Hills*, by Frances Parkinson Keyes. *Saturday Review of Literature*, 5 February 1944, 26.

Vance, Rupert B. "Tragic Dilemma: The Negro and the American Dream." Rev. of *An American Dilemma: The Negro Problem and American Democracy*, by Gunnar Myrdal, with the assistance of Richard Sterner and Arnold Rose. *Virginia Quarterly Review* 20, no. 3 (Summer 1944): 435–45.

Van Doren, Carl. "Howells His Own Censor." Rev. of *The Vacation of the Kelwyns, an Idyl of the Middle Eighteen-Seventies*, by William Dean Howells. *Literary Review*, 23 October 1920, 3.

Van Doren, Dorothy. "Into the Wilderness." Rev. of *The Great Meadow*, by Elizabeth Madox Roberts. *Nation*, 12 March 1930, 300–301.

———. "The Making of a Boston Brahmin." Rev. of *The Late George Apley*, by John P. Marquand. *Nation*, 16 January 1937, 77–78.

Van Gelder, Robert. "Escape from Labor." Rev. of *No Stone Unturned*, by Josephine Lawrence. *New York Times Book Review*, 4 January 1941, 6.

———. "Lynch Mob." Rev. of *Night at Hogwallow*, by Theodore Strauss. *New York Times Book Review*, 17 October 1937, 7.

———. "Neuroses in Athens, Michigan." Rev. of *The Inheritance*, by Allan Seagar. *New York Times Book Review*, 18 April 1948, 7.

Van Vechten, Carl. "Fitzgerald on the March." Rev. of *The Great Gatsby*, by F. Scott Fitzgerald. *Nation*, 20 March 1925, 575–76.

"Vulgarity Triumphs." Rev. of *The Old Enchantment*, by Larry Barretto. *New York Times Book Review*, 18 March 1928, 9.

Wallace, Margaret. "*East By Day* and Other Recent Works of Fiction." Rev. of *East By Day*, by Blair Niles. *New York Times Book Review*, 19 January 1941, 7.

———. "A Fine Novel of Revolution." Rev. of *Trumpets of Dawn*, by Cyril Harris. *New York Times Book Review*, 28 August 1938, 6.

———. "A Hollywood Story." Rev. of *City of Angels*, by Rupert Hughes. *New York Times Book Review*, 9 March 1941, 7.

———. "A Romance of the Navajo Country." Rev. of *Laughing Boy*, by Oliver La Farge. *New York Times Book Review*, 24 November 1929, 4.

Walton, Eda Lou. "A Modern Navajo." Rev. of *People of the Earth*, by Edwin Corle. *New York Times Book Review*, 18 April 1937, 21.

———. "A Return to the Soil of Maine." Rev. of *Neighbor to the Sky*, by Gladys Hasty Carroll. *New York Times Book Review*, 16 May 1937, 2.

Walton, Edith H. "Josephine Herbst's New Novel." Rev. of *Satan's Sergeants*, by Josephine Herbst. *New York Times Book Review*, 4 May 1941, 6.

Weaver, William Fense. "Southern Negroes' World." Rev. of *Without Magnolias*, by Bucklin Moon. *New York Times Book Review*, 10 April 1949, 4.

Weeks, Edward. "The Negro as Our Neighbor." Rev. of *Peaceable Lane*, by Keith Wheeler. *Atlantic Monthly*, January 1961, 152.

West, Herbert F. "War's Smell and Taste." Rev. of *The Strange Land*, by Ned Calmer. *New York Times Book Review*, 5 February 1950, 4.

Whipple, Leon. "Forecasts of Change." Rev. of *The Good Society*, by Walter Lippmann, *Divided We Stand*, by Walter Prescott Webb, and *The Folklore of Capitalism*, by Thurman W. Arnold. *Survey Graphic* 27 (January 1938): 47–48.

" 'The White Girl' and Other Recent Works of Fiction." Rev. of *The White Girl*, by Vera Caspary. *New York Times Book Review*, 20 January 1929, 8.

Wilson, Edmund. "Mr. Wilder in the Middle West." Rev. of *Heaven's My Destination*, by Thornton Wilder. *New Republic*, 16 January 1935, 282.

——. "Return of Ernest Hemingway." Rev. of *For Whom the Bell Tolls*, by Ernest Hemingway. *New Republic*, 28 October 1940, 591–92.

Winterich, John T. " 'The Popular Book.' " Rev. of *The Popular Book*, by James D. Hart. *Publishers' Weekly*, 9 September 1950, 1042–46.

Young, Stanley. "A Wide-Sweeping Novel of American Generations." Rev. of *American Dream*, by Michael Foster. *New York Times Book Review*, 27 June 1937, 2.

MISCELLANEOUS

Aldridge, John W. "Two Communications: Manners and Values." Reply to "American Fiction and American Values," by William Barrett, in *Partisan Review* 18 (November–December 1951). *Partisan Review* 19 (May–June 1952): 347–50.

Asheim, Lester. *Report on the Conference on Reading Development, January 20–21, 1951.* Committee on Reading Development, American Book Publishers Council, 1951.

Barrett, William. "The Liberal Mind: Two Communications and a Reply: Art, Aristocracy, and Reason." *Partisan Review* 16, no. 6 (June 1949): 658–65.

Basso, Hamilton. Letter. *New Republic*, 30 June 1937, 225.

"Best Sellers of 1941." *Publishers' Weekly*, 17 January 1942, 174–76.

"Best Sellers of 1942." *Publishers' Weekly*, 16 January 1943, 242–44.

"Best Sellers of 1943." *Publishers' Weekly*, 22 January 1944, 290–92.

"Best Sellers of 1944." *Publishers' Weekly*, 20 January 1945, 223–24.

Boyd, James. "The Prospect for American Literature." Editorial. *Outlook*, August 1929, 587.

Caldwell, Taylor. Letter. *Saturday Review*, 7 February 1953, 24.

Canby, Henry Seidel. "American Values." Editorial. *Saturday Review of Literature*, 16 September 1939, 8.

——. "Better Books, Better Men." Editorial. *Saturday Review of Literature*, 2 February 1935, 456.

——. "Books and the Radio." Editorial. *Saturday Review of Literature*, 15 February 1936, 8.

——. "Critic and Writer." Editorial. *Saturday Review of Literature*, 11 July 1936, 8.

——. " 'The Critics Be Damned.' " Editorial. *Saturday Review of Literature*, 18 May 1935, 8.

——. "The Ethics of Popularity." Editorial. *Saturday Review of Literature*, 9 May 1936, 8.

——. "Fiction Searches the Map." Editorial. *Saturday Review of Literature*, 24 August 1935, 8.

——. "Heroes for Sale." Editorial. *Saturday Review of Literature*, 19 September 1936, 8.

——. " 'Let the Republic Come to Harm.' " Editorial. *Saturday Review of Literature*, 25 November 1939, 8.

——. "The Present State of English Literature." Editorial. *Saturday Review of Literature*, 11 September 1937, 8.

——. "Significant Reading of a Literary Year." Editorial. *Saturday Review of Literature*, 8 August 1936, 8.

——. "Standardization." Editorial. *Saturday Review of Literature*, 12 February 1927, 572.

——. "Standards." Editorial. *Saturday Review of Literature*, 6 October 1928, 1.

——. "Standards." Editorial. *Saturday Review of Literature*, 18 October 1930, 237, 239.

——. "What's Wrong with Criticism in America?" Editorial. *Saturday Review of Literature*, 13 March 1937, 8.

——. "Why?" Editorial. *Saturday Review of Literature*, 1 December 1934, 324.

Canfield, Cass. Letter. *Harper's*, November 1959, 6.

Cantwell, Robert. Letter. *New Republic*, 25 September 1935, 188–89.

Chase, Richard. "The Liberal Mind: Two Communications and a Reply: Liberalism and Literature." *Partisan Review* 16 (June 1949): 649–53.

"Chaos in Literary Criticism." Editorial. *Catholic World*, November 1933, 129–38.

Cohen, Elliot E. "In Reply." *Commentary*, October 1947, 347–49.

Cousins, Norman. "Bystanders Become Active." Editorial. *Saturday Review of Literature*, 30 August 1947, 20, 26.

——. "The Time-Trap." Editorial. *Saturday Review of Literature*, 24 December 1949, 20.

Craigie, Annie Louise. Letter. *Publishers' Weekly*, 16 January 1937, 205.

DeVoto, Bernard. "The American Scholar." Editorial. *Saturday Review of Literature*, 26 December 1936, 8, 14.

——. "Enlightened Research." Editorial. *Saturday Review of Literature*, 10 April 1937, 8.

——. "My Dear Edmund Wilson." Editorial. *Saturday Review of Literature*, 13 February 1937, 8, 20.

"Fiction in the U.S.: We Need a Novelist to Re-Create American Values Instead of Wallowing in the Literary Slums." Editorial. *Life*, 16 August 1948, 24.

French, John R. P. Letter. *New Republic*, 25 September 1935, 188.

Gentleman's Agreement. Advertisement. *New York Times Book Review*, 27 February 1947, 19.

Gordon, Milton M. Letter. *American Journal of Sociology*, March 1949, 455.

The Great Gatsby. Advertisement. *New York Times Book Review*, 7 June 1925, 21.

Hanson, Lawrence E. "'The Crisis of the Middle Class.'" Letter. *Nation*, 8 January 1936, 45–46.

Hardwick, Elizabeth. Reply to letter of Cass Canfield. *Harper's*, November 1959, 8.

Hughstan, Thomas. "Who Are These Writers?" Letter. *Saturday Review of Literature*, 30 June 1951, 21.

Kain, Richard M. "The American Novel—1936 Models." Letter. *American Scholar* 7, no. 1 (Winter 1938): 121–24.

Lewis, Edward R. "Are Americans Hyphenated? A Reply to 'Big Bill Thompson.'" *Outlook*, 14 March 1928, 418–19.

Lewis, Sinclair. "Fools, Liars, and Mr. DeVoto: A Reply to 'The Literary Fallacy.'" *Saturday Review of Literature*, 15 April 1944, 9–12.

Loveman, Amy. "The Dilemma of the Novelist." Editorial. *Saturday Review of Literature*, 13 August 1938, 8.

Melcher, Frederic G. "Books in the Postwar World." Editorial. *Publishers' Weekly*, 9 October 1943, 1425.

——. "On the Optimistic Side." Editorial. *Publishers' Weekly*, 8 July 1944, 103.

——. "Radio vs. Reading." Editorial. *Publishers' Weekly*, 2 March 1940, 981.

"People Do Read." Editorial. *Publishers' Weekly*, 10 November 1934, 1747.

Pitkin, Walter, Jr. "Testament of Faith." Letter. *Saturday Review*, 16 May 1953, 23.

Pollak, Felix. "Books in Wartime." Letter. *Library Journal*, 1 January 1943, 3–4.

Pratt, Theodore. Letter. *Saturday Review*, 15 August 1953, 23.

"Regionalism or the Coterie Manifesto." Editorial. *Saturday Review of Literature*, 28 November 1936, 8.

Ross, Andrew. "Irving Babbit." In *Dictionary of Literary Biography*, vol. 63, n.d., n.p.

Schary, Dore. "Letter from a Movie-Maker: 'Crossfire' as a Weapon against Anti-Semitism." *Commentary*, October 1947, 344–47.

Smith, Harrison. "American Disillusion." Editorial. *Saturday Review of Literature*, 15 June 1940, 8.

——. "Culture in Soft Covers." Editorial. *Saturday Review*, 24 April 1954, 22.

——. "Defeatism in Contemporary Literature." Editorial. *Saturday Review*, 27 December 1956, 20.

——. "The New American Reader." Editorial. *Saturday Review of Literature*, 23 May 1950, 20.

——. "The Novel and the Facts of Life." Editorial. *Saturday Review*, 3 January 1953, 16.

——. "Only Half of Us Read Books." Editorial. *Saturday Review of Literature*, 5 August 1950, 22.

——. "Who Are These People?" Editorial. *Saturday Review of Literature*, 9 June 1950, 22–23.

——. "Writers—On Your Toes!" Editorial. *Saturday Review of Literature*, 14 April 1951, 32.

Stevens, George. "The Pulitzer Prize in Fiction." Editorial. *Saturday Review of Literature*, 7 May 1938, 8.

——. "What, No Books?" Editorial. *Saturday Review of Literature*, 11 March 1939, 8.

Trilling, Lionel. "The Liberal Mind: Two Communications and a Reply: A Rejoinder to Mr. Barrett." *Partisan Review* 16 (June 1949): 653–58.

Turbeville, Gus. "Communists Are Not the Only Saboteurs of the 'American Way' of Doing Things." Editorial. *Saturday Evening Post*, 8 May 1954, 12.

Whipple, T. K. Reply to letter of Hamilton Basso. *New Republic*, 30 June 1937, 225–26.

INDEX